The Commonwealth of the Kingdom of God.

Where God Reigns

2023 ©

Kieth (Bashar) Fansa

ledofgod@ymail.com

Table of Contents

Preface.

Proverbs 18:17 *The first to state his case seems right until another comes and cross-examines him* (Berean Bible).

I am but a man and I can err, only let my errors be proven by scripture and I will revoke my work and throw my books into the fire.

Unless I am convinced by scripture and by plain reason, and not by popes and councils who have so often contradicted themselves, my conscience is captive to the word of God.

To go against conscience is neither right nor safe. I cannot and will not recant. Here I stand, I can do no other.

God help me.

Martin Luther's speech before the Pope to excommunicate him (1521).

Myopia- 1/ A visual defect in which distant objects appear blurred because their images are focused in front of the retina rather than on it. Also called near or short sightedness. 2/ Lack of discernment or long-range perspective in thinking or planning:

Sometimes we can become a little short sighted, spiritually Myopic if you will. We see only what's close by while other things at a distance (especially in our peripheral) are out of focus. Often and usually over time, we tend to ignore those fuzzy things, things that are too difficult to understand, or things we don't think will affect us. Sadly, rather than correcting our sight so that we may see clearly much further down the road, many times, it is easier to remain Myopic. The reason is mainly if we saw things as clearly as we should, we would then have to face some facts we have ignored before. We mere mortals can be so fixated on our little corner of the world, our block, our church or group, our denomination or organization and completely miss what God is trying to do in *His* Ecclesia, whether it is down the road, in another state or overseas. God has always had the bigger picture in mind, and He wants us to see it, but it will require getting our spiritual eyesight tested properly and the proper corrective lenses adopted, so we can see things not just from God perspective, but through God's heart, not just the words in a book, but the spirit in which they were written.

Eve was the first person to suffer from Myopia, Genesis tells us, *And when **the** woman **saw** that the tree was good for food, and that it was **pleasant to the eyes**, and a tree to be **desired** to make one wise, she took of the fruit thereof, and did eat, and gave also unto her husband with her; and he did eat* (**Genesis 3:6**). She had a whole garden full of fruits and beautiful trees, but all she could see was that one tree she thought would be good for her and her husband. Satan blurred the lines then, as he does now, and instead of Eve just obeying God's word as given by her husband, she thought she could do better if she just had more knowledge or intelligence, to be an expert or have good success (desired- śâkal). We all know how that ended. God gave a garden and Eve focused on a tree. Humans have not changed in about six thousand years. Thankfully, neither has God.

Truth as it is written in God's word is always open to cross-examination. Those who are sons and daughters of God do not fear cross-examination, in fact, they welcome it. The apostle Peter makes the case for being able to answer any question as to why we believe what we believe: *But sanctify the Lord God in your hearts* (Kardia- thoughts, feelings, or mind)*: and **be ready always to give an answer*** (exculpate, to prove to be right and guiltless) ***to every man that asketh you a reason of the hope*** *that is in you* (he tells us how to give the answer) *with meekness and fear* (**1 Peter 3:15**). For a long time, I blindly believed what I was told, but soon found out that to search to see if what I was told was truth, was nobler to God than to blindly follow what we are told by man. Over the years, I have come to realize that I am not concerned with questions that cannot be answered, I am however, deeply concerned with answers that cannot be questioned.

In this book there will be many criticisms of a system I believe either to be non-biblical but portrayed as biblical or no longer fit with what is happening in our day and age. I am not criticizing the people who do them though many will think I am. This is because they have fully accepted the system and in the vast majority, will have accepted it with no research of their own. It will feel personal because they have identified with the system far more than they have identified with Christ and His word.

Phrases used by real disciples to grow in knowledge, wisdom and grace, whether in some form of leadership or not, are, *"In light of this new information I have changed the way I see things"*, *"I didn't know, I guess I was wrong"*, *"you make a strong case for me to rethink what I believe"*, *"I've always believed this, but didn't know how to put it into words"*. These show true leadership for a solid biblical perspective.

Church leaders will discuss many aspects of what is *available* in the Kingdom of God for those who believe in Christ as Messiah; answered prayer, joy, peace, holiness, power with God, healing, forgiveness, deliverance, and so on, however, I believe that a discussion on the *"Commonwealth"* aspect of the Kingdom of God is sorely lacking, well overdue and desperately needed. Commonwealth suggests voluntarily preferring and desiring wealth for the common people, giving up our earthly rights, and equally as important, the ludicrous idea that we own what we possess. Allow me to show the difference between own and possess. If I buy a car under finance, I possess the car, I must maintain the car and I can use the car for its intended purpose, however, I do not *own* the car. Only after I make the last payment and satisfied all legal requirements, and I receive the title, may I now say I *own* the car.

The discussion about who owns who in the Kingdom of God is not an easy one to have, even though Paul makes it clear in **Acts 20:28** *Take heed therefore unto yourselves, and to all the flock, over the which the Holy Ghost hath made you overseers, **to feed the church of God, which he hath purchased with his own blood.*** Hence the reason why most leaders and saints from Western church society are reluctant or find it difficult discussing such an almost taboo subject. If it is mentioned, it is done so in some ethereal and nebulously spiritualized way that it has little to no impact on the hearer with little to no real-life examples in the churches of today and has little to no actionable or tangible results.

The Ecclesia of today is so focused on getting a name for itself (coming up with catchy church names and catch phrases for our conferences or putting our denomination/organization name on our church signs or billboards for example) that we have, for the most part, either negated our purpose or think we cannot fulfil our purpose without a recognizable name or belonging to a reputable organization. I will be mentioning the purpose of the Ecclesia many times during this writing. First and foremost, the purpose is to make disciples of those God has drawn by His spirit. Secondly, God does this by disciples who have grown sufficiently to preach the Kingdom of God only

(Basileia Theos- the royalty, rule, and realm of the supreme divinity. All of it, not just the parts that so-called *'win souls'* or deals with our adaptation of holiness). Everything else the church does (the how, when, where, and to whom) must fall into either one of these two categories. If we are not preaching to the lost, we must be teaching the saints who sit in our pews daily (with our lives, not from pulpits for a few minutes once or twice a week).

We cannot think that we will live in God's heavenly realm (His Kingdom) upon our passing or His return if we neglect to live as if we are in His Kingdom today. His Kingdom is not defined by meetings, boards, leadership styles or the church's real estate portfolio or manifesto (what we believe). It is not defined by anything we can touch with our bare hands nor can conceive with our diminutive and finite minds (**Romans 14:17** *For the kingdom of God is not **meat and drink*** (something tangible); *but righteousness, and peace, and joy in the Holy Ghost* (intangible). **Acts 7:48-49** *Howbeit the most **High dwelleth not in temples made with hands*** (something tangible); *as saith the prophet, Heaven is my throne, and earth is my footstool: what house will ye build me? saith the Lord: or what is the place of my rest?* **1 Corinthians 2:9** *But as it is written, Eye hath not seen, nor ear heard, neither have entered into the heart of man* (intangible), *the things which God hath prepared for them that love him).* The more I hear men brag about their ministries or what they have accrued *'for the Kingdom of God',* here on earth, the more I wonder where their treasure is. The Renewed Covenant speaks one hundred times regarding the Kingdom of Heaven and the Kingdom of God, but not once does it equate the Kingdom of God with anything transitory. By the time the reader finishes this book, they will have come to a crossroads and decisions must be made. Will they remain in the status quo of church as they know it (only gathering in buildings, singing a few songs, pay their tithe and listen to a monologue, then off for a time of pseudo-fellowship to eat), or will they usher in a new era of exponential growth, trust, wisdom, faith, and experience in God, seeing daily His handiwork in their lives?

Search for truth.

No, I'm not talking of the flip-chart bible study some use to *"win souls."* The purpose of any good homicide detective is to discover who killed the victim, in what manner and why. The facts are there to be gleaned no matter what the situation. First, the detective must start with what they are initially presented. Sometimes it is not as clear cut as what they see in front of them. They must look at the body, its position, obvious signs of a struggle and the surrounding area. With this initial information, they now begin the task of asking the right questions of witnesses, piecing together what they say with what can be observed and verified. The answers to some questions come easy, but more often than not, the truth is hidden somewhere in their answers. Some answers are seemingly inconsequential but just as necessary to finding the truth. The killer is found by asking, listening, and collating the answers into a simple but profound conclusion. There will be many side tracks and some dead ends. However, unless the detective has caught the culprit red-handed at the time of the killing, it will require much time, patience, and resources to find the truth. Like prying open an oyster to find a pearl of great price, it is hard work. The detective finds satisfaction that truth has been sought, found, and brought to bear before a judge.

Truth that is worth basing our lives on is rarely accidently found. Jesus told the hypocritical Pharisees and Sadducees to, *Search the scriptures; for in them ye think ye have eternal life: and they are they which testify of me* (**John 5:39**). They were to Ereunaō- (through the idea of inquiry, searching out); to seek after, to investigate the scriptures. The scriptures we quote must testify of Jesus, not our group, pastor, or organization. The Pharisees and Sadducees had their extra-canonical writings they searched even before they went to God's word. Jesus pointed them back to the single source of truth (the Torah, the Prophets, and the Writings, also known as the Tanakh) and told them to see if what He was saying was, in-fact, from God. Through this searching, one of them realized that the Lord's word did come from God. *There was a man of the Pharisees, named Nicodemus, a ruler of the Jews: The same came to Jesus by night, and said unto him, Rabbi,* **we know that thou art a teacher** (Didaskalos- instructor) **come from God:** *for no man can do these miracles that thou doest, except God be with him* (**John 3:1-2**). The Lord's teaching lined up fully with God's holy and ancient word and was backed by signs and wonders that could not be explained. Our search for truth must not be allowed to be hindered because of what we already believe or is yelled down a microphone at church services. Nicodemus had the Tanakh but did not understand them from God's perspective. Based on the questions he asked the Lord, *Jesus answered and said unto him,* **Art thou a master** (Didaskalos- instructor) **of Israel,** *and knowest not these things?* (**John 3:10**). Jesus did not come to bring a new doctrine, but to restore what was given from the beginning but was covered by centuries of man-made doctrines and commandments of men.

My intention for writing this book is to restore the love commanded one towards another that we have neglected over the last few generations and to restore the viability of the world-wide Ecclesia (what the translators of the King James Version erroneously called *church*). However, to restore something, one must first admit that something is either broken or damaged. Broken or damaged parts must first be removed and either repaired or replaced. This requires much inquiry and a willingness to throw out the broken parts so the original parts may be inserted and after much blood, sweat, and tears, we will have an exact duplicate of the original (more on this later).

We have over spiritualized God's commands to such a degree that we cannot see the practicality of those same commands. I will use practical stories, history (both military and medical), the Hebrew, Greek and Aramaic translations of the word of God and everyday common sense illustrations to show how the Kingdom of God operates here on earth. Unless specifically mentioned, I am referring to the body as a whole. If any particular body you know is already doing what is written in this book, then the axiom *'If the shoe doesn't fit, don't wear it'*, comes to mind. But please, take a good hard look at your church or organization as a whole and your role in it with an honest heart and you will plainly see that the body (as a whole) has struggled with the concept of community for well over 1500 years and almost entirely neglected it in recent times. It has been since the Renaissance (15th and 16th centuries) which revived humanism (where it is all about using the mind and placating our earthly senses in our society rather than a sense of spirituality practiced in the natural and daily community), that the Ecclesia began its rapid decline. If we do not return to the original concept of Kingdom mindedness and daily community with God and one another in the Ecclesia, we will be doomed as a viable alternative to the kingdom of darkness to those who seek truth in this world.

I have often been called iconoclastic by many of my traditional religious leader friends, mostly by those of the Pentecostal and Apostolic movement because through my preaching, teaching, and writing, I often speak about or call out our cherished beliefs and institutions and how we have inadvertently strayed from the righteous path to seek a quick way of growth and acquisition through man-made rules, programmes, and traditions. I feel in good company though, as my Lord and Master was also accused of being iconoclastic. Though many people claim to live a life full of revelation from the living word of God, their traditional beliefs and understandings stop shortly after they were born again or *'ordained into the ministry',* and they remain stuck in the rut of traditions handed down to them by their leadership, often too frightened to question where these came from, why they were given and why they should not be continued. This proves they have not received anything fresh from the word of God they claim to venerate. The vast majority of believers listen to countless sermons and repeat what they hear, but do they really know how to do what they hear or is it a hit and miss affair? Sadly, today's *'sermons'* don't teach, they impart information (nothing wrong with that, but imparting without exampling does not last very long). God's word, which speaks in different ways at different times through different people, (though it always points to Him **Hebrews 1:1**), has been largely hobbled by those same traditions and commandments of men. It was so in the time of our Master's sojourn on earth, and it is so now. It is worth noting that no long-lasting change takes place until change is the only option we have.

I trust this book will open the eyes of those who seek more than what they have now. My goal is to challenge and tear down many man-made ideas, traditions and concepts that have insidiously replaced the commandments of God which inevitably and invariably make the *commandments of God of none effect* (**Mark 7:13, Matthew 15:1-9**). There is a marked difference between ideas and concepts. Ideas refers to plans formed by mental effort, while concepts refer to procedures. A leader may get an idea of how to grow *his* church, then *he* must come up with the procedures of how to put that idea into practice. And therein lies the main problem. God has already given us the procedures of how to grow *His* Ecclesia in His word. God does not leave that to men. The Master said, *I will build my church*, He also said, *I am the good shepherd, my sheep know my voice*. Then He goes on to say, *if I be lifted up, I will draw all men unto me* (**Matthew 16:18, John 10:27, John 12:32**). Yet, how can we think it is up to our ideas and concepts that the church will grow and function?

To the true seeker of God, a challenge to grow may seem scary but if growth is anticipated it will be refreshing. Common sense (a sorely lacking trait in many people, sadly, even within the Ecclesia) as well as a spiritually deep insight is what God desires of and for His Ecclesia. We may feel like all our cherished norms are being challenged and many will need to be revisited and some torn down so God can rebuild the original structure. This is not only okay but required of a true seeker of God. It is not my intent to pull down and not give the remedy for a complete return of the biblical Ecclesia. Anybody can cut down a jungle, the real art comes in irrigating the desert.

We mere mortals were created to live in a social environment and the Ecclesia is no exception. Allow me to define the word *social*.

1. Relating to human society, the interaction of the individual and the group, or the welfare of human beings as members of society.

2. Tending to form **cooperative and interdependent relationships** with others.

3. Living and breeding in more or less organized communities especially for the purposes of **cooperation and mutual benefit**. i.e., not solitary.

Many years ago, I was approached by a man who believed himself to be a socialist who tried to convince me that if we lived in a socialist country we would have no private property, no poverty, no crime, and very little sickness. I agreed with the premise, however, with the heart of man being deceitfully wicked (**Jeremiah 17:9**), attempting to live in this manner without God ruling our hearts and minds, the idea of socialism is doomed to utter failure as history has shown that everywhere it has been tried.

I preached a message in a large church in Sandton City, South Africa in 2008, where I told the people, '***The only place that true socialism works is in God's true community, by people who are*** *individually and collectively led of the Holy Ghost (not by selfish desires) to fulfil one purpose, to use their time, talents and treasures to preach the gospel of the Kingdom of God only and make disciples as commanded by the King.'*

Section 1

Chapter One.

In the beginning.

In order to be able to think, you have to risk being offensive.

Dr Jordan Peterson. Clinical psychologist, author, and professor emeritus at the University of Toronto.

I would like to add to Dr Peterson's quote by saying that in order to be able to think, you have to risk being offended by others and that truth that cannot withstand examination is not truth, it is a belief. Belief alone cannot produce anything of any value to anyone at any time. Contrary to common misconception, re-examining our faith is not a sign of weakness, but it strengthens it and forces us to grow in it. The reason is because of our proclivity to believe whatever we are told by what we consider trusted sources, whether it be from the media, the government, or the pulpit, and because these purveyors of information are merely human, we can safely assume that regular re-examination will realign us back to the word of God, the only trusted source of truth.

We ask people in the world to re-examine their faith to see if what we are telling them is, in fact biblical. So, why would we cease to do this once we come to the knowledge of Christ, Acts 2:38, One God, and holiness? In regularly re-examining what we think we know; we find out how little we really do know. This spurs the seeker of God to get to know Him even more, and the circle widens. It is imperative, nay, an obligation from the beginning, to take the mindset of the Bereans, in that we must search the scriptures *daily* to see if what we have been told (whether from a pulpit, a bible school, or anyone for that matter regardless of the position in the church) is indeed the word of God. God calls the Berean mindset *more honourable* than those who just believe what they are told (**Act 17:10-12**). And so, let the re-examining begin.

God has a history of taking the few out of the many and starting over again. He has done so throughout His word and history, and He continues to do so in our time. When He walked this earth, He took a few out of thousands who followed Him and out of those thousands, He took a few (He was left with twelve). He took one hundred and twenty believers and turned it into about three thousand people out of approximately six hundred thousand Jews, Romans, Greeks, and visitors in Jerusalem during the feast of Pentecost in 30AD. Out of all of Galilee (a very religious region of Judea) He took most of His disciples. Looking further back, God took eight out of the entire population of the world. He took two (Joshua and Caleb) out of an entire generation of those who left Egypt. He took three hundred men of Israel (out of 32,000) and defeated the army of the Midianites (approximately 120,000 in Judges 6-7. There are multiple more examples, but you get the idea).

God has no problem '*reducing to the ridiculous*' and starting again. God has always had a remnant who will follow His perfect way of manifesting His light and example of how to live for Him and one another. If the church we attend is so focused on everything but making disciples and those disciples going into all their world and preaching (Kērusso- proclaiming and publishing) the Kingdom of God and making more disciples, then we must seek the Lord and ask Him to forgive us for ignoring the great commission, just so we can placate our senses and selfish desires for happiness.

As a side note, the great commission is not going into all the world and trying to convince them that they must be baptized in His name or that God is one, that they must speak in tongues or that to live a holiness life pleases God. This is a man-made construct. Prayerfully and carefully read and study **Matthew 28:18-20** and you will see how far we have strayed from its purpose.

We must either ask God to place us with people who have the same passion as Christ (to preach the Kingdom of God only and make disciples) or ask Him to use us to start a ground up movement where the only creed is the bible (No, I really mean it. Just the bible, not the bible plus our articles of faith, book of ethics, set of standards, minister's manuals, what the leadership says is the word of God, what our traditions tell us or what we've grown up to believe is true), where the only message to preach is the Kingdom of God (*Basileia Theos*- the royalty, rule and realm of the Supreme divine One and Magistrate; not so much on what it offers) and the only teaching is the apostle's doctrine of whole life changes (not just the Fabulous Five- Acts 2:38, one God, pay your tithe, holiness and obey the man of God. The Israelites already believed in one God, tithed, lived a holy life, and obeyed the priest. So, this couldn't have been the apostle's doctrine that they were teaching in **Acts 2:42**). The real apostle's doctrine involves everyone, everywhere, every day in every way *observing all things Jesus commanded*, and involves sacrificial giving of all our lives (**Matthew 28:20**). In the Addendum of this book, there is a list of seventy-seven commands that Jesus taught the disciples. These are the foundation of the apostle's doctrine.

The Israelites in Jesus' day already had the word (in the form of Torah (the law), the Nevi'im (the prophets) and the Ketuvim (the writings), collectively known as the Tanakh, see **Luke 24:44**), what they did not have, was a visual example of how to live it in a hostile environment (under the rule of an oppressive government) and deliver it to the nations. They eventually ended up having the traditions and commandments of men as their false way of living it. That was one of the main reasons M'shiyach stayed so long. It was to fulfil the law (not do away with it) by showing mankind how to live it and to make (and teach how to make) disciples to continue His legacy. Then He said, *'follow me'*. He did not say follow Him to heaven (what is preached in many churches today. This is the false gospel Paul warns us of in **Galatians 1:8-9**) but follow Him to a rock in a garden where we sacrifice our own will, follow Him to the cross where we get on it and stay on it by denying our flesh, then follow Him to a lonely and empty grave. But He did not stop there. He told us that by going through this process we would give a lost world an example of how to live and die in a manner that pleases the Father as the M'shiyach did whilst on earth. Read John Chapter seventeen to see why He took so long.

I strongly believe the church today suffers from a malady I call *'destination disease'*. This is where we are so focused on heaven that we neglect to live in a manner here on earth that proceeds our prize. Our prize is not a destination, our prize must be that we have pleased God with our puny lives and He rewards us based on our works as John tells us, *And I saw the dead, small and great, stand before God; and the books were opened: and another book was opened, which is the book of life: and the dead were judged out of those things which were written in the books, according to their works. And the sea gave up the dead which were in it; and death and hell delivered up the dead which were in them: and they were judged every man according to their works* (**Revelation 20:12-13**) and Paul concurs with John when he writes, **Who will render to every man according to his deeds**: *To them who by patient continuance in* **well doing** *seek for glory and honour and immortality, eternal* *life: But unto them that are contentious, and do not obey the truth, but obey unrighteousness, indignation and wrath, Tribulation and anguish, upon every soul of man that doeth evil, of the Jew first, and also of the Gentile* (**Romans 2:6-9**).

Yes, all must hear the gospel of the Kingdom of God, as that was a command in **Mark 16:15** *And he said unto them, Go ye into all the world, and preach* (Kerusso- as a town crier, proclaim, publish, herald) *the gospel to every creature*. However, hearing rarely is enough, for the world must also see the good news of a heavenly Kingdom in action before their very eyes (the Aramaic translation of the phrase *Gospel of the Kingdom* is translated as *Hope of the Kingdom*). This is what the church has to offer. Hope that there is more to life than converting oxygen to carbon-dioxide for no apparent reason, of treading the same road day in, day out. Hope that we were born to be more than worm food. We cannot expect the lost to believe before they see; this is purely the domain of a disciple of Christ, one who has surrendered their own will and understanding to that of God's (**Proverbs 3:5-6**). If **Mark 16:15** is all there is to being a Christian, then God would not have told us to follow in His footsteps, for he did much more than just preach. It may astonish the reader to know that only about 15% of Christ's ministry (His recorded words) was preaching, 85% was teaching which incorporated signs and wonders where they were needed, in the general population, as proof that His teaching was from the throne of God.

He taught those who would listen how to live in the Kingdom of God here on earth (read the sermon on the mount and see how many times He tells them what it takes to live in the Kingdom and who will eventually inherit His Kingdom). Only about 6% of the Master's interaction with people was in a synagogue or temple, the rest was showing how to live what He taught where the real people were, in their homes, the marketplace, in the wilderness, on the road, by the seaside, or in the mountains. Of the thirty-six recorded miracles in the gospels (that did not involve happening to Himself) only a few were in a synagogue or the Temple, the rest were done where the people were (note: He did not corral them into a building by inviting people to the temple or synagogue to '*get their miracle or blessing*').

The Master walked everywhere except for a few short boat rides and a noticeably short donkey ride. Why is this? Because most people did not have the means to go in comfort and luxury. Jesus, though He was the Lord of life and the King of kings, *made Himself of no reputation,* so He could become as one of the common folks (**Philippians 2:7**). That was what endeared Him to the masses, and they heard His word gladly (**Mark 12:37**). He was the exact opposite of the leadership of His time. They wanted accolades, titles, honours, and praises of men, while He sought and received none of these things. Whose message has withstood the test of time, the religious elites, or the peripatetic preacher? The Master would not that He would have, while the people around Him did not have. He did not talk down to the masses and He did not demand they listen to Him because He was a Rabbi (a person with some authority). He had no permanent place to lay His head (**Luke 9:58**), His family were all those that *did* the word of God, not just heard it (**Matthew 12:50**) and in the end, He hung naked on a cross, while sinners gambled with what little He owned throughout His ministry (His robe. **Psalm 22:18, Matthew 27:35**). All these things are the exact opposite of what we do in today's Ecclesia. We fight to get a reputation in our communities and organizations, we fight to get better houses to live in, we build temples in the name of God but place our organization's name on the front to bring people to, our leaders get to eat before the others, and special gifts during "*pastor appreciation month*", they sit in the upper places (on our platforms), we gather stuff so that we have more when we die, and we are happy to have people come to just hear the word of God and don't show them how to love and live it, and somehow, we have been conditioned to think that if we have nothing or lose everything, we are out of the will of God. Was the man, Jesus, out of the will of God on the cross? Yet this homeless and materially poor man infected about 120 people with such determination to make disciples, that they would turn their world upside down (**Acts 17:6**). They went and made more of Him to show the world what God really wanted from the people who are called by His name. Just because we have been baptized in His name does not mean we are honouring it with our lives. This takes study, true worship, and passion to emulate the one whose name we call on and make others who desire it, to be like their Lord.

Have we become so fickle that we would cheapen the gospel of the Kingdom by reducing it down to sound bites or video clips like news outlets? A few songs in an hour, while hearing a few words from the same man about the same subjects every week? We give the people in the world a synopsis of what we believe via a quick run-down of our core doctrines, (one God, **Acts 2:38**, holiness, giving, and how important it is to have a man of God in our lives. But then we tell them that if they want to hear more, they should stay tuned (come to our church) for the full story on Sunday at 10am or for the really '*deep seekers*' they can hear the good news repeated on Wednesdays at 7pm.

God did not show up around 2000 years ago, perform a few huge miracles (i.e., stop the sun, withhold the rain or dew, or even have the Roman Empire set His people free. Why not? He's done it before, right?) and preach in a synagogue or the temple to get His message across. He took years to show what the Gospel really was and how it should be lived, not just preached (He started to teach and ask questions at the age of twelve, that is when young Jewish boys became a '*Son of the Law*'). The Torah was on earth for about 1300 years in the hands of prophets, priests, and holy men of God (**2 Peter 1:21**), yet God still needed to show up in the flesh for the world to see its manifestation and fulfillment (**Matthew 5:17**). If the writings and preaching alone were sufficient, if the reading of the word of God in buildings (synagogues and the Temple {now churches}) was sufficient, if going to the Temple and giving to the Temple treasury on Shabbat were sufficient to save the world, would there be a need for a visible manifestation of the writings to appear for us to be saved? All the things God said to do in and for His Kingdom as well as for one another came with a visible example that many men and women, throughout history, recorded for posterity through their lives.

We do not need another church reformation, these only last at the most about 50 to 75 years before we get stuck in that revelation. Today there are many leaders who claim they are reforming the church. We don't need a reformed church, but a restored Ecclesia. Look at the difference between reform and restore. The former means to: improve by alteration, put into a better form or condition (how does one improve on God's perfect church?), whilst the latter is to: bring back into existence or use; re-establish, to bring back to an original or normal condition.

To bring back to an original or normal condition. We are in dire need of a church revolution (a single complete cycle of such orbital or axial motion), that will lead to a complete restoration of the purpose of the Body of Christ as was lived by the Book of Acts Church, and this comes about by a fresh, not necessarily a new, revelation. Luther, Zwingli, Knox, Wycliffe, Huss, Waldo, Booth, Urshan, Tyndale; all these and many more did not bring a new revelation, they only uncovered what had been hidden under years of man's well-intentioned but erroneous traditions and doctrines (teaching) and neglect of the function of God's word (above the formulary) through His church and its purpose. Sadly, this is the same thing that birthed the lukewarm church of Laodicea and has been reproduced today, whose only priority is how much blessing they can get (spiritually, materially, financially, physically, and numerically). The people mentioned above, sought, and fought hard to return to the purity of God's word, took the baton of the Gospel of the Kingdom and passed it on to the next generation of truth seekers, while the comfort seekers were more than content to remain in their local church buildings and continue to take from God while giving little of their precious time and resources. This is not a fellowship; this is a façade.

The definition of a *façade* is- *the front of a building, **especially a large or attractive building**, an artificial or deceptive front or appearance.* Behind the façade of church as we know it today (the emotional, blessings and carnal nature of the majority of our services, this is not to say we don't *feel* God, just that that's not what it's all about) is the real church, just itching to break forth and show His glory and majesty to the world, not so much through songs and how much freedom we say we have by running the aisles, jumping and shouting, speaking in tongues, nor to show how many churches we have or what beautiful head office buildings we can acquire, and especially not within the four walls of our modern tabernacles or temples, but within the market places, school rooms, offices, neighbourhoods, and halls of government. To take and show the real doctrine of Christ on the highways, byways and to those who live in our neighbourhoods. This would make us all a walking tabernacle of God, as Peter puts it in **1 Peter 2:4-5** *To whom coming, as unto a living stone, disallowed indeed of men, but chosen of God, and precious, Ye also, as lively stones, **are built up a spiritual house,** an holy priesthood, to offer up spiritual sacrifices, **acceptable to God** by Jesus Christ.*

The definition of spiritual house is interesting in that is speaks of a Pneumatikos Oikos- a non-carnal, supernatural, regenerate family. Within our communities, the light (revelation) we receive would then be revealed to the lost where they live, and we would have no need to coerce them (via block parties, potlucks, or festivals, special Christmas/Easter services and gimmicks) into coming to our buildings to see what we believe and what we do; they would see it in our daily lives (see also **1 Corinthians 3:16**). We do these things purely from a convenience standpoint, but where does the word say we are to preach the gospel conveniently. To preach and teach the Kingdom of God places us at risk of not only being inconvenienced but if done correctly, also being persecuted. Mainly because we have invaded the enemy's stronghold with a message of another Kingdom. This ticks ol' slewfoot off and he will not take it lying down. Perhaps this is why we do not do it as the Book of Acts Ecclesia did it. The cost is too high.

There are so many groups and organizations claiming they have the truth, but the truth will stand out, not when it is scrutinized by bible scholars who sit in their bible college offices and board rooms high atop their ivory towers, who have forgotten how to interact with ordinary folk with any meaning (both in and out of the pew). It will be verified by people who do not know God. The best testimony that we are real *'little Christs'*, comes from those around us outside of our church circle. They see us for who and what we really are based solely on how much of the word we live in front of them (not just know or can quote on social media) and by the love we have towards one another. Nor will it be by trying to prove we have the anointing by how much we can scream in some effected voice down a microphone in our buildings. They will either be drawn by and to God by our spirits and actions (as we behave more like sheep amongst the wolves, prepared to be slaughtered if necessary. See **Acts 1:8**), more than just by scripture or how well we can argue scripture, or they will be repulsed by the likeness, character, and actions of the Lord we serve.

The average person outside of our churches cares extraordinarily little about scripture. They care about the state they are in and want to see a visible working model of what and who we say we belong to. When this occurs, we have captured their attention, not so much with miracles which are short lived (the people will still die of something and no matter how much they may be financially blessed, they will still go down in the long box and decay), neither by our invitations to our church buildings for functions, but with open hearts and invitations into our lives, our families, and our homes. How many church people invite others to their churches and how few invite people into their lives? Which do you think will have a greater impact on an unbeliever? Sharing a sermon, or showing and sharing Christ where they are? Will they see Christ in a polished and metronomic liturgical (a prescribed form or set of forms for public religious worship) church service or seeing us for who we really are, warts and all, or will they see Christ in our struggles and eventually being victorious? Perhaps that is why we do not invite them to our homes because we are not as victorious as we sing and shout about. It is when we become acquainted with their lives and they with ours, that we can give them the answers to the age-old question, *what must I do*? Anything and everything else, is just an expression of our opinions or offering of explanations about an event, situation or why we do what we do, in other words- a commentary. People do not get born again and stay in the body by this method, just like reading Matthew Henry's Commentary of the Bible doesn't substitute for the word of God.

We like to think we can *win souls* for the Lord through our church services better than through our lives, mainly because it takes much less effort to get people to come to a church service and let the professionals do the work. This is trying to produce a painless Pentecost. It is not only those who must submit to the word of God regarding salvation that will experience pain and loss, but those who claim to want people born again must experience this same pain and loss daily. Loss of time, resources and being humiliated for the gospel is all a part of being called by His name. Being baptized in His name is just the first breath of a life that will suffer for His name's sake, *And ye shall be hated of all men for my name's sake: but he that endureth to the end shall be saved. Then shall they deliver you up to be afflicted, and shall kill you: and ye shall be hated of all nations for my name's sake. But before all these, they shall lay their hands on you, and persecute you, delivering you up to the synagogues, and into prisons, being brought before kings and rulers for my name's sake.* (**Matthew 10:22, 24:9, Luke 21:12**). As it was written of Paul in **Acts 9:16** *For I will shew him how great things he must suffer for my name's sake,* then Paul tells us, *be ye followers of me as I am of Christ* (**1 Corinthians 11:1**)

We are told how the world will hear and see the gospel in **Revelation 12:11** *And they overcame him by the blood of the Lamb, and by the **word of their testimony*** (Logos Hautou Marturia [from Martus]- evidence given, a record or report, a martyr)*; and they loved not their lives unto the death.* Modern explanation: *your recorded testimony will cause you to be martyred and you will be okay with it.* Our lives testify and is evidence of what we say. We are constantly being judged by the world and so we should be. What we say in a court of law must be backed up with physical evidence or it is only hearsay, thus it is inadmissible.

Let us look to the Bard from Stratford-on-Avon for an analogy? I may be able to explain many of Shakespeare's writing in a way another person may generally understand, but to convince them that his writings have bearing today, I must do more than tell them what his writings are. I must do more than just print books explaining his writings, his meanings, and ideas, or give seminars or college classes espousing Shakespeare's wonderful talent of exposing the darker side of humanity or the lighter side of the foibles of mankind. I may be able to understand Shakespeare's ability to describe love and its infinite joys, but I may never experience that kind of love from another person nor could give that same kind of love.

If I genuinely believed in his writings as much as I say I do, then I would not only spread the ideas and thoughts of Shakespeare through words and books, festivals, and plays, but begin to live as he and others of his time lived. I would truly stand out from the rest of society, not just in my clothing or speech (that would be strange enough) but in my mannerisms and life. People would think me crazy, something to ridicule perhaps, but I would have given them a glimpse into what it would be like to live in Shakespearian times, and if they chose to, they could align themselves to doing the same (watching a Shakespearian play or movie for a couple of hours is not enough to convince a real thinking person to change their life). Watching a person living like Shakespeare over a long period of time would make it easier to become like what they see, because they have had a living representation of Shakespeare's writings. They could ask questions and I could show them (not just tell them) what the answer was.

"To be, or not to be" (Hamlet, Act 3, Scene 1, the opening phrase of a soliloquy given by Prince Hamlet, in William Shakespeare's play) is one of Shakespeare's most famous lines. But to be what? This question is open ended. It could mean to be or not to be a cowboy, a doctor, a mum, or a clown. As a believer in Christ as Lord (master, controller, ruler), I think the question should be asked, *to be or not to be a disciple of Yeshua*, with a follow up question of *how, o how to be a disciple of Yeshua*? This is the very essence of the Ecclesia; to help each other find how to be what God has called each and every one of us to be and do from before the foundation of the world (**Ephesians 1:4**).

It is our actions that convince others of the rightness of our cause, actions that prove we can truly deliver what we preach. Even with the mistakes we make (whether bad judgement calls or slip-ups), God still allows His word to shine through a seeker of His will. Our words have minimal effect on people today. Running the aisles in church, speaking in tongues, and weeping at the altar every week does not show anyone other than those in the building anything of our lives (and even then, only a modicum of what we display in a church setting is real. Why? Because being real risks vulnerability and most Christians are not good at that sort of thing). Mighty works and miracles are only one small aspect of knowing the truth (which is Jesus Christ, not a scripture). These things are what every person claiming the name of Christ should actually be doing as a natural part of their *daily* lives as the sovereignty of God wills it. People in the end will say to Jesus *...in that day, Lord, Lord, have we not prophesied in thy name? and in thy name have cast out devils? and in thy name done many wonderful works? And then will I profess unto them, **I never*** (Oudepote- not even at any time, that is, never at all: - neither at any time) **knew you: depart from me, ye that work iniquity** (Anomia- violator of the law. **Matthew 7:22-23**). The law Christ is speaking of here is what we will address shortly. The Lord knows who His people are. They are the ones who *seek first the Kingdom of God and His righteousness* in their own daily lives and who have devoted themselves to collectively and individually making disciples (**Matthew 6:33** and **28:18-20**). Doing mighty signs and wonders, casting out demons and prophesying in His name is not the first, second or even the third thing Jesus is looking for. He is looking for people who know Him and His will for His Kingdom. He is looking for people who show His Kingdom where they live and actually go out and teach the things He commanded to those who have answered the call to follow Christ to the cross. Mighty signs and wonders (which are a small aspect of our daily lives) will follow us no matter where we are.

Jesus said it.

Phrases like *'Jesus said'*, *'The Lord said'*: *'He commanded them'*, and *'He spake'*… are powerful words, but do we really understand how powerful they are? They are so powerful that they formed the basis of the great commission; *And Jesus came and **spake unto them**, saying…* (**Matthew 28:18**). Please note this statement. He didn't send an emissary after He died and resurrected, He came and spoke Himself. He *Proserchomai Laleō Legō*- uttered these words… *Go ye therefore and teach all nations… Teaching them to observe* (Tereo- fulfil) *all things I commanded you…* (**Matthew 28:19**). The Lord only gave us two commandments: to love God and love our neighbour as ourselves, right? Well, yes and no. There is only one way to love the Lord our God, but there are many ways we can show our love for our neighbour. Christ did not leave us to our own understanding nor our own devices of how to obey His word. He did, however, give us instructions, allowing for personality and character differences, on how to fulfil His word.

In the Old Covenant, God **told** humanity what He wanted from His people, while the Renewed Covenant **explains** and **shows** how it is to be fulfilled. Kind of like telling a young child to clean their room, then taking them by the hand and showing them *how* to clean their room.

Here are a couple of examples.

1: Loving thy neighbour was not a new idea. **Leviticus 19:18** *Thou shalt not avenge, nor bear any grudge against the children of thy people, but **thou shalt love thy neighbour as thyself**: I am the LORD*. The Master goes one step further by telling us, *A new commandment I give unto you, That ye love one another; as I have loved you, that ye also love one another* (**John 13:34**). The Master unearthed this commandment and restored it to its rightful place, right up there with loving God with every ounce of our being.

2: Taking a gift to the altar is not new. *And the priest shall take the basket* (carrying the gift) *out of thine hand, and set it down before the altar of the LORD thy God* (**Deuteronomy 26:4**). Yet, once again the Master tells us that when we do this, we must also, *Leave there thy gift before the altar, and go thy way; first be reconciled to thy brother, and then come and offer thy gift* (**Matthew 5:24**). Once again, the Master explains the scripture in a natural way.

Many times, Jesus gave the Logos and other times He gave a Rhema (the spoken word of God and the revealed word of God. Sometimes He told them what He wanted, other times He told them how and why He wanted it) and we must be able to differentiate between the two. An employer can sit down and have lunch with an employee (who is also a friend) and speak of what direction he wants the company to go in the next year (a logos), but after lunch, the boss now directs the employee (who is still a friend) how to achieve the goal (a rhema).

Who was the Great commission given to?

When carrying out the great commission it is important to understand that it was given to all who are His disciples (**John 17:20**). Sadly, it has been interpreted as it was meant for the ministers, pastors, and leadership team. Those who are not willing to take up their cross daily and follow him, are disciples in name only (nominal Christians), for only a true disciple will desire and be able to obey the great commission. The Lord did not give it only to the twelve or the one hundred and twenty in the upper room on the day of Pentecost, for had this been the case, at their death, the commission would have been completed, He did not give it to those who *want* to do more for God while the rest just coast along. He gave it to all those that come to God through obedience to their word (not just Acts 2:38, one God and speaking in tongues, but the whole word).

He commanded them to teach only what He commanded … *Teaching them to observe* (Tēreō-fulfil a command, maintain) *all things* **whatsoever I have commanded** *you...* (**Matthew 28:20**. See addendum). The Pharisees and Sadducees had their preferences and that is what they taught. Have we done the same thing today, ...*teaching for doctrines the commandments of men*? (**Matthew 15:9**). These are the things the disciples were told to teach, and this is what **Acts 2:42** speaks of as *the apostle's doctrine*). This is as imperative to every disciple as, *Thou shalt have no other gods*. We cannot utter the words '*I am a Christian*' and not burn with passion to fulfil the greatest directive given to mankind since God told Adam and Eve to tend His garden and go forth and replenish the earth. He told them to go and make more of that which was made in His image. The great commission is just that. Making more of Him. Not making more meetings, churches, more rules, more conferences, more ministries, or even more converts and mistaking these for obeying the great commission. Just because someone gets converted in one of these venues (born again according to Acts 2:38), does not mean they are like Christ. This is a lifelong affair called sanctification (being purified or made holy; conformity of the heart and life to the will of God) and this is fulfilled in discipleship which cannot be remotely or effectively done from behind a pulpit.

We cannot make people like Him of those in the world, but of those who are called to His purpose, those who have answered the call, submitted themselves to that purpose and are being made into His image (**Romans 8:28-29**). We are to make citizens for the Commonwealth of the Kingdom of God, not pew warming spectators who come to see what God will do for them, becoming weekly consumers of preaching, and definitely not making more people who would die for their organization or their pastor, but not for each other. This is not what God had in mind when He gave the great commission. If leaving the great commission to the professional ministry were truly the way of God, it would have taken more than seventy-five years for Jerusalem to hear the gospel let alone, Judea, Samaria, and the uttermost parts of the world. History has proven the word got to the far eastern parts of Syria within three years and all the way to India through Thomas, within twenty years of the resurrection as shown by historical records and verifiable traditions. Thomas was later martyred and buried there after being a witness to the Indian people. The tomb of St. Thomas is in Mylapore, India. There is still a large group of people who adhere to the teachings of this apostle. As the entire Ecclesia fulfills the great commission, God draws those who will be drawn by His spirit (**John 12:32**) as they watch our lives and love for one another, then, as they respond, He adds them to the Ecclesia (**Acts 2:47**). The responsibility of the Ecclesia is not to build churches, but to be and make lively stones in the church that Christ is building.

Paul writes of the Commonwealth of Israel and God's desire to have His people live as one in this Commonwealth, and it must be made clear that we, as believers in Y'shua as the M'shiyach, did not replace Israel but are grafted into it. God did not and does not have two separate people, but one people bound to each other by His spirit and born into His service to show the world an alternative to the Kingdom of darkness.

Five questions come to mind, the answers of which must be found in God's word if we are to live with Him and for each other. They are:

1. What is a Commonwealth?

2. How does it work?

3. What are one another commandments?

4. To whom were they written?

5. Are these prerequisites to becoming a member of the Commonwealth?

The answers are in the word of God if we will make time to search diligently for them. They will become apparent if we will only get rid of our worldly or traditional paradigms and preconceived ideas of who and what *church* is and submit ourselves to the teachings of the Master through His own words and of those who followed in His footsteps. This book is only an attempt to point the reader in the right direction to find the answers to the above questions.

But what about me?

In this first section I will dispel the ludicrous idea of *Christian individualism* and the false concept of the *'me and mine blessing'* doctrine which has permeated almost all the Apostolic pulpits predominately in the west. As author and speaker, Wendell Berry, so eloquently put it; *A proper community, we should remember also, is a commonwealth: a place, a resource, an economy. It answers the needs, practical as well as social and spiritual, of its members - among them the need to need one another. The answer to the present alignment of political power with wealth is the restoration of the identity of community and economy.*

The Art of the Commonplace: The Agrarian Essays of Wendell Berry. (Page 63).

Just as the name Commonwealth is read, it is meant to be lived. The wealth of knowledge, power and goods is meant to be shared with and amongst the common people (pertaining or belonging equally to an entire community) of the Ecclesia. If there is an aloof hierarchy within our church and or organization, then more than likely *'commonwealth'* is not a word that can be placed in front of it, no matter how much we speak in tongues, jump or shout that we have the victory or how many altars we cry at every week. It is when we help each other (not just those of our social circle) meet the commandments of God, that we have proven to the world that we are His children. Speaking in tongues is not proof to the world we are His, our love and service to one another however, is. I know many people who speak in tongues from all kinds of denominations and organizations who are more selfish than many people of the world and these people have deceived themselves into believing they are somehow right with God. They gossip, backbite, withhold love, refuse to restore relationships, or revile others behind their backs, then speak to God in tongues. The old saying goes, *it's not good enough if you speak in tongues, but can't speak well of the brethren in English.'*

The suffix 'ism' denotes a distinctive belief, theory, system, or practice and is placed on the end of words such as Catholicism, communism, despotism, Pentecostalism, individualism and so on. I will show individualism within the Ecclesia, is a tool the enemy uses to weaken the body of Christ and to lessen its impact on the world at large. There are hundreds of examples of things to believe of, do to, for and with one another and I will focus on just a few. After years of travel around the churches in the West, I have found these to be sorely lacking, ones that the world will notice immediately should we return to our roots and put them back in place. A further personal study is highly recommended to grow in God's character and His actions- Dikaiosune- righteousness.

The Ecclesia is a group of individuals who are not only called out from the world but also from the spectator churches of today. They are surrendering their selfish individuality so they can gather anywhere, anytime for one purpose (more on the biblical definition of church shortly), and once it has returned to its roots, the body will regain its glorious purity and splendour, not to mention the power to once again daily command the spiritual and natural world. Then, and only then, can we offer the world a viable alternative to the darkness it dwells in. You will see the term *viable alternative* many times in this writing because that is what the world is looking for: a real working model in function not just in form, of the Acts Ecclesia in the 21st century, not just a church that preaches **Acts 2:38,** but one that also lives **Acts 2:42-47, 4:32-37, 20:20-21.** The Book of Acts is both descriptive and prescriptive in its application. It describes what happened in the beginning and what is prescribed to maintain its effectiveness today.

Aldous Huxley wrote in his book *End and Means* that …*The function of the well-intentioned individual, acting in isolation, is to formulate or disseminate theoretical truths. The function of the well-intentioned individuals in association is* **to live in accordance with those truths, to demonstrate what happens when theory is translated into practice,** *to create small-scale working models of the better form of society to which the speculative idealist looks forward* (emphasis added). To put it in today's terms; individually, we can only share things *about* the Gospel of the Kingdom of God (the very basic form of information dissemination), but by living collectively in Commonwealth, we can *show* the Gospel of the Kingdom of God. Individually we only have a theory of God's community, however, by living the Kingdom of God collectively we prove the theory.

Allow me to expound. Someone can postulate what it's like to live in North Korea (a completely reclusive country), but until they have spent time living with the people under such a repressive regime, all they can tell us is what they have read or seen in media (information only). To really know what it is like, we must speak to those who have escaped and are willing to tell their story. It is when we learn from these people, we know the truth of North Korea. An individual (or even a group of individuals) can only theorize what a commonwealth is and how it operates, what they have heard of it or read about it. To get the reality of it, the individual must become a part of a commonwealth and all the responsibilities and privileges that go with it. It is hard work; it will not be easy and anyone that tells us that it is easy living for God in a broken world is self-deluded at best or outright lying. The Commonwealth of the Kingdom of God is a group whose sole purpose is to strengthen itself from within, fighting the urge to seek their own comfort before that of others. Additionally, it is that others may join and learn to function in the Ecclesia. No one is called to just come and sit.

Chapter Two

DARPA and the Church.

The Defense Advanced Research Projects Agency also known as DARPA in the USA, has one aim; to find fascinating and innovative ways of destroying humans. This agency puts out ideas of what kind of weapons it feels it will need 10-15 years in advance, then thousands of clever people come up with ideas and plans to build them. The designers of the weapons (both offensive and defensive) must first show that their concept or idea works under normal, combat, and harsh conditions, be cost effective and built from readily available materials. This is called Proof of Concept (PoC) also known as Proof of Principle (PoP). Then comes the realization of the concept or idea in the form of a prototype to demonstrate its effectiveness and feasibility in theory, principle, and practical applications. A PoC is generally small, but the idea shows its validity. However, even an agency with seeming inexhaustibly deep pockets like DARPA will shortly thereafter want to see a complete working model under combat conditions before it puts down billions in taxpayer dollars.

If the world wants to see a working as designed model of something prior to buying it, why do we expect to get the world to come to us (the church) and buy what we have, when we don't have working models of the original church in action in their neighbourhoods, workplaces, classrooms and marketplaces. Instead, we make them leave their neighbourhood and come to ours. Sure, we have many churches, of all creeds and flavours, colours, and sizes. We have Black churches, Hispanic churches, Asian churches, cowboy churches, even family or youth-oriented churches. We have churches where they only sing out of the *'Red book'*, and churches where it's so dark you can't see the saints beside you. We have churches where you can shout *amen* and *preach it,* and churches where if they were any more laid back, they'd be in a coma. But are they the real Ecclesia as given by the Holy Ghost and propagated by the early believers in the Book of Acts? Are the lives of the congregation based upon the lives of the people they claim to be spiritual ancestors of and not just what they believed? There are hundreds of churches in our respective areas, all of which claim to be the real church of God, but they can't all be right, because they each have their own thing going. Some focus on youth, family, music, outreach, or social issues, while others are all about the gifts or prophecy. Many churches focus on deliverance or on grace. There are churches designed to attract a certain group or class of people with the occasional token outsider to prove they are not prejudice? There may be churches with different demographics because of locale but we find no church in the bible seeking after a certain demographic. Are the believers self-sacrificing for one another, does the great commission passionately burn within the very depths of the hearts of *all those who sit in the pews **for** all those who sit in the pews?* For those who claim His name, is the so-called ministry doing all the work while the ordinary saint sits back and pat themselves on the back for how they have told the world of their doctrines, prayed for their pastor, how many missionaries they support and how many church visitor cards they were instrumental in filling out?

I live in a small town full of wonderful people in Southern Texas on the Gulf of Mexico (population- 4985), we have seventeen denominational churches ranging from Catholic to Protestant to Pentecostal/Apostolic and non-denominational with approximately 12 different types of separate smaller churches that meet in homes. None larger than about 80 in regular attendance with an average of around 10-25. That works out to be one church for every 178 people. We are not shy on places to go and find out something about God. The vast majority are just gathering and going through the motions of church, because that is what they do on Sunday's and midweek. That is where they hear about what God has done or will do for them. The problem lies between the meetings. Are their lives changed so radically that their friends and neighbours notice it? With this many churches, shouldn't we either have revival or riots?

Church is where they go to accept Jesus as their personal Saviour or be saved according to Acts 2:38, while others just go because their religion dictates it. Do most of these people have some kind of love for God? Undoubtably so, but rarely will their love for God translate to each one biblically discipling one another or experience the Almighty Himself on a daily basis. I have visited several of them many times and my heart breaks at the deadness and religiosity of their services. Whether they were clapping and shouting or sedate, there was little to no growth in the people past their initial experience. The reason is that the people live their lives during the week and gather to hear about God on the weekend and the enthusiastic ones meet on the few mid-week meetings.

Church becomes like doing laundry on Thursdays and taking out the trash on Tuesdays; routine, it's just what they do. It would benefit the town infinitely more if the committed believers were to go from family to family (or as the book of Acts puts it Kata Oikos- *household to household*) in their precincts (Temple- Hieron- entire precincts, i.e., neighbourhoods **Acts 2:46**) and discipling those that are seeking God, not just placating the need for routine, or going because they feel guilty. It would behove the real believers in our town (of which there are a committed few) to break the mould and mantra of *'come to our church'* (one of twenty-nine) and adopt an old but proven strategy of helping the residents to come to Christ. This is a microcosm of what happens in innumerable towns and churches around the world, mostly in the affluent West. We dance around the issue, but eventually, we must face the fact that we have very little impact in our towns, cities, and regions. Yet, we strut around as if we have achieved a great thing by opening another church.

Are we Apostolic/Pentecostals in danger of following in the footsteps of the dead or dying religions, denominations, and traditions of the past or are we really showing (not just preaching to) our towns and cities how a real working model of a Book of Acts church operates, not just in a meeting, but in our homes and businesses, in our dealing with the saints and the lost in our neighbourhoods? In most cases the honest answer to the latter part of this question would be a resounding NO! We Apostolics may have the right doctrine of salvation and can prove that God is one, and that baptism should be in His name, but we are light years behind regarding the Commonwealth aspect of the Kingdom of God. According to Jesus Himself, He commanded us to preach (Kērusso- proclaim, publish and herald as a town crier) the Kingdom of God, repentance, and remission of sin in His name to the world (**Mark 16:15-18**, **Luke 24:45-49**), not the doctrine (teaching) of why we do what we do, i.e., our standards or all the goodies one gets once they get *"born-again"*.

We have somehow confused coming to Christ with *'you must come to Christ through our organization or church, or their experience isn't real.* A harsh thing to say, but please, prove me wrong regarding the church universal. If you're not a Baptist, Methodist, Presbyterian, Apostolic etc, are you really even saved? Do the lost have to belong to our denomination/organization to be saved? We sometimes belittle other's experience in their search for God instead of building on it by adding more truth to what they believe, *And he* (Apollos) *began to speak boldly in the synagogue: whom when Aquila and Priscilla had heard, they took him unto them, and expounded unto him the way of God more perfectly* (**Acts 18:26**). Shortly thereafter, Apollos is a travelling companion with Paul (see **Acts 19:1**) and he watered where Paul had sown. Paul tried to help the growth of believers, *...covet earnestly the best gifts: and yet shew I unto you a more excellent way* (Huperbolē- a throwing beyond, far more exceeding, and beyond. **1 Corinthians 12:31**). There's a difference between having an experience once or occasionally and experiencing change in our daily lives in every aspect.

The Taste Test.

We offer salvation to the world like a small booth in a large grocery store offers samples of food they have on sale. We hope they will stop by our booth, have a small bite and if they like it, they will go to that aisle and buy a bag or a box of what we offer. Salvation is not handed out to people to try. The fierceness of the King and His Kingdom is proclaimed (**Acts 17:30** *And the times of this ignorance God winked at; but **now commandeth all men** every where **to repent***) and those who are drawn to His message will ask, *'Men and brethren, what must we do?'* (**Acts 2:36**). We have slowly but surely left preaching what our Master preached (the Kingdom of God- the royalty, rule, and realm of heaven) and now, almost exclusively, our preaching is about the God/Man Jesus Christ and what He can do for the sinner (fill you with the Holy Ghost, forgive your sins, heal your body, give you power and bless you in all manner of ways). Preaching what the Kingdom offers may bring many people *to* the Kingdom of God, but it doesn't bring many *into* the Kingdom of God. In far too many cases it only brings those who want the goodies that the Kingdom of God offers and not the God of the Kingdom. Many times, we *preach* submission to the church (via its representatives) before we *teach* submission to God Himself.

Coming into the Kingdom of God is a death-assuring, self-defying act. It is a Kingdom that promotes selflessness and shuns selfishness. Let me give you an example of how selfish we humans really are. We cannot help it; we were born with the selfish bone and have become proficient in its use by the time we are two years old. We use it to our advantage at every opportunity. Imagine yourself as a nine-year-old orphan. You feel sad and lonely because you don't have what other children have; loving parents, a happy life, toys, food whenever you want it. One day, two couples come in and say they want to adopt you. Both tell you they will love you and care for you. During the interview period, you find out James and Cindy are hardworking farmers and can only offer you the basics of life such as food, shelter, clothing, and the occasional gift but they will love you tremendously. The other couple (John and Elizabeth) are very wealthy executives, who live in a mansion in the city, and they have promised to take you to Disneyland, buy you the latest toys and fashion clothing and you'll want for nothing. Which one would you choose? Remember, you're nine years old, and all you've known is loneliness and stuck in a rut at an orphanage. This inbuilt selfishness is what a biblical disciple faces every single day, and it is the responsibility of the more mature members of the Ecclesia to teach the younger believers how to overcome this carbuncle on the backside of humanity that needs to be excised from the church, by and through example in prayer, study, teaching, fasting, discipleship, and worship.

Just another doctrine.

There are millions of doctrines in the world all claiming to be the right one that leads to Nirvana, Jannah, Utopia, Heaven, Paradise, or the promised land. All the places that bring happiness and wealth. People are not lacking choices of doctrines (teachings) but are sorely lacking a viewable, touchable, and viable alternative to the kingdom of darkness known as this world's system. *Telling* someone of a way of getting out of their darkness by raising their hand if they want heaven (preaching/proclaiming our doctrine) but not *showing* them what the Kingdom of God actually looks like and how it works, is tantamount to telling a thirsty man in a desert what a cold glass of water looks and feels like, then explaining how refreshing it is, but not showing him (better yet, taking him by the hand) to where the supply is (hint: it's not in the pews in our church buildings) so that he can drink from the tap once or twice a week (**John 4:14**). It is not only about the water, but the kingdom where the water is. We rarely tell them of the cost of this water, which is obedience to the King's word, loving Him and one another, and sacrificing our own will for the King's inclination. Many would rather die of thirst than give up their lives.

How can these thirsty souls make an informed decision about how they must endure all kinds of hardship in order to remain in the Kingdom of God, if all they are told is all the goodies they will get in the Kingdom? *And whosoever doth not bear* (Bastazō- lift, endure, sustain, or receive) *his cross, and come after me, cannot be my disciple. For which of you, intending to build a tower, sitteth not down first, and* **counteth the cost***, whether he have sufficient to finish it?* (**Luke 14:27-28**) They must just blindly follow us to who knows where? (I know, I see the irony in that statement). How can we brag on a King or a Kingdom we only visit, have only read, or heard about once or twice a week?

Mark, the disciple, comes straight to the point by telling us what the most important thing an unbeliever needs to hear, *Now after that John was put in prison, Jesus came into Galilee, preaching* the **gospel of the kingdom of God***, And saying,* **The time is fulfilled, and the kingdom of God is at hand: repent ye, and believe the gospel** (Mark 1:14-15). He said nothing about salvation, forgiveness, mercy, grace, healing, deliverance, love, joy, peace in or receiving the Holy Ghost. The Lord's preaching and teaching were what the Kingdom of God is and how they are to conduct themselves if they were to be in this Kingdom. That was the purpose of the Sermon on the Mount. The *goodies* will come as a natural consequence of that conduct and submission to the King.

As mentioned earlier, the AENT, (the language spoken by Jesus and His disciples) beautifully translates the word *Gospel* as *Hope*. The true meaning of the *Gospel of the Kingdom of God* is therefore translated as the *Hope of the Kingdom of God.* This hope can be seen in our love for God and for one another, our care for one another, sacrificing one for another, forgiving one another as God has forgiven us, giving to one another and much more (see **Matthew 5-6** and **Luke 6** as examples). None of these are prevalent in this ever-darkening world. The Hope of the Kingdom of God is what we are to proclaim and when the world sees us living that hope, they will follow us following Him. We then move from preaching to teaching these followers by showing and sharing our lives (biblical discipleship) and how it works whilst dealing with the effects of sin in this world of darkness and degradation with the help of the Holy Ghost and wise elders.

I am reminded of a seminar I taught in Maryland back in 2015 to a group of church leaders (about thirty in total). The subject was on prayer and its purpose and how the early church understood it. I told the leaders near the end... *What good is preaching salvation if we have not the Kingdom of God with all the gifts and fruits of the spirit as well as the responsibilities of the saints operating within the people of God?* We would be likened to these young impressionable people who have been sold a false narrative that capitalism is evil, and socialism/communism is the answer to all the world's ills. All while they text each other on the $1000 iPhones made in Chinese sweatshops, wearing their $200 Nike shoes also made in Chines sweatshops, $150 ripped jeans and driving their car that burns gasoline to the save the planet protests, holding up signs made of cardboard and wood that say *protect the forest* while sipping their $5 lattes made from cows whose flatulence supposedly adds to greenhouse gases. I could not make it clearer how their hypocrisy stands out like a peacock's tail in a yard full of peahens. These people's lives undo all they are trying to say. In like manner, the church is as susceptible to the same hypocrisy when we preach a Kingdom only a few elite operate in.

Notice what the Master (our perfect example) did not preach? He did not tell people of all the rights and privileges someone gets in the Kingdom but the Kingdom (the royalty, rule, and realm) itself. The Master did not tell the people that when they become born-again, they would be forgiven, have joy, be healed, and delivered, have happy marriages and obedient children, nor that they would have plenty of money and always have jobs and customers for their businesses. On the contrary, He told us that we would be hated, reviled, persecuted, be hungry in spirit, live lives of meekness and sacrifice, that even our families would reject us, that if someone takes our shirt, we must give them our coat too and that we are to lend and not expect it back in return (**Matthew 6:34-35**). This is supposed to be 'good news?' It sounds more like slavery. Yes, yes it does. And now we are getting to what God called us to be. Slaves to righteousness (Dikaiosune- equal with God in character and actions). He told us our forgiveness was contingent on our forgiving others (**Luke 11:4**), that the mercy we daily receive is a result of the mercy we daily give to others (**Matthew 5:7**), and the right to ask for anything in His name is based Christ's works being done through us (**John 14:12-13**) and if we are not bearing some kind of fruit, we will be cut off and cast into the fire (**John 15:2**). These do not sound very pleasant, do they? Yet they are the things our Lord majored on.

Why did our Master call it the *"good news"*? Because those of this world are living as the walking dead and do not really know that there is another kingdom outside of this present world and that their kingdom will not last for eternity and will one day be destroyed. Oh, they've heard of some vague place people talk about on Sundays, but where is the evidence of it the other six days? They even have sayings for this place like, *'oh for heaven's sake'*, *'my grandma went to heaven'*, and songs are written about it like *'Knockin' on heaven's door'*, *'Stairway to heaven'*, and *'Pennies from heaven'*. And the opposite is also true with sayings things like, *'I'm going through hell this week'* or *'the devil is in the details'*, or *traffic was hell today"*, but it's all ethereal to them. They don't know because the prince of this world keeps the Kingdom of God ethereal and vague in their minds. They have nothing solid to compare it to. However, when they are told *and* shown the evidence (as mentioned earlier, speaking in tongues is not evidence of the Kingdom, just evidence that you have received His spirit), they will flock to us like ants to a picnic on a hot summer's day.

What is that evidence that we know what we're talking about? *A new commandment I give unto you, That ye love one another; as I have loved you, that ye also love one another. By this shall all men* **know** (Ginōskō- understand, perceive, are aware of and can speak to) *that ye are my disciples, if ye have love one to another* (John 13:34-35. See also **John 15:12,17, Romans 12:10,13:8, Galatian 5:13, Ephesians 4:2, 1 Peter 1:22**). It doesn't help the lost to argue about one God, baptism in Jesus' name or our doctrine, if we can't show them what the Kingdom looks like. Other denominations can argue their point of view quite successfully. I used to sell Kirby vacuum cleaners back in 1992-3 (back then the cheapest model was about $1500-2000) and if I didn't demonstrate it correctly, why would someone spend that kind of money on something that moves dirt from one place to another? I could extol its virtues all day long, but before someone hands out over $2000, they want to see how it works in their house. The sad part is that many come into our churches because we've convinced them to. We believe that because they come to our church services, that they will 'get saved'. Why? Well, because we have the right doctrine, right? The problem is that they see as much partisanship, grudges, the haves and have nots, the neglected in our pews, the selfishness, pride of the leadership and in the pews, lack of love for one another as well as the gossiping and back-biting amongst the so-called believers as they see in the world. Sadly, they walk away disappointed. Consequently, when someone does come along later and wants to share the real Kingdom of God, they have already shut down because of the bad taste they have from their previous experiences.

Our job is not to convince sinners our church/organization is the right one to get to heaven. Our sole job is to preach the Kingdom of God only (Kerusso- proclaim, publish, and herald as a town crier, this we do with our mouths and prove what we say by how we live), and if they are true seekers, He will draw them unto Himself (**John 6:44, 12:32**), not to our church or organization. When they ask, *'What shall we do?'*, we tell them the answer, and when they follow through, then, we personally teach them with our lives what living in the Kingdom of God looks like and how they can live it too. Until then, the lost are spectators of our lives. What we portray to the lost cannot be different to how we treat the brethren in our churches. I cannot say I love the lost but love my brother and sister less than I love God.

Millions are trying to convince people to go over to another way for salvation, but those don't exist. The Kingdom of God actually exist and only an active participating member of this Kingdom can show it. That's *'The Good News'*. We were meant to live in it here and now, not just prepare for the rapture by reading all the signs like a medium reads the tea leaves for omens. We say the Kingdom of God is at hand (nearby), but much of our lives are such that we live as though it is something that has yet to come. There is an alternative to living in the prince of darkness' world, however, words alone will rarely, if ever, suffice in convincing someone seeking an alternative. That is why Jesus said that signs and wonders would follow them that believe, not follow a believer to the signs and wonders. He did not say that we would use them to draw a crowd or that we should get people to come to our buildings where signs and wonders will hopefully happen leading to sinners becoming believers. This is putting the cart before the horse.

Paul tells us in **2 Corinthians 3:17** *Now the Lord is that Spirit: and where the Spirit of the Lord is, there is liberty,* yet we daily act that the spirit of the Lord is only in a building on certain days at certain times. If we claim to be filled with His spirit and baptized in His name, should not the spirit of the Lord be ever present with us and should not the supernatural (miraculous) be a natural part of our natural daily lives? It need not be miracles of supernatural healing or a financial blessing, it could be a sacrificial giving of helping another soul to walk closer to the Lord, or of helping a of a mind change from selfish sinner to selfless saint or enjoying the miracle of a new day. We live far below what God has called us to because we hear a short sermon from an individual on what God has done for us and what we can expect from Him in the future once or twice a week. How does any of this help a hurting soul? The answer is simple, it doesn't. Using our lives to teach one another is the biblical way of showing the Kingdom of God to the lost and those who seem lost in our pews.

Jesus did not advertise that people should come to Temple or the synagogue in the town where He was speaking to get their healing, deliverance, miracle, or if they wanted to know more about Jehovah. No! He took what they needed (the Kingdom of God) to where the sinners and ignorant people were, showed them the Kingdom of God, proved what He was saying is real with signs and wonders and the people chose whether they would follow Him or not.

Neither did Jesus come to pop up a tent and operate a side show where miracles are performed to gather a crowd so that he could set up His own group of people in a building somewhere. He did the miracles when He went about His normal daily life amongst the normal people, dealing with normal everyday problems but showing a paranormal (beyond the range of normal experience or scientific explanation) God. We spend too much time focusing on the extraordinary moments (thinking this is God) whilst we let the ordinary opportunities to love and service slip through our fingers. Remember Elijah and the earthquake, fire, and wind? God was not in any of these, but in the still, small voice (**1 Kings 19:11-13**).

Belief in God is not mere mental assent, singing songs about that belief, gathering with those with the same belief or even recruiting others to that belief. Mental Assent is a subtle form of self-deception, pride, and hypocrisy, and only one step removed from the demonic leaven (yeast) of idolatry. Mental assent is believing something in our mind, something we agree with, approve of, and confirm it is right, proper, and righteous. It rarely comes from our heart with actionable consequences (I'm not talking of our feelings). However, what we believe and hold in our hearts, is what we put into practice, *...for out of the heart proceed evil thoughts, murders, adulteries, fornications, thefts, false witness, blasphemies...* (**Matthew 5:19**). If the bad things proceed from the heart, so do the good things. Therefore, if we believe we are right and have no real need to go any deeper in God than what we know right now, our actions will prove our belief. Ipso facto, out of the righteous heart (Dikaiosune- being equal with God in character and action) comes forth pure thoughts, giving life, fidelity, purity, giving to others, truth, sacrificing for His disciples and glorifying God.

To believe in something is to act in a manner that displays that belief in every area of one's life. Someone who has mental assent with their political party, will place signs in their yard for their particular politician or party affiliate. One who truly believes in the cause of their party, will show that belief by giving of their time, talents and treasures actively promoting the political party/politician. They do not just put signs in their yards and register their names with their part. It is not just signs and wonders of healings and deliverances (a minor part of a believer's life) but also of lives that used to live for themselves in this world and now live for Christ and others in this world, for the Kingdom of God. Just because we go to a church building regularly, put money in the bag and sing God songs, does not mean we have been delivered from the scourge of selfishness.

This world is looking for a kingdom run by a benevolent King, who's people behave like their Sovereign toward one another and will not just live and die for their King but live and die for one another- the King's subjects. The Master's words ring ever so true today... *Greater love hath no man than this, that a man lay down his life for his friends. Ye are my friends,* **if ye do whatsoever I command** *you* (**John 15:13-14**). We can sing, *I am a friend of God,* but unless we are keeping His commands, we are hypocrites of the highest order and not His friends. Church, as we know it today in western society, rarely reaches those in the pews with this kind of living and dying for each other, let alone those in this ever-present world of darkness, those who live in our neighbourhood or go to our schools and businesses. What we do or do not do to, for and with one another we do or do not do to, for and with the Master (**Matthew 24:40**).

Chapter 3

Admit it, then change it.

Proverbs 14:15 *The simple* (Pethîy- seducible and foolish) *believeth every word: but the prudent man looketh well to his going* (KJV).

A simple man believes anything, a clever man ponders his course (The Jewish Study Bible).

One of the greatest killers of discipleship is not the attacks of the enemy. It is being distracted from doing the will of God daily.

Kieth Fansa. 2011, Charlottesville, North Carolina.

When we are told by people that we are right with God because we have kept a set of rules handed down by our church leaders (and we do so without first checking with God), we have become seducible and foolish. To properly and contextually search out what we are told does not mean that we walk around second guessing every move we make just in-case we have made a mistake. It means that we cannot rely solely on the word of *anybody*, no matter who they are or claim to be, their position in the church or how long they have been in the church. That judgement belongs wholly and solely to the Spirit of God, and His word will guide us into all truth as well as the paths of righteousness if we allow it (**John 16:13, Proverbs 2:20, Acts 2:28**). People may guide us, counsel us, make us aware, even help to correct us, but the truth is no man can put anyone in heaven or in the lake of fire. It is up to us to do something about what we have heard from the Spirit through the word of God. It is impossible to fix a problem we do not know or will not acknowledge we have. We cannot be saved until we admit we are lost and in need of a saviour, but even when we realize we need a saviour, unless we act, we cannot be saved. We do not just need a saviour, but a Lord, one who rules our lives. Just like any problem, it helps to break it down into manageable pieces and tackle each one separately and spend time reviewing where we have come from and where we desire to be.

Within the first section of this book, we will find four major problems within today's western style Ecclesia that conflict with and contradict the word of God. We will also find the remedy, which, if applied, will shine the light of God into this dark world. They are boiled down to:

1. Hierarchy of individualism.

2. Lack of commonality in passion and goods.

3. Christian individualism and it's destructiveness within the Commonwealth.

4. Lack of the fear of God.

These despicable viewpoints have manifested themselves in this modern-day expression of Christianity we euphemistically call *church*. The western church, over the last few decades, has fundamentally changed its DNA and consequently, its course as well as its ability to replicate its original purpose. When an altered DNA is introduced into the body it will replicate itself and eventually mutate into something other than what the original DNA was, which consequently changes its purpose. Thus, mutation will cause malfunction thereby reproducing greater mutations eventually leading to a different form of life. It has become blatantly and painfully obvious that today's Christian Ecclesia as a whole has lost its power to influencing the cities and towns they reside in. There certainly are pockets around the world where the Ecclesia still has some influence on the surrounding population (these are almost exclusively not in the West) however, they are in places where Christianity is at best barely tolerated, and at worst persecuted and has gone underground on pain of imprisonment or death. But this does not excuse most of the churches and their leaders, mainly in the affluent West, from having to face the fact that church as we know it, is no longer relevant to most of our communities. I reiterate, we cannot fix a problem we cannot see nor will admit we have. We also cannot blame the world for our failure to be the powerhouse we were called to be. Not the powerhouse that brings down governments, but the powerhouse to make biblical disciples and change lives. This is a tragedy.

Something must change and the answer is not more outreach programmes, bigger, more, or renovated buildings or platforms, it is not more Sunday school rooms, or more updated songs, licencing more preachers, better head office buildings, greater or more conferences, more buses, or greater missionary outputs, better choir robes, or (dare I say it) putting on more revivals and other extremely short-term man-made fixes. The answer lays first and foremost in the pews (where the real power is, for in them is, *the chosen generation, the royal priesthood, the holy nation, God's peculiar people; that we should shew forth the praises of him who hath called us out of darkness into his marvellous light* [paraphrased] **1 Peter 2:9**) as well as behind the pulpit (which is meant to be the example of how **1 Peter 2:9** is to be accomplished). It is when those behind the pulpits begin to disciple the bible way, that their influence will change what happens in the pews. However, this will only happen when those who sit in our pews demand more than the Fantastic Five and demand that the leadership actually lead by daily example, not by osmosis from behind a pulpit.

In Paul's letter to Timothy, we are told, *For the time will come when they will not endure sound doctrine* (teaching- note: it did not say sound preaching) *but after their own lusts* **shall they heap to themselves** *teachers, having itching ears; And they shall turn away their ears from the truth, and shall be turned unto* **fables** (2 Timothy 4:3-4). Notice. It was the people who heaped to themselves teachers who teach what they want to hear. This was not written about the world but the church. The law of supply and demand is in play here. If the people do not want to endure sound doctrine, they will heap to themselves (Episōreuō- seek out and accumulate) teachers (Didaskalos- masters, instructors) having itching (knēthō- to scratch their) ears and we all know how good it feels to scratch an itch. They would rather listen to fables (Muthos- from the idea of tuition [a sum of money paid for teaching or instruction], storytelling, fiction) than endure sound doctrine. By *endure sound teaching*, it does not just talk about the doctrine of salvation, whether God is one, whether holiness is right, to pay the tithe, obey the man of God or whether to be baptized in His name. It has to do with the doctrine (teaching) of the apostles, which is to teach what Jesus commanded (**Matthew 28:18-20**). We are to preach the gospel of the Kingdom of God but teach (Didaskō- doctrine) the commands of Christs (see **Galatians 6:8-9**, **Mark 11:1, Acts 5:28, 42, 1 Corinthians 4:17, 1 Timothy 4:10-11**).

If enough people sitting in the pews would make it known that they want more than just a sermon or two a week (mainly on the Fabulous five topics), more than just token visits from the leadership when there's a problem, more than programmes, more than just teaching of the same things from the same voice and hold the leadership accountable as to why people are not personally discipled, there would be a fundamental change from bottom to top.

The people require the whole doctrine of the Apostles, not just their preacher's favourite go-to scriptures which keeps them in a state of religious euphoria. Preaching mostly on The Fabulous Five will not suffice (*Acts 2:38, one God, holiness, tithing and obey the man of God*). They need teaching on things like how to endure and grow through afflictions instead of trying to constantly pray them away (see **Acts 4** for an example of how to pray during persecution), how to seek the will of God and hear from Him for themselves (**1 John 5:14-15**), or how to not think it strange that they have hardships (*Beloved, think it not strange concerning the fiery trial which is to try you, as though some strange thing happened unto you: But rejoice, inasmuch as ye are partakers of Christ's sufferings; that, when his glory shall be revealed, ye may be glad also with exceeding joy* (**1 Peter 4:12-13**). They need to know how and when to do the work of the ministry, (make full proof, show evidence of your life **2 Timothy 4:5**) for all the saints are meant to do this work (see **Ephesian 4:11-13**). There is a saying that fits this scenario rather aptly that goes: *Cometh the hour, cometh the man.* When people are only interested in hearing the same thing every month, that is what God will send them. Conversely, when the people want nothing but the word of God (all of it, not man's opinion or their organization's interpretation of the word of God or what has been rehashed in our bible schools), the Master will bring someone who will fulfil His will to help them grow past the current knowledge of the leadership and become who they are called to be and do the work of the ministry.

There is a common lie going around the Ecclesia that a saint cannot grow past their pastor's knowledge. Where is that in God's word? What if their pastor chooses to remain in the understanding God gave him 5 years ago and has not grown deeper, are the saints to suffer in ignorance because of him? Look at the life of Apollos in the book of Acts and First Corinthians for example.

The reason why the Joel Osteen's, the Creflo Dollar's, the Kenneth Copland's, the Joyce Meyers', and the Angela Whites are so popular in the West and shunned by the persecuted believers in other countries is because they know that their self-serving, self-aggrandizing, idolatrise and man-centred message doesn't work in the real Kingdom of God, the Kingdom where life and death are left in God's hands and people are dying for His word and Kingdom. Their message mainly resonates in the West because there are plenty of people willing to have their corrupted and perverted ears scratched with these messages. If the people paying money to hear these purveyors of perversion would walk out of these sideshows that pretend to be church, and seek the real word of God, not one that tells them they can have their *"best life now"*, or cry Jehovah Jireh while showing the preachers Rolls Royce or new house, or saying that God will supply all their needs while the preacher has no needs, they would experience (the overwhelming majority for the first time), the liberating power of having a relational walk with their Creator for a purpose higher than their bank account or real estate portfolio.

These purveyors of this putrid corruption who call themselves pastors, preachers and bishops would soon lose their followers because the people in the pews have become followers of Christ rather than putting their trust in the arm of flesh and become followers of their organization (see **Psalm 146:3, Jeremiah 17:5**). Paul warns us of these vile villains of half-truths and delusions in **2 Corinthians 11:13-15** *For such are false apostles, deceitful workers, **transforming themselves into the apostles of Christ**. And no marvel; for **Satan himself is transformed into an angel of light**. Therefore it is no great thing if **his ministers also be transformed as the ministers of righteousness**; whose end shall be according to their works.* These people make themselves something they are not. Real disciples will see through this fog and will use the wind of the Holy Ghost and the word of God to blow away the lies.

From this group of real biblical disciples, God will raise up elders who are fully aware of the dangers of a self-seeking gospel and would be more likely to see when the enemy would try to sneak his vile doctrine of selfishness back into the Ecclesia. It is easier to listen to a veteran who has fought many battles and carries many scars than to listen to a young pup who got all his learning from books or from sitting in pews listening to sermons but has no idea how to live the word in a practical way.

I've heard of young people going straight from bible school into some form of ministry (be it music, youth, or pastoral. They think that because they are in the music ministry that they do not have to disciple anyone. That's the pastor's job), yet they have not even discipled one soul. Disciple is who they are, discipleship is for all and sundry in the Ecclesia to do, *"their ministry"* is just their task in the Ecclesia. They don't know what it feels like to pour their lives into another soul, the tiredness, the misunderstandings, the pain when one of their disciples walks away from God. And now, they tell people to follow them?

The Ecclesia must radically and fundamentally erase the selfishness of the saints (this includes leadership for they are saints also) which pamper themselves in the belief that it's all about God blessing them and theirs, that spend precious resources on pimping the building (bigger or more is better), the inane idea of a personal saviour (the pup-tent Christian theology), and the ludicrous concept of the *'us four and no more'* mentality (only allowing people into our groups who believe exactly as we do. Sure, this lessens the chances of strife or contention; unfortunately, it also does not challenge anyone to think, change and grow. This is called living in a confirmation bias bubble, and God loves to burst them).

To achieve this type of fundamental change within the Ecclesia will require commitment of the highest order to something greater than ourselves, our families, our organizations, or our bank accounts. It will require that a man or woman lay down their life (and all their personal desires and aspirations) for *His* friends (**John 15:13**). C.S Lewis wrote in his book The Four Loves, *"Friendship... is born at the moment when one man says to another "What! You too? I thought that no one but myself..."* This will be the litmus test of the Ecclesia; nothing less is acceptable in His Kingdom. For the Commonwealth of the Kingdom to be successful here on earth, it must be embraced and taught by and to the common man or woman.

If all the wealth of knowledge, power and resources is held in the upper echelon of church or organizational hierarchy, it is more than likely that they have misappropriated the word Ecclesia and is a commonwealth in name only. The Master came to set mankind free from sin, not to create a group of religious elitists.

He's my personal Saviour. Wait, what!

To quote Frank Viola's book, *Pagan Christianity* (Tyndale House Publishers Inc. 2008), *"The phrase personal Saviour is yet another recent innovation that grew out of the ethos of nineteenth-century American revivalism. It originated in the mid-1800s to be exact. But it grew to popular parlance by Charles E Fuller (1887–1968). Fuller literally used the phrase thousands of times in his incredibly popular 'Old-Fashioned Revival Hour' radio program that aired from 1937 to 1968. His program reached from North America to every spot on the globe. At the time of his death, it was heard on more than 650 radio stations around the world."*

Viola goes on to say, "*This relationship* [between Jesus, the God/man who walked this earth and His followers- Author's notes;] *is corporate just as much as it is individual. All Christians share that relationship together. In this regard, the phrase 'personal Saviour' reinforces a highly individualistic Christianity. But the New Testament knows nothing of a "Just-me-and-Jesus" Christian faith. Instead, Christianity is intensely corporate. Christianity is a life lived out among a body of believers who know Christ together as Lord and Saviour.*"

The concept of humanity accepting Jesus is as absurd as threading a ship's anchor chain through a sewing needle. A.W. Tozer once said, '*And so, in this view, our poor Lord Christ stands hat-in-hand, shifting from one foot to another looking for a job, wondering whether He will be 'accepted'*, and again, Tozer says, '*The question ought not to be whether I will accept Him; the question ought to be whether He will accept me.*'

When one has done wrong, the offending party does not wait for the offended party to offer forgiveness. It is the guilty party that repents, shows real contrition with works, then it is up to the forgiving party to see if this contrition is true or just sorry the offender got caught. At this point, the offended party chooses to either reject or accept the offering of repentance of the offender. Both parties then deal with the consequences of the offense and or unforgiveness. Remember that unforgiveness and not restoring the relationship is just as offensive to God as the original offense (**Galatians 6:1-3**).

Jesus dispelled the notion of we mere humans receiving Jesus or choosing to accept Him in **John 14:3** *And if I go and prepare a place for you, I will come again, **and receive you unto myself***; *that where I am, there ye may be also.* He also clarified who chooses who. **John 15:16** the apostle writes **Ye have not chosen me, but I have chosen you**, *and ordained you* (Tithēmi- to place in a horizontal posture. This is the opposite of what we have come to believe 'ordained' means. Today we think it means to lift up into a high office), *that ye should go and bring forth fruit, and that your fruit should remain* (Menō - stay continue, abide, and endure)*: that whatsoever ye shall ask of the Father in my name, he may give it you.* As a side note, when we bring in fruit but cannot keep it, is it really bringing in fruit?

To choose something means that we are given two or more alternatives. I can choose between my eggs being over-medium, poached or scrambled and when I receive them at my table, I enjoy the choice I have made. There are many who claim to be the saviour of mankind, (government, cult leaders, World Economic Forum, and the U.N for example) but to claim Lordship is another thing all-together. To say we choose Jesus as our Lord implies that there are other Lords out there on offer (notice the capital L). During our lives, many things happen and present themselves as our saviour; for example, when I was on my way home from Brisbane Airport in May of 2010, I was involved in a multi-car pileup. I was trapped in my car for a fair while, there was petrol all around me, until the fire brigade came and cut me out using the jaws of life. So, in essence, the fire brigade was my saviour in that instance. Was I going to submit my life to the brave man that cut me out as my Lord? Of course not. We only submit to one Lord. It so happens that this one Lord is also our Saviour. In the world, we can have a saviour but not a lord, but in the spirit, we cannot have one without the other.

In the second reading of the law, God only gives two choices to His people. Moses says in **Deuteronomy 30:19-20** *I call heaven and earth to record this day against you, that I have set before you **life and death, blessing and cursing**: therefore choose life, that both thou and thy seed may live:* As we can see, we are to choose between life and death, but that is not where the story ends my friends. Nay, Nay, read on, for there is a purpose to our choice. It is so that ...*thou mayest love the LORD thy God, and that thou mayest obey his voice, and that thou mayest cleave unto him: for he is thy life, and the length of thy days*: (there is reward for doing these things) *that thou mayest dwell in the land which the LORD sware unto thy fathers, to Abraham, to Isaac, and to Jacob, to give them.* There is a purpose to every choice we make. We serve either by choice or by default. If we choose to serve God, then all else pales into insignificance. By rejecting service to God, we, by default serve ourselves which, by default, is service to the god of this world (**Joshua 24:14-15**). If Israel chose not to serve God, they would, by default, be serving ...*the gods which your fathers served that were on the other side of the flood...*

John Baptist took repentance (Metanoia- compunction for guilt, including reformation, a reversal of decision, the idea of thinking differently) so seriously that he sent the leadership of his day away until there was some kind of inward/outward change as a sign (fruit) that their repentance was real in order for their repentance to be accepted by God (we don't repent and accept God, we repent- to think differently or afterwards, that is, reconsider (morally to feel compunction- Metanoia, and if the heart has truly repented, then God excepts us). Going down in the waters of baptism (Mikvah) alone does not cleanse someone who is just sorry for their sins. We see this in **Matthew 3:5-7** *Then went out to him Jerusalem, and all Judaea, and all the region round about Jordan, And were baptized of him in Jordan, confessing their sins. But when he saw many of the Pharisees and Sadducees come to his baptism,* (now John calls out their hypocrisy) *he said unto them, **O generation of vipers, who hath warned you to flee from the wrath to come**?* These religious hypocrites could see the writing on the wall, people were starting to follow John Baptist instead of them. They felt something was happening and wanted to get in on it. John saw that the leadership were not repentant, just going through the motions of the Mikvah (the Jewish ritual of cleansing) to be a part of the crowd. It was here that John tells them there is something they must do in order to make their repentance acceptable unto God, *Bring forth fruits **meet*** (Axios- deserving, suitable even worthy) *for repentance* (**Matthew 3:8**). They didn't even know if John's baptism was of God or not (see **Matthew 21:24-27**).

The heavens will not be filled with those who never made mistakes but with those who recognized that they were off course and who corrected their ways to get back in the light of gospel truth.

Dieter F. Uchtdorf

I once was asked by a man what he would get when he got baptized. God showed me his heart and the purpose he wanted to get baptized. He asked me if he would he get health, happiness, righteousness, would he get into heaven or receive the power of God, would he get peace of mind and forgiveness? I told him he would get wet. That is all, no more, no less. He did not want to be a living example of Christ on this earth, he wanted to be healthy, have a good marriage and to stop feeling guilty for his sins and get on with his life. He did not want to follow Christ to the paradoxical life of death on the cross, to be His disciple, and be a part of a living body where change is mandatory to become like the Master (**Romans 8:29**). He just wanted relief from the suffering he was enduring through the normal trials of life and guilt for his sins.

Baptism is not a way of escape from hell, though it is an essential part of the salvation experience. It can be described as a mandatory death and a burial in order to begin the journey of becoming like the one who died for us. This is what eventually brings about the resurrection and newness of life, *Therefore we are **buried with him by baptism** into death: that like as Christ was **raised** up from the dead by the glory of the Father, even so we also should walk in newness of life* (**Romans 6:4**).

It is vital we understand why so many believers lead ineffective lives within the Ecclesia (church attendance, tithing and obedience to the man of God *alone* is not an effective life of a biblical disciple). It is because many have an erroneous view regarding salvation. So, I offer the reader this biblical definition: *Being born-again is the first step of the way of getting into God's presence. It is the initial experience required to becoming like the one whom heaven is fashioned after, therefore making us fit to be in His presence. Thus, we are eventually saved from the wrath which is prophesied in the word of God for all those who chose not to become like the God of heaven.* If being born again was all that was necessary to enter into His presence for eternity, then what do we do with, *But I **keep** under my body (my flesh), and bring it into subjection: lest that by any means, when I have preached to others, **I myself should be a castaway*** (Adokimos- unapproved, worthless, rejected, a reprobate. **1 Corinthians 9:27**). The Master Himself told us of the requirement to gain access into His eternal presence once we are born-again in **Matthew 10:22** *And ye shall be hated of all men for my name's sake: **but he that endureth to the end shall be saved***. The endurance aspect is the journey of denying our own flesh and submitting to His spirit and being hated of all men for doing so.

Being hated of all men, (the reason we are hated is *'for His name's sake'*, because we are becoming like our Master, not because we are behaving badly) is sometimes painful but always a necessary requirement for citizenship in the Commonwealth of the Kingdom of God. Acknowledging our utter dependence on Him (being poor in spirit **Matthew 5:3**), having a healthy fear of God (**Luke 23:40, Acts 13:16, Romans 3:9-12, Ephesians 5:21**) and repentance (**Acts 2:38, Matthew 9:13, Romans 2:4, 2 Corinthians 7:10**) is as essential as breathing. Even after a time of failure, repentance brings His mercies to bear anew every morning, as we are reminded by the Prophet Jeremiah in **Lamentations 3:22-23** *It is of the LORD'S mercies that we are not consumed, because his compassions fail not. They are new every morning: great is thy faithfulness.*

Now you are the body of Christ, and each of you is a member of it (**1 Corinthians 12:27**). Our true individuality is found only in relationship to Christ, but it is manifested through His body. An individual cell does not last long outside of the body (I am talking of the living body of Christ not one that is only manifested in church functions and meetings). For the single cell to remain alive and viable, it must remain connected to the entire body, for on its own it will die. If a rogue cell (such as a virus, a cell devoted only to its own survival) is introduced into the body, one of two things will happen. It will eventually be surrounded by healthy cells, and it will die or, as has been happening over the last few decades, it will infect the surrounding cells with what made it rogue. Every now and then, an extraordinarily strong cell that lives for itself will begin to destroy the other cells surrounding it causing cancerous cells to grow and destroy the whole body. Each cell must realize that though it is an individual cell, it cannot exist outside of its place in the entire body, nor can it do as it pleases within the body and expect to remain in the body for long. Just to clarify, I am speaking of the body worldwide, not an individual gathering of saints you happen to know which makes up the body worldwide.

Scientists have concluded that the average human body contains approximately 37.2 trillion cells. That's 37 with twelve zeros behind it. Allow me to give you a visualization of what that looks like. A bundle of US$100 notes is equivalent to US$10,000 and that can easily fit in your pocket. 1 million dollars will probably fit inside a standard shopping bag while a billion dollars would occupy a small room of your house. With this background in mind, 1 trillion (1,000,000,000,000) is 1000 times bigger than 1 billion and would therefore take up an entire football field (Courtesy of labnog.org). It would take a little more than thirty-two football fields worth $100 stacks to make up what you are made of. Consider this, the world's population in 2022 was 8 billion and each one has 37.2 trillion cells. That means that there were approximately 297.6,000,000,000,000,000,000,000 cells living on this planet in 2022. God placed each one in a particular body and that body was meant to love, honour, and serve Him. No wonder King David said, *I will praise thee; for I am fearfully and wonderfully made: marvellous are thy works; and that my soul knoweth right well* (**Psalm 139:14**).

Though each one of those cells has life in and of itself, we cannot take one cell out of its place, put it in a Petri dish and introduce it to the world as Mary or Bob. We can keep human cells alive outside the body for years if it is cryogenically frozen and stored properly. Allow me to put this in perspective. To freeze something cryogenically is to place it in a container at -238° Fahrenheit (-150° Celsius). These cells will remain in a state of dormancy and will eventually lose their viability to replicate and multiply. With each human intervention, outside of its normal pattern created by God in its DNA, the cells become less and less viable for modelling normal human tissue growth.

God's ways are simple. As a cell is born and with its DNA in-tact, it automatically finds its place within the body and fulfills its function (to help facilitate the growth of surrounding cells and pass on its genetic information to the next generation), when it dies, a new cell is created to replace it. A cell that is not fulfilling its purpose is called a *dormant* or *rogue cell* and nothing good comes from one of these. Dormancy is a stage where the cell ceases to divide and replicate itself. It survives in a quiescent or inactive state while waiting for appropriate environmental conditions to begin proliferation again. Quiescence is the state where cells are not dividing but at arrest in the cell cycle. The same applies to many church goers. They remain dormant during the week and go to church waiting for the right conditions to worship the Lord and give little to nothing to Him or the saints during the rest of the week. I am sure you can see where this would naturally lead in the body of Christ if allowed to continue.

As each person finds their God given place and begins to multiply and function within the body, then we can honestly say that we have a person functioning within a greater community of persons. If I take an individual cell out of my body and try to grow another me out of it, I will fail miserably.

Man has been trying to clone a human for decades and with each attempt we have only succeeded in making a distorted/mutant gene. Why are we messing with natures ways? Because we are not satisfied with the way God made things. In like manner, many churches constantly try out new ways of having, doing or growing the church with new programmes, ideas, gimmicks, and copying the ways of the world by operating our churches more like corporations or small businesses with boards and CEO's and annual general meetings. We use food banks, block parties, inviting evangelists to build up numbers (equivalent to a company hiring a motivational speaker to get the people motivated to believe and sell their product even more. I can attest to this because I have been an evangelist for over 30-years). We hold classes offering all manner of subjects (like anger management, alcohol/drug abuse etc), all in the name of getting people coming to the church building with the aim of growing it, but this has damaged the Ecclesia in far more ways than we can imagine. None of these tricks or 'secrets of church growth' methods beat getting a new believer involved in discipling others from the very beginning (sticking them in a so-called discipleship class that meets once a week for information impartation without someone for imitation has only a minimal effect on their growth. Some studies have shown that up to 80% of these new converts do not make it past eighteen months in this type of church) and as they find their place in God, not only will they allow God to deal with their issues with the help of older and wiser saints, but they will greatly enhance the entire body through their successes and failures.

The Ecclesia is a binary system composed of two main entities: the Creator and His creation. When either one tries to operate independently, the results are considerably less than optimal. For example, God can show His majesty and power in any form He chooses (angelic beings, the pillar of fire and smoke, earthquakes, wind, fire for example), yet He has chosen in this dispensation to show His love and power to the world via His Ecclesia. On the other hand, the Ecclesia cannot operate as purposed without the spirit and power of God flowing through it and manifesting His love to its members, thereby, showing the world who He is. This then, becomes a symbiotic or binary relationship. Symbiosis (a phrase first coined by German mycologist (the study of fungi) Heinrich Anton de Bary in 1879) comes from the Greek word *syn* meaning *with* and *biosis* meaning *living*.

For example: Coral Clownfish secrete a substance that protects them against the sting of sea anemones (their habitats). They can pass through the anemone tentacles harmlessly, this keeps them safe from predators, and the clownfish attracts other fish which the anemones then catch and eat. Another example of symbiosis is the crocodiles on the Nile in Egypt. They replace their teeth sometimes 2-3 times a year and when food gets caught in their teeth it causes serious infections. Enter the Egyptian Nile Plover, which loves to eat the decaying food found in the crocodile's mouth. The crocodile opens its mouth and allows the Plover to feast on the decaying food with no fear of the obviously larger and predatory animal eating it. These two animals need each other to survive. They work in synergy to help each other to not only survive but thrive. To do the job that the Ecclesia was created to do, we must be in the will of God displaying His presence and power. That is why the Master said we need both spirit and truth in order to be a worshipper of God (**John 4:24**). But who's spirit and who's truth? The spirit of God and the truth of the entire word of God, not just the Fabulous Five.

We use external means (so-called 'necessities', such as coloured lighting in the background of our stages/platforms, soundboards, and video screens to bring an atmosphere of worship and prepare to hear the word) thinking this will somehow help us to draw closer to the presence of God in the service, or draw God into our buildings, but actually, it diminishes His presence. All it does is pamper the hearers of the word into a false sense of peace and security. For example, if the people see the word on a screen, there is no need to bring a bible, if they don't handle the bible in church, you can bet your bottom dollar, the vast majority are not handling it at home either. These so-called necessities take away from the fact that just our love and worship of Him and our passion to be like Him and helping one another in like manner will draw the presence of God. We have made convenience into an idol, and we are paying the price for it today. I fully believe comfort and convenience have made much of the church into an idolatrise entity because that is what it is seeking in the name of God. We place comfort and convenience before worship and discipleship.

This is like trying to catch shrimp, just so we can use it as bait to get the bigger fish to use as bait, to catch a bigger fish ad nauseum. We seem to have convinced ourselves into thinking that the use of these "things" will somehow entice the people in our buildings to worship or grow more and the more they grow and the bigger the crowd, the more it pleases God, then the more God is pleased, the more the people will get their healing, miracle, blessing etc. Instead of multiplying that very presence to every member of the body during the week via fellowship, discipling, and personal teaching outside of church functions, we now focus on other things (like keeping the so-called *'necessities'* going). We have become a generation of easy seekers, in other words, *'let's make it easier to come to church and hear the word'* or as I have seen lately, *"Let us create a generation of Christian Consumers"*. What type of people are we helping to create in our churches?

Both *Easy Believism* and *Christian individualism* are the act of making it easy to become believers whilst still living for one's own self-interests, have no place within God's Ecclesia, yet they both thrives in man's ecclesia. Yes, we are individuals with our own personalities, quirks, and characteristics, faults, failings, foibles, and victories, but God uses all of these to benefit the entire body of Christ. We are what we are as a result of all the things that have happened to us, whether it was by our doing or not, for a much higher purpose than just *"getting to heaven"* or *"getting our blessings"*. God uses our uniqueness to benefit and further the Ecclesia, not the Ecclesia to further our uniqueness.

Paul writes of different body parts and the essentiality of each part in **1 Corinthians 12:14-16** *For the body does not consist of one part, but of many. If the foot should say, "Because I am not a hand, I do not belong to the body," that would not make it any less a part of the body. If the ear should say, "Because I am not an eye, I do not belong to the body," that would not make it any less a part of the body....* (Berean Study Bible). Each member, though independent, cannot **operate** independently, but rather is **interdependent** and must operate within the whole body. Those who seek fulfillment without seeking the Kingdom of God and where God wants them (not where man has decided or ordained) only find frustration and unfulfillment. Self-dependence within the Ecclesia is a hindrance to its growth just as it would be in a four-man relay race. Each must run their best but only so they can pass the baton to their teammates. When the rewards for running the race are handed out, the entire team is on the podium, not just the one who carried the baton across the finish line.

Chapter 4

Hierarchy of individualism

Everything you know now, you did not know 5, 10, 15 years ago. Everything you know now is not all you will know 5, 10, 15 years from now. Spiritual maturity looks to dig deeper wells, where the water is fresher and purer, but this takes hard work and commitment.

The first step to addressing the problems within the Commonwealth of the Kingdom of God here on earth (the Ecclesia), is to accept responsibility for our lukewarm, lazy, and selfish ways (wanting what we want, when we want it, letting someone else carry the burden of ministering to one another). We have put all our problem solving and teaching onto a separated and, in many but not all cases, a hired/paid clergy and their appointees (many are volunteers) and thus we have created a hierarchical society and a class-based power system which the bible does not condone (in fact it utterly repudiates it). We have done this for three main reasons.

1. Any group (whether religious or secular, governmental, or corporate) with a problem will find those that can solve the problem (see **Acts 6:1-6**). The unintended consequence arises when these people stay there and no longer remain an intimate part of the body collective. There is now a permanent separation within the main group, a bureaucracy if you will, which now consumes vital resources to maintain it, because of or in case the problems arise again (mainly because bureaucracy mostly deals with symptoms, rarely with the root causes). In many instances the problem that is fixed is immediately replaced with another problem. If the problems and the leadership are the same year in year out, the problem is the leadership.
2. This bureaucracy has now created a lazy sub-section within the body who now believe that if they give their money/resources to the church or organization, government, or corporation it releases them from the personal obligation of caring for and sacrificing one for another. This also creates a dangerous and prideful sub-section of people who now believe and act as if everything they say is unquestionable truth. At this point threats or intimidation are used (if someone does dare to question their motive or means) to maintain the status quo of superiority and decision-making power over the lazy subsection.
3. When only a few people try to do the work meant for the whole, both the doer and the receiver suffer lack. The responsibility for the well-being of the Ecclesia is and was always meant to be spread across and throughout the entire Ecclesia, with the help of wise elders, via personal and corporate discipleship. In so doing, we have a correctly functioning body which God can use to fulfil His purpose. This is called *Body Ministry,* and this is how it was done in the first two and a half centuries until the advent of *'professionally trained ministers'* introduced by Emperor Constantine I, the human originator of the Roman Catholic church. Body ministry is a phrase that many institutional leaders balk at, mainly because it is the Spirit of God that operates in the body and control is wrested from the ministry. They are still to be overseers but not to control.

A business theory, ironically called, *The Peter Principle,* has permeated the Ecclesia of today. It states that, *a hierarchy is where every person rises to their level of incompetency and then remains there. An employee is promoted based on their talents or success in previous jobs until they reach a level at which they are no longer competent. As skills in one job do not necessarily translate to another, and situations often change rapidly, they remain where they are and have now become incompetent.* The leader is expected to know everything about everything and eventually this puts undue pressure on any leader, consequently they become proficient in some things while becoming dangerously ineffective or incompetent in others. The spirit of God can do amazing things, but He requires us to admit that we are not the be all and end all. The *Peter Principal* stifles growth in the group because it does not allow for corporate input. Many church leaders do not believe that God talks to anyone but the leadership, so corporate input has not value. According to God's word, all those within the Ecclesia who have submitted to the leading of the Holy Ghost and God's word, have a voice and God uses corporate input as a buffer against pride or arrogancy.

A *Peter Principle* in action. A brilliant computer programmer writes the perfect code to solve a long-standing problem. They spend their days, weeks and even months coding with amazing efficiency and prowess. After a couple of years, they are promoted to lead programmer, and then promoted to team manager. They may have no interest in managing other programmers, but it is the reward for their competence. There they remain, having risen to a level of competency and staying there. Sadly now, their technical skills lie dormant while they fill their days with staff meetings, department strategy and planning meetings, budgets, and reports. This brilliant programmer is no longer utilizing their skills, neither are they getting and sharing ideas from and with other programmers, thus dis-allowing personal growth. Because of the speed with which technology changes and due to a lack of hands-on work in coding, they now become incompetent in what they were once great at. They are still stuck on how they did things when they first became a manager and are now in a cocoon with no way to extricate themselves.

Changing the setting does not change the problem. Translating this to church settings we find that there is a person who could sort out issues in a church and they are voted in to do the job (whether that is preaching, administration, so-called evangelism, or a myriad of *'ministries'* we have dreamt up). They can pray, plan and they can do. Great, just what the church needs, right? Well, yes and no. If we take away the necessity for the whole church to pray, plan and do what they must do, then people being people, now have an excuse not to pray, plan and do. The leader is now out of touch with what's happening because they no longer have much time to do things with the regular folks in the pew other than church functions or when there's a problem. They must now spend inordinate amounts of time, energy, and money trying to coax the people into doing what should have been done in the beginning by everyone. The few are struggling to do what the many were created to do. And then we wonder why our churches are not growing and being as productive as we desire.

Biblical leadership has been around since God first told Eve that Adam would rule over her after the fall (**Genesis 3:16**). Eve was created equal in the eyes of God, as a help meet. Adam was not to tend the Garden while Eve made lunch. They were to work the garden together, not as a worker and a foreman. God told Adam what He wanted and Adam past on *ALL* the information to Eve (he did not give her snippets once or twice a week) and together they were to live **for** God **with** each other filling the earth with more images of God. Leadership has been put in place by God within the Ecclesia to show by example how to be and make more images of God (disciples). Nothing more, nothing less. A true leader has the ability to see a problem from a different perspective than the majority, then organize the resources (people, time, and material) at hand to implement the solution. This does not elevate the leader above any other member of the body nor are they to be revered or cared for above other members of the body (there is a huge difference between honouring and pampering leadership). When an elected leader is not in constant contact with those they lead (all, not just the leadership team), they are not a biblical leader, no matter how many pieces of paper they have on their wall. They are an administrator. That is, in fact, one of the gifts of the spirit. Governance- Kubernēsis- Kubernaō- to guide or administer to the needs (**1 Corinthians 12:28**).

We are to honour those that sacrifice their time, treasure, and labour among us (whether in some form of elected/appointed leadership role or not), but honour does not equate to elevation, receiving gifts and power (see who really gets the honour in the Ecclesia in **1 Corinthians 12:23**). In **Matthew 7:28-29** we read about biblical authority, *And it came to pass, when Jesus had ended these sayings, the people were astonished at his doctrine* (Didachē- instructions)*: For he taught them as one having* **authority** (Exousia- in the sense of ability, that is, (subjectively) force, capacity, competency, freedom, or objectively- mastery), *and not as the scribes* (Grammateus- professionals, highly educated). Please note what astonished the people. It was His ability to instruct with authority, not to preach, rule or administer with authority.

The Ecclesia is a finely tuned mechanism in the hands of God and relying on one or two nuts to hold it all together shows a design fault. The enemy cannot take down an Ecclesia in any area if all are functioning in their God-given roles. In almost every church today, if the leadership were to be taken out, fall into some kind of sin or die, the church would either close down or function considerably less until they bring in someone from the outside to fulfil the *'role'* of pastor/bishop. If everyone were contributing to the Ecclesia as God intended in His word, God would have someone who already is a part of the lives of the people to step in, and life/growth would continue unabated. That way, the Ecclesia would be a part of the solution for that community and not seek a solution from outside. Sadly, today if the leadership is gone, the vast majority would have no idea how to feed themselves the word nor how to hear from God directly.

The overwhelming majority do not know how to love one another as Christ loves us and give ourselves for the body as Christ gave Himself. The congregation is told weekly, but precious few congregations have someone who will sacrifice their time talents and treasures to daily show them how to do what they have heard for many years. Why? Because we have groomed the body into believing that the pastor is to do this for them, after all, that's his job, that's why he studies and shows himself approved and that's why he is paid, right? The body relies on one person to do all the work. The dangerous thing here is that the enemy can take out one man or a small cadre of leadership much easier than if the whole body were doing the whole job of the Ecclesia. Sadly, much of the Ecclesia is unaware or remains deceived into thinking that church planting and growth is the purpose of its existence. Biblically though, it only has two directives, 1/ Preach the Kingdom of God only. 2/ Teaching all things Christ commanded via personal and corporate discipleship (**Mark 16:15, Matthew 28:18-20, Acts 2:42**). Starting other gatherings and growth is a tertiary and organic outcome of doing the first two things.

As mentioned earlier, if the leadership of a group are constantly having the same problems every year, then the main problem is not with the group but with individualistic leadership. Not everyone can solve every problem, that is why the early believers had a group of elders to maintain the Ecclesia in a city (not on a block in the city) and the elders would then fellowship with the gatherings (Ecclesia) and disciple those with the passion to solve particular problems in God's Spirit, while not neglecting the others in the gathering. The skills to maintaining the Ecclesia are right under our noses. For example, **Acts 6:3** *Wherefore, brethren,* **look ye out among you** (Episkeptomai Ex Humōn- go to and see from amongst your own selves, in order to relieve) *seven men of honest report, full of* *the Holy Ghost and wisdom, whom we may appoint* (designate or conduct, nothing about elections or ordaining) *over this business*. Remember, almost all there were new believers and Peter said the answer was amongst them. What?!?!? New believers doing God's work? What a novel idea. The disciples didn't advertise outside of the group for people with the skills to do a task, the skills were within the group, they only needed to look for those *of honest report, full of the Holy Ghost and wisdom*. Not those who had the right organizational affiliation, degree, or pedigree. The wisdom of the collective that loved and honoured God and each other was utilized by God to solve many problems by many people which also lessened the chances of pride or arrogance in the leadership.

The elders were to serve in any capacity the Ecclesia needed, whether that was to teach, visit, admonish, pray, serve, and lay down their lives for the great Shepherd's flock. They were to be an example of what being a son/daughter and servant of the Most-High entailed. This is why James writes, *Is any sick* (Astheneō- to be feeble (in any sense) be diseased, impotent folk [lacking power], weak) *among you? let him **call for the elders** of the church; and let them pray over him, anointing him with oil in the name of the Lord:* (**James 5:14**). Why call the elders and not the pastor or bishop? Because at the time of James' writing (the Book of James is probably the oldest book of the New Testament, written perhaps as early as A.D. 45, before the first council of Jerusalem in A.D. 50), this was still a fairly new work and thousands of converts had entered the Ecclesia, some Jews, some Gentiles, and the elders were the ones who had the most experience in obeying the Lord and serving the saints by discipling them. Our understanding of modern-day pastors did not arrive on the scene until well into the third century. Shepherds (Poimēn- pastors) did not have a high position in the church until Emperor Constantine 1, (the human instigator of the Roman Catholic church) returned to the priesthood of the Old Covenant for a template and began using pagan priests who had become born-again and appointed these priests in the church (they were not called pastors until after Martin Luther's split from the Roman Catholic church). Martin Luther changed the title to differentiate his movement from the Roman Catholic, but unfortunately, he kept the same format as the Roman Catholic church, which we have kept to this day.

The more, the merrier.

The multitude of elders to the Ecclesia, must be a sort of God with skin on, not they are to walk around and behave as mini gods whose word must be obeyed or there will be hell to pay, but they are to exhibit the righteousness of God to those in their care. They are to teach us how to represent God here on earth, the sole reason for our existence. The elders should be *a chip off the ol' block* so to speak. The task of representing God here on earth is given to all spirit filled believers within the Ecclesia, it is just that the elders have been displaying it longer and have more wisdom because they have been hearing from the spirit of God longer (or should be) and have learnt how to deny their own selfish desires (flesh) for longer. However, this does not separate nor elevate them, it does not give them special privileges, or supreme power over the people, just more responsibility. An elder's function/task is to teach people in such a manner that those in their care will be able to move on and begin teaching others. In other words, it is given to the leadership to pass on to others those same skills and to teach others how to hear from and through the word and spirit of God for themselves so that they may perpetuate that same growth of God's Kingdom here on earth.

However, in far too many instances this wisdom has been withheld and reserved for an elite group within the church and spoon fed (in short 35–45-minute bursts of frenzied information impartation) to a congregation two to three times a week with just enough spirituality to satisfy them for another week but not enough to change them so they no longer require spoon feeding. The very things every disciple needs to grow closer to God are in the hands of a few individuals in a hierarchy. Is this really how God wanted His Ecclesia to operate? Did Christ not rebuke the scribes, Pharisees, lawyers, and chief priests for doing the same thing? Keeping the meat of the word for themselves and having perks (seats in the upper rooms, big robes, and chief seats in the synagogues/church, wanting to be called rabbi/pastor etc. **Matthew 23:4-7**).

Within the Commonwealth of the Kingdom of God, the opposite is true. As much information and inspiration with someone for imitation as possible, is given to the Ecclesia as quickly as possible so that all may fulfil their calling with as little supervision as possible. The early Ecclesia did not meet weekly as we do today (we only do this because it is convenient), but daily from household to household, teaching the apostles doctrine (those things which Christ commanded, **Acts 2:42-46, Matthew 28:18-20**). Even after Paul's third missionary journey, almost 20-years after his conversion, he writes, *And **how I kept back nothing that was profitable unto you*** (he gave everything to them, so he could move on to others), ***but have shewed you*** (not preached to you), ***and have taught*** (Didaskō- cause to learn- not preached) ***you publickly*** (Dēmos- as bound together socially, [not hidden from view until certain days]), ***and from house to house*** (Kata Oikos- family to family, household to household), *testifying both to the Jews, and also to the Greeks, repentance toward God, and faith toward our Lord Jesus Christ* (**Acts 20:20-21**).

We can see that Paul believed in empowering whole families (the essence or building blocks of the Ecclesia) to performing the works of the ministry still from house to house. Paul tells us, *I beseech you, brethren, (ye know the house of Stephanas, that it is the firstfruits of Achaia, and that they have addicted themselves to the ministry of the saints,) That ye submit yourselves unto such, and to every one that helpeth with us, and laboureth* (**1 Corinthians 16:15-16**).

We all have a responsibility to teach one another how to love, give, share, pray, worship, sing, study, pay bills, cook healthy meals, visit the infirmed, raise children, help the homeless, the elderly, the widows and the orphans and be involved in the broader community in a godly way. Since our society has left the principles of the village caring for the village (biblically described as body ministry within the Ecclesia), we also have left the very principles of showing young couples how to raise children in the natural as well as things pertaining to the Kingdom of God, helping the elderly in times of need, and visiting with them even when there isn't a need), sacrificing our time visiting the infirmed and most of all teaching the younger saints how to hear from God (not just so they can feed themselves but feed one another. This is more important and infinitely more beneficial to the Commonwealth of the Kingdom of God than any 35–45-minute sermon once or twice a week (see **Colossians 3:16** for an example of the elder teaching the younger). We have come to rely on the voice of an individual or an oligarchy (a small group of people having control of a country, organization, or institution) to do that which the village (Ecclesia) ought to do.

Discipleship is not something someone does on their own if they have spare time. The enemy will make sure we have no spare time. He will keep us busy, doing things of very little value to the Kingdom of God, that we will miss God's opportunities daily. We are to make as much time as possible and necessary (not as convenient) to strengthen the entire body daily. Biblical disciples sacrifice some things to make time, not complain because they can't find time. Every member of the Ecclesia is tasked with being hands on involved in building the Ecclesia from within and as a natural consequence, souls will be added daily to the church by God as the lost seek Him and see Him in us and He draws them, not through any man-made structures, contrivances, or programmes, but because God has a body of disciples He can trust to care for the newborn babes in Christ (see **Acts 2:47**).

Jesus said of people who believed in him, "*You are truly my disciples **if** you remain faithful to my teachings* (**John 8:31** NLT). Did Jesus teach much on how to be saved (He only mentioned being born again to one man in one instance), or did He teach on how to have a happier life, how to have a better marriage, have more money, on being too blessed to be stressed, or on the blessing of getting things? No, He taught them how to follow Him to the cross of self-denial and beyond. He explained the importance of how to take a slap and be hated, how to go the extra mile, how to react after we've been ostracized. He taught that when we are reviled, we are not to revile back, that laying up treasures (things) here on earth is the height of folly and that being poor in spirit is actually a great thing. He taught on giving out of sacrifice directly to those in need and of sorting out problems between brothers (see **Matthew 5:24**). He taught that submission to the Father was to be given far beyond submission to men (Peter and John and all the apostles understood this concept in **Acts 5:29** *Then Peter and the other apostles answered and said, **We ought** to obey God rather than men*. The phrase- **We ought**, is the Greek word Dei, and it means needful, binding, necessary, must, it behoves us). Christ gave instruction on how, why and to whom to pray. He allowed room for mistakes and proper correction and told us how many times we are to forgive as well as what to look forward to when troubling times come. Does any of this have anything to do with individual "*blessings*" here on earth? The Lord **preached** about the Kingdom of God, but He **taught** on what God expects from and for His people **in** His Kingdom. These are just a few of the things the Ecclesia is to teach the younger saints (not necessarily in age).

Pauls letter to Titus exemplifies passing on knowledge and leadership skills to one another. *The aged women* (Presbutis- [where we get the word presbyter from], this is not instructions for someone in an office but instructions for the older person, whether male or female, to teach the younger) *likewise, that they be in behaviour as becometh holiness* (Hieroprepēs- meaning reverent: this word has nothing to do with wardrobe or a list of dos and don'ts), *not false accusers* (slanderers, backbiters), *not given to much wine, teachers of good things* (Kalodidaskalos- to teach the right way to live, not just the spiritual); *That they may teach the young women to be sober, to love their husbands* (Philandros- affectionate as a wife, this helps the husband tremendously and helps bond him to the wife), *to love their children* (Philoteknos- to be maternal), *to be discreet* (Sōphrōn- self-controlled), *chaste* (Hagnos- clean in body and mind, modest), *keepers at home* (Oikouros- domestically inclined, good housekeeper), *good* (beneficial), *obedient to their own husbands, that the word* (Logos- that which is the divine expression) *of God be not blasphemed* (Blasphēmeō- spoken impiously, defamed). Please note, all of the above are things concerning the natural as well as spiritual.

Paul moves on to the men, *Young men likewise exhort* (Parakaleō- invite or invoke) *to be sober minded* (Sōphroneō- moderate of opinion and passion, self-controlled). *In all things **shewing** thyself* (Parechō- furnishing occasion or **exhibiting**, [not preaching]) *a **pattern of good works*** (Tupos Kalos Ergon- stamp or scar, statue, **model for imitation**): *in doctrine **shewing** uncorruptness, gravity, sincerity, sound speech, that cannot be condemned* (we cannot effectively **preach** these principle); *that he that is of the contrary part may be ashamed, having no evil thing to say of you* (**Titus 2:3-8**). There is more but you get the idea. How can one be a **model for imitation** if one is only seen for a couple of hours a week? The above is the perfect definition of biblically discipling someone. How does a single person (pastor/bishop) do all of these things to all the people? The answer is simple, HE CAN'T AND HE DOESN'T.

Wisdom in leadership is to be passed from one to another personally and impartially, not withheld for a moment behind a pulpit or for those who seem to have a talent to lead. There are many people who are content to just sit in the pews and be a spectator. The unfortunate part is that much of the leadership preaches to these masses while those with a passion to grow, must be spoon-fed pablum (a trite, insipid, or simplistic writing, speech, or conceptualization. A form of cereal for infants. A diet that does not require chewing) with those not interested in much growth. This invariably creates a church of milquetoast believers (very timid, unassertive, spineless person, especially one who is easily dominated or intimidated). These types of churches are filled with constantly sick people, always in need of another miracle or blessing to get them through to the next meeting. They are not ground-breakers or territory-takers, they do not know how to pray for one another nor know how to give the scriptures to others outside of the Fabulous Five. Why? Because the leadership does it all. They do not understand the commands of God past the Fabulous Five and are constantly in need of diaper changes even after many years. They do not have the skills to maintain their own growth neither do they take any responsibility for their own growth or that of others. They are a group of individuals who gather for their own purposes. This is not the Ecclesia Christ left almost 2000 years ago.

The main reasons these skills have not been passed on is either that this has not been exampled to the leadership or that the leadership wishes to remain aloof, fearing a loss of power, honour, or privilege. They erroneously believe that familiarity breeds contempt. So how did Christ disciple His followers? Was Christ aloof, did they need to make an appointment to see Him? That is our example. Christ was only ever aloof to the leadership of the day. The mark of a good leader/discipler is that they will work themselves out of a job as quickly as possible and move on to the next person or group that needs to grow in Christ. We fight like two little children over a lollipop to hold on to people to make them stay where they are when they could be more useful elsewhere once discipled the bible way. Somehow, we have come to believe that if we start in or with a group, we must be with that group until we die or unless we *pass on the mantle* and send someone out into the field. Where is that in God's word? If we don't promote growth for eventual leaving of the nest, we are even going against nature itself. If we are trained to live as and for community, this strengthens the whole body for ministry work no matter where or how God calls a saint.

Chapter 5

Commonality in Passion and Goods.

Acts 2:44 *And all that believed were together, and **had all things common**; And sold their possessions and goods, and parted them to all men, as every man had need.*

Acts 4:32 *And the multitude of them that believed were of one heart and of one soul: neither said any of them that ought of the things which he possessed was his own; but **they had all things common.***

To the saints in the church in western society, the above verses are amongst the scariest in the bible, right up there with, *...depart from me, I never knew you...,* and when God told the priests, *Behold, I will corrupt your seed, and spread dung upon your faces, even the dung of your solemn feasts; and one shall take you away with it* (**Matthew 7:23, Malachi 2:3**).

The story of the rich young ruler would have been told to the new disciples on a regular basis and these new saints of God obviously took the story to heart and made sure they would not walk away sorrowful as did this young man. We read in **Matthew 19:21** *Jesus said unto him, **If thou wilt be perfect** (Teleios- complete of labour, growth, mental and moral character), go and sell that thou hast, and give (Didōmi- to put in the palm of the hand) to the poor, and thou shalt have treasure in heaven: and come and follow me.* Jesus said that if we wanted to be perfect (Teleios- complete in labour, growth, mental and moral character), we would do well to do what He commanded of this man.

In **Exodus 4:29** we read, *And Moses and Aaron went and gathered together* ('âsaph- gather for any purpose) *all the elders of the children of Israel.* God didn't just gather the children of Israel for the sake of gathering. There was a specific purpose for the gathering. This is taken up in **Acts 20:7-8** *And upon the first day of the week, when **the disciples came together to break bread** (Sunagō- lead together, that is, collect or convene, specifically to entertain as in hospitably, accompany, assemble themselves together, to bestow upon one another, to gather to eat), Paul **preached** (Dialegomai- had dialogue, discourse, questions and answers, discuss in argument or exhortation [this was not preaching like we know it in church, it was dialogue between ALL there. Free and open exchange of spoken words between two or more people]) unto them, ready to depart on the morrow; and continued his speech (Logos) until midnight. And there were many lights in the upper chamber, where they were gathered together.* They gathered for more than to hear the word of God, but to discuss it, to learn from others, and doing it around the enjoyable past-time of food. We have somehow misunderstood what it means to be *together*. It is a combination of two Greek words- Epi Autos- superimposition (of time, place, order, etc.), as a relation of distribution over, upon and towards them or those. They gathered (Ecclesia) together for distribution (hospitality, giving one to another of their talents, resources, time, and wisdom) which was common to all.

We cannot follow Christ if we store up treasures on earth where moth corrupts and thieves can steal (**Luke 12:33**), but by going, selling, and giving, we can transfer our earthly treasures into heavenly treasure where neither Satan nor man can steal nor corrupt (**Matthew 6:20, John 10:10**), then we will have the capacity to take up our cross and follow the Master. We cannot carry our treasures and the cross at the same time.

This is just another reason the church has diminished in much of its impact in our communities today. Over time, it has neglected its obligation in the commonality in passionately giving knowledge and goods, and doing it in love one toward one another. Giving has become like *'once I give of my tithes and offerings, I can do what I wish with the rest'*. We seem to have lost the concept of one accord, (Humothumadon- being one in heart, mind, passion, and goods), in the 21st century western church. We see this important aspect of the Ecclesia in action at its very inception at the first Pentecost post resurrection in **Acts 2:44-45**. This is where the Commonwealth of the Kingdom here on earth truly shines to the world as Paul wrote to the Corinthians, *Being enriched in everything to all bountifulness, which causeth* (flows) *through us thanksgiving to God*. **For the administration** (Diakonia- from Diakonos- to run errands, an attendant, (generally) a waiter (at table or in other menial duties); specifically a Christian teacher and pastor) **of this service** (Leitourgeō- to be a public servant, to perform religious or charitable functions (worship, obey, to relieve, to minister) **not only supplieth the want** (Husterēma- deficit, poverty, that which is lacking) **of the saints**, *but is abundant also by many thanksgivings unto God*. (**2 Corinthians 9:11-12**). Is Paul talking of the leadership or the whole body?

Paul writes, *And don't forget to do good and to share with those in need*. **These are the sacrifices that please God** (**Hebrews 13:16** NLT) and in **Romans 12:13** he tells us that we are to give via, **distributing to the necessity of saints**; *given to hospitality*. This is not speaking of impersonal giving through a church or organization, this is specifically speaking of giving directly to those in need. How can one have hospitality to a building or an organization? Solomon tells us that, *He that hath a bountiful eye* (generous in giving) *shall be blessed; for he giveth of his bread to the poor* (**Proverbs 22:9**). It is not only faith that pleases God, but also sacrificial giving to those in need that pleases Him. Let us be brutally honest, is this even an option in most of our churches or organizations today? In some Apostolic/Pentecostal organizations, you are forbidden, or strongly advised not to safely send funds directly to a missionary in another country, it must go through their head office first. I know they have their reasons, but doesn't this make the giving quite impersonal? This takes away from each believer to obey God and put man's traditions (everything must go through head office) first. You are sharing in the missionary's struggles vicariously through a third party. By giving directly to the person in need, whether in another country or in the next pew, there is also the added benefit of none of the money being wasted through bureaucracy. I have had many tell me it is too hard to figure out how to do this, to which I answer, *"so giving must be convenient in order for us to do it?"* What else must be convenient before we do it? The number of excuses we have to NOT do something God's way is beyond imagination.

Paul tells his son in the Lord, *charge* (Paraggellō- transmit this message, enjoin, command, and declare to) *them that are rich in this world, that they be not highminded* (Hupsēlophroneō- lofty, arrogant, hold onto, portioning of the body; [the have's and have not's]) *nor trust in uncertain riches, but in the living God, who giveth us richly all things to enjoy*. Unfortunately, this is where most saints stop reading, and as usual a text taken out of context becomes a pretext (a reason given in justification of a course of action that is not the real reason. In other words, *'I want to believe this, so I will find a verse that agrees with what I say or believe'*). To get the full meaning we must read on *...That they* (who have riches) *do good, **that they be rich in good works, ready to distribute, willing to communicate** (financially liberal. **1 Timothy 6:17-18**). Paul says that we are to be *rich in good works*, not rich in our bank accounts or our real estate portfolios, or by how many toys we can accumulate, and that those who have much, must be willing to communicate, *ready to distribute* (Eumetadotos- good at imparting, that is- being liberal in giving, not stingy).

Paul is telling his disciple to charge them that are rich. (In context with the rest of the chapter, I truly believe it is not just money that is being conveyed here, but rich in knowledge, time, talents, and resources. For example, verses 1-2 speaks of servanthood, verses 3-6 is about wholesome words and teaching according to godliness leading to contentment and great gain, verses 7-8 speaks of humility and our basic needs, following after righteousness, godliness, faith, love, patience, meekness which are traits taught and shared within the Ecclesia, laying up eternal foundations, not earthly riches. They who have of these things have a greater responsibility to those in need of these things within the Ecclesia. We can clearly see that it is the responsibility of all the believers to distribute what they can to those in need.

To the best of my knowledge there are three places where money or goods were collected in one area for distributing at the genesis of the Renewed Covenant Ecclesia. **Act 4:37** *Having land, sold it, and brought the money, and laid it at the apostles' feet* (by the way, they did not store it up, build their own synagogue, bank it, pay themselves salaries or save it for another day, they did however give to *every man as they had need*), and when the gentile churches took up an offering to help the saints in Judea during a time of famine in (**2 Corinthians 8:14**). Paul rounds it off well when in verse 14 he says, *But by an equality, that now at this time your abundance may be a supply for their want* (where they fall short, have a deficit), *that their abundance also may be a supply for your want: that there may be equality* (likeness in proportion). The supply of needs didn't go just one way. For example, it wasn't just the pastor or leadership that got their needs met. A family of six got more than a family of three. If a person was single, they were brought into a family and catered to as they needed. Every other time supply was given; it was people looking after people within the body. After the Ecclesia was finally established and a system of caring for one another was set up, we do not read of mass offerings being taken up, just that God did not record it in His word. This is not to say it may not have happened, or that it may not be necessary at certain times today. The need was met *by* the people directly *to* the people, it lost none of its effectiveness through bureaucracy. A shekel given was a shekel received. The third instance is in **Philippians 4:15-18**.

In many of our organizations today, sometimes as much as between fifty and sixty five percent (even more in a few organizations) of every dollar given is swallowed up in handling, maintenance, and other expenses (bureaucracy). This leads to the overstretched pockets and purses of the saints having to give even more in order for the money to be effective. The early church had no such problem. A concern was brought to the attention of the body in that area and those with the ability to help actually went themselves and helped. The homeless person in their neighbourhood, the sick mother or father, the orphan needing a home: the blind and lame were taken into the family, and the wayfarer was helped along their way, all were catered to by each member of the body. Nothing was lost. And through these acts, the Gospel of the Kingdom was preached, demonstrated, and spread like a wildfire.

I would like to give you two scenarios for your consideration.

1. A traveller comes into your village, he is approached by a disciple of Christ, befriended, and taken to their home for a meal, a conversation, a cup of cold water and the offer of a bed for the night. While they are in the disciple's house, they see the Kingdom of God in action in the everyday doings of the family, how they love and interact with one another and their neighbours. They ask questions and receive not just scriptures about what the family believes, but a word from God also. As he prepares to leave, someone puts a few shekels into his hand or a bag with some dates, some olives, a loaf of bread and a small flask of olive oil.

2. A traveller goes into your village and finds a synagogue, knocks on the door, and explains his plight and asks for help. The man is given a few shekels from the weekly offering for charity's sake. He then finds an inn, pays for it with some of the shekels given to him, spends the night alone. On his way out of the village in the morning, he stops at the market, buys a loaf of bread, a handful of dates, a small flask of olive oil, and gets a cup of water from the village well on the way to continue his journey.

Which scenario do you think had the greater impact on this man's soul and which do you think spread the good news of the Kingdom of God from one village to another?

With all the *'wonders and signs'* taking place in the book of Acts such as miraculous healings, amazing prison breaks, angelic visitations, survival of shipwrecks, demonic exorcisms and much more, I have come to see that the greater miracle was when materialistic and naturally self-seeking, self-serving men and women gave of what they had, many sold their property and shared the proceeds of their hard-earned labours with those whom God had called in their midst. Surely, here we see a truer miracle and the proper operation of the Ecclesia of God. I have seen more miraculous healings and deliverances than I can write about in this book, but sadly, I can count on two hand the amount of times I have seen the type of miracle where people were willing to renounce ownership and control of their possessions, wisdom, influence and knowledge and share with those who have material, physical and spiritual needs by going to where the need is rather than having those with needs go to them?

I must stress how the early Ecclesia operated was not a form of communism or socialism. We must understand that this giving was not under compulsion nor duress, it was not as a result of hearing countless messages on tithing and offerings, being threatened with a curse nor coerced in any way. They were not told if they didn't give, they would go to hell, or it proved that they didn't *'really love God'*. Clearly Peter tells us of Ananias and Sapphira: *Whiles it remained, was it not thine own? and after it was sold, was it not in thine own power? why hast thou conceived this thing in thine heart? thou hast not lied unto men, but unto God* (**Acts 5:4**). The land legally belonged to Ananias and Sapphira. No-one had tried to coerce them out of it. They did not have to sell the land, nor were they forced to give any or all of the proceeds to be used for the poor. Their sin was that of deception, of lying to the Holy Spirit, of saying one thing while doing another, of pretending to be a part of the body, then showing who really came first in their lives: themselves. The upshot of their death culminated in **Acts 5:11** *And great fear came upon all the church, and upon as many as heard these things.* Miracles increased in magnitude and the influence of the Ecclesia grew mightily. This is a major part of what truly separated the Ecclesia from the rest of the world. Their doctrine of salvation of one God (the Jews were already one God people) was not the main reason thousands came to know them as *'people of the way'*, their application of their doctrine in their daily lives was.

Jean Vanier, CC GOQ, a Canadian philosopher, theologian, and founder of L'Arche, in his book, *Community and Growth*, points out that *"...Individualistic material progress and the desire to gain prestige by coming out on top have taken over from the sense of fellowship, compassion and community. Now people live more or less on their own in a small house, jealously guarding their goods and planning to acquire more, with a notice on the gate that says, 'Beware of the dog'."*

It cannot be more clearly stated that when we get, it is not so that we may keep or save for a rainy day, but it is so we can distribute to the body of Christ as and when needed. We keep telling the saints that we are to be good stewards of God's money, but we only seem to major on it when it comes to tithing or offerings. Good stewards' means being good with everything God gave us, not just the money. Our time, our talents as well as our treasures. It is when we let go of the concept of *me and mine* that we will show that His Kingdom has come to earth and operates as it does in heaven.

Back to **Acts 2:44** *And all that believed were together, and had all things common;* We need to break down this statement and address what it means to **believe**, have **all things** and what is **common**. All that *believed* means (Pisteuō), they had faith and entrusted their lives to the will of God. How was their belief shown? It was shown in action as stated by the very next part of the verse. They were together (this was not at the temple or the synagogue but in their homes). One cannot say they believe then only manifest that belief on Sunday and or Wednesday. The term *all things* is defined in the Strong's as *Hapas,* meaning absolutely all, everyone, all manner of means, daily or whole. This comes from the root meaning *Pas* defined as whatsoever and whosoever. This word, *Pas,* is the same word used by the Lord when He said, **All** *power is given unto me in heaven and in earth* (**Matthew 28:18**). All means all, it doesn't matter what we think, feel, believe or have been told, even from the pulpit or the bible college professor. Either Jesus has all power, or He doesn't. We either give all to Jesus or not, they had *all things* in common, or they didn't. No amount of mental gymnastics is going to change this truth. We must stop telling the world that we have the truth of Acts 2:38 but ignore or try to explain away the truth of Acts 2:44-46. The world is not dumb, they will see through our hypocrisy if they come to our churches.

Just as baptism in Jesus' name and the indwelling of the Holy Ghost with the evidence of speaking in tongues were fundamental and non-negotiable to the early Ecclesia, so the issue of sharing their resources, experiences, knowledge, and personal lives was fundamental and non-negotiable. Rich and poor alike, all contributed what they could out of a grateful heart that they were chosen to be a part of the bride. Remember, **John 15:16** *Ye have not chosen me,* **but I have chosen you,** *and* **ordained** you (Tithēmi- to place (in the widest application, literally and figuratively; properly in a **passive or horizontal posture**, to give, to kneel or bow down, lay (aside, down, up), make, ordain, purpose, put, set (forth), settle, sink down) *that ye should go* **and bring forth fruit,** *and that* **your fruit should remain**: *that* (Hino- so as, in order that, the result will be) *whatsoever ye shall ask of the Father in my name, he may give it you.* Verse seventeen goes on to say, *These things I command you, that ye love one another.* Love is shown by action not by mere words. A preacher can preach about love from a pulpit every week of the year, but unless he becomes intimately involved (biblical fellowship- Koinōnia- partnership, (literally) participation, or (social) intercourse, or pecuniary benefaction [financially support], to communicate (communication), communion, contribution, distribution) in the lives of those he is preaching to, he is only a distributor of biblical information (today we have many software programmes that do the same thing that does not cost ten percent of someone's income). He may as well just print out his notes and give them to the people as they walk in the door. All the yelling, sounding like he has emphysema and crazy antics will not get the message of love across. The wealth of the disciples (whether it be of time, resources, or abilities) became the wealth of the body of Christ, the Ecclesia.

Chosen or ordained?

We have given a meaning to the word *ordained* that did not exist in the early Ecclesia. Today, ordained means to be lifted up for something special, or that someone has been through a programme or institute, to invest with ministerial or priestly authority; confer holy orders upon, such as to ordain a priest or to be entitled. The most common definition of ordains is the process by which individuals are consecrated, that is, set apart and elevated from the laity class to the clergy, who are thus then authorized (usually by the denominational hierarchy composed of other clergy) to perform various religious rites and ceremonies. Political parties ordain their next leaders prior to elections. This is how we see it in churches and organizations today. For example, we ordain preachers, pastors, bishops, and evangelists. Let's see what Jesus meant when He used the word *ordained*, shall we? It may surprise you how much pride we have injected into this word.

To ordain was, in fact, the exact opposite of today's meaning; as mentioned in the previous paragraph, Tithēmi means to place (in the widest application, literally and figuratively; properly in a *passive or horizontal posture*). God has placed each and every one of us on an equal footing regarding our place in God's Kingdom. God ordains someone for a task, a job and if done well they may be honoured (respected) but honoured/respected does not equate to elevation or special privileges. Our task within the Ecclesia (the gathering) does NOT determine our status in the Kingdom of God. The newly born-again person is just as vital to the mechanics of the Ecclesia as the veteran saint or those in the so-called ministry. Unfortunately, we do the opposite to the words of Jesus when we ordain someone. We lift them up. The antithesis of Tithēmi- a *passive or horizontal posture.*

God chooses whom He will whether it be for president, prime minister, king or governor, Sunday school teacher, pastor, CEO, or director General of the U.N. A sister or brother who humbly goes about their Father's business of making disciples is more effective and highly prized in the workings of the Kingdom of God than all the preachers who spend all their time behind a pulpit and very little if any time with their feet under the dining table of the saints. Pastor/preacher/presbyter/superintendent are jobs like gardener, waiter, and bus driver. They are chosen to fulfil a task (God's will) in manifesting the Kingdom of God here on earth. Paul mentions this to Timothy, *But in a great house there are not only vessels of gold and of silver, but also of wood and of earth; and some to honour, and some to dishonour. If a man therefore purge himself from these* (verses 14-19 explain what *these* are), *he shall be a vessel unto honour, sanctified, and meet for the master's use, and prepared unto every good work* (**2 Timothy 2:20-21**). Being ordained is supposed to engrain someone into the body, not place them above to be seen on certain occasions. The body cannot work together if it is only convened for scheduled services or conferences. It is slowly becoming a sideshow and one of the main reasons is we are not connected 24/7 to one another. Think this is too hard to do? Then we must hand back the button and the piece of paper we got from our organizations until we can learn to love and serve each other as Christ and the disciples did, then perhaps, we can say we are approaching a facsimile of the first century Ecclesia.

Many have fallen in love with the idea of church or are bound to the idealism of church (unrealistic expectations of church), especially the false thinking that belonging to *a church* (modern definition) will solve their problems with little to no pain or inconvenience. If the Ecclesia is being real, church is where problems are exposed, struggled with and then, with love for God and one another, are dealt with. It is where we learn things about ourselves which we despise and as we deal with these things, we find ourselves helping others through their awful findings and we allow others to help us through ours. It is also where we learn to become selfless and give to others as Christ gave to us. This goes against the very grain of human nature, yet this is exactly what our God commanded of us when He told us to follow Him, to love one another as He loved us, to lay down our lives for one another as exampled by Christ Himself. If we will do this, then we will, by the community principles of giving our lives to one another in every area, begin the journey of becoming the community God is seeking. This can only be done by denying ourselves (**Matthew 16:24**), which prepares us to live in the community that will exist under the New Heaven on the New Earth in New Jerusalem and the people who will lead in this endeavour will be those who have been chosen (selected- Tithēmi- placed in a passive or horizontal posture) by God and not ordained (lifted up) by men.

Luke 6:38 *Give, and it shall be given unto you; good measure, pressed down, and shaken together, and running over,* **shall men give** *into your bosom. For with the same measure that ye mete withal it shall be measured to you again.* This verse in context in no way states or even implies that it is our finances we are to give in good measure, but whole of life, every area, holding nothing back (you will read this statement several times as you go through this book). The chapter clearly speaks of love, time, skills, talents, loving our enemies, of planting, in wisdom (and where necessary, in finances) and fruit, and all for the sake of the Kingdom of God. God gives through man as He finds willing vessels who will give of what they have on His behalf.

The main reason that the followers of Yeshua the Nazarene stood out from the secular community is that they took care of each other in every way conceivable. We must remember that people worshipped hundreds of gods and this *"god of the Jews"* was just another one. It was how they lived for their God and each other that made people take notice of what they were saying. The first believers in Yeshua truly believed the Lord's parable of the sheep and the goats which ended with, *And the King shall answer and say unto them, Verily I say unto you, Inasmuch as ye have done it unto one of the least of these my brethren, ye have done it unto me.* They took to heart the forty fifth verse which reads, *Then shall he answer them, saying, Verily I say unto you, Inasmuch as* **ye did it not** *to one of the least of these, ye did it not to me.* (**Matthew 25:40, 45**).

They believed, and rightly so, that by caring for *one another* they were actually caring for Christ. He and His own, are one and the same. If we love God and would be willing to do anything for Him, then why would we not transfer this love and action to each other? As Jesus said in **Matthew 7:12** *Therefore all things whatsoever ye would that men should do to you, do ye even so to them: for this is the law and the prophets.* I find it interesting that the very next verse tells us what we must do to enter into the Kingdom. *Enter ye in at the strait gate: for wide is the gate, and broad is the way, that leadeth to destruction, and many there be which go in thereat* (**Matthew 7:13**). *Doing unto others* in the same breath as *entering heaven*. A coincidence? I think not! Strait here means narrow from obstacles, standing close about, it means that it will not be easy to do the things God is asking us to do for one another, but it is necessary. In other words, the Golden Rule is immediately related to the narrow way which leads to the Kingdom.

Dietrich Bonhoeffer in His book, *Life Together:* writes in, *"The Classic Exploration of Christian Community* (Harper One. 1978), of the importance of understanding brotherhood and community: *'What determines our brotherhood is what man is by reason of Christ. Our community with one another consists solely in what Christ has done to both of us. This is true not merely at the beginning, as though in the course of time something else were to be added to our community; it remains so for all the future and to all eternity. I have community with others, and I shall continue to have it only through Jesus Christ. The more genuine and the deeper our community becomes, the more will everything else between us will recede, the more clearly and purely will Jesus Christ and his work become the one and only thing that is vital between us. We have one another only through Christ, but through Christ we do have one another, wholly, for eternity.'* Bonhoeffer also states that, *"The role of personal prayer, worship in common, everyday work, and Christian service is treated in simple, almost biblical, words. Life together serves as bread to all who are hungry for the real life of Christian fellowship".*

Remember when the Lord met Saul (soon to be known as Paul) on the road to Damascus in Acts chapter nine? Jesus called him by name and asked *Saul, Saul, why persecutest thou me?* (**Acts 9:4**). Who was Saul actually persecuting? Jesus had been killed and was already risen and returned to His throne. The Master was telling Saul, *"By hurting My people you are hurting Me".* Ipso Facto, *'if you care for My people, you are caring for Me'.* This is yet another parable manifested and explained.

Paul had experienced this kindness of care from non-believers also in **Acts 28:2**, *And the* **barbarous people shewed us no little kindness** (Philanthrōpia- benevolence, fondness of mankind, love towards man). These barbarians did not just wish Paul and his entourage well, but they had an action to go with the kind thoughts, *for they kindled a fire, and received us every one, because of the present rain, and because of the cold.* As we read on to verse seven, we see, *In the same quarters were possessions of the chief man of the island, whose name was Publius; who received us, and lodged us three days* **courteously** (Philophronōs- friendliness of mind and kindly). This unbeliever had many possessions before he became a believer, it would be safe to assume that he began to give of those possessions to others who had need. It seemed like the barbarians had shown Paul greater kindness than many religious people. The result of this kindness shown to a servant of God is rendered in verse eight, *And it came to pass, that the father of Publius* (the governor's father) *lay sick of a fever and of a bloody flux* (dysentery)*: to whom Paul entered in, and prayed, and laid his hands on him, and healed him.* The Master made a statement in **Mark 9:41** *For whosoever shall give you a cup of water to drink in my name, because ye belong to Christ, verily I say unto you,* **he shall not lose his reward.** The man gave to Paul, and God rewarded him with healing. This is a win-win situation. Care for His people and He cares for you. In its simplicity, we find the sublime. The enemy has us so busy caring for ourselves, building or getting a bigger or better (...insert desire here...), that we miss the blessing of caring for Christ through caring for the saints in our midst.

The responsibility of the saint's care rests upon the saints as the supply of God flows (yes, pastors and leaders are saints too and care means more than just preaching, paying the church bills, doing bible studies, and running the programmes of the church. These are all impersonal and require no vulnerability by allowing others to see who we really are). This is tested during times of persecution and has much power to draw the lost to Christ, but it is truly tested during times of plenty when we dig in our heels and resist digging into our savings and perhaps give away or sell some of our *"stuff"* in order to help those less fortunate than we are, *As we have therefore opportunity* (Kairos- an occasion arises)*, let us do good unto all men,* **especially** (Malista- in the greatest degree, chiefly and most of all) *unto them* **who are of the household of faith** (**Galatians 6:10**). Is this what is happening in our gatherings today? If not, then is it God's gathering, for God's purposes or are we gathering according to the traditions of men?

In ancient days (and in many religions today), people used to take food and other offerings to the temple/shrines of their gods and leave it on an altar. This food would be either consumed by the priests (who were very well fed indeed) or left to rot. The people had a desire to please their god, and this was the only way they knew to do it. But Jesus has no need for food, clothing, buildings, real estate, or money, so He confirmed an Old Covenant concept of giving to Him by proxy. There are over one hundred verses which speak of this, but here are just a few. **Deuteronomy 15:7-10** *If there be among you a poor man* ('Ebyôn- of want (especially in feeling) destitute, beggar, needy [in the natural or spiritual sense])*, of one of thy brethren within any of thy gates in thy land which the LORD* *thy God giveth thee, thou shalt not harden thine heart, nor shut thine hand from thy poor brother:* **But thou shalt open thine hand wide unto him, and shalt surely lend him sufficient for his need, in that which he wanteth** *(has need). Beware that there be not a thought in thy wicked heart, saying, The seventh year, the year of release, is at hand; and thine eye be evil against thy poor brother, and thou givest him nought* (when or how is he going to pay me back)*; and he cry unto the LORD against thee, and it be sin unto thee. Thou shalt surely give him, and thine heart shall not be grieved when thou givest unto him: because that for this thing the LORD thy God shall bless thee in all thy works, and in all that thou puttest thine hand unto.*

The next verse tells us, *For* **the poor shall never cease out of the land**: *therefore I command thee, saying, Thou shalt open thine hand wide unto thy brother, to thy poor, and to thy needy, in thy land* (**Deuteronomy 15:11**). I've asked God multiple times many years ago, why He doesn't just bless everyone so that they don't have these types of needs. His answer went something like, *I gave the resources to my Ecclesia, and I expect the Ecclesia to use them for the benefit of the Ecclesia.* Remember, *...shall* **men** *give unto your bosom* (**Luke 6:38**). God is saying, *When you do directly to them, it's as if you did it directly to me.* Since God is spirit (**John 4:23-24**) and does not dwell in buildings made by hands anymore (**Acts 17:24**), nor has He need of anything physical, it would be a natural course that when believers are filled with His spirit, by serving and caring for the believers (all believers, not just leadership), it is tantamount to serving and caring for God. Allow me to give you a personal example; My wife (who has severe back problems) and I would frequent a fish restaurant called *Fishville* in our little community of Boca Chica, Texas. The owner and friend, Michael, would see us coming and he would go get a more comfortable chair for Shelly. This made me feel great because he was caring for someone I cared about by just a simple act of kindness.

Most countries have special programmes for families of soldiers who are killed or wounded whilst in service. This is like saying, *'since your husband/father/wife/mother was wounded or gave the ultimate sacrifice for our nation and as they cannot or are not here to care for you, we will care for you* (their family) *on their behalf'.* This translates directly into the principles of the Commonwealth of the Kingdom of God. Since our Lord sacrificed His life for the Ecclesia and He is no longer here in the flesh (see **Ephesians 5:25**), we will care for His family and by so doing we recognize and acknowledge His sacrifice for the Kingdom of God.

Let us look at **Luke 6:38** again, *Give, and it shall be given unto you; good measure, pressed down, and shaken together, and running over, shall men give into your bosom. For with the same measure that ye mete withal it shall be measured to you again.* So, by the same way we love the brethren, we love God, by giving to the brethren, we give to God, by clothing, feeding, helping the brethren in both the natural and spiritual sense, we do the same to God and ultimately His Kingdom, and the wild side of this scripture shows that it is people God uses to give of their time, talents, mercy, grace, wisdom, and resources. The end game is this, if people do not give, it doesn't get given and if it's not given, then the Kingdom of God suffers.

Give to every man that asketh of thee; and of him that taketh away thy goods ask them not again (**Luke 6:30**). As mentioned earlier, nowhere in all of chapter six does Luke mention money. The terms *'of thee'* and *'thy goods'* are both one-word, (Sos- meaning singular). Thus, verse 30 is translated as *Give to every man that asketh your singular or entire Christian life.* Christ gave Himself singularly for us and we are to do the same for one another. The Kingdom of God is already set up in heaven, it is the Kingdom of God here on earth He wants to set up in this fashion.

The Jewish believers in Yeshua began to care for one another as never before. They began to give directly to the needs in their midst and in greater proportion than before. They would not just give of their alms in the marketplace while they were shopping for the day's groceries, or a few coins at the temple, but they began to actively seek out the needs of others so they could fulfil the words of their Master. They sought to please their Master in all areas of their lives, not just look pious on the Sabbath with their tithe and a few coins given to the beggars on their way to the temple or in the offerings.

The wealthier ones would dine and fellowship with the poorer ones on an equal level (Tithēmi- on an equal footing or placed horizontally. Same word as ordained) for they knew that all their riches, power, and influence here on earth (even if obtained in the name of good or of God) meant nothing in the eternal matters of the Kingdom. They were just copying their Master who ate with sinners and publicans, harlots, beggars, blind, lame, and diseased, those in the synagogue who had no office or seemed the least in the body (**1 Corinthians 12:20-23**). Jesus did eat a few times with the leadership in the Sanhedrin because He was not a respecter of persons. In **Mark 2:16** we can see, *And when the scribes and Pharisees saw him eat with publicans and sinners, they said unto his disciples, How is it that he eateth and drinketh with publicans and sinners? When Jesus heard it, he saith unto them, They that are whole have no need of the physician, but they that are sick: I came not to call the righteous, but sinners to repentance.* (Take note, the Lord called sinners to repentance while eating with them, not from some form of synagogue (church) service on a stage or platform behind a pulpit. He met them where they were and ministered to them in a familiar place). The new well-off believers understood that they were headed to the same separation from God (the Lake of fire) as the poor wretched ones on the street. They brought the poor into their homes and treated them as family, which, to the consternation of their friends, would have seemed inconceivable prior to their being born again of water and spirit. They no longer operated in the spirit of the world but the spirit of God.

To cite Jean Vanier again in *Community and Growth*, "*Community is a sign that love is possible in a materialistic world where people so often either ignore or fight each other. It is a sign that we don't need a lot of money to be happy- in fact, the opposite.*"

They did these things first to the brethren, then to the lost as Paul wrote, *As we have therefore opportunity, let us do good unto all men, especially unto them who are of the household of faith.* (**Galatians 6:10**). As they cared for the brethren it increased their faith and they were able to take their faith to the lost. As they cared for the lost, they (the lost) saw in the disciples a Kingdom that was not of this world, and they followed them back and submitted to this new form of life. None of this would have happened if they (the disciples of Yeshua) had remained in the spirit of the world, taking care of number one, and remaining under the hypnotic spell of the pseudo-fellowship of religion. They fulfilled Pauls words that God had given them regarding a new nature, *And that ye put on the new man, which after God is created in righteousness and true holiness* (**Ephesian 4:24**). *In righteousness* (Dikaiosune- character and action of God) **and** *holiness* (Hosiotēs- piety and consecration, with mercy. Nothing to do with a set of standards given by our churches). Our holiness is viewed by the world through our God-like character and actions, not by our lists of dos and don'ts nor by our wardrobe (we are to be modest in our dress because of our love for God, not because it separates us from the world), the scriptures we use or the types of church meetings we have.

James 2:19 *Thou believest that there is one God; thou doest well: the devils also believe, and tremble.* Modern translation: *Do not get cocky, believing in one God is nothing new or something to* *brag about, you don't believe any more than the devils. The enemy believes in one God too, but they have the good sense to tremble.* The Hebrews have believed in one God since the days of Adam (though many generations had forgotten it until Abraham had reawakened this truth about God to mankind). As the relative newcomers on the block of believers in one God, we Gentile Pentecostal/Apostolics have nothing to boast of. The enemy does not care if we believe in one God. He could not care any less if we wear the apostolic uniform, whether we shout *amen* or *preach it* while running down the aisle during a sermon, or even if we tithe to the 'enth' degree. He is however, incensed when our belief in one God causes us to live as one body in the form and function of the first Ecclesia after the first Pentecost post the cross. Old slewfoot is in the destruction business and his main target is not so much the individual who believes in one God, it is the body that operates as one kingdom with no schisms, separations, or partitions, and without partiality. He cannot destroy God nor His word, but if he can weaken the concept of the body ministering to the body, then he has accomplished his desires. If he can distract us with the shiny, the new, the bigger, the better, getting us focused on numbers instead of caring for the numbers we already have first, if he can get enough individuals to focus on themselves or their little cliques, groups, and organizations then he has accomplished something far greater than wars, famines, persecutions, or diseases ever has or could.

Self, me, and *mine* have no place in the Kingdom of God. The only self, me and mine that is acceptable in God's Kingdom is to examine *myself*, take responsibility for *me* and what I do for the Kingdom, and whatever I think is *mine* is God's. Like the tiny country of The Vatican (.2 sq miles/.5 sq klms, population 900), when we are focused on *self, me,* and *mine* then we are kings in our own miniscule and irrelevant kingdom. In the end we will either say to Him, *thy will be done,* and live with the consequences or God will say to us, *thy will be done,* and we will live with *those* consequences. Those to whom God gave them their will, they will regret it on the Day of Judgment. Those who searched out God's will, said and followed through with, *thy will be done,* will have it so for eternity in the New Jerusalem. God's will does not change from age to age. As it was in the early Ecclesia, so it must be now.

Churches in western society have been deceived into believing that the early Ecclesia suffered through horrific persecution so that we (especially in the west) may have it easier. As we used to say back in Oz, this is a **furphy** (an Australian slang for an erroneous or improbable story that is claimed to be factual). They suffered so that we may have an example of how to live together when persecution comes to the Western church. If we do not practice this now, while we still can, we will not know how to do it later when it is forced upon us.

In **Acts 2:44**, when Luke wrote *...And sold their **possessions*** (Ktēma- acquirements, estates, provisions) *and goods* (Huparxis- proprietorship [ownership], wealth, substance), *and parted* (Diamerizō- partitioned thoroughly, parted, distributed) *them to all men, as every man had need,* he was not saying that all should live like paupers on the street, but that all should help to raise the poor (especially of the household of faith **Galatians 6:10**) to a higher level by showing them how to serve God through service to each other. Those that sold to give to those who did not have, did not move to living on the street in poverty. They showed that the giving was spread throughout the entire body and giving was not only a reward in and of itself, but the words of Jesus made sure they had enough to give again in the future by seeking first the Kingdom of God and all their necessities were taken care of (**Matthew 6:31-33**). They worked, not to gain for themselves, but in order to give, *Let him that stole steal no more: **but rather let him labour,** working with his hands the thing which is good, **that he may have to give to him that needeth*** (**Ephesians 4:28**). At one time or another, we have all stolen from either one another or God. We stole time, grace, mercy, some stole money or goods while others stole love and honour from someone. Now we must work so that we may give these things.

We, the people who are called by His name yet still live for ourselves, have stolen from God His rightful place in our lives. In order to remedy this, we now live for God through service to the fellow believers (this is NOT limited to only those of our little cliques, churches, or organization. This shows partiality and God hates this kind of treatment of His people). We do not steal from God by withholding a puny 10 percent. We steal from God by withholding ourselves and living to please ourselves rather than living for the one who sacrificed Himself for filthy sinners like you and me. You can tithe of your mint and anise, eat kosher if you want, and even hold the Sabbath sacred, but living for yourself makes whatever you gave or the list you adhered to, null and void. The money you gave becomes filthy lucre, bribe money (anything given or serving to persuade or induce a favourable outcome) we give so that we may do as we please with the rest.

First century Kingdom thinking goes like this; God initially blesses the few in order to give to the many (this does not necessarily speak of money. The disciples were blessed with revelation, wisdom and understanding, not with money). This teaches two lessons. First, for those that have, that God bestowed the blessing on them in the first place. Paul rebukes the carnal Corinthian church, *For who makes you so superior? What do you have that you did not receive? And if you did receive it, why do you boast as though you did not?* (**1 Corinthians 4:7** Berean study Bible). Notice what is conspicuously absent in Paul's question? Pauls ask **who** makes you superior, not *what makes you superior*. Things do not make someone superior. Things can be stolen, lost, burnt, or worn out. We ourselves mistakenly think we are better because we have more, bigger, or better things, or pews filled with faithful tithe payers and church attenders and for some insane reason, people actually look up to those who have these things and class them as a raging success, and we look down on or disregard those who do not. Someone may have all of the above, but if there is no personal discipleship, giving, and sharing of lives with one another, they are not successful as far as the word of God is concerned. The Pharisees and Sadducees had the numbers, but their hearts were wrong.

Paul writes the opposite to the Philippians; he writes, *Yea doubtless, and I count* (Hēgeomai- judge, esteem, think and deem) ***all things*** (Pas- whomsoever and whatsoever, the whole, everything) *but loss* (Zēmia- a detriment and damaging) *for the excellency* (Huperechō- supremacy, superiority) *of the knowledge of Christ Jesus my Lord: for whom I have suffered the loss of* ***all things*** (Pas- whatsoever, whosoever, the whole, everything), *and do count them but dung* (as what is thrown to the dogs, [ordure- morally offensive], excrement) *that I may win* (gain) *Christ...* (**Philippians 3:8**). Those things that Paul gave up or lost were nothing but excrement, fertilizer to be scattered in the fields, fit only for dogs, compared to gaining God's Kingdom.

Second, it teaches others (by example, not by sermons or textbooks) who do not have as many earthly goods, that even what little they have is meant to be shared and that those that have not, are not lower in ranking or deserving less honour than those that have. When it comes to giving to the body it is always from the heart of gratitude for what God has already given to us ...*Every man according as he purposeth* (Proaireomai- to choose for oneself before another thing, to prefer) *in his heart* (Kardia- the thoughts or feelings, the mind), [so let him give] is not in any of the original texts. It is inferred through context from the beginning of the chapter]). No mention of money, but whole life service, which starts with, *For as touching the ministering to the saints* (Diakonia, from Diakonos- attendance an attendant, that is, (generally) a waiter (at table or in other menial duties); specifically, a Christian teacher and pastor, deacon, minister, servant), *it is superfluous for me to write to you:* Why was it superfluous? Because they were already ministering to one another. In verse five he speaks of preparing a bounty, but once again it has nothing to do with money. Pauls says that we are to prepare our consecration, our largess of patronage, supporting one another (Eulogia).

Paul goes on to say we are to give of ourselves, *not grudgingly, or of necessity* (Anagkē- must needs, or of obligation [compulsion]): *for God loveth a cheerful giver* (**2 Corinthians 9:7**). The AENT adds a little more clarification to the giving of our substance, *Every man, according to his own views, not with sadness, not by constraint, for Elohim loves a joyous giver.* The second half of the above verse is almost always taken out of context when it comes to paying tithes and offerings, that God loves a cheerful giver, but we must do the first half in order for the giving to be effective to the body. To give according to conscience as we purpose or determine.

Though a saint may not be able to offer financial aid to others, they may be able to offer their skills, time, and effort to help an aged, infirmed, or just plain exhausted person clean house, mow the yard, a stressed mother who is dealing with a sick child or unemployed brother or sister find a job, to pray with a brother/sister/friend who is going through a rough time just to name a few things. These are more important a part of giving than monetary, for these also encompass one on one fellowship. Think about it for a moment, giving someone a hand around the house or caring for a sick brother or sister, taking a weeks' worth of food to a saint who is struggling is infinitely more important than keeping the church doors open. What will we do when the government closes the church doors, what will be our purpose then?

The priority of the Ecclesia (not the lifeless stack of brick-and-mortar we call church) must be put back into perspective. The word tells us in **Mark 14:58** *We heard him say, I will destroy this temple* (lifeless stack of stone) *that is made with hands, and within three days I will build another made without hands* (see also **Daniel 2:34, 45, Acts 7:49**). After Christ rose from the dead, He manifested the new temple and fulfilled the prophecy in **Leviticus 26: 11-12**, *And I will set my tabernacle among you: and my soul shall not abhor you. And I will walk among you, and will be your God, and ye shall be my people* (see also **John 14:23, 1 Corinthians 6:19, 3:16-17**). The point being that it is not just our finances that we should have in common, but our skills, time, effort, compassion, and passion to share our experiences, knowledge and wisdom which builds the Ecclesia, the people doing the gathering.

Ask yourself this question. In the following two scenarios which would benefit your soul more. If you were very sick and I came to your house and gave you $200 and stayed for a cup of tea, said a quick prayer then left, or on the other hand, I came around and helped you clean house, did some shopping for you, ran your errands, bought you $100 worth of food, stayed with you for a cup of tea, prayed with you and left you $100.00 cash. Which would show the greater sacrificial love? In scenario #1 you might have $200 but no way of getting the groceries, no clean house, none of your errands done and still be lonely for fellowship. If we are to do unto others as we would have them do unto us, then scenario #2 would show a greater degree of love and sacrifice. The same effort that we use to care for ourselves must be used to care for one another. The saints cannot pay their rent, buy food, care for a sick child or parent, look for a job or care for themselves effectively, if they are broken in heart or mind, sick, or exhausted. This is not an either/or situation. We can, to a certain degree, do both (care of the natural and spiritual through loving fellowship). They will not be healed by us giving our *thoughts and prayers* or just typing *'praying'* on their Facebook feed. Giving our money to a church, rarely translates to the concerns of the people in the pews. Action is required in all forms and as we are the world's largest body of social care networks, counselling groups and educational facilities, the resources to care for each other are somewhere within that body (...*shall men give unto your bosom... Luke 6:38*). We must seek the Lord first and foremost as to what our part is in each situation. Somewhere in His Kingdom, an obedient servant will fulfil the will of God. Our first question ought not to be, '*Lord, who is it that will give?*', rather it must be, '*Lord, can it be me?*'.

Our shared passion to serve God in any and all ways becomes contagious and all within our sphere of influence become infected. The same passion Christ manifested in the Garden of Gethsemane to follow through to the bitter yet glorious end in order to save others (Sōzō- to make safe that is, deliver or protect (literally or figuratively), to heal, preserve, to do well, be or to make us whole) is our example of how to lay down all we think we are or possess for a greater purpose, the Ecclesia in His Kingdom.

Being in the body and not contributing to it in every way possible is like having a long-term houseguest who expects to be waited on hand and foot and does not even clean or help with the cooking or maintenance around the house. These guests are very quickly looked upon as leeches or freeloaders and soon become unwelcome in our homes. How much more within the household of God?

In the movie, *Star Trek, The Wrath of Khan*, Spock said "*The need of the many outweigh the needs of the few*". This is not to say that the few do not have needs, but if the view of today's Ecclesia would be the same as the early Ecclesia, there would indeed be very few that would have great needs. In the Torah, Israel is commanded to care for those who have joined themselves to God's people in this manner; **Leviticus 19:34** *But the stranger that dwelleth with you shall be unto you as one born among you, and **thou shalt love him as thyself**; for ye were strangers in the land of Egypt:* then God signs it to make sure we get it *...I am the LORD your God.* This Old Covenant principle did not change in the Renewed Covenant. Jesus even suggested that our loving the Lord with all our being was lived out/manifested by loving our neighbour as ourselves (**Matthew 23:36-40**).

The notion that once we believe in Christ, obey Acts 2:38 and live according to our holiness standards, we have nothing more to do in regard to our salvation or that of the saints in our midst, is at best, deceiving ourselves or at worst propagating lies. This in no way means that we work in order to obtain salvation, rather, we show (prove, display evidence, manifest) the works of God in order to prove salvation has been given and accepted on the King of King's terms. It is evidence of having rather than bribing with works in order to get ('*I'll do something for you if you do something for me*'). The Creator did not create us to be an ornament around His neck, but to be an instrument in His hands to fulfill His desires. Just as parents hope to create a child that will display their attributes to the world, thus making more people who think and act like them, God created us for the same reason. We all find it amazing when we know a family well and one of the children does something that brings shame or dishonour to the family. We use terms like '*boy, the apple certainly fell far from the tree, didn't it?*' or when they bring honour, '*she really is her mother's daughter,* or *he is his father's son.*'

Is it any wonder that God would want His creation to have the same character and actions as Him (the very definition of righteousness)? Even Jesus said we would do the same works as Him in **John 10:25** *Jesus answered them, I told you, and ye believed not: **the works that I do in my Father's name*** (Onoma- character and authority), *they bear witness of me.* In the same conversation, He goes on to say in verse 37 *If I do not the works of my Father, **believe me not**.* In other words, if I do not display the works given to me by the Father, then flapping my gums and giving my testimony proves I do not have the truth. If this is true of our example (Christ) of how to live and die for His body, how much more is it true for us today?

But then our Master takes it to another level for us mere mortals by commanding us in **John 14:12** *Verily, verily, I say unto you, He that believeth on me, the works that I do **shall** he do also;* Jesus puts on the pressure even further and says...***and greater works** than these **shall** he do; because I go unto my Father.* How can we mere mortals do greater works? Allow me to elucidate; Christ was God robed in flesh with the self-imposed fleshly limitations of time and space, in that being fully human, He could only be in one place at one time. The word *greater* (Meizōn from Megas) means larger in application, more spread out, in years. So, as a worldwide body cooperate, we are larger, more spread out and have been around for almost 2000 years. If we were doing the will of God (preaching only the Kingdom of God and making disciples, with signs and wonders following us, not asking others to follow the signs and wonders to our buildings), the whole world, our cities, towns, and neighbourhoods (**Acts 1:8**), would see the real Christ, and though many would reject Him, the real seekers of God (**John 4:23**) would have found and still find the real Ecclesia of God. By doing the good works of our Master, we would accomplish greater things because His body is spread out to all the world, starting at Jerusalem, then to Samaria and Judea and then to the utter most parts of the earth (**Acts 1:8**).

We were created to perform acts of righteousness as evidenced in **Ephesians 2:8-10** *For by grace are ye saved through faith; and that not of yourselves: it is the gift of God: Not of works, lest any man should boast.* Sadly, far too many uninformed or lazy preachers, pastors and believers stop there, but please read on (the same thought is carried through), *For we are his workmanship* (product, fabric)*, **created in Christ Jesus unto*** (Epi- for, towards) ***good works**, which God hath before ordained* (this is not Tithēmi, but Proetoimazō- to fit up in advance, to be prepared beforehand) *that we should walk in them* (good works). These works are already there for us to do, and it is up to us to be in tune with the spirit of God and do them to whomever, whenever, and wherever the opportunities present themselves.

To all the Churches in the Book of Revelation chapters 2 and 3, John writes the words of God, *"I know your **works**"*, *"Do the first **works**"*, *"You hate the **deeds*** (works) *of the Nicolaitans"*, *"As for your **works**, the last are more than the first"*, *"according to thy **works**"*... and *keeps My **works** until the end"*, *"For I have not found your **works** perfect before God".* Based on the last two paragraphs as an example, it would seem God is as interested in our works as much as what we believe.

Grace Received, Grace Given.

The gift of salvation offered to mankind was truly a remarkable act of grace. Let me explain how this amazing grace translates into our salvation and equally as important, our daily lives. Salvation is not just for when we die, but for how we live. Paul writes that *...you hath he quickened, who were **dead in trespasses and sins;** Wherein in time past ye walked according to the course of this world, according to the prince of the power of the air, the spirit that now worketh in the children of disobedience:* (**Ephesians 2:1-2**). Paul is saying that prior to submitting to Christ as Kurios (master, owner, controller, supreme authority), we existed and submitted according to the dictates of the prince of the power of the air (Satan, and his hoards), and we were dead, without life or meaning;

we were children of disobedience, doing our own thing and living a selfish life. For all intents and purposes, though we were vertical and walking, we were as dead men in the grave. A very bleak existence at the very least. Enter the Creator of the universe into our worthless and pitiful lives, and without you or I seeking to be like Him, freely gives us this amazing opportunity to be like our Creator, to go back to the beginning and walk and talk with the Creator, awakening us to who we are meant to be.

Grace is not salvation! Grace is a gift given that brings us to the knowledge that we are in need of salvation. Then we act in a manner that leads to salvation. He gave His word, which is spirit and life, free of charge, to you and me, and as always, the choice is ours to obey or not. We were not born asking for it and we did not deserve it, but we mere mortals were given the opportunity anyway. In my humble opinion, this is grace's perfect definition. When we take up God's word that was freely and without merit given and obey its commands, it leads to salvation after enduring all things (**Matthew 10:22**). It was not that we were deserving (by our works) of receiving His word.

Of all the nations in the world, God gave the children of Abraham His word. They did nothing but be born in sin, but God's word was given by grace without asking and as they obeyed, they were saved from wrath. This is what the first half of **Ephesians 2:8** means, *saved by grace and not of works*. In essence, grace is not salvation, grace leads us to the God of our salvation (**Psalm 18:46**) and our continued obedience to His word allows us to be forever with Him.

Our works through obedience to His word proves that we have taken up this amazing grace and becoming what grace has called us to be via the cross; Holy Spirit led children of the most-high God (**Romans 8:14**). Without these works, grace has not done what it was given to us to do. Just as a map of where to find water in the desert is not a thirsty man's salvation, the map gives him directions, if he follows it by going in the direction it tells him to and he keeps going, he eventually gets to the well, thereby receiving the life-giving water (he is saved from dying of thirst). In like manner, grace (the awakening of our consciousness to the filthiness of our sin and corruption) is not salvation but points us to the one who saves. What God did for us prior to and on the cross, ultimately raising from the dead, is not the culmination of our salvation (for if we don't do what He says, His death is meaningless to us) but just the beginning of the plan to get us to see our salvation come to fruition, otherwise He would not have told us to endure until the end, or that we must *strive to enter in* (Agōnizomai Eiserchomai- to struggle, literally (to compete for a prize), to contend with an adversary [which is our flesh- remember, Christ already defeated the works of the devil **1 John 3:8**], to labour fervently, endeavour to accomplish something- so that we may arise and come into). If being born again means we are already saved and guaranteed heaven then what is the need to strive to enter into the Kingdom of God or enduring all things or having our faith tried as in a fire? (**Luke 13:24, Matthew 10:22, 1 Peter 1:7**).

We cannot enter into what we cannot see (**John 3:3-5**). The last step of realizing our utter filthiness brings us to the starting point of being justified by our faith in God and with continued obedience to God's word and spirit, we are being sanctified (a lifelong process of denying our flesh), which leads to our ultimate salvation, being with Him for all eternity. Obeying the apostle Peter's command (**Acts 2:38**), however, is only a birth certificate, not a diploma. We must remain in Him and His word in us for our lives to culminate in our final destination (ruling and reigning in Him in the New Jerusalem), in other words, salvation (see **John 15:4-6**).

Paul would not have said, *But I keep under my body, and bring it into subjection:* (subjection to what? I believe it is in subjection to God's word) **lest that by any means**, *when I have preached to* *others, I myself should be a castaway* (1 Corinthians 9:27). If being saved by grace as we understand it today were fact, then what need is there to continue to walk with God in obedience. Unless he had to do something to keep his life on the right path, he would not be saved and all he had done would be in vain. To be a *castaway* (Adokimos) means to be rejected, worthless or unapproved. God does not let anything unapproved into heaven. One cannot be castaway if one has already reached their destination, i.e., *already saved.*

Paul goes further here and says, *Among whom also we all had our conversation* (lifestyle, behaviour) *in times past in the lusts of our flesh* (Sarx- the body, human nature, with its frailties (physically or morally) *and passions.* [Christ defeated the works of the enemy, we defeat our own flesh with the help of the Holy Ghost and the saints]), *fulfilling the desires* (Thelēma- will, inclination, choices, purposes) *of the flesh and of the mind* (Dianoia- our imaginations and understandings); *and were by nature the children of wrath, even as others* (Ephesians 2:3). For what purpose is this grace given? Verse seven picks up this point, *That **in the ages to come** he might shew the exceeding riches of his grace in his kindness toward us through Christ Jesus.* Paul is writing of something in the future. If God's grace has made us *saved* (past tense), then we have already seen the exceeding riches of His grace and kindness, right? If we have already received, there is no need for further participation in our walk with God and no need to endure anything. What then do we do with, *My brethren, count it all joy when ye fall into divers temptations* (trials and tests); *Knowing this, that the trying of your faith worketh patience. But let patience have her perfect work, that ye may be perfect and entire, wanting nothing* (James 3:2-4)? It is true that no man is *justified* by works or the law (Galatians 2:16, Romans 3:20) but by our adherence to God's word (such as the Law of Christ to love God and one another) and our works, we become sanctified (changed into His image. Romans 8:29).

Grace enlightens us to God's will and our initial response and continued obedience to His word makes God's will happen in our lives, whether they are nice things or harsh things. If we are being transformed into the image of the Son, we can expect all things to work together for good according to His purpose (Romans 8:28-29).

Indulge me another example. If I meet a homeless person on the street, I see their misery and lostness in their eyes, they tell me their story and I am moved to give them $10,000. After giving them some much needed advice on how to get off the streets and become a successful and contributing member of society, does the $10,000 guarantee them a successful life? Does it guarantee they have made it, are saved from a hard street life, and will die happy? Not at all. All I did was give them an opportunity and a roadmap to do something with the money I gave. If they squander the gift given to them, how could they possibly be saved from a life of destitution on the street? Once again, not possible. They had to do the right thing with what was given to them, take the gift ($10,000) and seek help from those who have also come from the street, learn from their failures and successes, and when their life is over, then it will be judged a success or failure as Paul says in Hebrews 9:27 *And as it is appointed unto men once to die, but after this the judgment.* Did they do anything *for* me in order to receive the $10,000 other than be poor and destitute? Not at all. Did the $10,000 guarantee their success (saved from street life)? Not at all. Whether they succeeded or not, did that lessen the grace by which the gift was given? Also, of course not. It is the grace of God (His love and word) that helped us get to the one who offers salvation, it is our obedience to following the instructions on how to be born again and live in the Kingdom of God (instead of living on the streets of this world) that eventually brings about salvation (Sōzō- healing, deliverance, protection).

As mentioned earlier, we were created to be like Him in our good works, but sin kept us from our purpose. *And let ours also learn to maintain* (Proistēmi- practice) **good works for necessary uses,** *that they be not unfruitful* (**Titus 3:14**). Being born again but not practicing good works for necessary uses is useless for the Kingdom of God. God intervened in humanity to restore our purpose and if you and I do not act on that purpose, then Christ died in vain for you and me.

When we love and serve one another, we prove that God's grace, love, and mercy truly does operate in our lives. We do not serve in order to obtain grace, love, and mercy, rather, we serve because we have been given these things. Paul warns of this in **Galatians 2:20-21** *I am crucified with Christ: nevertheless I live; yet not I, but Christ liveth in me: and the life which I now live in the flesh I live by the faith of the Son of God, who loved me, and gave himself for me.* **I do not frustrate the grace of God:** *for if righteousness come by the law,* **then Christ is dead in vain.** We can learn two things in the above verse.

1. That we can frustrate (Atheteō- set aside, violate, or neutralize) the grace of God in our lives.
2. There is righteousness that can be worked by the law (the Jews were doing it for about fifteen hundred years), through sacrificing animals to receive forgiveness and obeying the Mosaic laws to receive blessings, but that is not how God intended for His children to fulfil the law after the perfect sacrifice (Himself) was given. Rather we do the works of righteousness because He gave Himself for us, not work so we might get Him.

We are no longer children of disobedience, living for **me and mine**, but now letting Christ live through us performing the same good works He worked, only now through a willing vessel.

We can tell that God is with us by remembering what Peter told the first gentile believers in **Acts 10:38** *How God anointed Jesus of Nazareth with the Holy Ghost and with power:* **who went about doing good,** *and healing all that were oppressed of the devil;* **for God was with him.** He is our example of doing good despite persecution, rejection, being misunderstood or the possibility of not having good done to us.

With all the fake news, fake politicians, fake preachers, fake churches and fake believers in this generation, people are not convinced by what we say we believe about being in the Kingdom of God anymore (those days are long gone), but by watching how we interact with and care for one other and how we treat those still living under the power of the kingdom of this world. Signs and wonders are what makes a difference. Not only miraculous healings, demons exorcized, money coming from strange sources or even people being raised from the dead. These are only temporal miracles. If these are the only miracles performed in our midst, then we of all people are most miserable. Once we have their attention, then what? We tend to rely on signs and wonders because they take extraordinarily little input from us. All that is required is just a little faith (see **Matthew 17:20**). But to give of ourselves, to share this same grace with one another takes acts of faith far greater *and* sacrifice beyond our own means and understanding. I can tell what someone really believes, not by what they say, but by what they consistently act out over a long period of time. How they treat those who can offer them nothing, by how and on what they spend their money etc. The Master said that by our fruits we would be known, not by our beliefs, our list of holiness standards, by what church or denomination we belong to, by how many miracles happen around us or even by how much money we give or get (**Matthew 7:16**). Fruits take time from planting to harvest. When we have a basket full of fruit, it is evident we have laboured hard to produce it. Bragging about our tools (tongues, Jesus' name baptism, preaching etc,) is not showing fruit.

Many consider a sign and wonder such as a cancer cured, or a broken leg healed or a sudden influx of finances as a huge thing, but it is not. In the grand scheme of things, they are miniscule and likened to a vapour in a fan factory. These are only temporary because death (no matter how it happens) will eventually come to claim everyone, even those that received the miracle, and those miracles will be left behind on earth. The true signs and wonders wrought amongst us are that our life was changed from spiritual darkness and slavery unto sin, to walking in the light and becoming a slave unto righteousness (character and actions of God. See **Romans 6:19**). This is a miracle that will be taken with us when we stand before God. *Know ye not, that to whom ye yield yourselves servants to obey,* **his servants ye are to whom ye obey**; *whether of sin unto death, or of* **obedience unto righteousness?** (**Romans 6:16**). Do I believe that miracles are over and no longer available in this dispensation? Absolutely not! Just that they have been given a place in our gatherings that is not consistent with scripture or early church history. The real miracle is that God can take a miserable selfish sinner and turn them into a cross bearing, self-sacrificing saint by the power of His blood, guidance of the Holy Ghost and their obedience to His word given by revelation through His spirit (see **Romans 12:1-3**, **1 Corinthians 13**, **John 5:36, 10:35-38, 16:13, Matthew 16:17**).

As S.D Harris, D.Div., puts it, "*As love is essentially self-abnegation, sin is essentially self-assertion: a practical affirmation of the absurdity that a created being is sufficient for himself; therefore, a repudiation, by the sinner, of his condition as a creature, and an arrogating to self of the Creator's place. It has four principal manifestations, in each of which this essential character appears. It is* **self-sufficiency**, *the opposite of Christian faith. It is* **self-will**, *the opposite of Christian submission. It is* **self-seeking**, *the opposite of Christian benevolence. It is* **self-righteousness**, *the opposite of Christian humility and reverence, the reflex act of sin; putting self in God's place as the object of praise and homage.*"

Going to a church service once or twice a week, singing God songs, shouting *amen* and *preach it*, even dropping in an offering does not a member of the Commonwealth of the Kingdom of God (also known as a disciple of Jesus Christ) make. These are all something that take a relatively short time to perform (about two to three hours each time, and we can all do that. We behave in a certain manner when we go to work, so long as we can go back to our lives shortly thereafter, we seem to be okay). It is how we share, not just the Gospel and our doctrine of God, but our lives with one another that makes the case for the Commonwealth of the Kingdom of God impossible to overlook. It is never about *my ministry, my pastor, my organization, my church, my money, my* (...insert whatever we laughingly think is ours here...), but about His Kingdom, His people, His will. It will take sacrifice and time to change our thinking and eventually our vocabulary, but the concept of Commonwealth will catch on and when it does, the world will take notice and realize that where they are living (the kingdom of darkness) has a way out. The Good News is not what is in the Kingdom of God. The Good News is that there *is* another Kingdom and that through the death and resurrection of Christ, adherence to His word by following Christ to the cross and getting on it, there is a way out of the kingdom of darkness into the Kingdom of His marvellous light (**1 Peter 2:9**). The Messiah's actions proved His words, changed the face of the Middle East in His time (see **Matthew 4:24-25, Mark 5:20**), and His followers, being just like him, changed the face of the world, one household at a time. Our actions prove our words, just like our Master.

Chapter 6

Defining Christian Individualism.

The fruit of Christian individualism (this can also mean little factions or cliques in an organization) is not that the gospel of the Kingdom of God will be laid aside or that our pews will be covered with dust and cobwebs. Neither does it mean that giving to keep our building's operation going will diminish. On the contrary, it will mean that the majority of believers will continue to go to a church building, go through the ritual of service, feel the emotions, and believe that it can help them find and express who they believe they are or can be in Christ. Religion does not disappear; it metamorphs into an adaptable kind of *whatchamacallit* that can be understood with the worldly mind and embraced on our own terms (*we* decide what we will do and if, where or when we will do it). Faith in God and His will is no longer our focus based on reality or something true from God's word in context with other scriptures, history, and the lingua franca of the day. It does, however become an ersatz-therapeutic/psychosomatic crutch in much of our pursuit of self fulfillment or to feel good about what we are doing. We become self-absorbed and self-exultant because of our doctrine or how long our church/organization has been in operation which brings about selfishness and pride, all under the guise of going to church and being an obedient and faithful Christian and growing the church. But obedient to who and faithful to what? In the vast majority of cases, it will be obedient to the pastor and faithful to church attendance and giving so the church doors stay open. God may be involved in our doings, but He and His Kingdom are no longer the focus. The word of God is now filtered through traditions and commandments of men and manifest to the world and each other as standards and methods of having church.

I have spoken to hundreds of people about the things we do in the name of God and when scripture in context is applied to show an error, a vast majority have told me that it doesn't matter, they're going to continue the practice because it *feels right,* or they've been told by their leadership that it is right and that settles it. The word is fast being replaced (as the standard for truth) by our beliefs or stubbornness to hold fast to the traditions of men (**see Mark 7:8, Colossian 2:8**). These things, if allowed to continue unabated or un-challenged, will soon, and I believe unintentionally, replace our relationship with God and each other within the Ecclesia outside of the confines of a church building or church functions.

This type of thinking fills the pews with people who see 'their' church (please note: *their* church, not *The* church) as just another expression of their own self, an aid, if you will, in the pursuit of happiness of self/family and the blessings of material goods, health, a happy marriage, a better job or to get into the ministry and eventually gaining heaven, and any left-over energy or resources in this pursuit, will go towards growing '*their church*'. The concept of self-gratification above that of the body ministering to the body has become entrenched in our churches recently. This can be seen by our prayers and what we focus on, what we will give up for others and what we will pursue on behalf of others. The pursuit of happiness for self becomes the idol which destroys the very purpose of the Commonwealth of the Kingdom of God.

To paraphrase C.S Lewis "*I didn't go to church to make me happy. I always knew a bottle of Port* (wine) *would do that. If you want a church to make you feel really comfortable, I certainly don't recommend Christianity.*"

Finding your balloon.

To illustrate the antithesis of selfishness and the Ecclesia, I would like to recount a story I heard some time ago. A professor gave a balloon to every student in his class (about 100). He had them inflate it, write their name on it, and throw it in the hallway. The professor then mixed all the balloons. The students were given 5 minutes to find their own balloon. Despite a hectic search, no one found their balloon. At that point, the professors told the students to take the first balloon they found and hand it to the person whose name was written on it. Within 5 minutes everyone had their own balloon. The professor told the students: *"These balloons are like happiness. You will never find it if you are looking for your own. But if you care about other people's happiness, you'll find yours too."* (Unattributable). These students found their own fulfillment in making sure others found theirs. Happiness is not our ultimate goal, but you get the gist of the story.

This next paragraph is not written to denigrate the United States Declaration of Independence (it is just as important as the Cyrus Cylinder (first charter of human rights. 539 BC), the Magna Carta (the Great Charter of Freedoms. 1215 AD) or the Emancipation Proclamation (the freedom of the slaves. 1863 AD), all amazing documents which have saved countless lives and helped millions around the world), just that I wish to show the difference between the earthly and celestial kingdoms. The Declaration of Independence was drafted by Thomas Jefferson and further edited and adopted by the Committee of the Whole of the Second Continental Congress on July 4, 1776. It came about after a bloody war of independence from England. The second paragraph contains the following, *"We hold these truths to be self-evident, that all men are created equal, that they are endowed by their Creator with certain unalienable rights, that among these are Life, Liberty and* **the pursuit of Happiness."**

These are great words given by great men as an experiment in government that had never been tried before, but they were given for the formation of an earthly nation. We do not follow the edicts of a document made by men concerning temporal life, pseudo-liberty, and the pursuit of happiness in order to become a part of the eternal Commonwealth of the Kingdom of God. Our document is the word of God (all of it, even the bits we don't like, don't agree with, or don't understand), we seek the eternal life giver and in finding Him we find freedom from sin, and we pursue the will of God (not happiness) which ultimately brings about joy. However, we cannot pursue the Kingdom of God *and* happiness on earth at the same time as these two are diametrically opposed. They cannot coexist in any form or fashion. Happiness comes and goes like a fickle cat and cannot be relied upon for any reason at any time.

We are to live in, with and for the Ecclesia (the body of Christ) for the King of the Ecclesia's sake because that is what the King has chosen to use to manifest Himself to the world. The Ecclesia has limited, if any, real authority in the believer's life today. All authority has been surrendered to a few people with pieces of paper on their walls after reading a bunch of books recommended by their denomination/organization. Do these people love God and want to serve Him? Undoubtedly so, but these are not the ways that God chooses His servants. He chooses servants whose passion to serve others (Diakoneō- to be an attendant, that is, wait upon (menially or as a host, friend or [figuratively] teacher); technically to act as a Christian deacon, teacher, pastor, minister) exceeds and outweighs their desire to serve self and want to go deeper into self-sacrificial-service than ever before. They abhor the idea of being reverenced or lifted up just because they chose to serve and will fight so as not to be elevated into elite status amongst God's people. The saints hand authority over to these people (like a person getting mugged for their wallet) for fear of losing their salvation (you know the threats are real, '*If you don't have a man of God in your life you won't make it, if a man of God can't tell you 'no' then you're not being pastored*' and other such threats). All decisions are made based on *how this will affect me and my church* (modern definition) rather than what will this do to and for the entire Kingdom community and how will this be seen as Kingdom living by those who dwell in darkness. Building a bigger building does not show how the saints live, love and sacrifice for one another. When the almighty *me, my* and *ours* stays enthroned, the body tends to be self-absorbed rather than becoming selflessly Kingdom minded.

Like parents who tell two squabbling siblings to work out their differences then show them how to do it, so is the body meant to sort out the majority of the body's issues with the elders (like parents) being called in when there is an impasse. Before this can happen, the body must be *shown* through the Spirit of God, the word of God and wise elders, not just a sermon on the matter, how this is achieved in real life. When one member of the body is exulted over another within the community (a definite no-no in God's word, see **James 2:2-4**) the other member, who feels slighted, will leave, and take their family and money with them. Why is this? Because their individual feelings were slighted and that is not why they joined the church.

As mentioned earlier, the only self that is acceptable in the Kingdom minded Ecclesia is *self-sacrifice, self-denial, and self-examination*. Paul tells us… *to present **your bodies** a living sacrifice, holy, acceptable unto God, which is your reasonable service* (note, we do not present or force others to sacrifice). Jesus told His disciples… *If any man will come after me, let him **deny himself**, and take up his cross, and follow me,* and the ever unpopular, *Examine yourselves, whether ye be in the faith; prove your own selves. Know ye not your own selves, how that Jesus Christ is in you, except ye be reprobates?* (**Romans 12:1, Matthew 16:24** and **2 Corinthians 13:5**). How can we examine ourselves if we are so busy examining others to see if they are living according to what we believe God wants. We are warned by Jesus in **Matthew 23:12** *And whosoever shall **exalt himself** shall be abased; and he that shall **humble himself** shall be exalted,* and we are told that *Whosoever therefore shall **humble himself** as this little child, the same is **greatest in the kingdom of heaven*** (**Matthew 18:4**). We notice a total lack of individual glory or elevation in all of these statements.

Just because the Lord gave the keys to the Kingdom to Peter (**Matthew 16:19**), did not make him any better than those Jesus commanded to fulfil His will (**Matthew 28:18-20, Acts 1:8**). If we followed that line of thinking, we would have to also believe that Peter's ministry was more important than James' because James was killed earlier in the Ecclesia's history. Of all the epistles attributed to Paul, only three were written to individuals (Titus, Timothy, and Philemon) which leans towards Paul's interest in communicating to the body in a city or region. He knew that major problems or concerns would arise (after all, he is dealing with frail and fallible people), and that the majority of problems would be sorted out by the body led by the Holy Ghost with the wisdom and insight of older saints (elders), with minimum intervention from an outside source. If the body was wrong in a certain doctrine or practice, then the body must be addressed and the body must sort it out.

Consider this; When we pray after a disaster or a sickness and ask God to intervene and when little to nothing happens, we need not wonder why. Many times, God is waiting for us to do what we can with what we have. The Lord said, *Give, and it shall be given unto you; good measure, pressed down, and shaken together, and running over, shall men give into your bosom. For with the same measure that ye mete withal shall be measured to you again* (**Luke 6:38**). **How can we give if we do not already have something to give?** The body most likely has within it what it needs to fix or correct what has gone awry. Where the body lacks, God makes up, but not until the body has done what God has commanded it to do, *Give, and it shall be given unto you; good measure, pressed down, and shaken together, and running over,* **shall men give into your bosom.** *For with the same measure that ye mete withal shall be measured to you again.* In context with the entire chapter, these verses have nothing to do with tithes or offerings. The body is to minister to the body under the general overseership of wise and humble elders, pastors and bishops who show, by example how the Ecclesia is meant to live with and for each other. It is not to just sit back and pray then do nothing about it, expecting some miracle to fall from the sky. Miracles, like our lives, are reserved for the glory of God, for they are things outside of nature's laws. Constantly asking for a miracle in place of what we are meant to do is the epitome of spiritual laziness, carnality, and babyhood.

That is why the vast majority of the Epistles were written to the *Church of* Corinth, the *Church* of Ephesus, the *Church* of Philippi, the *Church of Galatia* and so on and why the letters in Revelation were addressed to the Church of Ephesus, Smyrna, Pergamum, Thyatira, Sardis, Philadelphia, and Laodicea (see also **Philemon 1:2, Colossians 4:16**). They were not written to the *churches* in the city of Ephesus, Thyatira etc. The church was many different gatherings but one church. They were not written to *a* church or to the pastor of *a* church, but to *THE* church in a region. The wise elders in those gatherings were to break down what the letters said and as mentioned in the previous paragraph, give it to the rest of the Ecclesia and show them, by example, how those things are to be corrected and lived. As each member of the Ecclesia grows, each person, over time and as wisdom grows, becomes an elder in their own right and passes on any and all information and experiences they receive from God through whole of life teaching. This is how the early Ecclesia grew so rapidly. (If a church has been operating for years and still has the same elders, then it is more than likely it has become stagnant, one where the waters of revelation are not flowing freely). A healthy gathering has new elders constantly coming in because real growth comes with responsibility. If a church has one hundred people and only three or four elders, this is not a healthy church. Reliance on a small cadre of *'leaders'* actually hinders the miraculous within the body and robs the body of involvement in God's plan for that town, city, or region.

Today, the churches suffer from a new malady called *'pastor burnout'*. The expectations that people put on pastors, and a great majority of pastors put on themselves are enormous. Pastors are expected and expect themselves to be right on target, first time every time. They must give exceptional leadership, be a bottomless pit of compassion, every sermon and prayer must be anointed and that they must come pre-programmed with words of encouragement and be able to operate in the gifts at the drop of a hat. This is not a pastor; this is a robot.

We have this problem because we do not understand the concept of heavenly community on earth. To paraphrase Peter and Paul, the three foundation stones for the ministry of God's people are: The priesthood of all believers, the gifts of the Holy Spirit as He gives the gifts, and the servant-hood example of Jesus (**1 Peter 2:9, 1 Corinthians 12:4-7, John 13:15**). Many pastors have taken it upon themselves (mainly because that's what they've been told by their leadership and has been passed down from past generations) that they are in charge of and must therefore control almost all aspects of the sheep's lives; of where they can or cannot go, of who they can and cannot see, what they can and cannot do in the body and they have convinced themselves (and sadly, the rest of the gathering) that they are indispensable, infallible and have an inalienable right to govern and are a *force majeure* (an over-powering force) in the church. They have persuaded themselves that they are responsible for the outcome of saint's lives, and in an extremely broad and shallow sense, this belief has a modicum of truth in it. They are a force, but they are a force multiplier not a force majeure. In military terms, a force multiplier is a small group of people that, when added to and employed by a combat force, significantly increases the combat potential of that entire force through training and thus enhances the probability of successful missions.

The Green Berets of the United States Army are such a group. Comparatively speaking, they are a small group of men that go into an area and train a larger group of local or native people with special tactics and weapons of war. They do this by living with, working with, and getting to personally know the ones they are training. Special forces are called on to undertake tasks that most soldiers would not be able to do. Their military doctrine is, *rather than sending in a battalion of Green Berets, they will go in company size and train about a thousand men with their special way of soldiering, thus they have now created a thousand highly trained and motivated men out of about a hundred of the same types of men.* The philosophy is that men will fight harder as a united group for, not just their own families, but for each other's families also. If my family had to rely on just me for survival, the chances are low, but when I know if I fall in battle, my fellow soldier will fight just as hard for my family as for theirs (and vice versa), my focus would be on winning the battle, not on what would happen if...

They will be tenacious in their fighting and wise in their tactics and use of the materials at hand, if they have the knowledge and weapons to do so, rather than just being cannon fodder. It is better to train a village to fight than to send men in later to liberate a village that has been overrun by the enemy. The Green Berets do not train and send only, they go into battle *with* the greater force as equals, not as superiors over inferiors. In this manner, a bond is built that lasts way beyond the conflict at hand.

The pastor does have a responsibility to the Ecclesia and it is not to do the work of God alone, but it is to deliver the word of God to God's sheep (sit in Moses' seat so to speak, but then , unlike the Pharisees and Sadducees who were all talk and no action of how to be a living example of how to love and live the word of God to the saints) they are to personally disciple and watch over them in prayer and fasting, in personal one on one teaching as the saint's attempt to follow Jesus. To be their friend and fellow labourer in the same battle with the same purpose: to build the Kingdom of God here in earth as it is in heaven. That is where their responsibility ends. To be accountable today means *subject to the obligation to report, explain, or justify something; responsible; answerable.* Yet, in **Hebrews 13:17** the phrase, *to be accountable,* in the Greek is *Apodidōmi Logos*- meaning to *give away, give over, give back, to deliver, restore and render the word of God* (it's true, check it out) and they are to do it without grudging. I address this in greater detail in my book, *To Obey Or Not To Obey, That Is The Question.* The responsibility of the hearers is to learn from the older saints how to live, love and die to self and die with honour and dignity in the natural, if necessary, in the service of Christ in a Christless world. The responsibility of pastors/elders is to give, to deliver, to declare the word of God and show how it is lived.

The congregation on the other hand, cannot abrogate their responsibility to care for one another and still say they are a part of the body. Yet many in the Ecclesia have instead, placed that responsibility on the overworked pastor. As these concepts are only traditions of men, with no biblical nor early church historical basis, there is no valid reason to allow either one of these erroneous practices to continue.

The idea that one person has the responsibility to care for more than he can personally disciple is foolish at best and thoughtless at worst. The Almighty created Eve because He knew it was not good for man to be or do a job alone. Not just because Adam was lonely, but that Adam's task to tend the Garden was a huge one. God commanded them to multiply and replenish the earth. Why? So, there would be many more to tend an ever-growing garden. We need others, we need community, and we need to stop behaving like we are self-sufficient in most areas and only need God or the church when times get really tough or when a miracle is needed. If the pastor belongs to an organization (man's woeful attempt to build community) in many cases, he still must go it alone as these usually only intervene when there is a crisis or when ministerial dues have fallen behind (do not believe me, when was the last time someone from headquarters called just to check on a pastor and see if he needs anything whether spiritual, mental, physical, or emotional?). Bureaucracy and protocol have all but destroyed the free movement of the Holy Ghost, learned wisdom and personal care of many in the Ecclesia. The best way to restore the Ecclesia is for every member to learn to hear God's voice for themselves from wise pastors and elders, then, with the counsel of multitudes and help from humble elders/overseers/pastors move forward to obey His voice and walk in the light they have been given (see **Provers 11:14, 15:22, 24:6, Romans 8:14**).

The whole community of believers (Ecclesia) is to be involved (not ruled, judged, or condemned, but guided and supported) in every aspect of the saint's lives. They watch out for each other, feed each other (in both the natural and spiritual sense), help each other with bills (or even teaching how to pay bills as these concepts are not taught in schools) or housework, mowing, shovelling snow, giving rides, and when the opportunity arises, counselling, teaching, looking after a sick or injured child, caring for the aged in their midst, visiting the shut-ins, the prisoners and so on. This is community living at its finest. Before the government wrested this job from the Ecclesia (and became our nanny), ordinary people were the major players in the lives of most communities. We have let the government/bureaucracy steal our job and therefore our blessings to be used of God.

Being involved in each other's lives was the way the early Ecclesia demonstrated the love and power of God to the community around them. How did God reward them for their efforts? ...*He added daily to the church* (Ecclesia) *such as should be saved* (**Acts 2:47**). He added people, all with the experience, wisdom and resources needed that come with each person to the group which in turn made the group stronger, being capable of handling more people which God then adds daily to.

A schoolteacher is only responsible to give factual information (not their opinion- be it political or religious) and in a manner the student will understand, teach the children how to think and learn for themselves and how to apply said information to normal everyday living. They are not responsible for the outcome if a student did nothing with the information given to them.

American economist and social theorist, Thomas Sowell says it elegantly, "*The problem isn't that Johnny can't read. The problem isn't even that Johnny can't think. The problem is that Johnny doesn't know what thinking is; he confuses it with feelings.*" Johnny is only taught *what* to think and feel about what he thinks. Johnny is not taught *how* to think.

A pastor has only one more responsibility than a secular teacher for the outcome of a saint's life. That is to guide them, and as long as he is giving the word of God and serving them in every way possible by being a visible example of how to live for Christ (not just behind a pulpit), and if he has done this, then he has fulfilled his task. The community of believers (Ecclesia), then steps in and ensures that saints have a place within it (and that they function in that position) and keep the fundamentals of maintaining harmony through caring one for another with the guidance of the Holy Ghost and wise elders.

Being connected or having meaning?

Being connected is not the same as having meaning. Someone can be connected to a group of people, but still have no meaning, no worthwhile purpose. To live without meaning creates a longing so powerful that if not fulfilled, it creates a separation between the spirit and the mind. This is a form of dismemberment. Every new believer must, with the aid of those surrounding them, find their meaning, their raison d'etre, at the earliest possible time. Sadly, where they find themselves in the beginning is where they will stay until the urge to go past the initial born-again experience either moves them on or they lay down for their final rest. A stagnant saint is precisely where God's enemy wants them. He steals their purpose. No matter how Christ gives life, without a purpose it is pseudo-life. Christ brings life abundantly- animated and dynamic, not coma like. A person in a coma, has breath and blood flowing through their veins, but is unable to think and do anything. *The thief cometh not, but for to steal, and to kill, and to destroy: I am come that they might have life, and that they might have it more abundantly* (John 10:10).

To experience exponential, effective, and permanent growth, with meaning in the community of God's people, we need all five of the essentials mentioned in Ephesians chapter four. We also need all the gifts of the spirit to be in operation within all God's community (not just in the leadership), all while exhibiting all nine aspects of the fruit of the spirit in all members of the Ecclesia. This will not be easy as there are not five steps to being spiritually fulfilled or twelve steps to operating in the gifts. Every congregation and city/town demographic are different. God is not into cookie cutter Christianity. We all live for God the way our convictions dictate and over the years, if there is growth in the spirit, our convictions also change. But we all try to serve the same God being led by the same spirit looking for the same results; God adding to the church daily as we do our part (see **1 Corinthians 12:7-11**). It is a daily walk with God and His disciples that teaches us these things, and it is when we practice on each other ...*That the man of God may be perfect, throughly furnished unto all good works* (**2 Timothy 3:17**). By connecting a new believer with a mature or maturing believer, they begin doing what God called them to do and fulfil their reason for being born-again. Growth that is solely based on numbers in pews, the size of a bank account, how much a congregation submits to their pastor, or the church's real estate portfolio is either superficial, fictitious, or misleading. With enough money, advertising and free stuff, anyone can fill a room, but only a community bound by the same spirit, can help each other build a healthier body.

Regarding the fruit and gifts of the spirit, if they are meant to be in operation at all times within the Ecclesia for the Ecclesia and the surrounding communities, wouldn't it be wrong to expect one man (the pastor for instance) or even a few people (the leadership team) in the church to have them all at all times? It would make sense that God would distribute these gifts and fruits to be in operation in *all* or at least as many of the members of the Ecclesia as will allow themselves to be used, and we display them all at different times, in different manners to different people as the Spirit of the Lord sees fit (**1 Corinthians 12:11**).

We must return to the concept of biblical community that existed prior to the industrial revolution (circa 1760). After the initial explosive growth in mechanized industry (with such innovations as the steam engine and using coal in large quantities to keep them going), people began to leave their communities and villages to make what they believed to be a better life for themselves in the crowded cities, only to find that very few ever did. The 95% of the population who did not rise to the top, lived in squalor and extreme poverty at the bottom, so much so, that they did not even have the wherewithal to go back to their villages or towns. Sadly, all too late, many realized that though conditions were poor and sometimes harsh in their village, it was the community that cared for them and gave them a sense of purpose and well-being outside of themselves. For the multitude in the cities, their moto was *'every man for himself'*. Growth within the Body of Christ (spiritual, physical, and least of all numerical) is not only limited but governed by the community's ability to care for each member. Each member only exists to care for the community of God's people and the care and feeding of its young, thus perpetuating natural and organic growth without the need of outside contrivances (man's ideas and traditions). As people outside the community saw how they cared for one another, they would have a basis to believe our preaching and come and join the community, bringing with them valuable life experiences, talents, and resources, and much more in the Holy Ghost. Remember, ...*shall **men** give into your bosom...* (**Luke 6:38**).

Jesus was speaking of **His** flock in **John 21:15-17** when he told Peter to feed **His** lambs and **His** sheep. This is how Peter could prove his love for the Lord. The Lord did not tell Peter to grow the flock, get bigger pens to hold the flock or produce identical looking flock through genetic engineering (messing with God's DNA or demanding all robotically look and behave alike). He told Peter to feed (which means to pasture) the flock. In Timothy Witmer's *The Shepherd Leader, Achieving Effective Shepherding in Your Church*, he says that, *Shepherding is broken down into a scriptural and practical approach for performing four things on two levels. "Know the sheep," "feed the sheep," "lead the sheep," and "protect the sheep" are the shepherd's four broad responsibilities. The shepherd must perform these four jobs on a large and small scale* (P&R Publishing. 2010). These things must be done daily for how can a shepherd *'know, feed, lead and protect,* if the shepherd is only with them once or twice a week for a couple of hours?

In Peter's encounter with Jesus in the Gospel of Jon, all three words for feed mean to pasture and tend to, care for (none mean to rule over or to force feed). It means to make sure they have plenty of room to move around, there is plenty of grass available for the sheep to eat, water must be reasonably nearby and that he was to watch out for predators. We can see this in **Zechariah 11:7** *So I pastured the flock marked for slaughter, **especially the afflicted*** (ʻânîy- depressed in mind or circumstances, lowly, needy, poor) ***of the flock**. Then I took for myself two staffs, calling one Favour and the other Union, and I pastured the flock.* This is the pastor's job description in a nutshell.

Christ's sheep and lambs cannot be cared for from behind a pulpit or meeting on a weekly basis. This would be like a shepherd caring for his flock from inside a truck, barking out orders at the sheep. This is totally ineffective and unlike anything the great Shepherd did to show us how He wanted them cared for. The real community of God will do all in its power to protect the young and teach them to be a part of a well-functioning and productive flock. The older ewes teaching the younger ones how to be mothers, the older rams teaching the younger rams how to protect the flock (see **Titus 2:3-4**). The younger ones do not learn as much by being corralled into segregated classes, but by including them into the everyday life of as many members of the community as possible, exposing them to experiences, ideas, and revelations from God's word.

The case for community is also made by King Solomon, *Go to the ant, thou sluggard* (ʻâtsêl- indolent, averse to activity, effort, or movement); *consider her ways, and be wise: Which having no guide, overseer, or ruler, Provideth her meat in the summer, and gathereth her food in the harvest* (**Proverbs 6:6-8**). Each ant has a purpose and will fulfil its purpose until it dies, whether naturally or by a predator. It exists for the nest. It gathers during the times of plenty so that during lean times the nest/colony may survive. It needs no prodding, cajoling or convincing to do what its creator placed inside it to do. Within each nest there are forager ants, soldier ants, nursery ants, cleaning ants, ants that guard and protect those who gather food, ants that store and disseminate food, but no ant is more vital than another.

Paul writes in **1 Corinthians 11:14-16** that we should let nature take its course and allow a woman's hair to grow because that is the way God made it, but it can also be applied in the case for the Ecclesia. Let nature (God's nature, not our old nature) teach us how we are to live with one another with older wiser saints (elders) as examples. Peter tells us that we are now partakers of the divine nature of the Kingdom of God, where we have new instincts (which goes against our old instincts of taking care of number one) as opposed to the nature of this world; *Whereby are given unto us exceeding great and precious promises:* **that by these ye might be partakers of the divine nature**, *having escaped the corruption that is in the world through lust* (**2 Peter 1:4**). To be a partaker is to Koinōnos- to be a sharer and a companion of the divine nature, in other words- real biblical fellowship.

Elephants, for example, will surround and protect a wounded member or calf of the herd against any predator. They will keep the wounded or young in the middle while facing outward toward the threat and each member of the herd (whether bull or cow) will give its life to protect the young or injured. They teach the next generation how a herd of elephants is meant to live by teaching them how to find water, feed themselves, which trees and what types of grasses are good or bad, how to mate, give birth, and care for the young, and the process starts all over again. These are natural instincts given to the animal by its creator so the created may continue to propagate the species and thrive.

Sadly, man is one of the few species on earth that tries to destroy its own weak or wounded (either actively or passively via neglect or segregation), and most pitiful of all, this attitude has crept into the body of Christ and perpetrated in the name of God and holiness standards (if you don't believe in our standards [television, rings, length of dresses, facial hair, stockings, closed toed shoes etc.], then we won't fellowship with you).

The sole purpose of the Ecclesia, (which is defined as a calling out, concretely, a popular meeting, especially a religious congregation (Jewish synagogue, or Christian community of members on earth or saints in heaven or both), is that we have been called to leave the thinking of the dog-eat-dog, looking out for number one world behind and gather as a Christian community both here on earth and eventually to rule with Christ in the New Jerusalem. This leaves precious little to no room for the individual to be exulted or where one gift is raised above another. Each gift has its place and has been given to use at different times by different people at the discretion of the Holy Ghost all for the same purpose by the same spirit, the same Lord, the same God (**1 Corinthians 12:4-6**). The community of God here on earth is supposed to be a foretaste of what is to come upon His return as we rule and reign with Him on the New Earth from New Jerusalem, the capital of the restored creation of God.

One does not find God's community as if it is stumbled upon like some hidden treasure, one puts all their effort into building the community that has God, His word and Spirit as its centre and people (not programmes, property, possessions, or position) as its main purpose.

One of the greatest definitions written on the Christian community (the Ecclesia) comes from Dietrich Bonhoeffer. He writes, "*Those who love their dream of a Christian community more than they love the Christian community itself become destroyers of that Christian community even though their personal intentions may be ever so honest, earnest, and sacrificial. God hates this wishful dreaming because it makes the dreamer proud and pretentious. Those who dream of this idolized community demand that it be fulfilled by God, by others and by themselves. They enter the community of Christians with their demands set up by their own law and judge one another and God accordingly. It is not we who build. Christ builds the church. Whoever is mindful to build the church is surely well on the way to destroying it, for he will build a temple to idols without wishing or knowing it. We must confess he builds. We must proclaim, he builds. We must pray to him, and he will build. We do not know his plan. We cannot see whether he is building or pulling down. It may be that the times which by human standards are the times of collapse are for him the great times of construction. It may be that the times which from a human point are great times for the church are times when it's pulled down. It is a great comfort which Jesus gives to his church. You confess, preach, bear witness to me, and I alone will build where it pleases me. Do not meddle in what is not your providence. Do what is given to you, and do it well, and you will have done enough.... Live together in the forgiveness of your sins. Forgive each other every day from the bottom of your hearts."*

The Master told us in **Matthew 16:18**, *And I say also unto thee, That thou art Peter, and upon this rock,* (please note who Jesus said would do what) ***I will build my church****; and the gates of hell shall not prevail against it.* He did not say He would send us out to build churches. The Master said He would build His church; we are only the lively stones He uses to complete the task (see **1 Peter 2:5**). What was the command the Master gave the disciples after His resurrection? To go into all the world and preach the Gospel to every creature, then make disciples of them (**Mark 16:15** and **Matthew 28:19-20**).

We are told in **Deuteronomy 7:6** *For thou art an holy people unto the LORD thy God: the LORD thy God hath chosen thee to be **a special people** unto himself, above all people that are upon the face of the earth.* God did not call an individual to be a special person, but to be a part of a special people ('âmam- as of huddling together, as a congregated unit; specifically, a tribe). Each person is a part of the congregation of God's people, that is what makes them special, not the other way around.

Chapter 7

Christian individualism.

Corinthians 6:19 *What? know ye not that your body is the temple of the Holy Ghost which is in you, which ye have of God, and* **ye are not your own***?*

There's an old 15th Century rabbinic story about a group of people traveling in a boat on a large and deep lake. One passenger takes out a hand drill and begins drilling a hole under his own seat. The other passengers, quite understandably, complain that this action may cause the boat to sink. *"Why should this bother you?"* this man responds, *"I paid for this seat, it's mine and I'm only drilling under my own seat."* The others cry out, *"But the water will rise up and flood the ship for all of us!"* It is painfully obvious that we have far too many people who think that church is there for them, to entertain them, to give them a way to heaven, to get their blessings, a place where, for at least a few hours a week, they can leave their troubles behind or a place to help them find their happiness. The church has become their boat to salvation. But they are blissfully unaware that their actions affect others in ways they cannot or refuse to comprehend.

Christian Individualism is an oxymoronic term (like civil war, freezer burn, militant pacifist, or honest politician- for any politician to be successful, they must compromise which is being untrue to their principles) and does not work towards fulfilling the great commission, as it has no basis in the word of God nor in Ecclesiastical history and therefore must not be found in the Ecclesia today. Christian Individualism is doomed to utter failure, for the Kingdom is never about one person, one group or one organization, but about an entire assembly of people (the Ecclesia) willing to submit their lives, not only to the head of state (God) but to each other. We can read how the *opposite* of Christian individualism was played out in **Acts 1:14, 2:1, 46, 4:24, 5:12, 8:6, 15:25,** and **Philippians 2:2.** Just because we gather together in a building, sing the same songs, and pay the same percentage of our income does not mean we are in one accord. If our hearts, wants, and desires are for ourselves, for better jobs so we have more money for example, and not towards seeking first and foremost the Kingdom of God and His righteousness, we may as well put all our efforts into good community clubs like the Boy Scouts, 4H, Rotary, Lions clubs or even a book club. However, because we Christians like using spiritual words, we may as well call it the *Open Heavenly Windows Bless Me Club.* This club has millions of members scattered around the world and they meet once or twice a week to *'fellowship'* but at the end of the day, the overwhelming majority of its members are just looking to get what they need not what they can also give.

Please explain to me, if everyone gives of tithes and offerings, what are we giving more than anyone else? The widow with the two mites far outgave the religious leaders and the woman with the spikenard whose name has been memorialized throughout eternity just for a couple of examples **(Mark 12:41-44, 14:3-9).** These gave to God more than required, what do we do that is more than required of us.

Here is today's definition of a club: you decide if it is what we currently portray as church; *an association or organization dedicated to a particular interest or activity. It can be church activity, going to a place to do the same thing on a regular basis. A book group/club is a group of people who meet regularly to discuss a book that all the members are supposed to be reading.* Jesus did not do all He did, said what He said and die like He died, so that we might join a book club where we meet regularly to discuss (though very little discussion is actually entered into) what is in the bible, a collection of sixty-six books!

We can see that the Ecclesia was more than a gathering (strictly speaking, parliament and congress is also an Ecclesia [a gathering] and we can see how much unity they have, right?), it is a knitting together for a singular purpose and that purpose is not to grow bigger but to grow stronger, and I must say that bigger is not always stronger. I could have two hundred baby Christians in a gathering or twenty seasoned, self-sacrificing, Holy Ghost taught and led disciples, which do you think will have the greater impact on their community? In **Colossians 2:2** and **19** we see the Ecclesia of Colossae were *knit together*, they were, in fact, as we are meant to be, in Sumbibazō- (driven or forced together, to show, teach or instruct one another), and this is what makes the Ecclesia strong enough to not only withstand the gates of hell (the authority of the grave) but to take ground from it.

The error here can be more serious still if the majority of church goers think they can serve God without connection with His body whether spiritually or naturally (I am not only speaking of only being connected by going to weekly meetings). In my years of travel around the world, having attended anything that even resembles a church, I have come to find that ninety percent of the people that gather in this manner know little to nothing of the daily lives of those they gather with and yet they have the audacity to call themselves a *fellowship,* (defined as Koinōnia- partnership, participation, and *social intercourse*). Most stay within their little clique of friends even within the larger group without venturing past their current spiritual or socio-economic station and will many times sit in the vicinity of someone and are blissfully unaware of the suffering deep inside their neighbour. Why? Because the vast majority of people are wholly invested in themselves and not in the Kingdom of God. In what universe is this fellowship, social intercourse, or partnership? In many instances, it is a group of individuals who happen to be in the same building at the same time to get what they need from God (as defined by statements like- *come to church to get your healing, your miracle, get your praise on, a word from God* etc.), then go on their merry way to live their lives in a manner they see fit. I have just described a concert (whether worldly or religious) and this is what Christ died for? Plato and Aristotle ended many of their arguments with *Non ergo videtur,* I don't think so!

"Hey, He is my PERSONAL saviour, and it is just between me and Jesus." While this is a popular notion taught in many churches today, it is not a biblical one. Scripture calls us into fellowship (Koinōnia- partnership, social intercourse, contribution, and distribution) with God **and** with one another. **1 John 1:7** tells us, *But if we walk in the light* (walk in Jesus), *as he is in the light,* **we have fellowship one with another,** *and* (Kai- therefore, then, likewise) *the blood of Jesus Christ his Son cleanseth us from all sin.* In other words, if we do not have Koinōnia, do we really have God's light or are we really cleansed from all sin? *One with another* is one Greek word (Allēlōn) which is defined as *mutually* and *with each other.* The plain fact is that we need each other desperately and we are to be mutually dependent on one another or we will not make it. The poor in spirit (who by the way will inherit the earth as opposed to the spiritually prideful, those who think and believe that because of their born-again experience, or by how many degrees they have on their walls, or the amount of preaching they do, that they are somehow superior to others) have much to give to the church, but sadly, are usually overlooked, neglected, or dismissed. These people, who do not sit on any of the boards that run our churches or on our platforms, neither are they asked their thoughts on any matters of any importance, have much life experience if we will just sit long enough, listen, and pay

attention. Why is this? Mainly because much of the leadership relegated these believers to filling pews, performing menial tasks in and around the church building, inviting people to church and paying tithes. I do not believe for one minute that this is done intentionally, but it is being done.

Christian individualism presupposes that the higher the individual is in their church or organization the more valuable they are to that church or organization and consequently to the laity. This value translates to elevation and inordinate praise and or honour to the individual. This then negates the necessity of the brotherhood (a group of persons formally joined together for some common interest) of all believers working together for a common goal and promotes competition where there is only one winner. Before Paul goes into the importance of faith in his letter to the Hebrews, he begins with a curious statement (please note the letters in bold print), *Wherefore seeing **we** also are compassed about with so great a cloud of witnesses, let **us** lay aside every weight, and the sin which doth so easily beset **us**, and **let us** run with patience the race that is set before **us*** (**Hebrews 12:1**). The AENT puts it this way, *Therefore, let **us** also, who have all these witnesses surrounding **us** like clouds, cast from **us** all impediments and sin which is always prepared for **us**, and let **us** run with patience the race that is appointed for **us**.* Who was this written to, laity, leadership, or the whole Ecclesia?

Paul commands **us** to run with patience a race (Agōn- a contest, an effort or anxiety, conflict, contention, fight). The only person I must be better than is my yesterday's self. The word patience is Hupomonē- cheerful (or hopeful) endurance, constancy: - enduring, patience, patient continuance (waiting). This is clearly not a 100m dash or a marathon where its every man for himself. As mentioned earlier, it is more like the world's longest and most gruelling relay race. When the race is over, the entire team gets to celebrate and partake in the prize.

Paul speaks of another race in **1 Corinthians 9:24** *Know ye not that they which run in a race run all, but one receiveth the prize? So run, that ye may obtain.* However, this *race* means Stadion from Histēmi meaning to abide, to stay a course. In context with the entire chapter, we can see that this race means to stay the course of suffering and ministering for His name's sake, speaking of winning a prize because of our stamina or endurance (see **Matthew 10:22, James 1:12**). We must remain faithful and have stamina in running the race, but this is a group effort where each individual knows they are not running solo but for, with, and in a group and if one falls, it affects the entire group. In like manner, Christian Individualism goes against the ethos of the Ecclesia.

If our faith does not change our behaviour, if our faith does not produce fruit and that it remain, if our faith is just something that we have and does not have an outlet in actions towards the saints, and if our faith does not cause others to question what we do, then do we really have the faith of the apostles and their disciples.

Chapter 8.

The Church and the Circus?

Give the masses bread and circus, and the people will never revolt.

Decimus Junius Juvenalis, (Juvenal), Roman poet. The Satires.

(Translation: give the people food and entertainment, and they won't leave or try to change the status quo).

Both Shelly (my beautiful wife) and I have heard variations of the following statement and it sickens not just us but also the Spirit of God; *'You may never be called on to preach or sing a 'special', but you can always pray'*. The arrogance of this statement is mind-boggling and especially egregious to the workings of the Holy Ghost within the Ecclesia. That is tantamount to telling a 10-year-old to *'be quiet, you don't know anything, and won't do anything important'*. This statement and those like it totally negate all the knowledge and life experience the disciples have and leads them to believe they are dumb and useless and unless you have some kind of formal education or are one of the chosen of the leadership, there's not much else you can do but pray. This lowers prayer to some kind of menial task that the leadership is too busy to do. It hinders the saints from striving to become something better than their current status or to grow in knowledge because there will always be someone who knows more.

This is what Paul warned us not to do, *Quench not the spirit* (**1 Thessalonians 5:19**). Statements and attitudes like the one above undermines and weakens the saints. It belittles and hinders their efforts to be a participator as well as a partaker in the Kingdom of God and relegates them to spectator status. It tells people that unless you are on the platform, you are virtually nothing, that *all you can do is pray and if you really love God, invite someone to church"*. In other words, God has no place for you in the machinations and maintenance of His Kingdom (except for church attendance and maybe cleaning the church building). A most pitiful existence indeed considering Christ promised life more abundantly (Perisos- beyond, superabundant (in quantity) or superior (in quality), by implication excessive).

So much for, *The thief cometh not, but for to steal, and to kill, and to destroy: I am come that they might have life, and that they might have it more abundantly* (**John 10:10**). Those who have stolen, killed or destroyed the hearts of the saints to be an active participant in the Kingdom of God because they do not have some kind of *'formal'* certificate from an organization or even not a part of an organization, have limited their own growth and that of the Ecclesia. I was told when I was a teenager in high school in Australia, that information is retained, and growth is accelerated when what is learned by listening is repeatedly practiced and taught to others willing to learn and to do it as soon as possible.

These unrepentant and insufferable leaders promote church as a spectator/entertainment affaire where one or two perform while the congregation enjoys what the one or two has prepared. They say God can use anyone, but only those with the required education level or from the leader's family or select few. They rob God's people of unknown riches in wisdom and talents which God placed in each pew. Do not believe me? Search your heart and your church and see if what follows has any validity. If not, then Praise God. However, what if what you are about to read is happening to some degree in our churches, under our very noses, what will you do?

The Three Rings.

Today, much of church as we know it, has become a one-man dog and pony show. This is defined as a small, traveling circus featuring animals as entertainment or a presentation or display that is overly contrived (prepared beforehand) or intricate. Have our church services inadvertently become a kind of circus act, where people go and watch a man lead a few other people in a well-choreographed and eye-catching event meant to hold paying customers so they will come back next week. If you think this is not true, ask yourself this question. What is the battle-cry of most pastors? COME TO CHURCH! I have yet to hear, with the same enthusiasm and passion; *Go and visit one another, study the word this week alone and with the saints, find someone in the church who has a need and fill it, pray for and with each other in each other's homes.* Like the Catholics of old, church as we know it today has become a place we must go to, rather than something we must become. Should we gather? Of course, we should. But we gather for more than to watch a metronomic programme that, if all went well, was a good service.

Back to the show. There is an entrance fee (voluntary tithe and offering), there are greeters and singers, musicians and of course the ring master. There are those people behind the scenes we know nothing of, who keep the show going. They put up the tents, keep the toilets operational and clean and welcome the paying customers, keeping them occupied until the show. When they hear the music, the patrons know the show is about to start. That is when the emotions begin their inextricable and inexorable move towards the wow factor, such as, *'wow, the choir really sang beautifully today'* or *'wow, what a great sermon we had today'* and just like all circuses, the best is left to the end and we hear *'wow, what a great altar-call'.*

Also, just like the circus, the church has many of the same formats (a plan for the organization and arrangement of a specified production). The traditional format of the circus, in which a master of ceremonies introduces a variety of choreographed acts set to music, has been copied by the leaders of the modern western church for the last three to four generations (about 100 years). We have music while we are waiting for the show to start, then the master of ceremonies introduces the choir, after a pre-set number of songs (if the spirit is really moving, we'll keep singing that last song for a while), the leader then introduces the giving segment of the show after which the leader may call for another song or two (what we commonly call *'a special'*). The leader (ringmaster) then comes on to *'wow the audience'* with their stories and biblical knowledge many times with much shouting/screaming and showmanship (like the effected speech pattern they put on for the sermon mistakenly believing that this is the anointing. This is intended to get the people's mind on God with enough anointing that the message will stay in the hearts and minds of the audience until the next service), sticking to a basic formular that has worked for decades (in the case of Apostolic/Pentecostals it will include the Fabulous Five- preaching **Acts 2:38**, one God, holiness, tithing and the all-important obey your pastor). After all, *If it ain't broke, don't fix it, right?*

However, human nature decrees that after a while, the acts must get more daring, showier, better food must be offered, comfier seats, newer carpet, newer songs (which nobody but the younger generation really knows), prettier platforms, nicer choir costumes, fancier lights and even fog machines in many churches and bible colleges now, and so on, must be acquired or only the die-hard fans will continue to show up.

Can someone please tell me where and what is the audience doing throughout this entire show, both in the circus and the church? They are spectating. They have been reduced to watching what has been decided will be good for them with very little if any input or opportunity to ask questions. They are told when to sit, when to stand, they are told when the praise component is over and the worship is about to start. The audience leaves the show on a high (hopefully) and go back to their daily humdrum lives, (some will drive back in their nice cars, others will catch a bus or walk home) all the while looking forward to the next show to break the monotony of life and hopefully learn a little bit more about God and His scriptures. They have yet to be shown how to implement these little snippets of scriptures because there are very few available for daily imitation. The reason is because we have conditioned the people to only see each other at service times. We have NOT stressed the importance of meeting each other outside of church service times to help each other grow.

There is no doubt that most in the church audience really do feel the Holy Ghost and certainly the majority do love God, and a miracle or two may even occur, but in far too many instances, it is the excitement of being in a crowd and being entertained, wowed by the latest songs that move our hearts and emotions, knowing deep down we are not singing reality, we are using mental assent put to music. The spectators know they will never be performers on the stage and are content to let others do the work while they pay their tithes and participate in the show as much as they can. However, I have spoken to countless believers in Christ in the last thirty years on all continents who, in their quiet times, ask themselves, *'is this really all there is to church?'* I have had deep and meaningful conversations with believers of all levels, some in so-called ministry, most not, who say they have not heard anything of any real depth for months or even years at a time, and even if they did, they have very few people they can ask to personally help them put the scriptures into practice.

Every human being born on this earth questions within themselves at one time or another, *"What is the purpose of my existence?"* They need a meaning for their life. They must come to the realization that they were born to do more than just convert oxygen to carbon dioxide for 70-80 years, then go into the long box to feed the worms. The church is to help each and every member of the Commonwealth of the Kingdom of God in their search for that God-ordained meaningful existence within a body. This passion must be greater than for numerical growth (which will occur naturally). Then, together as one body, we help each other fulfil that purpose. In doing so, those outside of our community see what real life is because we have not cloistered ourselves from real life and those experiencing real life in their communities. The seekers will gain hope and ask questions, and if we have done our jobs, they will ask the question, *'what must I do to be like you?'* (**Acts 2:37**). Natural and organic evangelism with nary a board meeting, planning session, diploma, musical instrument, sermon, or title in sight. Just people caring for people, or as Luke puts it *'in one accord'* (**Acts 1:14, 2:1, 2:46, 4:24. 5:12, 8:6**).

Don't try this at home Folks.

Have you ever seen stuntmen or a science programme doing amazing and death-defying acts? As we watch we say within ourselves, *wow, how do they do that?* We *ooh* and *aah* at these amazing feats, and secretly know that we will never be able to do those things. Usually somewhere at the beginning we hear a disclaimer saying, these things are done by professionals and under strict supervision and then comes, *"Don't try this at home folks."* Much of the church has been reduced to being entertained by professionals and warned not to try these stupefying things at home.

The main body of believers in most churches in Western society has been hobbled into spectator mode rather than being helped into participation mode. As mentioned earlier, their participation has been reduced to showing up, filling seats, singing songs, inviting people to come to *their* church, a bible study or two is also helpful and the all-important tithes and offerings. They get to see the show and the only food many will get is popcorn, peanuts, and candy (empty calories) and though enjoyable every now and then, can make a person weak and sickly if that is all they eat (see **Hebrews 6:1-2, 1 Corinthians 3:1-2**). The sights, the sounds, the atmosphere and the 45-minute sermon on living right (holiness standards), the importance of having a man of God in their life who can tell you 'NO', why we speak in tongues and baptize in His name, how God cannot be a trinity, are the staples they go there for. We have dumbed down the Gospel to catchphrases and so when someone asks the audience what they believe, only what has been put in, comes out. *I'm Apostolic, I'm holiness* (what does that even mean to a normal person?), *I believe in* … (fill in catchphrase here) … *I'm a holiness preacher.* No wonder most people invite sinners to church rather than answer the questions where the answers actually mean something. We bring them to church because we cannot articulate what we believe, so we bring them to hear the pastor, evangelist or bishop tell them. The vast majority have no idea how to present let alone show the gospel of the Kingdom of God to outsiders. Teaching them how to do a flip-chart bible study does not answer a sinner's questions about their life's struggles. When the demoniac ran to Jesus at Gadara, Jesus did not do a bible study with him. Jesus talked to the man for a short while, asked a few questions, then solved the man's problems. Jesus did the same thing to the woman of Samaria at the well, with Jairus, with the centurion's servant (**Mark 5:1-9, 5:22-23, 35-43, John 4:1-30, 5:4-8, Luke 7:1-10**).

Satan has snuck into the body of Christ and hobbled the saints into watching the ministry, instead of being and doing the ministry in their daily lives in the midst of sinners. The old saying, *Satan, isn't trying to shut churches down, he's actively joining them'*, comes to mind.

Big elephants, little ropes.

Speaking of being hobbled, have you noticed how circus elephants are just standing around the circus tent? These 8-11 tonne behemoths can easily kill a fully grown man, yet there they are, passive and docile, *easily moved by one man with a small stick and a few catchphrases*. If we look closely at their feet, we will notice they are held in place by a small chain and sometimes even a small rope. How is this even possible? They could easily break what is holding them there, but these huge pachyderms, that can stand up to 11 feet tall, are hobbled by an inferior object. The way they are trained to be so passive and obedient is rather interesting. Read on and see the correlation.

While they were yet young, they had a large chain placed on one of their feet, their movements were heavily restricted to what the trainer wanted them to do and no more. As they struggled to be free and do what their creator placed in them (to be at large and reproduce), the chain would bite into their leg and eventually the pain of fighting became so great, they stopped trying to be free from their bonds. They became compliant and docile because it was easier than fighting the nature given to them by their Creator. They were also kept away from constant contact with the herd, only seeing them during the show or training sessions. These huge animals were trained not to be scared of the lights, the music, the fireworks. They were trained to do unnatural things (elephants don't naturally stand on each other's back) and eventually to look forward to the few treats they got during the show. After years of such treatment these giants, powerful enough to crush a car, lose their instinct on how to be an elephant, to roam free and multiply. These giants of the bush have been hobbled into submission.

The enemy of Christ has repackaged and rebranded the circus format and sold it to the western style church, which we gladly try to reproduce on as many street corners and strip malls in towns and countries as possible, then pat ourselves on the back and boast that we now have X number of churches more than last year.

Many believers, who have a calling to help the body of Christ (maybe not in that particular group), have been hobbled into being nothing more than mere spectators, or in the case of those with a modicum of talent (which is not what God looks for anyway), are placed into menial tasks that give them some sense of belonging to something greater than the main audience. The people are treated with the occasional peanuts, popcorn, and candy to placate their desire to serve in the Commonwealth of the Kingdom of God. These spectators, who want more than, as Wolfgang Simson in, *Houses that changed the World, (Authentic Publishing. 2000)* so eloquently puts it, CAWKI (Church As We Know It), must be biblically discipled then set free to fulfil their purpose, which according to Jesus, Paul, and Peter, is to minister reconciliation to the Ecclesia through discipleship as God sees fit, based on their submission to the Spirit of God and His word first and foremost (**2 Corinthians 5:18** *And all things are of God, who hath reconciled us to himself by Jesus Christ, and hath given to us the ministry of reconciliation*). Having a group of compliant people sitting in pews is not a sign of a successful church nor of church growth. On the contrary, it is a miserable failure if they are not doing the word of God the other 164 hours in the week. As we care for and disciple one another, we build a place where God can then add, *to the church daily such as should be saved* (**Acts 2:47**), not just *our church.*

Yet, it is to these same people whom our Lord said in **Luke 4:18** *The Spirit of the Lord is upon me, because he hath anointed me to preach the gospel to the poor; he hath sent me to heal the brokenhearted, to preach deliverance to the captives, and recovering of sight to the blind,* **to set at liberty** *them that are bruised, To preach the acceptable year of the Lord.* Hold the phone! Set at liberty to do what? One needs no liberty to observe or be a spectator, to sit in a pew and pay money to the church. Each born-again believer who strives to live a sacrificial life on the cross is a true member of the Ecclesia and is thus united with Christ in passion and purpose which needs to be fulfilled.

The Ecclesia becomes united, not when they are in one place, singing the same songs and all thinking the same things, but when all are allowed to fulfil their purpose. A lone elephant is not as dangerous as a herd moving through the land. In order to change the status quo and return to the format of the Book of Acts Ecclesia, we must change our 21st century ways and pray, *Thy Kingdom come,* but first we must pray, *my/our kingdom die.* Unity is not based on unifying (I call it segregating) into our socio-economic, age or affiliate sub-groups (cliques or classes) and remain there. One of the hardest things that will be required of a new believer is to not fall into a special social group and then remain there until their socio-economic circumstances change.

Let me show the dangers of groups within a group. A young new believer in a church is funnelled into the youth group until they are about twenty-one or so, then, all of a sudden, they are moved into the young adults' group where they hardly know anyone, and they are expected to find their niche and behave like a young adult. Yet sadly, they have not been around any young adults (other than the youth leaders, even then it is only for a few hours a week) in order to learn how to live like young adults. They have had the scriptures told to them in a way meant for children from the ages of about 12-13 years old. Then, suddenly, they are in a group who has a somewhat deeper understanding of the same scriptures (or at least, should have) and they still understand them like a young teen. They now feel even less capable of doing the will of God, than before. As they stay in this group, they eventually fall in love and get married. Now they don't fit into the group they have just spent years in, so they are shuffled off into the marrieds group and expected to know how married people behave, yet, once again, they have had precious little if any interaction with any young or more experienced married people in order to learn how young married people live. They stay in this group, make friends, and get in a rut (which I describe as a grave with both ends dug out).

As they get older and hit their senior years, they are then shuffled off to join the golden years group until they die. None of the groups interact with one another other than through church services, the younger cannot learn from the elder because they are in a separate group doing separate things, but they are somehow expected to know how to be a part of the body? The older saints do not get to experience the enthusiasm of having younger people around them and they cannot impart the copious amounts of wisdom these elders have accumulated over the years, both in and out of the Ecclesia.

Then every Sunday and mid-week meeting they stand and tell each other how united they are and go home deluded into believing they just had *'fellowship'*; Koinōnia- partnership, that is, (literally) participation, or social intercourse, or pecuniary (financial) benefaction: communion, contribution, distribution, to be a part of the household). How have we come to this end? It is because we have swallowed hook, line, and sinker what has been handed down from generation to generation without questioning if this is even how God want's it done. Even though these people are in groups, they are still not living in biblical *community*- (a composite of two words- **compact unity**).

Sadly, we have become disingenuous to the people we claim to preach the gospel to when we promote a personal saviour to the detriment of the Commonwealth (the body of Christ) in that we have neglected the needs of the community of believers as a whole to learn from each other (both young from old and vice versa), from their failures and successes, and thus have exchanged the power of the whole for the blessings of the sole. I have heard many times (and many years ago I even caught myself saying it on occasion) *'if nobody but you believed in God, He still would have come and died for you'*. This sounds tempting, and makes us feel loved, but a quick search of the scriptures soon shows the deficit in promoting this thinking over the purpose of the body.

The body of Christ is to care for itself and has no need of ideas, programmes, gimmicks, and promotions from the world. Festivals, block parties, trunk or treat, potlucks, and invite a friend to church day, Christmas/Easter special services is not how Christ envisaged His people growing to be the world's largest and most effective jail-breaking tool. The Ecclesia is the greatest body of counsellors, philanthropists, educators, homecare and social welfare workers in the world, and its primary purpose is to grow and sustain its members to promote the Head of the Organization's message (the King and His Kingdom). The Ecclesia is self-sustaining thus promoting a Kingdom far greater than anything this world's system has to offer.

Everyone that God adds to the Ecclesia (**Acts 2:47**) has a purpose to fulfil whether it be in our little gathering or in the gatherings around our cities, across the state or around the world. When this purpose is thwarted in *any* individual be they in the so-called ministry or in the pews, by holding on to or holding back God's people, we rob not only other members of valuable experiences, but also our group loses out by not gaining valuable experiences in ministering to one another. Will we make mistakes? I refer the reader to the theory of *'Duh'*. But fear not, God will mitigate honest mistakes and use them for His glory and use all things to increase His Kingdom. We either take **Romans 8:28-29** seriously or not.

We have taken on the traits and machinations of the world and operate our churches more like a worldly business, where an employee is forbidden to share ideas with a rival company or take the initiative and do something they feel will help without getting in trouble with management because they did not get permission. Many churches won't let their people fellowship with members of the body who meet elsewhere for fear of losing them. If a person is growing and being biblically discipled, they are more inclined to stay where measurable growth is happening with the eventual hope of going and fulfilling God's will for their lives. The way we run our churches today is similar to large companies and corporations who make their workers sign an NDNC (non-disclosure, non-competition declaration) so that competitors don't grow at the expense of their labours. Another area we run our churches like corporations, is our management styles. We have a CEO and board members (pastor or bishop and the leadership team) who make all the decisions and the shareholders only get a say once a year at the general board meeting (which is compulsory by law) and the shareholders get a pittance in return for their investment. The CEO and board members may be voted in or voted out and if the shareholders do not like where the company is going, they can pull out by divesting their monetary share in the company and find somewhere else to invest. In an oxymoronic way, we have taught the people that they must seek truth then tell them that only that group has the truth and that they must stay. In other words, the Ecclesia is only located on the corner of One God Lane and Praise the Lord Boulevard.

God's Ecclesia doesn't operate using the world's ideas of *me* and *mine*, rather it is a deep and personally intensive fellowship group where anyone and everyone can and must contribute to the growth of others, where we share ideas, revelations, victories, failures and mistakes and help one another sort out our problems (regardless of which localized gathering we belong to, *So we, being many, are one body in Christ, and every one members one of another* **Romans 12:5**). Let me ask a couple of questions. Why is it that people who come to our weekly gatherings are discouraged from fellowshipping with people from other gatherings unless it is sanctioned (by the leadership) such as a rally or conference? Either meeting with others is bad or good. It cannot be both. Why can't someone from *our* group who has something to offer *their* group not help that *other* group grow and vice versa? The answer is because of the *"me and my"* disease.

It is mainly because of the three italicized words, *our* group, *their* group, and *other* group. We have commandeered God's people and withhold their contribution to the Commonwealth of the Kingdom of God because we do not have a biblical concept of what it is we are doing here on earth. We are block minded (some would say block-headed) rather than Commonwealth minded. We set up a church building on a block then try to get as many people to come to our block and if someone from our organization wants to set up another church on *our* block or too close to *our* block, we get upset as they may take potential people from *our* block to *their* block or that people from *our* block would go the to *their* block. We have allowed our pride to control the people's thinking into believing that only in our little gathering will they remain safe and make it to heaven (plus, I would venture to guess, many of the leadership are not keen on losing the tithes and offerings). If someone is growing, loved, and being discipled, why would they want to leave unless it is to fulfil their passion to serve God where He wants them?

It is Christ who bought us with His blood and yet, many times the saints are treated as chattel and forbidden to fellowship with others, even of the same organization. This causes schisms within the body and Paul specifically forbids these faction-oriented groups. Merriam Webster's dictionary explains faction this way: [noun] a party or group (as within a government) that is often contentious or self-seeking, a clique. We are told in **1 Corinthians 12:25** *That **there should be no** (ō mē- could, would, must never be) schism (a split or gap (schisma), literally or figuratively: division, rent) in the body; but that the members should **have the same care one for another**.* How can a broken and fractured body be an example to a broken and fractured world?

Like the elephants in the circus, many have given up fighting against the chains that bind them to the pews and have just submitted themselves to a life of biblical tradition and mediocrity. However, the numbers are steadily increasing of people who are seeking to be what their creator made them to be, whether it is where they are or elsewhere in the body. To go further in God is a drive that He put in all believers filled with the Holy Ghost and who want more than CAWKI. However, it has been slowly but surely squeezed out or as Paul puts it, quenching the Holy Spirit (**1 Corinthians 5:19**).

There are people who are content to just show up, pay their money, sing the songs, listen to the same rehashed sermons about the Fabulous Five, then go home. But there is a growing number within the Ecclesia, who want more than being kept in stasis (equilibrium or inactivity caused by opposing equal forces. In pathology, it is the stagnation in the flow of any of the fluids of the body), and who want to allow the gifts God gave to all men to flow freely (see **Romans 11** and **12, 1 Corinthians 12:1-31, 14:1-4, Ephesians 4:7-8**). God is starting a movement in this generation where God's people will have spiritual freedom (led by God's spirit and overseen by wise elders) to serve God by their conscience and the word of God. True seekers of God's will are not looking for more church services, conferences and ministries that suit their needs. They are looking for God to fulfil His will through biblical, one on one discipleship and interaction with the body of Christ. They do not need wine or circus (wine is a stimulant while circus is entertainment), they need to find and fulfil their raison d'etre.

There was a man mentioned by John in his third epistle, who had the '*us four and no more* or *me and my church*' mentality and refused to accept any other fellowship except of those within his own little clique. John quills from Ephesus; *I was wanting to write to the assembly* (Ecclesia) **but he who loves to be foremost among them**, *Diotrephes, did not receive us. Therefore, if he comes, remember those deeds of his, that he treated us with evil words; and this not enough for him, he also refused to receive the Brothers; and those who would receive (them) he forbade, and even rejected them from the assembly* (Ecclesia) (**3 John 1:9-10** AENT). This man had not only rejected John the Apostle but also the brethren that travelled with him, and anybody that wanted to share their lives with them, were ostracized from *his* church.

We can see six main attributes in Diotrephes that have made themselves quite comfortable within the overwhelming majority of churches in western society today including the Apostolic/Pentecostal church. These are not only detrimental to the body, but also aid the enemy of our Lord. Regarding Diotrephes-

1) He loves to be first.

2) He refuses to welcome other ministries into *his* church.

3) He maliciously spreads gossip about others he disagrees with.

4) He withholds hospitality from other believers.

5) He requires others to follow his poor example.

6) He excommunicates anyone who crosses him.

Valuable life experiences, finances, food, and spiritual growth were blatantly withheld and robbed from the assembly because Diotrephes either did not have the biblical concept of body ministry or, as John puts it, he loved to be number one in his little group. Having the apostle John show up would have shown he wasn't as great as he pretended to be as evidenced by the statement, w*ho loves to be foremost among them.* The KJV uses the term *preeminence among men*, which means one who loves to be number one and cannot stand when one greater than themselves shows up on the scene as it rattles their miniscule world. These are the same traits as a narcissist). Diotrephes was a legend in his own lunchbox or as the old saying goes, he was, *a big frog in a little pond*. He wanted to be highly esteemed amongst men and neglected what God was thinking of him.

Diotrephes robbed the body of the all-important opportunity to minister to another part of the body. In other words, he took a cell out of the whole body of Christ and erroneously called it church (Ecclesia). Many, mainly in the west, have unashamedly done the same thing today. How many Diotrephes' are there in our churches today? How many people have not been ministered to because we don't have the right understanding of what the Ecclesia is here for? Isn't it about time that we make it about the Lord and the Commonwealth of His Kingdom and not about us and our little group?

Isn't it about time that we shut down the three ringed circuses we call churches in the west and return to the roots of our humble beginnings, where God does not need big things to show how big and powerful He is? Where we become less reliant on things and instruments and learn from God's word and wiser disciples how to be an instrument in His hands?

Chapter 9.

He came to save the Kosmos.

Proverbs 8:17, 20-21 *I love them that love me; and those that seek me early shall find me. I lead in the way of righteousness, in the midst of the paths of judgment: That I may cause those that love me to inherit substance; and I will fill their treasures.*

God is love, right? So, God loves everybody, doesn't He? The above scripture, and many others like it, would seem to cast doubt on that ideology. Let us once again put on our thinking caps and search the full word of God to see how far we have strayed from who and what God is and what and who God loves. Not so we can beat ourselves or each other up, but so we may find our way back into His will.

Our emotional concept of a grandpa type God, who will forgive any transgression just because He loves us, is slowly but surely eroding the sanctity of the God/man relationship and killing us. It subconsciously gives license to sin (any sin, not just what we or our church/denomination/organization counts as sin), knowing that this god we have created in our own miniscule minds will kiss our boo boos and always forgive us. If we saw God, not just as a God of love, but a God who has, as well as will, do to humanity the horrific things written in the book of Revelation, we would view sin, His sovereignty, righteousness, and holiness considerably different. The wrong concept of God breaks Him down to a fickle supernatural being who behaves almost in a schizophrenic manner. I believe many Apostolics/Pentecostals see God as a vengeful God in the Old Covenant, as a loving God who dies for the world in the Gospels, as a correcting God in the Epistles, who then reverts to an angry God in the Book of Revelation in order to carry out judgement on those who did not obey Acts 2:28, had the wrong doctrine on the oneness of God, did not live a holiness life, were disobedient to their pastor, didn't go to church every time the doors were open and pay their tithe.

If all we see is anger in the Old Covenant and love in the Renewed Covenant, then we are not seeing God as He truly is. We have missed all the times in the Old Covenant God showed compassion, grace, and mercy to not only His people, but even His enemies. We have also missed how He showed much anger in the Renewed Covenant by, for example, calling the leadership blind guides, pretty graves, hypocrites, murderers, fools, a generation of vipers and swallowers of camels and strainers on gnats, and even excluding those who refuse to be born again from His Kingdom. He is the same God who does what He does for His purposes, and we had better get in line with those purposes or we will continue to have a wrong concept of the Creator God.

If we really believed in life after this body dies and that there will be a judgement of our works as well as our beliefs, we would not be behaving in the manner we are towards any of the saints in the Ecclesia let alone to a lost and dying world. Yes, He is a loving and forgiving God, but we must show all of God, not the grandpa part we love (see **Roman 2:3-6, 2 Corinthians 5:10, 1 Peter 1:17, Psalm 62:12. 1 Corinthians 3:8, Proverbs 24:12, Revelation 20:12**).

Yet, without batting an eyelid, we quote **John 3:16, Romans 5:8, 8:28,** that God loved the world so much that He died for it, even while we were yet sinners and will work all things for our good. We have misrepresented God and His love so much that it will take persecution of the church to show who and what He really is. Unlike the common misconception preached from a vast majority of pulpits, persecution is what God sends to grow the church, not our ideas of blessings. The Master tells us that, *Blessed* (Makarios- supremely blessed, fortunate and well of) *are ye when men revile* (Oneidezō- defame, [cause to] suffer reproach, rail against), *and persecute* (Diōkōyou- cause you to flee) *and shall say all manner of evil for my sake* (**Matthew 5:11**). Has this happened to the Ecclesia in the past? No doubt. Is it happening to the western style Ecclesia in any meaningful degree today? Not yet. Before He can add to the church, (for He has in the past and will do so in the future), He will perform a cutting off of the branches that have not or no longer produce fruit, *I am the true vine, and my Father is the husbandman.* ***Every branch in me that beareth not fruit he taketh away****: and every branch that beareth fruit, he purgeth it, that it may bring forth more fruit* (**John 15:1-2**). Even John Baptist knew this when he said in **Matthew 3:10** *And now also the axe is laid unto the root of the trees: therefore every tree which bringeth not forth good fruit is hewn down, and cast into the fire.*

Jesus echoes His cousin's words in **Matthew 7:19-20**. The Master tells us in no uncertain terms what will happen to those who do not bear good, healthy and nutritious fruit, *Every tree that bringeth not forth good fruit is hewn down, and cast into the fire. Wherefore by their fruits ye shall know them.* As we continue to read (remember, it's the same subject matter), Christ tells us what 'fruit' he does not consider important. The Lord says those that *do* the will of the Father, He does not say that those that only *believe* the will of the Father. Casting out demons, prophesying and miracles are not what God is looking for, though this is what has been heavily promoted as the will of the Father. The works/will of God can be found in Matthew chapters 5-7 and Luke 6. When we are bearing this kind of fruit, we will be where we need to be, right in the middle of His will and we will suffer for it, but the reward for such suffering is far greater than anything our puny minds can comprehend this side of Judgement Day (see **1 Corinthians 2:9**).

The greatest blessing God can bestow on the Ecclesia is growth through hardships, struggles, trials, and persecution. Growth through blessing never lasts longer than until the next blessing is desired or required. He does not look and feel like a God of love to those He is cutting off, but of course, He is, none-the-less, God. Scripture and history are rife with examples of God cutting loose those that say they love him with their lips but refuse to submit to His word with their actions. He gives time to repent, then He removes them and moves on (see **2 Peter 3:9**), and many times the unrepentant don't even know God has left, because they are going through the motions of living for God, but it is in vain.

We have a couple of examples of this terrifying situation, *And she* (Delilah) *said, The Philistines be upon thee, Samson. And he awoke out of his sleep, and said,* **I will go out as at other times before, and shake myself**. *And he* **wist not** (Lôh Yâda' - for want of intimate knowledge) **that the LORD was departed from him**. Saul's continual disobedience to God led to *...the Spirit of the LORD departed from Saul, and an evil spirit from the LORD troubled him. And Saul's servants said unto him, Behold now, an evil spirit from God troubleth thee* (**1 Samuel 16:14-15**). The spirit of God left Saul; others could see it but he could not. Does this sound like our modern version of God's love? So, what does love really look like?

John 3:16 revisited.

God robed Himself in flesh and came to save, or a better word would be to redeem (to take back what was once His) the world (Kosmos- the orderly arrangement including its inhabitants), to its former glory, because, honestly, man has made a right royal mess of it all.

It wasn't just for man that he came because ...*we know that the* **whole creation groaneth** (Sustenazō- to experience a common calamity) *and travaileth in pain* (Sunōdinō- as in pregnancy resulting in childbirth) *together until now, And not only they, but ourselves also,* (a distinction between man and the rest of creation) *which have the firstfruits of the Spirit, even we ourselves groan within ourselves, waiting for the adoption, to wit, the redemption* (Apolutrōsis- the act of paying ransom in full, riddance) *of our body* (**Romans 8:22-23**). He came to restore balance over His creation and His Lordship over man. God had no trouble wiping out almost all mankind during Noah's time. He was going to wipe out all Israel for their rebellious and complaining ways toward Him and start again until Moses stepped in. **Deuteronomy 9:13-14** *Furthermore the LORD spake unto me, saying, I have seen this people* ('Am- a tribe, a congregation or flock- in other words, the church) *and, behold, it is a stiffnecked people: Let me alone,* **that I may destroy them**, *and* **blot out their name** *from under heaven: and I will make of thee* (Moses) *a nation mightier and greater than they.*

God allowed the entire nation of Israel to be taken captive three times even though many in Israel did not bow their knee to the gods of other nations. He punished the nation not just the individuals, clear evidence that God is Kingdom centred. He caused an entire generation of the Nation of Israel to perish in the wilderness for their lack of faith in His promise (see **Jude 1:5**). God deals with the entire Ecclesia. We are to work together as one, however, we cannot do that if we have individualistically focused believers permeating the body of Christ. Assuming we Love God, if our thinking would be more like, *If I do this, how will this affect the entire body of Christ,* our actions would be markedly different from what they are now, but then again, our results will reflect that of the early church also. We would see entire towns and cities in an uproar (Acts 17), or whole households becoming disciples (Acts 10, 16), we would see the heathens delivered and healed (Acts 16, 28) and even demons proclaiming that what we preach is the way of salvation (Acts 16). We would be brought before kings and generals (Acts 25), and sinners would identify us as Christians (Acts 11).

We must not get big heads that it was just for us as individuals that God has come to restore to Himself. He started a garden community with Adam and Eve and told them to populate the earth (make more of themselves who are made in His image), to make families and work together to tend an ever-growing garden. If He was only interested in having fellowship with an individual or a small group such as Noah and his family or Adam and Eve, He would not have told them to procreate (*go forth and multiply.* **Genesis 1:27-28, 9:7**), He would also not have created the nation of Israel (which is nothing more than an extremely large community) out of nothing but a group of tribes and clans who were once slaves, then give them Commandments and Laws on how to please Him and how to live well with one another.

There's a word that we have rejected because we think it is a Roman Catholic word. The word is *eucharist* (a late Middle English word derived from the Old French Eucariste, based on ecclesiastical Greek Eukharistia meaning thanksgiving and grateful. It has its origins from Charis where we get the word *grace* from. This word is sometimes called communion) which basically is a community meal held in each other's homes regularly, where thanksgiving and celebrating the sacrifice of the God/Man (Christ) to redeem a broken world back to Himself takes place. Paul Tells us of such a meal held in fellowship with one another in **1 Corinthians 11:20-26.** He made a point in saying that, when we gather together to eat and drink, we do so in His honour. Sometimes we make something out of a word that it doesn't really mean. Breaking bread has come to mean formal celebration of communion, when in reality, it is an adaptation of a Greek word meaning a wonderful meal. This is what took place daily in the households of believers as mentioned in **Acts 2:42-46, 5:42 and 20:20** and many other places.

As we love each other and gather deliberately to celebrate Christ in this manner, we fulfil the definition of the Agapē (love) of God or as it is written, we celebrate an *affection or benevolence; specifically (plural)* **a love feast***, feast of charity, to hold dear.* Christians exhorted each other to love one another, serve one another and sacrifice one for another based solely on what Christ had done for them, as we can plainly see in the books John wrote in his old age whilst in Ephesus (**1st, 2nd, 3rd John**). John knew what a love feast was, he was in the supper room when the Master showed the disciples what love is by ministering (washing their feet and feeding them, expounding the word, and singing) to them *at a feast.* He saw the results of loving and having it turn on the giver of love when they fell asleep three times after Jesus asked them to pray. When Judas had betrayed the Lord with a kiss, when John and Peter ran away, and yet He continued to the cross. John heard the words of the master as He begged the Father to forgive the ones who had placed Him on the vilest instrument of torture and death known to mankind. John saw what a love feast was when the disciples came back from fishing after the burial of their Lord, and Christ had prepared a feast of fish for them, when He could have taken revenge on them for turning their backs on Him or going back to their old lives. Yes, above all men (even Peter) John knew what it means to love till it hurts. This is the love John is writing about when He says, *if we say we love God but hate* (Miseo- love less) *the brethren, we are a liar, and those who hate* (Miseo- love less) *their brother is a murderer.* In God's eye's we are murderers if we do not love the brethren as Christ loved them. Yes, John knew of what He was writing.

John also understood (as much as man can understand) how love was to be given fully toward our fellow man, especially those of the household of faith (**Galatians 6:10**). He wrote, *And hereby we do know* (we are aware) *that we know* (are sure we understand) *him, if we keep his commandments.* **He that saith, I know him, and keepeth not his commandments, is a liar, and the truth is not in him.** *But whoso keepeth his word, in him verily is the love of God perfected: hereby know we that we are in him* (**1 John 2:3-5**). Yes, it really does say that we show our love for God by doing something, such as keeping His commandments, and that if we do not keep His commandments, yet say we love Him, we are a liar. It doesn't get much simpler, clearer, and concise than that.

John reveals how we can be so contradictory when he says, *If a man say, I love God, and* **hateth** (Miseō- to detest (specially to persecute); by extension **to love less**) *his brother, he is a liar* (Pseudomai- falsifier, utterer of an untruth or attempt to deceive by falsehood), *for he that loveth not his brother whom he hath seen, how can he love God whom he hath not seen?* What does it mean, *by extension, to love less*? John is telling us, to say we love the brethren any less than we love God is the height of self-deception. To give anything less than a feast of love to the brethren is a falsehood, regardless of how much 21st century *'pseudo-fellowship'* we have in church, how many amens we shout out in the sermon, how many times we run the aisles or jump and dance during the services, or (dare I say it?) even if we tithe to the enth degree. We know John understood the idea of love (Agape- love feast) because he mentions the love of God and the love of the brethren thirty-nine times in one hundred and thirty-three verses. This works out to be about one third of his epistles. John is speaking of God's love within the brethren and not loving the things of this world.

Paul was many times in trouble and one of the troubles he had was *false brethren* (Pseudadelphos- a spurious brother, that is, a *pretend associate* **2 Corinthians 11:26**). Those who say they have fellowship with one another but in reality, only have meetings with one another are pretenders- to speak and act so as to make it appear that something is the case, when in fact, it is not. A spurious brother according to Webster's Dictionary is defined as, a bastard, brother (born to parents not married to each other) or outwardly similar or corresponding to something without having its genuine qualities). When we belong to a healthy family, we do all in our power to make sure that all in the family are cared for, helped in times of need, visited regularly (whether there is a problem or not) and shown love.

This next statement may sound harsh, but I believe that contextual scriptural research bears this out. *Pseudadelphos* belong to a Western style church, but not to The Ecclesia. The Lord told us that... *he that is not against us is on our part* (yet we treat others who are not sitting in our pews or carrying our organizational card almost as lepers). *For whosoever shall give you a cup of water to drink in my name, because* **ye belong to Christ,** (not because we belong to an organization or a particular church) *verily I say unto you, he shall not lose his reward* (**Mark 9:40-41**). Did you notice whom we belong to? We belong to Christ; we do not belong to a church, a pastor or organization. When we neglect or treat with disdain those who are not of our group, our church faction, or our organization, we are in fact, *Pseudadelphos*- a spurious (bastard) brother or sister, a pretend associate. "*But they don't believe like I/we do, they won't submit or tithe, they left our church/organization.*" Irrelevant! Are they for the Gospel of the Kingdom of God, are they doing their best to give cups of water to the saints? Are they, to the best of their ability, showing the love of God to the saints and the world? Then, by rejecting them we are a spurious brother or sister (not being what we purport to be; false or fake, a bastard) in the church. Regardless of their faults and foibles, we are the ones in the wrong, and we must repent now for our petty attitudes and trying to force unity.

The suffix *'ian'* denotes belonging to a group such as a politician (a person in a group concerned with politics), dietician (belonging to a group who are concerned with the healthy eating habits of people), electrician (group of people concerned with all things electrical) and so on. So, as we can see, an individualistic Christ-*ian* cannot exist in the Commonwealth of the Kingdom of God. The only individual that exists in this Commonwealth is God Himself. This is not a new phenomenon for even the prophet Elijah fell for the *'I'm the only one'* misconception in his own mind. He thought he was the only one who was serving Jehovah but was put straight when God told him He had seven thousand other prophets who had not bent the knee to Baal, Elijah just wasn't aware of them (**1 Kings 19:18**). Even Jesus told the disciples in **John 10:16** *And other sheep I have, which are not of this fold: them also I must bring, and they shall hear my voice; and there shall be one fold, and one shepherd.*

Paradoxically, people can behave as a singular selfish Christian even while attending a church of any size on a regular basis (although the larger the congregation, the easier it is to hide in plain sight and live alone), paying tithes and offering, even praying, and giving gifts to the pastor on *'pastor appreciation month'.* How can we truly call for unity in the church when we spend more time taking care of ourselves or our little group, thinking only of what pleases us and our family, sacrificing very little to nothing for the saints who are *unable* to give even a little or nothing in return and then, with a straight face, spin a yarn (we have a uniquely Australian idiom, *to tell a phurfy*: a way of saying that something as an exaggerated story, a false report or a rumour, to tell a lie or only part of the truth), that we are a copy of the Acts chapter two church of God just because we have the same doctrine of salvation and believe that God is one God? It must not be so my brothers and sisters.

We can speak in tongues until they fall out of our mouths, we can shout about our one God doctrine but live separate lives, dress so modestly that we can only see our faces and hands, but we will only ever be the church of God when we live for each other and not just our little group (though that is where we start). The Ecclesia cannot function as designed while we exclude others who are not exactly like us or from a different organization or while there are those with needs in that group that deliberately, selfishly, and continually go unmet. Excuses won't cut it with God. If we don't have the resources in our little group to help someone, we must reach out to others. We are all in the same family, are we not? We call each other brother or sister then act like third cousins twice removed, or like a totally dysfunctional family each vying for the last piece of pie at Thanksgiving dinner and wonder why we can't impact our communities as much as we claim we want to.

As briefly mentioned earlier, *God's desire for unity only comes in community. Anything else is a poor imitation and leads to nothing but confusion and frustration. The word 'Community' is a joining of two words with the same meaning to emphasize each word; com- meaning integrated with intensive force such as compact or compile and unity meaning the state of being joined as a whole with nothing missing.*

By its very definition, Kingdom is a community, a country, state, or territory organized and ruled by a king, (regarding the spiritual as well as the natural realm) in which the king's will is paramount. A country without people is not a country. The Antarctic is a huge tract of land (about 5.5 million square miles) and there are a few scientists on it (1000, during the winter, 5000 during the summer), but is it a country? Not at all. The reason is there is no king or head of state.

We cannot blame Satan when our congregations become spineless, insipid, and powerless in our communities at large, mainly because it is us that has formed the weapon against ourselves which will cause our downfall. We did this by accepting the whispered lie Satan has propagated to the church, that everything is all about, me, my and ours. One of the main weapon God's enemy uses is selfishness, and it comes pre-programmed into every human being. It takes submission to God and each other to remove it from our lives (**1 Peter 5:5**). We have somehow become divided by our factions, ministries, socio-economic or special interest groups. We are not being united in the light. United in doctrine of salvation and outward appearance (standards) possibly, but this is such a small part of being in His Kingdom. Is it important, yes, in as much as a standard car needs four wheels to go anywhere. Concentrating on standards is likened to only maintaining one wheel on a vehicle while neglecting the others. We will soon find ourselves with an inoperable vehicle, standing on the side of the road, scratching our heads, and wondering what went wrong.

As alluded to earlier, the enemy cannot kill the true community of God if its inhabitants live for God and each other first and foremost, (*But seek ye* (plural of you, all of you) *first the Kingdom of God and His-* Dikaiosune (to be equal with God in character and actions- *righteousness...* **Matthew 6:33**) even though the enemy may buffet and lash out at it. The church's selfishness, however, will prove to be its own demise if we do not repent and do the first works (**Revelation 2:4-5**). We are to behave in a manner that mimics the teachings and examples of Christ whilst He was here on earth (not just His power in heaven) as well as the apostles and disciples that followed after them before a watching world and to do anything less would be as hypocritical as the Pharisees, Sadducees and other religious leaders who sat on Moses' seat and gave the word then lived a different life, a life that only cared for their little group, to have the best seats in the upper rooms, to be called rabbi and pray long winded prayers (**Matthew 23:1-4**).

These pseudo-believers in one God went about in fine clothing, ate regularly and always first, slept in comfortable beds, would not mix with the poor in their midst, sat in high places and seeking and having the praises of men and being known by their titles and yet in the eyes of God, they had nothing worthy of praise. They put so many rules upon the people (all in the name of holiness) then stood in the door and stopped others from going in, *And he said, Woe unto you also, ye lawyers!* (experts in the word of God), *for ye lade men with burdens grievous to be borne, and ye yourselves touch not the burdens with one of your fingers. ...But woe unto you, scribes and Pharisees, hypocrites! for ye shut up the kingdom of heaven against men: for ye neither go in yourselves, neither suffer ye them that are entering to go in* (**Luke 11:46, Matthew 23:13**). They were the blind guiding the blind, they were swallowers of camels and chokers on gnats, they were like cemeteries- pretty on the outside, everything neat and tidy, but just below the surface they were full of death, they played church (Hupokritēs- an actor under an assumed character, a stage player), and they sought titles, perks, seats in the upper rooms (like our platforms) and the praises of men. They gave publicly and prayed long prayers in the square to look good to others. They were selfish, prideful, arrogant, and worst and most sadly of all, truly believed with all their heart that they were right with God. Sadly though, they were lost and didn't know it. Is this not the very definition of self-deception? They had separated themselves from the real world, from the real people and as such from the real heart of God. Yet, somehow, each sect claimed they were the light of the Torah and had the truth. How about instead of trying so hard to prove that we have the right doctrine, the right amount of holiness standards and that our organization is the right one, that we spend more time living what we say and showing the love of God to our brothers and sister. This behaviour will bleed into our communities, and they will ask us, *what must we do?*

Let me describe selfishness to you: Selfishness- adjective: (of a person, action, or motive) lacking consideration for others; concerned chiefly with one's own personal profit or pleasure). Got the picture yet? In reality, selfishness is as idolatry, placing ourselves before God, His Kingdom, and His people. The opposite of community is not disunity as we have been erroneously told for many generations from many pulpits. It is indifference. Selfishness manifests itself as indifference to the needs of others, whether they be spiritual, natural, physical, emotional, or mental. Indifference to the sufferings of those in our pews (shown by a lack of compassion, inaction, and biblical fellowship). Indifference places me before thee in lines when it comes to receiving. Indifference says, that's not my problem, they should have (...insert miserable excuse here...) while ignoring what we should have done to, for and with them.

We all deal with selfishness from time to time and when we recognize it, we must repent as quickly as possible. Allow me to give you a few synonyms from several dictionaries for selfishness that may put this destructive trait into proper perspective. Selfish people usually display one or more of these traits regularly: *superiority, egotistical, greedy, narcissistic, self-centred, miserly, narrow-minded, out for number one, prejudiced, self-indulgent, self-interested, self-seeking, self-absorbed, stingy, ungenerous, wrapped up in oneself, power-hungry, demanding respect, or service.* Any of these ringing a bell? None of these traits are conducive to a bible community seeking to please God and no amount of preaching or verbal/mental gymnastics we do with these traits in the Ecclesia will have any positive effects on our communities. It is hard to hear someone preach of the grace and mercy of God who constantly exhibits these above traits (we all have bad days, weeks or even months, but as we repent from our selfishness, God removes the stain it leaves on our lives). It is painful to hear someone try to explain that God is one and that He is their all in all, while they live for themselves and refuse to share this same God (with all his generosity in time, talents, or treasures) with others. Remember, that selfishness, like any other sin (adultery, murder, backbiting, unforgiveness or gossip for example) will eventually manifest itself, as Jesus said in His sermon on the mount, *For every tree is known by his own fruit. For of thorns men do not gather figs, nor of a bramble bush gather they grapes. A good man out of the good treasure of his heart bringeth forth that which is good; and an evil man out of the evil treasure of his heart bringeth forth that which is evil: for out of the abundance of the heart his mouth speaketh* (**Luke 6:44-45**). With the same breath He told the people to build on solid rock not on sand (**Luke 6:46-49**).

Lucius Annaeus Seneca the Younger (a Stoic from the 1ˢᵗ Century) once wrote, *"What I advise you to do is, not to be unhappy before the crisis comes. Some things torment us more than they ought; some torment us before they ought; and some torment us when they ought not to torment us at all. We are in the habit of exaggerating, or imagining, or anticipating, sorrow."* We bask in our sorrows and anticipated sorrows and beg for prayer at every opportunity to be released from such horrors as *normal life*. Have we not read, *There hath no temptation taken you but such as is common to man: but God is faithful, who will not suffer you to be tempted above that ye are able; but will with the temptation also make a way to escape, that ye may be able to bear it* (**1 Corinthians 10:13**)? The way of escape is not the getting out of it as has been erroneously taught in our churches. It is the Greek word Ekbasis meaning that eventually there is an exit after completion of the trial.

Peter tells us quite plainly, *Beloved,* **think it not strange** *concerning the fiery trial* (Purōsis-ignition, that is, (specifically) smelting (figuratively conflagration, calamity as a test), *which is to try you, as though some strange thing happened unto you: But rejoice, inasmuch as ye are partakers of Christ's sufferings; that, when his glory shall be revealed, ye may be glad also with exceeding joy* (**1 Peter 4:12-13**). We look to our own sorrows and hardships (many are perceived or anticipated) as if we are being personally attacked by Satan himself and that these hardships ought not to be so. Yet, we have scant regard for the troubles of others, especially of those in the household of faith (**Galatians 6:10**). We have convinced ourselves that our prayers to get out of these trials ought to take priority in the annals of heaven (mainly because we've been led to believe that we are special, and that sorrows, hardships and disappointments should not be a part of a real Christian's life, when in fact, they are proof of a real Christian's life (see **2 Timothy 3:12**). All the while we completely ignore the struggles of life (many, much worse than ours) of those around us we claim to *"fellowship"* within our church services every Sunday and Wednesday. This is the very definition of selfishness.

The antithesis of love is not hatred, but indifference. We cannot live in communion with one another without love for one another. The same love that Christ gave for you and I is the same love we must give to one another. *As we have therefore opportunity, let us do good unto all men, especially unto them who are of the household of faith* (**Galatians 6:10**). As we live indifferent lives, we prove our hearts are not for God nor for His Kingdom, *...for he that loveth* (Agape- love feast) *not his brother whom he hath seen, how can he love God whom he hath not seen?* (**1 John 4:20**).

The real heroes of life are not those with superpowers, wear capes or their underpants on the outside. The real heroes of life do those things which others will not do nor learn to do. Real heroes stand in the gap for others, they get bruised, bleed, and take up for those who cannot take up for themselves, they listen and love when others do not. They sit next to the lonely, the hurting and the struggling and will take up their cause for no other reason other than it would please God and help destroy their own flesh. They Koinonia fellowship with any and *all* the saints and teach others to do the same. They go out of their way to personally minister to the saints and become vulnerable (with all the risks that come with it) so that they may empathize with others. They allow themselves to personally feel the plight of others and fight for them in both the natural and the spiritual. These heroes are ordinary folks within the Ecclesia with knotted up lives themselves but will help others untangle the mess their lives are in, and in so doing, they (as part of the Ecclesia) get their own knots untangled. With the Spirit of God and wise elder's help (without cape nor mask) we become superheroes to the lost, lonely, scared, dying, the spiritually and physically poor and broken, those underutilized and forgotten saints that sit weekly in our pews hoping beyond all hope that there is more to God than church as they know it now.

Sometimes, we believers get stuck on the '*Me Mode*', where our prayers become akin to a me-fest (bless me, heal me, I need, give me and so on). But this is one of the greatest forms of self-delusion within the church. It is where our lives implode rather than becoming a blessing to one another. Are we to ask for the things we feel we need? Yes, but the Kingdom of God must come first (**Matthew 6:30**-34). The '*See Mode*' stops us from going into the '*See Mode*' where we see the hand of God move mightily in, on and through the entire body. The '*Me Mode*' removes us from the body of Christ faster than many of the devil's devices because it makes us like a rogue cell which, left to itself, will become malignant and replicate itself, infecting the body which then begins to take on a life of its own. It will use the body as a host and begin taking life from other cells in order to feed itself (this is exactly how a parasite works). When a parasite is done with its host, the host usually dies a horrible and painful death. What do we do when we have a virus or cancer cell? We try to destroy it with radical medicines or invasive procedures. Why would God put up with people who willingly remain selfish or arrogant and are in danger of poisoning His body? He will inject some truth into the body (which is usually a foreign object. Someone from outside the body) to bring the lie of self-centredness to a quick and usually painful death.

The '*Me Mode*' and many other modes like it (*my/our group, my/our organization, my/our pastor* and the disreputable and equally as deadly *we/us only* mode) are all the ways of the world and not *The way of holiness* (see **Isaiah 35:8**). Neither is it how the followers of the God incarnate, the Messiah, operated. Paul tells us of the new nature we are to strive to get (**2 Corinthians 5:17**) when we become born again of water and spirit. Paul told the Ecclesia in both Ephesus and Colossae that they must put on the new man which is created in His image not in the image of anything here on earth (**Ephesians 4:24**). One cannot put on the new man if one is still wearing the old man, *Lie not one to another, seeing that ye have put off the old man with his deeds; And have put on the new man, which is renewed in knowledge after the image of him that created him* **Colossians 3:9-10**).

Yet when these malevolent attributes of selfishness are prevalent within the Ecclesia, we show that we do not have a true revelation of the body of Christ, neither do we have a proper revelation of eternal life with our God. We have resurrected our former self-centred lives, which once again, was meant to be crucified (**Romans 6:6**). When we live in the manner of our former self (the old man), we have dug up the corpse of our former selves and are walking around giving a corpse what it wants in the hope that it feels better. When the *I* and *me* becomes the us and we (the entire Ecclesia, not just our little closed group), then we are beginning to get an idea of Kingdom living/loving and what, who and why God came to save. The old saying, '*think globally and act locally*' seems to be missing in many believers today.

Kingdom living brings about a pleasure that many Christians seek in all the wrong places. David tells us in **Psalm 133:1** *Behold, how **good and how pleasant it is** for brethren to dwell together in unity!* (Yâchad- to be or become one). David tells us that we become pleasant or Nâˁiym- delightful, sweet, and agreeable, when we dwell together. The term *to dwell* here does not speak of seeing each other once or twice a week in a building to go through the liturgy of *pseudo-service* to God. To dwell speaks of community, of living with and for one another and of having the same mind to accomplish a daily task. It goes deeper than the surface level *quasi-fellowship* we have in much of our western style churches where *feelings* are predominant. Feelings have become so prevalent that we are loathe to say something to each other for fear of causing strife. We set our so-called services so that everyone gets something from it, but in God's economy, only those who continuously put in get an output (the story of the five wise and five foolish virgins is a great example). I am not speaking of tithe and offering, attendance or church cleaning days. I am specifically speaking of input into each other's lives personally and as often as possible, sacrificially.

What are the only two tasks given to the body of Christ? To preach the Kingdom of God only and make disciples. When we do these in **one accord** (Homothumadon- together with passion and fierceness), we organically become the Body of Christ. No programmes or gimmicks needed.

Picture a husband and wife seeing each other regularly once or twice a week and occasionally at the store or gas station while they try to talk about important matters like rent or mortgage, or how they will raise the children, and see if you can imagine a happy and productive marriage. They must dwell together, share a breakfast or dinner table, have the same focus and goals. They must see things from the perspective of producing healthy and well-adjusted children. They must pool their resources in order to maintain a healthy lifestyle. They must be living in the same house at the same time. This promotes unity and makes for a good and pleasant marriage. The actionable love of God for one another is that condition in which the fulfillment and growth of another person is essential to our own. Anything else is commentary.

To quote a famous line from *Devotions upon Emergent Occasions* by John Donne (1624), '*No man is an island, entire of itself; every man is a piece of the continent, a part of the main. If a clod be washed away by the sea, Europe is the less, as well as if a promontory were, as well as if a manor of thy friend's or of thine own were: any man's death diminishes me, because I am involved in mankind, and therefore never send to know for whom the bell tolls; it tolls for thee.*' Without each member being connected to another on more than just Sundays and midweek services or special church functions such as conferences and camp meetings or so-called revivals, we only pretend to dwell together in unity. If we are to dwell in this pleasant unity as told to us by king David, then we must be real with each other, perhaps face rejection, or misunderstanding. Those who become real with each other, stand a far better chance of learning how to be real in the world, and when the world rejects them, they have a community, whose love and acceptance is beyond question. A community where they can go for the healing balm of Gilead, prescribed by the Master physician, and dispensed by His people. **Jeremiah 8:22** *Is there no balm in Gilead; is there no physician there? why then is not the health of the daughter of my people recovered?*

Loving others for the sake of God brings about a unity that cannot be manufactured from a board meeting, a conference, or a revival. The restoration of the Ecclesia is beginning, and we must be ready to lay down our selfishness or this restoration will pass us by, and we won't even know it. We must grow in God so that we may be a more useful instrument in His hands to grow the Ecclesia.

I would like to close this chapter with a slightly paraphrased version of Kent M. Keith's book, The *Silent Revolution. The Paradoxical Commandments*:

People are illogical, unreasonable, and self-centred. Love them anyway.

If you do good, people will accuse you of selfish ulterior motives. Do good anyway.

If you are successful, you will win false friends and true enemies. Succeed anyway.

The good you do today will be forgotten tomorrow. Do good anyway.

Honesty and frankness make you vulnerable. Be honest and frank anyway.

The biggest men and women with the biggest ideas can be shot down by the smallest men and women with the smallest minds. Think big anyway.

People favour underdogs but follow only top dogs. Fight for the underdogs anyway.

What you spend years building may be destroyed overnight. Build anyway.

People really need help but may attack you if you do help them. Help people anyway.

Give the Ecclesia the best you have, and you will from time to time get kicked in the teeth. Give the Ecclesia the best you have anyway. Why not? Jesus did.

Christian individualism is the antithesis of the Commonwealth of the Kingdom of God and should therefore be avoided like the plague. It has no ability to heal nor help to consecrate anyone for service unto God's people in God's Kingdom, done in God's name, receiving God's results. Becoming vulnerable places us in a position where God becomes our defender, our buckler and shield, *He shall cover thee with his feathers, and under his wings shalt thou trust: his truth shall be thy shield and buckler* (**Psalm 91:4**). If we love and serve those that love God, it places us with that which God came to save.

Chapter 10.

God is into community.

When the Stranger says: "What is the meaning of this city? Do you huddle close together because you love each other?" What will you answer? "We all dwell together to make money from each other?" or "This is a community"? Oh my soul, be prepared for the coming of the Stranger. Be prepared for him who knows how to ask questions."

From The Rock, by Thomas Stearns Eliot. Poet, Essayist, Publisher, Playwright, Literary critic, and Editor.

Being asked questions that challenge our paradigm is never comfortable. It feels like we're being personally attacked, sometimes causes us to think we're dumb, or we're called lazy. Yet asking and being asked questions is how we grow, how we separate truth from tradition, fact from fiction. When confronted with more or deeper truth, we have only two choices. Either we accept or reject the challenge to search deeper. Whichever way we choose, who we are in God will be different tomorrow than we were yesterday.

As mentioned earlier, the only individual that matters is God, that's why He called Himself *I AM that I AM* (not we are that we are) to Moses (**Exodus 3:14**), neither did He introduce Himself as the, *I AM what you want me to be*. It was the descendants of Adam, Noah, and Abraham that God wanted to set them free from their Egyptian slave masters and bring them into a new land. He wanted to be their King so they could live in community with one another, hence the Kingdom of Israel. Moses (a murderous wanted felon) had left Egypt 40 years prior to the Exodus, so he was already free from Egyptian rule. God wanted His people back. He wanted to be their King and their Lord. Man needs to be ruled by something higher than himself (not by other men). For instance, when God created the universe, He made the planets, He made the stars to revolve around their given paths without deviation. If left alone, plants will grow, drop seeds, and grow again, animals will reproduce naturally, water will always follow the path of least resistance and the tide will always change every 12 hours and 25 minutes. These do not need a Lord.

Man, on the other hand, with the ability to set, change and achieve goals, use tools, reason, fall in love, and create ever bigger and better ways to live and then kill each other, needs a Lord. Why, with all these wonderful and unique attributes, do we need a Lord? Because left to our own devices we would have destroyed ourselves millennia ago. We humans are in desperate need of directing and correcting. You will notice that once God told the animals and trees to multiply, He never had to give them another command. Man, on the other hand...?

It is clear God always intended to have Utopia, a place where mankind could live and work (for we must have a purpose) in peace and harmony and a special place in community with one another and our Creator. There was an Eden in the beginning of God's word (**Genesis 2:8** *And the LORD God planted a garden eastward in Eden; and there he put the man whom he had formed*), and an Eden at the end of God's word (**Revelation 2:7** *He that hath an ear, let him hear what the Spirit saith unto the churches; To him that overcometh will I give to eat of the tree of life, which is in the midst of the* **paradise of God***.* (Paradeisos- of Oriental origin, a park, that is (specifically) an Eden (place of future happiness). As we lost our access to the first Eden through rebellion by the first Adam, so will have access to the same Eden through obedience to the Last Adam.

A quote attributed to author and correspondent, Tom Bodett states; *A person needs just three things to be truly fulfilled in this world: someone to love, something to do, and something to hope for.* All three are prerequisites for a normal Christian living in the Kingdom of God. Love your neighbour, do the word, and share the Gospel (Hope) of the Kingdom. If we love only by emotions or words without clear actions, then our love is baseless, pretentious, and inconsequential in the long run. True love requires hard work and much sacrifice and for no other reason than for the benefit of the object of our love. Sometimes we see little to no return, yet if it is true love, it will continue until the end. Easy? No! Do-able In Christ? Yes!

A person who is idle eventually loses all respect for themselves and for others. During the world-wide Great Depression of 1929-1939, men were so despondent about the lack of work and their inability to care for their families (a micro community) that many thousands committed suicide. They did not want a handout; they wanted a job to fulfil their purpose, to care for their family. The Great Depression lasted 10 years, but after it was over, hope was restored, and the community began to function again. Men were able to fulfil their purpose and suicide rates plummeted to the lowest level in generations. World War 2 ushered in a time of extreme hardships and sacrifice, but the community in many nations banded together and sacrificed for each other for a common goal via rationing, recycling, working 12-14 hours a day to make munitions, equipment and farming for food and sending their young men and women into harm's way. Why? Because they had a common goal; to gain the victory over an evil enemy, who, by the way, also wanted community, but they wanted a community ruled by fear and intimidation and forced adherence to laws and rules set by men and forced giving of the finances to a bureaucracy, rather than by voluntarily allowing the people to care for one another.

We have the same need today to work together to take advantage of the victory God has provided over an evil enemy. God's enemy still uses our own selfishness to slow or prevent our growth in God. Our enemy tries to have God's people ruled by men who sometimes use fear, coercion, and intimidation to enforce laws and rules set by them all in the name of God. If we do not or will not live, sacrifice our will, and even die, if necessary, for God and His community here on earth voluntarily, how can we ever live in it after we have shuffled off this mortal coil?

Though the word commonwealth, meaning *public welfare, general good or advantage*, is a term used only once in the Bible, it is written about many times using other words and terms by Paul, John, Peter and James, Isaiah, Jeremiah, Samuel, Hosea, Elijah, and many other writers in both the Old and Renewed Covenants. Other terms meaning Commonwealth for example are, *His people, The Congregation of the Lord, The Congregation of the Children of Israel, The people of God, the Nation of Israel* and so on. The word *congregation* is 'êdâh and it means a stated assemblage (specifically a concourse, or generally a family or crowd).

Paul wrote in **Ephesians 2:12** *That at that time ye were without Christ, **being aliens from the commonwealth of Israel**, and strangers from the covenants of promise, **having no hope**, and without God in the world.* This clearly states that outside of the Commonwealth of Israel we are strangers and aliens having NO HOPE. The word alien is the Greek word, Apallotrioō, meaning estranged away or a *non-participant*; this last definition is important as we will soon see. It does not only mean one from another country, but one who does not participate in the lives of their fellow-citizens (see also **Ephesians 4:1-6, 16, 1 Peter 3:8, Colossian 3:14, Acts 2:42-46, 1 Corinthians 12:26**). When only a few in the church are getting the good, both spiritually or materially, in knowledge, wisdom or revelation, how is that the general good of the church?

Chuck Swindoll in his summary of the book of James called, *The General Epistles,* puts it rather succinctly when he writes: '*In the opening of his letter, James called himself a bond-servant* (author's note; Doulos- a slave in subjection or subserviency to) *of God, an appropriate name given the practical, servant-oriented emphasis of the book. Throughout the book, James contended that faith produces authentic deeds. In other words, if those who call themselves God's people truly belong to Him, their lives will produce deeds or fruit. In language and themes that sound similar to Jesus's Sermon on the Mount, James rails against the hypocritical believer who says one thing but does another'.*

I would add they would say one thing and then do *nothing.* I have an acronym that aptly describes to these types of people. ABNA- All Belief, No Action. Does this mean that they are unfaithful to church attendance, giving of their tithe or not obeying the pastor? Not at all. But almost exclusively, the people that see this type of faithfulness are those within their own group. Our belief and faithfulness to God is proven to the world by our love for one another in the real world (**John 13:35**), not in the sterile, cloistered environment of church services. The world sees how we drop anything and everything to help one another to achieve the purposes that God has given to our fellow-labourers in the Ecclesia.

Paul chose the phrase wisely regarding **the Commonwealth of Israel**- Politeia- meaning *citizenship and community.* In order to obtain citizenship, one must live in and for the community. Their allegiance is to the whole country of their citizenship, not just parts of the country, their state, city, or block. The latter is how gang warfare starts. Rival gangs fighting over the same *turf*, trying to sell their form of high, family or meaning to those on their block, which somehow, these gangs have taken ownership of. This usually ends with many innocent victims getting killed or wounded and people staying away from that part of town.

During the early military history of the United States of America (War of 1812, American Indian Wars, Revolutionary War, Civil war etc.) soldiers fought in militias, small armies based on what states they came from and in some instances even based on what cities they haled from. Texas units, Mississippi units, Virginia units and so on. However, it was not until the U.S. entered WW1 in April 1917 and fought as a single cohesive nation, that they began to win battle after battle and war after war. The Australians in the Boer War in South Africa fought bravely as militias from different states, but it was not until WW1 that they fought as a nation, that they were called The Australian Army. Both the USA and the Aussies learnt to fight no longer *in* a small unit for a state but fought *in* a small unit *for* a nation. The whole purpose of an army is to fight for the safety and freedom of the people of their nation, most of which, these soldiers will never meet.

Kingdom living goes against everything we have been taught during toddlerhood. Let me illustrate; while we were toddlers, we were taught to play nice, then, as we grew up, we were taught to be tough. As toddlers we were taught to share, then we were taught to accumulate. As toddlers we were taught to trust each other, then we were taught to not trust until… No wonder Jesus said that …*Except ye be converted* (go back to)*, and become as little children, ye shall not enter into the kingdom of heaven* (**Matthew 18:3**)*.* Most children are naturally inquisitive, resilient, and greedy and they must be taught how to share. Therefore, we are to be like little children. We must become teachable and ready to forgive and ready to share with others.

We have robbed today's Christians of a sense of community with non-sensical statements like, *your **personal** saviour, God wants to bless **you**, open up the door of **your** heart, come to the front and get what **you** need, come, and get **your** blessing* and my all-time favourite misunderstanding, *my God shall supply all **your** need according to His riches in glory* (**Philippians 4:19**). More to follow on this verse shortly.

The first five have no basis in scripture and the last is taken completely out of context. There is no mention of a personal saviour, of God wanting to bless *you* alone without some input from you, of Jesus standing at the door of *your* heart (Jesus was standing outside the church of Laodicea trying to get back in) and of going and getting *your* whatever. These are all sales spiels used to entice many into the church and then once in, to get them to the front, only to leave people dissatisfied and disillusioned with the word of God. We have attempted to entice them into the church building and in two hours, we hope they'll buy the package. These are the same tactics that timeshare salespeople use. Show them all the goodies they can get, the pool, the amazing views, the fantastic room but neglect to tell them of the ongoing costs and they may not get the goodies they want when they want them.

"A proper community, we should remember also, is a commonwealth: a place, a resource, an economy. It answers the needs, practical as well as social and spiritual, of its members - among them the need to need one another. The answer to the present alignment of political power with wealth is the restoration of the identity of community and economy.

Wendell Berry, The Art of the Commonplace: The Agrarian Essays. Racism and the

Economy.

Chapter 11

Is it Biblical or just scriptural?

'You can't judge me', don't judge me and I won't judge you, the bible says so'. How many times have we heard this from someone who wants to continue in their sin? Is there a bible verse that tells us that? Well, yes and no. There is a verse that uses the words *'judge not'*, so yes. Should we not judge then? Of course not, because the rest of the verse finishes the sentence *...condemn not, and ye shall not be condemned: forgive, and ye shall be forgiven* (**Luke 6:37**). We may judge a situation to be wrong, but we are never ever to condemn, for this is not our domain.

First, let us see how taking a verse out of context from the scriptures makes it unbiblical and thus powerless. The word *judge* has two definitions, one we are to do, the other we are forbidden to do. *Judge*- Krinō- 1. is to distinguish and decide, or 2. to pronounce guilt, condemn, and punish. Depending on the context, we will know which one we are to do. If we do the latter, we make ourselves judge, jury and executioner which is a definite no-no in God's Kingdom. There is only one in the universe who has that responsibility and that is God Himself, *But God is the judge: he putteth down one, and setteth up another* (**Psalm 75:7**). There are several words that have been translated as judge, such as discern, search, and observe, these have their own similar definitions.

Before we go any further, I feel I must define what *Biblical* means as we have unwittingly adopted a 21st century religious understanding rather than a theological one based on the ancient document itself. Biblical means that it can withstand scrutiny by checking it with the entire collection of Holy writ, not just what our organization, pastor, bishop, teacher, family, or friends say about said Holy writ. The Bible (from Koine Greek τὰ βιβλία, Tà Biblia, meaning- 'the books') is a collection of smaller books and letters whose authors were given divine unction to write what they had seen and heard by the Holy Ghost (**2 Peter 1:21**). God used their lives, personalities, failures, and human limitations to bring His message to a lost and dying world. For God's word to be read, understood, and obeyed correctly, He commanded that the reader have the same spirit that the author had (the Holy Ghost), thus reading the bible while looking through the eyes of the writer's inspiration and life (via the Holy Ghost). Not doing this gives a different understanding resulting in false beliefs and shallow living. This collection of books must be studied via an open mind through the lens of the author, while keeping with His nature, the times, location, and language of the day.

Scriptural, on the other hand, means that a text is found in the Holy writings of God we call the scriptures. Just as a medical textbook is broken into chapters and paragraphs and its information is vital for a student to learn how to tend to a broken or diseased body, a student must understand that just because something is written in the textbook doesn't make it valid for every situation. For example, the medical textbook says that a splint must be applied to a broken arm (in essence a splint is scriptural), but that doesn't mean a doctor applies a splint to someone who has appendicitis. Is a splint in the textbook? Yes. But is it medically sound for the patient with appendicitis? Obviously not, because upon further reading of the medical book, it would reveal what the procedure is for appendicitis. Scriptural is text, and when read and understood with the whole, makes the scripture Biblical and helpful.

Because something is scriptural doesn't mean it is for everyone, everywhere, every time. Just as there are certain things every doctor must do to and for every patient (listen to them, observe symptoms, prescribe the right medication for the right ailment etc.), there are certain universal verses in the bible such as, *we must be born again of water and spirit, we must love God and our neighbour as ourselves, obey the Ten Commandments* and so on. For example, there are literally hundreds of scriptures that refer only to the Levitical priesthood. They are scriptural but not for us today such as how and when to sacrifice the animal and in a manner that pleases God, what type of clothing the priest must wear and so on. They are scriptural, but not in accordance with how we sacrifice today.

In Mosaic Law (**Leviticus 15:19-30**), it is stated that a woman undergoing menstruation is perceived as unclean for seven days and whoever touches her shall be unclean until evening. She must remain outside the city for seven days and then return home. Is this scriptural? Yes. It is plainly written in the bible. Is it biblical and for women today? Of course not. Another example is when a family joined themselves to Israel, the man was to be circumcised in the flesh before he and his family were counted as Israelites (**Exodus 12:48-49**). Is this scriptural? Yes. Is it biblical for us today? No. Paul tells us that it is infinitely more important to be circumcised in the heart than of the flesh (**Romans 2:28-29**). The Tabernacle/Temple was clearly God's meeting place with man (**Exodus 25:9**) with a priest as the mediator (**Exodus 28:1**). Is this scriptural? Of course. Is it for the believers today that they must meet God in a building through a priest or pastor as mediator in order to show their piety or faithfulness? Absolutely not! Jesus prophesied that the temple was only a temporary thing and Paul concurred (see **Acts 17:24, 1 Corinthians 6:19-20**). The disciple Stephen tells us about this in **Acts 7:48-49** *Howbeit the most High dwelleth **not** in temples made with hands; as saith the prophet, Heaven is my throne, and earth is my footstool: **what house will ye build me**? saith the Lord: or what is the place of my rest? ... Jesus answered and said unto them, Destroy this temple, and in three days I will raise it up* (**John 2:19**). Was the Temple and mediatorial priesthood scriptural? Of course. Is it biblical for the true disciples of God today? No!

Paul writes to Timothy regarding the abolition of the old-style priesthood in **1 Timothy 2:5** *For there is one God, and **one mediator between God and men, the man Christ Jesus.*** God would not have destroyed the only place He said He would meet with men (the Tabernacle in the wilderness or what replaced it- the Temple), if He was not going to be our high priest from now on. He still dwells with man, only now it is in the hearts and minds of man, and He is our high priest and mediator.

The problem with using just one or two scriptures to make a point is, it eventually leads to disaster. Look at what is said of one of the disciples in **Matthew 27:5** *And he cast down the pieces of silver in the temple, and departed, and went and hanged himself.* Is this scriptural? Of course, it is. Should we go and hang ourselves when we have done something so bad that we think we have blown it with God? No, because it's not in accordance with the whole bible, in other words, it is not biblical. The word biblical just means that it's in accordance with the whole biblia (the books) in context with itself, the character of God and historical evidence based on the language and times it was written. Commentaries, bible dictionaries, and books such as the one you're reading now may be helpful, but it is still God's word in context with itself that has the power to change us from inside out.

Earlier I cited a much misquoted and misunderstood verse in the bible, *...But my God shall supply all your need...* (**Philippians 4:19**). This is indeed written in the bible; however, it has been taken completely out of context and given to a church populace that is generally ignorant of God's word and therefore has lost much of its efficacy. This verse was written to a group of people (the Ecclesia at Philippi) who cared for the need of another group of people (the Ecclesia travelling with Paul). For example, let's just look at that scripture in regard to this blessing being a solely individual one in context with the whole scripture, *But my God shall supply all* **your** (Humeis- plural of you-yourselves) *need* (note also: the singular word *need*, not *needs*) *according to his riches in glory by Christ Jesus*. This cannot be used to seek a blessing or a miracle just because we want or need one. It can and should be sought by the Ecclesia for a member or members in need and when the miracle or need has been met, it benefits the Ecclesia. Why? Because now we have fully functioning members who are not distracted by circumstances out of their control. It therefore goes, that it was the *body* that received the miracle, it just happened to land on a part of the body and spread out to the rest of the body. So, I ask again, who was this written to and why? And individual or the '*Church of Philippi*?

Paul wrote this to the elders of the church (the Ecclesia) in Philippi, to be read to the entire church in a city of about 10,000-15,000 people in a town of about 100 square hectares (about half a square mile). To understand the context of verse nineteen, we must go to verses fourteen and fifteen when Paul writes, *Notwithstanding* **ye** *have well done, that* **ye** *did communicate with my affliction* (burdens and troubles). *Now* **ye** *Philippians* (notice once again, not written to a particular person, but to the Ecclesia at Philippi) *know also, that in the beginning of the gospel, when I departed from Macedonia,* **no church** (Ecclesia) **communicated** (Koinōneō- to share with others (objectively or subjectively) to distribute, be partaker.) *with me as concerning giving and receiving, but* **ye** *only*. Here is the difference between *ye* and *you.* Remember, words in the bible have specific meanings for specific purposes. In 17th century old English, thee, thine, and thou are singular, while ye, you and your, are plural. When *ye* or *your* are used, think the church, not an individual in the church. For example, *O clap your hands, all* **ye** *people; shout unto God with the voice of triumph* (**Psalm 147:1**). To whom did David write this to? He wrote this to his subjects, the nation of Israel.

We can see that the people of Philippi *communicated* (Sugkoinōneō- to share in company with, that is, co-participate in: have fellowship with, be partaker of or with) Paul, even when he went to Thessalonica (about 160 km/100 miles away) they sent an emissary (a person sent on a special mission, in this case it was Epaphroditus) with goods to meet their necessities, not once but many times (verse 16), even to the point where he says that he abounds in all (they were given more than enough for the upcoming journey) and that their gift, *became an odour of a sweet smell, a sacrifice acceptable, wellpleasing to God* (verse 18). Please note, the gift was a sacrifice, meaning that it hurt to give it. Paul goes on to say, *But* (De- now, moreover) *my God shall supply all* **your** (Humon- from Humeis plural of you- yourselves) *need* (Chreia- employment, lack, necessities) *according to His riches in glory by Christ Jesus*. When we sacrifice and go out of our way for the need of others, it becomes an acceptable and wellpleasing smell to God, **then** God will meet our need. It was the Ecclesia that met Paul and his fellowlabourer's need and it was the Ecclesia that benefitted, not an individual. All this was done in and for the love of God and His disciples.

The problem with individualism in Christianity (the church) is that it flies in the face of the Kingdom of God. Christian individualism poses an existential threat to the proper operation of the Kingdom of God here on earth in that we've been commanded and commissioned to proclaim a message that is God-centred. The true gospel of the Kingdom of God replaces the "*I*" with the "*I Am*". The social gospel of the '*I*' and '*me*' is a self-centred, self-satisfying message, that parades on platforms and performs weekly rituals in the hope that it will please God. The '*I*' centred message is all about what God can do for me and mine, my little group or organization and is diametrically opposed to the Gospel of the Kingdom of God and makes us an enemy of the cross of Jesus Christ (**Philippians 3:14-18**). A gospel that is centred around individuality is precisely the gospel Paul warned us about, *But though we, or an angel from heaven, preach **any other gospel** unto you than that which we have preached unto you, let him be accursed* (**Galatians 1:8**). He is not specifically speaking of a gospel of three Gods in one or the wrong baptism (these did not come about for over 250 years). Paul was warning of a gospel where God was not the centre, and we can see this in context with the rest of the letter to the Galatians.

To the best of our knowledge, the great commission was given to approximately 120 people, not 1 or 12 but 120. These were people from diverse backgrounds and differing ages; teenagers, men, women, fathers, mothers, some educated, the vast majority were not, few were wealthy, most were poor, slaves and freemen, both Jew and Gentile but all had walked with or experienced the Master in some way and had been affected by the Messiah and His message at some point in His earthly ministry. Their diversity of background and experience was an asset to be embraced not a hindrance subjected to forced unity. One cannot encounter the real Christ (remember, there were false Christs also, *For there shall arise false Christs, and false prophets, and shall shew great signs and wonders; insomuch that, if it were possible, they shall deceive the very elect* **Matthew 24:24**, see also **Acts 5:38-39**) and not have the same passion and burning desire to fulfil the will of the Father. The commonality of passion, experience and shared lives brought about an organic change in their lives by the Holy Ghost, with no need of browbeating or coercing someone into living holy for God, which then led to an organic unity in vision and outreach and sharing all they had with each other. This passion to be like their Lord was breathed on them when they received the Holy Ghost. This in turn made them effective in their world and their generation. They were in one accord (Homothumadon- from Homou and Thumos meaning at the same place or time [for a purpose] in passion- as if breathing hard, fierceness, indignation), and therefore they could accomplish so much in such a relatively short space of time. We can be in the same place at the same time, but without the passion of Christ for one another and to fulfil the great commission, it's just a club meeting.

What is the purpose of being in one accord? Like any carpenter, mechanic or surgeon, a single tool at one time in their hand, is how they ply their trade. A carpenter can use a hammer, a saw, or a level, but he will not use a hammer to level a piece of wood or a saw to drive in a nail. One tool for one aspect of his job. A surgeon will deftly use a scalpel, a clamp, or a suture, but not at the same time (one cuts, one holds and the other joins together), one tool for each aspect of their job. When we are in one accord, God can use each of us for our intended purposes. We have become many tools in the Master's toolbox that *He* uses to build *His* church at *His* discretion not at the discretion of man (**Matthew 16:18**). As we strive to be an effective instrument in His hands at the right time and right place, we show the world the difference between the kingdoms of this world and the Kingdom of God, and why He left the Ecclesia to finish the job He started (see **John 14:12**).

Colossians 2:2-3 *That their hearts might be comforted, being **knit together** in love, and unto all **riches of the full assurance of understanding**, to the **acknowledgement of the mystery of God**, and of the Father, and of Christ; In whom are hid all the treasures of wisdom and knowledge.* Do you see any reference here to riches and wealth of money or real estate? No! The riches are an assurance of understanding (wisdom) and being able to discern the mysteries of God. It is when our hearts are knit together (Sumbibazō- to force; causatively [by reduplication i.e. discipleship] to drive together, unite (in association or affection), (mentally) to infer, show and teach: compacted assuredly, gather, instruct, and to prove) that we receive the blessing of full assurance of our understanding (Sunesis- to put together with intelligence, to comprehend and **act piously**) and to acknowledge or recognize the mystery of God, whose treasure is not gold, fame, land, prestige or position, but wisdom and knowledge. We get these things for one purpose only; for the furtherance of our great King's message to a lost world as evidenced by our lives together.

Remember, the suffix *ism* is described as an oppressive and especially discriminatory attitude or belief. Christian individualism or group sectarianism is the complete antithesis of our calling. Being in one accord *will* bring strife and pressure, it can and will cause arguments because we must fight our own selfishness and lusts, our own pride and arrogance, our own thinking or understanding, and many times we must fight the traditions of men which hinder the commandments of God. As we submit one to another, humble ourselves and do things someone else's way, we work it out for the sake of the Kingdom of God (**1 Peter 5:5-6, Romans 12:10, 1 Timothy 5:21, Philippians 2:12**). It will be difficult or frustrating sometimes, even seemingly impossibly at other times, but we strive to enter the gate that leads to Christ which is ...*narrow and few there be that find it*. We don't kick out those who don't fit into our mould and hide it under the guise of unity. We become one (with freedom of expression and free to grow at the pace God has chosen) so the world may see that we truly do serve One indivisible and incorruptible God who rules us as well as the universe.

The ways of the world tell us that we should look inward, take care of number one, blow our own trumpet, while the gospel says to look outward and upward, take care of the Kingdom and let God lift us up. Paul reminds us of our priorities in **Galatians 6:9-10** *And let us not be weary in **well doing**:* (not just good doctrine) *for in due season we shall reap, if we faint not. As we have therefore opportunity, let us do good unto all* [**men**] (the word *men* is not in the original letter, it was added by the translators. The word is actually *De-* meaning *but* or *moreover*), **especially unto them who are of the household of faith**. The Aramaic English New Testament adds a little more clarification to the word *opportunity* when it says, *Now therefore, **while we have time**, let us do good to every person, especially to the members of the household of faith. While we have time-* that is the problem. We foolishly believe we have lots of it, however, this is a self-imposed delusion that we have copious amount of 60 seconds, 60 minutes, 24 hours, 30-day allotments, and when we find out we don't we cry and bemoan our lot. These are all man-made constructs we feel we have mastered. Time (according to our clocks and calendars) is a misconception, for we only have now in time. There will be a time when we run out of time to be used for the Commonwealth of the Kingdom of God, after that, time is up and we must answer the question, "*What did we do with the time we were given?*"

We can earn money, fame, influence, power, or prestige but we cannot earn time. It is the only thing we ourselves can redeem. Paul tells the Ecclesia of Ephesus, *Redeeming* (Exagorazō- buying back wasted or rescue from loss) *the time, because the days are evil,* he goes on to say, *Walk in wisdom toward them that are without, redeeming* (Exagorazō) *the time* (**Ephesian 5:16, Colossians 4:5**). When the opportunity has passed to do good, it will be too late and then we must answer to God for the time we wasted. *And that, knowing the time* (Kairos- occasion, opportunity) *that now it is **high time*** (Hōra- the day, hour season, as in tide) *to awake out of sleep* (Hupnos- spiritual torpor [inactivity, lethargy or apathy], subsilence (a combination word meaning substance and resilience): *for now is our salvation nearer than when we believed* (**Romans 13:11**). Paul tells us that now (not later or tomorrow) is our salvation even closer than we think. Selfishness robs us of time we can, should, and must spend on preparing the Ecclesia, (and as we are a part of the Ecclesia, we prepare ourselves) for the Kingdom which is to come down in the New Heaven and New Earth, with the New Jerusalem as its capitol in which we will reign and rule forever with Him. It was focusing on self that got Satan expelled from God's presence. Individuality of want and desire, mimics Satan and his kingdom, why would God tolerate it in His Ecclesia on earth let alone in His presence.

Chapter 12.

Altruism and the Commonwealth of the Kingdom of God.

Before we go down the road of servanthood through altruism, it is important to know that there is no such thing as purely altruistic thoughts, if they do not end in altruistic actions. If there is no action, the thought was merely a nice idea or a good intention. Nobody gets comfort, healing, or deliverance by sending good thoughts. The same goes for the unbiblical idea of a *"special unspoken prayer request"*. Even a quick search of the bible tells us that it was when someone spoke, prayed, or asked that God intervene in a situation that something happened. Jesus healed all those whom He asked what they wanted, such as the leper, blind Bartimaeus, at the sheep's gate pool (Bethesda), the ruler of the synagogue's daughter and many others (**Matthew 8:2, Mark 10:51, John 5:6-10, Matthew 9:18**). Even the woman with the issue of blood didn't offer up a silent prayer, She got on her knees and crawled to God.

It is noted that the bible speaks of an altruistic society (the Ecclesia) in which the well-being (in mind, body, and spirit) of all within it is the core of its existence. Just like we are told in the safety instructions on an aeroplane, that we must place the oxygen mask on ourselves first before we help others, so the Ecclesia must care for its own sick, weak, hungry, and poor before it expends even more time and resources bringing in more of the same from the world. Who will look after those who come in if there isn't anyone to personally feed and care for the new babes in our churches now.

This well-being is directed by the head of the Ecclesia because no-one but the head knows the beginning from the end, no-one but the head of the Ecclesia is the alpha and omega and the author and finisher of our faith. Allowing the Spirit of the Ecclesia (God Himself) to rule it, was a radical way of living and proving the beliefs of the early church (33 AD to middle-to-late second century AD). It was only after the forced acceptance of the then state religion of Rome (which became known as the Roman Catholic church), that the Ecclesia lost its ability to be ruled by the God that bought it with His precious blood (**1 Corinthian 6:20, 7:13**) and began to be ruled by men. We must return to the Ecclesia's core value if we are to be relevant again today and change the zeitgeist of our time. Core beliefs shape a person's world view, and this then is subconsciously acted out. If we think that God is more interested in blessing the individual than in placing each individual into a fully functioning body, where all are equal and where God gives gifts to ALL men, that He can use at His discretion, thus *being* a blessing, then we are most sadly deceived.

Altruism is best described in general terms as an individual whose behaviour aims to benefit another individual in need (with no thought of personal gain); one with whom the altruist has a connection (whether spiritual or natural) and if enough people in the Ecclesia have an altruistic outlook on their purpose here on earth, the Ecclesia turns into an egalitarian society (this doctrine is generally characterized by the idea that all humans are equal in fundamental worth or moral status). This is the characteristic of the social welfare function of God's Ecclesia. (As an example of the Ecclesia's altruistic leaning, we see that the tithe consisted of produce and livestock and only one tenth of the tithe was given to the tribe of Levi as we are told in **Leviticus 27:30-32**. This was given to the Levites for their support for ministry as they were not allowed to own business or work in secular employment, see **Numbers 18:21-2**. The Levites, in turn and in gratitude gave a tithe of the tithe to the priests for their service in **Numbers 18:25-28**). The worshipper could eat a portion of the sacrifice with his family and the Levites in **Deuteronomy 12:17-19** and **14:22-27**. Lastly, another tithe was taken every third year to help the poor, the strangers, the orphans, and the widows. This tithe was comparable to a social welfare system for the most unfortunate in society.

As we can see, the Children of Abraham, Isaac, and Jacob and all the subsequent generations knew that taking care of others was a way to show God their love for Him. In **1 Corinthians 10:1-11** we can see that Paul tells us to use what happened to and through Israel as an example to us that we might learn from them and their history.

When the world, which is individualistic by nature, sees another group living and loving in a manner so totally removed from their own, it will peak their spirits, and many will be drawn to the spirit of God in this society which is meant to be the same in earth as it is in heaven.

Core beliefs come in all shapes and sizes, ranging from the ultra-negative to the Pollyanna type hyper positive ('*No, my leg did not just fall off my body*') and neither are healthy to the individual nor the Ecclesia. A positive example of core belief would be a runner in a marathon who has trained for months for the race. If they focus on Usain Bolt and his achievements, it will motivate them to continue running. On the other hand, as they start getting tired and begin thinking that their legs are made of bricks, they will soon slow down. Neither one of these scenarios would have made a difference if they had not trained in the first place, but their mindset in the race does help in determining the outcome.

The core belief of altruism is more finely characterized as: *the belief in and practice of being interested, selfless and concerned for the well-being of others. Its practitioners advocate,* **using evidence and reason,** *as the most effective ways to benefit others within the group.* Within the Ecclesia we add the dimension of prayer and fasting. People whose core belief is altruistic are not hyper positive *Pollyannas* running around saying all's well when it is not. They see things for what they truly are but are dedicated to improving the lives of others in every area (spiritual, mental, material, emotional, and physical) using all the resources at their disposal with and for the whole group. Altruism does not believe in a class of elites within the group (defined as having special privileges and segregated from the main group). This does not negate the need for leadership, just that leadership is recognized as having information and abilities to share with all and sundry and they may be honoured but are not elevated or segregated because of said information and or abilities.

Ego: 1/ An exaggerated sense of self-importance; conceit. 2/ The self, especially as distinct from the world and other selves.

Egoism: 1/ The belief that self-interest provides the proper basis for moral behaviour. 2/ A doctrine that individual self-interest is the valid end of all actions. 3/ Excessive concern for oneself with or without exaggerated feelings of self-importance.

The antithesis of altruism is egoism, can also be defined as, *the moral concept that composes self-interest as the substance of morality.* The primary thinking is, '*if it seems good, looks good or feels good for me, then it must be good, therefore, I should have it or do it*'. We only need to look at the Garden of Eden and the Tree of knowledge of Good and Evil: '*it looks good for me; therefore it must be good for me*', said Eve (paraphrased **Genesis 3:6**). Egoism uses coercion, intimidation, ostracization/silent treatment, cold shoulder, and ultimatums to achieve self-interest (many times under the guise of doing good for others) and does not accept that others within the group may have a differing view or perhaps a better way of doing things. Egoism imposes change by force (whether overt or covert) rather than proposes change through example. In leadership, egoism's main catchphrase is, *I'm in charge, do as I say!* When the flesh leads it tells the spirit it's in charge, just do it. Egoism seeks out and preys on the weak-minded and weak-willed and is highly intimidated by others who have a strong will to do anything other than fall in line with the egotistical mind.

The Commonwealth of the Kingdom of God is an altruistic society, fuelled by love for one another, which mirrors what is happening in their future home. Are there examples of looking to a future home on earth in recent centuries? Yes, it can be seen in the migration of peoples throughout history. When people leave their country (whether because of persecution, famine or as refugees from war), after a long and arduous journey, they will find a suitable place to live that will sustain their community (availability of water, food, shelter, farmland, building materials) and over time they will transform this new land to resemble the community they lived in prior to being forced out. These immigrants do this to restore their sense of well-being and to root themselves in the past and in fond memories. This can be seen initially by some of the names they choose for their new homeland such as New South Wales, New Brunswick, New York, New Jersey, New Hampshire, New Zealand, New Mexico, New Caledonia and so on. They bring with them vestiges of their former lives in order to make it feel more like home. This is how the church has lost much of its power in the community. We have brought ideas and concepts into the church from our former lives in the world and incorporated them into our church lives. Rather than saying the old land was full of death, pain and destruction and we will start a new life, putting new practices in place, so the new will not become like the old.

Commonwealth minded people come with a different mindset. The Ecclesia also has a place they seek. It is mentioned in **Revelation 21:1-2** *And I saw a **new heaven** and a **new earth**: for the first heaven and the first earth were passed away; and there was no more sea. And I John saw the holy city, **new Jerusalem**, coming down from God out of heaven, prepared as a bride adorned for her husband.* This place has yet to be seen with the naked eye, yet we know it exists. We will take with us the experiences (but not the practices) which we have lived here on earth as citizens of the Commonwealth into the new land where there will be peace and security in God. We are no different than any other people born on the planet, we only seek to have the mind of Christ as opposed to the mind of the world we dwell in.

The pioneers and refugees that went to these new lands looked back at what once was and changed their surroundings to remind them of a kinder past. The body of Christ, on the other hand, looks at a Kingdom that has yet to physically come, they look for a city whose builder and maker is God Himself and no hand has made (**Hebrews 11:10**), who's King cannot be seen with the naked eye right now (**1 John 4:12**), and it changes itself into the image of its creator (**2 Corinthians 3:18**) in order to prepare for a time in which they will dwell in a future land. The words of the Messiah Himself, *Thy Kingdom come **in** earth* (not **on** earth) *as it is **in** heaven* (**Matthew 6:10, Luke 11:2**), should give us a clue as to what we are to look for, and we must do all in our power to prepare ourselves.

Please note the often mis-quoted word in what is commonly (but erroneously) called the Lord's Prayer. The Lord did not say **on** *earth* but **in** *earth*. The Kingdom of God is not operating on earth as it is in heaven today because sin and Satan still rule this planet. The death, burial and resurrection of Christ has defeated Satan and sin only for those who choose not to dwell in sin or who choose another master (Christ). However, Pauls words remind us that we are vessels made *of* earth to contain a treasure (His word), and shows that His Kingdom can indeed, be **in** *earth* while we are still *on* earth. But we have this treasure *in* earthen vessels, that the excellency of the power may be of God, and not of us (**2 Corinthians 4:7**).

An altruistic society does not merely focus on the bare necessities of life such as food, water, clothing, and shelter (we have many charities throughout the world that provide these free of charge to hundreds of millions of indigent people on a daily basis). Sadly, man's attempt to be altruistic in their own strength only causes the need to arise again tomorrow, for they will be hungry, thirsty, and cold, necessitating the continuance of these services, *For ye have the poor always with you; but me ye have not always*, **Matthew 26:11**). Altruism is focused on the whole being (natural and spiritual) and endeavours to lift each person, regardless of their socio-economic, educational, or spiritual status, to a higher level of being for the good of the community, in our case, the Kingdom of God. They seek the well-being of other members of their group through actionable empathy, tangible compassion and striving for all to have access to the same resources, information, and opportunities, not so they may feather their own nest, but to give back to the group. All teaching and resources are given on the same level, (nothing is held back for an elite few) regardless of length of time in the group or on someone's ability to input into the group (be it with time, talents, or treasure).

When, on occasion, the group has excess (more than its basic needs), it does not needlessly store it up or squander it on nicer, newer, or bigger things. The group (in our case, the Ecclesia) turns its attention onto others outside of the Ecclesia as a way of showing how the Kingdom of God operates here on earth. They practice these same qualities to potential members outside the Ecclesia, hoping they will see the love of God in and for the Ecclesia. Thus, it can now fulfil the outside portion of the mission of the Ecclesia, and those who are drawn to this way of living (as seen by our treatment of each other, see **John 13:35**) will become a part of the Ecclesia. We then teach them how to live and work within the framework of God's word for the Ecclesia. This has a two-fold benefit; first, the Ecclesia grows, thus increasing the life experiences and wisdom brought in by the new members. Second, it increases the labour resources and spreads the burden amongst a greater area, which in turn raises the level of productivity and the cycle begins again. This is church growth in its simplest, most effective, and most lasting form.

This sounds an awful lot like the group that Jesus had around him and how they practiced their lives after He left them. I use the word practice in its literal sense meaning- the actual application or use of an idea, belief, or method, as opposed to theories relating to it. I also use the word practice, because very few people get it right the first time every time. God allows for mistakes and missteps, that is why we have on going grace and mercy, and as long as we keep going, our mistakes make us stronger and wiser. Not allowing people to do things in-case they make a mistake is stopping one of the most powerful ways people learn.

The Lord focused on households, not houses, the occupants not buildings. The heart, mind, and body voluntarily giving to one another, not an institution which robs the group from fulfilling its purpose by taking from one source, running it through a bureaucracy, and giving to another. Christ is more interested in each member of the Ecclesia fulfilling their God given purpose within the Ecclesia (learning from and teaching one another) than each member handing over their responsibility to a few, all the while hoping they are pleasing God. Christ's burden was that we would get His burden and live it out so others may see Him through us. This type of community will stick out like a frog in a tutu. Altruism and Commonwealth are two wings connected to the same bird and it is how the Ecclesia will soar through any storm (whether natural or through persecution) headed its way.

I feel a definition of bureaucracy is warranted at this point. The Encyclopedia Britannica defines it this way: *it is a specific form of organization defined by complexity, division of labour, permanence, professional management, hierarchical coordination and control, strict chain of command, and legal authority.* Bureaucracy is a beast that once it has established itself is constantly in need of feeding and when it is starved of its preferred food will turn on those who cannot or will no longer feed it. It robs the people of personal responsibility of caring for one another and thinking for themselves. Bureaucracy demands that all goods and service come under its control and tells others that only they have the answer to the dilemma that created the bureaucracy in the first place.

The Kibbutz.

In Israel, they have had small communities called Kibbutz (literally meaning a gathering or clustering), the first being called *Deganya Aleph* (meaning *the first grain*) and has been around since 1909 (almost 40 years before the Nation of Israel was formally re-established by the U.N.). Each member contributes as best as they can and all benefit from what the community produces. All contribute and all gain. Sounds a lot like **Acts 2:42-46** and **Acts 4:32-37,** doesn't it? These communities are not cloistered groups nor have secluded themselves from interaction with the outside world. They trade, barter, and interact with the world so that others may see a different kind of community in operation. They have open arms to accept any and all into their community on the understanding that they will be a part of a working body designed by its creator to eventually fulfil His will here on earth. They must be made aware prior to joining that their new Lord and Master expects much from them and that servanthood is a prerequisite to remaining in this Kingdom.

I've spoken about this to many pastors and leaders and have been told this sounds an awful lot like socialism or communism. A few even told me it was pie in the sky stuff I was proposing, and that it's too hard to implement today. I beg to differ. Too hard is not impossible. I would also hear these same people tell the congregation that nothing was impossible for God. Wait a minute, does that not seem contradictory? When Christ filled His Ecclesia, He sent them into a hostile world under the rule of a brutal dictatorial empire where famines and wars were the order of the day. And yet, somehow, they not only survived, but thrived. Through their persecution and death came freedom and life. This is **Romans 12:1-3** explained. This is our blueprint on not only how to survive, but to thrive.

I would like to make a clear distinction between altruism led by the Spirit of God and communism/socialism which is a construct of frail and fallible man. In the most direct form, communism's main criticism is that it entails every individual completely abandoning his or her own well-being for the "good of society". All **must** contribute (under pain of, prison, death, or excommunication from the community), but not all necessarily gain from the contributions made. It's kind of like, all must give their money to the church, but when they need some money, the church does not reciprocate. How is it that in all communist countries there are still poverty stricken and sick people and those that are in the upper echelon of society always have what they need and more?

Communism/Socialism states that we do all for the good of the state, while neglecting the sense of self. The Ecclesia states we do all for the good of our brother and sister at the same time and in the same manner we care for ourselves, *And the second is like, namely this, Thou shalt love thy neighbour as thyself. There is none other commandment greater than these.* (**Mark 12:31.** See also

Leviticus 19:18). Communism states that all goes to a central bureaucracy then doled out as the state defines the need. The Ecclesia states our help is interpersonal without the need of a central bureaucracy to move goods and services to those in need (time, talents, or treasures). Communism states that all laws and rules are made by a central committee led by one man. The Ecclesia states that the Lord makes the rules, and we all exhort and provoke one another in love to keep them for the health of the community which in turn pleases the Lord (**Matthew 22:39, Hebrews 10:24-25**).

Biblically based altruism has a different outlook in that it is the ideal spiritual and socio-economic society of "*from each according to his ability, to each according to his need*". The community is still focused on each member; however, the sharing is done as whatever we input into the community we will also benefit from, (I am not speaking just financially). For example, if one member of the community is injured or sick, whether physically, mentally, or spiritually, all will work a little harder to help the sick or injured get better whilst still performing their own duties, this then allows the group to go back to full productivity and lessens the workload of all (see **Galatians 6:1-3**). If the community has a mechanic and a farmer, they will help each other to achieve the goals that will increase the input of the community. The farmer has equipment that needs a mechanic, and the mechanic has need of grain and meat. If one member is good at teaching while another has much insight/wisdom in parenting then these would be greatly advantageous to the group and each other. If a member of the community is good at administrating while another is good at cooking, they will both use each other's strengths and teach each other skills that did not have before, thus minimizing the groups weaknesses and helps keep everyone on the same footing. This works in all areas of community and Ecclesiastical life.

If a member is unwilling (not unable) to input into the group, this puts an undue burden on all members. The unwilling member cannot expect to benefit from the eventual reward. A common problem with communism is all benefits go to a central location, where bureaucracy swallows up a great portion of the input, and what is left is doled out to all and sundry. The problem now arises that what remains is not enough to sustain growth within the society. In a communist or socialist society, the bureaucrats who receive the outputs of society are never poor. It is never the community that decides who needs what, but the bureaucrats, who rarely have much interaction with those lower on the totem pole, so they do not have firsthand information as to the needs of others. Altruism works on one's desires to better oneself (spiritually, mentally, physically, emotionally, and financially) for the sake of the community and where all (regardless of what status they have within the group) are raised from where they are and helped to better themselves for the benefit and goals (depending on the central theme) of the group and all done in the name of Jesus.

It is no longer working *for* one's own self-interest but working *on* oneself for the interest of those within the group who have needs (not necessarily wants), for those who need what we have to offer, not just in resources but in experience, compassion, wisdom, and revelation. It is allowing the Holy Ghost to make us who we are meant to be for a greater purpose than self or even heaven. Paul tells us in **Ephesians 4:28** *Let him that stole steal no more:* (we've all stolen from society and God in one way or another) *but rather let him labour,* **working with his hands the thing which is good, that he may have to give to him that needeth.**

Since this book is being written in the United States of America in 2019-22, I will use a more local example than that of the Kibbutz' of Israel. The closest we must look to regarding community living remotely similar to the Kingdom of God in the U.S would be the Amish or Mennonite communities. Though their doctrine of salvation is not in accordance with the bible, their understanding of Ecclesia (called out and gathered) is closer than any mainstream Christian organization in western society and therefore worthy of study.

Their doctrine of community encompasses five fundamental rules: humility, modesty, obedience, equality (of opportunity), and simplicity. These fundamentals must be supreme within the Ecclesia of the living God.

Let us look at these and see how they are meant to be manifest in God's Ecclesia.

1. **Humility**: One cannot be self-centred and humble at the same time. Let's face it, we don't have to struggle to be self-centred, it comes naturally. But being humble, like loving, is a choice we make. The maxim is true that, *Humility is not thinking less of yourself, but thinking of yourself less.* Humility's definition can be described as a freedom from pride and arrogance; lowliness of mind; a low estimate of oneself; an attitude of spiritual modesty that comes from understanding our place in the larger order of things, modest opinion or estimate of one's own importance or rank. Humility is always looking to have others recognized or cared for before self. It is knowing that self may have talents, but without God and others, those talents would be detrimental to the group in the long term. It also recognizes that talent without humility will manifest as inordinate pride. In the Amish and Mennonite community (as it is meant to be in the Ecclesia), one does not brag about one's own achievements and goods but lifts the group's ability to give to others through the grace and mercy of God. Remember the words of the Master come to mind, *And whosoever shall exalt himself shall be abased; and he that shall humble himself shall be exalted*, and then James' admonition, *Humble yourselves in the sight of the Lord, and he shall lift you up* (**Matthew 23:12, James 4:10**).

2. **Modesty**: This is closely related to the former in that it does not draw attention to any part of the body or soul. Modesty is defined as the act of showing reserve in behaviour or clothes. Those that live ostentatiously are drawing attention to certain parts of their lives (mainly their bank account) and those who dress immodestly are drawing attention to certain parts of their body, rather than living in a manner that draws attention to the character of God. Wearing non-revealing clothing that costs a small fortune is still not modesty. IT IS PRIDE! The Amish dress, spend money and behave modestly because their desire to let others see God first, trumps their desire to look good before the world.

3. **Obedience**: Though their understanding of obedience is a little askew, their purpose is to be obedient to God in every area of their lives, starting from the time they rise to the time of their evening repose. They understand that one cannot show their faith without obedience to the Faithful One and His word. Their obedience to God's work and work ethic is guided by wise elders who have been around the block a time or two and are willing to impart their knowledge to those willing to listen and heed time proven advice. A young farmer would do well to heed the words of an older successful farmer. Hence heeding and obedience have the same outcome. Forced submission does not help the individual nor the group.

4. **Equality**: No one person or family is rich nor poor, in either a natural or spiritual sense. Older and wiser, perhaps, but all receive the same input. One may have more by dint of years of labour, but it is not hoarded nor flaunted but shared when needed. When one has a need, it becomes the need of the entire family or community. One does not boast about personal ownership for all belongs to the community. The holders of the goods, information or wisdom are only stewards of what God has granted to the community which shares in the wealth. If one has a need of a plough, fabric, lantern,

or flour for example, it is the community that makes sure the need is taken care of. This cannot happen via forced socialism but through a voluntary and joyful deference to the community. The way much of Christendom lives today, can be paraphrased from George Orwell's book, *Animal Farm: A Fairy Story,* **All saints are equal, but some saints are more equal than others.** (Secker & Warburg: London, 1945).

5. **Simplicity**: The Amish live with basic needs, and this removes the temptation of hoarding. Their clothing, transport, housing, and food are of a basic nature to ensure that all within their community have, not only enough food and shelter, but also, spiritual, mental, and physical well-being. Paul writes in **2 Corinthians 11:3** *But I fear, lest by any means, as the serpent beguiled Eve through his subtilty, so your minds should be corrupted from the* **simplicity** *that is in Christ.* This simplicity is Haplotēs- singleness, that is, sincerity (without dissimulation or self-seeking).

Financial, shelter and food security come from the community itself. This can be seen in small part in the famous Amish barn-raising. A barn raising is an example of what the Amish call a *frolic*, a work event that combines socializing with a practical goal. The barn raising fulfills a practical need as well as serving to tie the Amish community together, reinforcing Amish society through a very visible expression of the principle of mutual aid. When a project, such as a barn, shed or major house repairs needs to be undertaken, the entire community chips in to help. Not so much the giving of money (though this is a part of the giving in case the community does not have what they need, they may buy what they need from the outside world), but of time, skills, labour, and resources. In essence it is the community that builds the barn, not just the farmer with the help of the community. The men use their skills as carpenters, blacksmiths, architects, and labour while the women keep the workers fed and hydrated. Even the children help when it is safe to do so, and they are taught how to build, not just a barn, but community with every barn-raising or public project the community does. This is a team effort and all share in the fact that the community has a new barn to store the fruits of their shared labour to share with an ever-growing community.

"We look forward to raisings," said one Amish man. *"There are so many helping, no one has to work too hard. We get in a good visit"* ("The Barn Raising", Gene Logsdon, Chelsea Greene Publishing, 1995). Amish feel a deep sense of security in knowing that the community they are a part of will be there for them if they ever find themselves in need, not just for a barn, but for counsel, wisdom, and spiritual aid also.

The Amish have also created other ways to help community members in times of need. In Lancaster, Pennsylvania, USA for example, an Amish Aid Society was formed whereby members are assessed and money collected to help rebuild after a disaster (a type of fire and storm insurance). Those with medical bills are helped by the community taking up alms (as a side note, alms do not necessarily mean cash, it is more akin to compassionateness, that is, (as exercised towards the poor) beneficence, being generous or doing good deeds), or more concretely a benefaction. Biblically speaking, alms equates to deeds. For example, **Proverbs 11:24** *There is that scattereth, and yet increaseth; and there is that withholdeth more than is meet, but it tendeth to poverty*). Jesus also rebuked the religious leaders by saying, **But rather give alms of such things as ye have**; *and, behold, all things are clean unto you. But woe unto you, Pharisees! for ye tithe mint and rue and all manner of herbs, and pass over judgment and the love of God: these ought ye to have done, and not to leave the other undone* (**Luke 11:41-42**). Jesus started this verse by saying, *'do what you can with what you have...'* We cannot give what we do not have.

Doing alms in the bible means fulfilling any need a poor person has, whether spiritual or physical. An Amish Church Aid was developed for serious problems as an informal version of hospitalization insurance. Self-sufficiency is the Amish community's answer to government aid programs (which leads to government control), this way they are not beholding to the government. When the government eventually collapses (as all governments eventually do), these communities will be fully self-sustaining and, though the world be in chaos, life will go on with far more normality for these types of communities. World politics does not affect the workings of the community dedicated to God and each other, even if their doctrine is not quite right. Just as the principle of sowing and reaping are immutable i.e., it doesn't just work for believers, and the sun and rain affect the sinners and saints alike, so is the principle of community that will strengthen them towards outside forces.

All members of the Amish community are accountable to the entire community, unlike our western style churches where we are told we are accountable to one man (a proper study of the Greek and Aramaic definitions of Hebrews 13:7 and 17 shows a complete deficit in this thinking). When something happens to or someone does anything that affects the entire community, then the entire community becomes a part of the solution or suffers the consequences.

When it comes to popular leisure activities, the Amish seem to like visiting one another (household to household **Acts 2:44, 20:20**). This may include everyone from relatives and the sick to non-Amish friends. The Amish have long been known for taking care of their own members. This has many people outside their community looking on with amusement and some with derision, but the end will show who are less stressed due to outside forces. These types of communities have far less illnesses, have an extremely lower rate of cancer, asthma, heart disease, and allergies. Autism and ADHD are virtually non-existent, their immune system is far healthier than that of the general public and divorces are almost unheard of (mainly because when a problem arises within a marriage, they have a community they can go to for help and the wisdom of the whole community is available to the couple). Out of control children are rare, as they are taught more self-control than in most communities in western society. Retirement communities or nursing homes do not exist; in most cases, each family takes care of their own elderly and infirmed, and the Amish community gives assistance as needed to other families. Even the children care for the elderly and infirmed, showing from an early age that it is the responsibility of all to care for each other regardless of age or ability to input. The young are included in all family matters which is essential to their growth. The concept of community purported in **Acts 2:42-46** and **4:32-37** is alive and well within communities such as these.

If there is a problem between two parties within these communities, it is brought before the community, and with prayer and guidance of wise elders, the community decides how best to handle it. The spiritual welfare of the whole community is taken into consideration, and no-one is excluded from the decision-making process; everyone of age is allowed a voice (Acts chapter 15 tells us how this was manifested in the early church). All teach what they know to the level of their competency under the watchful eyes of a wise and benevolent eldership, and all are asked to participate in one form or another within the community.

In effect, this is a visible way **Acts 2:42-46** is placed before the lives of the surrounding communities today so they will have no excuse, saying they didn't know. We (the Ecclesia) through the leading of the Holy Ghost, are to be more concerned for the needs of others (especially those of the household of faith- **Galatians 6:10**), than we are for ourselves. Jesus tells us in **Matthew 6:33** *But seek ye **first** the kingdom of God,* [His community] *and his righteousness; and all these things shall be* *added unto you*. For something to be first, there must be a second and a subsequent third. This is what it means to prioritize. Paul writes of how a community is to care for itself in **Philippians 2:3-5** *Let nothing be done through strife or vainglory*; **but in lowliness of mind let each esteem other better than themselves.** *Look not every man on his own things, but every man also on the things of others.* **Let this mind be in you, which was also in Christ Jesus**: These are the five fundamentals in one scripture. Paul is saying that these things are the mind of Christ and that we ought to have it also.

Let each esteem is Allēlōn Hēgeomai and it means to strengthen and lead by mutually reduplicating one another and making others better than ourselves. Is this not the very definition of biblical discipleship? The NLT puts in into a clearer perspective: *Don't look out only for your own interests, but take an interest in others, too.* This is self-explanatory and when we finally understand the importance of being in the community God has ordained to spread His gospel via the medium of love and obedience to Him and one another, we will see the desperate need we have for each other. There is not one group or church that has the answers to all the needs of their communities.

Jean Vanier says again, in his book *Community and Growth*; '*A community that is growing rich and seeks only to defend its goods and its reputation is dying. It has ceased to grow in love. A community is alive when it is poor and its members feel they have to work together and remain united, if only to ensure that they can all eat tomorrow!*" This is even more relevant within the Ecclesia where most are well off and keep most of the wealth within the four walls of their little corner of their little kingdom. Our need for one another in the Commonwealth of the Kingdom of God trumps our need for selfish rights, wealth, and blessings. It is the community that has the power to withstand any onslaught of the enemy, not one individual or one group/organization. **Matthew 16:18** *And I say also unto thee, That thou art Peter, and upon this rock I will build my church* (Ecclesia); *and the gates of hell shall not prevail against it.* As mentioned earlier, the only I, me, my and mine that are acceptable regarding the Ecclesia is when God speaks of it of Himself. Please note the Master's words. *I will build **my** church.* Contrary to popular church doctrine, it is Christ that raises up gatherings as a result of His people loving, sacrificially serving, and submitting to one another.

Today, we do things backwards in out attempt to spread the gospel. We gather a group of people, get a building as quickly as possible, hold as many meetings as the people can withstand and try to do outreach to "*win the lost*", thereby growing numbers and proving we are of God. This is NOT how God started the Renewed Covenant church. As we gather with each other daily, as we sacrificially give to one another, as we share our revelations from God's word and experiences with one another, as we care for the sick, the poor, the neglected in our own midst, God adds to His church daily such as would be saved. Peter tells us that however God is going to judge the world, He is going to start with His own people first, so why shouldn't we start with our own people first? *For the time is come that judgment must begin at the house of God: and if it first begin at us, what shall the end be of them that obey not the gospel of God?* (**1 Peter 4:17**). He grows His Ecclesia organically and daily as we do our part. He did not tell us to go and start/build *churches*. He sent the disciples into towns and cities to preach the Gospel of the Kingdom and as a result, gatherings would raise up and those within the gathering would disciple one another as the spirit of God leads under the general oversight of wise and humble elders.

This is not a new idea. David wanted to build the Tabernacle for God (even the prophet agreed at first), but God told him that if a building was to be built, it would be by God, not man, (**1 Chronicles 17:1-5, 11-12**). God said there would be a house (Bayith- especially family, household), but that it would be God building it. We have become so focused on building churches, that we have neglected to let Him build HIS CHURCH, His way in His time and manner. Different locations have different needs, yet we do not cater to those needs. Instead, we build cookie-cutter churches, all with cookie-cutter church formats and liturgies and force people to become cookie-cutter Christians. Why? Because this is easier than going to where the people are and ministering to them where the people need it, in their homes, their places of work and their schools. Cookie-cutter churches only produce cookie cutter believers. Our over-reliance for order and regulation has stifled the move of God we so desperately claim we want. God is not interested in the order of our services, but whether He can order His saints to serve the saints as and when He pleases.

The competitive spirit of the world within the Ecclesia is counter-productive to the Spirit of God. It is counter-productive to the spirit of altruism (just so I make myself clear, there is not a spirit called altruism). Take what Paul said for example, *For, brethren, ye have been called unto liberty; only use not liberty for an occasion to the flesh* (selfishness)*, but **by love serve one another**. For all the law is fulfilled in one word, even in this; Thou shalt love thy neighbour as thyself. But if ye bite and devour **one another**, take heed that ye be not consumed **one of another*** (Galatians 5:13-15). We may have liberty, but it is not liberty to cater to the flesh. So, do we gather to hear the word, or do we gather so we can freely exercise our divine purpose to freely ***love and serve one another***?

Liberty for occasion to the flesh is a Shakespearian English way of saying, *I have rights and I'm entitled to live the way I feel is right for me.* When we live for ourselves, we end up fulfilling the second part of verse fifteen: biting and devouring one another. Interesting choice of words chosen by Paul. *If you bite* (Daknō- to thwart) *and devour* (Katesthiō- eat or wear down) *one another, take heed* (Blepō- beware) *that you be not consumed* (Analiskō- used up or be destroyed) *one of* (by) *another.* Paul happily gives the cure to the deathly malady of self in the next verse. *This I say then, Walk* (Peripateō- be at large (especially as proof of ability); figuratively to live, deport oneself, follow [as a companion or votary- as one who has made a vow to do something], go, **be occupied with things**)*, in the Spirit, and ye shall not fulfil the lust of the flesh* (Galatians 5:16). In context he is speaking of the Spirit of Christ which is the spirit that dominates in the heavens (God's community) that we must walk in.

There is a myriad of reasons why people gather. Many out of loneliness, desperation, grief, divorce, sickness, financial need, or the need to rule or be ruled, but we all gather somewhere, sometime, because it is in our nature. There are relatively very few hermits around today and when we hear of them, we view them as an anomaly in society. Yet, we have been gathering into cities since shortly after the fall in the Garden of Eden, **Genesis 4:16-17** *And Cain went out from the presence of the LORD, and dwelt in the land of Nod, on the east of Eden. And Cain knew his wife; and she conceived, and bare Enoch: and **he builded a city**, and called the name of the city, after the name of his son, Enoch.*

In my view, cities are the greatest paradox of life. Even though millions of us live in cities, we live alone and rarely have much to do with our neighbours. We double deadlock our doors, build fences, and stay within our perimeters, place keep out signs on our yards, get home video security systems to see who's at the door, and only invite those with the same views as we have (or the pizza delivery person) or have something to offer us. Why? Because we don't like to be challenged, we want to live in a homogeneous society, meaning of the same or similar nature or kind of lifestyle, with little if any conflict. As we become more affluent, we move to suburbs where other affluent people live so we can be with our kind. This, however, also results in living in an easily burst bubble. This is not what God intended for such a varied and divergent group of people as His Ecclesia. To live in a homogenous society defeats the purpose of God calling a diverse group of people, *After this I beheld, and, lo, a great multitude, which no man could number,* **of all nations, and kindreds, and people, and tongues**, *stood before the throne, and before the Lamb, clothed with white robes, and palms in their hands; And cried with a loud voice, saying, Salvation to our God which sitteth upon the throne, and unto the Lamb* (**Revelation 7:9-10**).

Gustavo Gutiérrez explains what and who a neighbour is and is not ...*a neighbour is not he whom I find in my path, but rather he in whose path I place myself, he whom I approach and actively seek.* (Translated from Teologia de le Liberacion. Orbis Books 1973)

This modern counter-intuitive view of life has embedded itself into the body of Christ in western society and has kept it from performing its task, that of being salt and a light to an ever-darkening world. We have relied on the few to do the work of many. Not because we are evil, but because the vast majority have either not been shown nor allowed to minister to one another in any meaningful way. This robs the many of the blessings that come with being able to fulfil their purposes in God. Though we do not earn our way (by works) into His good book, we do these things because we have assurance that we are already written in it once the requirements for being biblically born-again have been met. We are to live in reverent fear of a God who, through our continued disobedience, will remove our names from His book (**Revelation 2:5** *Remember therefore from whence thou art fallen, and repent, and do the first works;* **or else** *I will come unto thee quickly,* **and will remove** *thy candlestick* **out of his place, except thou repent**). This is not well-accepted by the majority of denominational churches, but it is a fact nonetheless for the Lord tells us in **Revelation 3:5** *He that overcometh, the same shall be clothed in white raiment; and* **I will not blot out his name out of the book of life**, *but I will confess his name before my Father, and before his angels.* If Christ overcame the world (**John 16:33**) and overcame the devil (**1 John 3:8**), then it stands to reason that the only thing left for us to overcome is our own flesh (**Colossians 3:5**). We remain in His book *if* we overcome, and it is Christ who gives us as much strength as we seek in order to fulfil our purpose in, for and through Him.

What is it that we must continue to overcome? Not our neighbours, our enemies, those with differing views in our churches, or those from another organization, but our selfishness, pride, arrogance, and such things as are detrimental and counter-productive to the Commonwealth of the Kingdom of God. The Lord dictated those letters to John who wrote them to the Ecclesia, the body of Christ, in those regions, not to an individual with individual problems, but to a body with body problems which required the body's participation to secure a solution. God provided the answer, we do the work, it's not brain science or rocket surgery.

God's word calls us to live in harmony which is very difficult to do when we have so many individuals striving for different things. At this point I would like to differentiate between harmonious and homogeneous. Harmonious is showing accord in feeling or action, while homogeneous is of the same kind; alike, similar, a clone if you will. God didn't call us to be robots programmed to function, look, act, dress and speak in the same way as each other. This is why He gave many different gifts to men (**Ephesians 4:8, 1 Corinthians 12:1-11**). The scripture tells us many times that they (the early Ecclesia) were in one accord, however, one accord does not necessarily mean in one place at the same time or that they were robotic or clonish. We are exhorted to have the same mind and follow the same book. This leaves much room for personality differences and doings the same things just in a different way, while still working to achieve the same goals. We can celebrate our uniqueness within the body of Christ and strive to use our personalities and character traits to strengthen the Ecclesia.

There is a stark difference between individualism and uniqueness. Individualism is relating to a single person or thing as opposed to more than one, while unique is (not comparable) being the only one of its kind; unequalled, unparalleled, or unmatched. We are to remain unique in God's Kingdom while we surrender our selfishness (individualism- the belief in the primary importance of the individual and in the virtues of self-reliance and personal independence) for the sake of the Kingdom of God.

Chapter 13.

Learning the Fear of God.

Leviticus 25:17 *Ye shall not therefore oppress* (suppress, maltreat, or hold back) *one another;* **but thou shalt fear thy God**: *for I am the LORD your God.*

2 Corinthians 7:1 *Having therefore these promises, dearly beloved, let us cleanse ourselves from all filthiness of the flesh and spirit,* **perfecting holiness in the fear of God.**

We cannot call ourselves holiness people and yet not biblically fear God. All of our outward holiness becomes a millstone around our necks, a filthy rag in His sight, if the fear of God is of little concern to us. Here we find that those who fear the Lord have a much less chance of oppressing, suppressing, depressing, maltreating, or holding one another back from doing God's work. Having a fear of God also aids in **perfecting** holiness. Please, do not shout to me or the world of your holiness standards if you do not **FEAR** Him in all He is and can do and showing that fear in everything we do. In many of today's churches, the believers have lost the ability to fear God (a prerequisite to holiness, wisdom, knowledge and serving Him). We must once again learn how to fear God and just as importantly, teach one another how to fear God. Over time, we have confused fearing God with fearing the consequences of our actions (both are good to have, though the former is greater). For example, *if you don't tithe, it proves you don't love God and you'll go to hell* or *if you don't live a holiness life, you won't get the blessings of God* (I've heard this from more pulpits than I can remember).

Even one of the malefactors on the cross understood this, *But the other answering rebuked him, saying, Dost not thou fear God, seeing thou art in the same condemnation?* (**Luke 23:40**). We are told to fear God in many books of the bible, none more so than in Deuteronomy, Psalms and Proverbs with much mention in the minor and major prophets. *Specially the day that thou stoodest before the LORD thy God in Horeb, when the LORD said unto me,* **Gather me the people together** (Qâhal- to assemble- equivalent to the Greek word Ecclesia), *and I will make them hear my words,* **that they may learn to fear me** *all the days that they shall live upon the earth, and that they may* **teach** *their children* (**Deuteronomy 4:10**). Learning as a community as well as an individual how to fear God is essential to the assembly of God's people, as this enables us to maintain a sense of right and wrong. Not based on our feelings, perceptions, man's understanding, whims, fashion changes or who happens to be in charge at the time, but on what is written in His word and what pleases or displeases God. What an awe inspiring and fearful thing it is to learn and understand the same power that created the universe, now dwells in flesh, and that those who yield to the Spirit's calling are but mere vessels in the hands of this same creator.

Because we humans have such a varied sense of right and wrong based on our past experiences, our feelings (for example: if we felt slighted, then we were slighted), where we grew up and who had the most influence in our lives and our communities, we have ended up becoming a mish mash of perceived right and wrong. But when all are focused on one entity (God and His community, for they are truly one and the same) we become attuned to God's sense of right and wrong. A.W. Tozer wrote, *"We don't get 100 pianos in one accord by tuning them to each other, but by individually tuning them to another standard. That 'standard', that 'fork', is Jesus Christ! When man tries to create unity, he employs all manner of 'forks' to bring people into one accord."* This reinforces Paul's words that we are to have the mind of Christ, not the mind of man.

As we look to be like our God in His righteousness (Dikaiosune- the character and actions of God) in fear and trembling, we find that unity is a natural consequence. Ironically the greatest enemy to Ecclesiastical unity in the Church is actually the Church's *pursuit* of unity. When a part of the Church pursues an isolated form of unity along sectarian/organizational lines, it only accomplishes the opposite. It becomes divisive to the larger body of Christ. The Master said that *...if a kingdom be divided against itself, that kingdom cannot stand* (**Matthew 3:24**). In fact, the sectarian/organizational pursuit of unity is one of the most ineffective practices the Church regularly engages in.

The fact remains, that even though God desires unity in His Ecclesia, it is not His primary concern. Rather, it is a secondary matter. Unity comes to fruition as His people primarily seek a singular goal, one that has a much higher and greater objective, i.e., His kingdom and His righteousness (that of conformity to Jesus Christ. **Matthew 6:30-33, Romans 8:29**). In other words, the unity that He seeks comes about as a fruit of the Spirit, not something contrived in boardrooms and conferences. As we fear God together, we become united in Him and His will (Thelēma- a determination choice, specifically His purpose, decree and volition or inclination, His desire or pleasure).

This also gives us the ability to hold each other accountable for our actions, attitudes, words, and ways. When trivial matters distract us from our purpose, we can remind each other of **Micah 6:8**, *He hath shewed thee, O man, what is good; and what doth the LORD require of thee, but to do justly, and to love mercy, and to walk humbly with thy God?* We humans are easily distracted and being reminded that all God really requires is that we live *justly* (do justice- do right, follow God's word), *love mercy* (be kind towards God's people, live piously and have pity) and *walk humbly* (to be lowly- the opposite of prideful) with God and we are to do it all in the fear of God. This is so simple; the vast majority miss it.

There are more important things to concern ourselves with, like are we being what God has called us to be, are we where we are supposed to be and doing what we are supposed to be doing according to God's word? All of us, not just the *"ministry team"*. Or as is the case in most churches in western society, are we trying to force our sense of right and wrong onto others, forcing them to think and behave as we want them to, forcing someone to worship like we do and burying them under mounds of traditions of men. If they do not conform to our standards, do we call them rebellious, wayward or backsliders? Do we have less fellowship with them all in the name of unity?

Church traditions, like laws and certain government or business regulations, have, over time taken on a life of their own and lifestyles are changed in order to comply with the traditions. Once implemented, these traditions and regulations take on a life of their own and almost invariably live forever unless someone purposefully looks at the tradition objectively, finds it wanting, and then willing to remove it from the books. This is considerably harder to do than we think. If courage to examine our beliefs and structures is not engaged regularly, especially in our churches, we end up with factions of people, some wanting to adhere to certain traditions, while others see the need for strict adherence to different traditions. This creates a divided house which, according to Jesus, will fall from within. We cannot blame Satan for what happens when we behave like this. We seem to fear pastors, bishops, and superintendents a great deal more than we fear disobeying God's commands to us.

Consider this for a moment. Have we set up a community where we can be honest with each other about our strengths and weaknesses without fear of rejection or recrimination? Sadly, I believe these are far and few between. We know that the Ecclesia of God has problems because we are all dealing with some kind of issue at one time or another, but the real Ecclesia of God has chosen to not hold it against His people. Much of the organizational church on the other hand, does not allow for freedom of thought and expression, weaknesses, or differences in opinion, and it tends to shoot its own wounded. Our measuring rod (God) must once again become the standard (not our standards) that all must strive to adhere to with the same level of passion, and we hold each other accountable for the sake of the community called the Commonwealth of the Kingdom of God.

Biblical accountability goes both ways. Just as children should be taught to have a healthy fear of law enforcement officers, (this is beneficial for the whole community in the long run) so should the Ecclesia have a healthy fear of God. Those children who, through bad parental/leadership exampling, are taught to disrespect the law and those who enforce it, will be the ones who will be the greatest thorn in the flesh of any community. It will usually be the law breakers that complain bitterly to their cell mates how life is unfair. There is an old adage of, *if you don't break the law, you need not worry about going to prison.*

The ideal manner of maintaining right and wrong will be the community of God that is focused on God and His Kingdom and not distracted by the new, the shiny, the big or the better thing. It will police itself in love (with the help of humble and wise elders- older saints), using the same grace and mercy shown to them by the Great Judge. They allow themselves to be led by the Holy Ghost and use only the word of God as their measuring rod, not an individual, their church or organization's definition of the word of God (see **Romans 8:14, Hebrews 4:12**). This is accomplished by operating in the gifts of the spirit while displaying the fruits of the spirit for the edification of the body. The ultimate purpose is to influence the lost, by example, outside of the community to become a part of God's community. Of course, we will have wise elders that will guide us, but it will be a healthy fear of God that will motivate us (not a fear of man and how they will punish, ignore, or ostracize us), and an undying love for His word and each other that will keep us on the straight and narrow way. We will not need to be ruled with an iron fist by an oligarchy, or a few self-righteous, autocratic people, but by example of humble and wise elders, by much prayer and fasting for one another and wise counselling, using the tools mentioned in **2 Timothy 3:16-17**. We will be able to confront one another in love (both ways- up and down) when things are not going according to God's word, not just for the benefit of the one out of sorts, but for the entire community. We will search out those within the community who will use their skills to benefit the community and not make them jump through a myriad of hoops in order to meet their approval before they can use those God-given skills at His discretion. There will be such a holy reverence and fear that displeasing God (the object of our love) and disobeying His word would be unthinkable. For the sake of the community of God's people, we will help those struggling to get back into the will of God. We will use the tragedies and failures as well as the strengths of all members of the Ecclesia as opportunities to restore and release the fallen and broken, back into the service of God for His Kingdom's sake.

We are commanded and commended to fear the Lord and speak of that fear to one another. *Then they that feared the LORD* **spake often one to another: and the LORD hearkened, and heard it, and a book of remembrance was written** *before him* **for them that feared the LORD,** *and that thought upon his name* (**Malachi 3:16**). God pays particular attention to those that fear Him and speak of Him often and He hears their prayers. Please note also, there is a book written for those that fear the Lord.

This fear is not the fear that paralyses, but that motivates, a fear (Hebrew: Yârê'- to morally revere, to dread, to see as terrible- 17th century definition- dreadful, awesome, formidable, powerful) that moves those in God's community to do the right thing because it pleases God and teaches the new believers how to dwell with each other. This brings about a natural and organic sense of Holy Ghost driven morality. This is a set of rules that a community lives by in order to live a harmonious life within that given community. It is doing the right thing because it is the right thing to do with no guarantee of reward.

The Top Ten.

Enter the Ten Commandments. These are broken down into two sections. The first four have to do with our direct relationship with God (*no other Gods, don't make any images of God, don't take God's name in vain and keep God's sabbath*), the remaining six are the basics of how to dwell with each other in love (*honour your parents, don't murder, don't steal, don't commit adultery, don't lie, don't covet your neighbour's wife or things*).

Paul tells us in no uncertain terms in **Hebrews 10:30-31** *For we know him that hath said, Vengeance* (Ekdikēsis- vindication and retribution) *belongeth unto me, I will recompense, saith the Lord. And again, The Lord shall judge his people. It is a **fearful thing*** (Greek: Phoberos- frightful, formidable) *to fall into the hands of the living God.* I am concerned that we now have a generation of believers who behave more like Pharaoh than like Moses. Pharoah was more frightened of the plagues, than the God who sent them, as evidenced by his statement ...*Who is the LORD, that I should obey his voice to let Israel go? I know not the LORD, neither will I let Israel go* (**Exodus 5:2**). Each time Pharaoh asked Moses to stop the plagues it was not because he feared God but because his people would have revolted (Pharaohs were considered gods to their people). As Pharaoh of Egypt, he was taught the history of the God of the Hebrews but did not fear God and it eventually cost him his first-born son's life. This is also the beginning of the decline of the greatest empire of its time.

The Lord told us in no uncertain terms whom we are to fear in **Matthew 10:28** *And **fear not THEM*** (many) *which kill the body, but are not able to kill the soul: but rather **fear HIM*** (one) *which is able to destroy both soul and body in hell.* Please note; we are not to fear THEM (men) but to fear HIM (God) that can destroy the body and the soul. Man can excommunicate and ostracize, revoke our licenses, and take our lives, but only God can destroy (Apollumi- to destroy fully (reflexively to perish, or lose), cause to die, mar) both body and soul. Those who fear men more than they fear God also go against the prophets warning, *Thus saith the LORD: Cursed is the man that **trusteth in*** (places confidence in) *man, and maketh flesh his **arm*** (strength)*, and whose heart departeth from the LORD* (**Jeremiah 17:5**). Our confidence is in God, who uses man, not in man whom God uses. We can't put all our trust in man and God at the same time. If we put our trust (strength) in man, our hearts eventually depart from the Lord. Jesus told us in **Mark 6:21** and **Luke 12:34** *For where your treasure is, there will your heart* (Kardia- thoughts, feeling and mind) *be also.*

One thing that is needed in any group of people with many differing backgrounds and lifestyles is wisdom. It takes wisdom to sort out between right and wrong, just, and unjust, when to speak and when to remain silent, if, when, and where to do a thing, how to deal with broken hearts and marriages, the sufferings of loss through death or divorce, the agony of a seemingly never-ending sickness, the distortion of mental illness or the correct dividing of the word of God for the body.

David gives us an insight into this wisdom in **Psalm 111:10** *The fear of the LORD is the beginning* (Rê'shîyth- firstfruits) *of wisdom: a **good understanding have all they that do his commandments**: his praise endureth for ever.* David passed this powerful insight to his son Solomon, who tells us that the fear of the Lord is wisdom, knowledge, and confidence (**Proverbs 8:13, 9:19, 14:26**).

Once again, we see that the fear of God brings wisdom and the doing of God's word is what gives us understanding. As a side note, for those who claim to be holiness people, please understand that standards do not automatically equate to holiness. We must dress and behave modestly indeed, but we must understand how holiness is perfected; *Having therefore these promises, dearly beloved, let us cleanse ourselves from all filthiness of the flesh and spirit, **perfecting holiness in the fear of God*** (2 **Corinthians 7:1**). One does not *perfect* holiness through, wardrobe, language, behaviour modification, or church attendance. These are modified as we fear the Lord. These are just one of the myriad of outward signs that God is working on the heart, mind, and spirit of man. It is far easier to change our wardrobe than it is to change our attitudes to match Christ's. Faith, clean thinking, edifying speech, sacrifice, mercy, grace, loving the brethren and joy during trials are the things that will perfect and prove the fear of God infinitely more than standards given to us by men. Two people keeping standards look the same, but it is only after we spend time with them, we will be able to tell which one walks closer with God by the way they treat and speak to and of others, whether they have pride or arrogance or are humble and willing to serve.

We are told that while the disciples were with their Rabbi in the boat, He calmed the storm, *And he said unto them, Why are ye so fearful? how is it that ye have no faith? And they **feared exceedingly,** and said one to another, What manner of man is this, that even the wind and the sea obey him?* (**Mark 4:40-41**). They feared the storm more than they feared God. Their fear was something they discussed amongst themselves. Fear of the Lord and fear of damaging each other are two immensely powerful motivators to keeping an eye on each other (though our fear of God is motivated by our love for God and His people), not to spy or to pry, but so we can help each other make it. We commend certain types of fear- fear of crossing the road with oncoming traffic, fear of falling from great heights, and fear of wild animals. Fear is essential in the walk of a disciple, but it must be the right kind of fear.

The following verses in Isaiah speak of the Messiah and as we are to imitate Him in all His ways (*But as he which hath called you is holy, so be ye holy in all manner of conversation; Be ye Holy for I am Holy* **1 Peter 1:15-16**), they are also speaking to us today. *And the spirit of the LORD shall rest upon him, the spirit of wisdom and understanding, the spirit of counsel and might,* **the spirit of knowledge and of the fear of the LORD**; *And shall make him of quick* **understanding in the fear of the LORD**: *and he shall not judge after the sight of his eyes, neither reprove after the hearing of his ears: But with righteousness* (Tsedeq- the right (natural, moral or legal); also equity or to cause to prosper) *shall he judge the poor, and reprove with equity* (Mîyshôr- straightness, evenness) *for the meek of the earth: and he shall smite the earth with the rod of his mouth, and with the breath of his lips shall he slay the wicked* (**Isaiah 11:2-4**). The first part of this speaks of God manifesting as six different spirits connected to the Ecclesia. They are the spirit of wisdom, understanding, counsel, might, knowledge and fear of the Lord. With these we operate the Ecclesia and not with the six spirits of man- they are man's ideas, man's philosophies, man's commandments, man's traditions, man's beliefs, and man's programmes.

The Psalmist David puts light on what is *meant* to happen when the saints gather. **Psalm 89:7** *God is greatly **to be feared in the assembly*** (Sôd- company of persons (in close deliberation); by implication intimacy, consultation) *of the saints* (Qâdôsh- those made sacred by God), *and to be had in reverence* (Yârê) *of all them that are about him.* David tells us that God is to be 'ârats meaning; *to awe* or (intransitively) to dread, be affrighted (afraid, feared, terrified), break, oppress, prevail, shake terribly as well as Yârê meaning; morally to revere; causatively to frighten: - affright, be (make) afraid, dreadful, put in fear, to see as terrible, when we assemble. Do we fear the Lord greatly in our church services? I have been to thousands of churches worldwide over the last thirty-five years and I can truly say the number of meetings I have been to where they fear, and reverence God is miniscule. Oh, they love Him greatly, they praise Him with all their heart, they run the aisles and jump and dance, they see Him as their way maker, miracle worker, promise keeper, light in the darkness and creator of the universe. But fear Him, be in dread and awe of Him where they cannot stand in His presence? Not so much! If there is no fear of God in our services, is there really any wisdom in them either? I'm just asking.

Truth is truth, no matter whom God chooses to bring it even if it goes against what we believe, feel, or been told by our leadership. The only thing that suffers destruction through exerted examination of our beliefs is error. If we are more frightened that we may find ourselves not being as right as we thought or of what others will think as we claim to pursue not only truth, we have our priorities out of order. If the fear of God does not change us based on what we have found to be truth in God's word, then we have no right to be preaching or teaching others. Many are frightened to search deeper into God's word because it will cause them to be at odds with years of tradition handed down by men and women they have trusted. I once met a spirit filled pastor who, after we did a bible study on the name of Jesus in baptism and that God is one, realized he was genuinely mistaken in his doctrine, but refused to change to accommodate the word. When I asked why, he told me it is was because he would have to tell his congregation of about 100 that he had baptized them incorrectly and that the word commanded them to be rebaptized. His pride not only stopped him from entering into more truth, but it hindered the congregation also. The fear of man has terrible consequences.

The enemy uses the terror of man to keep us in an error. But by regular self-examination of our belief, structures, programmes, and spirit, we can quickly fix an error before it becomes established. This can only happen if we fear God more than man and decide to put away pride and arrogance and admit that change may be necessary. The fear of man (and what they **can** do) should be minuscule compared to the fear of God (and what He **will** do) should we reject more truth, regardless of whom God chooses to bring it. A donkey saw into the spiritual realm more than a stubborn prophet and saved his life (see **Numbers 22**). If we do not listen to the donkey, we will deal with a sword wielding angel.

A divided Kingdom lacks the fear of God.

When the Commonwealth of the Kingdom is divided between the haves and the have nots (both in the sense of spiritual wisdom/authority and material), between groups with different initials before or after their name, or divided because of differing *holiness standards*, it causes the Kingdom to be divided and Jesus said that this kind of kingdom would fall. The Master was accused of using something bad (the devil) in order to do something good (cast him out). *And Jesus knew their thoughts, and said unto them, Every kingdom divided against itself is brought to desolation; and every city or house divided against itself shall not stand: And if Satan cast out Satan, he is divided against himself; how shall then his kingdom stand? And if I by Beelzebub cast out devils, by whom do your children cast them out? therefore they shall be your judges. But if I cast out devils by the Spirit of God, then the kingdom of God is come unto you* (**Matthew 12:25-28**).

The Lord was a relative nobody when He showed up in Jerusalem, yet here is this nobody casting out demons, healing the sick, calming storms and raising the dead. The religious elites could not see a man of God right in front of their eyes because he was not of their denomination or organization, so they attributed what he did to the devil. We haven't changed much of the years, have we? I believe it is because we do not fear God the bible way. The fear of the Lord will eliminate any chances of operating outside of the six spirits of God (wisdom, understanding, counsel, might, knowledge and fear of the Lord. **Isaiah 11:2**).

As a side note the definition of *Kingdom divided* in Greek is Basileia Merizō- the royalty, rule and realm being parted, literally to apportion to some but not to others, to disunite, to differ one over another, to deal with difference between, distribute differently or unevenly. In other words, to treat with partiality the brethren in the Ecclesia. This is a definite no-no in God's Kingdom, and it will cause the downfall in those who practice such foolishness. If we feared God as we are meant to, this would not even be an option in His Kingdom here on earth.

The importance of not having any divisions or partitions within the body cannot be overstated, whether they are division in wealth of goods, health, finances, spiritual gifts, knowledge, wisdom, understanding or between so-called leadership and regular saints. *"Regular saints"*, is an oxymoron. Saint is defined as Qôdesh [Heb] meaning- a sacred place or thing, consecrated (thing), dedicated (thing), hallowed (thing), and Hagios [Gr] meaning- an awful thing, sacred (physically pure, morally), blameless. Is there anything *regular* about God's people who are sacred and consecrated unto Him? The fear of God and wisdom are given to us all to share within the Ecclesia fully and continually which is well pleasing unto God. As we continue to fear Him, He manifests himself through us to a world of darkness, giving them the same opportunity He gave us to come out of it.

Chapter 14.

One another commands. What are they?

As we begin our search for how to interact with one another within the Ecclesia, in a manner that pleases God, we must first define what **one another** means in God's Kingdom. What does, "*Love one another*" even look like from God's perspective? Though the term has two words in English, it is one word in Greek; Allēlōn which means *each other, mutual or together*. When someone else is involved, we cannot put ourselves first. We cannot focus our care for another while we focus on caring for ourselves at the same time. For example, just like in physics, two atoms cannot occupy the same space at the same time, a parent washing their newborn cannot do so and wash themselves at the same time or when washing someone else's feet, I cannot wash mine and theirs at the same time and vice versa. Jesus said in **John 13:14** *If I then, your Lord and Master, have washed your feet; ye also ought to wash* **one another's** *feet*. As a side note, why have we relegated this important act of humility to a once-a-year ritual? I have been told it is because they wore sandals, and their feet were dirty all the time and because we primarily wear closed shoes, it is not necessary. Great excuse, but it won't wash (pardon the pun) with God. Jesus did not say that we ought to wash one another's feet until we get closed in shoes. This humbling act of getting on our knees before another human makes this sacrament important to the body, not the ritual. Do this often enough and pride seems to melt away.

We have done the same thing with communion and yet both these practices were daily occurrences within the body of Christ for hundreds of years. What excuse have we come up with for communion being a once or twice a year ritual? I believe it is because we know that we are not right with each other most of the time and our spirits couldn't handle the conviction that would come upon us if we did this regularly or when God calls it. I have even heard pastors and bishops give a month's warning that they will have communion and foot washing so people can get right with God and each other. What would happen if the pastor called for a foot washing and communion a few minutes before service? If the people really knew the purpose of these things, most would not be able to take part because they know their hearts are not right with God or each other. Will God give a month's warning before His return or our death so we can get right with Him and each other?

If the Ecclesia is to be like Christ, then it would behove the disciples of Christ today to wash each other's feet, a symbol of love, humility and meekness which mimics the life of Christ perfectly and to have communion with each other (outside of the church ritual) to get things right. It would force us to repent for our awful attitudes daily. For how can we say we fellowship with each other, yet secretly hold, grudges, unforgiveness, bitterness, anger, malice, greed, or partiality in our hearts, then have the audacity to stand up and sing with gusto that we love God with all of our hearts?

Back to *one another*. In certain context to the scriptures, one another can also be interpreted as one above or one better than another as in **Philippians 2:3**, *Let nothing be done through strife or vainglory; but in lowliness of mind* **let each esteem other better than themselves**.

There are many attributes of the body of Christ which show the community aspect of God's plan for the world. Following this section is a list (by no means exhaustive) of some things God requires of His body to do for, with and to one another. One another verses are almost always directives, or commands, if you will, on how to interact with one another in the body of Christ. A lost world is watching, and they want to know what we claim is real is, in fact, real, or what is a put-on show once or twice a week. It is imperative that the body of Christ begins to disciple one another (to make duplicates of our Lord, well versed in the scriptures (not just memorizing them or to show off what we know, but so we might live what we know) as we are commanded to in the word of God (see **Matthew 28:18-20, 2 Timothy 2:2, Ephesians 4:16, Titus 2:3-12, Colossians 1:28-29**). By believing God's word of salvation for the Kosmos and its method for being born again (**John 3:3-6, Acts 2:38-40**), we are brought to the gates of the Kingdom of God, but by doing God's word we become fellow citizens in the Commonwealth of the Kingdom of God and make the crossing.

Jesus' brother James makes it quite plain that faith alone in God is woefully inadequate to maintain a walk with the Creator. In fact, he tells us that faith alone equates to death and leaves us alone (see **James 2:18-26**). To say we are one body and not act accordingly is as useful to the Kingdom of God as an inflatable dart board. *If a brother or sister be naked, and destitute of daily food, And one of you say unto them, Depart in peace, be ye warmed and filled; notwithstanding ye give them not those things which are needful to the body; **what doth it profit**? Even so faith, if it hath not works, is dead, being alone. Yea, a man may say, Thou hast faith, and I have works: shew me thy faith without thy works, and I will shew thee my faith by my works* (**James 2:15-18**). If obedience manifested by action does not follow our belief and faith, then both are self-deceit and self-defeating.

There is an old saying of the early believer's attitude, '*What must we do to be saved*', while many modern believers in the western churches have adopted a somewhat ambivalent attitude. Theirs is '*What can I do and still be saved?*' God did not create the Ecclesia to dwell in comfort and blessings (that will come after we have fought the fight, run our course, kept the faith and a crown is placed upon our heads after the judgement (**2 Timothy 4:7**), but to comfort one another and be a blessing. As in every age, Satan will soon be loosed on the Ecclesia of today as never before, and if we have not prepared each other, we will fall, and it will be our *Mea Culpa*. John warns us in **Revelation 12:12** *Therefore rejoice, ye heavens, and ye that dwell in them. Woe to the inhabiters of the earth and of the sea! for the devil is come down unto you, having great wrath, because he knoweth that he hath but a short time*). This is done to keep the church on its toes and be ever ready to perform the will of God. Peter tells us to *...sanctify the Lord God in your hearts: and **be ready always to give an answer** to every man that asketh you a reason of the hope that is in you **with meekness and fear*** (**1 Peter 3:15**).

This generation, as all generations before us, are in a battle, and we must either be fighting or preparing to fight. In any of today's major conflicts by major nations like the US, UK, or Russia they will first gain air superiority, however, this does not equate to occupying ground. Like the Gulf War on the 1990s, the politicians of the 35-nation coalition thought they could win the war using their obvious superior air power. This softened up the enemy with their marvellous whiz bang gadgets of destruction, but eventually they had to send men and material and build a cohesive ground force into hostile territory to maintain several bases of operations in order to take further ground, being vigilant and always expecting the enemy to counterattack. They did not build a fort on some piece of ground then wait for the enemy to come to them. The purpose of the fort was to send soldiers ever deeper into enemy territory.

The days of building a castle surrounded by a moat and outlasting the enemy are long gone. Our adversary has become far more sophisticated and proficient and, as mentioned earlier, is infinitely more wrathful because he knows his time is short (**Revelation 12:11-12**). If we do not build a cohesive fighting team, one where we have each other's back, where we use each other's strengths and protect each other from being blindsided, we will soon be overrun, and our enemy does not take prisoners. He does not subscribe to the Geneva Convention on the treatment of prisoners. He is vengeful and brutal with no sympathy to traitors (you and I were once a slave to sin, now we are becoming a slave to righteousness. We have not been set free to do as we will, we have just switched masters. **Romans 6:16**). The U.S Marine Raiders of WW2 had a motto that saw them through some of the toughest missions in the Pacific Theatre of Operations (PTO). They trained together and fought together under the banner of *'Gung Ho'*, a Chinese term meaning to *work together*. In every engagement these men not only came out victorious, but with fewer casualties than any other unit in the PTO.

Air superiority equates to the power we have in prayer in the spiritual realm, but until we learn the art of war, practice what we have learned with our own people (love one another, not love the world), don the boots and hit the ground, lay our lives on the line for a greater cause than ourselves, we are just playing army. By dealing God's way with each other with all our faults and failures, the enemy will always try to come back after the prayer is over and occupy his former territory, but we will be victorious in the end. Jesus spoke of such a cataclysmic event when He told us that... *When the unclean spirit is gone out of a man, he walketh through dry places, seeking rest; and finding none, he saith, I will return unto my house whence I came out. And when he cometh, he findeth it swept and garnished. Then goeth he, and taketh to him seven other spirits more wicked than himself; and they enter in, and dwell there: and the last state of that man is worse than the first* (**Luke 11:24-26**). This is a warning that we are not only to have a clean and furnished house but that it must be occupied, and we must be employed in our Heavenly Father's business.

The following section, comprising of some dos and don'ts are hard work, and it will separate the chaff from the wheat. God Himself said He will gather the chaff and cast it into the fire (see **Matthew 3:12**). It will test the mettle and the commitment level of every saint. Not commitment to more church meetings in more purpose-built structures (we seem to have that down pat), but commitment to meeting the needs of those in the Ecclesia, whenever, wherever, with whatever and to whomever, whether those needs be spiritual, physical, emotional, or mental in nature. We must first gain superiority in the spiritual realm through prayer and fasting for one another (by following the edicts of fasting as laid out in Isaiah chapter 58), then put what we are told by the Holy Ghost into practice, and we will eventually gain the victory. Let us now go on a journey to learn how we are to live for God here on earth by living with and for one another.

Don't just tell them we love God, let our love, compassion and empathy be so great, that they will say of us, *'Wow, they really love God'*.

Section 2.

Chapter 15.
Have peace with one another.

*Mark 9:49-50 For every one shall be salted with fire, and every sacrifice shall be salted with salt. Salt is good: but if the salt have lost his saltness, wherewith will ye season it? Have salt in yourselves, and **have peace** one with another.*

John 14:27 Peace I leave with you, my peace I give unto you: not as the world giveth, give I unto you. Let not your heart be troubled, neither let it be afraid.

First and foremost, peace does not mean staying away from a brother or sister with whom we disagree so that there is no tension. It does not mean that someone can leave a spouse just because there is no peace in the house. It is easier to ignore or run away from a person whom we deem has done or believes wrong. Any lowlife coward can ostracize someone, but it takes courage to face someone and talk it out. This is harder than many people think, but when we get rid of the erroneous worldly concept of peace, it becomes clearer what Jesus was commanding His disciples to do. The Lord was telling us to have and be Eirēneuō- (to be and act peaceful: to be quiet, *to set at one again.* This last definition is vital in explaining peace within the Ecclesia). This peace is not the absence of conflict or troubles, but inner peace in the midst of conflict and troubles. It is our behaviour during conflict and troubles especially with one another that the world will determine whether we have the peace of God or not. Did Jesus shy away from dealing with troubled or troubling people? I don't think so. In fact, He lived His life to please the Father, and this brought conflict.

Relationships are by nature hard work with many setbacks as well as successes, and we would be foolish to believe that they will be easy just because we believe in One God, are baptized in His name, and filled with His spirit. Are we not still dealing with fallible and frail human beings, even the ones who are born again, or who stand behind our pulpits and sit on our boards, trying to serve God to the best of their ability? Is grace and mercy not a prerequisite, first and foremost towards one another in the Ecclesia *then* to the world?

Our understanding of God is greatly enhanced when we purposefully choose to live and be at peace with one another. Many times, when there is conflict, we withdraw ourselves or ostracize others, when Jesus is telling us to set at one again. Set what at one again? Our relationship with one another, which, when done God's way, will in turn, eventually brings about an end to the conflict and restores God's community and its ability to function as purposed. One cannot set at one something that has not been broken. It may take days, weeks, months and even years. There is no timetable to being at peace with one another. As a side note, we must not confuse unity with peace. They are often not synonymous. Peace eventually brings unity, but unity does not guarantee peace. In our endeavour to have unity with the brethren, very often we have conflict, but in the pursuit of peace we eventually triumph and have the unity God commands us to have. The reason is because the peace we seek from God brings a common purpose and with this common purpose, unity is assured.

This will require maximum effort and sacrifice on each member's part, mostly in the putting down of pride and admitting we don't know everything. The question we must ask ourselves is, *will this conflict,* (with the right amount of submission to the spirit of God, prayer, and effort on our part to resolve it)*, strengthen the community of God's people?* If truth be told, many times we are usually just ticked off because it is causing us some inconvenience or challenging our world view? Many times, we shy away from making peace because our pride has been bruised, our egos injured, our leadership has been challenged, we were embarrassed, or the other person has revealed things in ourselves we are either unable or unwilling to deal with and so we project onto others what we feel in ourselves (usually anger and disappointment), rather than going to the Lord and asking for help to face it and release it.

Tension brings and reveals conflict, not so much with other members of the body, but within us, and robs us of the ability to set at one again, the members of the body whom God has chosen to help us deal with these issues. If God has placed all the gifts of the spirit within the body, (both local, regional, and international) then common sense (a rare commodity these days) tells us that the help we need to deal with our issues lies somewhere within the body. By ostracizing members of the body with whom we disagree, we are cutting off our own noses to spite our own faces. We may not like what they believe, did, or said, but does that mean they have no value within the Ecclesia to help in other areas? Or have we reverted to the Roman Catholic version of church, where we believe that if you don't agree with me, then you cannot be of God. This smacks of pride and arrogance, two traits that will keep us away from God and His Kingdom far more than what others have done or not done to us.

To repeat an earlier statement, all but three epistles were written to the Ecclesia, and not to individuals. The main reason was that the Ecclesia was meant to solve the problems within it with the guidance of the Holy Ghost, God's word, and wise elders (both men and women) who teach and help us how to deal with the beams in our own eyes. These wise elders do this by example of how they dealt or are dealing with theirs. (wisdom is not just saying *'Just pray about it'*. This is a cop out and they who blithely spruik this abhorrent cliche do more harm than good). As all members of the Ecclesia learn to hear the voice of God, they go and teach others to do so for themselves. In other words, disciples making disciples.

There are two different types of peace mentioned in God's word. The peace that the Master gives (**John 14:27**- Eirēnē- to join in peace, to set at one again) and the peace we are to have between each other (**Mark 9:50** Eirēneuō- be at peace with or live peaceably with). Not only are they different in their application, but they are equally as important to the correct functioning of the Body of Christ.

Let us look at the peace the Lord gives first. The Master slept in the boat during a raging storm because He knew that His time to die was both not yet and not by drowning. The disciples did not avail themselves to the fact that they were with their Messiah and rest in His peace. They were more concerned with their own lives and thus questioned, *Master, carest thou not that we perish?* (**Mark 4:38**). Everything Jesus did and the parables He told illustrated and demonstrated the Kingdom of God and this situation was no different.

The Master rose from his repose and said, *Peace be still* (verse 39). But consider for a moment, who was He talking to? Was He just talking to the wind and the waves or was He talking to the disciples also. The wind and the waves heard His command and became calm. They had to, for the Master had spoken. His command was used to illustrate who He is and what power He has, even over the elements. When the point was made, the wind and the waves need not be stormy anymore. The disciples interpreted it as He was only talking to the wind and waves, but they experienced the same peace as the forces of nature. Peace was restored to the hearts of the disciples which created an ever-deeper bond between them all. Can you imagine the stories around the campfires over the years about when their hearts failed them for fear, but just three words from the Messiah brought peace?

This kind of peace cannot be dragged out from the depths of our own being because we do not innately have it. This kind of peace only comes about because of the Prince of Peace. We have this peace because we are one with Messiah. If we do not have the Lord indwelling our very being, ordering our very lives and fulfilling His very purpose in us, how can we possibly have peace with one another. The Master prophesied about this kind of *Peace* (Eirēnē- quietness, rest, to set at one again) when He said *Peace I leave* (Aphiēmi- send forth) *with you, my peace* (same word) *I give unto you: not as the world giveth, give I unto you. Let not your heart be troubled* (Tarassō- agitated), *neither let it be afraid* (Deiliaō- timid, from Deilos- faithless) (**John 14:27**). This is the peace, the inner quietness and rest He gives to the individual believer who is seeking first the Kingdom of God and His righteousness. To live in peace within the body is a peace for which we must strive, swallow much pride, eliminate elitism and many times lose much now in order to gain much more later.

Peace is not something that humans are born with. Since the fall of mankind, we have been born to struggle. To paraphrase Job, *As sure as sparks fly upwards, man was born to struggle* (**Job 5:7**). We will end up in conflict and war, no matter how many times we try to avoid it. We set up organizations to bring unity (for example, the senate during the Pax Romana- 200 years of relative peace during the Roman Empire period, The League of Nations [1920-1944], and the U.N. 1945 until now), but most only last a generation or two then we have differences and splits and end in even more bloody conflicts. Man's organizations fall woefully short of their goals because they are attempting to fulfil the will of God (to live in peace) without submission to God alone. They interject submission to men and their rules as much as unto God, saying that by doing so, others will find peace. A delusional fantasy at best and it always ends as a pox on humanity.

The League of Nations was an international diplomatic group of 41 nations who convened after World War I to resolve disputes between countries before they erupt into open warfare. That lasted less than twenty-five years. After yet another devastating world war (60 million deaths and 100 million wounded with another 30 million dying from disease and starvation), The United Nations was formed with the same mandate as the League of Nations, and we have had more than 30 major wars (civil and international) since World War 2 as of 2020. (This does not include border or territory wars as these number in the hundreds). There have been over 187,000,000 deaths due to wars in the last one hundred years alone. As we can see, peace is not something that comes naturally to us mere mortals. It is obvious that the United Nations is not as united as they claim to be, or that they are as impartial as their manifesto claims. They are an abject failure in the truest sense at bringing unity to anyone in the world let alone bringing peace to them. The main reasons are that bureaucracy swallows up the vast majority of resources and they are using man's ideas to bring about something that only God can bring by and through His Ecclesia.

For thousands of years, nations have intermarried to try to bring about peace. King Solomon was a perfect example of marrying for peace. The European royal families intermarried for the same reason for hundreds of years and there were still wars culminating in World War I. The Hundred Years' War (1337–1453) between Britain and France was nothing but a family squabble about some land and who was boss. Mankind hasn't changed much in the last 800 years. We still squabble over who's boss and over stuff. Mankind cannot bring about peace because mankind (outside of obedience to God's word) is broken in pieces. When people are restored to the Prince of Peace (**Isaiah 9:6**) then we can have peace amongst ourselves. As we find peace in the Creator, we take that peace and give it to one another.

As we will see in a following section, God does not command us to do something we are already doing, that is why God **commands** us to be *peacemakers, have peace with one another, follow peace with all men* (**Matthew 5:9, Mark 9:50, Hebrews 12:14**) because we cannot do it on our own. A command requires input from the one commanding. We need to have the new nature God has promised His true biblical disciples who are led of the Spirit, in order to fulfil this command. *And to esteem them very highly in love for their work's sake. And be at peace* (live peaceably) *among yourselves* (**1 Thessalonians 5:13**). This is a directive from Paul to the people of Thessalonica, the region where the greatest conqueror of the known world, Alexander the Great, came from. He fought many great battles and brought about a pseudo-peace to the squabbling tribes and nation-cities wherever he went.

Ezekiel makes it abundantly clear what God expected of Israel regarding their wrong ways of living, *Therefore I will judge you, O house of Israel, every one according to his ways, saith the Lord GOD. Repent, and turn yourselves from all your transgressions; so iniquity shall not be your ruin. Cast away from you all your transgressions, whereby ye have transgressed;* **and make you a new heart and a new spirit:** *for why will ye die, O house of Israel?* (**Ezekiel 18:30-31**). Paul says the same thing, only now 550 years have passed, and the problem of man's sinful heart remains, but the solution remains the same, *That ye put off concerning the former conversation* (manner of life), *the old man, which is corrupt according to the deceitful lusts; And be renewed in the spirit of your mind; And* **that ye put on the new man,** *which after God is created in righteousness and true holiness* (**Ephesians 4:22-24**).

Some churches and organization have been deceived into thinking that the world will know that they are His disciples by their doctrine, manner of dress, programmes for the poor, by how big, bountiful, beautiful their buildings are, or how many missionaries they support. They brag in their annual reports of how many churches they have started in the last year (I have noticed a conspicuous absence of reports as to how many churches have closed during the same period) or how many pastors they have ordained. This is just the opposite of what Jesus was trying to convey.

Today, we have many denominations (sects if you will) and at the time Jesus spoke these words in **Mark 9:49-50**, there were many sects of the Jews (Pharisees, Sadducees, the Essenes, the Zealots, the Hellenists, and the Stoic Jews, just to name a few) and they each had their own thing going. It was very confusing as to who, in reality, had the real word of God. They each held different beliefs, dress codes, programmes, and doctrines (teachings) regarding everything from heaven and hell, authority, piety, the written as opposed to the oral law and many other things. Each one said they adhered only to God's word and that the rest were off kilter. So, how did Jesus say that the world could differentiate between His disciples and the other sects of the Jews? The obvious answer is by our love. The question must then be asked, how can we have peace with one another if we do not love one another? If we are separated by denominations, organizations, priest/pastor separated from the lay believers, rich in the body sitting beside the poor in the body week in week out not affecting one another or infighting between factions in the church or organizations?

We spend a lot of time arguing about who's definition of holiness standards are right and other such drivel. Holiness is right, but holiness standards without a right relationship with God and each other is hypocrisy, not holiness. It is a *show* of godliness rather than *exampling* the character and actions of God (Dikaiosune- righteousness). It is swallowing camels while gagging on gnats. We will allow bitterness in our hearts towards one another, but as long as we dress right and say amen often enough during the preaching, don't go to movies, or watch television, pay tithes and offerings, we are still holiness people. This is a lie and we must repent of it, NOW! We allow the treatment of some people better than others sitting in our pews, we allow *sharing for prayer* (Christian version of gossip) and we remain silent. We allow other matters such as pride, arrogance, slander, division within the body to slide, as long as we go to church, obey the man of God, don't cut our hair, stay clean shaven and don't indulge in worldly pleasures we are somehow we still claim to be holiness people? Do I have that right? We build beautiful buildings and fill them with people who choose to have ugly hearts, who speak in tongues but can't speak civilly to one another, who give to the building fund, but can't make the time to build each other up in God. Since when is this okay with God?

The first mention of peace in the Renewed Covenant proves that we have the power to give peace as a matter of choice. **Matthew 10:13** *And if the house be worthy, **let your peace come upon it:** but if it be not worthy, let your peace return to you.* We have the option to be at peace, to give peace, to bring peace with us and leave it there. Peace in the Old Covenant many times is translated as Shâlôm meaning safe, well, happy, friendly; welfare or fare well], health and prosperity, favour, rest, safety, salute, all is or be well. It was spoken on Abraham at his death bed and a promise that he would lay with his fathers in peace. Jacob sought this peace while bargaining with God to go back home in **Genesis 28:21-22.**

David wrote an injunction to the Sons of Korah, *Depart from evil, and **do good;** seek* (Bâqash-strive after, procure) ***peace, and pursue it*** (run after it, hunt it down. **Psalm 34:14**). We need not strive after something that comes naturally. In **Psalm 85:10** we read that, *Mercy and truth are met together; righteousness* (Tsedeq- equity, justice) *and peace have kissed each other*. We can see that God also puts mercy and truth, equity, and peace in the same class. David states that mercy and truth have met (meet each other and concur) while righteousness and peace have kissed, Nâshaq- to fastened together through the idea of fire and they are, *equipped as with weapons to rule*. If righteousness and peace are to kiss, we must fight for it.

To us Apostolics who continue to shout we have *the truth*, but neglect mercy, peace, and righteousness, I must issue a warning that our hypocrisy will only shout louder than our statements of holiness or articles of faith. Peace is not easily obtained; we must fight for it (I see the paradox of this statement). One cannot have the righteousness of God and not seek to dwell in peace with the brethren. **Romans 14:17** tells us that ...*the kingdom of God is not meat and drink; but **righteousness, and peace,** and joy in the Holy Ghost* (Paul's citation from **Psalm 85:10**). Paul clearly says that righteousness and peace go together. Once again, Paul tells us to, *Follow* (Diōkō- pursue, press toward) *peace with all men, and holiness, without which no man shall see the Lord* (**Hebrews 12:14**). When we wait for peace to come to us, our enemy, ol' slewfoot himself through the help of his minions (sadly, some of them sit in our pews and stand behind our pulpits), will do all in his power to keep us from it, but we are commanded here to pursue or press toward peace, not wait for others to bring it to us. To pursue peace is not a passive statement but a directive to action, just as to love our neighbour as ourselves is not a passive statement but a call to action, so we must pursue peace with all men.

It is clear in God's word that being at peace does not mean the lack of conflict but a way of life. *For he that will love life, and see good days, let him refrain his tongue from evil, and his lips that they speak no guile: Let him eschew evil, and do good;* **let him seek** (to endeavour after and require) **peace**, *and ensue it* (follow after, press hard toward, be given to. **1 Peter 3:10-11**). If we genuinely love life, we must not only stop doing the bad things, but we must also desire and require peace.

For those readers who claim to be holiness people, who dress modestly and do not partake of any of the world's vices, I would like you to read **Hebrews 12:14** again. Did you notice that Paul said, *Follow peace, **and** holiness...?* Some holiness people are so busy following holiness standards that they have neglected to first follow peace with all men (this includes the brother and sister with whom they disagree). The word Kai is also translated as *even, therefore, indeed, then,* and *yet.* So, we can read **Hebrews 12:14** thus, *follow peace then holiness, follow peace, even holiness, follow peace, therefore holiness* and so on. There are no degrees in following peace, and with the same tenacity we choose to follow Jesus and follow holiness, we are to follow peace. Jesus said 19 times in the gospels to *'follow me'* and the prophet tells us in **Isaiah 9:6** M'shiyach is the Prince of Peace, so by following Jesus but not following peace we have contradicted our own holiness testimony.

The apostle writes, *But glory, honour,* **and peace, to every man that worketh good,** *to the Jew first, and also to the Gentile* (**Romans 2:19**). Please note the order in which we are to do good- to the Jew (God's people) first, then to the gentiles. He uses the word Ergazomai for *worketh good,* meaning to be engaged in, to be occupied with and to toil in doing good. Peace is not a state of mind, but a conscious state which, by deliberate effort, attains a state of brotherhood with our fellow man and Paul tells the Galatians the same thing, *As we have therefore opportunity, let us* **do good** (same Greek word as *worketh good*) *unto all men,* **especially unto them who are of the household of faith** (**Galatians 6:10**). We cannot attempt to win the world to the peace of Christ if we will not fight our own selfishness and feelings-based faith to be at peace with those of the household of faith.

Paul writes to the Philippians, *And be found in him, not having mine own righteousness, which is of the law, but that which is through the faith of Christ,* **the righteousness which is of God** *by faith* (**Philippians 3:9**). James tells us that... **the fruit of righteousness is sown in peace** *of them that* **make peace** (**James 3:18**). Notice the words *make peace,* not find peace? To *sow* is through the idea of extending as well as to scatter. The prophet tells us that God ...*will extend* (Nâṭâh- stretch forth, spread out. This speaks of deliberate action) *peace to her like a river, and the glory of the Gentiles like a flowing stream: then shall ye suck, ye shall be borne upon her sides, and be dandled upon her knees* (**Isaiah 66:12**). If we are to be like God in His fulness, we also are commanded to sow (extend) peace to one another. So, how can we claim to have the righteousness of God through His blood (**Romans 5:9**) if we are not proving it by sowing in peace?

We must also remember that one of the fruits of the spirit is *peace* and it is imperative that we have these fruits as a part of our testimony. To rely on organization/church affiliation or attendance, outward appearance, tithing and obedience to the pastor without pursuing peace with the brethren first, then those outside the Ecclesia, is once again, to negate our testimony before the court of heaven.

We are even told that peace is a part of the gospel in **Romans 10:15** *And how shall they preach, except they be sent? as it is written, How beautiful are the feet of them* **that preach the gospel of peace,** *and bring glad tidings of good things!* Remember the Aramaic word for *gospel* is translated as *hope.* When we pursue peace, we bring hope to those without it. We are told to walk in shoes of peace in **Ephesians 6:15** *And your feet shod with the preparation of the **gospel of peace***; To have our feet shod is to Hupodeō, meaning to bind onto one's foot. These are not slip-on shoes; they take effort to bind them on tight, so they stay on.

Paul tells his young disciple in **2 Timothy 2:22** in no uncertain terms to ...***Flee** also youthful lusts: but **follow** righteousness, faith, charity, **peace, with them that call on the Lord** out of a pure heart.* The word follow is Diōkō- pursue, press, be given to, press toward and is the same word Paul uses in **Philippians 3:14**, *I press* (Diōkō- pursue, press toward) *toward the mark for the prize of the high calling of God in Christ Jesus.* Paul is writing this to his son in the Lord, Timothy, about those who already have the right doctrine of salvation but are lacking in other important matters concerning their lives. He is telling them to follow the doctrine (teaching), about righteousness (having God's character and actions), faith (assurance, persuasion, reliance in Christ and fidelity), charity (God's love feast), **and** peace with a pure heart. If one does these, one will eventually find their way into a deeper understanding of God and the Ecclesia. Paul tells Timothy (and by extension, us) that we must flee one in order to follow the other. The peace of God must not be a weekend visitor, but it must rule as Paul told the people of Colossae: *And **let the peace of God rule*** (Brabeuō- arbitrate and govern) *in your hearts**, to the which also ye are called in one body; and be ye thankful* (**Colossians 3:15**).

I must reiterate that to belong to the Kingdom of God does not entail meat and drink (our natural needs) but... *righteousness* (Dikaiosunē- equity of character or act [with God])*, **and** peace, **and** joy in the Holy Ghost* (**Romans 14:7**). Notice that righteousness (being like God) comes before peace then comes joy. Many are seeking joy hoping it will bring them peace which will make them like God (holiness). If this is not putting the cart before the horse, I don't know what is. Furthermore, we are also told in **Ephesians 4:3** *Endeavouring to keep the unity of the Spirit in the **bond of peace**.* The *bond of peace* paints a rather interesting picture. Sundesmos- a ligament or joint tie, a binding principle (a basic, fundamental, foundational belief or behaviour). Two bones cannot work together unless there is a ligament holding them together. That is the entire purpose of a ligament. Seriously, is this what we are doing in our churches today, or are we just playing the church game like people meeting weekly to play card games and have partners for the duration of the game?

Ephesians 4:3 is interesting in that it uses the same Greek word in another verse, **2 Timothy 2:15** *Study to shew thyself approved unto God, a workman that needeth not to be ashamed, rightly dividing the word of truth.* Both the word **endeavour** and **study**, come from Spoudazō meaning to use speed, that is, to make effort, be prompt or earnest: do or give diligence. We cannot claim that we are students of the word and can rightly divide the word if we are not ...*endeavouring to keep the unity of the Spirit in the bond of peace* also.

Peace with one another is one of the things that edifies the Ecclesia, as is written in **Romans 14:19** *Let us therefore follow after the things **which make for peace*** (one word- Eirēnē)*, and things **wherewith one may edify another**.* Making peace, not keep the peace, will edify one another. Division within the body is just another sign that we need to make peace with God who, with much forethought, made each and every one of us (not just the leadership) to function in the Commonwealth of the Kingdom of God for His glory.

For those who say, and rightly so, that without holiness no man shall see God, please read the first half of that verse again, FOLLOW PEACE. Holiness is our way of being in the same state of mind as our Lord, but peace with one another shows in what state we are within the Ecclesia. We are given the opportunity to be at peace with God through His sacrifice (see **John 14:27**), where we struggle is to be at peace with one another. It is not just without holiness that we will not see God, but without righteousness (Dikaiosune- equal with God in character and actions) *and* peace, (with holiness coming in a close third), we shall not see the Lord. All three are a necessity if we are to see God.

We can be so holy that we look like Swiss cheese, we can speak in tongues like we work in a Lebanese bakery, and we can baptize someone in Jesus' name everyday of our lives, but this will not help us to see God if we do not pursue peace first. Zachariah's prophecy on his newborn son, John (soon to be known to the world as the Baptizer), ended with this admonition, *To give light to them that sit in darkness and in the shadow of death,* **to guide our feet into the way of peace** (Luke 1:79). He led people to the Prince of Peace. We, on this side of the cross, have been given the same mandate as John the Baptizer. We are to be guided by God and wise humble elders/leaders in the ways of peace with one another then guide others to the Lord.

The Risk of the Status Quo.

I feel I must end this chapter with a warning. The overpowering desire to keep the status quo has destroyed many more churches than any device the devil has in his arsenal. When we see that things are not right within the body, we are tempted or sometimes warned to say nothing, to do nothing or only give token efforts in being a part of a solution, because we have been lied to and told we are to be peacekeepers, to keep the unity under almost any circumstance. Nowhere in God's word are we ever called to be peacekeepers, but peacemakers.

There is a bias that has crept into this last days church that not only prevents growth but retards it in any organization (regardless of its purpose). *Status Quo Bias* is one of the most dangerous, and common biases in our decision making. It was popularized by Nobel Prize winning economist Richard Thaler. This bias in decision-making, also commonly called inertia, prompts people to prefer for things to stay the same by doing nothing or by sticking to a previous decision. This bias becomes a problem when the expected value of a change, one that may only have small transition costs, is higher than the reward for sticking with the status quo. It is also a considerable problem with big decisions, where the benefits of change could be quite substantial.

One reason people do not challenge the status quo is *concept of commitments*. Diverging from the status quo could force people to withdraw from previously made commitments. Individuals are likely to keep commitments to avoid reputation damage or cognitive dissonance (the perception of contradictory information). In the latter case, breaking with committed strategy would be subconsciously inconsistent with the initial commitment to the strategy and the reasoning that drove the initial commitment. *"I have to stay here, because this is where I started"*. Humans suffer from a crippling malady called *loss aversion*. This is where we run the risk of losing what we have in pursuit of what we want. This has brought about the demise of many marriages, churches, and friendships. In the pursuit of a biblical Ecclesia, where one that is totally submitted unto God, we may need to let go of something that has worked for a long time in order to benefit from what God is trying to do in these last days.

To pursue the God of Peace that passes all understanding we will need to let go of the pseudo-peace we have at the moment. The *"don't mess with me and I won't mess with you"* approach only ever works for a short time. How do we know when it's time to change the status quo? Test the status quo. Often and regularly. If we find ourselves resisting change, we know we are on the path to derailment, one which causes far more grief and pain than the initial peace we had in the status quo.

Not pursuing peace has a deleterious effect on the Ecclesia and many times politics comes into play. We don't want to be on the wrong side of an attempt that may fail. Most people are reluctant to pursue a strategy that breaks from existing dogma (*we're right and they're wrong*) because they fear if a change they support fails, it will be blamed on them while benefits from a successful shift will not be directly attributed to them. This sounds like our modern-day politicians. These people are thus making a rational, albeit sub-optimal decision not to support changes to the status quo. *"Better the devil you know, than the devil you don't"* comes to mind. In the long run, maintaining the status quo actually is more detrimental than the small loses we have had to endure to benefit from the changes necessary to grow.

Jesus told us of a man who was changing the status quo (from not having a tower to having one). There was a risk that he may not complete it and Jesus said that it is wise to calculate that risk. However, once the risk was calculated, the man could either move forward with what he had, or he must get more in order to build. The moral of the story was not to build or refrain from building, but to make sure he had enough resources and gumption to start and finish the tower. Many tower builders have been ridiculed for not finishing what they started or are complainers because they don't have new towers. The purpose of this story was not about towers, but about the cost of discipleship, about cross bearing, and about becoming like our Master (being Holy as He is Holy). How can we call ourselves disciples, if we will not challenge our status quo and sacrifice ourselves and our dainty feelings in pursuit of peace with one another?

Peacemakers, not Peacekeepers.

The definition of peacekeeper is, *to maintain the status quo which is to keep the existing or previous state of affairs*. Where would we be if Jesus came to keep the status quo of His people? His very existence brought turmoil to the Nation of Israel, to Rome and eventually to the whole world, yet His death, burial and resurrection brought peace to those who would embrace the manner of life He championed and lived.

United Nations Peacekeepers, for example, are sent into an area of conflict under a ceasefire and told to keep the status quo, to make sure no one rocks the boat, to keep warring factions apart. This only works for a brief period. Peacekeepers are easy targets for the warring parties because they know they cannot go past their pitiful man-made mandates. Being a peacekeeper is not what Christ was when He came and walked amongst us, neither is it what Christ called us to be.

A peacemaker, on the other hand is someone who shares the perspective that peace must first be disrupted in order to allow for greater peace to enter. They speak up, anticipate discomfort, and hang on because they know that it has to get worse before it gets better. Peacemakers take initiative to create spaces for brave conversations to happen resulting in conflicts being settled and not ignored.

The great Peacemaker Himself came to show us how to make peace. How to confront wrong and make it right. He said He came to bring a sword (which rightly divides truth from fiction- **Hebrews 4:12**). The Master said, *Think not that I am come to send peace on earth: I came not to send peace, but a sword* (**Matthew 10:34**). In fact, Christ told us in the Beatitudes, *Blessed are the **peacemakers**:*

for they shall be called the children of God (**Matthew 5:9**). Peacekeepers are not called children of God, but *Peacemakers* are. This word is a combination of two words, Eirēnopoios and Poieō meaning to band together, to commit, to lighten the ship, to perform or provide, to work towards quietness, to set at one again and bring prosperity. It also means to bear and carry, to agree and to avenge. We read in **Acts 7:26** that even Moses tried to restore peace between two fighting brethren, *And the next day he shewed himself unto them as they strove,* **and would have set them at one again**, *saying, Sirs, ye are brethren; why do ye wrong one to another?* His attempt at being a peacemaker cost him the crown of Egypt, but it won him the crown of the Nation of Israel and a crown when he is resurrected. His attempts to make peace were not ignored by God, just that the reward was not what he had expected.

We may keep all the holiness standards of our little group, but if we are not endeavouring to be peacemakers, by Jesus' own words, we cannot call ourselves children of God. He told us to promote peace. To promote a business, one does not sit, and hope customers come to the business. One must actively go into a hostile area (a community where we don't know whether our business will be accepted) and promote what we feel will be beneficial for the community. There will be people who will reject our offers, some will remain neutral, while others will gladly accept what we have to offer.

The body of Christ is to make peace with its own members first, then when we have *MADE* peace with the brethren, we can now say we have a tried and proven peace we can now export to the wider community. They will see a hard fought for peace and will come to receive from us what God has offered to all. Our Lord told us in **Matthew 10:8**, *Freely ye have received* (Lambanō- to take or seize, to get a hold of), *freely give* (Didōmi- bestow, to minister, to bring forth). We were never called to be peacekeepers, but we are blessed when we become peacemakers.

Chapter 16

Every one members of one another.

Romans 12:5 *So we, being many, are one body in Christ, and **every one members** one of another.*

Men are free when they are obeying some deep, inward voice of religious belief. Obeying from within. Men are free when they belong to a living, organic, believing community, active in fulfilling some unfulfilled, perhaps unrealized purpose. Not when they are escaping to some wild west. The most unfree souls go west, and shout of freedom.

D.H. Lawrence. English writer and poet.

We, being many, is a term used in the bible for God's people. It is the word Polus where we get the polis (like metropolis, from Greek meaning "chief town or capital city of a province") and it means, *we being altogether, common or plenteous*. It can also be combined with Ecclesia, as we are being gathered together with the common, hence, the Commonwealth of the Kingdom of God. This is also something Jesus alluded to when speaking to the leadership in Jerusalem. He called them whited sepulchres which can be likened to a necropolis, a large, designed cemetery with elaborate crypts and monuments. The name hales from the ancient Greek word νεκρόπολις, literally meaning "*city of the dead*". The term usually implies a separate burial site at a distance from a city, as opposed to tombs within cities. I have been to many a mega-church (and some not so mega) in my travels, where the overwhelming majority are there to get something from God and give very little back. They are there in a traditional sense, not in a relational sense. These people were not connected to each other, save for church meetings and functions. I felt like I had entered into a necropolis.

In **Romans 12:5** and other verses like it, God is telling us that we are *Melos* or be connected to each other as a limb is connected to the body, to put it another way, as mentioned in the previous chapter, we are connected via a ligament or tendons to one another. The main difference between ligaments and tendons is that tendons join bone to a skeletal muscle and ligaments join bone to another bone. Either way, whether we are muscle, bone, tendon, or ligament, without recognizing and behaving as members of the same body, the body is useless for any worthwhile purpose.

When we see a person, whose limbs are deformed or missing, we instantly think that something has gone wrong, whether by trauma, disease, or birth defect. We may feel sorry for that person and pity their dilemma but walk away knowing there is little if anything we can do about it. The world may be lost and evil, but it is not blind and stupid. When they see a group of people claiming to be the body of Christ but have members who are out of sorts with each other, not working together for a common purpose or trying to operate with missing parts, they will see that there is something wrong and pity us.

When we care for other members of the body, though they may not be directly connected to us, we show the world and new believers in Christ that there is a viable alternative to the dog-eat-dog existence they have now. Many non-believers have seen the church hurt that far too many saints have endured and would not even consider what we have to offer. Paul told us in **1 Corinthians 6:1** *Dare any of you, having a matter against another, go to law before* (Epi- superimpose, in front of) *the unjust, and not before the saints?*

What happens in a court? A case is presented before the public and a decision is made based on clear evidence (not hearsay, circumstantial evidence, or conjecture) and judgement is pronounced. After that, all actions done by the guilty party will be tainted by their past as far as the public is concerned. When a felon is released from prison, his crimes are on public record for all to see and they struggle to return to normal life. When we go to law with one another, we are just proving how carnal we really are, and we also show how little we understand forgiveness and restoration.

Society at large has dumped these people on the garbage dump of life, then we wonder why, in the US alone, 83% of prisoners go back into prison within 9 years of their release (the numbers are similar around the world, author's note).

(https://www.bjs.gov/content/pub/pdf/18upr9yfup0514.pdf table 3 page 6).

Prison is the only place many have found what we laughingly call family and have some kind of social structure. We were all criminals, lawbreakers, workers of iniquity in the eyes of God before His grace gave us a different choice. These people (we call them sinners) are members of the criminal element of the world's system and until we show them a real working model of the body of Christ (not how good our church is) and what family really means, we cannot become members one of another in the eyes of God. We may be members of a church, but not the body of Christ. The people we claim to be seeking will remain where they are, or if they do come in, many find it not as advertised (where it's the same as in prison and its every man for himself, only we use the name of Jesus to get stuff for ourselves), and they will go back into the world.

I believe we have taken an extremely narrow view of what Paul told us **1 Thessalonians 5:21-22** regarding proving all things and abstaining from all appearance of evil. We have come to believe that evil is sexual immorality, alcohol, drugs, cheating or lying and so on, but the true definition of evil in context also means hurtful, especially (morally) culpable, derelict [of duty to one another], vicious, facinorous [bad deeds], mischief, malice [in heart and deeds], grievous, harm, lewd, malicious-Greek- Ponēros. It also means that we have the ability to do good but withhold it, and for some reason we choose not to help. We are behaving like the world and telling people we live in a different world. The hypocrisy screams louder than our testimony. If I break my arm, the brain will send a message to my other arm to protect it, at the same time it tells my legs to move away from what hurt it and go to seek help from others to help fix it. All of this is done organically and without hesitation. Is this what is happening within much of the western Ecclesia today? How then do we have the audacity to call others backsliders and wonder why they won't come back, when all that happened was, they were hurt or they were ignored? How can we bring them in or back in and incorporate them into the body when many times we are as divided as the world, and many times within the same church let alone denomination or organization? How can we call ourselves members, when we allow the enemy to whisper into our ears, accusations about the brothers and sisters? How can we judge their motives without even talking to them? We are a greater fool than the devil if we think the world does not see these things? Do we think God does not see these things? Are we so blinded by our pride, arrogance, and love of our doctrine (just because we have Acts 2:38 and one God), that we have somehow stepped into a higher plain and all others are just people who should want what we have? As my mother used to say, '*phooey on that*'.

There are risks that come with full integration into the body. Will we get hurt? More than likely, yes. Will we be misunderstood? Undoubtedly. Will we sometimes have feelings of regret? Most definitely. Will we be taken advantage of? As we say in Australia, *too right mate!* Were we any different than those we struggle with when we were strangers and aliens from the Commonwealth of the Kingdom of God? (**Ephesians 2:1**). Or when we came into the body, did we immediately and instinctively know what to do or did we grow into what we now know? God took a risk on us hurting His body, (which, if honesty were to prevail, we have done countless times since we have come to Him) and actually died from the rejection of the very people He came to show love to and to save.

When there is strife within the body (of which we are all members one of another) we must deal with it as though that member's actions/inactions or pain and suffering were to affect all the Ecclesia not just ourselves or our little clique. By strife I do not mean that we don't agree on every point of doctrine, they have done something wrong, annoying, or made us mad or threatened our authority. These are things we must deal with as a matter of course in normal life. Maybe they just disagree with the way we do things; they see things from a different perspective or that they have issues they are struggling with. We must learn to work as a body to sort out any differences we have in love and humility, then (and here comes the sticky bit) we must instigate **Galatians 6:1-2** for those who are no longer a part of our body, no matter who's fault it is. *Brethren, if a man be overtaken in a fault* (Paraptōma- a side slip (lapse or deviation of judgement), that is, (unintentional) error or (wilful) transgression, fall, offence, sin, trespass)*, ye which are spiritual* (Pneumatikos- non-carnal and regenerated)*, restore* (Katartizō- repair, fit and perfectly join together) *such an one in the spirit of meekness; considering thyself, lest thou also be tempted. Bear ye one another's burdens, and so fulfil the law of Christ.* Instead of writing people off because we either disagree or they have broken one of our moral codes, they don't believe like we do or they did something wrong, we are *Commanded* to **repair, fit, and perfectly join together** the members of the body.

Why would God command a restoration of this kind of fallen saints? The same reason when someone loses a leg, or an arm and doctors try to fix the problem by using a prosthesis. If man and his wicked ways can come up with a second-rate attempt at restoration of a broken or missing body part, how much more should the body of Christ, with the healing, regenerative, and restorative power of the Holy Ghost do to and for itself? Christ alone can heal the physical body at any time He chooses, but to restore a member (just because they are a member, not because they have paid their dues in the penalty box) back to the body to function as a member, takes the body itself. We are to remember the members and that we are members one of another.

Messed up thinking.

BIID or Body Integrity Identity Disorder, also known as Xenomelia, is a mental disorder characterized by a desire to be disabled or having discomfort with being able-bodied. It is a condition in which there is a mismatch between the brain's image of the body and the actual physical body and is characterized by an intense desire to amputate that part of the body. Even something as unbiased as a mirror cannot convince people with Xenomelia that what they see, and feel is not reality. We rightfully view people with this kind of mindset as mentally unstable and not to be trusted with sharp objects or any major decisions. This desire for *dismemberment* refers, in general terms, to the act of cutting, tearing, pulling, wrenching, or otherwise relieving the limbs from a living thing, and shows a major malfunction in the cognitive thinking of the person. Sadly, many churches perform this hideous practice (BIID) on people with whom they disagree or have fallen from *their* graces almost on a weekly basis. The only grace these people have fallen from is of men, for the grace of God does not so easily right someone off.

There is nothing physiologically wrong with the limb of a person that suffers from Xenomelia other than it is *perceived* as superfluous, deformed, or mismatched. When a member of the body of Christ is considered as either non-functional, non-essential or just does not fit in with our clique and we treat them as such, it will not be long before we cease to care if they are with us or not, and all too soon, we will lose them and all their life's past and future experiences that could and would be beneficial to the body. Far too often, we will say they never really wanted God anyway (which in almost all cases is wrong at best or an outright lie) and point out all the wrong they have done while totally neglecting or downplaying any good they may have done or tried to do. Would we stay where we were not wanted, thought of as superfluous, or treated with contempt?

How is it that we say with our lips to unbelievers, we believe that God would accept and use any person into His eternal Kingdom, but we will not do the same for those already within His body here on earth? God does not neglect to reach out and care for a saint who is struggling with a past they just cannot seem to defeat, while we (the church) give them a certain amount of time to 'get over it' or 'get their act together', then unceremoniously remove them from fellowship whether forcefully or through neglect. This is usually done covertly and many times without the person's prior knowledge. Is there one worthless saint in the Kingdom of God? If so, this would mean that God has made a mistake. I would venture to guess that it is our narrow mindedness that has failed to see the worth of a saint within our midst, and more is the pity for us. Some of our so-called saints and leaders are so narrow-minded that they can look through a keyhole with both eyes. Some churches have outreach programmes but won't reach out to people in their own midst unless it is in their clique.

To be a member of a body means that when one member goes through a trial, all do so. Paul admonishes us in **1 Corinthians 12:25** *That there should **be no schism in the body**; but that **the members should have the same care one for another**. And whether one member suffer, **all the members suffer with it**; or one member be honoured, **all the members rejoice with it**. Now ye are the body of Christ, and members in particular*. If we are NOT caring for the members the same way, we are being partial, and God hates that (**James 2:1-4, Leviticus 19:15, 1 Timothy 5:21, Deuteronomy 1:17, Job 32:21, Romans 2:11**).

Please allow me another military analogy. Let us look at how military forces train, function and succeed. These men and women are no different than any other citizen, save they have joined a community of people with the same goal, to protect and serve their nation. They take in all kinds of people and train them to be one kind of people (with individual skills and ability to think for themselves and using those abilities to complete the mission), ones who know and function in the place and job they were trained for, within the entire corps and recognize their role is just as important as each other's.

Their term of service begins with a pledge to protect the nations constitution. Then indoctrination (teaching) of the core values of the service, to prepare for war and serve during times of emergency in peace. Their training is not just to toughen them up, but to teach them that they are an integral part of a whole. All soldiers, sailors and airmen respect the rank of any branch of the armed forces not just their own. This is to show that all have the same responsibility to the nation and respect each other based on each other's willingness to give up a relatively easy life in the civilian world and choose a much more restrictive and less comfortable life of service.

Special operations unit, *Joint Task Force 2* (JTF2) in Ottawa, Canada, for example, have a motto, *Facta Non Verba- Deeds Not Words*. This is biblically confirmed in **James 1:22** *But be ye doers of the* *word, and not hearers only, deceiving your own selves.* A doer is one that sees what needs to be done then, with all the resources they have on hand they Poiētēs- from Poieō- perform the task, they avenge, band together and bear, they commit and continue, without delay, they execute and exercise, they journey, they lighten the ship, they observe and provide, they have a purpose, they secure, and they yield. These are the definitions of the word *doer*. The training of JTF2 teaches that the individual does not mean as much as the unit when it comes to the mission. Yet they recognize that the unit is made up of individuals working in unison. They are taught to improvise and act on current information and conditions and change when change is necessary. The task/mission is the main focus, and the individual is only important in that they must know their job and complete it in a timely manner. They work together to see the mission accomplished and to get as many members of the team home as possible. Where the individual matters greatly are if they are wounded or injured, then all resources at their disposal are used to care for them. War is dangerous and they do not leave someone behind if they are killed or wounded. It is not just those that are in harm's way that are performing the task, but those who are supporting them with food, equipment, logistics, maintenance, and family services. Without these backing them up, the mission would not get planned nor executed.

The training is harsh and, many times, even seems brutal to outsiders, but it is necessary in order to prepare for the service required of everyone. The person wishing to join this type of family is made fully aware that they will be trained as an individual but treated as an integral part of a larger body with a specific purpose and will be a part of an eternal fraternity of people who have given themselves to the service of others no matter what their job is in the corps. They are made aware of the dire consequences not just for themselves but for all the members of the body should they not perform to the best of their ability.

All members of the armed forces (even elite special forces with all their toughness) would not be able to complete their mission without land, air or naval insertion/extraction, medical staff on hand to return the wounded prior to mission completion, intelligence services, surveillance, food and water preparation for the mission, munitions supply, even something as seemingly innocuous as knowing their pay and families are taken care of.

So, we can now see what Paul was writing about in **Romans 12:4-5** *For as we have many members in one body, and all members have not the same office: So we,* **being many, are one body in Christ, and every one members one of another**. If we have no purpose other than to go to a building, sing a few songs and give some money for the upkeep of said building and leadership, invite a few people to church, then go about our business, we are not the Ecclesia, we are a club (see earlier definition of club).

Gang members in New York were asked in 1995 after an outreach programme that seemed to be successful, why they stopped *"going to church"* several months after they were *born again*, and their answers were deeply disturbing. Almost to a person, they said that when they met Christ, they felt like there was hope, but eventually left *the church* because they did not feel like they were a part of the family. They were encouraged to come to church and even picked up from their homes and returned, but that they were not included as a family member nor had a purpose other than to hear a sermon and told to *'witness for Jesus'*. Sadly, when many returned to their old life, they were immediately accepted back and treated as family members in their old gangs even though they knew it was not right.

The lack of integration into the body (other than church or new believer's class), being treated as not much more than a wallet with a life support system, a number to brag about or trying to turn everybody into a robotic automaton, worshipping, praying, dressing as the rest of the congregation, is stifling the Ecclesia, and stunting its growth spiritually (numerical growth is not a reliable indicator that God is blessing a gathering). I do not think for one moment that we are doing these things consciously or deliberately, but I do believe it goes on in far too many of our western style churches. I believe the reason we do not include these lost in the pew or underutilized saints, is because we do not truly understand what Christ has done for us when we were reprobates. Many times, it can be because of pride that we are high in God's Kingdom and that is a dangerous place to be.

I believe we have forgotten that in all our filthiness, He brought us the offer of salvation (truly an act of grace) and we began to see our own righteousness (character and actions) for what it really is, filthy rags in His sight, and yet, with all that going against us, He openly welcomed us into His family (the Ecclesia) and works with us to change us into His image until we got to where we are today. However, He did not do all of that so that we can be spectators watching an elite few doing all the work in the body. If we felt such great love and gratitude for God, we could not help but treat each other as He treated us, with respect, kindness, and dignity. To God, the Ecclesia was the purpose of His death, burial, and resurrection, a way of showcasing His attributes to a lost and dying world. The Ecclesia is a tool God uses to train His disciples to reign in the Kingdom to come.

Hearing a one-man monologue every week has some benefit for information impartation and it tends to stick for a few days if the message is an *"inspiration or anointed"*. However, without someone for imitation, how will the new followers of Christ learn to deal with life's frustrations? Most hearers, experience aggravation, which unfortunately leads to many members living a life of deprivation in the spirit. They can sing they have the victory all they like, but victory has fruits which will be evident to others.

Our lack of community is intensely painful. A TV talk show is not community. A couple of hours in a church pew each Sabbath is not community. A multinational corporation is neither a human nor a community, and in the sweatshops, defiled agribusiness fields, genetic mutation labs, ecological dead zones, the inhumanity is showing. Without genuine spiritual community, life becomes a struggle so lonely and grim that even Hillary Clinton has admitted "it takes a village".

David James Duncan, American essayist.

Chapter 17.

Kindly affectioned to one another.

Romans 12:10 *Be **kindly affectioned** one to another with brotherly love; in honour **preferring** one another.*

I believe that the community - in the fullest sense: a place and all its creatures - is the smallest unit of health and that to speak of the health of an isolated individual is a contradiction in terms.

Wendell Berry, The Art of the Commonplace: The Agrarian Essays. Health is Membership.

The above scripture by Paul is powerful indeed, but as usual, scripture must compel us to ask, *how does this scripture affect me today and what must I do to align myself to this scripture?* So, what does kindly affectioned one to another really mean in today's world? It is, in essence, that kindness is shown within the community (whether in our neighbourhood or within the Ecclesia) for the greater good of the community, not for self but because God desires and requires it. According to *mayoclinichealthsystem.org*, in *Hometown Health*, their studies have shown, *"Kindness is more than behaviour. The art of kindness means harbouring a spirit of helpfulness, as well as being generous and considerate, and doing so without expecting anything in return in this life. Kindness is a quality of being. The act of giving kindness often is simple, free, positive, and healthy..."* Steve Siegle, Licensed professional counsellor in Behavioural Health in Menomonie, Wisconsin.

Even the people living in this dark world can see the powerful benefit of this command. Sadly though, in much of today's church, we seem to have lost the art of kindness. It is more than shaking someone's hand at church meetings and more than smiling at visitors. It goes beyond the superficial or trivial greetings deep into the psyche of humanity. Many times, kind people are accused of having ulterior motives but in reality, they just know how to be kind and we would do well to watch and learn from these kinds of people (pardon the word play), practice it and we will see a greater response to our efforts to preach the gospel to every living creature (**Luke 4:18, Mark 16:15**). Kindness is a learned attribute, like mercy, grace, and forgiveness, but we must choose to practice it on each other for it to become a natural part of our lives.

In **Romans 12:10,** Paul commends us to be, *kindly affectioned* to each other and though the King James uses two words here, it is actually one Greek word; Philostorgos- which comes from one of the definitions of love; Storgē- cherishing one's kindred, especially parents or children; fond of natural relatives, that is, fraternal towards fellow Christians, the other being Philo- of man.

Sadly, affection today has been twisted to mean some kind of physical or emotional attraction when in its truest form it means, a gentle feeling of fondness or liking. The archaic meaning of affection is... *the act or process of affecting or being affected.* Being affectionate has a positive effect on people. As nouns the difference between affection and effection is the former is the act of affecting or acting upon, while the latter is creation, it creates somethings. For example, God so loved (had affection) for the world **that He gave** (it had an effect on the world) His only begotten son. His affection had an effect on the world.

As mentioned earlier, there is a science to kindness and affection. When we are kind to one another, it has a physiological effect on the body in a positive way. The communication of affection towards others has been proven to have tremendous health benefits which includes but is not limited to, lowering stress hormones, cholesterol, blood pressure and aiding in producing stronger immune systems. Studies have also shown that just one act of kindness a day lowers the chances of depression and anxiety. It also floods the body with hormones that produce a calming effect on both the giver and the receiver. It increases serotonin which heals wounds, helps us to relax and makes a us feel good. It also raises the levels of endorphins which help to reduce pain and increases oxytocin which helps to reduce blood pressure. In contrast withholding kindness and affection has a deleterious effect on both parties.

'In summary: Like all interpersonal behaviours, affectionate communication has biological and physiological antecedents, consequences, and correlates, many of which have implications for physical health and wellness. In particular, there are observable genetic and neurological differences between individuals with a highly affectionate disposition and those less prone to communicating affection, suggesting that variance in the tendency to engage in affectionate behaviour is not entirely the result of environmental influences such as enculturation, parenting, and media exposure. In addition, the expression of affection is associated with markers of immune system competence and appears to help the body to relax and remain calm. The biological effects of affectionate communication are perhaps most pronounced in situations involving either acute or chronic stress. Specifically, highly affectionate individuals are less likely than others to overreact physiologically to stress-inducing events.... Further, it aids immunocompetence and promotes relaxation and calm. Unsurprisingly, therefore, the lack of adequate affection is associated with a host of problems, many of which have specific biological roots.*

Kory Floyd and Colter D. Ray. Oxford Research Encyclopedia.

These benefits are more internally noticed when the emotion is expressed and not merely felt. Even if affection is not returned from the receiver, the effects of the affection are still felt by the giver. It raises the endorphin levels (a neurochemical occurring naturally in the brain and having analgesic [pain relieving] properties) thus perpetuating a greater desire to show affection. The natural mimics the spiritual. If this is what the effect of kindness and affection has on the human body, how much more could, and should it have on the spiritual body of Christ? Our being *kindly affectionate towards one another* has an effect on our lives in that it gives hope that others are fond of us and leaves us with a gentle feeling. The harshness of the world is reduced by our kind affection for one another.

When people see acts of kindness, it makes them feel good and more likely to perform acts of kindness themselves. There are many studies that have shown that, *there are three primary learning styles: visual, auditory, and kinaesthetic (seeing, hearing, doing). It has been proven that 10% of what we read, 20% of what we hear, 30% of what we see, 50% of what we see and hear, 70% of what we say or discuss with others, 80% of what we experience personally and 90% of what we say and do tends to stick with us and effect ourselves and others.*

Glaser, R. (1983, June). Education and Thinking: The Role of Knowledge. Technical Report No. PDS-6. Pittsburgh, PA: University of Pittsburgh, Learning and Development Centre.

So, what if someone in the Ecclesia does not reciprocate our acts of kindly affection? Let us briefly go to the second half of **Romans 12:10** which tells us to *...prefer one another*. Paul was telling us that we must lead the way for others or show deference to one another (to prefer- Proēgeomai). By showing deference (to yield to someone's opinions or wishes out of respect for that person) we place ourselves in a position that is usually extremely uncomfortable for our egos, thus preferring one another has the added benefit of keeping our pride in check.

When we are witnesses to an act of kindness, we may go through what Abraham Maslow, famous American psychologist and creator of **Maslow's Hierarchy of Needs,** called a *"peak experience",* those moments of wonder, amazement, and a sense of what is right that make us feel immeasurably thankful to be alive. The Lord is the one who saves our souls; this is undeniable; however, we (the Ecclesia) help to build the community that will rule and reign with Him in the New Jerusalem on the New Earth. We invite people to see what the Kingdom of God looks like every day, not just on Sundays and Wednesdays. How do we do this? By our daily acts of kindness and affection. We show them how the Kingdom will operate when all the lights are turned off, the music stops, the doors are locked, and the dust has settled. We, as sinful humans, do not have the innate ability to do these things, that is why we must put on the new man that Christ has given to all those who are called by His name. Baptism in Jesus name only changes our status, from rebellious sinner to justified believer by removing the guilt and penalty of sins committed prior to baptism, it does not change our nature. That is the sanctification process which takes place until we die.

If we are still operating from our old nature, then it is obvious, we have not put on the new man, whether we speak in tongues or not, whether we live so-called holiness standards or show up at church every time the doors are open. Not being kindly affectioned to one another is one of the signs that shows we are yet to fully comprehend what Kingdom we have joined so we may promote it to the world.

We cannot call ourselves *holiness* people if we do not follow scriptures like **Ephesians 4:22-24** *That ye put off concerning the former conversation* (behaviour or lifestyle) **the old man,** *which is corrupt according to the deceitful lusts; And be renewed in the spirit of your mind; And that ye* **put on the new man,** *which after God is* **created in righteousness and true holiness,** and again, *Lie not one to another, seeing that ye have put off* **the old man** *with his deeds; And have* **put on the new man,** *which is renewed in knowledge after the image of him that created him* (**Colossians 3:9-10**). We can dress right and say the right things at the right time, but if we are still embracing, *the former behaviour of the old man,* we are just putting lipstick and a bow on a pig. When we say we love someone but do not show kindly affection to one another- WE LIE.

The world has robbed many people of the concept of giving affection mainly based on the fear of it not being returned or misinterpreted. However, the true disciples of Christ within the Ecclesia, who operate in the spirit of Christ to fulfil the law of Christ, have a different mindset. Theirs is a mindset of change by example regardless of personal reward.

There is an instance mentioned by Paul to Timothy where preferring is mentioned in a negative sense. **1 Timothy 5:21** *I charge thee before God, and* (Kai- even) *the Lord Jesus Christ, and the elect angels, that thou observe these things without* **preferring one before another** [now he explains what he means by that] *doing nothing by partiality* (proclivity to favouritism). Here Paul warns Timothy of Prokrima- prejudgment [a predisposition or bias) that is, prepossession (preconception) meaning prejudice). Rather than using the encouraging phrase *one to another,* in context, he uses the harmful phrase *one before another.* This is a directive of what *not* to do to one another (more on the not to's will follow shortly).

James condemns partiality in the Ecclesia as outright and openly promoting sin in his letter to the saints, *My brethren, have not the faith of our Lord Jesus Christ, the Lord of glory, with* **respect of** *persons* (Prosōpolēpsia- partiality, favouritism [nepotism- advantage, privilege, or entitlement granted to relatives or friends in any occupation or field, or discrimination). *For if there come unto your assembly a man with a gold ring, in goodly apparel, and there come in also a poor man in vile raiment; And ye have respect to him that weareth the gay clothing, and say unto him, Sit thou here in a good place; and say to the poor, Stand thou there, or sit here under my footstool: **Are ye not then partial*** (Diakrinō- to separate thoroughly, to discriminate, to withdraw from, to contend) *in yourselves, and are become judges of evil thoughts?* (**James 2:1-4**). He rounds it off with, *If ye fulfil the **royal law** according to the scripture, Thou shalt love thy neighbour as thyself, ye do well: But if ye have respect* (Prosōpolēpteo- favour an individual or show partiality) *to persons, ye commit sin, and are convinced* (at fault and convicted) *of the law as transgressors* (**James 2:8-9**). James tells us the *royal law* is Basilikos Nomos- the sovereign and preeminent prescription of the scriptures.

James then tells of the result of such partiality, *For he shall have judgment without mercy, that hath shewed no mercy; and mercy rejoiceth against judgment* (**James 2:13**). To those who show no mercy they shall receive no mercy, but judgment. Ouch, that's gonna leave a mark. Read that last part again. MERCY REJOICES AGAINST JUDGMENT. Ever wondered what to do in a sticky situation? There is your answer. Lean on the side of mercy. Mercy looks not only to forgive but to restore. I have seen and heard of many people who have been hurt by someone and they say they have forgiven. Truth be told, if everything possible was not done to restore the relationship, forgiveness and mercy were not biblically applied. Only our earthly concept of mercy and forgiveness, not God's was applied. Not sure if God's forgiveness was applied? Ask yourself, what if you did to God what they did to you? Would you be happy for God to do to you that you have done to others after you repented and sought forgiveness and mercy? Would He restore your relationship status with Him to prior the sin or write you off? That is how you are to read *For he shall have judgment without mercy, that hath shewed no mercy; and mercy rejoiceth against judgment.* Jesus gives us something to think about when He says in **Matthew 6:12** *And forgive us our debts, as* (in the same manner as) *we forgive our debtors.* This is your gauge of forgiveness and mercy.

The NLT puts the first part of **James 2:1** this way, *My dear brothers and sisters, how can you claim to have faith in our glorious Lord Jesus Christ if you favour some people over others?* Putting one *above* another is *double-minded hypocrisy* according to the Aramaic English New Testament. This comes directly from **Deuteronomy 1:17** *Ye shall not respect* (show partiality to) *persons in judgment* (Mishpât- divine law and justice)*; **but ye shall hear the small as well as the great**; ye shall not be afraid of the face of man; for the judgment is God's: and the cause that is too hard for you, bring it unto me, and I will hear it.* Today we will only hear (listen to) pastors, bishops, great speakers at our conferences and camp meetings and ignore the little-known ones who also have something to give from God. This is the partiality that Paul and James rail against.

If we are going to be what we claim to be, the true carbon copy of the disciples of Christ, then we must see things the way they truly are not through rose-coloured glasses handed to us by our denominations and organizations. How can God show impartiality of judgement to a lost world, when His own people do not show it within their own ranks. We cannot say, 'Yes, but not my church, my group or my organization', then still only fellowship with the same people while ignoring others. This alone shows the deficit of our understanding of the Commonwealth of the Kingdom of God. It is painfully clear that partiality (preferring one before/over another) has permeated the Apostolic/Pentecostal movement and is diametrically opposed to preferring one another. Preferring one another (putting others before self) has a healing effect on the body while the former will eventually weaken the soul of the Ecclesia, thereby rendering it useless for the purpose for which it was created, to be salt and light to a sick and dark world. Partiality will also destroy those who are quick to judgement, who judge without asking questions, or who judge solely by what they hear from others. These will find themselves being judged without mercy.

Though it is human nature (the old man) to expect reciprocity for kind acts or showing affection, it has no place in the Commonwealth of the Kingdom of God. I find it rather amusing that when we pray that reciprocity be not forthcoming when we do wrong, but crave it when we do right. This, in itself, should show where our hearts are in the Commonwealth of the Kingdom of God.

Kindness that looks for reward is not God's kindness, but is, in fact, disguised selfishness which according to God's word is also idolatry. This is one of the issues of the flesh we must fight against daily and with the help of the Holy Ghost, wise elders, and the brothers and sisters in the Ecclesia, we will defeat this scourge that hinders our growth in God. Seeking reciprocity cheapens the act of kindness and lessons its impact. Kindness can be and sometimes is misinterpreted as manipulation, but this is usually done by people with an unkind heart. However, this in no way releases us from acts of kindness just for kindness's sake towards one another. Each act of kindness done for kindness' sake no matter who is receiving the act of kindness is recorded in the archives of heaven and will be rewarded in due time as Paul tells both the Galatians and Thessalonians, *...And let us not be weary in well doing: for in due season we shall reap, if we faint not.* **As we have therefore opportunity, let us do good unto all men, especially unto them who are of the household of faith** (**Galatians 6:9-10**), *But ye, brethren, be not weary in well doing* (**2 Thessalonians 3:13**).

Chapter 18.

Edify one another

Romans 14:19 *Let us therefore follow after the things which make for peace, and things wherewith one may **edify** another.*

As Michele, my wife, regularly asks after I make a statement on what God wants for His Ecclesia, *"Ah, yes, but what does that look like?"* Jesus came to *show us* what Torah looks like when it is lived by a human filled with God's spirit. When He left, He did not give us a pat on the back, give us two thumbs up and say, *'Hope you make it'*, but told us to be filled with the same Spirit that enabled Him to live the word of God and teach others how live it. We have mistakenly come to believe that we receive the Holy Ghost because we cannot get to heaven without it. Once again, partial truth portrayed as full truth. He told us to live it like He lived it and our submission to the Holy Ghost is what gives us the power to live it as He lived it.

Paul was an integral instrument in the business of building God's Kingdom in the first century. He was, in effect, one of the foundation layers of the Renewed Covenant Ecclesia reaching mainly the gentiles after several failed attempts to reach his own people, the Jews (**Ephesians 2:20** *And are built upon the foundation of the apostles and prophets, Jesus Christ himself being the chief corner stone...*). Remember the words of Jesus when He said in **Mark 6:4** *But Jesus said unto them, A prophet is not without honour, but in his own country, and among his own kin, and in his own house.* Many times, a person will be fought the hardest by those who know or *think* they know them well. These *know it all's* are aware of the faults and failings of others and the enemy uses these fools to stifle what God is trying to do through people by their so-called inside knowledge. But they have forgotten what God can do with a dangerous dealer of death and destruction turned daring disciple. These *know it all's*, get upset because someone else's sin is different from theirs or that God could use someone who has not been vetted by them or their organization. These types of people cannot understand how God can use someone so blatantly underqualified to build God's Ecclesia God's way. The religious frauds thought it back in Jesus' day and they that think it today have increased exponentially.

The Architect.

An architect has information at his fingertips on what structure can and should be built, on what type of ground, with the building materials and technology he has at his disposal. That is why the architect's plans are the most important part of a building. All things are measured according to the architect's original plans, and nothing, not even the expert knowledge nor experience of a builder, is to be used to change what the architect's plans have determined. We can and should use knowledge and experience, but as an aid to help one another fulfil our purpose in God. Any fit and proper builder will fight the temptation to make changes they think will help the construction or make the building *"better"*, and they will constantly refer to the blueprints.

If a structure has collapsed or is in danger of doing so, the city or town officials will always refer to the architects plans to see where the error in the building is and how they can correct it. We, the Ecclesia, are called buildings and lively stones in **1 Corinthians 3:9** *For we are labourers together with God: ye are God's husbandry, **ye are God's building**,* and *Ye also, **as lively stones, are built up a*** *spiritual house*, *an holy priesthood, to offer up spiritual sacrifices, acceptable to God by Jesus Christ* (**1 Peter 2:5**) and as such we have an architect who had a vision of what He wanted built and put that vision in written form we call the Bible. Even the least read book in the Renewed Covenant tells us, *But ye, beloved,* **building up yourselves** *on your most holy faith, praying in the Holy Ghost* (**Jude 1:20**).

When we are encouraged to edify one another, Paul is stating that we must build each other up, but to do so according to the architect's plans. To edify is to Oikodomē- meaning architecture, that is, (concretely) a structure; confirmation: a building. Notice, the focus is on building people, not people building buildings. It is the duty of every member of the Ecclesia to edify each other, to build each other up, to create a structure strong enough that nothing can bring it down, though it be buffeted daily (see **Matthew 7:24-27**). Each brick in a building not only has its place but also strengthens the bricks it is connected to.

This edifying of the body is a major way that we combat many of the devices of the enemy, whether they be the stresses of life, sickness, or persecution. Imagine hiding from danger behind lattice. Easily seen, easily caught. But behind a brick wall there is safety, the enemy knows you are there but cannot get to you as easily as he desires (I'm not referring to the false sense of security we get from being behind the wall of a church building). When we edify each other, it must go up and down and side to side in equal measure. The bricks at the bottom are just as important as the bricks at the top and to edify each other is to strengthen the entire structure. Any time a building becomes top heavy, it is prone to cracking and eventual collapse, in like manner, when more resources (e.g., wisdom, knowledge, finances or time) are spent on the church's hierarchy than on the congregation, that church will begin to show signs of stress and cracking and will be prone to collapse/failure. I have spoken to many pastors who have bragged about the success of *their* church by telling me how many people *they* have in their leadership team.

Many of us have seen videos of how skyscrapers are brought down by strategically placed explosives and how they cause the building to implode. It takes a long time to build such structures. However, it takes only a few weeks of planning and placing the explosives in the right places, then, at the push of a button, in a few seconds, the entire structure comes down. After the dust has settled, we see nothing but a pile of rubble where once stood a mighty building occupied by many workers or families.

Webster's defines edifying as, *instructing or improving (someone) morally or intellectually [to enlighten]*. The opposite would be to misguide, mislead, or misinform (whether intentionally or unintentionally, verbally or through actions not consistent with truth- author's note). Holman's Bible Dictionary defines edification as- *building up which includes encouragement and consolation, with the focus being the goal to establish unity of faith, knowledge, maturity, and the full measure of Christ. Edification is not all talk, however, but involves the demonstration of love (**1 Corinthians 8:1**) and consideration for those weak in the faith.* We are to place within the body a system whereby all within the Ecclesia are building one another by instructing, improving, and enlightening each other to the knowledge of God (and each other) until it becomes so normal that we will not give place to our enemy to perform his evil deeds. **2 Corinthians 2:11** *Lest Satan should get an advantage of us: for we are not ignorant of his devices.* During any war, the enemy would try to sow discord among the troops via misinformation or disinformation. He will misguide and mislead us into looking for what we might gain here on earth instead of looking at what is going on inside the body, mind, and heart and how we may be of use to the King to heal, edify and restore. The enemy will distract us from searching for God's will by keeping us focused on the small or irrelevant matters instead of allowing justice, mercy, and righteous judgment to pass through us. If the Ecclesia are encouraging each other, building each other up and strengthening one another, the enemy has no chance of breaking down morale or the structure.

Paul tells us of Christ's example in **Romans 15:1-3** *We then that are strong ought to bear the infirmities of the weak* (the antithesis of selfishness), *and not to please* (Areskō- through the idea of exciting the emotions, to seek to be agreeable to) *ourselves.* **Let every one of us please** (Areskō) **his neighbour for his good to edification.** *For even Christ pleased* (Areskō) *not himself;* (this is where most of us fall) *but, as it is written, The reproaches of them that reproached thee fell on me.* William Tyndale's Bible (written in 1535 directly from Hebrew and Greek a full seventy-six years before the KJV) says, *Let every man please his neghbour vnto his welth and edyfyinge* (yes, this is the actual spelling). It is not about us as individuals, but the body of Christ and those we hope will enter that body. To bear the infirmities of the weak is to Bastazō Asthenēma Adunatos- (through the idea of removal); to lift, endure, declare, sustain, receive, to carry or take up the diseased, feeble, or impotent folk [this speaks of both the natural and spiritual], those who are unable to take up for themselves. Paul ends his letter to the Corinthians with this final note; *Therefore I write these things being absent, lest being present I should use sharpness, according to the power which the Lord hath given me to* **edification** (Oikodomē- architecture, structure), *and not to destruction* (**2 Corinthians 13:10**).

If what we call edification of the body leads to the destruction of anyone in that same body, then we have either lost, misunderstood the meaning of biblical edification, or have a wrong spirit. Anybody can pull down, cast down or put down, but to edify takes much prayer, fasting for others, effort, time, sometimes many resources, letting go of hurts, offences, and a passion to see another restored.

In Paul's second letter to the Corinthians, he tells them that he does all things for *their* edification, not his own edification (**2 Corinthians 12:19**) and he does not mince his words when he says he edifies **before God in Christ**. We cannot edify someone else and we, as members of the same body, not eventually get the benefit from it though we do not edify with our benefit foremost in mind. I must make it clear that how we edify is done in full view of Christ. This should give us reason to pause before we jump in there to edify according to our standards or what we want people to believe or do. Paul writes to Timothy and tells him not to be distracted by people's frivolous fables and genealogies (who or what group you belong to) but rather minister Godly edification (building) in faith (**1 Timothy 1:4**).

As mentioned earlier, we can also build ourselves up, *But ye, beloved,* **building up yourselves** *on your most holy faith, praying in the Holy Ghost, Keep yourselves in the love of God, looking for the mercy of our Lord Jesus Christ unto eternal life* (**Jude 1:20-21**). Paul poses a question then gives us a command; *How is it then, brethren? when ye come together, every one of you hath a psalm, hath a doctrine* (a teaching), *hath a tongue, hath a revelation, hath an interpretation.* **Let all things be done unto edifying** (**1 Corinthians 14:26**). If we are coming there to posture, show our leadership, how long we've occupied a pew or position, then we have misconstrued the idea of building each other up. It is up to each of us to edify one another, through scripture, teaching, revelations God has given us, through praying for each other, mainly because long lasting edification rarely comes from the pulpit (information and inspiration- perhaps) and if it does, it is usually in a rather generic sense (meant to reach a wide variety of listeners) with extraordinarily little if any instruction to the congregation on how to use said information, considering each one's personal struggles, strengths, and weaknesses. Nebulas messages only result in nebulas lives.

The main difference between edification and encouragement is, the former builds up while the latter incites to action, to mentally support, to motivate, to give courage, hope, and the Spirit of God to one another. However, how can we incite others to action when we have not built into them how and what God wants to do in, for and through His people. We hear encouragement in a sermon for a few minutes then go back to the real world where we are buffeted and reviled and have soon forgotten the words in the sermon. But when we make time to go and see one another, call one another, and enter each other's world specifically to edify one another, we have not just fulfilled the scriptures, but possibly rescued someone from a needless time of extreme hardship or exhaustion.

Hardships will always come to the true saints of God, however, being edified during those times is like giving a glass of cold water to a thirsty man in the desert. They will follow you to where there is more and can get the life-saving water for themselves. Jesus Himself said such in **Matthew 10:42** *And whosoever shall give to drink unto one of these little ones a cup of cold water only **in the name of a disciple** (because they are a disciple), verily I say unto you, he shall in no wise lose his reward.* Edifying others for its own sake, gives us a reward for our effort whether here on earth or in the hereafter.

We must be careful what we use to edify. Paul warns us in **1 Corinthians 10:23-24** *All things are lawful for me, but all things are not expedient* (conducive or advantageous): *all things are lawful for me, but all things edify not. Let no man seek his own, but every man another's [wealth].* Loosely translated it means, *just because something is good for me does not make it good for others. Just because something worked for me in a particular manner doesn't make it a one size fits all solution.* We must seek the Lord's will on how to help each believer within the Ecclesia as this will guarantee success in the end. Jude tells us that we all have different temperaments and God uses these to bring the seeker in, *Keep yourselves in the love of God, looking for the mercy of our Lord Jesus Christ unto eternal life. And of some have compassion, making a difference: And others save with fear, pulling them out of the fire; hating even the garment spotted by the flesh* (**Jude 1:21-23**).

We must use the tools given to us by God for each member of the body. As mentioned in the introduction, if the only tool we have is a hammer, then we will more than likely treat everything as if it were a nail. To edify means that we will give a part of ourselves necessary for the building up of others (whether that be knowledge, finances, time, prayer, fasting, wisdom, etc,) and the only *guaranteed* benefit we get on earth is to see another member of the Ecclesia be successful in fulfilling their purpose in Christ.

English politician, Sir Richard Cecil (1495-1553) is known to have said, *The man who labours to please his neighbour for his good to edification has the mind that was in Christ. It is a sinner trying to help a sinner. Even a feeble, but kind and tender man, will affect more than a genius, who is rough and artificial.*

Many times, God allows things to happen to people that breaks them so He can remake them in His image (not the image of man, a church, or an organization) and His instrument of choice to restore and grow the saint is overwhelmingly the members of the Ecclesia which submit one to another (see **1 Peter 5:5**). He uses us to help rebuild them and integrate them even deeper into the body. I have mentioned it before, but it bears repeating; Paul writes of the importance of the *seemingly* lesser parts of the body in this manner...*But now are they **many members**, yet but **one** *body. And the eye cannot say unto the hand, I have no need of thee: nor again the head to the feet, I have no need of you. Nay, much more those members of the body,* **which seem** *(Dokeō- we think, we deem)* **to be more feeble***, are necessary: And those members of the body, which we think (Dokeō) to be less honourable, upon these we bestow more abundant honour; and our uncomely parts have more abundant comeliness. For our comely parts have no need: but God hath tempered (Sugkerannumi- comingled, combined or assimilated) the body together, having given more abundant honour to that part which lacked: That there should be no schism (Schisma- split, gap or division) in the body; but that the members should have the same care one for another. And whether* **one member suffer, all the members suffer with it***; or* **one member be honoured, all the members rejoice** *with it. Now ye are the body of Christ, and members in particular* (**1 Corinthians 12:20-27**).

The Aramaic English New Testament puts verse 22 like this, *But rather, those members which are accounted as weak, are indispensable.* It does not say they are weak, but they are *accounted* or *considered* to be weak, but to God they are indispensable and essential, with the body being incapable of functioning at full capacity without them.

God is not interested in what we think is important as we can see when Samuel comes to anoint the new king in Jesse's house (see **1 Samuel 16**). David was considered so insignificant that he was not even worthy to be brought to the feast to stand before the prophet. But Samuel would not let the family sit down until the insignificant was brought into their midst. To rub salt into their wounded pride, he anoints this insignificant young lad to be their king, to whom they, in the not-so-distant future, would have to bow down and pay homage.

We must be careful not to right off, neglect or underutilize any members, for they are more than likely the ones who are chosen to do the real work of God in the real world. Pulpit time, board, and planning meetings and such is not the real work of the Kingdom. God is interested in promoting the Gospel of the Kingdom to a lost and dying world and He delights in using the neglected, the weak and uneducated to do it, as He bypasses our arrogant, pride-filled, overly educated, and tenured for life leadership. God heals the physically broken body, but He edifies the soul through His body. He will fulfil His ultimate purpose and reward these humble souls who edify and sacrifice for their service.

Chapter 19.

Like minded one toward another.

Romans 15:5 *Now the God of patience and consolation grant you to be **likeminded** one toward another according to Christ Jesus:*

The Aramaic English New Testament adds clarification to this verse, *...And may the Elohim of patience and consolation grant you to **think in harmony with one another** in Y'shua the Mashiyach.* We seem to struggle with this one a lot, mainly because we all have our own ideas of what is proper, what is right, what is ethical and what is unacceptable thinking or action. But the answer to this quandary is in the last four words of this verse, *according to Christ Jesus*. Please don't tell me you don't personally interpret the word of God and try to put your interpretation onto others, because we all tend to do this to one degree or another and without allowing the Holy Ghost to check us and correct us, we would continue to do so. We all want people to think like we think and tell them that this is what Christ wants. That is the struggle Paul speaks of in the flesh. To deny ourselves and what we think is right and submit to Christ's idea of right.

We have been fed a steady diet of a false narrative that to be likeminded means we are to be exactly like each other, where one cannot think for themselves (come to the same conclusion in their own time, way, or manner) or have their own personal conviction towards a certain thing, to be robotic or a clone of our pastor/bishop, church, or organization. This is in no way what Paul was writing to the Romans regarding like-mindedness. God made each of us with our own personalities and character traits, but we are to use those for the Kingdom of God. As mentioned briefly earlier, God has never been into cookie cutter Christianity, where we are locked into *groupthink* and to have a dissenting opinion is to be rebellious or bucking authority. Why do we think Christ chose 12 young men from such diverse backgrounds, families, and occupations as Peter the hot-headed fisherman, Levi the methodical tax collector, Philip the lover of horses, Simon the Zealot, James, and John the sons of Thunder, Saul a Pharisee and tent maker, Lydia a wealthy seller of purple, Timothy a young man with medical issues, Cornelius a roman soldier, Philemon a runaway slave or Aquilla and Priscilla learned Jews? Like minded means that we are working toward the same purpose, building the same Kingdom of God, helping each other fulfil our purposes in God, not mindless robotic automatons who are coerced or forced to submit to whatever they are told, badgered into giving *'because that is just what we do'* or we must worship in this or that manner otherwise there must be something wrong with us.

The Perils of Groupthink.

Likeminded in no way means *'groupthink'* which Webster's defines as, *a pattern of thought characterized by self-deception, forced manufacture of consent, and conformity to group values and ethics.* When one is *forced* to think like the group in order to either remain in the group or feel safe from expulsion from the group, then one has been dragged into *groupthink*. This type of worldly like-mindedness is extremely damaging when forced upon the Ecclesia. Please allow me to explain.

Investopedia Dictionary defines Groupthink as, *a phenomenon that occurs when a group of individuals reaches a consensus without critical reasoning or evaluation of the consequences or alternatives. Groupthink is based on a common desire not to upset the balance of a group of people.*

This desire creates a dynamic within a group whereby creativity and individuality tend to be stifled in order to avoid conflict.' Quite the opposite of what Christ commanded in **Luke 14:28-30.** He told us to use the grey matter between our ears He gave us at birth. Once again, I want to reiterate, we are individuals, with individual personalities, characteristics, and convictions, but we are to use these things to benefit the Kingdom of God as the Holy Ghost directs (see **John 16:30**), not to demand our individuality be catered to do so that we benefit. We are special because of who we belong to, not who we belong is special because of us.

There are three main detrimental consequences with groupthink that we must be mindful of.

1. Groupthink is a phenomenon in which individuals overlook potential problems in the pursuit of consensus thinking. The *"Don't rock the boat crowd"*. Remember, it was the consensus of the people to crucify Christ. Just because most people believe or want to do something doesn't make it right.

2. Any dissenters in the group who may attempt to introduce a rational argument are pressured to come around to the consensus and may even be censored and or censured.

3. Groupthink actively promotes non-critical thinking in a group. This has been the cause of many disasters in lives which many times are irrevocably changed. The Challenger Shuttle disaster, the Bay of Pigs, Watergate, and the escalation of the Vietnam War, are all considered consequences of groupthink. Somebody knew it wasn't right, but they were too afraid of losing their jobs or position within their organizations. Another more recent example was the war in Iraq. Soon after the war began, it became clear that groupthink had, in fact, played a major role in the government's (and the press') eagerness for military conflict. Although incompetence and dishonesty were part of these war preparations, the quasi-automatic process of "*groupthink*" unconsciously swept many along into conformity with "*expert*" opinion. The Groupthink dynamic can lead to bad decisions. Consequently, many thousands of people needlessly died.

A group of individuals may consider themselves experts and thus infallible, thereby perpetuating falsehoods under the guise of unity. They see themselves as a group always right regardless of any facts presented to them even if it comes from their own ideology. A person who is not a part of the groupthink that presents a different point of view or facts that contradict the group is instantly dismissed as having anything of value to input into the group. In other words, if it doesn't come from the hierarchy of the group, it cannot be right.

Groupthink is one of the most dangerous forms of manipulation known to man. It has caused this generation of young people to accept many ideas that contradict basic science and history. Men can be women, women can be men, a baby is nothing but a bunch of cells, homosexuality is biological, communism makes people free and happy, humans originated from rocks and so on. None of these have any validity in facts, whether scientific or historical, but even if one were to use scientific and historic evidence to expose these fallacies, it will be viewed as dangerous to the group mentality and the bringer of facts will be shouted down, ostracized, or physically harmed. Here's a couple of examples of groupthink in the church; *"If you say something about my Pastor, I'm liable to fight you"* (this one has been making the rounds recently from young men enamoured by their leaderships personality/preaching style or position, *"My organization/pastor knows what its/he's talking about, and if you disagree, then we cannot fellowship"*, *"If you don't believe 'the truth' like we believe, we cannot fellowship together"*.

Groupthink is what caused the murderous atrocities of the Nazis, the Roman and Japanese empires, and the Russian/Chinese communist revolutions, where over 200 million people needlessly died in just the last 100 years. Groupthink is an insidious enemy that has, as recently as 100 years ago, re-emerged and invaded the church, mainly through our organizations and filtered down through our bible colleges into our pulpits and settled into our pews. People who have doctorates from bible institutes have made themselves infallible and to challenge anything they say is almost likened to challenging God Himself. Why? Because groupthink has told us that those with PhD's are infallible. To think differently is to be radical. The Lord was openly against groupthink because He did not quietly submit to the elders, priests, and the duly elected officials of His time, but brought truth and lived truth in its purest form. He riled up the leadership of His time, by bringing back the word of God (*"it is written, but I say, as the prophet says"*) and because of His meddling with their paradigm, programmes, and prestige, He was ridiculed, accused of collaborating with the devil and eventually killed (see **Matthew 12:24, Mark 3:2, Luke 11:15**).

The destructive apostacy of groupthink robs a saint of all responsibility for personal growth and personal discipleship. It is always easier to just go along with the group than to say something that will incur the ire of the leadership of the group or the group as a whole. As briefly mentioned above, in essence it goes like this, *'If you don't think like us, look like us, teach/preach like us, give, sound like us, or belong to our organization, you are an enemy (or at least have nothing of any real value to offer) and therefore not to be taken seriously. If you leave our group, you must be backslid, rebellious or never really belonged to the group in the first place and therefore not worthy of our time and or resources. We will openly try to destroy your testimony or negate what you did with us in the past because you now think differently to us, there can be no deeper revelation other than what comes from our leadership or group.'* Unfortunately, this exists in the vast majority of our organizations and churches. One cannot be a truth-seeker if they are caught in the control of groupthink. One cannot be a truth-seeker if they are unwilling to challenge, be challenged, or changed when truth is presented even and if it is presented by a *'so-called'* enemy of ours. Truth does not become less truthful just because it comes from a source we dislike.

I have had many pastor friends of mine who disagreed with certain aspects of their organization's teachings and or dealings with people. They saw with their own eyes what was being done or said, and it was not biblically correct and struggled for many years with it. They were told to grin and bear it for the sake of unity and stop being rebellious. When, after much prayer, introspection, tears, and counsel from wise elders within the Ecclesia, they left with no malice in their heart for their former associates. They knew they had made the right decision when many of their lifelong friends within the organization/church turned on them like a pack of rabid dogs on a defenceless animal. They were vilified on social media, many pastors told their church members to ostracize them, the work they had done was minimized and maligned and they were told their walk with God is either non-existent or they were completely backslid. They thought and had different convictions or ideas of how they felt from God to do something and were labelled as not being like-minded or unsubmissive.

Sadly, many gullible church members believed what was said about them based solely on the groupthink of their church or organization, and these people were given no avenue to check for themselves. The ones who were cut off were rarely given any recourse. In fact, most church members were told to take at face value what they were told and that to question their leadership was to be in danger of receiving the same treatment (this may not have been verbally spoken; however, people are not stupid, they can see what happened to someone who went against the flow). They were told to be likeminded to the pastor/bishop/organization, but the scripture says we are to be *likeminded according to Christ Jesus*. **According to** (Kata) means after the manner of, or the intensity of Christ Jesus. When someone disagreed with Jesus, did He vilify them, tell them to leave, or have nothing to do with them? Let's use this example of *according to Jesus.* The one's in these churches that did check and voiced their concerns, were labelled as rebellious also and called into the pastor's office for a dressing down. Is this really what Paul meant in **Romans 15:5, Philippians 2:2, 20**? These so-called leaders sound more like sheepdogs than shepherds.

William H. Whyte Jr (who coined the term *groupthink* in 1952) wrote an article in Fortune Magazine entitled *Groupthink,* where he highlighted what he saw as an outgrowth of the increasing focus on the social nature of human beings by social engineering, *the management of human beings in accordance with their place and function in society* (Websters). George Orwell's writing on the dystopian world in his book, *1984,* is a perfect example of groupthink (social engineering) when left unchecked and unchallenged. There is social engineering going on in most of the western nations today and only the gullible ones cannot see it. Groupthink is also the psychological manipulation of people into performing actions to comply with certain standards of a group or organization, usually against their better judgement or for fear of retribution. Uniforms worn by fast food chains for example are a non-malignant or benign form of social engineering, however, when they finish work, they have the freedom to wear what they choose. Cults are a perfect example of Groupthink that overtakes the entire life of cult members. A brief summary of a cult is simply, a small, unestablished, non-mainstream religious group that typically revolves around a small cadre or a single leader. The American Heritage Dictionary defines "cult" this way: A religion or religious sect generally considered to be extremist or false, with its followers often living in an unconventional manner under the guidance of an **authoritarian, charismatic leader**. Groupthink is what gives cults their sense of power and moral compass.

Likeminded is the antithesis of groupthink. William H. Whyte Jr raised concerns that a new philosophy was taking over America (and in my opinion, most of the world) in which a *rationalized conformity* was the norm. It was so in 1952 and it is worse now. It is a philosophy he felt that presented humans as *"creatures completely of our environment, guided almost totally by the whims and prejudices of the group and incapable of any real self-determination of our destiny."* It is also a powerful enemy of learning. Lack of critical thinking only leads to gullible people believing anything that a person with some form of authority tells them. Aum Shinrikyo. (a Japanese doomsday cult in 1987), Jim Jones (1978), The Nazi's (1932-45), The Branch Davidians (1993) and many more can be traced back to charismatic leadership which led many to groupthink. These people and many others like them (maybe not as severe) believed that they alone had the answers, and all ended in the deaths of their followers.

The only one who has the right to socially engineer us mere mortals is God Himself, however, even He doesn't force people to believe or behave in a certain manner. He does it via voluntary submission to His idea of Kingdom. He does this because He is preparing us to live in a totally different environment (the New Jerusalem in the New Heaven on the New Earth which will be under New Management).

When people in the Ecclesia value **conformity** (*the act of changing behaviours in order to fit in or go along with the people around them, a form of cultural holiness, social influence which involved agreeing with or acting like the majority of people in a specific group, or in a particular way in order to be perceived as "normal" by the group*), over biblical unity, or cohesion over creativity, which usually leads to condemnation from the group rather than conviction of the Holy Ghost, we run the risk of becoming our own worst enemies. I am not saying that we should not conform or be cohesive, but that if we are to conform it must be to Christ and our cohesion comes from our submitting to the leading of the Holy Ghost and one another (**1 Peter 5:5-6**) and with guidance from humble and wise elders we can and must be interconnected (cohesive, well integrated) with one another. We think that following a set of standards set by a man or board of directors leads to more people living a holiness life, when in fact, it is when we become so much like Christ that His Holiness exudes from our pores that people will see His Holiness. Groupthink leads to *"cultural holiness"* (forced or coerced behavioural change in order to belong) whereas likeminded leads to natural and organic behavioural change to suit God (real holiness). Being likeminded is a choice one makes in order to please the Lord. I want to be likeminded according to Christ not the government, pastor, friends, or family (**Romans 15:5**). This true form of holiness (a passion to be like Christ in ALL areas, not just wardrobe and speech change) comes from the depths of one's soul and remains forever.

Even God cannot penetrate these misguided groups, whether religious or secular, as they have insulated themselves from any ideas or revelations that does not originate from that group and almost always from the head or leadership of that group. The Ecclesia is not run by consensus formed by an elected hierarchy, as this is Pharisaical in its purest form, but by the Holy Ghost who challenges, and commands change. These people ask God to speak to them, but they do not hear Him because He does not say what they want to hear nor does He always say it from their own leadership, which in many cases is bound by the same groupthink mentality.

Likeminded one toward another is not a command to think and behave like a robot. Likeminded is having the same disposition and purpose; it is when we are animated by the same spirit or temperament of Christ, working toward the same goals with similar (not identicle) thoughts and tendencies. It is relinquishing our desire to make carbon copies of ourselves as we allow God to make carbon copies of Himself using His Ecclesia as His instruments at His discretion in His time. When Paul said, *Be ye followers of me, even as I also am of Christ,* He was telling us that as He imitates Christ, so should we (**1 Corinthians 11:1**). He was not telling us to be like Paul in mannerisms but by imitating His desire to be like Christ. Groupthink annihilates all possibilities of this happening thus making the Commonwealth of the Kingdom of God nothing more than an echo chamber (another term is confirmation bias,) where we only hear the same thing we've always heard, by the same people who always say it thereby continuing getting the same weak and insipid results and not the abundant life Christ promised us (**John 10:10**).

Psychology Today reports, *"groupthink* in this manner; *Groupthink occurs when a group **of well-intentioned people** make irrational or non-optimal decisions spurred by the urge to conform or the discouragement of dissent. This problematic or premature consensus may be fuelled by a particular agenda or simply because group members value harmony and coherence above rational thinking. In a groupthink situation, group members refrain from expressing doubts and judgments or disagreeing with the consensus. In the interest of making a decision that furthers their group cause, members may ignore any ethical or moral consequences."* (Author's note: I would add spiritual consequences also).

"When groups feel threatened—either physically or through threats to their identity—they may develop a strong "us versus them" mentality. This can prompt members to accept group perspectives, even when those perspectives do not necessarily align with their personal views. Groupthink may also occur in situations in which decision-making is rushed—in some cases, with

destructive outcomes. To minimize the risk, it's critical to allow enough time for issues to be fully discussed, and for as many group members as possible to share their thoughts. When dissent is encouraged, groupthink is less likely to occur. Learning about common cognitive biases, as well as how to identify them, may also reduce the likelihood of groupthink."

Psychologytoday.com/us/basics/groupthink.

According to Paul, to be likeminded is to Phroneō- to exercise the mind, that is, entertain or have a sentiment or opinion; to be mentally disposed (more or less) earnestly in a certain direction, intensively to interest oneself in with. It seems today that to entertain a sentiment or opinion that is not precisely like that of our group is almost like committing spiritual suicide. The apostles tried to break down the groupthink of some Jewish believers when they defied the ideas of how the Gentile believers were to behave and what to think, *As many as desire to* **make a fair shew** (Euprosōpeō- look good, make a display) **in the flesh***, they constrain* (they compel, try to force) *you to be circumcised* (a Mosaic law meant for the Hebrews)*; only lest they should suffer persecution for the cross of Christ. For neither they themselves who are circumcised keep the law; but desire to have you circumcised* (proven hypocrites)*, that they may glory in your flesh* (count how many proselytes they have made- this is still going on today in our false idea that the more people we convert, the more it proves we are right. **Galatians 6:12-13**). Peter broke with groupthink by going into a gentile's house and eat with them and preached to them. And to rub salt into the religious leader's mindset, he stayed several days in that house. What was the result of this rebellion from groupthink? The first gentiles received the same command to be baptized in His name and were filled with the spirit as the Jews were (**Acts 10:8-48**). Who was Peter to obey? The spirit of God in Joppa or the groupthink of the leadership at head office at Jerusalem? (See also **Acts 5:29**). As we can see, groupthink has been around in many guises for a long time (*The thing that hath been, it is that which shall be; and that which is done is that which shall be done: and there is no new thing under the sun* (**Ecclesiastes 1:9**) and when it enters into a group it can be called a wolf in sheep's clothing.

According to Encyclopedia Britannica, *"Groupthink is a mode of thinking in which individual members of small cohesive groups tend to accept a viewpoint or conclusion that represents a* **perceived** *group consensus, whether or not the group members believe it to be valid, correct, or optimal. Groupthink reduces the efficiency of collective problem solving within such groups."*

Britannica.com/science/groupthink.

Faith in God's word and critical thinking are not antithetical. Critical thinking is being responsive to variable subject matters, issues, and purposes which present themselves in our daily lives. We ask others to think critically when it comes to their misconceptions regarding the Godhead, or which name to baptize in, why would it not be okay for people to think critically regarding other matters within our own group, church, or organization. We have conditioned others to think that dissent is evil when all it really means is to have or express an opinion different from a prevailing or official position; in essence it is to disagree, which does not negate being likeminded to one another for the Gospel of the Kingdom. Disagreement may just mean that things need to be discussed further or other issues need to be considered.

When someone disagrees, this should cause us to use critical thinking and do further research and pray on the matter. We all, in one form or another, use critical thinking to decide what we must do each day, based on what we are presented with. We weigh up priorities and opportunities and discard those things we think will not be conducive to a productive day. When we have faith, we take our options, use our God given abilities to think critically about what we have been presented with, search the word for ourselves (not blindly believe what we have been told is the word of God), and through prayer, meditation, and counsel, we commit our works unto the Lord, at which point He will establish even our very thoughts. We then take those priorities and place our faith in God's word that backs up what He has told us in the spirit and move on from there (see **Proverbs 16:3**). True faith in God means my ability to step into the objective truth (facts) that is much greater, much stronger, and much higher than our subjective experiences (opinions).

The scriptures also tell us to not be **conformed** to this world but to be **transformed**. Metamorphoō- to change and transfigure. There is a marked difference between those two words. Being conformed is to act in accordance with expectations; to behave in the manner of others, especially as a result of social pressure: like conforming to the norm that we are to show up for work on time and stop at traffic lights when they are red. While being transformed is to change greatly the appearance or form of something or someone almost exclusively from within. Conforming is usually done under external pressure (abiding by the law), coercion or duress, while transforming is an internal operation which permeates the entire person.

The world has placed enormous social pressures on mankind to conform for the sake of so-called unity or community cohesion and recently *social justice*, and any dissention is highly frowned upon at best and condemned with character assassination, persecution, and isolation.

Cancel Culture in the Church.

Cancelling is not a new phenomenon. It has been around in many guises for thousands of years. John the Baptist was cancelled because he went against what King Herod wanted to do with his sister-in-law, almost all the prophets were cancelled because they went against the status quo of their time, Paul was cancelled because he left the Sanhedrin and joined the Nazarenes, and Jesus was no exception. All the apostles were cancelled because they came to their own people with a different outlook on what God wanted rather than sticking with the status quo. Martin Luther was cancelled by the Roman Catholic church and the United Pentecostal Church International was cancelled by the Assembly of God Church. The only thing one must do to be cancelled is think differently from the group they are currently in.

So, what does being cancelled really mean. It is an individual or group's volitional act of publicly rejecting and actively pursuing physical harm, destroying employment opportunities or character assassination against a perceived transgressor. It is a way the group *'cleanses'* itself from those with differing views or perhaps the same views but different perspectives on how to do certain things. It is a complex individual act that spreads to groups and causes much harm. We Apostolics use biblical terms such as, *sowing confusion* or *discord*, (simply by questioning the rationale of a decision). In almost all cases, this results in an active and public rejection such as calling those with whom we disagree out, usually followed by punitive, socially visible actions, vilifying, and ostracizing the one being cancelled (getting them fired, shaming them, ruining their reputation, or careers etc.).

According to Psychology Today, *"a core characteristic of cancelling (relative to other rejections) is that to many (but not all) observers, the canceler's punitive actions appear disproportionate to the magnitude of the transgression. Relatedly, when cancelling someone, the canceler bypasses the legal due process. There is no complaint, no trial, no prosecution, no conviction, and no presumption of 'innocent until proven guilty.' The canceler's judgment that the transgressor is at fault is sufficient to trigger punitive action."*

The science behind behaviour, 2007. Psychology Today.

Anyone can cancel, and anyone can be cancelled for any reason as long as enough people think that the target has transgressed, and they are willing to act punitively on their beliefs. Is this really what God had in mind for His people? To look for and find reasons to NOT commune with each other? I know of several churches who cancelled many people who disagreed with what colour the hymn books should be or what colour the carpet or paint should be in their church building. The Amish cancelled the rest of the modern world because of differences of opinion regarding what is good for their families and what is not.

We all conform in one way or another for the sake of societal cohesion, obey traffic laws, stand in line at the airport etc., yet Paul tells us that we are to be transformed from the thinking of the majority's point of view (this doesn't just mean the sinful things, dressing wrong, smoking, drinking etc., but also thinking in the same manner as the world which may not necessarily be sinful acts but behaving like the world in mannerisms and styles). Why? Because he knew that the majority would be in the wrong almost all of the time. As we look at what Jesus said in **Luke 17:26** *And as it was in the days of Noe* (Noah), *so shall it be also in the days of the Son of man.* And verse twenty-eight, *Likewise also as it was in the days of Lot; they did eat, they drank, they bought, they sold, they planted, they builded*; we can see the righteous will not be in the majority. In verse thirty, Jesus said, *Even thus shall it be in the day when the Son of man is revealed.* The strait and narrow way is the only way and *few* (Oligos- puny in number, somewhat small) there be that find it (**Matthew 7:14, Luke 13:24**). Jesus is not interested in groupthink, the majority opinion or in the opinions of men with more degrees than a thermometer. These woefully inadequate people cannot even tell the temperature of a soul who is struggling right under their noses. Instead of trying to help, they cut them off at the knees or try to get others to do so. There is a special place in the Lake of fire for these miscreants. God is interested in what He commands, our obedience to those commands and that we be likeminded according to Christ Jesus, for the sole purpose of fulfilling those commands (see **Matthew 28:19**). Paul tells us, *That your **faith should not stand in the wisdom of men**, but in the power of God* and that we are to, *have the mind of Christ* (**1 Corinthians 2:5-16, Philippians 2:5**). Why did Paul command this?

One of the fundamental issues for the people in the Philippian Ecclesia was they were at odds with each other. At least two of the women, Euodias and Syntyche, were fighting amongst themselves and their disagreements were affecting the rest of the congregation, more than likely with people taking sides with either Euodias or Syntyche. Grumblings, divisions, and arguments were fast becoming the markers by which the Philippian Ecclesia were known. And yet, Paul's answer to this division was not to start a different gathering down the street, cast people out of the gathering or brow beat them into submission. It was in fact *...that they be of the same mind* (Phroneō) *in the Lord* (**Philippians 4:2**). Paul does not say one thing to one group, then another thing to a different group, neither does he take sides. He tells them to put their differences aside and focus on the mind of the Lord. The only thing that stops this from happening is pride.

Paul is not interested in which faction is more right or more wrong. He does, however, exhort the Philippian Ecclesia to follow the examples of humility and service to others that their Master portrayed and commanded. Paul underscores that the community will find its strength and direction to fulfil its purpose by modelling the character and life after their Master, Jesus. This is what brings about being likeminded. If all are fulfilling the law of Christ *(Bear ye one another's burdens, and so fulfil the law of Christ. For if a man think himself to be something, when he is nothing, he deceiveth himself* and, *Owe no man any thing, but to love one another: for he that loveth another hath fulfilled the law* **Galatians 6:2-3, Romans 13:8**) then, just by sheer coincidence we will be likeminded.

Being likeminded (Phroneō- to exercise the mind, that is, entertain or have a sentiment or opinion; to be mentally disposed intensively, to interest oneself in, with or concern oneself, to set the affection on, being careful for, regarding, to think- *one towards* another) is the biblical opposite to groupthink. It is not to be robotic or lose one's own personality, character, or ability to think for the sake of unity, but to be predisposed *one toward another* for the purpose of the Kingdom. To use our uniqueness for the purpose of edifying the body of Christ. God does not condemn uniqueness, neither does He discourage intelligence or critical thinking, otherwise He would not have asked us to count the cost (Psēphizō- to use pebbles in enumeration, that is, to compute) before building a tower or search out whether we should go to battle with only ten thousand, whilst another has twenty thousand or to search the scriptures for ourselves (**Luke 14:28-32, John 5:39**). He would not have told Moses to send 12 spies ahead of the main body to find out what they were going to deal with or called the Bereans more noble because they searched the scriptures daily to see if what they were being told is in fact the truth in context with the whole word of God (**Acts 17:11**). This is using our critical thinking to come to a right conclusion (in line with God's will) then adding faith to that conclusion and seeing it through to its glorious end.

Our thinking is determined by what input we have had in the past and what and who we currently allow to influence us. Through this bias (also known as confirmation bias), we tend to favour information that reinforces the things we already think or believe to be true and dismiss anything that may challenge our ideas and beliefs. This only helps to protect our self-esteem by making us feel that our beliefs are accurate. After all, who relishes being wrong? Yet Paul tells us through his letter to the divided Philippians, *Let nothing be done through strife or vainglory; but in lowliness of mind let each esteem other better than themselves* (**Philippians 2:3**). Having our thinking, understanding, authority, and paradigm challenged is not the works of the devil, but a natural part of human growth, be it physical, emotional, mental, financial, or spiritual.

If we are not careful, we can fall prey to a different kind of bias known as Anchoring Bias. This means that we can be overly influenced by the first piece of information that we hear. For example, *"Doctors can become susceptible to the anchoring bias when diagnosing patients. The physician's first impressions of the patient* [after the patient has begun to tell of their symptoms. Author's note] *often create an anchoring point that can sometimes incorrectly influence all subsequent diagnostic assessments"* (Saposnik G, Redelmeier D, Ruff CC, Tobler PN. *Cognitive biases associated with medical decisions: A systematic review* (2016).

If we have been heavily influenced by our denomination or organization, listening to the same preacher over many years, then we will think likeminded according to our set of standards, protocols, articles of faith, code of ethics, minister's manuals, and our preacher's own biases. This however does not always corollate to *according to Christ Jesus.* (Just because it is in a book from head office or bible school does not make it gospel). If this were the case then we would all be Roman Catholic in our thinking and doctrine, mainly because, for 1200 years the Roman Catholic church dominated almost all religious activities in western society. Many men over the centuries began to think critically using the bible as their central source of information and the leading of the

Holy Ghost as their inspiration. It was only after people began to think like Christ that they were able to break the stronghold over the Roman Catholic church.

Paul exhorted the carnal Christians in Corinth, *For who hath known the mind* (Nous- the intellect, that is, divine or human; in thought, feeling, or will, by implication meaning, understanding) *of the Lord, that he may instruct him? But we have the mind* (Nous) *of Christ* (**1 Corinthians 2:16**). It is clear Paul was saying that not one person (and I would venture to guess, not one denomination/ organization) has the complete mind of Christ, but together, with all our different life experiences and pure hearts, searching through the pure word of God for the pure will of God and being submissive to the Holy Ghost and each other (**James 4:7, Ephesians 5:21**), will doubtless find our purpose. We have this promise from God through His prophet in **Jerimiah 29:12-13**. Paul told this to the Corinthians who were recorded as the most carnal of all those that he had written to. He continues, *And I, brethren,* **could not speak** *unto you as* **unto spiritual, but as unto carnal** (Sarkikos- temporal, unregenerated), *even* **as unto babes** *in Christ* (**1 Corinthians 3:1**). This is a church that was born-again of water and spirit, filled with the Holy Ghost, spoke in tongues, baptized in His name, were believers in One God, operated in the spiritual gifts and yet he warns of carnality (unregenerated thinking) to this church more than any other.

Let us see what it means to be carnal in the context of being likeminded *according to Christ Jesus.* Carnal- Sarx, meaning human nature (with its frailties: physically or morally and passions), or (specifically) a human being). This word is where we get carnival from (carne- meat, flesh. Levare- to lighten). Carnival is a western Christian festive season that occurs before the liturgical season of Lent, which is the 40 days (not including Sundays) from Ash Wednesday to the Saturday before Easter. This period is often oddly enough, described as a time of preparation and an opportunity to go deeper with God. The main events during a carnival (occurring during February or early March, during the period historically known as Shrovetide or Pre-Lent), typically involves public celebrations, including events such as parades, public street parties and other entertainments, combining some elements of a circus. Elaborate costumes and masks allow people to set aside their everyday individuality and experience a heightened sense of social unity. Participants often indulge in excessive consumption of alcohol, meat, and other foods that will be forgone during upcoming Lent (play now, pay later). The purpose of a carnival is to let the body enjoy all kinds of pleasures, to allow the pretty lights, the music, the unhealthy food, and rides to take precedence for a while. To forget the problems of life for a few hours and just do what pleases us. We will deal with the consequences of the cost and what we have eaten another day, but for right now, let us allow our senses (what we feel, see and touch) have their way. Sound familiar? (See **Luke 12:19-20, Isaiah 22:13**).

We are commanded to not think with the human mind rather, we must train, or as Paul puts it, *exercise* our minds to think and behave as Christ himself. *"Yes, but we do think like Christ in our church or our organization because we have thousands of churches and millions of believers"*, I hear many people say. If we use that criteria to judge our correctness, then we can come to the same conclusion regarding the Mormon and Jehovah's Witness churches. Or we could prove Christ was an abject failure because in His time he had neither churches nor many believers. The proof is not in how many believers or churches we have, but by what is happening within those towns and cities where these churches and believers reside. Is the spirit of God changing our towns and cities because of our lifestyle of loving Christ and one another as He loved us? Are we so much concerned with being likeminded one towards another that the unifying spirit of God has built a body so strong that there is an uproar or persecution in those towns and cities? Is there a church where no-one's ideas are dismissed simply because they are not in *'leadership'*? Are there still people suffering within our own ranks, who sit in our pews and are daily neglected (yet welcomed into our church meetings with a hearty handshake on Sundays or mid-week services?) Is the wealth of time, talents and treasure being distributed amongst those with needs we call brothers and sisters, or is it placed into buildings and programmes or kept for the ministry rather than benefiting the saints only on certain days of the week? Are the officials within that town or city, becoming members of that church also, if so, are they treated with greater respect than the so-called *ordinary saints*? If we answer these questions truthfully, we will see whether we have the mind of Christ or are carnal in our thinking no matter how big the church/organization portfolio is. The answers to these questions will also be an indicator if a church is predisposed to groupthink.

If we are proclaiming revival because we fill our churches, or when an evangelist shows up, but the people have the same lives when all the hoopla is over and the only thing we have committed to is more of what we're already doing (church attendance, giving of finances or inviting more people), then, by any empirically measurable and biblical standard or even any stretch of the imagination, this is not a revival. A true biblical revival is when the true saints of God are gathering in their own and each other's homes in order to pray in God's manner for God's will and heaven and earth are shaken (see **Acts 4:31**). Where lives are changed on a daily basis through personal and biblically derived and sustained discipleship and God is adding **daily** to the church (not necessarily to the church meeting) such as should be saved (**Acts 2:47**).

A true biblical revival is when the saints are gathering to pray for one another daily (not just at the 'altar' but in each other's homes), and meet each other's needs, to manifest to a lost world what God looks like with skin on and what He expects from His creation. A true biblical revival is when the youngest or newest saint is being personally discipled and after a *short time*, is beginning to disciple others, and changes of hearts and souls are occurring in and outside the pews. A true biblical revival is when each saint is engaged in being about the Father's business, from the one-week-old saint to the elders, to preach the Gospel of the Kingdom of God only and look for opportunities to serve God and each other daily. We can have a church filled with carnally minded, tongue talking, holiness standard keeping, baptized in His name, pastor obeying, tithe paying people who are there for what they can get and have no input into the lives of other believers, and we will be as lost as we were before we heard the good news of the Kingdom of God.

However, when we have a gathering that is filled with people who not only do the works of Christ in signs and wonders (a minor part in a Christian's life) and repented of their lackadaisical and selfish ways, but also are likeminded by showing the compassion and sacrifice of Christ and allows the thinking and deeds of Christ to permeate into the pews in spite of the persecution they receive from the world (and sometimes even from others who call themselves saints), then we can truly say we are on the way to being revived.

The Lord and Paul warn us of the dangers of being carnally minded in **Romans 8:6-9** *For to be* **carnally minded is death**; *but* **to be spiritually minded is life** *and peace. Because the carnal mind is enmity* (hostile and in opposition) *against God: for it is not subject to the law of God* (which is to love God, to love one another and bear one another's burdens **Matthew 22:38-40, Galatians 6:2**), *neither indeed can be. So then they that are in the flesh cannot please God. But ye are not in the flesh, but in the Spirit, if so be that the Spirit of God dwell in you. Now if any man have not the Spirit* (which also encompasses the mind) *of Christ, he is none of his.* Why do we preach that to be in the flesh means to dress wrong, speak wrong, not pay tithes, disobey the pastor, be sexually immoral, lie, steal, or cheat? To be carnally minded means to *think* as we did (not necessarily or only *what* we did) before we were filled with His spirit which includes thinking as the majority who have not submitted themselves to the Holy Ghost and each other as Christ commanded.

We need to have the mind of Christ, but we must also be careful not to let it go, *Ye therefore, beloved, seeing ye know these things before,* **beware lest ye also, being led away with the error of the wicked, fall from your own stedfastness**. *But grow in grace, and in the knowledge of our Lord and Saviour Jesus Christ. To him be glory both now and for ever. Amen* (**2 Peter 3:17-18**). This growth is measurable by ourselves, *But we all, with open face beholding as in a glass the glory of the Lord, are changed into the same image from glory to glory, even as by the Spirit of the Lord* (**2 Corinthians 3:18**), and visible to others by letting... *your light so shine before men,* **that they may see your good works**, *and glorify your Father which is in heaven* (**Matthew 5:16**). What is the purpose of this growth? It is so that the whole body will benefit (see **Ephesians 4:14-16**). But not all grow at the same pace and to force or coerce others to grow at a pace they cannot sustain, nor has been instigated by the Holy Ghost, is to be carnally minded and not Christ minded.

The highest calling a sinner has, is to be born again of water and spirit. But, once this has occurred, and they begin working through God's spirit and word to become a new creature in Christ, they move on to an even higher calling; *to have the mind of Christ*, which is the highest calling all believers have on this earth (**Philippians 3:14-15** *I press toward the mark for the prize of the high calling of God in Christ Jesus. Let us therefore, as many as be perfect,* **be thus minded**: *and if in any thing ye be otherwise minded, God shall reveal even this unto you*).

For those who think that to be called to be a preacher, pastor, bishop, evangelist, presbyter, or superintendent is the highest calling, are, in fact, mistaken. The highest calling is to be like Christ, the rest is just our job, our tasks, our service to the body (see **Philippians 3:12-16**). This high calling places us in heavenly places with Christ Jesus (**Ephesians 2:6**). It helps us differentiate between this world and the world that is to come and gives us direction regarding our actions to benefit the Commonwealth of the Kingdom of God. To have the mind or *Nous* of God is to indulge in His intellect, to imbibe in His divine nature, to be imbued with His thoughts, feelings and will. It is to walk away with His understanding and cultivate empathy with His creation. To achieve this means changing our understanding and lives to conform to His word (His point of view, not that of our pastor/church/denomination/organization) and His image (**Romans 8:29**), which will benefit those in the Ecclesia. To be likeminded one toward another is to think as Christ thought of each one of us.

When we separate into our cliques and uphold one school of thought or mindset, holiness standards or types of services above another claiming that we alone have the mind of Christ, we have just proven how carnally minded we really are and how far we have strayed from His word and will. How does this happen? Nobody wants to be in the wrong group, so we stubbornly stick with what we believe and automatically put down others (this is not usually done in an openly condescending way, but subtly, by our attitudes to those who do not think like we do nor belong to our little group).

Paul rebukes these carnal Christians in **1 Corinthians 1:12-13** *Now this I say, that* **every one of you saith** (please note, it was not just a few, but the whole of the church), *I am of Paul; and I of Apollos; and I of Cephas; and I of Christ.* **He shows this ludicrousy by asking a few questions,** *Is Christ divided? was Paul crucified for you? or were ye baptized in the name of Paul?* These carnal Corinthians were breaking off into sects based on different apostle's and teacher's thinking and focused on those things rather than on each other and the word of God. If you were of one sect, you would not fellowship with members of another sect, because they were not likeminded to your sect. We are not commanded to be likeminded to one sect, group, or organization but *according to Christ Jesus* (**Romans 15:5**).

This is partisanship (adhering to a party or faction; especially one who is strongly and passionately devoted to a party or an interest) and it is denounced in the bible as evil. We adhere solely to God's word and all else is a lie regardless of who it comes through. **Romans 3:4** *God forbid: yea, let God be true, but every man a liar; as it is written, That thou mightest be justified in thy sayings, and mightest overcome when thou art judged.* A lie is still a lie, even if it is debated and voted on in general board meetings, synods, or general assemblies.

To be carnally minded is diametrically opposed to how we are *commanded* to think. If we are filled to overflowing with the spirit of God, then we no longer ***impose*** our ideas on one another. We try to help each other think as Christ thinks, but we do not force it onto anyone. We ***propose*** the changes by manifesting change. We help each other behave as Christ would behave in any given situation. I cite Paul once again, *For to be carnally minded* (Phronēma Sarx- inclined to human nature) *is* ***death***; *but to be spiritually minded* (Phronēma Pneuma- inclined to Christ's Spirit) *is life and peace. Because the carnal mind is enmity against God: for it is not subject to the law of God, neither indeed can be* (**Romans 8:6-7**). These are extremely powerful words. To think in purely humanistic terms (the way we used to think before we came to Christ) brings death, separation from loved ones, isolation, corruption, and extreme sorrow. Is this not what happens when a loved one dies?

Paul then goes on to indict these carnal believers and calls them enemies (*at enmity*) of God. To be in enmity against God has a powerful meaning. It will determine where we stand with God. The word enmity is Echthra- in hostility; a reason for opposition, we would be odious to God and have a hatred (through actions or inactions, not necessarily in word) to all He stands for. To think in such a manner brings about death, not only to the individual but to the body of Christ.

When Mind over Matter, Matters.

Amyotrophic Lateral Sclerosis (ALS), also known as Lou Gehrig's Disease, is a disease that attacks nerve cells, called motor neurons, which control voluntary muscles (the muscles we can control with our thoughts). This disease leads to progressive weakness and disability in the connections between the nerves and the muscles. When these cells die, the person begins to lose control of voluntary muscle function and movement is lost. Some of the symptoms of ALS are, difficulty walking or doing normal daily activities, tripping, falling, and dropping things, abnormal weakness or tiredness in the arms, legs, feet, or ankles, hand weakness or clumsiness.

This is symptomatic of when the brain thinks one thing, but the body does another. The mind says pick up that cup, and the hand does its own thing. A normal functioning brain and body parts work in harmony to achieve a desired result. Unity between thinking and doing is minimised when the body is dysfunctional.

This gives us a lot to think about concerning how we think one to another. Are we thinking about one another according to Jesus Christ? Are we interested or concerning ourselves one to another, are we regarding one another, being careful one to another, are we mentally disposed one to another? If this is not the case, then we have inadvertently allowed ourselves to become like the dog-eat-dog system of the world that we are commanded to come out of (see **2 Corinthians 6:17**).

Contrary to popular belief, the pastor is not the brain, and his congregation is the body, whom he tells what to do and they automatically do it. There is only one head of the church and that is Christ (see **Colossians 1:18, 2:10, 1 Corinthians, 11:3, Ephesian 1:22, 5:23, 1 Peter 2:7**). So, when the head of the church tells the body we are to do something, and the body doesn't do it or does it differently, we have an ALS body.

When we hear something about another saint but have no personal knowledge of that situation nor what led up to it, yet we judge them based on what we have heard or what we would have done, we have forfeited our right to call ourselves by His name until we repent and go and make it right with the brother or sister. This is like handing our brain over to another to think for us because we are either too lazy or unwilling to think for ourselves. We are to be likeminded, to think as Christ would think. Yes, there are times that require severe judgement, such as when Paul wrote of a man sleeping with his stepmother and that he should be dealt with harshly (**1 Corinthians 5:1-5**), but these cases are rare, and these harsh measures should not be taken until *all* avenues are exhausted to rectify the problem. In the strongest terms I must say that disagreeing is not one of those things that require harsh treatment. To be likeminded one toward another is to have the same mind as our Lord and Master has towards the Ecclesia by reason that He gave His life for it as should we all, from head office to pulpit to the pew.

His mind and spirit are one as Paul tells us in **Galatians 5:22-24** *But the fruit of the Spirit is love, joy, peace, longsuffering, gentleness, goodness, faith, Meekness, temperance: against such there is no law. And they that are Christ's have crucified the flesh with the affections and lusts.* These fruits are the results of those who have crucified the flesh and the affections that go with it. If we do not have these fruits, have we truly crucified the flesh. What kind of things are we to have on our minds regarding each other? One of the last things Paul writes to the Philippians is on how to consider each other which is just as pertinent today as it was then. In context Paul is writing to fellow labourers, those who have chosen to walk the walk of Christ, who have given of their lives to the saints, and he tells them to let their *...moderation* (mildness and gentleness) *be known unto all men, The Lord is at hand* (**Philippians 4:5**). We tend to think the only way we deal with people who have either done us wrong or left us is to be harsh. The word then proceeds to tell us what and how to think in **Philippians 4:8** *Finally, brethren, whatsoever things are true, whatsoever things are honest, whatsoever things are just, whatsoever things are pure, whatsoever things are lovely, whatsoever things are of good report; if there be any virtue, and if there be any praise,* **think on these things**.

The phrases to *think on* and *these things* means to take an inventory, that is, estimate (literally or figuratively) to conclude, take account of, esteem, impute, reason, reckon, suppose (in other words, think critically). The term *think on* is Logizomai and it comes from the word Logos. We are to use the word to engage our thinking within the Ecclesia and have the mind and spirit of Christ (the word **John 1:1-3**), to be likeminded one toward another *according to Christ Jesus*.

Our own fleshly thinking is what got us into this mess in the first place, how can we now believe that our own ideas, our plans, and programmes is what will sort out the mess. Modern man's philosophies in their basic forms are this: that we can think our way out of this, we can see things as they really are, that somehow, we have the power to fix this, or through our own efforts we can grow and become wealthy, strong, or large. We can do these things, but they will not be of heavenly or eternal things. We are to think critically but according to Christ Jesus, not with our own worldly wisdom or understanding (**Proverbs 3:5-6**). How on God's green footstool is using our own understanding being poor in spirit? This is unacceptable to God in every way, shape, or form. When

Jesus said, *blessed are the poor in spirit for theirs the kingdom of God* (**Matthew 5:3**), He was saying that the poor, the indigent, those without the capability to care for themselves, those who cannot extricate themselves from their own situations (both carnal and spiritual), are truly blessed. Why is that? Because the poor must rely on the goodness, knowledge, and wisdom of another in order to just survive. It is they who are truly blessed. When we recognize that we, in our own spirit and strength, are just as poor as the homeless man or the beggar on the street, we will be ripe to receive the mind of Christ and to do so for and with one another. To think critically is to take what we know and submit it to God's word and operate in faith that God's word will come to pass.

Critical thinking is the ability to effectively analyse information and form a judgment. When this is done with the leading of the Holy Ghost, using solely the word of God as our foundation and a multitude of counsel from independent sources (not within our own echo chambers), the judgement will always be for the good of the Commonwealth of the Kingdom of God. Therefore, being likeminded one to another according to Christ and having the ability to hear from God of things pertaining to the Kingdom of God (**Acts 1:3**) is a definite benefit for the Ecclesia.

Chapter 20.

Receive one another.

Romans 15:6-7 *That ye may with one mind and one mouth glorify God, even the Father of our Lord Jesus Christ. Wherefore* **receive ye** *one another, as Christ also received us to the glory of.*

Following hard on the heels of being likeminded comes the command to *receive one another*. We cannot say we are likeminded but then have nothing or little to do with one another outside of the confines of a meeting in a church building or function. This behaviour is more like club-minded, where we only need to put up with people's faults and foibles for a set period of time, where all have the same interests anyway (knitting, motorcycles, sports, bible reading, conferences etc.), but are not involved in helping each other's lives change to be transformed into the image of our Lord and Master (**Romans 8:29-30**).

Unfortunately, more and more churches today have taken on a club-like attitude (and in many cases a club-like atmosphere) to one another. We all say we love Christ and want His Kingdom to grow, that we want to glorify God, we give of our offerings to keep the church doors open and pay the pastor, but that seems to be where it ends for a vast majority of believers. We then go on our merry little way and say unto them *...Depart in peace, be ye warmed and filled; notwithstanding ye give them not those things which are needful to the body; what doth it profit?* (**James 2:16**). This is the opposite of receive one another.

In the days of yore when someone was received into a palace, home or even a tent, they were to be treated with kindness. They were given food, shelter, provender for their animals or anything else that was necessary for their journey. When an emissary came from a foreign land or even a rival army, he was to be received and treated with respect and his message heard.

We are not only to receive those who are like us, but in like manner we are to receive strangers and even those who have fought against us, in the name of Jesus. We are commanded to *receive* one another in this light; Proslambanō- to take to oneself, that is, use food, to lead aside, admit to friendship or hospitality: take unto or instruct. We are even told in what manner we are to do it *...as Christ also received us...* Christ received all who came to Him. It does not get much clearer than this, does it? Before we try to do mental calisthenics and figure out how we are going to receive those with whom we vehemently disagree, let us start small and receive those who sit in our pews that that are neglected and mostly unseen, that we don't really know, those who live in our neighbourhoods that we call the brethren. Once we have begun to master these, we can then receive the lost. To receive the lost and not receive the brethren is the height of hypocrisy. Why? Because those that do come in and see how we treat each other will see how we will eventually treat them. It is as glaring as staring into the sun.

We have seen throughout scripture that Christ does not give us commands without giving us the plan on how to accomplish them with His help (see **Matthew 19:23-26**). For example, *Husbands, love your wives* (**Ephesians 5:25**). Very good advice indeed, but it is also a command. The vast majority of men would say they truly do love their wives, but still struggle in many interpersonal areas within their marriages. How could this be? The answer is in the second half of that verse... *even as Christ also loved the church, and gave himself for it.* The command then the instructions. Is the husband giving every ounce of himself for his wife, holding nothing back as Christ did for the church? Is he doing his best to protect her from harm and unnecessary suffering? If not, then he has not fully obeyed the command as given by God. There are times when the church is not being the bride she is meant to be, yet Christ still loves her and cares for her. He still heals, delivers, and provides for her. He still corrects, exhorts, reproofs, and rebukes her, when necessary, but His love for her does not diminish based on external circumstances.

The answer lies in the husband's willingness to admit his inability to keep the command without help from the Spirit of the one who gave the Command. He knows that to love his wife as Christ loves the church takes a supernatural intervention in *his* life which he must be willing to submit to, thus giving him the strength to fulfil the command.

The same goes for a wife. *Wives, submit yourselves unto your own husbands* (**Ephesians 5:22**). Many wives do obey their husbands and yet many times there is tension within the marriage regarding submission. Again, how can this be? The answer is also found in the second half of the verse *...as unto the Lord.* Does she willingly and lovingly submit to her husband as though she was submitting to the Lord, or does she submit grudgingly, or only after she has fought with him or even just so there won't be a fight? Does she continually argue with him about the decisions he makes? If so, she probably does so with the Lord also. Does this mean that the husband should not talk to his wife on many matters, get her opinion at the very least? Definitely not, but the final decision is his as it is with Christ and His Ecclesia. Many times, Christ does not tell His church what He is planning on doing, but the church must trust that whether He tells the church or not why He does something, the church must still obey.

Where does it say the wife submits only if she agrees with her husband's decisions or if he is showing her love. There are no conditions to her obedience just as there are no conditions for a husband to love his wife. A wife's obedience to her husband is the same as the church is to Christ. We obey because we are commanded to obey and because of our love for our Lord, not because Christ gave us what we wanted or because we *feel* His love. And once again we find the answer is in the wife's willingness to admit that in herself, she does not have the natural ability to obey her husband (even though she feels he is wrong), so she goes to God and asks for help to fulfil the command. Eventually learning how to submit in love.

In like manner, we receive one another, not because we must (grudgingly or even under suspicion), but because we get to, as Christ received us (willingly and joyfully), and we do so out of loving deference to our Lord. Sometimes it will be hard. Sometimes it will seem impossible, and we will be tempted to argue with and resist the Spirit of God, but that is when we go to God and admit that in ourselves, we do not have the capacity to receive others as Christ received us, but with the help of the Holy Ghost, we will receive them in like manner. Again, this is what it means to be poor in spirit (**Matthew 5:3**). To receive a saint in the name of the Lord is to receive the Lord Himself (**Matthew 25:40**).

Look how Paul finished his letter to the Romans. It is full of salutations, greeting and receiving people. **Romans 16:1-2** *I commend unto you* (Sunistēmi- introduce you favourably to and stand by) *Phebe our sister, which is a servant of the church which is at Cenchrea* (a city near Corinth): *That **ye receive her in the Lord**, as becometh saints, and **that ye assist her in whatsoever business she hath need of** you: for she hath been a succourer of many, and of myself also.* Notice how Paul commends her to be received? *In the Lord.* These exhortations are throughout Paul's writing, in particularly when he closes his letters. Many times, Paul uses a deeper understanding of receive than Proslambano. He says that they were to Prosdechomai- to admit, to intercourse, to have close dealings between individuals or groups, communication or hospitality, credence, with endurance); to await upon with confidence or patience, accept, to allow. Webster's defines non-sexual intercourse as "exchange especially of thoughts or feelings: COMMUNION. Connection or dealings between persons or groups." This states that we are to look for ways to receive each other, to exchange ideas, gifts, and our lives through and with hospitality, having endurance, confidence, and patience. Instead of looking for difference that would Keep us apart, we must look for similarities that unite us.

Paul uses another word in verse twelve, *Salute* (Aspazomai- as a particle of union, to enfold in the arms, that is, to welcome, embrace, greet) *Tryphena and Tryphosa, who labour in the Lord. Salute the beloved Persis, which laboured much in the Lord.* He also uses the word *greet*, which has the same meaning as salute. The entirety of Roman 16 is about how to deal with people who are saints and those that cause disunion and bring in ...*offences contrary to the teachings of Christ...* (verses 17-18, these are people who are **all talk, no action**).

We are also commanded to *greet one another with an holy kiss* (**Romans 16:16, 16:20, 2 Corinthians 13:12 and 1 Thessalonians 5:26**), a tradition dating back thousands of years. This is used to show friendship, familial relationship, perform a greeting, confer congratulations, to comfort someone or show respect and affection. It was performed in Jesus's day, and Judas used it to betray the Master on that fateful night. It is not practiced much in the west, but many countries that were once ruled by ancient civilizations such as, Rome, Greece, Mesopotamia, Persia, and Ottoman still practice this form of greeting. If you go to Italy, France, many South-eastern European, Arab or Southern Mediterranean nations, you will still be greeted with a kiss on both cheeks or the neck.

I understand that it is not considered customary in the western influenced nations, but the point is that the closeness of the community was especially important to them. Judas betrayed Jesus with a kiss and that is why he was so reviled. He took something that was meant to show love, friendship and acceptance and used it for evil. If one did kiss an enemy in order to betray them (commonly called a Judas kiss) they were reviled. But if it was done in honour and love for those in the Ecclesia, they were considered family and treated as such.

I would like to insert and excerpt from my book, self-published 2019, '*Get Up and Do Something*'. In the chapter, *Who Really Fed the Five Thousand?* I write, *"On a much larger scale, but to be carried out within the Ecclesia, Christ received the four and five thousand that followed Him into the wilderness. This is, once again, an example of how we are to receive strangers as well as those who are fellow believers in Christ as Messiah. In Luke 9:10-11 we read,* And the apostles, when they were returned, told him all that they had done. And he took them, and went aside privately into a desert place belonging to the city called Bethsaida. And the people, when they knew it, followed him: and **he received them**, and spake unto them of the kingdom of God, and healed them that had need of healing. *The first thing Jesus did was to receive them though they were spiritually lost and naturally hungry even though He did not know them personally."*

*"The word **received** is rich with meaning. It is the word Dechomai, and it tells us- He accepted them both literally and figuratively, He did not refuse friendship with them, He showed them hospitality, He received them as into one's family to bring up and educate, He took it upon Himself to sustain them, He instructed them. When was the last time we Dechomai (received) someone in this manner, whether a member of our church or not?"*

Jesus speaks to us of receiving only those whom we either like or will receive us in return and tells us how useless that is. *For if ye love them which love you, what thank have ye? for sinners also love those that love them. And if ye do good to them which do good to you, what thank have ye? for sinners also do even the same. And if ye lend to them of whom ye hope to receive, what thank have ye? for sinners also lend to sinners, to receive as much again* (**Luke 6:32-34**). Here Jesus uses the term, *what thank have ye,* which is translated from the Greek as graciousness of manner or act especially the divine influence upon the heart, and its reflection in the life, pleasure. In today's vernacular the term would be, *'What good are you to the Kingdom?'* Yes, according to Jesus we get joy and pleasure by receiving those who cannot return the favour.

Moreover, we can see that when we receive others, we have a divine influence upon their heart which reflects in their lives, yet we gain favour and liberality from it. But, doing it for the wrong reason is like not doing it at all in the eyes of the Almighty. Jesus is just as interested in *why* we do the word of God as *how* we do the word of God. To Him, our attitude in receiving one another speaks volumes within the Commonwealth of the Kingdom of God.

I have been involved in many church foodbanks where we gave away food to those in need. In almost all cases, the church was using it as an outreach tool rather than a way to become a real part of those people's lives. We meet check-out employees for a few minutes at a time in a store, that does not mean we became a part of their lives or they in ours. We did not influence them in any meaningful way. We did not engage in their struggles nor offer them hope of a Kingdom that is different from the kingdom they live in now. In these foodbanks, when I mentioned that we could pray for and minister to the people in need while they were there, I was hit with a lot of legal mumbo jumbo about how these churches get the majority of their food from some government sources, and they won't allow us to mention God or offer them prayer at the distribution place. All we can do is invite them to church. Can't we do the same just standing on a corner and hand out church invitations? So, how is this an outreach tool when we can't reach out to the people? Why are we reliant on the government to get the food when the disciples fed 4000 and 5000 people with just a handful of food that Jesus increased? If we're not going to find a way to interact in their lives past the handing out of food, then we must not call it an *"outreach"* tool. This just shows how we have come to rely on government to do a job that the Ecclesia was meant to do from household to household. It shows our lack of faith (not our lack of desire) and lack of understanding on how we are to allow God to work through us His way.

Jesus received and cared for the multitude through the hands of the disciples. He has lost none of His power to increase what is given to Him nor His passion for the people, be they believers or unbelievers. There was no distinction between the followers of the Messiah and the towns people who came to hear the Messiah's message. Luke's gospel says He, *received them all.* He healed and delivered all that had need regardless of their spiritual status. He treated all as family and preached the Kingdom of God to all who came. If Jesus did this to the multitude who were not His disciples, should we not receive, in the name of our Messiah, those whom we call brother and sister then those in our neighbourhoods?

We sometimes have the attitude of the young disciples in **Mark 9:38** *And John answered him, saying, Master, we saw one casting out devils in thy name, and he followeth not us: and **we forbad him*** (Kōluō- to estop, prevent (by word or act), to hinder, keep from doing or going, to disallow or withstand)*, **because he followeth not us**.* This happens today, more than we think. Seems like the opposite to receive one another, doesn't it? *"If you're not like me/us you must not be of God", "If our/my rabbi (pastor) didn't give you permission, then you can't do the things we do", "If you don't follow our denomination/organization, then are you really even holiness/saved".* Jesus' answer to

John is unequivocally clear. *But Jesus said, Forbid* (Kōluō- to estop, prevent (by word or act), to hinder, keep from doing or going, to disallow or withstand) *him not: for there is no man which shall do a miracle in my name, that can lightly speak evil of me. For he that is not against us is on our part* (**Mark 9:39-40**). Do we really claim to be the only ones God is using to perform miracles or preach the true gospel? If God is using other people to do His work, what right have we to not receive them as Christ received us? How can they see what we believe if we won't fellowship (Koinōnia- partnership, that is, (literally) participation, or (social) intercourse, or (pecuniary) benefaction [investment], communicate, communion, contribution, distribution) with them.

The Master even told *how* we are to cater to the needs of others who are doing things in God's name, *For whosoever shall give you a cup of water to drink **in my name,*** (why do we give to them?) *because **ye** (we) belong to Christ, verily I say unto you, he shall not lose his reward* (**Mark 9:41**). Giving to someone just because *we* belong to Jesus? Now there's a novel idea.

We read that Jesus expounded to the multitude that followed Him, things concerning the Kingdom of God. He did not speak of what they would get in the Kingdom but about the Kingdom itself. He accepted them so that He could tell them and personally show them His passion and His power. To receive someone as Christ received us is to include them into our lives and make decisions with others in mind. Let us begin to receive all those of the Ecclesia first and get that right, then we will have learned what true love to our fellow man really means. We will then have a working model to take to the world we desire to see born-again.

Chapter 21.

Forbearing one another.

Ephesians 4:2 *With all lowliness and meekness, with longsuffering, **forbearing** one another in love;*

Here we are commanded to not just forbear one another but to do so with longsuffering and in love. OUCH! This one's gonna hurt. God does not command us to be something He is not Himself nor things He has not shown us as we can see in **Psalm 86:15** *But thou, O Lord, art a God **full** of compassion, and gracious, longsuffering, and plenteous in mercy and truth* (see also **Numbers 14:18, Exodus 34:6**). If we claim to have the Spirit of God who is full of *compassion, and gracious, longsuffering, and plenteous in mercy and truth,* should we not be exhibiting the same things at the very least, one to another? We seem to have forgotten that God's *longsuffering* is what leads us to our repentance as Paul tells us in **Romans 2:4** *Or despisest thou the riches of his goodness and forbearance and longsuffering; not knowing that the goodness of God leadeth thee to repentance?* We humans are a most impatient and fickle creature. We behave in such a superior manner by expecting others to be just like us and if they are not, they had better get there quickly, because we are too busy and do not have time for their petty problems. Whether we admit it or not (and sadly, many will not) we battle the metaphorical demon of pride and arrogance daily. We want things our way, when we want it, how we want it, and anything that precludes it, will be the target of our secret (and sometimes, not so secret) scorn and indignation.

Case in point #1: We get frustrated with little children just for being little children. We want them to start talking, crawling, and walking as soon as possible, we buy them a bicycle, skates, and other such toys, but as they get older, we tell them to sit down and be quiet because it's not what we want them to do right now.

Case in point #2: A new employee joins our company, and we give them three months' probation to learn the ropes and if they don't cut it, out they go. They may have what it takes but it better not take more than three months to find that out. We are so impatient because the almighty dollar beckons to be increased in the shortest amount of time as possible. We potentially lose an excellent long-term employee because we did not forebear them.

Case in point #3: A new saint comes into our church meetings and we expect them to learn how to be a disciple by osmosis from a once or twice a week pulpit sermonizer or we stick them in 12-week *'discipleship classes'* (unfortunately, this gives them a false sense of security, mainly because all we've given them is a bunch of scriptures, possibly explained them a little bit, but not shown them how to live those scriptures) then we expect them to behave, dress, speak, worship or give as we do or the tongues start to wag faster than the tail of a dog with a bone in its mouth.

Longsuffering is so rare amongst the modern western style church today, it ought to be considered a superpower. A church that does not teach its members to have forbearance with longsuffering is a church that foolishly believes that God approves of its selfishness. Sadly, the lack of these two traits have made the church weak and powerless in society today, and if we continue to behave in a manner that contradicts our Lord's forbearance and longsuffering, we will not only become weaker, but also continue to produce churches where growth in numbers is valued above the spiritual growth of the Ecclesia. Oh, don't get me wrong, we will still have people coming to our services, the odd miracle or two and even produce a few preachers. The question remains, is this what God really expects to receive for all He has done to purchase us.

The bible was written to Middle Easterners, by Middle Easterners, for the people of the Middle East, with Middle Eastern problems, concepts, and solutions. It was written in the days of despotic empires and slavery was predominant. Changing the verbiage and meaning to fit our western mindset and selfish lifestyle, has only defiled the word of God and made it of little to no effect within our own communities. Have we become so arrogant that we now falsely believe that our way of worship, *'having church',* and so-called evangelism is not just the right way, but the only way. We live in a complex world with complex problems, but the truth is that the bible offers simple solutions which translates to, *anybody, anywhere* can receive the knowledge, wisdom, power of the Spirit of God as well as a word from God in context with corresponding revelation. Then they can have the audacity to live it with the help of the spirit of God and wise counsel (see **John 16:13, Psalms 32:8, 143:10, John 14:26, 1 John 2:27, Proverbs 11:14, 15:22, 19:20, 24:6**). Changing an ancient document to fit our ideas and traditions based on our western understanding of governments, hierarchies, sovereignty, makes this same document as useless as fireproof matches.

Some readers will say that to allow the people the freedom to hear from God for themselves and get help from those who are willing to sacrifice their time, talents and treasures will only lead to anarchy. To this I say *PHOOEY*. God is not interested in robotic service or rote understanding of His will. He understands us better than we understand ourselves and He has much longsuffering and forbearance for us and He expects us to have it for each other.

Will mistakes be made? Once again, I refer to the theory of *Duh!* Yes, this is one of the ways we learn and grow and that is one of the reasons we need longsuffering. This long-misunderstood trait of a biblical disciple is explained thus, *the ability of having or showing patience despite troubles, especially those caused by other people*. Did you catch that? *Caused by other people*. Sadly, we have come to believe that forbearance means that we will put up with pastor's long sermons or the choirs off notes during worship. We mistakenly believe that longsuffering is still shaking hands with those that we disagree with or have hurt us in the past. This is the childish longsuffering that keeps us chained to mediocrity and self-exultation. Many of us (though we may not like it) will have a fair amount of patience when troubles are caused by our own foolishness or mistakes. Where we struggle is when others cause us to practice this biblically necessary trait.

Forbearance symbolizes tolerance and restraint in the face of provocation; the act of giving a debtor more time to pay rather than immediately enforcing a debt that is due or, the cessation or intermission of an act commenced, or a refraining from beginning an act. Did you note that forbearance is an act not a feeling?

The modern definition of longsuffering goes a long way to showing how little we all do it. It is defined as- patiently enduring lasting offense or hardship, enduring injury, trouble, or provocation and doing it patiently. Biblically speaking, we are to *forbear one another* but to do it in the spirit of longsuffering (Makrothumia- longanimity, fortitude, patience, with long enduring temper or **leniency**). Leniency: this sorely lacking characteristic within the Ecclesia needs to make a long-awaited return. What is leniency? In plain and simple terms, it is the act or quality of being more merciful or tolerant than expected. Leniency has all but disappeared from our thinking, our pews and sadly our pulpits and boardrooms. It has been replaced with the harshness of retribution, and by strict adherence to our laws and standards. It is expecting almost instantaneous results from people to whom we have preached. Have we forgotten how much leniency God has shown us with all our faults and failures, our times of weakness and outright disobedience? Remember, longsuffering is one of the fruits of the spirit (**Galatians 5:22**).

We are told not only that we are to forbear, but also in what manner we are to forebear. This is going to be the one that tests whether we really have submitted to the Holy Ghost or not, whether we are all talk and no action. Forbearing describes the attitude of, *holding oneself up against, figuratively to put up with, endure, suffer,* Anechomai (Greek). Christ had to forbear twelve teenage boys with all their over zealousness, moodiness, hunger for power and sometimes laziness, yet after only a relatively short time (about three and a half years), they were ready to take on and conquer the greatest empire the world had known (The Republic and Empire of Rome lasted almost 700 years). Have we forgotten how to suffer, to put up with and to endure the normal frustrations of life without the luxury of complaining about it? The definition of complaining describes us humans rather well: It is to express dissatisfaction, pain, or resentment **usually tiresomely.** There's nothing wrong with saying the way things are, our problem is when we do it with resentment or constantly and tiresomely. Also, I would like to add that complaining encompasses telling when something is wrong, but nothing can be done about it. i.e., the weather, workmates, traffic, regular occurrences, inconsistent food at fast food restaurants etc. Complaining re-enthrones self and demands that things be the way WE want and expect them to be with little to no forbearance for the situation or the struggles of others.

On our morning commute we complain about the traffic, though it is the same every day, we complain about our workmates though they are the same every day, we complain about getting up to go to our jobs, about how our car is getting kind of old and not looking or running as good as it used to, about waking up and making breakfast for our loved ones when we're exhausted, about cleaning the house or taking out the trash, we complain about every sniffle or ache and pain. We complain about our weight or about our health, yet we do little to nothing to resolve the things we complain about. We complain when it is too hot or raining for several days. We complain about the pastor or teacher that they went a little longer than normal, about how the song service was too loud or not loud enough, about how our spouse is having a particularly bad day, week, month or even year, about how the service at the restaurant was not up to par, about how sister Elsie or brother John dropped the ball again with the cleaning, about how bible study was boring for the third week in a row. Got the picture yet? Where is our forbearing and longsuffering?

Life is a series of ups and downs, joys, and sufferings but in most cases, it is a time of mind-numbing mundaneness. The old saying, *suck it up buttercup,* is more apt than what we like to think. Consider the farmers of old, who would walk behind their bullocks for ten to twelve hours a day and the view never changed (let's face it, looking at the south end of a north facing bullock is no fun), but they did it because their family needed to eat, they did it without complaining because complaining wasn't going to change anything. Even when tractors became available, they still had to get up at the same time to do the same thing day in day out, only now they had to feed the tractor with diesel and now they have the added stress of maintaining the tractor instead of feed the bullock with hay. That's life, with or without God.

Suffering, putting up with, and endurance are some of the hallmarks of a real follower/disciple of Christ. These are not automatically found in the vast majority of humans and thus must be taught and nurtured by those who are living it. Enter biblical discipleship, the art of transference of biblical traits and principles from one person to another via daily contact. Christ is our example as Paul writes in **Hebrews 12:2** *Looking unto Jesus the author and finisher of our faith; who for the joy that* *was set before him **endured** the cross, despising the shame, and is set down at the right hand of the throne of God.* How much is there to endure doing something twice a week for a couple of hours? *Looking unto Jesus* means to consider Jesus in order to emulate Him. He endured; (Hupomenō- stayed under, remained, to undergo, that is, bear (trials), have fortitude, persevered, **took patiently**, suffered, **waited for**) the cross. He had a plan and He put up with whatever it took to see it through to the end. Jesus told us in no uncertain terms in **Matthew 10:24-25** *The disciple is not above his master, nor the servant above his lord. It is enough for the disciple that he **be as*** (Hos- in like manner, according to, with all speed) **his master**, *and the servant as his lord. If they have called the master of the house Beelzebub, how much more shall they call them of his household?* If our Master had to suffer the foolish antics of His disciples, the Sanhedrin, and the Romans, who are we to think that the disciples of Christ today are to behave in a perfect manner so that they do not ruffle our feathers?

Christ did not endure the cross so that we may not suffer loss nor endure hardships. He endured so that we may have an example of how to suffer loss and endure hardships for the same reason (the cross). He had to suffer long in order to bear with endurance, not just our iniquities but also our constant failings in obedience to His word. He gave us an example of obedience being a learned response, *Though he were a Son, **yet learned he obedience** by the things which he suffered*; (**Hebrews 5:8**). He learned or as the Greek (Manthanō) puts it, He *came to understand* through suffering what obedience as a human was. Learning something takes time for most of us and our impatience with others while they learn speaks more about our rotten attitude than it does about their inability to understand. A saying that is all but ignored by most saints is *'suffering teaches obedience'*. Where are the sermons on this subject in our western style churches? We have been erroneously taught that when suffering occurs, we are to pray it away in Jesus' name. Then how are we to learn to forbear one another with longsuffering? Once again, *suck it up, buttercup.* If we want to be like our Master and Saviour (like we sing we do), then we must endure what He endured for the sake of others.

Okay, but how?

So, how do we forbear one another in the same manner as Christ? First, we are told to forbear in *lowliness* (Tapeinophrosunē- humiliation of mind, that is, modesty) or as the Webster's puts it, *free from self-assertive pride, ranking low in some hierarchy, a lack of vanity or self-importance.* This leaves no doubt as to whom the burden of forbearance rests upon. When someone does us or our loved ones wrong or irks us with their mannerisms, it is we who must remain humble. Sometimes it's not that others are doing wrong, it's just that we are busy right now or have other things on our minds and now they're just getting on our nerves. Enter lowliness, which shouts its characteristics from the towers and ramparts of our churches and it tells others whom we really serve. Do we serve self and our feelings or the Christ that taught us how to live a lowly life?

Paul told the disciples of the City of Colossae, *Put on* (Enduō- to invest with clothing, literally, to endue or tolerate,) *therefore, as the elect of God, holy and beloved* (now he tells us what it is we are to clothe ourselves with and tolerate), *bowels of mercies* (pity and sympathy), *kindness* (usefulness, moral excellence in character or demeanour, gentleness), *humbleness of mind* (humiliation and modesty), *meekness* (being mild-mannered), *longsuffering* (fortitude in patience); ***Forbearing one another***, *and **forgiving one another**, if any man have a quarrel against any: **even as Christ forgave*** *you, so also do ye. And above all these things put on charity, which is the bond of perfectness* (**Colossians 3:12-14**). In most instances, forbearing and forgiveness go hand in hand.

Jesus spoke of this as a trait His disciples are to exhibit in **Matthew 5:41** *And whosoever shall compel thee to go* (one word- Aggareuō- press into public service) *a mile, go with him twain.* It is said that under Roman rule a soldier could compel a Jewish citizen to walk a mile carrying some of his gear. Jesus exhorted His disciples to go two miles, hence the phrase, 'going the extra mile'. This is a character trait that God can only develop in us under trying circumstances. We need not have forbearance when things are going our way, do we? We must recognize how much Christ has forbearance toward us and in like manner, we are to have forbearance one toward another. Jesus even brings it down to our personal clothing, *And if any man will sue thee at the law, and take away thy coat, let him have thy cloke also* (**Matthew 5:40**). To put it colloquially, *"you want my shirt? Okay, take my coat too."*

Second, we are to forbear in meekness. But let me first set the record straight. Meekness is not weakness. The meekest man that ever walked this earth was also the strongest man to do so. The word has come to mean weak and insipid, but this is not what the original meaning was. It is Proates- meaning mild, humble, gentleness. For example, a 300lb weightlifter gently holding a baby in the crux of his arms is displaying meekness. He has the power to hurt the child, yet he is gentle because he knows he has the power to hurt the child. Its ancient meaning is that, *even though we carry a sword, we keep it sheathed.*

A perfect example is when Peter was in the Garden of Gethsemane with the Master, *Then Simon Peter having a sword drew it, and smote the high priest's servant, and cut off his right ear. The servant's name was Malchus. Then said Jesus unto Peter, Put up thy sword into the sheath: the cup which my Father hath given me, shall I not drink it?* (**John 18:10-11**). We do not know why Jesus allowed Peter to have a sword, but we know that Peter used it to defend Jesus's honour. Jesus' response was, *Put up thy sword into the sheath.* There was a time to use it and there was a time to keep it sheathed. There is a time to speak out and a time to shut up, and unless we are actively seeking God's will and willing to submit to it (**1 John 5:14-15**), we will not understand when each of those times comes, nor will we walk in meekness. When we use our authority to get what we want (even if it for Jesus) we are not showing meekness.

We sing about the baby Jesus in the manger being gentle, **meek**, and mild but this could not be further from the truth. The bible dictionary puts meekness this way; *Sensitivity of disposition and kindness of behaviour, founded on strength and prompted by love, a quality of gentleness.* Gentleness, meekness (Gr. Praus- humble), and mildness are attributes that display a character trait which is described through observable actions or responses during certain situations. Webster's dictionary describes it as, *the quality of being kind, tender, or mild-mannered.* How is a baby displaying kindness, tenderness, behaving mild mannered or being humble? It is a baby! One of the most demanding and selfish creatures known to mankind. Being mild mannered is something that is consciously done and is defined as behaving in or having a mild or gentle manner, moderate in type or degree, effect, or force; far from extreme. Does this sound like a new-born baby to you? Babies are the purest definition of demanding, extreme and chaos. They want what they want, and they want it *NOW!* They push parents to the very limits of their endurance and often, their sanity. They rob their parents of sleep, of eating hot food, and when they are toddlers, even going to the bathroom is no longer a solo and restful experience to any parent and any personal time they wanted no longer exists. Being mild mannered or humble is a choice. Babies have no choice.

Displaying meekness and forbearing to the brethren is also a choice. These are all choices we must make and when Jesus grew up, He chose to display those attributes and gained the love, admiration, and affection of millions. If we are to emulate our Lord, then we will also receive the same reward as our Lord on that final day.

The meekness of Jesus was on display when, though He was being falsely arrested, accused, mocked, and condemned, scourged, and spat upon, He had the right to defend Himself, both in word and with twelve legions of angels set for His defence, yet He withheld these vengeful angels so that He might suffer for the sake of others.

Christ knew He would soon be on an instrument of death so vile that it was reserved for the most violent of criminals and political miscreants. It was a slow and agonizing punishment ultimately culminating in death by asphyxiation. A death that involves not only excruciating pain, but dehydration and exposure to the elements. The suffering began before he was arrested because He knew it was coming. The emotional stress was incalculable and what made it worse was that one of His closest friends brought it about by turning Him into the authorities (Judas thought that the Messiah was going to overthrow the Roman Empire and when he saw this was not going to happen when he wanted it to, he felt a betrayal like many of us have felt). To add insult to injury, the rest of His disciples had fled for fear of guilt by association. Moreover, the Lord is placed in front of a tyrant who hates Him (so He knows He will receive no leniency). The Lord was from a class of people that the government of the time would love to destroy. The king knew He was innocent, and the overwhelming majority of people knew it too, but instead of releasing Him, the people choose a known felon to be released in His place. There were twelve legions (36,000) angels with swords drawn and nothing but the utter destruction of humanity on their minds. And yet, Christ displayed *sensitivity of disposition and kindness of behaviour, founded on strength, and prompted by love, a quality of gentleness-* He displayed meekness and forbearance with longsuffering, topped off with exorbitant amounts of forgiveness for those who harmed Him. WOW!

Paul showed longsuffering when the saints tried to get him to not go to Rome (**Acts 21:10-13**. See also Paul's comments regarding obedience to forgive in **2 Corinthians 2:9-10**, and when someone grieves us in **2 Corinthians 2:5-7**). Peter showed meekness and did not grandstand and demand obedience because he was the *"chief apostle"*, when he stood against the Jewish believers and the other apostles. Through calm argument, he showed that the Holy Ghost could fall on the gentiles as well as the Jews (see **Acts 11**).

According to The Holman Bible Dictionary, the opposite of meekness is, *"a harsh and proud wickedness that insists on **immediate self-vindication** (see **Proverbs 3:33-34, 16:19, Isaiah 32:7**). Biblical meekness is usually not simply gentleness and humility, but those qualities displayed with integrity during times of trial. In the Old Covenant, God often promises deliverance or salvation to the meek who are righteous* (having His character and actions, do acts of justice in humility) *persons suffering injustice, poverty, or oppressions."* Jesus held off twelve legions of angels at his trial knowing He would have been **immediately vindicated**. This is meekness personified. We can see that showing meekness towards others has its own rewards (the salvation of those who choose to follow Him).

Meekness and gentleness, (Chrēstotēs- usefulness, moral excellence (in character or demeanour) and kindness, are an integral part of the fruits of the spirit which is grown in a disciple of Christ (**Galatians 5:22-23**) through the normal trials of life and the persecutions from the enemies of the cross (**Philippians 3:18**). Humility and gentleness go hand in glove when it comes to forbearing one another in lowliness and meekness with longsuffering. Adding forgiveness to the mix mimics one of Christ's greatest attributes.

The attitude of forbearance leads to just the thing we want from others, but in our haste to see things happen, we forget to inject the critical element of time. There's no such thing as instant forbearance (an oxymoron at best and idiotic at worst). Look at what Paul writes, *And thinkest thou this, O man, that judgest them which do such things, and doest the same* (the very definition of hypocrisy), *that thou wilt escape the judgements of God? Or despisest thou the riches of His goodness and **forbearance and longsuffering**, not knowing that the goodness of God leadeth to repentance* (**Romans 2:3-4**). He tells us that forbearance and longsuffering are attributes of God's goodness and when put into practice eventually lead to repentance.

He also warns us through **1 Corinthians 4:4-5** *For I know nothing by myself; yet am I not hereby justified: but he that judgeth me is the Lord. Therefore **judge nothing before the time,** until the Lord come, who both will bring to light the hidden things of darkness, and will make manifest the counsels of the hearts: and then shall every man have praise of God.* Paul is rather adamant that we should know that it is the Lord that judges us and even then, not before the time is right. To judge a situation without prayer and searching for the truth in that situation is judging before its time. God has allowed for our stupidity and weaknesses in His plans for us, and if for us then why not for others also? He allows us leeway to make mistakes and learn from them and to self-examine our heart over time, then, and only then, only *He* decides what is right and wrong based wholly and solely on His word in context. We must remember, more often than not, our judgment about another person says more about our own character than the character of the person we are pointing a finger at.

"In school we learn that mistakes are bad, and we are punished for making them. Yet, if you look at the way humans are designed to learn, we learn by making mistakes. We learn to walk by falling down. If we never fell down, we would never walk."

Robert T. Kiyosaki, Rich Dad, Poor Dad.

Paul does not stop there. He warns of what will happen to our hearts without this crucial element of time. He goes on to say, *But after **thy hardness** (callousness and stubbornness) **and impenitent heart** treasurest up* (reserve) *unto thyself wrath against the day of wrath and revelation of the righteousness of God* (where God's righteousness- His character and deeds will be revealed); *Who will render to every man according to his deeds:* (this puts the asinine idea that we don't have to do works after we believe right where it belongs, in the grave). ***To them who by patient continuance in well doing seek for glory and honour and immortality, eternal life;*** He continues to tell us what happens to those who do not have the above mentioned qualities (in bold print): *But **unto them that are contentious*** (two words; Ek Eritheia- intrigue [plots and schemes], to stimulate factions, i.e. **belonging to separated groups),** *and do not obey the truth* (more than just the truth of salvation, one God and holiness), *but obey unrighteousness* (the opposite of God's character and actions), *indignation and wrath, tribulation and anguish, upon every soul of man that doeth evil, of the Jew first and also of the Gentile* (**Romans 2:5-9**). Forbearance, longsuffering, and forgiveness in love are tools that God uses in His willing servants in order to build up the Ecclesia.

Chapter 22.

Bear one another's burdens.

Galatians 6:2 *Bear ye one another's burdens, and so fulfil the* **law of Christ***.*

The unexamined life is not worth living.

Plato quoting Socrates at his trial in 399 BC.

As we regularly examine what we believe regarding the law of God to see if we are fulfilling it according to His word, we find if we are in line or have drifted from not just the word, but the spirit of the word. Just believing what we are told by pulpit preachers and bible schoolteachers is not enough to defeat the enemy when we are confronted by issues in our lives. Just telling someone to have faith doesn't explain what God means by faith. Just telling someone to believe for a financial blessing doesn't make one come about. Our belief must be based on God's word and will combining to produce God's results. If our prayers are going unanswered it may mean we need to examine what we believe and why we believe it, and then see if what we believe is in contextual alignment with the whole word of God. It is by doing this we also find out if there is something that we must do to bring about what we are asking for.

For example, the word '*law*' conjures up all sorts of nasty ideas in most believer's minds and has people standing up, proudly and loudly proclaiming, '*We are no longer under the law, but under grace!*' However, just like all false doctrine, that statement has a smidgeon of truth. The Gentiles may not be under the 613 Mosaic laws handed down to the Children of Israel in the wilderness at Mount Sinai, however, we are under the law of Christ. This law requires much more from the citizens of the Commonwealth of the Kingdom of God, mainly because it requires a 24 hour a day commitment to obey the word of God in the spirit.

Paul is telling us the *law of Christ* is something that can and must be fulfilled. The question now arises, how? In this instance, by bearing one another's burdens. This is not a passing request, for in context with the rest of chapter six it comes across as a **command** to fulfil (Anaplēroō- complete or accomplish by coincidence or obedience) the law of Christ. It is noteworthy that Paul (an expert in the law) calls what he tells us to do for one another, *The* **Law** *of Christ,* (Nomos- the principle, the prescriptive usage). This puts *the work* of the whole Ecclesia (not just the leadership) as an integral part of preaching the Gospel of the Commonwealth of the Kingdom of God, and it is, to a fairly large degree, accomplished by bearing one another's burdens.

The law of Christ goes further than the Mosaic laws and encompasses our hearts, thoughts, will, and intentions not just our actions. For example, Jesus told of the seventh commandment in **Matthew 5:27** *Ye have heard that it was said by them of old time, Thou shalt not commit adultery:* He proclaimed the Law of Moses to be true. But He did not leave it there. He went even deeper into the heart of man and said in verse 28 *But I say unto you, That whosoever looketh on a woman to lust after her* **hath committed adultery with her already in his heart.** God is greatly interested in our heart's motives not only our actions. This brings a greater condemnation than the law when it is ignored.

Another example, in the second reading of the Law of Moses we read the command concerning giving to the poor and needy, *If there be among you a poor man of one of thy brethren within any of thy gates in thy land which the LORD thy God giveth thee, thou shalt not harden thine heart, nor shut thine hand from thy poor brother: But thou shalt open thine hand wide unto him, and shalt surely lend him sufficient for his need, in that which he wanteth.* Modern translation: *If we have someone in our midst with needs (regardless of what they are), we will tend to that need until the need has been fulfilled* (**Deuteronomy 15:7-8**). This was a command to be obeyed as much as, *thou shalt not steal or commit adultery.* In the continuation and explanation of Torah in the Sermon on the Mount, Jesus makes it a heart issue, *Take heed that ye do not your alms before men,* **to be seen of them: otherwise ye have no reward of your Father which is in heaven.** *Therefore when thou doest thine alms, do not sound a trumpet before thee, as the hypocrites do in the synagogues and in the streets, that they may have glory of men. Verily I say unto you, They have their reward. But when thou doest alms, let not thy left hand know what thy right hand doeth* (**Matthew 6:1-3**). Giving is good but giving with a right heart attitude has a greater impact and reward in the eternal.

The law in the Old Covenant was a law of actions and consequences (if you did this, you get that) but the law of Christ addresses the heart even more so. The law of Christ is more than a set of rules that we obey and check off our list, and if we have enough checked off, we are somehow right with God and on our way to heaven shouting victory. It is a life surrendered unto God from the inner man which will eventually work its way to the outside. It is a walk with God that can be seen in action by others on more than just Sundays, midweek meetings, camps, and conferences. It is the heart condition of sin and selfishness which ultimately leads to rebelliousness that God is dealing with, the heart will always show itself outwardly given enough time.

I find it amazing that church people want to please God with their worship, tithes, offerings, obedience to their pastor and church attendance and yet neglect something that pleases God infinitely more and displeases Him far greater when we do not do it. **Galatians 6:2** *Bear ye one another's burdens, and so fulfil the law of Christ.* The Aramaic English New Testament sheds greater light on this, *And carry the load of one another, and become full in the instruction of Mashiyach.* Are we not to fulfil Christ's teaching/instruction? (See **John 14:15,23, Matthew 28:19**).

The way to fulfill the Torah (law of Moses) and please God in the Old Covenant was to obey Him, sacrifice, and tithe so the poor could eat (that was the purpose of the tithe, not to build anything nor the upkeep of the Temple. There was a special tax for that). The way to fulfill the law of Christ in the Renewed Covenant is to bear one another's burdens but to do it in love, to lay down our lives for one another by being a living sacrifice and by becoming the image of Christ (**1 John 3:16-18, Romans 12:1-2, 8:29, John 15:13-15**). As we are a Commonwealth, where all things (goods and services, time and resources, wisdom, and knowledge) are had in common, so we must share one another's burdens. Giving money to someone but not sharing in their burdens is only doing part of the job of the Ecclesia. It is like baking a cake and leaving out the main ingredient. Millions of people (both believers and unbelievers alike) give to charity and feel good about it but have little to no personal dealings with the burden's others carry. Throwing money into the offering but ignoring the plight of the brethren is as useful as lips on a chicken. People often give to assuage their guilt because they have plenty and others lack tremendously and by giving a few dollars here and there, they feel they have fulfilled a duty. God will use the money for His purpose, but it will not help the giver in their spirit at all. He wants the heart to be involved in as many instances as possible.

There are people who have dedicated their lives to the gospel (who do more than just preach good sermons, pay the church bills and counsel when necessary) who not only struggle financially but are also weighed down with sicknesses, family concerns, travel difficulties, demonic attacks and much more. Instead of just giving a few dollars, then sitting back and demanding good sermons, church bills paid and be ready for counsel, how about we find out their other needs and see if there is a way to alleviate them? I am not speaking of the need for another electronic tablet, a cruise or annual vacation, or car, but their personal needs. If we cannot (not will not) personally do so in the natural, then in prayer and fasting for them and seeking someone who can help is one way we can still act on their need. When the burdens and trials of another keeps us awake, and we lose our appetites, then we can honestly say that we have shared in their burdens.

"But don't we all have burdens that we need to carry?" Yes, that is the point, we all do, and if the Ecclesia followed this law of Christ, all our burdens would be met, many by ourselves and the rest by the Ecclesia. Then, as new believers come in, we would have more people bearing each other's burdens. Verse two states that we are to *bear one another's burdens* and verse five states that *each man should bear his own burdens*. Contradiction? In the words of Jesus, *I trow not*. To bear is to carry, sustain or endure and though the English uses the word *burdens* in both verses, the Greek definitions of both words are different. The *burdens* in verse two (Baros) means *abundant weight* or *heavy load*, while the *burden* in verse five (Phortion) means a *task, service,* or *a light load*. In essence, we are told that we are to carry our own task or service for the Kingdom, however, when that burden becomes too much, then we are to carry each other's heavy load until we can carry our own again.

This is essential to keeping the stress level down as low as possible for all members of the Kingdom. Just so we are clear, according to the truth in the word of God, there is no such thing as a stress-free disciple of Christ. Those who walk around saying they are 'too blessed to be stressed', are not living for God, but are living a man-made concept of church born out of traditions and dogmas. As they keep their traditions, they feel all is well. This *pie in the sky* attitude is harmful, mainly because when trials do come, they believe something is wrong and they will not have the wherewithal to withstand what is coming. They have forgotten Peters words, *Beloved, think it not strange concerning the fiery trial which is to try you, as though some strange thing happened unto you* (**1 Peter 4:12**). Does this mean we are to be constantly in stressful situations and living a frazzled life to prove we are disciples? Of course not. It means that because we live for God according to the bible and not our own ideas, in a world buffeted by sin and full of death, we will also be buffeted and we must endure if we are to be saved (**Matthew 10:22, 2 Timothy 3:12**).

Ask Paul, Peter, James, Stephen, Lydia, or the millions of martyrs throughout history if their lives were *"too blessed to be stressed"*. As we fulfil the law of Christ, life takes on different challenges and stresses and with the help of the Holy Ghost and humble godly men and women (biblical elders) as examples and counsellors, we can lessen, but never eliminate, the stresses of normal life. Anyone that tells you that being a Christian promises a stress-free life, is either self-deluded and have cut themselves off from any semblance of reality, or they are trying to hoodwink you. There will be times when stress is alleviated, but in reality, these are relatively short lived and to be enjoyed when they come, but if we are to continue to be involved with humanity and grow in grace and faith (which is tested in trials), stress is expected and to be used to push us closer to God for strength and endurance. Just as our Lord did and those that followed in His footsteps. Hence, the need for the *body of Christ*.

Sharing one another's burden is like reinforcements sent in when the battle seems the hottest and doesn't look like it's going the right way. These fresh soldiers are sent to relieve, re-arm and restore tired or wounded members of the body, they come with a fresh perspective of the battle and fresh supplies. To not do so allows the enemy to not only kill our people but also to take ground and set up bases in what was once our own ground. To remove our enemy then takes twice as much manpower, material and effort and is a great waste of time if you ask me.

When we say, *"I love you"*, but our actions say, *'it's not my problem'*, we have just lied to them, to God and sadly, to ourselves. By doing so we make things worse for the Ecclesia. Remember, it's not about you and me or our group, but about God's Ecclesia here on earth and about showing the Commonwealth of the Kingdom of God to those around us. If we take care of the fallen, the weak, the neglected that sit in our pews every week, those who have been hurt by the world or church members or are infirmed in both spirit and body and help restore them, we will have more saints to train someone from scratch. These restored members will pick up where they left off- seeking first the Kingdom of God and His righteousness.

Bearing one another's burdens is a prerequisite to understanding one another. The poem by Mary T. Lathrap, *Judge Softly* (1895) speaks of walking a mile in someone's shoes which in turn gives empathy to the wearer (more on empathy in a later chapter).

If someone truly does love the Lord, modesty will be a natural outcome of that love, so instead of trying to fulfil a list of dos and don'ts handed down to us by church officials or a group of people at the last general conference, or board meeting to prove we love God, we can, in a greater part, fulfil the law of Christ by bearing one another's burdens. Our wardrobe will fall in line as a matter of course. We would be helping to change people from the inside out and we will be able to eliminate *"clothes-line preaching"* altogether. As God adds to the church such as should be saved, they will see our abundant love for God and one another and as we disciple them, their outer appearance (modesty), language, giving and gathering will fall in line with God's desires naturally.

How, may you well ask? Let us look at the word *fulfil* again, Anaplēroō- to complete; to occupy, supply; figuratively to accomplish (by coincidence or obedience). We can see that to fulfil is not based on a check list thing as we see it in today's meaning (to carry out a task, duty, or role as required, pledged, or expected) but rather the purpose is to either to be complete by coincidence or obedience or to occupy, supply and accomplish the will of God here on earth.

Bearing a burden that is not our own shows us that we are more interested in the Kingdom of God and think more like Christ than our daily comfort. Christ bore the burdens of a rebellious (living for self and not for God) world so that He could fulfil and accomplish a promise made to Adam in **Genesis 3:15** *And I* (God) *will put enmity between thee and the woman, and between thy seed and her seed; it shall bruise thy head, and **thou** shalt bruise his heel.* Now He can **occupy** this planet with little images of Himself. Paul tells us that it is we, the Ecclesia, who use our heels to accomplish the same thing, *And the God of peace shall bruise Satan under **your** feet shortly. The grace of our Lord Jesus Christ be with you. Amen* (**Romans 16:20**). God in us fulfilling His will on earth.

Satan attacks the Ecclesia by attacking the saints on an individual level and is successful because of it, by trying to place unnecessary burdens on them. But when the Ecclesia responds as a whole, to carry one another's burdens, the effectiveness of our enemy's attacks become greatly diminished with fewer long-lasting effects.

Fulfilling the law (Nomos- prescriptive usage and principles) of Christ makes us law abiding citizens of the Commonwealth of the Kingdom of God here on earth. Our love for the Master (Didaskalos- instructor, teacher) and Saviour compels us to fulfil His law. Not through coercion, cajoling or condemnation, but purely because He has commanded the Ecclesia to do so (for its own benefit none-the-less) and because of His great love for us and our love for Him.

What kind of burdens do we needlessly carry? Well, for starters there's guilt and shame for past sins which, once Christ has indwelt a person through the baptism of the Holy Ghost and they have been baptized in His name (thereby remitting those sins), are needless and harmful to the body. Guilt and shame are tools that God uses with our conscience to bring us back in line (repentance) with His word, but once the sin has been dealt with through repentance, contrition, and a burning desire with action to change, these things (guilt and shame, if still present) become tools of our enemy (Satan and hypocritical, self-serving, and sanctimonious pseudo-saints who will not let past sins go). These malicious and merciless people will not acknowledge that the sin has been dealt with by the blood of the perfect sacrificial Lamb of God unless it is either done in their presence or until a penalty, they deem necessary, has been paid. They will do all in their power to continually resurrect other's sins while simultaneously hiding their own past sins.

This Roman Catholic attitude has set up a presence in some of our churches and organizations. Sad to say, even after that, they may not bring it up verbally but will continue to treat the person with less honour than they should. This, however, places them in a rather precarious position of having their own sins brought up and used against them, (see **Matthew 18:21-35**). If a sin is confessed and under the blood, the repentant person is cleansed and the guilt of said sin is removed from all records in the annals of heaven (**1 John 1:9,7**). Just as God uses willing people to bring healing and love to a searching soul, so Satan uses his servants to resurrect someone's past sins after they have been repented of (**Revelation 12:10**). Because we love God, and we have this pesky thing called a memory, we feel ashamed that we have done those things and remember them. But we not only have a memory, we also have a promise and to have a promise there must be a promise maker and because His faithfulness is beyond reproach we know He keeps His promises. We even sing songs about that aspect of Him. Our security is not in the promise but in the promise keeper. **1 John 1:9** tells us, *If we confess our sins, **he is faithful and just** to forgive us our sins, and to cleanse us from all unrighteousness* (Homologeō- to assent, to covenant, acknowledge: - con- (pro-) fess, to give thanks, promise). Guilt and shame are just tools in God's and Satan's hands. One uses it to bring us closer to Him, the other to drive us to despair, ruin and further from God.

Reminding me of my past sins is like robbing a house I used to live in. I don't care because I no longer live there. Lying, cheating, adultery, theft, incest, oath breaking to God and our spouses, embezzlement, dictatorial/authoritarian leadership, pride, arrogance, gossiping, backbiting, interfering, and meddling in people's lives, and such are sins people can plainly see. But what of the sins hidden within the depths of our souls that are just as evil in God's sight such as anger, malice, unforgiveness, greed, bitterness, tearing down other believers in our hearts and minds, withholding fellowship, causing others to refrain from fellowshipping with someone, clandestinely planning to break-up families and selfishness? All these and many more are contrary the character of God and all carry the same sentence: Death (separation from God). Unless we repent of these things, we are only deceiving ourselves into thinking we are okay with God.

Yet the enemy (and many times, false brethren who go to the same church buildings and conferences with us, and sometimes preach from pulpits as we are told by David, *For it was not an enemy that reproached me; then I could have borne it: neither was it he that hated me that did magnify himself against me; then I would have hid myself from him: But it was thou, a man mine equal, my guide, and mine acquaintance* **Psalm 55:12-14**). Sometimes we inadvertently take back the burdens God has relieved us from because we are not used to *not* having them.

Enter the real disciples of Christ, the Ecclesia. They will show by biblical example how to live the word of God and eventually have a victorious life. The real disciples of Christ will walk side by side with someone until they have the victory over both the sin and the corresponding shame and guilt, no matter how long it takes. If there's a time limit on our walking with someone, then we cannot be classed as a disciple. When we eventually come through the other side victorious with another saint, we will not be lying when we sing how we have the victory, but we will actually have the victory. Then as quickly as possible we will find others who have a heavy burden and help them get the same victory. Perseverance becomes reality.

Freedom? Sure, but from what?

In my years of traveling from coast to coast and around the world, I have found that most people do not really want the freedom God offers. The main reason is because freedom involves responsibility. Most people shudder at the prospect of being responsible for the well-being of another. Parents are responsible for the well-being of their children and, as the Ecclesia is the Bride of Christ and referred to many times as a woman, she is responsible for the well-being of the souls in her care. We are responsible through our actions and inactions for the care of others within the body of Christ. We are commanded to care for them as we care for ourselves. Freedom is not freedom if it carries no responsibility and that is why most people sing about their concept of freedom but rarely practice biblical freedom.

If we really have the testimony of freedom in our lives and we are honest with ourselves and each other (unfortunately, most of the time, we really don't. As Christians, we don't tell lies, but many times we put music to them and sing them), we will see such an explosion of God's presence that we will not be able to stand in our services. We will have freedom from the secret guilt and shame of already repented sin, the anguish, anxiety, insecurity, faithlessness, unbelief and partiality amongst the saints, stinginess and many more things that keeps us from interacting with the Spirit of God outside of sanctioned church activities. We will no longer have attitudes like, *'we're up here and you're down there* or *they don't speak the same language as we do* or *we have been ordained by our organization, we know more than you, so be quiet* (this is called a haughty spirit and we know what happens to these people in **Proverbs 16:18, 18:12, 21:24**).

Ever wonder why the vast majority of believers struggle to worship God and pray after we gather for a *church service*. The answer may surprise you. It is because in a church service we are surrounded by others who also have struggles and are trying to work them out (see **Philippians 2:12**). Then, as we go to our respective lives after a church service, the struggles are still there and usually they have grown in energy and intensity or, as we oldies used to say, *with vim and vigour*. However, when we purposefully see each other outside of church gatherings and we encourage, exhort, pray for and with one another, edify (build) each other up, give to one another and share one another's burdens, we have carried the ability to fight and win victories outside of the confines of our forts (buildings) and into each other's lives.

Think of the Ecclesia as a library in a community. When one needs information on how to tackle a problem, raise children in a godly manner, how to live as a witness for Christ, how to love and honour our spouses, how to behave in a work or school environment, how to trust God during a trial, what to believe or how to build one another up, one goes to the everyday people who are successful in these matters (remember that success is getting something right at least 51% of the time), where there is a veritable fount of information, knowledge and wisdom and a willingness to help one another to find answers. Answers to all of life's concerns are rarely found solely in the church building or leadership or especially from behind a pulpit. Information that comes from the pulpit (as important as that is, must have an outlet outside the pulpit to become realized wisdom). If biblical information impartation can be successful without the personal interaction of disciples, then all we need are sermonizers and self-help books.

For example, a single young pastor with no life experience might be able to tell us about the scriptures with inspiration and anointing, but it will be the wise elders (Presbuteros- an older person, wiser by dint of life experience) who have lived through the trials of life, that will be able to give wisdom and experiential counsel and show us the pitfalls of the enemy's devices. The Holy Ghost does tell and teach us these things, however, having someone watch over us, go to God on our behalf and *show* us, not just *tell* us, how to implement these things into God's Kingdom, is the job of the Ecclesia.

The other burdens that we encounter are the burdens of everyday life. Sickness of self or a loved one, loss of income, housing, transportation, bad working environment, schooling, mental stresses and so on, are all things that we encounter just from being alive. And though God promises that through prayer for His will to happen daily in our lives He would care for us, he has also chosen to use the church as the vehicle to help ease the vicissitudes of life which sometimes hinder us from carrying out our tasks in, for and through the Commonwealth of the Kingdom of God. By bearing one another's heavy burdens we are released to carry out our task for the Ecclesia.

Chapter 23.

Admonish one another.

Romans 15:14 *And I myself also am persuaded of you, my brethren, that ye also are **full of** goodness, filled with all knowledge, able also to **admonish** one another.*

Paul tells the recipients of this letter that we are to be (*full of*- Este- be or have) goodness, (*filled*- Plēroō- to make replete, that is, to cram or level up or to be furnish with) knowledge and to *admonish* one another. Today, to admonish seems to be the domain of only the leadership, but this has been hijacked from the saints. To admonish comes from the Latin word- Admonere meaning to advise or remind. Today's understanding of admonish has been used with an eye on reprimanding, scold, improving someone's behaviour based on another's understanding, set of laws or perceived morality, or even berating them. For example, if a child or subordinate is being admonished, it usually means they are being scolded, rebuked, chastised, or looked down on with an air of superiority. Once again, we have taken a modern definition of a word and attached it to an ancient document and thrust it upon an uneducated and unsuspecting church populace as truth.

The biblical word admonish, however, brings a different attitude to today's meaning; Noutheteō- to call attention to, to put in mind, that is, (by implication) to caution or **reprove gently**: a mild rebuke, warn. To reprove today means to disapprove of strongly; censure: to upbraid, chide or reprehend, to express disapproval to (someone), to criticize. Definitely not the bible's definition.

Please note the scripture does not say berate, belittle, criticize, scold, or reprimand, yell at, browbeat or put down, ostracize, cut off, or give the silent treatment to one another. This is not a part of Christian ministry in the Ecclesia and anyone who practices admonition in this manner whether they are in leadership or not, deserves little if any attention much less respect or honour. It is a part of the carnal church of today where making people do what they're told has become as normal as thinking that church attendance alone or tithing makes or keeps us right with God. This is not helpful even in a miniscule way. How we interact with God and His people (Ecclesia) is the real indicator of our walk with God. Having pieces of paper given to us by others who have pieces of paper proves nothing if we are not admonishing *each other* both up and down the chain of command God's way. In fact, more than likely it is a hindrance.

Another translation puts **Romans 15:14** this way, *Now I am persuaded, my Brothers, even I, concerning you, that you too are full of goodness, and are replenished with all knowledge, and are able also to instruct others* (Aramaic English New Testament. AENT). Replenished can only come into play if we have given out our knowledge, wisdom, and instructions to others. Paul was not interested in being someone's Holy Ghost, but he was greatly interested in the Ecclesia instructing and putting in mind the things of God to other members of the body. Nowhere is it written in the Renewed Covenant where instruction can only go down the proverbial ladder or chain of command. Paul was writing this to the entire church, not the so-called *ministry*. It was given to the Ecclesia *to help one another* achieve success in God. Success in God is measured daily by how much of God's will did we accomplish, how much revelation did we receive and live out today. We have attached a 21st-century definition of leadership to an 1800-year-old document and using it to brow beat people into submission. For the sake of all that is Holy in God, please stop! We are not helping.

The word admonish/admonishing and warn are only used six times in the KJV Renewed Covenant and both have the same meaning. Admonish is not used at all in the Old Covenant, however it's counterpart- *warn and warning* (admonishing) are used fifteen times. Four of those time were by the prophet Ezekiel to warn (admonish) the brethren (see **Ezekiel 3:18-20, 33:4-5**).

As we can see, to admonish one another is never for our personal benefit, to get someone to do what we want (even if we believe it is good for them) or punish them, to teach someone a lesson (*But the Comforter, which is the Holy Ghost, whom the Father will send in my name, **he shall teach you all things**, and bring all things to your remembrance, whatsoever I have said unto you* (**John 14:26**), or to make them repent to us. As mentioned earlier, those who think that others must repent to them before they can be forgiven by God may as well don the Catholic priest's robe and mitre and begin holding confessions in small boxes, telling the people how many hail Marys and our fathers they must say.

It is not easy to let things go, to allow God time and chance to work things out in other's lives. We were slighted or offended by someone, and somehow action must be taken immediately to remedy the situation or else they don't really love God nor are any of their words to be taken seriously. Nowhere are we told this in regards to repentance anywhere in God's timetable. What seems to be immediately, is in reality, a long chain of events leading to something happening in a timeframe that seems to be in our present. God gave us a multitude of chances to repent and make things right with someone we have slighted or offended and either we did it over time or we have yet to repent of it because we have forgotten what we did. Put the book down and truly examine yourself and see if there are times you have done others wrong, whether it was speaking to them in a condescending manner, a critical attitude, not giving of your time, talents or treasure as God commanded, or just being your selfish self for a time when others needed you. Do you honestly think these things did NOT affect others in a negative way or that they escaped God's notice?

Below are the Renewed Covenant verses which encourage us to admonish/warn one another, but when we do, it must always be with a grave and sober heart, many times with tears, out of love and to reiterate, never to punish. We are to teach one another (not teach each other a lesson), by our life's examples through discipleship, so that the body might be fitly framed and joined together (**Ephesians 2:21** and **4:16**).

*Therefore **watch*** (Grēgoreuō- be vigilant, rouse from stupor. A state of reduced sensibility or consciousness [apathy]), *and remember, that by the space of three years I ceased not to **warn*** (Noutheteō- caution and reprove gently- admonish) *every one night and day **with tears*** (Acts 20:31). He writes to the slack and carnal Christians in Corinth, *I write not these things to shame you, but as my beloved sons I **warn*** (Noutheteō) *you* (1 Corinthians 4:14). **Warning and admonishing are not meant to shame someone or get them to bend to our will nor into God's will!** To the disciples in Colossae he writes, *Let the word of Christ dwell in you richly in all wisdom; **teaching and admonishing*** (Noutheteō- caution and warning) ***one another** in psalms and hymns and spiritual songs, singing with grace in your hearts to the Lord* (**Colossians 3:16**). He writes twice to the Thessalonians, *And we beseech you, brethren, to know them which labour among you, and are **over you*** (Proistēmi- practice, stand before and help maintain. This has nothing to do with ruling over someone) *in the Lord, and **admonish*** (Noutheteō) *you; And to esteem them very highly in love for their work's sake. And be at peace among yourselves. Now we exhort you, brethren, **warn*** (Noutheteō) *them that are unruly, comfort the feebleminded* (faint hearted), *support the weak, be patient toward all men* (**1 Thessalonians 5:12–14**). *Yet **count him not as an enemy**, but **admonish*** (Noutheteō- gently warn and reprove) *him as a brother* (**2 Thessalonians 3:15**).

Notice, the scripture does not say, *Pastors admonish the saints*. We are commanded to *admonish one another*, and it is always for the purpose of helping each other stay on the straight and narrow (so to speak) and to grow in God. Many churches and organizations feel it is their God given duty to admonish the saints and do it with such gusto that it ends up damaging the saints rather than helping them find and fulfill their purpose within the Commonwealth of the Kingdom of God. Yet, we are to remind each other, then advise on correct understanding of the ways of God, we need to caution (not dictate) or gently reprove each other, and do it in love and humility, remembering that we ourselves do not have it as all together as we think.

In a nutshell, what the bible clearly states the seeker of truth's main purpose within the Ecclesia, are the six E's. We are to *edify, encourage, empathize, exhort, educate, and equip* one another into becoming like our Lord by making disciples. In doing this, we exalt our Lord far more than any song we can sing, any sermon we can preach (no matter how much anointing we yell into the mic) or any amount of money we can collect. When we focus on entertaining and enthralling the audience with fancy songs and fancy flowers on the stage, reading from fancy screens, while sitting under fancy lighting, we may fill fancy pews, but we will also have empty hearts, lonely lives, and unfulfilled purposes. It takes far more than a few songs and anointed sermons to fill a heart with passion to fulfil a purpose in the Kingdom of God. It takes learning from and teaching others in the Ecclesia daily how to live the scriptures they've heard in our sermons, not just learn where they are and what they mean.

I believe that in our attempts to have church growth, we have inadvertently made the church a theatrical affair where we go to be filled with *'whatever we need from God'* or the ever popular, *'Come and get your blessing/miracle'*. We tell the gullible people they can get these things with no input from themselves other than a little faith (y'know, like a mustard seed). We have preached mustard seed faith as if that is all we need, but that is not the point of **Matthew 17:20** or **Luke 17:6.** The point of these verses is, mustard seed faith is where we all start, it is not the goal. Mustard seed faith is for babes in Christ, but mature men and women of God have moved on to greater faith. Their goal is to one day be with the great cloud of witnesses whose faith moved mountains, changed the course of lives and that they may be counted worthy of the Name of Jesus. They have grown into men and women who ...*may be perfect, throughly furnished unto all good works* (**2 Timothy 3:17**).

Is it truly the purpose of the body of Christ to come to a central place to get from God when God can give anywhere, anytime through the disciples? The purpose of gathering is that when the body is in one place, that is where we can meet each other's needs and share what God has revealed to us through revelation, through our trials, our victories, and failures. A place where we will share what He has given to us in treasure, time, and talents and to impart love and wisdom in a meaningful manner. It is where we carry out the 6 E's of *edifying, encouraging, empathizing, exhorting, educating, and equipping* one another. If we meet and these things are not happening, are we really gathering to fulfil the words of Christ, ...*shall men give unto your bosom* (**Luke 6:38**)? We expect to be entertained (which other than the admission price- tithes and offering and joining in on the singing, has little to no input from the audience) just because we have taken the time to get out of bed and go to the church building (the amount of times I've heard variations of, *'If Christ can raise from the grave, you can get out of bed and go to church'*, or even, *'If you can go to work with a cold, you can go to church with a cold'* is beyond reckoning). We make not like it but this is mental brow beating.

The audience are told (not necessarily shown how) to pray, study, read, share, and love each other. However, the vast majority have either never or rarely had a visible example daily of how to pray, study, read, share, and love each other during the week where the metal meets the meat. They are *told* but not *discipled*. They are preached to but not shown how to. In the Kingdom of God, these two (knowing and showing) are as distant as sin is from righteousness. By our enemy inserting the word *'church'* into the word of God, (a pagan idea reinvented by the Roman Empire turned Catholic church and copied by the protestants in the King James Bible) instead of remaining with the biblical definition of Ecclesia/congregation, he has ensured that the silent majority remain silent. How? By making it that only one man speaks while the audience listens. There is little to no interaction between the speaker and the audience (save the occasional amen, preach it, hallelujah, perhaps an excited few 'running the aisles and dancing'). Where is the admonishing one another in Christ, (we seem to be too busy trying to get out of the parking lot to get to the restaurant) therefor there is very little personal growth though there may be growth in numbers. There is no long-term meaningful interaction during or after the *'service'* between the saints and yet, we proudly (and falsely) tell people we are a fellowship of believers.

We have left the *edifying, encouraging, empathizing, exhorting, educating, and equipping* to one man or a select few called the *'ministry team'* (a task meant for everyone) in less than two hours or so with no time allowed to ask questions and we wonder why we have lost the power to influence our towns and cities towards our One God. We sit separated in church with chasms between the saints, yet we say we are united. We only pray for one another at the front, but not in their homes. We give to the church funds, but rarely to each other. We sing of our love for God on Sunday's and mid-week meetings but ignore our brother or sister in whom God dwells the rest of the week. The only thing that our unity displays to the world is our one God doctrine, baptism in Jesus' name and the infilling of the Holy Ghost with the evidence of speaking in tongues, and that we know when church starts and what restaurant we want to eat in after church.

Sin will always increase in the world as we get closer to the day of judgement, that is its mandate, indeed, its obligation. However, the responsibility for the devastating state of our communities regarding the lack of personal and visible attributes of God rest wholly and solely on the back of the Ecclesia of our time, and within the Ecclesia, the responsibility must lay at the feet of the leadership and the members of the congregation who know or should know better (see **1 Corinthians 3:1-13**). We have allowed the Ecclesia to get so far away from God's blueprint of what a true *'gathering'* is meant to be and do (see **Acts 2:42-47, 4:32-37, 5:42, 20:20**), and yet, with impunity, we behave as the heathens of old, albeit within the boundaries of our holiness standards. If we cannot *edify, encourage, empathize, exhort, educate, and equip* one another, then we are leaving out a very important aspect of why we gather in the first place.

Back to admonishing, for those who feel that it is their God given right to punish or teach someone a lesson, here is a gentle warning (irony noted). We have just stepped into a most unholy place that only One (the Holy Ghost) has a right to be. We are in a very dangerous place full of pride and arrogance and I admonish you (once again, irony noted) to get out of there, repent, humble yourselves, stop trying to change people to think and act like you would, be about your Father's business of edifying (building) the Commonwealth of the Kingdom God the way you are admonished in the word, instead of letting your carnal thinking interfere with God's plan for the lives of the saints by wanting them to change to suit you or your church's vision. People change to come in line with God's word when the desire is there and when it is exampled in others in love and patience.

As mentioned earlier, we find no examples of Christ trying to change the hearts of men by *imposing* change. He did, however, *propose* change and showed what that looks like in real life and those who wanted to and did change, received the reward of that change. This is the example we are to follow and teach each new disciple. We would do better if we were to propose change, example change, and in due time, if the heart of the disciple desires it and with much prayer and a good dose of fasting for them, change will follow. This is the true definition of biblical leadership (not necessarily holding a so-called office, using titles like, pastor, bishop, presbyter, superintendent, or doctor to prove our superiority in knowledge, or having the right connection within our group or organization. Leadership is not so much conferred upon someone as it is God who chooses, we just agree with God's choice. Hint: whether we agree or not, they are still chosen by God to deliver His word, not to rule). To truly build a strong Ecclesia (all of it, not just the *'ministry team'*) we must recognize someone else's strength as a complement to our weaknesses, not as a threat to our elected or conferred position or authority.

You and I are no-one in our own selves and the sooner we recognize it and begin to live as though it was as true and as an important the Fabulous Five are, the further we will be in advancing God's Kingdom in earth as it is in heaven (**Matthew 6:10, Luke 11:2**). It is only the Holy Ghost that makes us someone in God's Kingdom and as He is impartial, He does not have better or worse, higher, lower, more, or a less useful someone. These someone's still struggle with weaknesses, but to write them off because of these weaknesses and not come along side and walk with them until they get the victory, is to tell God His choice was wrong. This is the embodiment of absurd. Like telling a five-year-old to unravel the mysteries of the human mind. Those who expect this are the absurd ones.

All those in the Ecclesia, following the Master to the best of their ability and passion are on the same road, just at different stages, and admonishing one another helps us all see things from a different perspective. If someone is living for God and their lives prove it, (sadly, many times, we look at the stumbles and not at the journey) then who are we to say that God is not speaking through them to admonish us.

We must take the beam out of our own eye before we begin to complain about the mote in our brother's eye (**Matthew 7:3-5**). We would be like a farmer who is telling another farmer how to run his farm. We are complaining that his tools are not up to our standard and that his methods are antiquated or too modern, or his crop is not to our liking. It would be tantamount to telling a farmer that he must plant potatoes and not wheat, because all the other farmers in that area grow potatoes. We are telling other farmers to have nothing to do with him because we do not like what or how he's planting. We have become the epitome of **1 Timothy 5:13** and **2 Thessalonians 3:11-12** *And withal they learn to be idle,* **wandering about from house to house** *(in a bad sense); and not only idle* (Argos- lazy, useless, and barren), *but tattlers* (Phluaros- a garrulous person [using or containing more words than necessary to express an idea], that is a prater [obnoxious talker]) *also and busybodies* (Periergos- officious [volunteering or excessive eagerness in offering one's services or unwanted advice where they are neither asked nor needed], meddlesome), *and, speaking things which they ought not. For we hear that there are some which walk among you disorderly, working not at all,* **but are busybodies** *(Periergazomai- meddlers, bustle about as with much activity, little to no long-term results). Now them that are such we command and* **exhort** *(gently warn you) by our Lord Jesus Christ, that with quietness* (Hēsuchia- desistance from bustle or language [talking too much]) *they work, and eat their own bread.*

In other words, *don't interfere without invitation, and be about you Father's business to build the Kingdom to His standards, not yours.* When we help one another in God's spirit and as we are members one of another, we will also get the benefit. If someone is unruly, have the courage to warn them in love (to their face, not to everyone else like spineless cowards do) then pray and fast for them and offer to help. Be the agent for change rather than the hammer of God or the messenger of doom that if they do not listen to you and change, they will end up in hell (I've heard leaders and saints tell members of their church this and it has always backfired). This has been the downfall of many a move of God and Jesus foresaw this and made provision for it. **Mark 11:25** *And when ye stand praying, forgive, if ye have ought* (anything whatsoever) *against any: that your Father also which is in heaven may forgive you your trespasses* (see also **Matthew 5:23-24**). How do we expect God to answer our prayers if we have unforgiveness or pride in our heart.

A biblical admonisher sees a bigger picture and can help to show (not impose) that picture to others. An admonisher doesn't just correct, they show and instruct by example. We all get trapped in our own tiny and insignificant world, where we are the head honcho, believing our worldview is the only right one and that view should not be rattled. To admonish someone or to be admonished is to open the mind to a different view regarding thinking or actions and possible consequences. The Lord admonished the disciples when they were arguing about who was the greatest among them, *And there was also a strife among them, which of them should be accounted the greatest* (**Luke 22:24**). They had Philoneikia- quarrelsomeness, a dispute. From Philo- of man or brethren and Nike- to have power over. They were arguing as to who would have power over the other brethren and the Master stepped in to sort them out. He not only admonished them but gave them direction to correct their erroneous thinking and pridefulness, *But ye shall not be so: but he that is greatest among you, let him be as the younger; and he that is chief, as he that doth serve* (**Luke 22:26**). He admonished them when they wanted to call fire down on a town that refused to hear the word of God (for example, *'If you don't do what God says, you'll all burn in hell'*). They wanted to impose God's word on that town, but Jesus said, *leave them alone and check your own spirit* (see **Luke 9:52-56**). An admonition always comes with instruction, an action plan to understand what the will of God is, and more often than not, it will be to serve the one being admonished in whatever area is needed.

If we only receive admonition from those above us within our circle, then we are not receiving biblical admonition. True admonition may come from friends, enemies, strangers or, more than we like to admit, even children. Limiting those that may admonish us creates echo chambers and biases that hinder growth. These are despised by God (see **Proverbs 11:14, 15:22, 24:6, 27:9,16, Isaiah 1:26, 1 John 4:1, Proverbs 18:17**), and we would do well to not allow this to happen as this is not a good way to learn.

If biblical admonition is an action and the heart of the admonished is seeking God, it will eventually and always lead to the three R's: repentance, rectification of actions and attitudes and restoration. If it does not, then either the admonished is not interested in the three R's or the admonition was not given in love with much prayer and empathy. We cannot be too hasty to throw these failures on others. We must check our hearts daily to see if we are being humble before God.

Sometimes we get impetuous, not just in judgement, but in our desire for a quick fix of the other person's behaviour or beliefs and we become harsh in our admonition. I am thankful that when God admonishes us, He does not do it rashly nor harshly. He sees the big picture and adjusts His admonition accordingly. God will always have our restoration as the central theme of any admonition He feels we need. If we are to have the mind of Christ (as we are commanded) then we must operate within the same parameters.

Chapter 24.

Tarry one for another.

1 Corinthians 11:33 *Wherefore, my brethren, when ye come together to eat, **tarry** one for another.*

"I wish it need not have happened in my time," said Frodo.

"So do I," said Gandalf, "and so do all who live to see such times. But that is not for them to decide. All we have to decide is what to do with the time that is given us."

J.R.R. Tolkien, The Fellowship of the Ring.

This command works hand in hand with the preceding chapter. To tarry comes with much sacrifice, labour, and patience. Tarry in this context also carries with it the idea of a farmer who awaits the harvest. He cannot speed up the seasons but must work the farm and wait for his time to prepare, sow, water, fertilize and reap. He is at the mercy of the weather and season and adjusts his day based on what he has been given. While waiting to do one thing, he works on other things, such as sharpening tools, maintaining equipment, buying supplies for the work to come, teaching others to work the farm etc. He eagerly looks for the smallest signs of growth then acts accordingly to help the next stages of growth, all with the final results firmly planted in his mind. When harvest time finally comes, he does not keep the fruit of his labours in the barns (for it will go rotten) but prepares it for distribution to the wider community. Note Paul's directive, *when you come together* (the very definition of Ecclesia. **1 Corinthians 11:33**) *to eat,* this can mean in the natural and the spiritual, we are to, *tarry one for another.*

As mentioned in a previous chapter, time is an extremely precious commodity, and it is something we tend to either waste for no heavenly purpose or we hold onto for dear life and will not share it with anyone outside our circle of family, friends, or organization. The way we view time today is a social construct of humanity. In ancient days, people viewed time by the seasons and the moons for planting and harvesting. Their lives revolved around great expanses of time (seasons, months). People then started to break time down to daily increments with the introduction of calendars by the Sumerians of Mesopotamia (circa 4100 BC), then people moved onto daytime hours using a sundial (3-hour slots, e.g., first, second, third watch etc). With the advent of the mechanical clocks in the 14th century and the steam engine in the late 17th century, we moved on to timing things by the hour and minutes as the need for a reliable timetable became necessary. This was not an entirely new concept as this division of the hour into 60 minutes and each minute into 60 seconds comes from the Babylonians who used a sexagesimal (counting in 60s) system for mathematics and astronomy. They derived this number system from the Sumerians who were using it as early as 3500 BC. As we gathered in cities, we tended to shrink time into watches, and we took time with us. Time as we know it was broken down by man and used for his purposes.

As we progressed through the industrial revolution and beyond, we became technologically savvy and fixated with speed (which is a measurement of time of an object in motion between two fixed points), we began breaking things down even further. From seconds into milli, micro and nano seconds (that's 1,000,000,000,000's of a second). We complain when things take even slightly longer than what we want. We get frustrated and replace a cell phone because it is taking too long to load the page (1-2 seconds longer) and acting up in little ways, the traffic light is taking *'forever'* to change, we want our pizza in under 15 minutes, and we expect others to keep to our timetable. Companies boast about how fast their equipment is or how fast their service times are. Download speeds on our internet is measured by how many gigabytes per second we can ram into our computers. Many people in the church have bought this package in full and unfortunately have used it to get people to do as they want, when they want, or else. This seems harsh considering God gives us time to repent and be restored to His will.

But how has this ridiculous concept of *our time* affected humanity and most importantly the Ecclesia? Mankind's internal clock has not changed from the days of Adam and Eve. God created them to live by seasons. We still require the same amount of daylight and rest in order to function at our best. A child still takes 1095 days to go from birth to its third birthday, the sun still rises and sets at the same time each day of each season of each year even though we have introduced the ludicrous illusion we call daylight saving (which makes as much sense as cutting 30 cm off the top of a blanket, sewing it to the bottom and saying we now have a longer blanket) and it still takes time for a husband and wife to get to know each other after the wedding day.

We squeeze our church service into a particular time frame and if somebody has not begun to change within a *'reasonable time'* (who's idea of reasonable are we using) we start to worry if they'll change at all, then we take over and try to fix them ourselves on our timetable or cast them of like a piece of rubbish. We have tried to speed up time for convenience's sake and all we have done is added stresses into our lives that our minds and bodies were not meant to bear. Releasing ourselves from this illusion, that we can ignore God's timetable and run our lives by man's timetable, is very liberating indeed. It allows us to enjoy the day and look forward to living in the season at hand. There is a reason why the seasons each last three months. We were not meant to have rapid and uncontrollable change in our lives.

Man's obsession with time only causes grief and fear. Allow me to explain. We fear the boss's demand to show up on time and because he stated the start and finish time, we are his mercy. If we are not on time often enough, we lose the job. Our minds then rush headlong into the future and see ourselves unable to pay the rent and feed ourselves and families. We revolve everything around a time frame set by someone. If anything interferes with it, we get frustrated, but we still carry on. All this so that someone else can have a nicer car, house, or bigger bank account. Unlike our bosses, God's timetable is for our benefit and we need not fear or get frustrated when things don't work the way we want in our timeframe.

So, when God tells us to tarry one for another, it flies in the face of our self-imposed prison of time. If God truly is the supreme being, knows all things and has all things in His control, and we use some of that critical thinking mentioned earlier, then it would make sense that time is also in His control. The only thing we control about time is what we do with it. Most of our frustrations come when, at a crucial moment in time, we want something to happen, and it doesn't. This is when we become acutely aware of how little control we have of time, and this creates frustration in our lives.

Tarrying one for another means getting rid of the ludicrous idea that we can impose our time concept and limitations onto others, and we patiently wait for God to do His thing in us and one another, and as we are members one of another, we will be acutely aware that we are to be there for each other when that time comes. We have forgotten that just as nature, we have been created to be born, grow and die in seasons. We would do well to remember Solomon's admonition of time. *To [every thing there is] a season* (Zemân- an appointed occasion)*, and a time to every purpose under* *the heaven: A time to be born, and a time to die; a time to plant, and a time to pluck up [that which is] planted; A time to kill, and a time to heal; a time to break down, and a time to build up; A time to weep, and a time to laugh; a time to mourn, and a time to dance; A time to cast away stones, and a time to gather stones together; a time to embrace, and a time to refrain from embracing; A time to get, and a time to lose; a time to keep, and a time to cast away; A time to rend, and a time to sew; a time to keep silence, and a time to speak; A time to love, and a time to hate; a time of war, and a time of peace* **Ecclesiastes 3:1-8**. The word *time* is translated as a final point in space or time, an end or extremity, a season.

Notice what Solomon says here? That God deals more with His seasons than He does with our clocks and calendars and if we are to be like Him then we must operate with the same mindset and within the same perimeters. Should we be on time for meetings, jobs, and such? Of course, that is just common courtesy, but if something happens outside of our control which delays or speeds up the meeting, we should not get frustrated or angry. God is more interested in the long-term result of what and why He does something than in the short-term frustration we have heaped upon ourselves because something did not happen when we wanted it to. If someone is struggling, it may be their season and we are to tarry for and with them, help them as much as God allows (not as much as we deem necessary or until it becomes inconvenient) and be there when the end of the trial finally comes so we can celebrate their victory with them. The term *"It came to pass"* is written 457 times, showing that what is now is not what will always be. In almost all incidences, it did not come to stay, *it came to pass.*

As God is sovereign, we must also acknowledge that times and seasons are truly in His mind when He declares something will happen. Look at what Paul wrote to the Galatians, *Even so we, when we were children, were in bondage under the elements of the world:* **But when the fulness** (Plērōma- repletion or completion,) **of the time was come,** *God sent forth his Son, made of a woman, made under the law, To redeem them that were under the law, that we might receive the adoption of sons* (**Galatians 4:3-5**). The Jews were waiting through many centuries and difficulties such as famines, droughts, exiles, pestilence, evil empires, and persecutions but when it was God's time, He showed up as their Messiah, though many did not take the time to recognize it.

The necessity of time can be seen in the story of, *Frog and Toad in the Garden,* by Arnold Lobel (Harper & Row, 1972) in which Toad finds Frog working in his beautiful garden. Toad wants to have what Frog has, so Frog shares with Toad a bag of seeds and tells him how to plant them. Toad follows the instructions on planting, then comes back the next day, and is annoyed that nothing has happened. He begins to tell the seeds to grow and when they do not, he yells at them demanding them to grow NOW! Frog hears Toad screaming at the top of his lungs at the seemingly non-growing rebellious seeds. Frog laughingly tells Toad that they will not grow out of fear. They must be planted and let the light shine on the ground and the rain go into the soil and in time, he will have a beautiful garden.

Toad then proceeds to read to the seeds at night with candles all around (to provide constant light) and serenade them with much music for many days in order to make them grow. Eventually out of shear exhaustion he falls asleep and when he wakes up, the seeds are showing a few signs of growth. He mistakenly thinks the artificial light and music he provided caused the seeds to grow. Toad did not understand the concept of time, nature, and nurture, all three combining to get God's results. All he needed to do was to keep the weeds away from the seed and make sure they got plenty of water (not too much or they will drown), whether it was from rain or by bringing water to the plants regularly. Then, watch as God does the rest. *And he* (Christ) *said, So is the kingdom of God, as if a man should cast seed into the ground; And should sleep, and rise night and day,* **and the seed should spring and grow up, he knoweth not how.** *For the* **earth bringeth forth fruit of herself;** *first the blade, then the ear, after that the full corn in the ear. But when the fruit is brought forth* (in its proper time)*, immediately he putteth in the sickle, because the harvest is come* (**Mark 4:26-29**).

Weeds try to take away the goodness from the soil. When a new believer comes into the Ecclesia, they come with a plethora of problems, weighed down with weaknesses, strengths, and many misconceptions about who and what God is. These things will try to take away from what God is trying to do to change them into His image. Weeds like shame, defeatism, loneliness, bad thinking, discouragement, pride, arrogance, self-reliance, selfishness, confusion and thinking they know it all, will try the patience of even a Job-like discipler many times over. These weeds need to be gently ripped away by the Holy Ghost, the word of God and gentle admonition, friendship and most importantly, time from the Ecclesia willing to give these essentials in order to see the seed of God flourish and grow.

The answers to their questions are to be placed around them as one would fertilize a garden, they need to be watered with much prayer and copious amount of fellowship outside of the *sterile church building* environment. The more time we spend with them outside of church times, the greater chance will be that change becomes permanent and they themselves will begin to bear much fruit and that it should remain (John **15:16-18**). All too frequently the older saint's impatience delays many changes that will last for a lifetime. Impatience will cause change, but that change will be out of fear not from the depth of their being and thus will be temporal. When the thing or person feared is not in the vicinity, the younger saint will often revert to old habits, thus bringing even more feelings of condemnation and shame and perpetuating the vicious cycle we are trying to break. When change happens because it has been modelled, in almost all cases, the change becomes permanent and usable in the Commonwealth of the Kingdom of God.

If each of us tarries for one another, as we are commanded to do, it helps us to grow, and the Commonwealth has been bettered. The Christian walk is not a competition against other Christians but with a disciple's former self. *For if we judge* (discern or examine) *ourselves, we should not be judged, but when we are judged,* **we are chastened** (Paideuō- educated, instructed, and disciplined) *of the Lord, that we should not be condemned with the world* (1 **Corinthians 11:31-33**). Our chastening is of the Lord not of the saints and leaders (who are only instruments). In **Hebrews 12:1** Paul calls it a race (Agōn- place of assembly (as if led), that is, a contest an effort, conflict, contention, fight) but it is not against another brother or sister. We are to help one another finish the race, to get to the great assembly where all the witnesses are cheering us on so to speak (see **Hebrews 12:1**).

To tarry, to Ekdechomai- means to accept from some source, that is to await: - expect, look for, wait for. The purpose of the body is to help get and keep each member in optimum condition, to help each other prepare for the great harvest that is to come.

Healthy people and athletes eat certain foods that aid certain parts of the body. Some examples of this would be carrots, a good source of beta-carotene, which the body converts to vitamin K (a crucial component of overall eye health), eggs that are high in natural calcium, leafy greens, and green tea brimming with a type of antioxidant called catechins, which are very beneficial for the liver. Then there's fish which is loaded with Omega-3 fatty acids, which help the brain and vitamin E which is necessary to keep skin thick, supple and moisturized and helps protect our skin against damage and inflammation.

Exercise of the body is just as important as the food it eats. Muscles that are left unused for an extended period become atrophied and eventually useless. The exercise spoken of in the word of God is more for the benefit of the body (Ecclesia) than for the individual. Look at what Paul writes in **Acts 24:16** *And herein do I exercise* (Askeō- Train and strive in) *myself, to have always a conscience void of offence toward God, **and toward men.*** Paul exercises his mind for the benefit of God and men. To Timothy he writes, *But refuse profane and old wives' fables, and exercise* (Gumnazō- to practise or train naked) *thyself rather unto **godliness**. For bodily* (physical) *exercise **profiteth little*** (for a little while)*: but godliness is profitable unto **all things*** (Pas- whatsoever and whosoever)*, having promise of the life that now is, and of that which is to come. This is a faithful saying and worthy of all acceptation. For **therefore we both labour and suffer reproach**, because we trust in the living God, who is the Saviour of all men, **specially of those that believe*** (1 Timothy 4:7-10). We will not always be liked or understood for what we do in Christ, but we labour anyway, *especially for those that believe.*

Each member of the Ecclesia is inextricably attached to each other and if there is thought and action apart from the brain (Christ being the head of the Ecclesia, not a man, such as Pope, president, pastor, or superintendent) we have a disease within the body which causes it to be dysfunctional.

Sadly, many churches are still operating in a community where its every man for himself, and not behaving in a manner that brings glory to the Kingdom of God in earth as it is in heaven. Rather than having a form of utopia (a place, state, or condition that is ideally perfect in respect of politics, laws, customs, and conditions), we will dwell in a dystopian society (a futuristic, imagined universe in which oppressive societal control and the illusion of a perfect society are maintained through corporate, bureaucratic, technological, moral, or totalitarian control). When we allow God to become the head and allow Him to work through the conscience of men and women, there can be no concerns that what has, is and will transpire within the Ecclesia is not for the benefit of the Kingdom of God. He, as the Creator of time, is also the Master/Controller of time. I may create a product but if I sell/give it to another, I am no longer in control of what happens to that product.

So, as we can see, it is up to the head's logic centre (brain) to order the body to care for itself. But when the body (the flesh in spiritual terms) dictates what it wants, then it gets weak and sickly or grossly overweight thus being unable to perform its normal function. The brain's logic centre here is the Lord Jesus Christ, telling the body (Ecclesia) how to care for itself and then how to perform its function. As mentioned in a previous section, Paul tells us how the body works together in **1 Corinthians 12:20-24** *But now are they many members, yet but one body. And the eye cannot say unto the hand, I have no need of thee: nor again the head to the feet, I have no need of you. Nay, much more those members of the body, which seem to be more feeble, are necessary: And those members of the body, which we think to be less honourable, upon these we bestow more abundant honour; and our uncomely parts have more abundant comeliness. For our comely parts have no need: but God hath tempered the body together, having given more abundant honour to that part which lacked.*

The body of Christ has inadvertently ended up with muscular atrophy, a gradual decline in effectiveness or vigour due to underuse or neglect of certain muscles in the body; (the leadership is doing all the work, while the body just shows up, sits down and consumes what the leadership has prepared for the service) and as a consequence the body has been unable to **stand** against the fiery darts of the enemy, nor has it recently been able to **run** the race that God has set before it, it has not **carried** one another's burdens to the extent that God commands, it has limited its **walk** in newness of life with Christ by its inability to walk with the brethren (all of them, not just the ones we agree with) and **lifting** up holy hands within the Ecclesia (**1 Timothy 2:8, Roman 6:4, Galatians 6:2, Hebrews 12:1, Ephesians 6:16**). **Running, standing, carrying, walking,** and **lifting** are the operative words here and when these are performed often enough, we become spiritually fit for the Master's use.

We were meant to take the gates of hell (in the bible, gates speak of where all political, financial, and judicial business was conducted and set into law. It is the place of authority of a city or domain. Thus, this verse tells us that the authority of hell [Hades- the grave] will not triumph over the Ecclesia that God builds) and proclaim the true gospel of the Kingdom of God. A question must therefore be asked, how can we proclaim a Kingdom we only visit once or twice a week for a few of hours? How can we preach a social gospel meant to make us feel good, placate our senses, build up our egos, and promote our little temporal empires and still expect God to intervene in our lives for the good? The Gospel of The Kingdom of God is a gospel that requires sacrifice, cross-bearing and enduring all manner of hardship to the end and doing it with and for one another. A people that does not tarry for one another cannot biblically be called His disciples no matter how big, small, rich, poor, or well-connected the church is. Remember the Church of Laodicea?

We are meant to wait **on** each other, **for** each other and **with** each other, expect more **from** each other, **hold** each other accountable to the promises we make to God, and **help** each other get to where each member of the body needs to be, then we are to **work** with one another to perform the task given to the body, which is to be the light of the world, the salt of the earth, the earthly manifestation of the body of Christ. We cannot do this if we are busy fighting one another because, *they do not go to our church any more* or *are not a part of our organization*, or *it's been a year now and they're still doing* (...insert problem here...). We defeat our own purpose if we refuse to fellowship with one another because their idea of holiness is different from ours, or because they left our organization. We are to be united in one accord (Homothumadon- unanimously, with one mind. From Homou- same place or time, together; and Thumos- passion, as if breathing hard, fierceness, indignation, wrath), regardless of the name on the 501c3, which bible school we attended or what the name of the organization we stick on our church signs. None of these have any impact on the dying, lonely or neglected souls sitting in our pews let alone those who are dying, lonely or neglected in our neighbourhoods.

The Ecclesia ought to be fierce in her love and protection of those who seem least in the body of Christ and should be indignant and wrathful if anyone gets left behind in growth or services. This is not a new problem. The early church dealt with the same thing in **Acts 6:1** *And in those days, when the number of the disciples was multiplied, there arose a murmuring of the Grecians against the Hebrews, because their* **widows were neglected in the daily ministration**. What was the apostle's response? See a problem, solve the problem. There was no need of a prayer meeting, a board meeting, a committee to be established to do a study of how to fix the problem, no elections held, no special classes required. The answer was in the congregation. **Acts 6:3** *Wherefore, brethren,* **look ye out among you** *seven men of honest report, full of the Holy Ghost and wisdom, whom we may appoint over this business.*

We ought to get mad when we see someone refuse to wait for and help another become who they are meant to be in Christ Jesus, *For as many of you as have been baptized into Christ have put on Christ. There is neither Jew nor Greek, there is neither bond nor free, there is neither male nor female: **for ye are all one in Christ Jesus**. And if ye be Christ's, then are ye Abraham's seed, and heirs according to the promise* (**Galatians 3:27-29**). How can we call ourselves *the church* (Ecclesia- a gathering of those with like passions and mind) when the only gathering we do is in a building and the only thing we are *waiting* (tarrying) on is our blessing?

How many times have we heard of a well-known brother or sister within our organization who has passed on, how heaven will gain another powerful saint and how they will be missed? We miss them for their contribution to the body. The reason we don't feel this way when an *'ordinary brother or sister'* passes away is we didn't see them as being a contributor to the body. Sadly, it is because we did not help them find their niche, their place or calling, within the body from the very beginning as the few who have passed that we revered. We just helped them find their pew and their comfort zone.

Many times, these sorry excuses of people who call themselves the church of God today, who have bitten off and written off their own members for the most ridiculous and insipid reasons, must answer for the callousness and indifference to those who are different to them. Here are just a few illegitimate reasons I've overheard the last 35-years, *they hurt my feelings, they didn't submit to the pastor, they don't believe the way we do, they went to another church, they're not spiritual enough, they're too spiritual, they committed a sin, they won't come to service regularly, they don't tithe, they won't contribute to the church building fund, they have a mixed marriage, they won't go the altar, they disagree with the church on points of doctrine or how that doctrine is portrayed, they have the audacity to think they can hear from God outside of the church chain of command, they speak out against sin in the church whether it be in the pew or the pulpit, they are too shy or too boisterous.*

I have heard all these and sadly, many more excuses and I could go on, but the point is made. Are any of these and many other frivolous and absurd reasons to be found anywhere in context with isolating, excommunicating, shunning or disfellowshipping anyone in the word of God? We all have our different ways of seeing things and of dealing with issues in our lives. Waiting on and for each other to become whom we are meant to be helps us to be united in spirit and is as essential to the body of Christ as breathing is to you and me.

How did the early disciples all have the same doctrine and faith despite the diversity that marked the early church, and despite the lack (at that time) of a written Renewed Covenant canon? Somehow there emerged a basic common confession of faith in *...one body, one Spirit, one hope, one Lord, one faith, one baptism, one God and Father of all...* as Paul clearly states in **Ephesians 4:4– 6**. In our day, formalized expressions of religion are often looked at suspiciously and rightly so. To early believers, however, the *"rule of faith"* was regarded as a yardstick by which they measured and shaped all thinking and conduct. The unity of the Spirit was paramount while the unity of doctrine was not forced but allowed to be injected into the Ecclesia by the same Spirit that led the people to God in the first place (see **John 6:44**). Elders (and eventually pastors and bishops) were there to oversee the flock, not just spiritually but physically as well. This power the Ecclesia had was embraced by recent converts and organically tailored apostolic authority, and thus it illuminated their search to understand and propagate this renewed faith in Jehovah. It was NOT contrived at some board meeting and funnelled down to the local gatherings via some bureaucratic system. It was people loving people and disciples making disciples under the watchful eye (not rulership) of wise and humble men and women (elders, pastors, and bishops- Presbuteros).

If all we're doing is showing up at the same time, at the same place, singing the same songs, hearing the same sermons, from the same people, giving the same lip service of worship in a one to two-hour time frame, then I would like to express my deepest sympathies to those who call this biblical unity. This is not unity, this is uniformity, and this is not healthy for a body as diverse as those called from ...*every kindred and tongue and people and nation* (**Revelation 5:9,** See also **Revelation 14:6**). The Ecclesia boils down to disciples obeying God's word when it is inconvenient. Don't speak of your one faith, one Lord, one baptism (a scripture taken out of context almost every time it is quoted in our circles) if you cannot do the verses that surround it. Please read on, *I therefore, the prisoner* (Desmios - a captive, as one bound, [a ligament of the body]) *of the Lord, beseech you that ye walk worthy of the vocation* (Klēsis- invitation, the bidding) *wherewith ye are called,* ***With all lowliness and meekness, with longsuffering, forbearing one another in love; Endeavouring to keep the unity of the Spirit in the bond of peace. There is one body, and one Spirit, even as ye are called in one hope of your calling***; *One Lord, one faith, one baptism, One God and Father of all, who is above all, and through all, and in you all.* ***But unto every one of us is given grace*** *according to the measure of the gift of Christ* (**Ephesian 4:1-7**). If we can't or won't do the first part of Ephesians chapter four but proudly proclaim that we have one Lord, one faith, one baptism and one God, then we are hypocrites of the highest order, surpassing that of the scribes, lawyers, Pharisees, and Sadducees of Jesus' day. We should find a rock to lay on and sacrifice our pride, arrogance, and the theft of scriptures that we have used as we please to promote our doctrine and not Christ and His Kingdom.

I find it amazing that only four verses later in Ephesians, Paul writes of the five essentials for everyone in the church to be edified and trained to do the works of God. And yet, we have hoarded the ministry to those who we think are capable, educated by our organizations or bible schools, connected to the right organization, know how to preach or been in church the longest. We have treated the Ecclesia like a businessperson finds employees. We look outside for those who can contribute to our church while almost entirely neglecting those who sit in our midst. Why? Because we have neglected to teach and train them for service in ALL aspects of ministry to the body. We have raised a group of religious consumerists by not tarrying for and with one another.

What is religious consumerism? This is evidenced by an inordinate preoccupation for the regard of self, and whatever goods and services are required to satisfy self. One evidence of religious consumerism is the "Pareto Principle" (thought of by Vilfredo Federico Damaso Pareto, an Italian polymath and economist) which states that, for many phenomena, 80% of the consequences stem from 20% of the causes. In western style churches, eighty percent of the people allow the remaining twenty percent to do eighty percent of the ministry. That leaves much of the congregation as spectators watching the show, in other words, religious consumerists, who consume, without question, what others have deemed is good for them. This is diametrically opposed to the ideas spread by the Master and His disciples.

When we tarry for one another, we find hidden talents within the Ecclesia that will help the Kingdom. Young, old, trained, not trained, freed or slaves, uneducated or learned, women, men, it didn't matter, Christ filled them all and Christ used them all as and when He chose. Some lived, some died, some stayed in towns, many left to spread the Gospel of the Kingdom as they were led of the Holy Ghost (**Romans 8:14**) or persecution made it impossible to stay. Now we hold them in buildings, only train those who we think have potential and the rest support the few, then we have the audacity to call ourselves a fellowship or the church of God. May God forgive us for sacrificing the power that sits in the pew so we may support the few. While looking for the talented or capable, we often neglect to use our gifts, talents, time, and treasures to make disciples and fellowlabourers for the Kingdom of God of all who have been born again.

As mentioned earlier, in **1 Corinthians 12:12-27**, Paul speaks of the necessity of the *entire body* and in verses 22-23 he makes the very strong case that all members of the body are important by saying, *Nay, much more those members of the body, which seem to be more feeble, are necessary: And those* [members] *of the body, which we think to be less honourable, upon these we bestow more abundant honour; and our uncomely* [parts] *have more abundant comeliness.* We certainly do NOT do this in the overwhelming majority of our organizations, in fact we do the opposite. We bestow more honour on people who have climbed the ministerial ladder or who can contribute to the church funds or as a member of the *'worship or leadership team'*. The higher they have climbed, the more honour we bestow. I'm not saying they should not receive honour for what they do, but we have robbed honour from the seemingly feeble and uncomely parts and given it to those who already have honour.

Some people erroneously think that the average person in the pew is meant to bring people to the church building by sharing their testimony, show up for service and church building cleaning days and provide the finances for the leadership to do the work of God. This is a lie from the centre of the lake of fire and those that perpetuate this drivel have a special place in it. These forgotten or neglected souls not only **are** the work of God, but it is **they** who **do** the work of God when discipled the bible way and given the opportunity. We're in such a hurry to grow numbers that we neglect to tarry for those who don't seem to have much to offer other than their voices during the *'worship service'* and their tithe and offering, instead of finding out what each member has to offer the Kingdom of God through their life by actually getting to know them outside of church times and tarrying, anticipating, and becoming a part of each member's journey to contribute to the Commonwealth of the Kingdom of God.

The so-called *'ministry'* (today's meaning is a misnomer at best) is there to teach and guide the so-called *'average'* saint (also a misnomer) how to do the work of reconciliation and what we call ministry (see **Ephesians 4:11-12**). Terms such as *ministry, average saint* and *lay people* are an abhorrence to God. In the beginning everything God created was good, not average, and when He made man, it was very good, not above average. How can there be such a thing as an average saint? We have created three classes of believers. The upper echelon of ministry, the local ministry, and the regular saints. Shame on us for dividing the body, for creating schisms and treating people according to where we think they are in the body. Many remain *average* because they don't know how to be anything else. The real disciples of God do not believe in average, or even good. They strive to help one another to become excellent in God, thereby showing His excellency to the world (see **2 Corinthians 4:7**).

They are born and born-again to finish an extraordinary task begun by their Lord. That would be like calling the Great Wall of China a nice fence, the mighty Nile River a backyard creek, Mount Everest a big hill, the Statue of Liberty or the Eiffel Tower pretty garden ornaments. These are great feats of ingenuity and natural resources to be marvelled over. Why? Because they are a one-of-a-kind creation, whether of man or God. Is not a person who has submitted themselves to God according to His word and their own conscience also not a one-of-a-kind creation of this same God? A saint, according to Gods word in both the Old and Renewed Covenant, is a feast of experiences and a natural resource for the Ecclesia if we will just wait on God and do what He tells us to help them unleash their potential in Christ. The *saints-* Old Covenant- Qâdôsh (seen as sacred and holy) such as in **Daniel 7:8**, *But the* **saints** *of the most High* **shall take the kingdom, and possess the kingdom for ever**, *even for ever and ever.* Take note, it does NOT say the *'priests or the ministry'* shall take the kingdom and possess it for ever. The *saints-* Renewed Covenant- Hagios (sacred, an awful thing) such as **Matthew 27:52** *And the graves were opened; and many bodies of the* **saints** *which slept arose.* There are many more examples in God's word which depicts the saints as more than average. Calling those who will take the Kingdom and who will rise in a resurrection *'ordinary saints'* is an insult to the One who makes them sacred and holy.

Treating them as anything other than amazing and holy or with the utmost respect is to disrespect God Himself. Forcing them to bow to our so-called authority or to recognize us as special because we happen to stand behind a pulpit is an insult to God and whom He chooses to call as Paul reminds us in **Romans 8:30** *Moreover whom he did predestinate, them he also called: and whom he called, them he also justified: and whom he justified, them he also glorified.* Is this only for the *'ministry'*?

Allocating the saints to funding the church and leadership, filling pews or someone to bring people to church is a total misallocation of God's resources and holy purposes for His Ecclesia. Daniel saw the saints, God's chosen people take God's Kingdom, not the princes, priests, or a separated leadership. When it comes down to taking God's Kingdom and bringing it to the world, God does not see a faction of the Ecclesia doing all the work. Those who know how, must disciple those who do not: personally, daily, sacrificially. It takes time, patience, love and honouring those who *SEEM* to be weak, to be a member of the worldwide Ecclesia, and those older in the Lord who don't know how must admit their ignorance and learn from those who do (be aware, they may not be from your church/organization who know how to disciple the bible way). Trying to do the works of Christ (**John 14:12**) any other way (via man's traditions- *this is the way we've always done it*) is doomed to utter failure.

To whom was Paul writing when he said, *And all things are of God, who hath reconciled* **us** *to himself by Jesus Christ, and hath given to* **us** *the ministry of reconciliation; To wit, that God was in Christ, reconciling the world unto himself, not imputing their trespasses unto them; and hath committed unto* **us** *the word of reconciliation* (**2 Corinthians 2:5, 18**)? Who is the *us*? Is it not all people who need to be reconciled by those who are being reconciled (Katallagē: from Katallassō- to change mutually, to become different, to restore)? The very idea of elitism defies this scripture. As we wait on, for and with each other, we eliminate any chance of elitism, of one member being lifted above another, which only leads to pride and returns us to our selfish ways.

The Lord draws people who are seeking Him in their hearts to us (**John 12:32**) and we integrate them into the body so they can fulfill their purpose within the body. As God sees us becoming the body He called us to be, He adds *daily to the church such as should be saved* (**Acts 2:47**). He does this, not because we have numbers in pews or because we have a great ministry team, amazing outreach or worship teams, Sunday school programmes, belong to the right organization, or we have buildings to bring them to (whether rented, mortgaged or owned), but because the saints meet daily and shared their lives, their goods, their wisdom and revelations. Nobody said it would be easy, quick, or convenient. It takes practice (with many failures along the way), patience, sacrifice of time, and resources to tarry one for another.

Church folklore.

This is a set of traditional beliefs, myths, tales, and practices of a people, transmitted orally. A body of widely accepted but usually specious notions about a place, a group, or an institution. Today's Ecclesia has become addicted to the twice a week sermon/worship fix and has become incapable of being the church where it really matters, in the pews and their neighbourhoods. Being the church in the building does not promote God's word in the greater community, neither does it equate to a room full of disciples. We must move the entire body from milk to meat as quickly as possible and train them to feed themselves from the word of God and to hear from God for themselves, whilst having humble and wise elders, pastors, and bishops available to help them (not rule them) in their endeavours to grow in God.

This does not happen by osmosis, or by church attendance. It happens when we fellowship one with another outside of church functions sharing life's experiences, revelations, our failures as well as our successes. There will be much patience needed as we wait on each other; teaching each saint according to their ability (which takes more than just an anointed sermon once or twice a week, more than daily bible devotions, or finding the right bible study). It takes more than giving everyone the Fantastic Five every week just because there are new believers in the pews, while the hungry saints who need more than milk, starve to death. This is not what God calls a healthy Ecclesia, no matter how many modest looking people we have in our pews. A woman can dress up and say all the right things to win a man, but the husband will know what she is really like on the wedding night. The old saying, *the proof of the pudding is in the eating*, paints a rather clear picture of this. When we spend more on the façade than on caring for who is on the inside, we are nothing but an empty shell or as Jesus so eloquently put it, *Woe unto you, scribes and Pharisees, hypocrites! for **ye are like unto whited sepulchres**, which indeed appear beautiful outward, but are within **full of dead men's bones**, and of all uncleanness. Even so ye **also outwardly appear righteous** unto men, **but within ye are full of hypocrisy and iniquity*** (Matthew 23:27-28).

When I was in Harare, Zimbabwe in 2008, I saw many little shops with brightly painted fronts, beautiful handmade signage and yet when I went inside the shelves were bear with only one or two items. This was a country which for over one hundred years was the breadbasket of Africa until it gained independence in 1980 after which it hit hyper-inflation (the inflation rate as of December 2008 at 6.5 quindecillion novemdecillion percent (that is, 65 followed by 107 zeros. A Zimbabwean $100 billion note was needed to purchase three eggs in July 2008), where a suitcase full of these $100 billion notes could by a can of soft drink and maybe a packet of gum. I got a haircut in Harare at my hotel which cost me $750,000,000,000 ZD and a pair of nail clippers was $275,000,000,000 ZD. In 2009 notes were being printed at $1,000,000,000,000 (one trillion) and it wouldn't even buy a loaf of bread. Big numbers on pieces of paper that were worth nothing to the nation. Sound familiar?

I saw hungry people going from pretty store to pretty store, looking for something substantial to eat and going home hungry. Everybody was a billionaire (and in the end, a trillionaire), they had suitcases full of 100 billion-dollar notes, but the vast majority were going hungry. A very small cadre of elites, government bureaucrats and well-connected people were living far above the 'ordinary people'. Many of our churches are struggling with a pretty façade, but their shelves are bear of anything nutritional (other than the Fabulous Five), with only a few sweet things on the shelves due to hyper-inflating ourselves (*come to our church, we have the truth.* We may have the truth regarding the doctrine of salvation and one God but are we living the truth according to the rest of the bible?). This happens when we use all sorts of temporary measures and gimmicks to prop up the church (as the Zimbabwe government, propped up its worthless dollar), and we do not have the supply of personally trained disciples to fulfil the demand these truth seekers require.

When church meetings become about shouting, running the aisles, constantly speaking in tongues, and preaching the same type of messages, culminating in the ritual mass migration of sheeple going to the front (*to get what they need from God*), then going home and doing it all again, tomorrow, next week or next year, with no visible change in their hearts, families or their communities, we have shown that hyper-inflation of our services actually reduces the availability of the bread God offers a hungry person both in and out of the pew. During times of hyper-inflation, it is every man for himself.

When we tarry one for another, we help fulfil the law of Christ. **Ephesians 4:25** *Wherefore putting away lying, speak every man truth with his neighbour: for **we are members one of another**.* This is translatable to; *stop lying about loving God, especially when we do not or will not love the members of the body as we love ourselves or as Christ loves them.* When we neglect what we consider to be the insignificant members of the Ecclesia, those who sit alone in our pews every week, those whom no one takes to a restaurant let alone to their homes, those whom the saints don't call just to see how they are going or if they would like some fellowship, we are lying and hurting ourselves in the long run. It is imperative that we remember that a chain is only as strong as its weakest link.

As we tarry for one another, we strengthen the weak links, thereby strengthening the entire chain. The greater the work, the heavier the load, the stronger the chain needs to be. A safe lift on a crane for example, depends on several people fulfilling their roles including operators, riggers, signal persons, crane owners, crane operators, lift directors and site supervisors, the man who checks the nuts and bolts are tight, that the wheel pressure is just right and many more seemingly innocuous or insignificant jobs, and the communication between all these people must be clear and concise. If one of these aspects is out of kilter, there will be a dangerous work environment and all work ceases until it is fixed. There seems to be a lot of activity on the ground, while others are standing by idly. However, the purpose of the crane is not utilized, thus a lot of money and time is wasted. The same is true for much of the body of Christ. We seem to have a lot of revivals and meetings, with a lot of commotion, but are we doing the works of the Lord in our own homes, the homes of the saints and greater communities as Christ did? Are we laying down our lives for His friends?

Going back to the subject of time for a moment, it is the only commodity that God asks the Ecclesia to redeem. He came to redeem man, but we are commanded to redeem the time, **Ephesians 5:15** *See then that ye walk circumspectly, not as fools, but as wise, **Redeeming the time**, because the days are evil.* Paul tells us to walk circumspectly (Akribōs- diligently, most straitest), remember, it is "*the strait and narrow*" that leads to God. Time is split into two distinct categories in the Renewed Covenant. Kairos and Chronos time. The former is an occasion, season, a while, such as in **Mark 1:15** *And saying, The time is fulfilled, and the kingdom of God is at hand: repent ye, and believe the gospel,* while the latter being a space of time, a day, an hour as in **John 14:9** *Jesus saith unto him, Have I been so long time with you, and yet hast thou not known me, Philip? he that hath seen me hath seen the Father; and how sayest thou then, Shew us the Father?* These two translate to God's time and man's time. When we look at things from our perspective, we tend to try to make things happen in our space of time, but God says He will do what needs to be done in His time.

When we expect something or someone to change in our time we are, more than likely and without realizing it, telling God that He may control the universe but not our time.

I'm sure that after the fall of man, God was eager to do something to restore the relationship, but in His omniscience, He knew exactly when to come. God saw man destroying themselves in war, hating one another, killing one another, robbing, and cheating one another and God's heart was breaking. He watched as a nation He formed from a nomadic, tribal, and clannish people and former slaves and raised up to become the greatest in His power, had turned its back on Him, *The beginning of the word of the LORD by Hosea. And the LORD said to Hosea, Go, take unto thee a wife of whoredoms and children of whoredoms: for the land hath committed great whoredom, departing from the LORD* (**Hosea 1:2**).

He could have intervened at any time by just showing up and rightly proclaiming Himself as King, not only of Israel but of the whole world. But the *Kairos* time was not yet. We have approximately four hundred years where we have no recorded prophecy (between Malachi and John the Baptist). How hard that must have been for Israel to not hear from God for so long. How they must have felt abandoned. Jesus showed Himself to Saul in Acts chapter nine rather than chapter four or six because it was not Saul's time. There was much Saul needed to experience before His conversion. He needed to see Stephen forgive those who were stoning him, or the arrested believers staying true to their testimony and praying for him. He needed to be on the road to Damascus with people who heard the voice of God also and saw how the light blinded him (**Acts 9:7**).

God expects us to tarry, to wait and be patient with each other because there are things that we know not of that only God's timing will reveal and eventually restore. Like every other one of God's creation, time is meant to bring about His glory. *The trees of the fields clap their hands* (**Isaiah 55:12**), *The earth* (God's creation which includes time) *is the LORD'S, and the fulness thereof; the world, and they that dwell therein* (**Psalm 24:1**) and God told Abraham and Sarah, *Is any thing too hard for the LORD?* **At the time appointed** *I will return unto thee, according to the time of life, and Sarah shall have a son* (**Genesis 18:14**).

If we are to do things in our timeframe, then there would be no need to tarry. The disciples were told to tarry for the Holy Ghost. No timeframe was given, just tarry (like the farmer with his crop, they were to wait with expectation. They did not know they had ten days to do the ordinary things of life like fetch water, cook meals, encourage one another, worship, and pray and so on) and when God was ready, it would happen (see **Luke 24:49** for an example of waiting on God). We tarry one for another in God's space and time for God's season and in expectation of what God will do to, for and with one another. Lao Tzu is believed to have said *"Time is a created thing. To say 'I don't have time,' is like saying, 'I don't want to"*, and should we take this to heart I believe it will change our thinking, our lives and the lives of those in the Ecclesia.

Chapter 25.

Consider one another.

Hebrews 10:24 *And let us **consider** one another to provoke unto love **and** to good works:*

Proverbs 6:6 *Go to the ant, thou sluggard; **consider** her ways, and be wise:*

Here we have a conflict of interest between the biblical and our modern definition of *consider*. The 21st century word, consider, means to think carefully about (something), typically before deciding, like buying a car or house, but the biblical word has a deeper meaning. Here, God is telling us to Katanoeō- to observe fully, to behold, discover, perceive (**to truly see beyond the surface**), but we are to do so with one another. Solomon tells us to *consider* (Râ'âh- to see and discern, to advice self). However, we are to do these things for a purpose. In Solomon's case it is to see how the ant lives, works, gathers food, and dies for the nest, not for itself. Paul tells us to see how we can provoke each other *unto love **and** good works*. Please note the connective word *and* (Kai-cumulative, it is also translated as- even, moreover, then, and likewise). It is seeing one another for who we really are, it is discovering how we are more alike than different, it is beholding God that is in the fellow members of the worldwide Ecclesia and then do something about it by helping each other achieve our goals which is manifested through love **and** good works. It is, in essence, doing all those things in order to provoke or as the Greek puts it; Paroxusmos, *to sharpen alongside and incite* unto love **and** good works and it comes with the deeper understanding of stirring up. We are to incite or inflame each other to love *and* good works.

Inciting a crowd to stampede by yelling fire in a crowded hall, a discontented group of people to riot and damage property or urging someone to kill another, carries with it severe punishments, and rightly so. However, inciting someone to love *and* good works carries a reward that lasts an eternity. Just as a riot or a stampede is almost impossible to stop, so is a group of people who are bent on promoting *love and good works* within His Ecclesia. This then translates to others outside the Ecclesia who, seeing what we are really all about (more than our ritualistic and metronomic services), will be drawn to the God that the Ecclesia is so excited about. We end up growing without the need for gimmicks such as Christmas and Easter programmes, trunk or treat, bring a friend to church day, potlucks, family games nights, special revival events or block/spring/fall festivals. To incite the church will try even the most dedicated leaders (mainly because the saints have been lulled into a false sense of security that all these works are to be done by the elites in the hierarchy). It will take time and patience to teach to the consumerist believer who is mainly there for what they can get from church and God, but persistence will ultimately result in a stronger and powerful body God can use at His discretion. For a while there may be no growth in numbers, in fact, we may even lose several lazy or false brethren (tare, sucking the goodness from the wheat), this is to be expected and it is okay with God. Once the believers are incited to *love and good works*, growth will begin naturally sans gimmicks and programmes. The savings on church funds can then be distributed to those in need, *first to those of the household of faith,* then to the surrounding neighbourhood (see **Galatians 6:10**).

The community at large will see dedicated disciples in their midst for who they really are and will be attracted by the word of God that dwells in them (**John 15:7**). How they live that word amongst the brethren will be how the new believer will be expected to live when they come in. How will this be evident? Primarily, these freshly minted disciples will have a deeper meaning of what it means to follow Christ and they will invite others into their lives, not the church building to witness a synchronized and metronomic show meant to portray our living God in under two hours. Second, the seeker will have real life questions and the real disciple will have real life lived answers, not pulpit platitudes we have collected on our twice weekly scriptural fixes.

According to **Hebrews 10:24** in order to *...**consider** one another to provoke unto love and to good works:* we must purposefully seek out, be proactive if you will, how we can provoke one another. There is scripture which tells us that we must not provoke one another in a negative sense, *Fathers, provoke **not** your children to wrath: but bring them up in the nurture and admonition of the Lord* (**Ephesians 6:4,** see also **Colossians 3:21**) but we will deal more on some of the not to's in the latter part of this book.

God told Moses that He was going to use the heathen nations to provoke, or motivate if you will, Israel into being what she was created to be. Paul quotes God in **Romans 10:19** *But I say, Did not Israel know? First Moses saith, I will **provoke** you to jealousy by them that are no people, and by a foolish nation I will anger you.* This was meant to provoke God's people unto repentance and become the light that God had called them to be in **Isaiah 49:6** *And he said, It is a light thing that thou shouldest be my servant to raise up the tribes of Jacob, and to restore the preserved of Israel: I will also give thee for a light to the Gentiles, that thou mayest be my salvation unto the end of the earth.* We have all heard of people being provoked into a frenzy such as food riots and political riots. There was a riot that was provoked by the leaders of the Jews in Jesus' day in **Matthew 27:20** *But the chief priests and elders persuaded the multitude that they should ask Barabbas, and destroy Jesus,* and **John 18:40** *Then cried they all again, saying, Not this man, but Barabbas. Now Barabbas was a robber,* while only 24 hours earlier these same people, *Took branches of palm trees, and went forth to meet him* (Y'shua)*, and cried, Hosanna: Blessed is the King of Israel that cometh in the name of the Lord* (**John 12:13**).

As these leaders provoked the people to do an evil thing, we are to consider how we will provoke one another to *love and good works.* Why is that? Well, Jesus said that the world would know we are His disciples by the love we have one to another and by the works that we do (**John 13:13, James 2:18**). It doesn't get clearer than that, does it?

Get in Sync.

Synchronized describes many of our church services perfectly. When did we begin to believe and measure a church service went off without a hitch, the singers were all on key, the message was anointed or, *"everyone"* came to the front, that we had great church? Synchronized means to represent or arrange (events) to indicate coincidence or coexistence (Merriam Webster). Synchronized swimmers put on a good show. We marvel at their ability to be at the right place, at the right time, doing the same thing until the show is over. They train for months and years and win all sorts of awards and accolades. Can you imagine, they got an award for being robotic. But at the end of the day, they go to their daily lives, doing their own thing and have their own struggles. Their unity is limited to a pre-set show for the public to enjoy or medals to be won (e.g., in the church realm it is which church or district gave the most, has the most people in their church or has the biggest or best buildings, missionary support, or youth group that we class as successes and people try to emulate). Our church services have become places where we try extraordinarily hard to look the same, have all the pieces of the service going off without a hitch (the sound, the musicians, the lighting, the flowers, the greeters etc.) so the public will see we have our acts together. Sadly though, most of the people go back to the daily grind and struggles after they've just sung how they got the victory, how He is the way maker and how they have the joy, joy, joy, joy down in their hearts. The real sad part is that most of the people in that church have no idea what the other believers sitting in the same pews struggle with daily because we do not consider (perceive or understand) one another as we are commanded to do. We *wow* and *marvel* at the synchronized service, the presence of the Lord and the anointed message. We say a quick hello, look each other in the face and boldly call each other brother and sister, then ignore each other until the next meeting. We have not considered (perceived nor understood) one another, let alone provoked one another to *love **and** good works*, yet we will ask God for things or worse yet, ask God to bring in more people that we can ignore. Tsk Tsk Tsk!

We all get distracted from time to time from our purposes by sickness, children, disasters, political climate, and just plain routine. The purpose of the body of Christ (not just the leadership) is to incite us, stir us up, sharpen our skills and bring us back in line with what we are meant to be (going to church, sitting still until we are told we can do something is not a purpose in life. This sounds more like being treated as a child). If it is to pray, worship, study, give, love, disciple one another, visit one another, then so let it be that a brother or sister can come alongside us and be used of God to put us back on track or help us move forward without us taking offense. God knows we struggle doing that ourselves, so He provided a mechanism to achieve this. The Master calls it His Ecclesia.

As we consider one another it is not on how to judge one another or decide how we will treat each other because somehow, they have disappointed us, but rather so that we can fully observe and perceive each other's needs through prayer and observation, their strengths and weaknesses and find a way to help each other to fulfil those needs. It is to look for ways on how to provoke one another to *love **and** good works*, first within the Ecclesia then to look further afield to the community at large. Look at the words of the Master in His Sermon on the Mount, Christ is talking to His people, the Jews, when He tells them, *Let your light so shine before men, that they may see your good works, and glorify your Father which is in heaven* (**Matthew 5:16**). He tells them that their works will make the world glorify God. He is inciting them to love *and* good works. We may hear a few sermons in a year on loving one another but precious few on good works, even fewer on provoking each other to do both.

As mentioned earlier, God does not command us to do things we are already doing. For example, we are commanded to love and give, because, generally, people struggle with loving and giving to one another. The reason Paul wrote the command concerning good works is because selfishness has permeated every aspect of society and, sadly the church is no exception. God knew that we would need to be provoked into doing good works for no other reason than for the good work itself. We are told to love and give, not necessarily to look for a return on that loving and giving.

As mentioned earlier, Jesus spoke of the folly of loving only those who love us back in **Luke 6:32** *For if ye love them which love you, what thank have ye? for sinners also love those that love them. And if ye do good to them which do good to you, what thank have ye? for sinners also do even the same. And if ye lend to them of whom ye hope to receive, what thank have ye? for sinners also lend to sinners, to receive as much again.* This type of loving and giving is of the world, but Jesus commands us to step up our game and go beyond the worldly norm when He says in verse 35, *But* *love ye your enemies, and do good, and lend* (Daneizō- from Daneion- a gift. This means to give with no thought of getting it back. Don't worry, if we really believe God is our supply, when we need it, God will resupply it)*, **hoping for nothing again***; and your reward shall be great, and ye shall be the children of the Highest: for he is kind* (Chrēstos- good and useful) *unto the unthankful and to the evil.* Notice, it is in our giving that we *...shall be children of the Highest.* Doing good to and for one another while looking for a return or gain is not the attitude which God looks for in His Ecclesia. He gives rain and sunshine to both sinners and saints. He gives for the sake of giving; it is up to us whether we will pass on that giving.

We have somehow come to think that good works is only giving food or money and other such things (the Jews throughout history were good givers to the poor and indigent. The tithe was specifically for the poor, the widow, the orphans and homeless. Only 1/10 of the tithe was given to the priests, and that is because they were not allowed to own houses, lands, or businesses), but Jesus adds to this in verses 36-37 *Be ye therefore merciful, as your Father also is merciful. Judge not, and ye shall not be judged: condemn not, and ye shall not be condemned: forgive, and ye shall be forgiven.* Mercy, grace, respect, honour, forgiveness, time, talents as well as treasures are just as important a good work as a hot meal and shelter. An important form of good works is of our precious time or talents. Sometimes it takes hard work putting down our flesh and doing what is necessary for others or giving mercy where we have been wronged or forgiveness to someone who has hurt us.

The Master then rounds it off with one of the most misquoted and misunderstood verses in the word of God. Remember, we are talking about the Sermon on the Mount which is all about what the Kingdom of God is like. In Verse 38 Jesus gives a command *Give, and it shall be given unto you; good measure, pressed down, and shaken together, and running over, shall men give into your bosom. For with the same measure that ye mete withal it shall be measured to you again.* Once again, we see no reference here (or anywhere else in chapters five or six for that matter) to money? He is speaking of an entire life of service manifested through giving and good works.

These are the things we are to look for (consider) in each other for the sole purpose of provoking each other to *love and good works.* It did not say good thoughts, good prayers, or good beliefs, good doctrines, but good works. *Works* is translated as Ergon which comes from Ergō meaning to work, toil (as an effort or occupation) by implication an act, deed, labour. This is also where we get the word ergonomics, which is defined as an applied science concerned with designing and arranging things people use so that the people and things interact most efficiently and safely. It is also the scientific study of people and their working conditions, especially done in order to improve effectiveness. It seems that God is a very ergonomic God.

Many people are frightened off by the term *good works* because they have had it shoved down their collective throats that good works can't save them and that is true, good works cannot get our names into the Book of Life. However, what then do we do with **Ephesian 2:10** *For we are his workmanship* (His product, His fabric, the thing that He made)*, **created*** (Ktizō- through the idea of the proprietorship of the manufacturer); to fabricate, that is, found or form originally) ***in Christ Jesus unto*** (toward, for, to) ***good works*** (Agathos Ergon- beneficial labour, toil, act or deeds)*, which God hath before ordained* (Proetoimazō- to fit up in advance) *that **we should walk*** (Peripateō- to tread all around, walk at large (especially as proof of ability), to live, deport oneself, follow as a companion, votary [to make vows of dedication to religious service], to go, be occupied with) ***in them***. How can we say we have a walk with God and not walk in the good works that were ordained (set or put down in advance) for us before we began our walk with God? As I have said for a long time now, we were not born again to become an ornament around the neck of God but an instrument in the hands of God.

What type of instrument? One that He can wield at any time for the purpose of showing Himself to the world. We must consider how we can provoke one another to walk in love and the good works He has ordained for us from the beginning.

Paul wrote to his son in the Lord, Timothy, *Wherefore I put thee in remembrance that thou stir up* (re-kindle) *the gift of God, which is in thee by the putting on of my hands* (**1 Timothy 1:6**). What gift of God is Paul talking about here? The gift of the Holy Ghost (who teaches and brings to remembrance **John 14:26**) and all the works that He does in, for and through the true disciples in the Ecclesia.

Chapter 26.

Submitting one to another.

Ephesians 5:21 *Submitting yourselves* one to another in the fear of God.

We are about to venture into a minefield, but please bear with me. If we tread through the word of God where the early Ecclesia trod, we will come through the minefield unscathed and armed with knowledge to help others through this needlessly stressful part of learning about and submitting to each other.

First, let me state what this passage does NOT tell us. It does not say that submission only goes in one direction, such as saints only submit yourselves to your pastors, pastors only submit yourselves to your bishops, bishops only submit yourselves to your district presbyters, district presbyters only submit yourselves to your state superintendent and state superintendent only submit yourselves to the national board. The fallacy of this type of hierarchical submission is not biblical and must cease, or we will go the way of the dodo bird, 8 track cassette players and all denominations that have died in their traditions having lost their power to make a difference in the broader world.

The term *submitting yourselves* is one word which is a combination of two Greek words, *Hupo* and *Tasso,* and together they determine what type of submission we are to have one toward another. Hupo means to be under or beneath and Tasso is to arrange in an orderly manner or to determine, and when we take the plural of yourselves (not of the word *you*), we get the phrase *to be beneath one another* (not beneath one) *in and for an orderly fashion*.

To be underneath or under something would be likened to supporting it. The foundation under a building is supporting it, holding it up so to speak. Do we think that the foundation of a building is somehow subordinate to the structure that rests upon it? To submit to one another is to support one another.

Romans 12:10 gives a clearer indication of beneath one another. *Be kindly affectioned one to another with brotherly love; in honour **preferring** one another,* (Proēgeomai- to lead the way for others, that is, show deference). The Berean Study Bible puts it succinctly by saying; *Be devoted to one another in brotherly love. Outdo yourselves in honouring one another.*

Let me give you a few examples of this touchy subject (though it is mainly touchy to those who are bound to and by their organizational/hierarchical/bureaucratic thinking). It is written of Jesus, our great example, in **Luke 24:28-29** *And they drew nigh unto the village, whither they went: and he made as though he would have gone further. But they constrained* (Parabiazomai) *him, saying, Abide with us: for it is toward evening, and the day is far spent. And he went in to tarry with them.* Here we see Jesus had a mind to go elsewhere but at their Parabiazomai- to force contrary to nature, their compelling by entreaty, He did what they wanted Him to do. He submitted Himself to their desire for more fellowship and teaching though they did not really know who it was they were talking to as evidenced in verse 30-31 *And it came to pass, as he sat at meat with them, he took bread, and blessed it, and brake, and gave to them. And their eyes were opened, and they knew him; and he vanished out of their sight.* Though He was the risen Saviour, He submitted Himself to the desires of others.

Another instance was when Paul was shipwrecked on the Mediterranean island of Melita (now called Malta) in Acts 28. The barbarians entreated him to stay with them, mainly because their need for teaching and prayer was greater than his need to get to Rome at that time. He submitted or placed himself under their desires for the common good of those on the island. He still fulfilled his mission to go to Rome, but his submission to others for a time was important for the whole island of Malta. In **Acts 10:19-20** we read of how Peter was to submit himself to three gentile strangers (which a Jew would never condescend to do) and not doubt they were sent from God. In verse 26 when Cornelius bowed down to Peter, we see his attitude, *But Peter took him up, saying, Stand up; I myself also am a man.* In other words, *"Don't bow down to me, I'm not better or worse than you, we are together in this journey"*.

After this wonderful gift of the Holy Ghost was bestowed upon the gentiles in Cornelius' household, we read in **Acts 10:48** *And he commanded them to be baptized in the name of the Lord. Then prayed they him to tarry certain days.* The word *prayed* is an interesting word because it does not mean that they prayed to him as one of lower station would pray to one of a higher station, but they requested, beseeched, desired, and entreated him, the word also means they interrogated or compelled him (Erōtaō) to stay, and he did. The apostle Peter had submitted himself to others who were within the Ecclesia. Peter, who was with Jesus from the beginning and was the first person to preach of the Kingdom of God after the resurrection, submitted to a gentile's desire for more time to know more of God and then stayed longer. We read of no word from God that Peter should stay longer. He stayed because they wanted him to stay. He submitted to their desires.

When submission goes only one way (submit to those above) the chances of abuse of power (whether intentional or otherwise, recognized or not) becomes prevalent within any organization, and sadly within the Ecclesia also. That is why Paul wrote that submission must go both ways. When we submit one to another (which Paul wrote to the entire Ecclesia), it is not handing over control, but a willing deference to learn from someone on a different pay scale so to speak. A military commander would be the greatest of dangerous fools if he did not heed the warnings of those in the lower ranks just because he is of a higher rank. Military history is replete with instances of high-ranking officers who did not heed warnings or first-hand information from men of considerably lower rank regarding tactical planning and the result turned into major disasters needlessly costing tens of thousands of lives (more on this shortly).

The leading maker of film for cameras for over a century was Kodak. No-one came close to their market share. But when digital cameras started to become popular in the late 90s, many engineers and people on the frontline of the company urged the CEO and the board of Kodak to change with the market. They refused citing that they were market leaders and that film would be the way of the future for a long time. They would not listen to those lower on the totem pole and in 2012 Kodak filed for bankruptcy. Who were these people that they, the ones who run the company, should submit to other's knowledge on a matter?

Submission one to another (down as well as up) does not lower our IQ nor our standing with God. It does not negate authority neither is it a sign of weakness. It shows a humility which is rare in much of the leadership in many organizations and in many churches today and, it can be said, has been the downfall of far too many civilizations and organizations, be they secular or religious. It is extremely difficult for us in our modern way of thinking to recognize, but Peter was introducing the Christian family to an entirely new community. He had learned from his Rabbi that there was to be a new way of operating God's Kingdom. He was about to start a group of people that transcended the rigid hierarchy of human institutions (the Sanhedrin, priests, bureaucracy, and Rome), and usher in a community in which submission is mutual, voluntary and all are free to express their thoughts, give and express their love for God and worshipping the creator through their own conscience (**2 Corinthians 9:7, 1 Timothy 1:5**). They were free to grow at their own pace with the help of this same community.

We must heed the advice given to us in the word of God regardless of whom it comes through. I have known many church leaders who were given great advice from people outside of their hierarchical pyramid and refused to heed it. Then, eventually when someone from their organization made mention of it, they took the advice. Sadly, in far too many instances, it was too little, too late. To the detriment of themselves, the congregation, and the surrounding community, the word of God was stifled. In many cases it was far more difficult than necessary to affect a turnaround. Much time, resources, and finances were needed and wasted when simple submission would have sufficed. The same goes with those who sit in the pews. Submission is for all, not just from the top. If they will only heed advice from their pastor (whom they barely know) while others who know them well are ignored, they will have placed themselves in a very precarious position. Those who see and pray for us regularly can help to prevent a great fall in all aspects of church functions.

Breaking the pattern.

History is replete with instances of men and women who refused to take advice from those who were not on their level, in their group or their organization. The example of Kodak is a most recent catastrophe, but this has been going on for centuries. Allow me to give you an example that cost almost 20 million lives. Before Germany invaded Russia (June 22, 1941), the dictator, Joseph Stalin, was warned more than ninety times over several months by the allies that Hitler was preparing to invade Russia. Even those in his own spy organization (NKVD) were too afraid to go against what Stalin believed to be fact. When they tried to tell him, he dismissed them or had them put in prison. Even though the information was verified multiple times, Stalin was unwilling to submit his thinking to those of lesser rank or trust any information from another spy organization, though they had the same purpose, the defeat of Nazi Germany. Because of his stubbornness to listen and respond to people outside of his normal sphere of influence, 8.6 million Russian soldiers were needlessly killed, wounded, missing in action, or captured in less than one year. This does not include civilians who were killed, tortured, or starved to death (more than 10 million). Just for perspective, this equates to a population the size of New York, 75% of the population of Australia or 30% of England's population, who died because one man would not submit to people he considered to be of lower status than himself. The statistics are about the same for the Germans and the Japanese during WW2. America was warned weeks ahead of the Pearl Harbour attack on December 7th, 1941, that Japan was planning something against the US, but because it did not come from a regular source, this information was ignored, and 2,403 Americans needlessly lost their lives in one day. America was plunged into a war for which it was ill prepared. Facts are facts, no matter who delivers them. Jesus brought truth to the Sanhedrin, but because He was not one of their own, an unknown with no earthly conferred authority, truth was rejected.

The inability of anyone to submit to those around them with the same purpose (the furtherance of the Kingdom of God for instance) shows not just pride but also the utmost of ignorance in God's word or worse still, arrogance that this part of God's word does not apply to them. God despises arrogance as the writers of **1 Samuel 2:3** and **Isaiah 13:11** tell us; *Talk no more so exceeding proudly;*

let not arrogancy (`âthâq- in the sense of license; impudence, grievous (hard) things, stiff [necked]) *come out of your mouth: for the LORD is a God of knowledge, and by him actions are weighed,* and once again, *And I will punish the world for their evil, and the wicked for their iniquity; and **I will cause the arrogancy*** (Gâ'ôn- pomp [and ceremony], pride, proud, swelling) ***of the proud to cease, and will lay low the haughtiness of the terrible*** (see also **Romans 12:3, Proverbs 8:13** and **Luke 11:9-14**). Biblical submission one to another is God's way of preventing arrogancy and maintaining humility in the Ecclesia. Submission to the word brings life no matter whose lips speak it.

One man or organization does not have all the answers and when we work together relying on the knowledge and experience of all members of the Ecclesia (regardless of what sticker they wear), we will be what God has called us to be, the light of the world and salt of the earth.

We submit to one another in the Lord so that we may learn from one another the intricacies of life's different stages. The younger ones in the Lord would be wise to listen and show deference (not military style submission) to those who are older in the Lord, those who have seen the hardships that the enemy would bring on a new believer. However, there is also much the older saints and leadership can learn and re-learn from the new disciples. We learn, if not for ourselves for now, perhaps for another time or perhaps for someone else. The modern church in western society has perfected the art of making certain people feel unnecessary or unimportant unless it is a means to an end (*we need you in church service because… your giving helps build the church, you have a talent we can use* and so on). Every member of the Ecclesia is necessary and important for who they are, not just what they can do, and the experience of their lives can reach and teach each one of us if we will only let it, no matter what position they hold in their organization, if any at all.

Submission is not to be done because of the fear of man, but as Paul rounded off the verse in **Ephesians 5:21** *…in the fear of the Lord.* We can submit for the wrong reason. The prophet Isaiah tells us, *I, even I, am he that comforteth you: **who art thou, that thou shouldest be afraid of a man** that shall die, and of the son of man which shall be made as grass* (**Isaiah 51:12**). When we do or do not do for the wrong reason, then it actually goes against us in the long run.

Here's an example of doing the right thing for the wrong reason.

Two people are waiting for a job interview, both find an envelope on a side table in the room. They open it and find three $100 bills. Their internal conversation goes something like this…

Person #1. I really need that $300 because my rent is due, and I need gas money for the next few days, but I'd better not take it because I might get caught and I'd go to jail for theft.

Person #2. I really need the money because my daughter desperately needs textbooks for school, but to take it would displease God and I love Him too much to do that.

Both did not take the money but for two different reasons. God is equally as interested in our heart condition as in our actions, mainly because the heart condition establishes and primes the correct action (to please God). Solomon warns us of this incorrect fear in **Proverbs 29:25** *The **fear of man brings a snare*** (Môqêsh- a noose for catching dumb animals, a hook), *But he who trusts* (Bâṭach- to hie (run) for refuge, be confident and sure) *in the LORD will be exalted.* Jesus Himself gives us a great picture of whom we are to fear in **Luke 12:4-5** *And I say unto you my friends, Be not afraid of them that kill the body, and after that have no more that they can do. But I will forewarn you whom ye shall fear: Fear him, which after he hath killed hath power to cast into hell; yea, I say unto you, **Fear him**.*

There are only three non-negotiable forms of submission that mainly go up in the Renewed Covenant.

1. *Wives are to submits themselves to your own husbands as they would unto the Lord.* In the home, men should and must lead, and women must comprehensively encourage and embrace his leadership. Leadership and submission do not start only when a decision is to be made; it begins long before. Husbands are not to abdicate their authority over their wives because it is easier than arguing with them. They are to put aside all selfishness and repressive dominance and lead with love. Husbands obey the Lord regarding their wives by laying down their lives for them as they tirelessly, selflessly, and most importantly, seek their wives' longest term and highest good (**Ephesian. 5:22-29**). This does not negate the need for a husband to sometimes submit to his wife when it is for her benefit.

2. *Children obey (submit) to your parents.* When children are allowed to run the household, they will eventually destroy the household (**Ephesian 6:1** and **Colossians 3:20**). Children are not capable of seeing past the moment and thus all decisions they make are based on the here and now and how it will affect them at this moment. They want the candy now because they feel like it, they don't want to go to bed because they don't feel like it, they don't want to do their homework because they want to play now and so on. However, by submitting themselves to the parents, they get a better view of future events based on wisdom gained from the parent's past.

3. And last, but by no means least, *demons are subject* (must submit) *to the Ecclesia in His name as they fulfil God's given purpose* (**Luke 10:17, Romans 8:28**). If we are not fulfilling our God given command to go and preach the Gospel of the Commonwealth of the Kingdom of God only and make disciples, then why would the demonic realm submit to us? First submit to God and His word, then the devil will flee (**James 4:7**). Submission must be towards God and His word as revealed by His spirit and it is only then that the demonic realm must submit to the disciples of Christ.

To paraphrase a well-known 16th century preacher; *"When a husband lovingly bears the burdens of his wife, is that not subjection? When a father [or mother] lovingly gives themselves for their children, there is subjection. When we assist one another, it is servitude or subjection to one another. Thus, there would seem to be a sense in which we all are mutually to submit to one another, without abandoning our roles of God-given authority. This would have Paul saying, 'Filled with the Spirit believers' relationships should be marked by joyful submission to one another out of the fear of Christ'."* (John Calvin, Banner of Truth, p. 561).

Submission one to another for the sake of the Commonwealth of the Kingdom of God will have a greater impact on the spiritual growth of the members of the Ecclesia than mindless submission to any one person or an organization. God knows the power of pride and has instigated a way of circumventing it when we submit to one another out of a willing deference to those whom God has bought with His precious blood. It is wisdom to submit to someone who has shown by their lives that they have a close walk with God so long as they are willing to *submit to one another* as the scripture clearly and concisely states when it is in the best interest of the Ecclesia.

Ephesians 5:21 is based on adherence to verse 18 *And be not drunk with wine, wherein is excess; but be filled with the Spirit;* When one is filled with the spirit, it is no longer about them, but being about the Father's business in building the Commonwealth of the Kingdom of God. The Father's business is more than starting churches, leading worship service, or going to conferences and camp meetings. The Father's business is more than pulpit time or board meetings. It is meeting the needs of one another in the name of Him who has chosen us to do the works He did whilst He was on earth. We will mutually defer to each other if it is done in the fear of the Lord and in His name, that is, they will submit to what is in accordance with pleasing God, not what is convenient or places us as number one.

We do not live in a spiritual democracy where we do what the majority votes for, neither do we live in a spiritual oligarchy (a small group of people having control of a country, organization, institution, and yes, that includes the Ecclesia). Neither is biblical and both are detrimental to the health and wellbeing of the Commonwealth of the Kingdom of God and its subjects. Submitting one to another just means that, *I am going to lay down my rights and privileges in order to help you grow in the Lord in a manner that best suits you and will also be best for the Commonwealth of the Kingdom of God here on earth.* Submission one to another in the eyes of God has a powerful affect in the spiritual realm.

Let me give you an example. A squad of marines or army (usually about 9 men run by a corporal) is on patrol and comes across a target of opportunity. They radio back to headquarters and call in a fire mission. The artillery base (usually a battalion run by a lieutenant colonel) drops what they're doing and pours whatever ordinance (high explosives, smoke, anti-personnel, phosphorus) is necessary in order to accomplish the mission (destroy the target, disrupt movement etc.). The one calling for the fire mission determines what is needed, not the one providing the shells. The lieutenant colonel is now doing exactly what a corporal is telling him to do. Does this make the corporal greater than the lieutenant colonel or lessen the rank of the lieutenant colonel? Of course not. It means that the eyes and ears of another can see and hear clearer than someone else and if the mission is to be achieved, submission must go both ways at different times. A ranking officer suffering from malaria is subject to fever delusions and a medic can order said officer to step down. He does so for the health of the officer, mainly in the interest of the unit, and because the medic knows more about a sickness or injury, the ranking officer will submit. It is not a power play, but for the health, morale, and overall wellbeing of the unit.

There may be differing views on issues within the Ecclesia and submission one to another allows all views to be considered and submission or deference to one another, assures that the unity of the Ecclesia and its mission takes the highest priority. Leadership does not say, *because I said so,* but rather, *talk to me about what you see, and I will humbly take it to God. His point of view is far greater than mine. When we have both taken it to God we can come together and fulfill the will of God.*

In the days when the Roman Catholic church was the only game in town, there was a devastating punishment laid upon people of differing views. If a parishioner had a different opinion from the leadership on *any* matter, they can be stripped bare of all earthly belongings and as devastating as that may be, a far greater disaster would befall them. They are stripped of their community (excommunication). We do this to one extent or another today in many of our churches. We ostracize others with differing views or personalities that don't fit our little group. It seems some of us have reverted to the ways of the Roman Catholic church. Biblically, excommunication was a last resort, after ALL options had been exhausted and even then, it was done to restore a person to the Kingdom of God, NEVER AS A PUNISHMENT. Please read that last sentence again.

That is why excommunication was a fate worse than death within the Roman Catholic Church. The church was the only community that had anything to do with the afterlife and to be isolated from that community was to be isolated from God Himself (or so the church told everybody). There was no listening to, let alone considering, another's view and so submission only went up and never down. This is why the church had such a hold on the common folk, until people like the Waldensians, the Lollards, the Hussites, the Anabaptists who showed the common people that they actually mattered, were more than just a means to an end (to build bigger and more ornate cathedrals and parsonages and fill the coffers of the church) and that their spiritual and physical health was the responsibility of each individual in the community first and all other matters a distant second.

By submitting to one another we learn from one another things that only another can teach through their life's experiences. This pleases God infinitely more than using authority to dictate or mandate to others what we feel is God's will. The results are that all will benefit, in one way or another, in the growth of the Commonwealth of the Kingdom of God manifested on this planet as it is in heaven.

For an in-depth understanding of biblical submission, please read *To Obey Or Not To Obey. That Is The Question?* My contact details are in the back of this book.

Chapter 27.

Comfort one another.

1 Thessalonians 4:18 *Wherefore **comfort** one another with these words.*

1 Thessalonians 5:11 *Wherefore **comfort yourselves** together, **and edify one another**, even as also ye do.*

Here we see two diverse ways of comforting. Comforting one another and comforting ourselves, but in doing the latter we must also edify one another.

There is much heartache, brokenness, and grief in this world and whether it be from death, trauma, substance abuse, illness, divorce or even loneliness, in the midst of all that we are commanded to comfort one another. Can there be a greater way to show a grieving person true biblical love than comforting them in their most trying times? Once again, we have a disparity between the modern definition of comfort and the biblical one. To comfort someone in this day and age is to offer someone a state of physical ease and freedom from pain or constraint. Though this is a start, the biblical meaning goes far beyond this superficial (though still necessary) explanation. Allow me to clarify.

We are told of a story about a woman's last-ditch attempt to avoid a horrible death by haemorrhaging and how her faith in God's word was eventually rewarded with more than just a miracle healing. *For she said within herself, If I may but touch his garment, I shall be whole. But Jesus turned him about, and when he saw her, he said, Daughter, **be of good comfort**; thy faith hath made thee whole. And the woman was made whole from that hour* (**Matthew 9:21-22**). Before The Master healer told her she was healed, He told her two other things. He called her daughter and to be comforted.

A woman, who had a death sentence due to illness, in her darkest hour, when all hope in the natural was gone and only had God's word left, saw that the word just walked into town (**John 1:1-2**). She was bound and determined to get to the manifestation of the word before it walked away. Being a Jewess, she knew the scriptures well and would have remembered **Malachi 4:2** *But unto you that fear my name shall the Sun of righteousness arise **with healing in his wings**; and ye shall go forth, and grow up as calves of the stall.* But she had a dilemma on her hands. Being unclean, she could not come within touching distance of others. According to the Levitical law, if a woman's issue of blood lasts more than seven days, she is to stay outside the camp until the issue had stopped (**Leviticus 15:25**). Her issue lasted twelve years. Every bed she laid on, chair she sat on, every item of clothing she owns and everyone who touched her, and she touched, became ceremonially unclean. Imagine having a severe and contagious flu (which normally lasts a week) that lasts for twelve years, and nobody wants to be near you for fear of catching it. The disease was bad, but the emotional toll would have been horrific. This woman desperately needs comfort, not just a healing. She covered herself with a cloth and crawled on her knees to trust God one last time.

Now, we move to the protagonist of the story. Every Rabbi wore his *tallit katan* (prayer shawl- a fringed garment traditionally worn either under or over the clothing of Jewish males and has special twined and knotted fringes known as *tzitzit* attached at its four corners). The Hebrew word in **Malachi 4:2** for wings is Kanaph meaning an edge or extremity, the uttermost parts; so, what she wanted to touch was the edge, the outermost parts of Jesus' prayer shawl also known as wings. She heard and saw in this Rabbi, power that was not in any other man and knew that in His *tallit* there must have been power also.

Think about it for a moment and put yourself in her shoes: twelve years of doctors, pain, sleepless nights, she had been isolated, alone and untouched for twelve years, she endured being ostracized by friends because she was unclean, spending all she had trying to get better, all to no avail. She musters the last bit of faith she has in touching a man she doesn't know, but has heard that God uses Him. Miraculously, she is healed and feels a sense of relief like never before. But life has a way of reminding her of all those years, and questions will arise; *'Why was I not healed all these years? I prayed, I sacrificed, I believed with all my heart. I'm broke now, how am I supposed to live?'* But the words of the Master physician will come to her mind, **Daughter, be of good comfort**... Not just did she receive a miraculous healing, but the Son of God called her *daughter*. This woman not only received healing for her body, but for her wounded soul also. She was sick and lonely and in one day she was healed and made part of a family (that is what Jesus meant when He said, *thy faith hath made thee whole*) that would last for eternity. If that doesn't bring comfort, I don't know what will.

The Lord said, *I tell you that he will avenge them speedily. Nevertheless when the Son of man cometh, shall he find faith on the earth?* (**Luke 18:8**). God is looking for faith (and the corresponding works that accompany it. See **James 2:15-16**), not for belief when he returns. God does not consider all who believe (which today is mostly mental assent), to be sons and daughters, only those who have faith and those who are led by His Spirit (and there is a vast difference). Note Paul's words to the Ecclesia, *Know ye therefore **that they which are of faith*** (Pistis- persuasion, that is, credence, a moral conviction (of religious truth, or the truthfulness of God or a religious teacher), *the same are the children of Abraham,* and his letter to the Romans, *For as many as are led* (Ago- reflexively move/go, be driven or induced) *by the Spirit of God, they are the sons* (children) *of God* (**Galatians 3:7, Romans 8:14** respectively). Not just faith that there is a God or that He is one God or that God can do anything, but a faith that is lived out so that others may see God through them. A faith that takes no risks is not faith, but mental assent (which garners nothing in the Kingdom of God). True faith costs us something dearly and daily, but the rewards are both tremendous and eternal. The woman with the issue of blood displayed a faith that we should all strive for.

Another example of faith gaining comfort, **Matthew 9:2** *And, behold, they brought to him a man sick of the palsy, lying on a bed: and Jesus seeing **their** faith said unto the sick of the palsy; Son, **be of good cheer*** (Tharseō- take courage, be comforted)*; thy sins be forgiven thee* (**Matthew 9:2**). A sick man was brought to Jesus by four friends and God showed His compassion on him, not just by healing him but also forgiving him. Once again, take note on what came first, forgiveness then healing. With God, it is not one or the other, but both and in almost all the miracles of Jesus, He either encouraged, comforted, or exhorted them, as a part of their physical needs. We Pentecostals seem to major on the physical miracles and sadly treat as secondary or tertiary the matters of the heart. Jesus came to heal the soul *and* body, not one or the other. This ex-palsied man had a story to tell about the day he placed his faith in his friends, about how the God of Israel intervened in his life and how this same God comforted both him and his friends. I have no doubt his testimony would have drawn many to God.

A blind man by the name of Bartimaeus, sat on his bedroll (the only thing of value he owned beside his cloak) by the side of the road for years begging from passers-by to have compassion on him and give him enough money to last until he came to do it again the next day. Rabbis and priests, government officials and members of the religious elite (the Sanhedrin) passed him by daily and did precious little to nothing for him. They were praised of men but were useless to God. They did not take him in nor help him find a family that would care for this blind man. Perhaps they tossed in a coin or two to assuage their miserable consciences, or as many people thought in those days (sadly and erroneously, many today also think), he must have sinned somehow, and this is his punishment (see **John 9:1-2**). His life was dismal, with nobody but a few kind people to take his hand and lead him to his begging spot every day. He began to hear these same passers-by talking of a Rabbi who not only spoke the word of God with authority (**Mark 1:27**) and in a manner all could understand (**Mark 12:37**), but also backed it up with signs and wonders (**John 3:2**). Then one day, he heard this same Rabbi was in his town and determined to not let this opportunity pass him by, like many of his fellow citizens did daily, he said within himself, like US Navy Admiral Farragut famously once said, "*Darn the torpedoes, full speed ahead*". He would put it all on the line. He took his meagre bedroll, cloak and faith and did something about his situation. He could not go to Jesus himself (he was blind). He could not send someone to Jesus on his behalf, he was just a beggar. So, he decided to use the only thing he had left. The thing he used to ask for money, he would now use it to get the attention of this Rabbi. His voice. He would not beg this Rabbi for money for he knew it would last for only a day. He would scream at the top of his voice with what little strength and dignity he had left to change his life.

Did he not know, beggars we meant to be seen and not heard? He more than likely said to himself, *after all, what do I have to lose*? He was already at the bottom of the food chain, right? We pick up the story in **Mark 10:47** *And when he heard that it was Jesus of Nazareth, he began to* **cry out** (Krazō- scream, shriek), *and say, Jesus, thou Son of David, have mercy on me*. Sometimes, our last act of courage is misunderstood as rudeness or arrogance as conveyed in the next verse. **48** *And many charged* (strictly forbade) *him that he should hold his peace* (in other words, shut up. He was out of order. Did he not know that a man of God was in the area and must not be bothered?) *but* **he cried the more a great deal**, *Thou Son of David, have mercy on me*. He began to *Krazo Polus Mallon*- to plenteously shriek to an even greater degree. It is this last act of squeezing what little is left of ourselves out, in defiance of other's opinions and our situations, just to be in His presence, that causes the miracles in our lives. However, we must not put all this story on the shoulders of Jesus or Bartimaeus.

Read on, *And Jesus stood still, and* **commanded him to be** *called* (someone else had to go and get Bartimaeus and bring him to Jesus). *And they* (the disciples) *call the blind man, saying unto him,* **Be of good comfort**, *rise; he calleth thee*. It was the disciples that had the task of getting him and telling him to *be of good comfort*. That is our task in the Kingdom of God today within the Ecclesia. We are to comfort anyone seeking the Lord with all their heart. Jesus did not yell across the street, send an invitation to come to the synagogue where He was to preach or tell Bartimaeus to go to Temple to get his miracle. He just indicated what He wanted to do with Bartimaeus there and then, and the disciples did the going, the getting, and the comforting, until the Master stepped in and did what man could not do. Though the miracle was done by Jesus, the work (including the going, the getting, and the comforting) was conveyed by the disciples.

The phrases *be of good comfort* and *be of good cheer* are the same word; Tharseō which tells us to have courage, to be bold, to have confidence, be comforted. Imagine this, the woman with the issue of blood, the palsied man and Bartimaeus now have their physical healing and courage to continue in God. This comfort (courage) is the one that Jesus gives as a reward for our faith, but the comfort that we are to give to one another has a different meaning. It is Parakaleō- to call near, to invite, invoke, beseech, call for, desire, give exhortation, intreat, pray. In Batimaeus' case, the disciples called near, invited and intreated him, to go with them to the healer.

The Ecclesia struggles with distance because we have conditioned ourselves that we are to travel to a place where we can meet in order to worship God together, get our healing, hear from God or give to His work. So, we leave our homes and communities once or twice a week on the pretence of fellowship (in almost all churches, we sit far apart from each other in the service and many of us don't actually fellowship with each other, we just see the same people for a short while then go about our normal lives) while at the same time, passing many saint's (or potential saints) homes to gather together. Why not do as we are commanded to do? Go from household to household, teaching each other, comfort, call near, invite, call for, desire, intreat and pray with *one another*? Not call near to the church building but call them near to our own lives and homes. This comfort is one that we are to give because it allows us to redeem the time wasted on frivolous things and we do so because the days are evil, and fear is gripping the world. When the world is consuming and devouring one another, the Ecclesia is comforting and encouraging one another.

The disciples did not tell Batimaeus they would pick him up and take him to the synagogue where their Rabbi would be preaching, and if he would just go with them and believe, he would get his miracle from God. Yet this is how we have structured our church lives today. Make the people wait until a certain day or time, at a certain place after they hear a certain message from a certain man before God will do a certain thing. This is in direct contradiction to the word of God, and yet, we call what we do biblical. This is also a dereliction of our duty as disciples of Christ. Are we not aware that every one of us who have obeyed the call to salvation, are washed clean in His name and filled with His spirit, has the same Holy Ghost that the apostles had, and that God has commissioned *all members* of His Ecclesia to do the works of Christ, anywhere at any time, to anyone who calls on that same name? The purpose of the gathering is so we may encourage one another, exhort one another, and share what God has done during the week, but we all are called to do the works of God seven days a week.

Where is God?

Ever doubt that God is not with you? Answer honestly. There is a way to *know* (not necessarily *feel*) beyond any doubt that He is. Certain things happen which draw God near to us and Paul tells the Corinthians in his final farewell what they are. *Finally, brethren, farewell. Be perfect* (Katartizō complete, thoroughly repaired, well-adjusted and prepared, restored), *be of good comfort* (drawn near, exhorted and intreated), *be of one mind* (Phroneo- mentally disposed to one another), *live in peace; and the God of love and peace **shall be with you*** (2 Corinthians 13:11).

The operative words here are *perfect, good comfort, one mind* and *live in peace*, but then the word **and** (Kai) is inserted which can also be translated as *then, indeed, moreover, therefore*, which means that after we have done the previous, becoming complete, having good comfort, being in one mind and living in peace and being well adjusted with one another, **THEN** we can expect the next statement to occur. Paul says this same God, **shall be** *with you*. This is Esomai which speaks, *of what will follow after*. As Jesus tells us in **Matthew 10:22** *And ye **shall be*** (Esomai) *hated of all men* *for my name's sake: but he that endureth to the end* **shall be** *saved*. To rewrite this verse in the positive sense, it reads; *because of me and my name, it shall be* (**it will follow**) *that all men will hate you:* **but** (De- moreover) *those that remain,* (have fortitude and persevere) *to the end of their persecution, the same will be saved.*

Comfort is often mistaken as consoling someone after a sorrowful time (this is the lowest form of comfort we can give to one another), but God is telling us that comfort means more than that. We truly are to console one another after a tragedy (even mammals in the animal kingdom do that for one another), but as citizens of the Commonwealth of the Kingdom of God we must learn to go further.

It means to be courageous, to be of good cheer, to be strong mainly because it is at these times, when things seem at their worst, when loneliness seems to be the way of the future, that we need the most courage. When we are at our weakest and most vulnerable, we are to be of good cheer with each other. But how do we do this? Paul tells us in **1 Thessalonians 4:18** *Wherefore* (Hōste- so too, thus, therefore. In other words- in this manner) *comfort one another* **with these words**. With what words? In verses 13-17 he writes about the second coming of our Lord, what to look and listen for, what will happen to us and our loved ones and where we will end up if we will endure, hold on to Christ and each other. Words that declare His Majesty, His will, and His sovereignty. Words that teach His commandments and the need to keep them. These are comforting words indeed to someone needing comfort.

If we are not enduring some kind of persecution, struggle, and hardship (outside of normal life trials or because of our dumb decisions) why would we be so eager to get out of here? We need courage in the face of trials for His name's sake and to be cheered up when things look bleak, the mountain seems too high and the valley seems too deep, when, for example, death, disease, or divorce looms like a shadow over our lives. It is at these times we need the Ecclesia to comfort one another even more.

Look at the prophet Elijah for a moment. After the Mount Carmel miracle, his spirit was riding high. Not only did he see Israel finally repent from their backsliding and idolatrise ways (after 3 years of prayer), but they also showed their contrition in a tangible way, (just as John Baptist told the Pharisees to, *bring forth therefore fruits meet,* [Axios- worthy, deserving suitable] *for repentance* [**Matthew 3:8**], by killing the prophets who had helped them backslide). Shortly thereafter, Satan speaks through his servant, Jezebel, in the form of a threat on his life and he flees into the wilderness. Elijah just stood against a small army of false prophets and a rebellious nation, he had seen God answer his prayers (with fire from heaven, no less) and the threatenings of a heathen queen had caused him to flee. After some time in the wilderness, he asks God to take his life. Some would say that Elijah suffered from depression, (yes, prophets are human, they feel depression and inner hurts just like all God's chosen) whether he did or did not is a matter of conjecture, but even if he did, God did *not* send an angel to *preach* to him, to tell him to get his act together, quote Torah to him or that he needed to pray more, to remind him of what God had done for him in the past or to condemn him for his lack of faith or how he was feeling. Not at all. God sent someone (a messenger- prophet, priest, or teacher) to comfort him.

How? By twice cooking him a meal, give him some drink and suggesting he take a nap. He was comforted in a tangible way. Elijah rested and in the strength of that comfort (rest, food, and nap), he was able to travel forty days and nights to the next leg of his journey. **Comfort in tangible forms gives strength to continue** (see **1 Kings 19:1-8**). I believe sometimes when we are under duress, it might be time to take the *Elijah Remedy*. Eat something, drink something and take a nap. We will usually see things clearer and then move on.

In modern terms, we could call the concept of comfort- *morale,* and its importance has been greatly underestimated or misunderstood within the Ecclesia. I have studied military history since the late seventies and found that low morale in any group inhibits its performance in the tasks the group was formed for. Morale in all ranks, in any organization, be it the military, business or church, will be one of the main contributing and determining factors to their successes or failures. In the face of adversity, boosting morale helps with the overall productivity, attention to detail and satisfaction in any position within any organization or group.

An Australian based business coaching firm, *iperform*, puts it this way: *"In order to improve staff morale, you need to understand what has caused the slump in morale in the first place. Arguments between team members, supervisory actions that intimidate, or the possibility of losing a job are among the common reasons why staff morale will drop. A heavy workload or feeling unappreciated are other reasons why people will leave the workplace. Listen carefully to your staff and see if you can discover the reason why morale is dropping."*

"So, how do you raise staff morale? Show concern, give appropriate feedback, and be enthusiastic and genuine in your appreciation for your team. These are basic facets of leadership. However, you can go further than that. Find out what motivates the individual staff member and give rewards that match that motivation. One individual may appreciate getting an hour off, while another will want a movie ticket. Of course, you need to know how to listen to, motivate, and show appreciation for the members of your team in order to raise staff morale." (**iperform.com.au/morale**). This does not mean that we are to use business practices to run the Ecclesia, just that people are people no matter whether they belong to secular or religious organizations.

Another reason morale drops off is, members seeing other members getting favours or promoted that either don't deserve it or being praised for less than satisfactory work. Even God himself rewards those who increase their gift (see **Luke 19:15-20, Matthew 25:14-23**) and those who do nothing get nothing. Can you imagine how the two in the parable of the talents who worked hard for their master to increase their talents would have felt if the one who did nothing but hide his talent got the same reward? That would have shown God as unrighteous or unjust (see **Romans 2:11, Deuteronomy 10:17, Acts 10:34, Psalm 62:12, 1 Peter 1:17, James 1:17**). Notice the wicked servant was not cast into outer darkness because he *couldn't* increase his gift, but because he *wouldn't* increase his gift.

Morale (also known as esprit de corps) in any organization and especially in the military, is the capacity of the group's members to maintain belief and momentum in the institution or goal, especially in the face of opposition or hardship. It is also defined as a feeling of pride, fellowship, camaraderie, and common loyalty shared by the members of a particular group. According to Alexander H. Leighton, 1908-2007, a well-known sociologist and psychiatrist, *"Morale is the capacity of a group of people to* **pull together persistently and consistently in pursuit of a common purpose.***"* Building the Kingdom of God is the purpose of the Ecclesia (people), not building, renting, renovating, or acquiring church structures (facades). If the common purpose is consistently material in nature, then all that will be gained is material things, with the occasional spiritual blessing. However, when the Ecclesia is persistently and consistently pursuing that which Christ and the early church focused on, we will reap the same reward, God adding to the church daily.

We know that the early church lived in a time of evil empires, greedy governments and much sickness. There was much comfort needed just to make it through the day. And so, they went from house-to-house teaching exactly what the Lord's disciples taught, caring for each other in all manner of ways and this brought comfort to one another. Comforting each other helps build esprit de corps and invigorates people back into purpose and action. Realistically, when a group or person has a purpose greater than the individual, it will come with many challenges and with many challenges come frustrations, heartaches, and hurts. Enter those in the Ecclesia who know how to comfort and share the ability to do so with others. This lessens the negative impact that accompany life and helps turn a seemingly impossible or tragic situation into one where God gets the glory, and we become disciples worthy of our Lord. This attracts the seekers who view our lives and see God, whom we then help turn into a disciple, not just a church attender/tithe paying liturgical consumerist.

Morale is important in the military, mainly because it improves unit cohesion (the ability to stick together under stressful times). Without good morale, a force will be more likely to fight poorly or even surrender. Morale is usually assessed as a collective, rather than on an individual level. In wartime, civilian morale is just as important. During the Blitz, Germany bombed England's civilian population for 8 months straight to try and break the fighting spirit of the Briton's. The Nazi's gave up because, although there was mayhem and destruction all around (41,480 civilian deaths and over 100,000 wounded), the people would comfort each other by telling them there will be an end to the destruction soon and that they would eventually prevail over the Nazi's. They would not let their morale break and give in to the enemy. They found those who had lost loved ones, homes and jobs and bound together to comfort and help each other through the blitz. Esprit de corps is an important part of a fighting unit, without it, the heart of the unit will eventually fail. It is equally if not more important within the body of Christ, because ...*we wrestle not against flesh and blood, but against principalities, against powers, against the rulers of the darkness of this world, against spiritual wickedness in high places* (**Ephesians 6:12**).

The allies wrestled against Nazi, Italian and Japanese imperialism, and because they remained united in purpose and kept up morale, though they fought in different ways, they were victorious. The Ecclesia fights an unseen enemy who uses the seen (people, material, positions) as weapons, but we will be victorious if we comfort, edify, exhort, and strengthen one another. Instead of looking for differences why we cannot stand together, why not seek out those things we can unite in, do our job, and let God take care of the outcome?

Hubert Renfro Knickerbocker (1931 Pulitzer Prize Author and journalist) writes, "*Morale is when a soldier thinks his army is the best in the world, his regiment the best in the army, his company the best in the regiment, his squad the best in the company, and that he himself is the best blankety-blank soldier man in the outfit.*"

When a unit's morale is said to be depleted, it means they are close to being useless. All training and financial input at this point becomes moot. During WW2, for example, hundreds of thousands of Italian soldiers in North Africa surrendered en masse because morale was so low (mainly because of an elitist leadership who kept the best food and comfort for themselves, and a lack of supply in both men and material to the front line soldier to do their job), while the German soldiers fought to the death because their leader was sending as much to the front as he could and withholding nothing from the frontline soldier, they believed they could win and unit cohesion was high and though the allies had severely curtailed the supply lines of the Germans, they understood it was a result of war not elitism. Eventually morale began to drop because the leadership had given up all common sense and allowed Hitler to run the war from his *ivory tower* (a bunker in Bavaria) and when the end of the war was at hand, only the most fanatical units fought on to the end. What was left either surrendered or deserted. There was no more unit cohesion and no more goals worth dying for. Trying to repair exceptionally low morale at this point takes drastic and expensive measures which are usually rushed into place (Hitler sent in boys as young as 15 and men as old as 65 into the firing line as cannon fodder), but unfortunately it was too little, too late. Unit cohesion had been lost and surrender with its inevitable defeat was all too imminent.

Paul encourages his disciple Timothy, by telling him ...*Thou therefore **endure hardness*** (one word- Kakopatheō- undergo hardship and afflictions)*, as a good soldier of Jesus Christ. No man that warreth entangleth himself with the **affairs of this life**; that he may please him who hath chosen him to be a soldier* (2 **Timothy 2:3-4**). *Affairs of this life* is an interesting choice of words; it is Pragmateuomai: to busy oneself with life. A soldier will endure all sorts of hardships if they are focused on their purpose and that they know they are not alone. The problems arise when a soldier is in the trenches, the enemy is bound and determined to kill him, and he's preoccupied with what's going on at home or the creature comforts he misses (the affairs of this life). We are all called to endure hardships, but to do so within a cohesive unit called the Ecclesia. It is in the trenches when we comfort one another that we have the greatest effect upon each other's lives.

Carl Philipp Gottfried von Clausewitz (1780–1831), a Prussian general and military theorist writes comprehensively on moral and the political aspects of war. He stresses... *"the importance of morale and will for both the soldier and the commander. The soldier's first requirement is moral and physical courage, both the acceptance of responsibility and the suppression of fear. In order to survive the horrors of combat, he must have an invincible martial spirit, which can be attained only through military victory and hardship. The soldier has but one purpose: The end for which a soldier is recruited, clothed, armed, and trained, the whole object of his sleeping, eating, drinking, and marching is simply that he should fight at the right place and the right time."*

Comfort from both the Lord and the saints builds morale, a backbone instead of a wishbone and endurance which eventually leads to crossing the line into the New Jerusalem (salvation) (see **Matthew 10:22**). As we comfort one another with God's word, as well as give of our time, effort, finances, prayers and fasting for each other, we will see the courage of every saint rise and then we can truly claim the words spoken by Jesus to Peter as our own, *And I say also unto thee, That thou art Peter, and upon this rock **I will build my church**;* (note: He did not say '*you will build churches*') *and the gates of hell shall not prevail against it* (**Matthew 16:18**).

Storms, trials, hardships, deaths, sickness, frustration and let downs are as much a part of a true believer's life as anyone living for the world. The difference is that when these things come upon us, we have the Lord, who controls the season and the reason they have come as well as the outcome which will *always work together for the good of those that love Him and are being changed into His image* (**Romans 8:28-29**). Add our faith to His sovereign will and the result will be that the world will see our works and glorify God (**Matthew 5:16**). As those who have taken on His name in baptism and filled with His spirit, obeying His word, and discipling one another to obey His commands (which includes comforting one another), we have a right to petition the Lord and expect an answer. What we don't have is a right to tell the Lord what He must do. He is the Sovereign of the universe, who knows all, sees all, feels all and because He does, He allows certain things to come and test, strengthen, and teach us how to live in a manner that shows the world who He is. To do this, He needs a vehicle: enter The Ecclesia. We are to comfort one another with His word and with our lives through the trials of life. The world does not have this ability and they will look to us when we show it.

We must be careful that we do not indulge ourselves in constantly seeking our own comfort. Comfort can become a drug. Once we get used to it, it becomes addictive. If we give a weak person consistent stimulation, good food, and cheap entertainment, they will throw their ambitions to the wind. The comfort zone is where obedience and passion to serve God and one another goes to die.

Chapter 28.

Kind, tender-hearted and forgiving one another.

Ephesians 4:32 *And be ye **kind** one to another, **tender-hearted**, **forgiving** one another, even as God for Christ's sake hath forgiven you.*

Here we see that Paul is writing about three things we are to do and be to one another, a triple whammy. Kindness, being tenderhearted and forgiving one another. Though we have discussed forgiveness in a previous chapter, we will attempt to go deeper on this subject in this chapter. These three commands are inextricably intertwined and trying to do one without the other only ends in frustration and failure. One cannot be kind but unforgiving, nor can one forgive and not be tenderhearted (not according to God's standard anyway). It is hard to get someone to see the Kingdom of God through our lives if we do not display these important traits within the Ecclesia.

Have you ever heard someone say, *'just be kind to me'*? All good and well, but who's idea of kindness are we talking about, ours or theirs? Every one of us has a distinct set of standards regarding what we like or dislike, what we feel good or bad about. Our understanding of kindness is viewed through the lens of our own personal history.

Paul is telling us specifically that by being kind we are to be Chrēstos- employed, useful and gracious to one another. Compared to Paul's understanding, today's meaning of kindness pales into triviality. For instance, one of the things I find kindness to be is Michele making me a cup of tea and some scones after a particularly busy day, while Michele feels it is listening to her, kind words and a good old-fashioned back scratch that mean more to her. We all have different hurts and fears that have accumulated in and on us through the vagaries of life, and kindness is a way of putting salve on those things. Pain and suffering go hand in hand with being alive, and these are only multiplied as we go deeper into the service of God and the saints. However, as they happen, they also teach us valuable lessons on what it means to be a biblical disciple of God. They help us to become more like our Master and others will see how, with the help of the Holy Ghost, we handle these hurts and use them to grow the Kingdom of God.

Being considerate of another's way of seeing things is putting kindness into action which tends to bring a little more sanity into one's life. To place oneself in a position to see what others see is not a sign of weakness and we do not have to agree on the minutia of another's view before we can fellowship with them or show kindness. A gentle word, a few moments of time, a listening ear, a phone call, a visit to a neighbour's home, a hospital bed or a lonely saint can open the heart of almost all people. We all need to *feel* kindness. This does not exclude carrying out an action to help alleviate a situation when it is within our means or the means of friends when possible, even if we don't *feel like it* (see **Luke 11:5-8**).

How far will we go to be tenderhearted one toward another? Is it a sign of weakness to show tender-heartedness? How did Jesus display this trait? This attribute within the body is the one that seems to hurt the most when it is unrequited. It is when we place our heart on the chopping block of life and pray like crazy that the knife does not cut it to pieces.

A quote (unattributable) I read a while ago defines a tenderhearted person as, *"one who would not willingly cause pain and one who is eager to relieve it."* To be tenderhearted does not mean that you always wear your heart on your sleeve, as the old saying goes, just that people's situations move you to actionable prayer and to provide a solution if and when possible. These people are sometimes viewed as weak and not very stable, but according to God's word, they are fulfilling an especially important task within the Ecclesia.

Years ago, in a meeting with some pastor friends, I heard a quote that has stayed with me and encouraged me to be more tender-hearted. *"An environment that practices tender-heartedness, goes beyond letter-of-the-law compliance with minimal biblical or church requirements. It goes to where the grace of the gospel sets a new tone and standard. It makes the Ecclesia outshine the world with divine beauty, it becomes a delight to its members, and able to persuade outsiders to come in."*

Being tenderhearted doesn't always have the outcome we desire but we continue to be tenderhearted because it is our way of showing Christ to a hurting, lonely or lost church populace. To be tenderhearted is to display the same compassion as Jesus in His years on this planet (though He was not received all that well, He continued) and to this day still does through the real disciples of the Kingdom of God. When we are tenderhearted, we display to the whole world, as Paul writes, that we are being transformed into the image of the Son of God. If read in context, those who are changing into the image of the Son of God are the ones for whom all things will work together for their good (**Romans 8:28-29**).

For example, Dr Luke tells us of the Master's heart while He was in a city during a funeral, *And it came to pass the day after, that he went into a city called Nain; and many of his disciples went with him, and much people. Now when he came nigh to the gate of the city, behold, there was a dead man carried out, the only son of his mother, and she was a widow: and much people of the city was with her* (**Luke 7:11-12**). There was much sadness in Nain that day, a small village of only 250 acres. It was quite clear that this woman had not only lost her husband earlier, but now her son, and to make things even worse, her only means of financial support.

As we continue the story in verses 13-15, we see what happened to Jesus as He came upon the funeral procession... *when the Lord saw her, he had **compassion** on her, and said unto her, Weep not. And he came and touched the bier: and they that bare him stood still. And he said, Young man, I say unto thee, Arise. And he that was dead sat up, and began to speak. And he delivered him to his mother.* He had Splagchnizomai- to have the bowels that yearn, that is to feel sympathy, to pity: to be moved with compassion. What does it mean *to be moved with compassion*? He felt sympathy and pity that led to inward affection and having tender mercy (mercy that does not have some kind of outward response, is not biblical mercy). This just means that He was moved to action, to alleviate the suffering of the one on whom the compassion was directed (the widow).

We can see that after the compassion and weeping came an action which restored a situation back to good. We must also see what happens when God does a miracle ...***there came a fear on all: and they glorified God, saying, That a great prophet is risen up among us; and, That God hath visited his people*** (**Luke 7:16**). As a side note, we can see that Jesus reached in and touched the body of the widow's son. This made Him ceremonially unclean. He was willing to become unclean to alleviate suffering. The Lord was willing to touch death to bring life to a situation. What would we be willing to do to achieve such outcomes?

We spend much of our time glorying that a miracle has happened, however, when the word of God in a vast majority of cases, speaks of a miracle happening, it ends with, *fear came upon all that saw and heard and all glorified God* or words to that affect. A miracle that does not have people in awe of God and glorifying Him (both saint and sinner alike), shows the heart of the Pharisees in our midst. For example, Jesus performed a miracle, and all the religious elites could do was complain that it was done on the Sabbath (**John 9:13-16**). Also, when people demand a miracle (a sign), to prove someone is from God, we can turn to **Matthew 12:38-39** ...*Then certain of the scribes and of the Pharisees answered, saying, Master, **we would see a sign from thee**. But he answered and said unto them, An evil and adulterous generation seeketh after a sign; and there shall no sign be given to it, but the sign of the prophet Jonas.* Jesus knew that any sign He did would not end with God being glorified. *And he sighed deeply in his spirit, and saith, Why doth this generation seek after a sign? verily I say unto you, There shall no sign be given unto this generation* (**Mark 8:12**). Sadly, much of the church in western society seeks (Epizēteō- demands or craves) after signs and wonders, rather than allowing signs and wonders to follow them in their daily living.

For example: *For we cannot but speak the things which we have seen and heard,* (they only copied the Master like a true biblical disciple does). *So, when they had further threatened them, they let them go, finding nothing how they might punish them, because of the people: **for all men glorified God for that which was done.** For the man was above forty years old, on whom this miracle of healing was shewed* (**Acts 4:20-22**). Peter and John did not go to the Temple to hold a service or perform a miracle. They went as a part of their daily lives in prayer and worship. God did what He did because they were doing what they were doing- living for God daily. Then there is, *And great multitudes came unto him, having with them those that were lame, blind, dumb, maimed, and many others, and cast them down at Jesus' feet; and he healed them: Insomuch that the multitude wondered, when they saw the dumb to speak, the maimed to be whole, the lame to walk, and the blind to see: **and they glorified the God of Israel*** (**Matthew 15:30-31**, see also **Matthew 9:8, Mark 2:12, Luke 5:26, 23:47**).

Back to the word tenderhearted, which is only used once in the Renewed Covenant, but it is used in conjunction with forgiveness which is tied to forgiving as we have been forgiven (**Matthew 6:12** and **Luke 11:4**). God was tenderhearted towards you and I, in that He saw our suffering from the weight of sin with its inevitable death and permanent separation from God and He came to alleviate it. If we are to be our Master's disciples, then we are to have Eusplagchnos- well compassioned, sympathetic: [benevolent or considerate, quick to feel pity]- tenderhearted, and whenever the need arises, we are to be at one with one another's suffering and if possible (by God's standards, not our own selfishness or convenience) be an instrument to alleviate or lessen the impact of such suffering, being careful that we may not be undoing what God is trying to do in the sufferer's life. Rarely are members of the Ecclesia to suffer alone, but if they must suffer, as Paul tells us we all must, then let us suffer with them, *And our hope of you is stedfast, knowing, that as ye are partakers of the sufferings, so shall ye be also of the consolation* (**2 Corinthians 1:7**) and... ***whether one member suffer, all the members suffer with it;*** *or one member be honoured, all the members rejoice with it* (**1 Corinthians 12:26**). When we go through the suffering with them, we will also rejoice when the suffering is over.

The opposite of this vital command would be as Paul puts it in **Ephesians 4:31** *Let all **bitterness**, and **wrath**, and **anger**, and **clamour**, and **evil speaking**, be put away from you, with all malice.* Bitterness is a slow acting, tasteless, odourless, and colourless poison which has permeated the Ecclesia via pride and unforgiveness and it not only erodes the soul of the individual but also destroys the essence of the Ecclesia. It slowly but surely erodes the purpose of the Commonwealth of the Kingdom of God here on earth. Wrath, (indignation) is also called vengeance and is the carrier of this destructive tool of the enemy. Anger (punishment), clamour, the (false) outcry of sins and bringing it to the public arena (under the guise of wanting to help or the Christian version of gossip- *'sharing because we care'*) and evil speaking, have but one purpose, to vilify someone which today means to speak or write about them in an abusive and disparaging manner without giving the other person a chance to answer the charges.

These opposites to tender-heartedness have crept into the body and are slowly but surely negating the power of God to influence and change the world around us. Tender-heartedness is an antidote to the wrath and malice displayed within the Ecclesia and is a pre-requisite to compassion. However, action-less compassion is not only useless, but dangerous. It leads us to believe that when we *feel* pity or compassion, (because we felt it in the depths of our hearts and maybe even said a prayer or two but fail to act upon it whenever and wherever possible), we think that it will satisfy God or the person in need.

Not only are we commanded to have sympathy with and for one another, but we are commanded to have empathy. This is the ability to understand by placing ourselves in another's position and share the feelings of one another. If we feel what others are feeling, we will be more likely to act accordingly. For example, when a close friend's parent or child dies, many of us sympathize because we have an idea of what that would feel like, even though many have not lost a close friend or child. So, we go to the funeral, cry with them, tell them that it will all be fine in God's time, maybe take them a dinner and call them after to console them (usually for a week or two, then we get back to our own busy lives). But if, on the other hand, we have lost a parent, child, or a close friend, we feel their agony, their questioning God's love, His wisdom, or mercy, we feel their emptiness and their profound sense of loss and loneliness, we then act accordingly because we empathize not just commiserate with them.

We go and sit with them, hold their hand, check on them regularly (for as long as it takes), take care of their physical needs, their mental well-being, those of us who are born again will pray and fast for them. The Ecclesia will help with the kids or the housework, mow their lawns, do the shopping for them etc. We become one with their sufferings and willingly do what is necessary, once again, for as long as it takes. When they get mad and yell at us, or go silent, it will not bother us, because that is their journey right now and we don't take it personally. It's their pain and anguish that must come to the fore and be allowed to heal. We will be with them as they come out of the darkness and begin the arduous journey of restoration to what is as close to a normal life as possible but with much more wisdom, empathy, understanding and a bond of fellowship considerably deeper than before. The rewards are self-evident. This is tenderhearted compassion in operation. It need not be a death; it could be anything that overwhelms a brother or sister in any field of life. An illness, loss of employment, church hurt, financial ruin or divorce are just some of the things that feel like a death has occurred. Some people face this darkness when they are about to retire, after an accident, or unplanned pregnancy, when a child goes wayward, or a spouse goes into depression through illness or caring for an ill loved one or breaks the bond of marriage through adultery. This is when compassionate empathy (tender-heartedness) is needed within the body. Going up to people and just telling them to get their act together or telling them to just have faith/believe, fast, and pray, or read their word is not necessarily the right thing to say. We must *show* them the word with tender-heartedness. There are many more situations that require the help of the Ecclesia, we only need to open our eyes and hearts, as well as our wallets, homes, and businesses.

Solomon wrote, *the human spirit of a man can endure a sick body, but who can bear a crushed spirit* (**Proverbs 18:14** paraphrased). Today we have hospitals, hospices, clinics, and rehab centres that deal with all manner of physical diseases, addictions, and the dying, but who, on God's green footstool, is there to deal with a wounded or broken spirit? Do we honestly think that just because we have the Holy Ghost, that we go to church and continue to listen to sermon after sermon that our broken spirits and wounded heart will just get better? Are we so foolish to believe that the effects of disease, drugs and family breakdowns are solely the domain of sinners? Thankfully, God has provided for the healing of life's disasters through the Ecclesia (when it operates in a biblical manner). There is enough healing, compassion, understanding and wisdom, financial and physical care sitting in the pews and in our head offices to cater to the needs of every single person who connects themselves to Christ, His word, and His body. Jesus said, *If ye abide in me, and my words abide in you, ye shall ask what ye will, and it shall be done unto you* (**John 15:7**). Where do we think these things come from? Do they rain down from heaven? The answer is in Luke's gospel, *Give, and it shall be given unto you; good measure, pressed down, and shaken together, and running over, **shall men give into your bosom**. For with the same measure that ye mete withal it shall be measured to you again* (**Luke 6:38**).

The criteria to having the needs of the Ecclesia met is that we **abide in Him** (not predominately in our churches or organizations) and His word (Rhēma- revealed utterance) abides in us, then we have God's ear. If we do not live according to the mandate of the Ecclesia as set out in **Acts 2:42-46, 4:32-35, 20:20**, and *preach* (Kerusso- proclaim and publish) the Gospel of the Kingdom of God only (not our standards and convictions) to the lost and make disciples, then why would God be obligated to add to our churches or intervene in our situations? **Remember, our own human endeavours can produce fruit, but will it be fruit that lasts and is usable by God to reseed His word into others?**

Tenderhearted people hurt much more than the rest of the church populace and they are enraged at the lack of justice and blatant unequal treatment of members within the body. But this is just what our Lord is to us (tenderhearted) and feels anger when we treat each other in like manner. Paul told us so in **Hebrews 4:15** *For we have not an high priest which cannot be touched with the feeling of our infirmities; but was in all points tempted like as we are, yet without sin* (Harmatia- offence, missing the mark and so not share in the prize). Not only does He know how we feel, but He also gives us the action plan to remedy what's wrong. In verse 16, when we come to that point where we need help... *Let us therefore come boldly unto the throne of grace, that we may obtain mercy, and **find grace to help in time of need**.* We do this not just for ourselves but for each other.

How does He do this? Through kind, tender-hearted and forgiving disciples. When we find tenderhearted people, we tend to dismiss them as easy marks. If this is truly the case, then let me be an easy mark, for I am emulating not just our Lord but also His disciples.

Peter writes, *Finally, be ye all of one mind, having **compassion** one of another, love as brethren, be pitiful, be courteous* (Philophrōn- friendly of mind, kind. **1 Peter 3:8**). This shows what and how we are to feel for others. It comes from Sumpaschō, and it means to experience pain jointly or of the same kind, to suffer **with** someone. How many times have we said we will pray for someone, only to forget or say a quick one-minute prayer? If we were the one feeling the pain, I would venture to guess our prayer would have more fervency. Fervency does not equate to length of time, shouting at the devil or the situation or waving our arms around like a head with its chicken cut off, but with how much passion we pray, how much of ourselves we are willing to put into the prayer and if possible, the answer to the prayer. When Christ was praying for you and me in the Garden of

Gethsemane, it is called *The Passion of Christ*. He prayed with such passion He began to sweat blood. Why? Because He was about to experience our sin and all the pain we will ever and have ever experienced or caused another.

Though I mentioned this parable briefly earlier, I want to deeper so we can see what true biblical compassion and tender-heartedness looks like. Jesus tells the story in Matthew chapter 18 of the ungrateful servant who was forgiven of 10,000 talents by a wise and benevolent king. The parable goes on to say when the king demanded what was rightfully owed to him (as God demands payment for sin), the servant begged for time to pay. Something happened to the king's heart ...*Then the lord of that servant was moved with* **compassion***, and loosed him, and forgave him the debt* (**Matthew 18:23**-26). The servant asked for time and instead, was forgiven the debt. This is how compassion works. It goes beyond feeling sorry or sympathy for someone. Compassion gives far more than is required or asked for. Compassion restores and relieves. It saved the servant from a life of debtor's prison. The king's bowels yearned for him, yes, the king felt sorry, sympathy and pity but he moved past these minimums and had tender mercy towards the servant. Then came an action, he did something about what he felt (verse 27). He forgave the servant and gave him his life though the servant did not deserve it.

Bishop John Davenant of Salisbury (1572-1641) is known to have said of compassion/tender-heartedness, "... *it is the real inward and unpretended affection of condoling* (grieving) *with another's woe. The phrase is a Hebraism, and is taken from the emotion, and, as it were, concussion which is felt in the stomach, in deep affections of the mind*" (**Genesis 43:30; Lamentations 2:11; Luke 1:78; Philippians 2:1**). *The apostle wisely begins with the expression of condolence; because from hence flows the act of relief; and because,*" ..."*it is more to compassionate any one from the heart, than to give: for he who gives what is external, gives what does not belong to his own person; but he who gives compassion, gives somewhat of himself.*" I would like to add that to have compassion in the heart and follow through with an act of giving has a deeper impact than that of just giving.

The difference between compassion and empathy is that compassion is an emotional response to empathy or sympathy and creates a desire to help. Empathy is an understanding of our shared humanity. It is the ability to see yourself in another person's shoes. Unfortunately, this servant had neither compassion nor empathy. We continue, *But the same servant went out, and found one of his fellowservants, which owed him an hundred pence: and he laid hands on him, and took him by the throat, saying, Pay me that thou owest* (**Matthew 18:28-30**). No Sumpaschō- No compassion, no bowels of mercy, no forgiveness of debt. These have everlasting repercussions, as we shall see.

When the other servant also begged for time, the forgiven servant, who had much compassion poured on him (by a king no less) would not have the same compassion on a fellow servant. Things went from bad to worse for the forgiven servant. The amount owed is not the main point of the story, but the lack of compassion and bowels of mercy to his fellow servants is. The response from the king was to *re-instate* the debt to the servant who would not pass on the compassion given to him. As a side note, the king called the unforgiving servant what he really was... ***O, thou wicked servant*** (verse 32). This is not a, *sticks and stones may break my bones,* name calling thing going on here. These words described what kind of person the unforgiving servant was. The king, who represented the Lord in this parable, called the wicked servant, a Ponēros: he was hurtful, degenerate, diseased, especially (morally) culpable, derelict, vicious, facinorous [atrociously wicked]; mischievous, full of malice, the devil, malicious. You are in trouble when a king thinks this about you. This rather strongly suggests that lack of compassion/tender-heartedness in God's eyes is wickedness, and those that continue to practice this wickedness would have their sins re-instated, doesn't it?

We see here that compassion, tender-heartedness, and forgiveness are inextricably linked (just as justice and mercy), and it is when we neglect to show these attributes of God that we deny our citizenship in the Commonwealth of the Kingdom of God, regardless of how many church services we attend, or how many times we sing that we have the victory, or that we are baptized in His name and speak in tongues when the Holy Ghost came, shout amen or how much money we drop in the bag. Our greatest victory is not over our lack of finances, sickness, or demonic attacks. Our greatest victory is overcoming our selfish nature, becoming Christlike and keeping His commandments. Claiming citizenship and proving it are two different things.

As a citizen of the Commonwealth of Australia living in the US, I can claim to be a citizen of the US to gain all the rights and privileges a citizen has, but when I am challenged and cannot produce evidence to prove what I claim, I will be evicted from the US and rightly so. I have attempted to use the US for my own personal gain without contributing to its growth. I must go through the process of becoming a citizen of the USA if I want to have its rights and privileges.

Evidence and proof.

I would like to digress for a brief time and focus on a word we rarely use when it comes to our testimony: *evidence*. We, who are of the Apostolic persuasion, (some of us are so Apostolic, we won't even eat a pizza unless it is delivered) believe that speaking in tongues is evidence that someone has received the gift of the Holy Ghost and there is much scripture to support this. But let us move past this initial baby form of evidence and go to adult evidence, shall we?

Jeremiah 32:14 *Thus saith the LORD of hosts, the God of Israel; Take these evidences,* (Siphrâh- writing; the art or a document, a record) *this evidence of the purchase, both which is sealed, and this evidence which is open; and put them in an earthen vessel, that they may continue many days.*

Hebrew 11:1 *Now faith is the substance of things hoped for, the evidence* (Elegchos- proof, conviction) *of things not seen.*

I would like to use the parable of the ten virgins our Lord speaks of in **Matthew 25:1-13** *Then shall the kingdom of heaven be likened unto ten virgins, which took their lamps, and went forth to meet the bridegroom. And five of them were wise, and five were foolish. They that were foolish took their lamps, and took no oil with them: But the wise took oil in their vessels with their lamps. While the bridegroom tarried, they all slumbered and slept. And at midnight there was a cry made, Behold, the bridegroom cometh; go ye out to meet him. Then all those virgins arose, and trimmed their lamps.*

We can see that all the virgins had the Holy Ghost when they were called to be brides. The problem was that when the cry was made that the bridegroom was coming, they all went to light their lamps ...*And the foolish said unto the wise, Give us of your oil; for our lamps are gone out. But the wise answered, saying, Not so; lest there be not enough for us and you: but go ye rather to them that sell, and buy for yourselves. And while they went to buy, the bridegroom came; and they that were ready went in with him to the marriage: and the door was shut.*

Note: the evidence that they were the wise virgins was their light. It was not their garments, for they all had wedding robes. It was not that they had lamps. The evidence was that the five wise had oil (representative of the Holy Ghost and they kept their lamps filled) while the five foolish relied on the oil they had when they were first chosen. The wise virgins proved their wisdom by the light they had. The foolish virgins proved their lack of wisdom by the lack of light they had. The foolish virgins once had oil and therefore once had light. The difference between the wise and the foolish, was one continued working to get more oil (resulting in continued light) while the others were satisfied with their initial allocation of oil and that same oil ran out. The five wise virgins had light because they bought more oil at the market (how could they buy more if they did not work. See **2 Thessalonians 3**:10). What was the response from the Bridegroom? *Afterward came also the other virgins, saying, Lord, Lord, open to us. But **he answered and said, Verily I say unto you, I know you not**. Watch therefore, for ye know neither the day nor the hour wherein the Son of man cometh.* The phrase "*I know you not*" is translated as *I don't see you* or *I don't consider you.* Jesus demanded proof that they have the light by actually showing it when called for.

Paul asks for proof of love from the Corinthians, and they asked Paul (rightly so) to prove that Christ was speaking through him (**2 Corinthians 2:9, 8:24** respectively). Paul also asks Timothy to prove his servanthood (Diakonia- attendance, aid, service, relief, ministry) and we can rest assured if evidence and proof was required of the first century believers, it is required of us today. Believing in Jesus, that He died and rose again, being baptized in Jesus' name and speaking in tongues is not evidence nor proof that we are what we claim we are. It only proves that at one time we heard the word and obeyed it to gain entrance into the Book of Life. But there is a caveat to remaining in this Book. Jesus spoke this to the church at Sardis, **He that overcometh**, *the same shall be clothed in white raiment; and **I will not blot out his name out of the book of life,** but I will confess his name before my Father, and before his angels* (**Revelation 3:5**). Note the phrase *I will not blot his name out of the book of life?* Obedience to the plan of salvation gets us into the book of life, continued disobedience can get us blotted out.

We claim we are people who have faith that Jesus is God, but where is our evidence? The evidence of our faith must be proven in the open court of our workplaces and communities, schools and marketplaces, our families and friends and especially those sitting in our pews. Is our faith proven because we go to church often? Committed Baptists go to church often. Is it that we dress modestly? The Amish dress modestly (they have church four to five times a week). Is it that we do not partake of worldly pleasures? Neither do devout Jehovah's Witnesses. Is it perhaps that we believe that God is one and not three? Muslims and Jews also believe in one God. Perhaps it is that we speak in tongues. So do members of the Assemblies of God. So far none of these is evidence that what we claim to believe to be truth is, in fact, truth. We are just a part of the cacophony of voices that shouts the same words that all churches shout, "*We have the truth because* (insert reason here)".

We do not need to perform acts of malice in order to do harm to the brethren, just the lack or absence of understanding, sympathy and especially empathy will suffice. The inclusion of kindness, tender-heartedness and forgiveness is as much and far greater evidence that we are filled with and led of the Holy Ghost as speaking in tongues is. How we treat one another, especially those of the household of faith (**Galatians 6:10**) and those who cannot return any favours proves we are being transformed in His image (**Romans 8:29**). The sign on the front of our churches or the name on the pieces of paper hanging on our walls had nothing to do with it.

When someone is drowning, our lack of action will be considered a contributing factor to their death. Turning our backs on those who suffer (spiritually, mentally, emotionally, or financially, first to those of the household of faith, then to those within our sphere of influence) shows our lack of love for what and who God loves. There is a time to pray and a time to act and we had better know the difference. If we walk past a large body of water and we see someone drowning, it is not time to pray, it is time to jump in and rescue them. *Yes, but what if I can't swim,* is not an excuse. Look for a rope, a branch, anything that can to save a drowning person. If in the end, the person drowns, you can rest assured you did all you could have done.

I was a member of the SES (State Emergency Service) in Queensland, Australia, in the 80s and I remember we were called to look for a man who was suspected of going to Morton Island (off the coast of Queensland) to kill himself. We had trucks, helicopters and hundreds of people combing the thick forest looking for him. We knew his state of mind and that he had a rifle, but our concern was to bring him back alive and get him all the help he needed. We walked from sunrise calling his name, hoping beyond all hope that it was not too late. We all carried canteens of water and medical equipment in case one of us found him. Moreton Island is a beautiful place, but it was not a day for fun and frolicking in the forest. We kept calling out his name until someone found him. Sadly, he committed suicide the day before. We did not know that, but we behaved as if there was still a chance. When we got the word over the radio, we had to walk back to the collection point and await our return to daily living. We were sad that a man had given up on life, and we talked amongst ourselves about how bad he must have felt to do such a thing. Even though it did not go the way we wanted it to go, we knew we did all we could, based on the information and resources (trucks, helicopters, ambulances, counselling staff etc.) we had at the time.

Now, put this scenario into those within the Ecclesia and read **1 John 3:16-18** again with this new insight, *Hereby perceive* (Ginōskō- are aware, understand, to be sure) *we the love of God, because he laid down his life for us:* **and we ought to lay down our lives for the brethren.** *But* **whoso hath this world's good, and seeth his brother have need, and shutteth up his bowels of compassion from him, how dwelleth the love of God in him**? *My little children,* **let us not love in word,** *neither in tongue; but* **in deed** (Ergon- to toil, an act, in labour) *and in truth.* John goes on in the same letter to say, *If a man say, I love God, and hateth* (Miseo- to love less) *his brother,* **he is a liar**: *for he that loveth not his brother whom he hath seen, how can he love God whom he hath not seen? And this commandment have we from him, That he who loveth God love his brother also* (**1 John 4:20-21**). I have said it before and will say it again now, if we say we love God and would do anything for Him, yet we will not love the brethren with the same kind of love, WE ARE LIARS!

Hebrews 11:1-2 *Now faith is the* **substance** (Hupostasis- the underlying essences) *of things hoped for* (Elpizō- expect with confidence), *the* **evidence** (Elegchos- proof and conviction) *of things not seen. For by it the elders obtained a* **good report** (from Martus- martyr). The evidence of their lives caused them to me martyred. The word *Elegchos* is only mentioned once in the Renewed Covenant and has been mistranslated into the English as evidence. In reality it means proof sufficient to establish a thing as true in open court, a conviction. The difference between evidence and proof is that the former refers to documentation or verifiable testimony used to strengthen a claim. It refers to an item of information, data or a fact that helps to establish the truth, testimony, or existence of something. Proof is the sum of much evidence which helps to prove something beyond a reasonable doubt. We even use terms like *"I want to prove my case in court!'* Then we proceed to bring as much evidence before the people as possible so they may differentiate between truth and counterfeit (which is making something as close to the real to deceive individuals into believing the fake is of equal or greater value than the real thing).

The proof of our testimony is that we are changing daily, with little pieces of evidence that others are seeing the Kingdom of God in our lives. Proof is more concrete and conclusive than evidence. A person can show one or two pieces of evidence in court, but they must provide a preponderance of evidence to prove their case. Speaking in tongues and being baptized in his name is evidence that at one time we had the Pentecostal experience. But since then, we have changed so much that others barely recognize us. Have we the works of Christ (**John 14:2**) and do we sacrifice our lives for the Ecclesia so the world may see the Kingdom of God in action here in earth as it operates in heaven?

A solicitor may produce evidence that a gun, purchased one week before a murder and was found at the scene of a crime, does, in fact, belong to the accused. This is evidence, but the accused may have been in another state at the time with video, airline tickets, hotel receipts and testimony of many people to prove it, thus these two pieces of evidence contradict each other and cannot prove the accused committed the crime. No judge in his right mind would convict a person on one or two pieces of evidence, but a preponderance of evidence is proof of guilt or innocence. More than tongues, more than baptism, more than one God, more than tithe paying, more than being able to argue the scriptures correctly and having a modest wardrobe is required to prove our beliefs to a naturally suspicious and sceptical world. The preponderance of love, longsuffering, forbearance, compassion, exhortation, forgiveness, mercy, and grace we have for one another (with their corresponding actions), is how we will convince the world that we have the truth, which is Christ, not a set of scriptures. If it were scriptures, anybody could quote a verse or two and say they have the truth.

Though we speak in tongues, dress modestly (correctly mentioned in the word of God) and go to church every time the doors are open, we may tithe to the enth degree, obey our pastor, and even give to missionaries and invite people to our church services, if we do not practice kindness, are tender-hearted and forgive one another, love one another, edify one another, all of the above will not be enough to prove our claim that we are members of the Commonwealth of the Kingdom of God. It only proves we belong to a group of people who belong to an organization that obeys the rules of dressing modestly and going to church every time the doors are open, paying tithes to the enth degree, obeying the pastor, gives to missionaries and invites people to their church services.

The Necessity of Forgiveness.

Hot on the heels of tender-heartedness comes one of the hardest things we humans find to do one for another. Not just to forgive as the world forgives (for they do forgive), but to forgive as Christ forgives. Why is this so important to God? Sadly, we treat people's sins as if they sinned against us, when, in all truth, we are not that important that any sin can be against us. Things people say and do may affect us in some way, which doesn't take away from how we feel when bad things happen, but we must realize that sin is when a law is broken.

Paul tells us that if it had not been for the law there would be no sin (**Romans 7:7**). In essence, it is a law that makes something a sin. God is the only lawmaker, and all sin is because we have broken His laws. Let us go back to the story of the drunk driver who killed those children in the car accident.

Automobiles started to become prevalent in the US by 1903. Driving while intoxicated was dumb but not illegal until 1910, when, in New York, a law was enacted to fine drink drivers. Many states soon followed suit, but until a law was made by the government which forbade drink driving, it was just plain stupid, not illegal. Anybody who broke the law had sinned against the state, but it affected others around them.

Let us read what the rebellious lost son said to the father after he came to himself in **Luke 15:21**, *And the son said unto him, Father,* **I have sinned against heaven**, *and in thy sight and am no more worthy to be called thy son.* Notice, the sin was against heaven (the highest authority) but he did it in the sight of his father. Even though he dishonoured the father, the sin was against God. Did his sin effect the father? By all means, but the son was breaking the 5th commandment of God, *Honour thy father and thy mother: that thy days may be long upon the land which the LORD thy God giveth thee* (**Exodus 20:12**), **he just did it in front of his father.**

You see, in a broad sense a sin is the breaking of a law enacted by a higher authority, this is called a transgression against a law maker. So, in essence, the only sin people can commit against us is when they have broken one of our laws. This is problematic because our laws are not eternal, nor are they impartial and cannot be relied upon to be consistent. They are mostly frivolous, transient, lacking compassion and mercy, tender-heartedness and are usually based on how we feel at the time of their enactment. Sometimes we say someone sinned against us by dint of it happening to us in the past. Our laws hold no weight in the high court of heaven and when we do judge it is usually based on who did what and at what time the infringement occurred.

Let me explain how the laws of man work. I am an Australian citizen (though now living in the United States) and I am bound to live by the laws if this country. If I keep the law all will be well, however, if I break the laws of the land (transgress), I cannot expect to get away with it just because I am a citizen of another land.

However, when I hopped on a plane to Dubai during the time of Ramadan (which I did in the mid 2000's) I was bound by another set of laws. One day I was walking from my hotel to a meeting that happened to be about a mile away, and I stopped to get a soft drink and some gum. While I was in the store, I opened the bottle, stuck the gum in my mouth and headed to the door to resume my walk. The store owner almost jumped the counter and shouted for me to stop.

My first thought was that he didn't think I had paid for the drink and gum, but he frantically tried to explain to me that it was Ramadan, and it was not lawful to eat and drink in public between sunup and sundown. Even though I was born into a Muslim family, I have been a Christian so long that I had forgotten about the laws of Ramadan. Unwittingly, I was about to break a cardinal rule and would have incurred the wrath of the UAE and rightly so. I was in a foreign land, and I must obey the laws of that land. However, when I got to Paris this law did not apply anymore. In all my travels (six times around the world and counting) I have learned that there are universal, national, state, and local laws that must be obeyed. Killing someone and stealing are pretty much universal laws (unless it is the government doing it) and punishable by prison or death. However, there are laws that transcend borders, such as the Ten Commandments.

There are also unwritten laws of decent behaviour, but once again these are regional and once again, I cite an incident that happened to me while I was in Narita, Japan. I entered a cab and began to chat with the driver about how long the flight was and how I was looking forward to a good night's sleep. He didn't say a word the whole trip. As I was leaving the cab, I gave him a tip.

Curiously, he frowned at me, and I thought the tip was too small, so I handed him some more money, but the frown got worse. I thought his day in the cab must have been worse than mine on the plane. It was only when I got to Johannesburg, South Africa, a few months later and was recounting my story to a friend, that I found out I was insulting the driver by talking to him and tipping him. Different people, different laws.

Here in the US, it is perfectly normal to chat to the driver and tip. I had broken an unwritten rule and earned the ire of an industrious cabbie in Narita. The same type of thing happens on a personal level each day, only we humans have a bad habit of changing the rules on an almost daily (an in some cases, hourly) basis. What ticks us off one day may not do so on another day. We unknowingly write and rewrite our own laws with such monotonous regularity and hubris, which, when we compare them to the laws of God, are the most frivolous and demeaning laws of all.

We only get upset if certain people get too close to us or invade our personal space. How fickle is that? I've preached at churches where if you don't shout, *"amen"* or *"preach it"*, you're deemed backslidden. On the other hand, I've preached at some churches where if you squeak out an *"amen"* they think you're trying to be hyper spiritual. In some churches, wearing a wedding band or women not wearing pantyhose makes you backslidden while others are not uptight about it. I have seen people get offended at a brother or a sister for doing something against them that they gladly let others (friends or family) do. How lame and pitiful is that? Therefore, we are to obey the laws of God and not worry as much about breaking the pitiful laws of men when they contradict His laws or have little to no mercy in their judgement.

Anyway, back to God's ways. God is the only law maker and as such only his law counts. He does not let one person slide while coming down like Thor's Hammer on another. His laws are eternal and impartial, they do not care if a saint or sinner commits (or omits) the breaking of them. He is not interested in being our friend just because He loves us. *"How can you say that, Kieth? I sing that song 'I am friend of God' all the time!"*

Please read the following very carefully.

If ye walk in my statutes, and keep my commandments, and do them; **Then** *I will give you rain in due season, and the land shall yield her increase, and the trees of the field shall yield their fruit* (**Leviticus 26:3**).

And it shall be, **if** *thou wilt hearken unto all that I command thee, and wilt walk in my ways, and do that is right in my sight, to keep my statutes and my commandments, as David my servant did; that I will be* (Hâyâh- it shall come to pass, it will follow) [in other words **then**] *with thee, and build thee a sure house, as I built for David, and will give Israel unto thee* (**1 Kings 11:38**).

Beloved, **if** *our heart condemn us not,* **then** *have we confidence toward God* (**1 John 3:21**).

Take the above verses and put them in context with God's character. Because God uses the words **if** and **then,** and God has not changed from the Old Covenant, then that would explain **John 14:15** and **John 15:14** regarding who are God's friends. He makes a statement then qualifies it shortly thereafter. Remember, it is part of the same conversation… *If ye love me, keep my commandments.* Following hard on the heels of all of this, just 30 verses later (same conversation) we read **John 15:14** *Ye are my friends,* **if** *ye do whatsoever I command you.* He uses **if** in both verses. The point being that if we say we love Him and are His friends then we must keep His commandments. Forgiving one another is a commandment of God.

Unlike the laws of man, God's laws are not finicky or dependant on how He feels. **1 John 5:3** *For this is the love of God, that* (Hina- to the intent) *we keep his commandments: **and his commandments are not grievous**.* His commands are not burdensome, they are in fact, quite liberating because we know that they remain the same and they are impartial. If we break them, we know we must repent and bring forth fruits meet (worthy of) repentance (**Matthew 3:8**), seek His forgiveness and because God, our creator, is such a stable God, He forgives impartially and completely. He can because it was *His* law that was transgressed.

He now commands that we follow in His character and His actions (Dikaiosune- righteousness). If God forgives us for breaking one of His cardinal laws, should we not forgive if someone broke one of our rules? We forgive them, not for the sin, but how it affected us. As stated earlier and must be brought up again, forgiving (Aphiēmi- forsake, to lay aside, to make payment or yield up) those, *that are indebted to us* (Opheileō- morally fail in their duty) is a prerequisite to our forgiveness for breaking God's laws. In doing so, we learn to live with and for God, and with each other. We read this In **Luke 11:4**, we ask God to *...forgive our sins for we forgive those who are indebted to us*. There are two different definitions of forgiveness, Aphiēmi and in the above verse it is Opheileō- through the idea of accruing; to owe pecuniarily [a penalty or fine], to be under obligation (as one who ought, must, should). *And forgive us our sins;* **for we also** (Gar Autos Kai- seeing as, for indeed and because) *forgive every one that is indebted to us*. Either way, forgiveness to others is the standard for our own forgiveness. In Matthew's version of the Lord's prayer, we are told that our forgiveness is based on the word **as** (Hōs- in the same manner, even as, as quickly as). We are forgiven of our sins: (Hamartia- trespass, offence, our missing the mark), as (Hōs- in the same manner, even as, as quickly as) we forgive those who have failed us or failed in their moral duty or have missed the mark we have set for today. Our forgiveness of those who have broken our puny laws will dictate what forgiveness we receive from the great law giver Himself. When we treat someone differently because of something they did wrong, embarrassed us, or let us down, we are exacting a penalty or fine from them. This is how our sins will be viewed and treated by God.

To be wronged is something that we cannot control. Yes, it hurts and may even leave scars. However, to not forgive, and restore moves the wrongness of what was done to us onto our slate, and we must now bear the brunt of God's wrath. Sometimes it hurts so much that we struggle with forgiveness. The pain is real, the feelings are real, the nightmares are real. Don't let platitude mongers, those who have the spiritual insight of an uneducated flea on a dead camel, tell you after you have been hurt that you must forgive instantly. Sometimes you can't. But here is where we go to the one who has forgiven us countless times and as we seek His healing, we find we can forgive others as we have been forgiven. If we choose not to forgive, (saying we forgive but still treat them differently is not forgiveness) then we will be held accountable for that choice. However, when we forgive (no matter how long it takes), we release the spirit of the one who said to, *forgive them for they know not what they do* (**Luke 23:34**). Do we really believe that those baying for the blood of Jesus did not know what they were doing? Of course, they did. They allowed themselves to be influenced by their spiritual and political leaders who were bent on maintaining power and influence no matter what their reasoning was. What Christ was saying was, *If they knew the **consequences** of what they were doing, they would not have done it.* Yet, this same Christ, whom we claim to love and emulate, commanded us to follow in His footsteps and love and forgive as He did. Anything else is hypocrisy, no matter how we dress or how many meetings we attend.

The word or law of God is as steady and reliable as the sun rising in the east and setting in the west, *for He maketh his sun to rise **on the evil and on the good**, and sendeth rain on the just and on* *the unjust* (**Matthew 5:45**). Forgiving only those who have gone through our repentance programme is as bias as a bought and paid for corrupt judge. They will soon be found out and receive the fall weight of the law coming down on them. Being tender-hearted, showing kindness, and forgiving one toward another as Christ has forgiven us is a good indicator that we are in the true Ecclesia of God.

Chapter 29.

Fellowship one with another.

1 John 1:7 *But if we walk in the light, as he is in the light, we **have fellowship** one with another, and the blood of Jesus Christ his Son cleanseth us from all sin.*

Hebrews 10:25 *Not forsaking the **assembling of ourselves** together, as the manner of some is; but exhorting one another: and so much the more, as ye see the day approaching.*

The latter verse has been misunderstood, misquoted and sadly, hijacked by many sincere believers to mean that, should we fail to meet at a church building every weekend, we are somehow backslidden and in danger of hellfire. If this were true, then all the true believers in Iran, North Korea, Somalia, Uzbekistan, The Maldives, Yemen, and many other places are out of the will of God, for they cannot gather in a purpose build structure to go through a liturgical service in full view of others. After all, what's good for the goose is good for the gander, right? The fellowship that John is talking about here is true biblical fellowship or Koinōnia, where lives intertwine and change. In fact, God calls this fellowship *social intercourse.* The fellowship the vast majority of churches have today is nowhere near the kind of fellowship the early Ecclesia had, and if we do not return to it, we are just playing church.

The neighbourhood bar is possibly the best counterfeit there is to the fellowship Christ wants to give His church. It's an imitation dispensing liquor instead of grace, escape rather than reality. But it is a permissive, accepting, and inclusive fellowship. It is unshockable. It is democratic. You can tell people secrets and they usually don't tell others or want to. The bar flourishes not because most people are alcoholics, but because God has put into the human heart the desire to know and be known, to love and be loved, and so many seek a counterfeit at the price of a few beers. (Source unknown.)

The word *fellowship* has been hijacked and held for ransom by the modern-day western style churches and seeker friendly *God clubs.* It has been stripped of its meaning and consequently its power and effectiveness to grow a mature and healthy disciple. True disciples of Christ will replicate the spirit of God in themselves to those around them by their lives, not only or necessarily their church life. Let me clarify with a brief recap of the definition of *fellowship.* Today, it has come to mean that the believers in Christ gather together at a specific time, in a specific place to do a specific thing, when in fact the correct biblical sense of fellowship has a far more reaching impact on the Ecclesia. To fellowship is to Koinonia- to be in partnership, that is to literally participate in another's life or social intercourse, pecuniary [giving of money] benefaction or distribution (*author's note- where is the distribution in our churches today?*), to communicate, communion, (*author's note- not the wafer and juice type*). How can one do the above by meeting once or twice a week for a couple of hours each time? When we biblically fellowship, we become a sharer and a partaker of one another's lives, having all things in common, shared by all.

Now ask yourself, is this what is happening where you are when you say, *'you had a great time of fellowship'*? If not, then fellowship has been hijacked and you are the unwilling hostage being taken to a foreign land. We now have *fast food fellowship.* Look at the menu of church people we like to spend time with. Do they have all the ingredients we like? We quickly eat then leave. Fellowship has been used as an excuse to corral the believers into one common place and spoon feed them on a steady diet of P.O.P.S (Pray, Obey, Pay, Stay), with a regular dessert of *'live a holiness life and win souls.'*

Fellowship is infinitely more than meeting together once or twice a week, stare at the back of someone's head for a couple of hours while we sing the same repetitive songs or become just another radio channel where the latest 'worship songs' are shoved down our throats, listen to a man or woman telling us what the bible says and then go home to do as we please with no accountability to one another. Fellowship is a 24 hour a day passion that must be satisfied or else it has no meaning.

Being told that if we do not show up for church services because we are somehow abandoning God, is getting people to come out of fear. Should we gather? Absolutely. But what are we gathering for? When we gather, are we exhorting one another, are we provoking one another to love and good works, are we edifying one another, are we giving to one another, or are we there to receive the word of God and give money to keep the church doors open? When we gather to give as well as receive, we will gather for love not out of fear. Fear is a great motivator, but it is not based on relationship. It is based on carrot and stick motivators (*if you come to church, you can get your blessing, miracle, answers to prayer, conversely, if you don't come to church, you will eventually be lost and go to hell*). Governments, schools, and corporations use fear to get the masses to toe the line for the sake of the country, school, or business. If there was a real biblical fellowship between the saints, where we could be real with one another without fear of rejection or isolation, show our weaknesses as well as share our strengths and revelations from God's word, there would be a love for the Ecclesia that no sickness, job, or family issue could prevent us from gathering. Fear only motivates until some greater fear replaces it. Biblically intimate fellowship stands the test of time, trials, and persecution. When we are given the real word of God and we disciple and share with one another our time, treasure and talents, all members of the Ecclesia will have *'skin in the game'*. As a result, all participate in service towards one another outside of so-called *'church-service'*. The *'service'* is not left to the professional or their appointees, but we gather to serve one another and by sheer coincidence we end up serving God.

John says, *But **if** we walk in the light* (which means we have a choice to walk in the light or not), *as he is in the light, we* **have-** (we possess or have contiguity with) *fellowship with one another* (**1 John 1:7**). Contiguity is the state of bordering or being in direct contact with something. Just as bricks in a wall have contiguity with one another, so are we to have fellowship with one another. If we look at a regular brick wall, pick any brick and you will find it is connected to six other bricks. Mortar, the thing that holds it all together, is a workable paste which hardens to bind building blocks such as stones, bricks, and concrete masonry units, and to fill, seal the irregular gaps between them and spread the weight of the bricks evenly. The ingredients used in mortar are water (likened unto Christ), cement (likened unto love that binds), lime (it helps break down our flesh), and fine aggregates like sand (likened unto abrasive people) but put together in the right mixture, they make a building able to withstand any storm. As a side note, we think that just because someone irritates us or challenges us, we have the right to withhold fellowship. This would be like trying to mix mortar with missing ingredients or not in the proper proportion. Continued use of this ill-mixed mortar will result in the building collapsing under duress, strong wind, or excessive water (see **Matthew 7:24-27**).

The mortar that holds the Ecclesia together is what we have one for another in the Holy Ghost. Peter even describes us as lively stones in **1 Peter 2:5.** This connection with each other is the fellowship the Ecclesia must have one with another and unlike the common misconception that the pastor or organization holds the church together, it is, in fact, the Koinonia fellowship that not only keeps us in the bonds of love both for God and one another (see **Jude 1:21**) but allows God to build onto what He has already built. It makes us strong enough to withstand the gates (government) of hell.

A group of bricks do not come together whenever the occupant wishes to dwell there, they are put in place by the builder and stay connected to each other awaiting the occupant who comes and goes as He pleases. They are bound together by mortar (it can also be likened unto the word, spirit, obedience, and righteousness of Christ- character and actions of God) and held together by pressure from all four sides.

Fellowship is nothing more than finding our place within the worldwide, regional, and local Ecclesia and putting all our energy into providing whatever we have to offer, so we might strengthen the saints. Paul addresses this very issue in **Philippians 2:1** *If there be therefore any consolation* [solace] *in Christ, if any comfort of love* (Paramutheomai- to relate near, encourage)*, if any fellowship* (Koinōnia- partnership, that is, (literally) participation, or (social) intercourse, or (pecuniary/financial) benefaction, to communicate, communication, communion, contribution, distribution) *of the Spirit, if any bowels and mercies, Fulfil ye my joy, that ye be* **likeminded**, *having the same love, being of* **one accord** (Sumpsuchos- co-spirited, similar in sentiment [i.e. not identical or robotic])*, of* **one mind**. To be likeminded as Paul tells the Philippian Ecclesia, is to exercise the mind, to entertain or have the sentiment or opinion, that of being mentally disposed one to another and to intensively interest yourself with the needs of others, to be concerned and obedient to His will and to set our affection on others. All of that is to Phroneō- to be likeminded. The fellowship of the spirit is to fellowship with others with the same spirit (not just the same interests/hobbies/activities) and have the same passionate Spirit our Lord had when He laid down His life for the Ecclesia. Paul is not talking to an individual but to the Ecclesia in Philippi and by extension, to us.

Paul tells of what kind of fellowship he is seeking in Christ when he continues to write, *That I may know him, and the power of his resurrection, and* (here's the part we don't hear explained much from most pulpits) **the fellowship** *of* **his sufferings**, *being* **made conformable** (Summorphoō- to assimilate and be rendered) *unto his death...* (**Philippians 3:10**). Paul was saying to be in Christ is to be in partnership (fellowship) with what Christ endured, not just His victories and resurrection (those who are the shouting, dancing, and singing type of believers but don't want to endure through the sufferings for Christ are fair weather friends, not the friends Jesus mentions in **John 15:13-14**). Koinonia type fellowship helps us to conform one another unto His death and if that is so, then we will be conformed unto His resurrection also (verse 11). Paul says that he wants to be one with the sufferings (Pathēma- hardship, afflictions, pains, the emotions, and its influences) of Christ. How does he say this? He tells the Corinthians twice and the Philippians also to follow Him as he follows Christ (see **1 Corinthians 4:16. 11:1**). In the western churches, many want to avail themselves to the saving, supplying, healing, and delivering power and resurrection of Christ but are not willing to die to themselves through sufferings, isolation, rejection, or the emotional and mental anguish that the Lord went through prior to the victory of the resurrection. In other words, they want a painless Pentecost, and since this creation of mankind is like the fabled unicorn, the Jackalope and the Abominable Snowman, in that it doesn't exist, chasing a painless Pentecost is a waste of time, talent and resources.

A Realist with Faith.

We must not be fooled into thinking that just because we go to church, we will be shielded from hurts and disappointments. In fact, these things will be added to us and many times it will be the ones closest to us within the Ecclesia that will cause some of the deepest hurts. This can only happen when we have true fellowship, when we become truly vulnerable to those whom we claim to have fellowship with. These hurts bring to the surface, things that are keeping us from fully interacting with the Kingdom of God and with continued neglect, will keep us from entering His Kingdom on that great day. Perhaps this pain we seem to want to run from is why we won't give ourselves to others as we ought to. The chances of getting hurt are all too real.

King David felt this kind of heartache and expressed it beautifully in **Psalm 55:12-14** *For it was **not** an enemy that reproached me; then I could have borne it: neither was it he that hated me that did magnify himself against me; then I would have hid myself from him: **But it was thou, a man mine equal, my guide, and mine acquaintance*** (Yâdaʻ- one in whom we truly know, care for, take instruction, advise, familiar friend). *We took sweet counsel together, **and walked unto the house of God in company.*** These were one God people, or in today's vernacular, they were the *one God, Holy Ghost, tongue talkin', baptized in Jesus' name, conference attending, shoutin', tithe payin', pastor obeyin'* church people. It was not the betrayal of the world and heathen kings or princes which David had agreements with that hurt David (he expected that), but a true friend with whom he went to church to meet with God. If he only saw this friend once or twice a week, it would not have hurt him so deeply. In true Koinonia fellowship, we can be both elated in each other's presence and devastated by disagreements in the same week, we can experience divine kinship and frustration with our kin in the same day, but that is what family is all about.

Once again, with all my years of traveling from country to country and church to church as an evangelist, teacher and twice pastoring, I believe this is one of the main reasons we will not become vulnerable to the brothers and sisters within the Ecclesia. Did not our Lord take that chance also? To love and serve His creation, risking rejection and yet still loving and serving.

We are constantly told by our leaders of Paul's words, *Not forsaking the assembling of ourselves together, as the manner of some is.* Sadly, this is where they stop, but please, for all that is good and holy, keep reading, *but exhorting one another: and so much the more, as ye see the day approaching* (**Hebrews 10:25**). Again, I would like to reiterate what was said earlier in this section. There are millions of people who cannot gather in church buildings in non-Christian aligned nations, furthermore, there are millions of shut-ins, people living in remote areas or have remote jobs, military and emergency personnel who also cannot gather in church buildings, people who have been devastated by dictatorial church leaders or who simply cannot get to church buildings for financial reasons. What of these? Are these *forsaking* (Egkataleipō- leaving behind or deserting) the body? Are they any less members one of another? Are they somehow less Spirit filled than you and me?

I know a lady who lived on a cattle station about 3 hours' drive west of Strathmore, Queensland (about 13 hours' drive from where I lived). We met in Cairns on her two monthly grocery shopping trips. We talked about the Kingdom of God for hours and she went home but we kept in contact for over six months. I got a call one day telling me she was ready to commit her life to Christ, but she couldn't come to Cairns for another couple of months. My friend Bunge and I drove to her cattle station, and she was baptized in Jesus' name and filled with His spirit. She was about 1000 klms (600 miles) from the nearest church. Her church attendance was sporadic to say the least. Was this woman *forsaking the fellowship of the saints?* Did God have a different set of rules for her? Of course not. We must stop painting everyone with the same brush and use scripture sparingly and in accordance with what God is doing. To forsake is to abandon. When a husband or wife divorces their spouse, they have forsaken their wedding vows, or when a mother or father leaves their children and goes away to *"do their own thing"* they have forsaken/abandoned their children. Is this what we are meant to feel if we cannot *"make it to church?"*

For those who no longer come to our meetings, have we spoken to them and found out why they are not coming or is it just easier to judge them as forsakers? Could it be that someone is not going to our churches because they are neglected or have been hurt by people in the pews and they don't know how to heal yet? Could it be that they are not being fed in the spirit and they sit in their pews spiritually starving to death. Are these even considered where we *"fellowship?"*

A misunderstanding of the word *forsaking* has permeated the pulpit and bible schools today and we must cease its false propagation. *Forsaking* is speaking of *refusing* to be with the saints at all, but if they are meeting in homes, workplaces, coffeeshops, schools etc. as often as possible, then where is the forsaking? The word does not say, *Not forsaking the assembling of ourselves together **in a purpose build structure to go through a liturgical service**, as the manner of some is; but exhorting one another: and so much the more, as ye see the day approaching* (**Hebrews 10:25**). Is it good to gather together? Of course. But if someone cannot be there or they've been hurt so bad that they can't face it one more time, then we should meet them on their terms for a while.

Have we narrowed down the purview of the Ecclesia so far that unless we meet at a sanctioned time and place, we have somehow forsaken the body? I know of countless thousands who meet every week and sit in the pews feeling forsaken, left behind or deserted by the body, but we keep silent about those, don't we? We are hypocrites of the highest order and should hang our heads in shame before God if this is happening in our gatherings.

If two or three gathered together (Sunagō- lead together, that is, collect or convene; specifically, to entertain (hospitably) to accompany, assemble selves), constitutes an assembly (a rather intimate way of getting to know each other, in other words, Koinonia- fellowship), then where is the forsaking? What is the purpose of trying to get as many as possible into as big a building we can afford, to join in a metronomic, liturgical service where everything is pre-planned and polished for a few hours a week, of which the ultimate aim is to hear a sermon about God and what He has done and can do? We then judge the *"service"* by how many people come to the front/altar. Who does this help? I'm sad to say that we have many weekly sermonizers, but very few daily exemplars of biblical fellowship.

Please read the rest of that verse about the real reason we are to gather... *but exhorting one another...* Are we exhorting one another when we gather or is only the pastor exhorting the saints? We want to tell people to do the first part of the scripture but neglect the rest. Why? Because showing up at a building takes little to no faith or vulnerability to one another, not in western society anyway. Exhorting one another takes becoming vulnerable, becoming accountable to one another, (not so much the pastor), to help each other and ask for help, letting others see who we really are by dropping the façade of *"too blessed to be stressed"* or the ever popular but equally insipid, *"God is good, all the time"*. Like the phrase *"I love you"* these phrases have lost all their meaning. Platitudes such as these are as useful to a hurting, confused or lonely saint as waterproof teabags. How can we truly exhort, encourage, spur one another on to *love and good works* (see **Hebrews 10:24,** yet another verse that is meant to be read with verse twenty-five) if we do not really know one another? It takes patience to listen to others, not so we can jump in with the answers or our point of view, but so we can listen and understand who and what our family is, so we know how to pray and follow through with God in actions to be a part of the answer. It will take making ourselves available to be used by the Spirit of God in the gifts of the Spirit to build one another up and edify one another without constantly asking permission from someone who is barely involved. Sadly, this does not happen in our western style church fellowship on the whole. There may be small pockets of it in some places, and for these I am infinitely grateful, but this is meant for the **whole** Ecclesia.

If we meet with the saints and are exhorting one another as we are told in **Hebrews 10:25** then we are fulfilling the reason of why we gather. We do not gather to hear a sermon or to collect money (this will be impossible when the government, takes away the tax breaks (from American churches) and eventually become openly hostile to those who are His disciples). Macmillan's dictionary puts fellowship this way; *a feeling of friendship and support between people who do the same work or have the same interests*. Nowhere in the scriptures are we told that it is more important to fellowship in a church building. Fellowshipping with one another is a lifestyle not a religious practice done once or twice a week. Biblical fellowship has a purpose, that of comforting, exhorting, and discipling one another, not to corral, extort and discipline one another.

Fellowship done on a weekly basis only is more like a modern-day club than the Ecclesia. Let us re-examine the definition of a club; it is an association or organization dedicated to a particular interest or activity such as "a photography club", a commercial organization offering subscribers special benefits, a group of people, organizations, or nations having something in common, the building or facilities used by a club. Sound familiar?

If we are not fulfilling our purpose as the Ecclesia of God (to preach the Gospel of the Kingdom [Basileia- the royalty, rule, and realm] of God only and personally making disciples), then we have inadvertently become the world's largest book club, which is defined as a group of people who meet regularly to *discuss* books they are reading (remember, the bible is a collection of 66 books). Perhaps this would be a step closer to what was in the beginning, because at least we would be *discussing* the bible not just hearing one person telling us what it says. In western style church services there is no discussion, it is a monologue.

Fellowship is far more than just meeting with people of the same belief. It is a meeting of the minds and hearts, of wallets and homes, of faith and family; it is a place where a difference is made in each other's lives that lasts longer than the memory of what the sermon was about. If you and I are not changed, even a little bit by being in each other's presence as we worship the same God, then please tell me, what's the point? Christ did not die so I could be in an association of people who believe the same thing. He died so I could become a part of His living, growing, and overcoming body, where all that I am and have can be shared with His body and all that the body is and has can be shared with me. Where I don't need a piece of paper to say whether I can contribute to the body, and I do not expect that only someone with a piece of paper can contribute to me. Where we don't all have the same job, but we are on the same level of commitment, with the same passion to see the body grow. It is a place where no one is honoured above another, just because they have a membership card or a degree. Where spectators become participators purely and solely because of the calling of the Spirit of God and their submission to the word and Spirit of God and each other. A fellowship where older saints teach with their lives as well as their lips, and younger ones are not frowned upon as though they know nothing or have nothing to offer.

Being in Koinonia fellowship is meeting together to change lives, it is when meeting each other brightens our days, helps us find solace and someone to point us to God through what they have experienced, it is encouraging one another to study God's word together and often, to pray and fast for one another and to give of our lives to those who need what we have to offer. It is about giving and taking, it is about sharing the most intimate parts of our lives together (where it is appropriate), about learning from each other's victories and failures. It is where everyone ministers to everyone else. It is where we have learnt as much if not more from fellowlabourers in the Lord (**Philippians 4:3**) than from a 45-minute polished, yelled or effected speech sermon that is so generic that it helps very few people. Pseudo-fellowship is where a small cadre does all the work and gets all the perks. It is where we walk away alone and the same as when we came.

Fellowship is being a partaker of each other's lives whether it is good, bad, ugly, or mind numbingly mundane. It is where a spouse caring for a sick spouse trigger those within the Ecclesia and alerts them that both are in dire need of fellowship outside the confines of a church service. Fellowship becomes a way of life to the body of Christ, so much so, that not seeing each other breaks our hearts. Biblical fellowship is about finding out all we can about our brothers and sisters so that we can interact with God on their behalf. Fellowship demands time, effort, material, fasting for one another, praying in the spirit and finances, and cannot be done half-heartedly, half-cocked, or half-spiritedly on Sundays and mid-week meetings. Fellowship must be sought out and carried out with determination, compassion, and passion.

Passion is wrongly thought of today as emotions or strong feelings, but according to God, passion (only mentioned once (**Acts 1:3**) *To whom also he shewed himself alive after **his passion** by many infallible proofs, being seen of them forty days, and speaking of the things pertaining to the kingdom of God*) has a much deeper meaning. Strong's defines it as Paschō- to experience a sensation or impression, usually painful, to suffer. It pains us to be apart. It pains us to see our fellow-labourers not just leadership suffer, or to see our brothers and sisters be alone during bone-crushing trials. Why is it that when leadership has a need, we take up an offering, but when a member of the congregation has a need, we are told to pray for them. Is this not incongruous or inappropriate in God's Ecclesia? Biblical fellowship sees us rejoice when others succeed, hurt when they hurt, weep when they weep and suffer with them. True biblical fellowship is not just what we can get from fellowship but what we can give that makes us look forward to it. During our times apart we have gone to the throne for one another, we have received revelation from the throne of God and are eager to share it, we have received a blessing and can barely wait to minister it to one another. This is biblical fellowship. All else is a façade that God is bringing down and the real Ecclesia is beginning to rise.

Biblical fellowship, as opposed to our modern western style church understanding of fellowship, i.e., something we go to once or twice a week, is becoming fellow labourers not just with Christ, but with each other. There are a few terms used in the Renewed Covenant for working together for the same goal such as in **Philippians 4:3** *And I intreat thee also, true **yokefellow*** (Suzugos- conjoined [picture Siamese twins], from Sun- companionship, resemblance, completeness), *help those women **which laboured with me*** (Sunathleō- to wrestle or struggle in company with, to seek jointly or strive together with) *in the gospel, with Clement also, and with other my* **fellowlabourers**, *whose names are in the book of life.* Why do we think that those with an elected or appointed office in the church are the only ones who labour in the Gospel? Paul even tells us that we are fellow workers **with** God in **1 Corinthians 3:9** *For we are labourers together* **with** *God: ye are God's husbandry* (cultivation), *ye are God's building* (Oikodomē- God's architecture, structure) (see also **Philemon 1:24, Colossians 4:11, 1 Thessalonians 3:2**).

We have a term in the Australian Army, *'He's a real Conchie Digger'*. The word *digger* has been synonymous with the Australian soldier since the Boer War in South Africa in the 1880s but was solidified in Battle of Gallipoli (17 February 1915 to 9 January 1916). The ANZACs (Australian and New Zealand Army Corps) were dropped off at the Gallipoli Peninsular to fight the Turkish Army in the vain hope of weakening the German Army's southern flank. The strength of the Turkish Army was greatly underestimated by the British and the ANZACs were caught on the open beaches. After several months of failed head-on attacks, they began to dig trenches to avoid the deadly machine gun fire and artillery shrapnel. Each soldier began to dig as if his life depended on it. They dug an elaborate system of trenches which kept them from artillery and sniper fire.

They did not dig a small hole for themselves and hide it. Each man dug until his hole joined the hole of his mate. They dug the trenches for the whole army. They were *conscientious* and purposeful in digging for themselves and others, hence the term *'Conchie Digger'*.

Fellowship is not a part-time activity we do twice a week like a hobby, but a full-time calling and career as though one were studying to become a doctor. It takes commitment and sacrifice; it takes study and practice, forgoing earthly pleasures and wants for the sake of others. Rarely does one become a doctor to heal themselves, but to help alleviate the sufferings of others. One would not readily lay down their lives for a stranger, someone we see once or twice a week, *For scarcely for a righteous man will one die: yet peradventure for a good man some would even dare to die* (**Romans 5:7**), but for a friend? Jesus said that laying down our lives for one another was the first sign of God's love; *This is my commandment, That ye love one another, as I have loved you. Greater love hath no man than this, that a man lay down his life for his friends* (**John 15:12-13**).

It would behove us to look at the words of Paul once again, *For scarcely for a righteous man will one die: yet peradventure for a good man some would even dare to die. But God commendeth his love toward us, in that, while we were yet sinners, Christ died for us* (**Romans 5:7-8**). While you and I did not deserve such grace, mercy, and love that one so pure of heart and sinless would die for us, should we not also follow in His footsteps and die for those He also died for? We must be willing to lay down our petty squabbles, selfishness, pride, and sacrificially give ourselves to His great cause through Koinonia fellowship one with another?

For to their power, I bear record, yea, and beyond their power they were willing of themselves; Praying us with much intreaty that we would receive the gift, and take upon us the fellowship of the ministering to the saints, or as the AENT puts it, *For I testify that according to their ability and beyond their ability, in the spontaneity of their mind they looked for us with much eagerness that they might participate in the ministration of the Set Apart ones* (**2 Corinthians 8:3-4**). This is biblical fellowship personified. When this practice is resumed, we, the Ecclesia of God, will be unstoppable.

Fellowship can be viewed as a group of fellows rowing together in a ship. If all are rowing together with the same purpose in mind, the destination will eventually be reached by all in the ship. Another way of looking at it is, *I cannot row you across a lake, and both of us not get to the other* side. Dietrich Bonhoeffer once said, *"The first service that one owes to others in the fellowship consists of listening to them."* If one or two are doing all the talking then it is a board meeting not fellowship. These types of meetings soon turn from a board meeting to a boring meeting. Fellowship can be quiet time with each other, a rousing time around the dinner table, a phone call just to see how we are going, a time of prayer, a time of counselling, sharing a burden or a revelation, times of joy or tears with each other or a myriad of things that bind us together in love.

Extraordinarily little of this is happening in much of the western Ecclesia at this time. I am not talking of cliques where we only meet or spend time with the same people week in, week out. This just shows immaturity amongst the Ecclesia. We are happy in our cliques because we will not be challenged to think differently, act differently, or hear any opposing views. That is why we gravitate to political groups (Republican, Democrats, Liberal, Labour) sports teams and yes, even ministry or non-ministry. Not wanting to be challenged is a human failing which not only hinders growth but actually causes it to shrink.

I used to commute on the train from Mt Dandenong to the Melbourne CBD in Victoria, Australia, (about 2 hours) every morning for over a year with the same people doing the same thing at the same time. I would say hi to a few people and every now and then I would strike up a very casual and superficial conversation with someone. Was I fellowshipping with them? Using today's understanding of assembling, I was. We were on the same train at the same time for the same purpose (going to work). If *fellowshipping* with the saints is not more than my commute, then it is NOT fellowship. Where else but biblical fellowship can we exhort one another and challenge (provoke) one another to *love and good works*, where we can grow into the full stature of Christ (see **Hebrews 10:24, Ephesians 4:13**). It is a place where we can edify and give a little of ourselves every time we meet one another. When we can do this, we can now say it is not a club we have joined, but the body of Christ.

Much of the western church has become a club-like group, and within each group we have sub-groups such as ministry and non-ministry, worship leaders and singers, musicians and soundboard operators, Sunday school groups, youth, marrieds, and oldies. It is when we crave the company of those not in our socio-economic group, but those with like precious faith (not like precious talents, time on earth or tasks) that we can truly call ourselves a part of the Commonwealth of the Kingdom of God. We must become addict-like when it comes to fellowshipping with one another.

Being a Christian addict.

An addict craves whatever they feel will fill the void in their lives at the moment. Being a part of the Ecclesia and not having a void that needs to be filled with believers is in and of itself an illusion at best and oxymoronic at worst. There are people who are addicted to church meetings because it fills a void in their lives, but not addicted to Koinonia fellowship as this would mean they would have to give more than a few hours or a few dollars a week, and this frightens many people. Have we become committed to church meetings but not to church people? The Ecclesia (people and their lives) is what makes us members one of another (**Romans 12:5, 1 Corinthians 12:25, Ephesians 4:25**). Meeting in a building but not meeting outside of one or meeting each other's needs is having church, not being church. The Catholic, Methodist, Baptist, Lutheran, Presbyterian, Episcopal, Assemblies of God and other denominations do the same. What must separate us is that we are to have Koinonia with one another. In this type of fellowship we grow through giving and receiving.

These biblical concepts teach what true fellowship is, and it is when we ignore or forsake these facts that we are forsaking the assembling of ourselves and we do this to our own peril. Look at how Paul finishes his first letter to the Ecclesia at Corinth, *I beseech you, brethren, (ye know the house of Stephanas, that it is the firstfruits of Achaia, and that they have addicted* [Tassō- appointed themselves, arranged themselves, ordained themselves, set] *themselves to the ministry* [diakonia- attendance (as a servant, etc.); figuratively (eleemosynary, [charity, alms]) aid, service especially of the Christian teacher, or technically of the deacon, administer, office of and for relief, service] *of the saints,) That ye submit yourselves unto such, and to every one that helpeth with us, and laboureth* (**1 Corinthians 16:15-16**).

True biblical fellowship is not interested in whether someone has something we need or want, or is affiliated with the right group, but rather being whom God created us to be so that we might fulfil the needs of others. This is a pre-requisite to entrance into the Commonwealth of the Kingdom of God. To be in biblical fellowship is what a disciple of Christ craves and feels miserable when they do not have it. They are addicted to serving the saints. They will arrange themselves and set themselves to fulfil the craving of fellowship as a drug addict will do *anything* to get what they need to make it through another day.

Not going to a church service regularly is not forsaking the brethren, meeting with them weekly and not getting to know them (Ginōskō- to perceive and understand) is.

We don't need meetings that don't meet real needs. Whether those needs be spiritual, physical, mental, or emotional.

Chapter 30.

Hospitable to one another.

1 Peter 4:9 *Use **hospitality** one to another without grudging.*

Romans 12:12-13 *Rejoicing in hope; patient in tribulation; continuing instant in prayer; Distributing to the necessity of saints; **given to hospitality**.*

This one will test how clean or mean we really are. It will show how much we treasure or surrender our own lives. This will be a crucial factor of how much of the Commonwealth of the Kingdom of God we possess and will share. First, we must distinguish the difference between hospitality from a Middle Eastern/Jewish/Biblical standpoint and western standpoint. Biblical hospitality is taking someone into our homes and lives when theirs is a mess or the vicissitudes of life have robbed them of one. Biblical hospitality is not dinner parties where we show off how God has blessed us, but the breaking of bread with someone who needs Him more than we do. I have long believed that true sacrifice is not when we give of what we have, but when we give what we have left.

In Old Covenant Judaism (our spiritual roots), showing hospitality (*Hakhnasat Orchim-* literally *"the bringing in of strangers"*) to guests is considered a mitzvah (a precept, a command or principle intended especially as a general rule of action). To a Jew (and from an engrafted Jew's standpoint- Gentiles who follow Messiah. See **Romans 11:17-19**) when one knows of strangers who are hungry or need a place to relax, it becomes a legal obligation. Most rabbis consider *Hakhnasat Orchim* to be a part of *Gemilut Hasadim* (giving of loving kindness). The Old and Renewed Covenants as well as a plethora of Rabbinic and archaeological literature abounds in recording and praising the practice of hospitality on behalf of travellers and indigents. It is even suggested that it is *"greater than welcoming the Divine Presence* [Shekinah].*"* As challenging as charity can be, *Hakhnasat Orchim* (inviting people to come to or stay at our home) is even harder. If money is personal, our home is hyper-personal. This is where our personal lives are challenged in an obvious way. Allowing someone to enter our space, our sanctuary, the place that we call our castle, is quite scary. Giving them the opportunity to be privy to the secret life we live in our home and perhaps discover a skeleton or two (the temper no-one knew we had, or how messy the house is regularly, how our kids behave when no-one is looking, how we treat our spouses, where we spend our money etc) can be gut-wrenchingly scary. There is no fear like that of having others see us for who we really are, not the façade we put on at church meetings or in public places. When the façade is torn down and we become real, is when hospitality can really fulfil its purpose. Hospitality is when we give of ourselves to the point where we have deprived ourselves of a luxury for the sake of another.

Hospitality and fasting.

Fasting is one way we can do this. The only in-depth biblical definition of fasting is found in Isaiah chapter 58. This is where the prophet of God breaks down the purpose of fasting and what the outcome of biblically fasting God's way will be. First of all, I would like to destroy a myth that the western church propagates. That fasting either moves God or makes God answer prayers in our favour, or that if we have an issue (whether spiritual, physical, financial, or mental) that God will deal with it. These are doctrines that were borne out of desperation and not from revelation. When we read it slowly and with an open mind, we will see that the fasting is done for the release of another's issues, to break strong bonds and set other people free, while giving ourselves to the needs of others, (taking them into our homes, feeding, clothing, and caring for their needs). It is only after we have done these things for others that God's light shines on us, and revelation ensues.

God says... *Is not this the fast that I have chosen? To loose the bands of wickedness, to undo the heavy burdens, and to let the oppressed go free, and that ye break every yoke? Is it not to deal thy bread to the hungry, and that thou bring the poor that are cast out to thy house? when thou seest the naked, that thou cover him; and that thou hide not thyself from thine own flesh?* **Isaiah 58:6-7.** The Jewish Study Bible shines a greater light on the subject; *No, This is the fast that I desire; To unlock fetters of wickedness and untie the cords of the yoke, To let the oppressed go free; to break every yoke. It is to share you bread with the hungry, and to take the wretched poor into your home; and when you see the naked, to clothe him, and not to ignore your own kin.* We may be fasting (doing without food) but are we doing what we are told *while* fasting? Are we giving the food we are not eating to others who have need? Are we neglecting our own families? Are we clothing the naked or bringing in a stranger into our homes (*Hakhnasat Orchim*)? To the overwhelming people in the west, this would be unthinkable, but we cannot say we have fasted if we have not done all in our power to fulfil the words of God on fasting.

We fast so others might be set free. Verses 8-10 tells us what will happen as a consequence of our fasting for others, **Then** ('âz- at which time, at that time, therefore) *shall **thy** light break forth as the morning, and **thine** health shall spring forth speedily: and **thy** righteousness shall go before **thee**; the glory of the LORD shall be **thy** rereward.* **Then** ('âz- at which time, at that time, therefore) *shalt **thou** call, and the LORD shall answer; **thou** shalt cry, and he shall say, Here I am. **If thou take away from the midst of thee the yoke, the putting forth of the finger, and speaking vanity; And if thou draw out thy soul to the hungry, and satisfy the afflicted soul;** then* ('âz- at which time, at that time, therefore) *shall **thy** light rise in obscurity, and **thy** darkness be as the noonday.* It is after we have fasted correctly (for one other) that we will receive what we need from God. This is Isaiah prophesying the words of the Messiah, *But seek ye first the kingdom of God, and his righteousness; and all these things shall be added unto you* (**Matthew 6:33**).

If the Ecclesia were operating according to God's standards, not our own selfish standards, I would fast for you and you would fast for me, no one is left out. We would be walking in the light as He is in the light because we are in Koinonia *fellowship with one another and* (Kai- cumulative force, then, moreover) *the blood of Jesus Christ cleanses us.* How can we claim to be washed, redeemed, and delivered via His blood, if we will not walk in the light we are given? (See **Revelation 1:5, 5:9, Ephesians 1:7, 1 John 1:7**).

The doctrine of hospitality has been around way before the children of Abraham became a nation. A midrash (a biblical exegesis by ancient Judaic authorities, using a mode of interpretation prominent in the Talmud. The word itself means "textual interpretation", similar to our bible commentaries such as Matthew Henry, F.B. Meyer, or commentaries by the leaders of our organizations) as well as devout Jews around the world presents the biblical patriarch Avram (Abraham) as the paragon of hospitality. He ranks high on the scale of Jewish hospitality because of his reception of wayfarers in Genesis chapter 18 among other places. Look at Avram's position at the entrance of his tent in the midday heat **18:1**, (this is interpreted as a proactive seeking out of passing travellers). Other elements of the story contribute to Avram's reputation: his eagerness **18:2**, his persistence for them to stay and eat **18:4-6**, His largesse by the size of the meal he gave them **18:7**, and his insistence on seeing his guests off as they departed **18:16**.

We can also see Jethro's (Moses' future father-in-law) disappointment at not being able to extend hospitality to Moses after he showed a great kindness to his daughters at the well (**Exodus 2:20**) and the Shunammite woman's unsolicited preparation of a special room for the prophet Elisha (**Kings 4:8-11**). We can see ancient hospitality in action via the inhabitants of Melita to Paul and his entourage (**Acts 28:1-2**), our Lord cooking breakfast for His disciples on a beach after they had just caught a huge hall of fish (**John 21:9**). It is even written in the Levitical laws, *But the stranger that dwelleth* (Gûr- to turn aside from the road for a lodging or any other purpose, that is, sojourn as a guest, to assemble [in other words hospitality) *with you shall be unto you as one born among you, and thou shalt love him as thyself; for ye were strangers in the land of Egypt: I am the LORD your God* (**Leviticus 19:34**). It is plain to see those sojourners on the road of life, when we offer hospitality, are to be treated as family members, with love, honour, and respect. We only need look at the multitude of examples in the bible and throughout history to find how important the hospitable treatment of guests is.

On a Shabbat service in many synagogues around the world, it is common practice for the worshippers to go to their homes for a meal, and for them to invite individuals and families as guests. Whether they are poor or well off, the idea is not to impress, but to fellowship (Koinonia) over food and drink, to learn about and from each other in a relaxing atmosphere. Many even open their Shabbat tables to visitors from out of town or someone they just met at synagogue. In many communities, the evening prayers are followed on occasion by a communal meal at the synagogue. Some synagogues regularly put off their Shabbat evening service until after the dinner hour so that each family can entertain strangers, the lonely or visitors and follow the service with unprogrammed socializing over light refreshments.

The one thing we all do whether we are rich or poor, from high society or from the wrong side of town, whether we went to Penn State or the state pen, young or old, is eat food of some sort, drink liquid of some kind, and need some form of company and these are the three main aspects of hospitality. Surprisingly, the modern English definition of hospitality is not that far removed from the ancient one. It means, *The reception and entertainment of strangers or guests **without reward**, or with liberality and kindness. The friendly reception and treatment of guests or strangers. The quality or disposition of receiving and treating guests and strangers in a warm, friendly, generous way.* Sadly though, today we have dumbed down hospitality to those who agree with us or like us. Being hospitable for no reward brings us to the parable of the feast for strangers. *Then said he* (Jesus) *also to him that bade him, When thou makest a dinner or a supper, call not thy friends, nor thy brethren, neither thy kinsmen, nor thy rich neighbours; lest they also bid thee again, and a recompence be made thee. But when thou makest a feast, call the poor, the maimed, the lame, the blind: And thou shalt be blessed; for they cannot recompense thee: for thou shalt be recompensed at the resurrection of the just* (**Luke 14:12-14**). Here we can plainly see when our reward for our obedience regarding hospitality will be given, ***thou shalt be recompensed at the resurrection** of the just* (Dikaios- equitable (in character or act) similar to the Greek Dikaiosune meaning righteousness. (See also **Revelation 20:12**).

This parable does not forbid calling friends, family, or the brethren, it states that the calling of those who cannot return the favour is far more beneficial and has a deeper reward at the resurrection of the *just*.

Though the word *hospitality* is only mentioned four times in the bible and all in the Renewed Covenant, its principle is found throughout the word of God. Hospitality comes from the Greek word Philoxenia which means to *entertain strangers* or *to be fond of guests* and we are told that a bishop (for and as an example in leadership) is supposed to be given to hospitality (**1 Timothy 3:2**) and not only hospitable to other bishops, pastors, or other leadership, but to all kinds of people. Perhaps that is why we struggle with Philoxenia as a whole. Can you imagine what would happen of our leadership would start practicing hospitality to those in our pews first, then to the stranger? How would this filter down to the rest of the congregation? This is our example of how we are to treat one another even though we may be strangers within the same group, if we are given to hospitality, we soon eliminate the stranger aspect of it.

The opposite of Philoxenia is Xenophobia which is described as fear and hatred of strangers or foreigners or of anything that is strange or foreign. When we take on the name (Onoma- character and authority) of Christ in baptism and claim to be filled with His spirit, we are also repulsed by our old nature. As we take on the nature of a member of the Commonwealth of the Kingdom of God, hospitality begins to become a natural part of our daily lives. This means that strangers and foreigners are no longer a source of fear to us. We welcome or Philoxenia all manner of people instead (not just those whom we agree with or are like us) and look for ways to bless and learn from and teach them. The current trend in the west is to have as little to do with strangers as possible, until we get to know them (which makes about as much sense as a transparent eye mask). We will not get to know them until we invite them into our lives (this includes our homes and families). I've even been asked, '*But what if I live in a small apartment?*' C'mon, we were called to surrender our sinful lives and our hearts, not our common sense.

I have seen several variations of the following statements on social media lately and I would like to offer a common-sense rebuttal. "*Being saved and not going to church is like being married and not going home*" is one of the cuter platitudes I have seen recently. However, this makes as much sense as, "*Being saved and going to church twice a week is like being married and seeing your spouse only twice a week.*" How long do you think this marriage will last? Without giving of ourselves to those who sit in our pews, or to those outside, we have little to no effect on the Kingdom of God. The world may come in for a short sojourn, check it out and the overwhelming majority will leave because what we say we are does not match what we do to, for and with one another. Why? Because when it comes to giving to one another, many of us stop at nothing. If, on the other hand they see a feast of love (the very definition of Agape), who in their right mind would not stay. There is not real love in the world, but ought to be, nay, must be, in the Ecclesia.

Peter commands us *...above all things have **fervent charity*** (Ektenēs Agapē- an intentional, breathing heavy and without ceasing love feast) ***among yourselves**: for charity shall cover the multitude of sins. **Use hospitality one to another without grudging*** (Goggusmos- without grumbling or murmuring). *As every man hath received the gift* (this could be speaking of the gift of the Holy Ghost, the gift of hospitality or the gifts of the spirit to edify the Ecclesia), *even so minister* (Diakoneō- to be an attendant, that is, wait upon (menially or as a host, friend or [figuratively] teacher) *the same **one to another**, as good stewards of the manifold* (Poikilos- various in character and divers) *grace of God* (**1 Peter 4:8-10**). Peter tells us to have charity (a feast of fervent and deliberate love) without ceasing, to stretch beyond the norm is to be good stewards. Using hospitality without grumbling or murmuring is showing ourselves to be good stewards of God's grace, time, and money. The number of times I have heard sermons on being good stewards of God's money (usually in regards to tithes and offerings) is beyond my recall. I have yet to hear from an apostolic standpoint about being good stewards of God's grace through hospitality. Why is that? Because so few understand its importance.

The western mindset puts an inflated price on our personal space and personal freedom and if we do something for others, such as invite them into our personal bubble it is usually for a set period, and we get anxious when they stay longer than anticipated. Yet the biblical definition of hospitality is defined as, *you're welcome until your journey moves you on*. I have had many long discussions with many organizational leadership friends, and each has dug deep into their bag of excuses as to why this is impossible in today's society. I agree, using a western mindset and our own carnal thinking would make this impossible. However, we are to have the nature, mind, character and actions of our Lord and Master, not those of the 21st century world.

Even when its inconvenient?

Yes, especially when it is inconvenient. The Lord tells the parable of a man whose friend showed up unannounced at midnight and he was unprepared to host him, but rather than telling him that now is not a good time and sending the guest on his way, the host went and borrowed what he needed from a neighbour in order to fulfil his duty and task as a Hospitaller (more on this word shortly). This story is a continuation of what we call the Lord's prayer (**Luke 11:1-4**). This is not a new thought but continues from Jesus's explanation of the Kingdom of God. The next words out of the Master's mouth after giving us the manner in which to pray is how to be hospitable toward one another. **Luke 11:5-8** *And he said unto them, Which of you shall have a friend, and shall go unto him at midnight, and say unto him, Friend, lend me three loaves; For a friend* (Philos, and associate, neighbour) *of mine in his journey is come to me, and I have nothing to set before him? And he from within shall answer and say, Trouble me not: the door is now shut, and my children are with me in bed; I cannot rise and give thee. I say unto you, Though he will not rise and give him, because he is his friend, yet because of his importunity he will rise and give him as many as he needeth.* Is this a coincidence that the Master would speak of hospitality straight after speaking of God's Kingdom, forgiveness, and supply? I trow not! Look at the attitude of both men, one was inconvenienced while the other wanted to serve a sojourner. Which do you think, lovingly served the Kingdom? Remember, *Use hospitality one to another without grudging* (grumbling or murmuring. **1 Peter 4:9**).

Why is this rarely mentioned from the pulpit? Because we preach a western definition of the bible, not the original version. We may use the King James bible, but we interpret it through our western societal lenses, which lessens the impact it has in our lives and the lives of those watching us.

The so-called Lord's Prayer and hospitality are one subject. They are a continuation of seeking God's Kingdom here in earth as it is in heaven. How do we behave with each other here on earth? That is how we will behave in the New Jerusalem, but as God is the King of heaven, He decides what type of behaviour is acceptable in His new capitol and we are tested here on earth to make sure we have what it takes to be a member of the Commonwealth of the Kingdom of God. If we cannot or will not show hospitality to the saints and strangers here on earth, we will not fit in the New Jerusalem.

Look at the next highly quoted verses about getting what we desire. Remember, Christ is still speaking on the same subject matter, The Kingdom of God and how to pray. **Luke 11:9-10** *And I say unto you, Ask, and it shall be given you; seek, and ye shall find; knock, and it shall be opened unto you. For every one asketh receiveth; and he that seeketh findeth; and to him that knocketh it shall be that opened.* The sojourner *sought* out his friend, who *knocked* on his door and he *asked* for aid, then he *received* him. His friend then did the same thing to his neighbour. We are to ask, seek, and knock-on doors to be hospitable to one another. Not one mention of money or blessings for ourselves is mentioned in this chapter, and yet, this is how it is preached from almost every pulpit in the west.

As we are getting our daily bread and being forgiven, we will be required to be hospitable, and asking and receiving, for a friend (even at a most inconvenient time such as midnight) not for ourselves. As we seek the Kingdom, God takes care of our needs (**Matthew 6:30-34**). This is no accident, no mere slip of the quill by Doctor Luke. This was deliberate and like all scripture, (which is all divinely inspired, not just the parts that agree with us or are told are true) it is meant to reprove, rebuke, exhort and instruct (**2 Timothy 4:2**). It is a wakeup call and when taken as challenge to change our selfish nature into the nature of God, we become citizens of the Commonwealth of the Kingdom of God. We are commanded to be like God; **1 Peter 1:14-16** *As obedient children,* **not fashioning yourselves according to the former lusts** *in your ignorance* (wanting what we want and when we want it)*: But as he which hath called you is holy,* **so be ye holy in all manner of conversation** (lifestyle)*; Because it is written, Be ye holy; for I am holy.* If we claim to be holiness people, then hospitality must be as much a part of our holiness lives as our manner of dressing, uncut hair, and speech.

Doing the above is becoming like God. Holiness is not just a manner of dress or obeying a set of rules. Holiness is becoming like the God of the universe as He demonstrated to us when He came to earth in the flesh. God created a planet with a beautiful garden, then invited Adam and Eve to share it with Him. When He came to earth as a man, He dwelt modestly in all aspects of life, not just clothing, and He has left us hundreds of thousands of examples on how to live in and for the Kingdom of God. As a side note: if we claim to be holiness people but are obese because of gluttony, then our witness is destroyed. Holiness means modesty (moderate) in food also.

Hebrews 13:1-2 tells us to, *Let brotherly love continue* (Meno- to stay (in a given place, state, relation, or expectancy) to abide, dwell, endure, be present, remain, stand, tarry for. *Be not forgetful to entertain* (Philoxenia- to be hospitable to) *strangers: for thereby some have entertained angels* (Aggelos- to bring tidings, a messenger, especially an angel) *unawares* (Lanthanō- unwittingly or ignorantly). We never know whom God is going to use and for what purpose. It might be a homeless person or a person from the Ecclesia that seems to be a no-one or not in the *"so-called ministry"* but mark my words, God speaks more through unexpected channels than He does through what or whom we normally expect, if we will only take and make the time to listen.

Abraham entertained angels believing they were strangers in Genesis 18, Jethro entertained a prince of Egypt and didn't know it in Exodus 2 and ended up travelling with the children of Israel, Samson's parents asked to let the man of God (though it was an angel) come back to them, then begged him to stay and eat and he came back in Judges 13. Lot took care of the servants of the Lord in Genesis 19; Gideon made a meal and fed a stranger who showed up out of nowhere which turned out to be an angel in Judges 6. People sat, ate, and talked with Jesus, not knowing He was the Son of God in John 21. Things are not always what they seem to be, but with a heart open to God's perspective we can see into and interact with the spiritual realm every day.

We never really know who we have in our midst, be they friend or foe, close relative, or total strangers, until we truly get to know them. This begs the question; how can we get to know them if we only have western style church fellowship with them? We are commanded to be hospitable at every opportunity and rely on God to supply our needs after we have done what we were asked to do.

When **Matthew 6:30-33** becomes real in our lives, we will not be able to use the excuse that we do not have what we need right now to show hospitality. Because hospitality is one of the aspects of the Commonwealth of the Kingdom of God which requires a physical move before God reacts, it is only fitting that when we seek the Kingdom and His righteousness (His character and authority) and do what the word says, that all these things (our needs for food, shelter, and clothing), shall be added unto us. He knows many of us would not use these things for His kingdom and so He adds them to us after we have first sought to fulfil His will.

Back to the man in Luke 11, he did not tell his friend who came to his door to go away because he didn't have what was needed or because he showed up at an inopportune time, neither did he send the sojourner to his neighbour's house. Quite the contrary, God brought the traveller to his house, so it was his responsibility to care for him. The host sought by any means possible to fulfil the word in **Leviticus 19:18** *Thou shalt not avenge, nor bear any grudge against the children of thy people, but thou shalt love thy neighbour as thyself: I am the LORD.* Many who are casual readers of the bible will not have realized the dangerous journey this man (the visitor) undertook. Due to highwaymen and robbers, people did not travel at night unless it was urgent. For this sojourner to show up at this time at his house proved that this was no ordinary visit. What risk this man took to travel at night and what love of the host to not only receive him but hassle another friend for food. He could provide the shelter and what he was lacking he sought from another, who for the sake of God and His Kingdom, rose up and gave it to the host. The host had showed his friend no mean kindness.

This story is just a continuation of another parable told shortly before, about a man who was robbed on the way to Jericho and left for dead (**Luke 10:30-37**). It is also about hospitality and kindness and going out of pocket for another. Jesus did not change the theme, just where the stranger was found, out on the street instead of on the doorstep.

What would we go through to show hospitality to one another? We are exhorted by John in his final epistle, *Beloved, thou doest faithfully* **whatsoever thou doest to the brethren, and to strangers;** *Which have borne witness of thy charity before the church: whom* **if thou bring forward on their journey** *after a godly sort, thou* **shalt do well**: (3 John 1:5-6). Once again, look at the order in which John tells us to do these things, **whatsoever thou doest to the brethren, and to strangers.** He is just reiterating what Paul wrote to the Galatians, *As we have therefore opportunity, let us do good unto all men,* **especially** *unto them who are of the household of faith* (**Galatians 6:10**). The Berean Bible puts **3 John 1:5-6** this way; *Beloved, you are doing faithfully whatever you might have done toward the brothers, and they are strangers, They have testified to the church about your love. You will do well to send them on their way* **in a manner worthy of God**. Did you catch that? **In a manner worthy of God.** These people had a reputation of the love of God shown through hospitality. *Thou shalt do well* (Poieo Kalōs) is a phrase that means *you will continue in a good place.*

The seven-word phrase, *If thou bring forward on their journey,* is a compound of the one Greek word Propempō which means to send forward, that is, escort or aid in travel, to accompany. This is more than just giving a meal or a few dollars to someone and send them on their way. This requires commitment to their journey and being grateful that God has brought them across our path so that we can play a small part in it. When our day to stand before God comes, it will be recorded as to whether we ignored or helped others on their journey. Not only will we receive our reward, but it will be accounted to all that helped as well. What would we do if God Himself showed up at our doorstep in a manner or fashion we are unaccustomed to? How would we treat Him as opposed to how would we treat the premier, mayor, governor of our state, pastor, bishop, presbyter, or superintendent of our organization? God showed up to the Jews as a newborn baby and they didn't recognize whom they were rejecting. They were expecting a David, a Solomon, and a Joshua showed up (a man fashioned after Moses' humble servant). Even His name, Yeshua- ישוע, is a contracted form of Joshua- יְהוֹשֻׁעַ. In like manner, as these religious people did not recognize God was amongst them, many times we don't recognize the presence of God in strangers or those we wouldn't give the time of day to, and we miss an opportunity to fellowship with God. These are indicators of how we treat the God that is in the people within the Ecclesia.

We are told three times what sort of things will lead us to doing well. **3 John 1:5-6** and **James 2:8** *If ye fulfil the royal law according to the scripture, Thou shalt love thy neighbour as thyself,* ***ye do well:*** and **Acts 15:29** *That ye abstain from meats offered to idols, and from blood, and from things strangled, and from fornication: from which if ye keep yourselves, ye* ***shall do well.*** *Fare ye well.*

The phrase *do well* in **Acts 15:29** is the compounded Greek word- Prasso which is to practise, that is, perform repeatedly or habitually. It is not an occasional or blasé thing we must do to be hospitable to each other, but a well thought out and deliberate, often repeated (habitual), and visible act which proves we are members of the Commonwealth of the Kingdom of God. **Matthew 7:20** *Wherefore by their fruits ye shall know them* (see also **Matthew 7:16**). This last scripture means that the life we claim to have and sing about in our church services must be proven outside of our church services.

I would like to recount something that happened to me in December 1990 not long before I came to the USA. I owned and operated a cobbler shop in Mareeba, not far from where the North Queensland rainforest meets the outback. I was on my way home after a gruelling day with boots, bags, and bad customers (I was a cobbler, it comes with the territory) when I saw a swaggie (unemployed wanderer carrying a sack with his belongings) hitchhiking along the road with his dog. I naturally stopped and picked him and his dog up. His clothing was pretty torn up and his hair was matted. It looked like he had not bathed in weeks. I asked where he was headed, and he told me that it didn't really matter as he was just wandering anyway. As we struck up a conversation, he let out that he had not eaten all day, so I invited him to my place to give him and his dog some tucker (food). While I was cooking dinner, I asked if he wanted to take a bath which he gladly accepted. While he was cleaning up, I checked his swag and found he had no other clothes. He was about my size, so I got several of my shirts, shorts, underwear, socks, a pair of boots and a warm jacket, (it gets cold at night in the outback).

When he came out of the bathroom he looked like a different man, his face was glowing, hair was combed, he was shaven and in clean clothing. I could hardly recognize him. We sat and ate and talked for hours about everything from his life and family to God and how to solve world problems.

We both laughed a lot, cried a little and reflected on life and its meaning. I asked if he wanted to spend the night, he said he had to go but would not tell me where. We prayed together, hugged and I gave him the few dollars I had in my wallet at the time. As he was leaving, he patted his dog, said something that made the dog bark and eagerly wag its tail, he turned and walked away without looking back.

Exhausted from the day's work and the late night with the swaggie, I fell into bed and promptly fell into a deep sleep. I woke up in the morning and went about my normal routine; more boots, bags and as it turned out, more bad customers. The next evening, I was driving to Cairns (about 60 kilometres/40 miles) to pick up some supplies, when I spotted a hitchhiker with a dog. As I drove by, I looked in the rear-view mirror and saw it was the swaggie and his dog. I thought he may have been going to Cairns, so I turned the car around (I had not gone more than about 100 metres passed him). Now, understand this, there were no trees, bushes, rocks, or other roads on that particular stretch of highway. By the time I had turned around, he and his dog were nowhere to be found. I got out of the car and walked around to try to find him. After a while I continued my journey, I thought that I had lost my mind and even began to question the night before.

I asked God what was going on and He told me, (and I quote verbatim) "I sent you one of my own from my throne room and you cared for him as though it was me and you didn't even think about it, you just did it. I am proud of you". I was gushing like a little schoolboy all the way to Cairns. To this day I do not know what the purpose of that transaction was, other than to show God's hospitality to a stranger. I never saw him or his dog again. The moral of the story? We must be ready and do what is right in God's eyes whenever, even, and especially when it is inconvenient or when we don't feel like it.

The sign of the Maltese Cross.

In 1099, Gérard de Martigues became the founder of the Order of St John of Jerusalem, also known as the Knights Hospitallers or the Knights of Malta. This order was formed specifically to provide care for sick, poor, or injured pilgrims coming to the Holy Land. The ensign of their order is the Maltese Cross, (pictured above). The eight points are a reminder of the eight obligations and aspirations of the Knight Hospitaller. They are, *"to live in truth, have faith, repent one's sins, give proof of humility, love justice, be merciful, be sincere and whole-hearted, and to endure persecutions.* The knights took in and cared for those who were on the long, arduous, and sometimes perilous journey from points as far away as Briton to Jerusalem, which took up to 6 months. These journeys were considered to be the culmination of their pious lives. Many of the world's religions also have pilgrimages to show their piety. Those that were sick or injured on their pilgrimage to Jerusalem and needed food or shelter, were given so, as an act of kindness shown to God by these Knights Hospitallers. The men who formed the order and those who tended for the sick, injured and poor were wealthy or well-connected men, who wanted to help others reach their goals. We don't need to be wealthy or high up in some organization to make a difference in people's lives and we are already well connected to the Body of Christ which has all the resources necessary to do what it takes to help others on their journey. If we are connected to Christ and each other's lives, helping each other is a natural and organic outcome of our lives. The change we seek in our and each other's lives will happen as a matter of course.

Today, though many make trips to Jerusalem, they are not doing so in order to show piety with God. They travel in the comfort of automobiles and aeroplanes; they stay in comfortable hotels on the way and most have some form of health insurance. Today, we need not travel to earthly Jerusalem, for we are all pilgrims looking for the heavenly Jerusalem as Paul writes in **Hebrews 11:13** *These all died in faith, not having received the promises, but having seen them afar off, and were persuaded of them, and embraced them, and confessed that they were strangers and pilgrims on the earth.* He tells us we are resident foreigners on earth (as I am a resident foreigner in the US). Peter also writes in **1 Peter 2:11** *Dearly beloved, I beseech you as strangers and pilgrims, abstain from fleshly lusts, which war against the soul;* We are all on a journey and hospitality one to another gives us strength and fellowship on that journey.

Section 3

Chapter 31

Do not stop now!

There are many ways the bible tells us to treat members of the Commonwealth of the Kingdom of God. Do not rely on just what the preacher, pastor, bishop or even this book tells you, but search it out for yourself. It will not only be far more rewarding, but you will grow exponentially and become a more effective disciple for the Kingdom you say you belong to. Saying you belong to the Kingdom, but not adhering to the rules of conduct amongst its citizens is not helpful to those looking for the Kingdom.

When I was in Washington state in the late 90's, I crossed several times into Canada. I had a wonderful time, but I always came back across the border. I could not tell you what Canada or Canadians were really like from a few visits. I would have to live there, embrace the culture, eat their food, enter the lifestyle of the people before I could extol the wonders of Canada, especially if I was trying to get people to go there. I tell my friends about what it is like to be an Aussie living in the USA, and they sometimes look at me strangely. But since I married, Michele Ann (I call her my BB-beautiful bride, and she's from Texas no less), I have embraced the culture, I have seen much of the country (37 states and counting) and dwell amongst its people. I have laughed, wept, preached, taught, been frustrated, infuriated, and agonized over its inhabitants and now I can frankly speak, not just about Australia (28 years), but the United States of America (16 years). An ambassador lives with the people they are sent to influence. Someone cannot be an ambassador to a nation or Kingdom the do not dwell in. We cannot be an ambassador of the Kingdom of God if we only visit it twice or three times a week.

Doing bad by not doing good.

What happens when we stop doing good? Evil begins to flourish. If we are not striving to enter into the strait gate, we are allowing our old nature to rise and keep us from it. At first, we do not see it, but it lurks beneath the surface of every one of us and is not far, is waiting for the right circumstances to sprout. It looks for and feeds on lukewarmness and apathy. It thrives on offences and convenience. It searches the hidden caverns of our hearts for selfishness and builds cliques, creating schisms and causes as much pain, grief, death, disease, and divorce as any of the devil's tools. Singing how much we love God and how baptized we are and how we are a one God tongue talking people, makes no difference in the Kingdom if we do not sacrifice ourselves for the Kingdom. The words of the Master come to mind, *Then said Jesus unto his disciples, If any man will come after me, let him **deny himself,** and take up his cross, **and follow me**. For whosoever will save his life shall lose it: and whosoever will lose his life for my sake shall find it* (**Matthew 16:24-25**). Deny himself, where are the *amen, preach it* shouting saints when this is read?

One way (of many ways) to show and grow the Kingdom is by being hospitable to one another. It is by far the greatest way of showing who we really are. Anybody can put on airs and graces for a time, but eventually, the reality of who we are comes to the fore and we either confirm or deny what we have been saying all along.

Lack of action is an action, and it stifles growth within the Ecclesia and makes it the laughingstock of the world. To not speak against evil is to give tacit approval of said evil. If someone in our churches is being neglected or underutilized and we keep silent (a form of injustice), we may as well be the one doing the neglecting/underutilizing. When we quit doing the right thing for, with and to one another, the enemy sees an opportunity to bring his weapons to bear on the weak, the lazy, the arrogant and the ignorant, thus robbing the Ecclesia of its potential strengths and growth. They become the weapons the enemy uses to buffet the church. *'Oh, how the mighty have fallen',* is an idiom used to describe the decline or failure of a person, group, or entity, who used to be highly successful, powerful, or important but now sit on the ash heap of their memories of their former glories. With the internet, jet travel, instantaneous global communication, printing hundreds of thousands of books in a month, bible schools coming out of our ears, a majority of the world's population is mostly non-plussed at our existence. Other than thousands of conferences, conventions, revivals, what lasting damage have we done to the kingdom of darkness in the last fifty years? We have more churches, but our people are lonelier than ever. We are busy (like Martha) but not learning from the Master. We are following our creed, articles of faith and denominations and organizations, but are we following Christ to the cross and denying ourselves.

The Sadducees and Pharisees were a force to be reckoned with for more than 75 years before Christ showed up, but they let their pride, arrogance, offices, and offences take over and blind them and others to the plight of the poor and neglected. They started out as a potential force for good, but they eventually lost their raison d'etre (their reason for being). They continually added more rules and protocol, not only to themselves but placed these burdens upon the backs of the people (**Matthew 23:4** *For they bind heavy burdens and grievous to be borne, and lay them on men's shoulders; but they themselves will not move them with one of their fingers*). After the disciples came and showed them what the Kingdom of God was really like, they began to lose all their power because they would not heed the words of these uneducated and lowly people. Now, even hearing the name Pharisee or Sadducee is a cause of derision. I have yet to hear a sermon where the praises of these leaders are extolled.

When we cease to build each other up, entropy (the second law of thermodynamics) comes into play, where things go from order to chaos. Once this has occurred, (if it is not too late) copious amounts of time, manpower, material, and finances must be spent to reverse it. There are warnings in the word of God on how not to behave in order to keep the body from *dis-integrating* (look at that word. The opposite to integrating, becoming one). Watch out for signs that will bring the body of Christ shame and nip it in the bud. One another commands are an important feature of the Ecclesia. Let us use them for the glory of God.

Chapter 32.

Apostolics Anonymous

There is a group of people who have helped millions for over 85 years overcome the bondage and destruction that the overuse and abuse of alcohol has wrought on society. This group has only one goal; To help those who want to quit abusing alcohol, do so successfully. They have no other agenda; they use an extremely simple format that has proven to be phenomenally successful. They are Alcoholics Anonymous, better known as AA.

Indulge me for a moment and I will show not only how they are successful but also why and how this relates to the Ecclesia in today's messed up society. Disclaimer: I do not subscribe to AA's doctrine that once an alcoholic, always an alcoholic, as I myself was delivered from alcohol abuse over 38 years ago by the Spirit of God. It is the structure of AA and how they have successfully adopted the biblical method of discipling a new member that I want to illustrate.

A brief history lesson.

Alcoholics Anonymous (AA) sprang from The Oxford Group, a non-denominational movement modelled after first-century Christianity and their ability to disciple those who desired to become like Christ. The Oxford Group was a Christian organization known as *First Century Christian Fellowship* founded by the American Lutheran Christian priest named Frank Buchman in 1921. Buchman believed that the root of all problems were the personal problems of fear and selfishness (people haven't changed at all in 102 years). Further, Buchman believed that the solution to living with fear and selfishness was to *surrender one's life over to God's plan*.

AA is not organized in the formal or political sense, and borrowing the phrase from theorist Peter Kropotkin, it is a *"benign anarchy*." In Ireland, Shane Butler (author of Benign Anarchy; Alcoholics Anonymous in Ireland) said that, *"AA looks like it couldn't survive as there's no leadership or top-level telling local cumanns* (Irish- can be described as non-political association) *what to do, but it has worked and proved itself extremely robust."* Butler explained that *"…AA's 'inverted pyramid' style of governance has helped it to avoid many of the pitfalls that political and religious institutions have encountered since it was established here in 1946".* (Carroll, Steven [26 March 2010]. "Group avoids politics of alcohol". The Irish Times).

AA has no dues or fees in order to attend or be a member of a local chapter. They do *pass the hat around,* so to speak, but no-one is pressured or coerced into giving or looked down upon on if they do not give. They have over two million active members and almost 180,000 chapters and their head office are staffed by one or two paid members. The general board, of whom four are ex-alcoholics and seven are non-alcoholics who just want to help, are all volunteers.

The members of AA have financed their own recovery plan and spend enormous amounts of time and not a little money in helping new members. Most Psychiatrists say that if an alcoholic is to be cured, they need a hobby. An alcoholic's old hobby was drinking. The hobby of most Alcoholics Anonymous members is to help each other recover from what was destroying them. Even though telephone calls, gasoline bills, buying meals for new members mount up for each individual, yet they continue because they remember when they were new members. Hospitality to new members is a given. A rule of the society is that each member's *latch string* (sponsor) is always out to any other member who needs to talk or fellowship, which may include a bed or a meal, at any time.

All members in any group sponsor a new member until that new member has the ability to sponsor a member themselves. The sponsor contacts the new member daily or more often if needed to make themselves available to do anything to help them break the cycle that keeps them alcoholics. The sponsor will stay up late, visit their charge anywhere at any time, mainly to pass on the tools necessary to live a life free of alcohol.

AA owns no buildings for local chapters to meet (they meet in rented buildings and more often in the homes of either recovering alcoholics or people sympathetic to their cause). They have no formal hierarchy (paid or volunteer) in each chapter and all members get to speak, ask questions, and share their lives in order to help one another. Each chapter recognizes that they are a part of a larger group within their town or city. They do not get upset if another chapter opens up in the neighbourhood as they believe the more chapters they have, the more they will reach. Each chapter gives the locations of other chapters in their vicinity and regularly meet with other chapters in order to fellowship for the benefit of each member of the group. They recognize that their group may not be the one where every member may get the help they need or that members can outgrow a group. Groups do not get large as this makes it possible for people to *slip through the cracks* for a lack of available sponsors and removes the ability to be accountable to one another.

If we cannot see the early church in the previous few paragraphs and how we have strayed from it, then we truly are blind and there is none so blind as he who will not see, or as the prophet Jeremiah puts it, *Hear now this, O foolish people, and without understanding; which have eyes, and see not; which have ears, and hear not* (**Jeremiah 5:21**).

The reason AA works is that each member begins to teach what they have learnt to a new member as soon as possible. Each member is accountable to their sponsor and more importantly the sponsor is accountable to the new member. This does not mean that the new member must ask permission to do everyday things, change jobs or whom they can see. The new member recognizes that their sponsor has been through the hell that alcoholism brings, and they seek advice on how to live without alcohol using the collective wisdom of their sponsor and the AA group. The new member watches the life of their sponsor and emulates what made them successful (see **1 Corinthians 4:16, 11:1, Philippians 3:17**).

This is biblical discipleship at its absolute finest and more importantly, simplest. The origins of the word disciple come from the old English *discipul* (fem. discipula), meaning- one who follows another for the purpose of learning. We get the word pupil from it, and as a pupil has to do with the centre of the eye, we learn by watching. In biblical Greek it is, Mathētēs- meaning a learner or pupil. We can see how the word has changed very little from the early days of the church. Today, it has come to mean a church goer, a believer or one who follows Christ. It really means, one who has watched another disciple and becomes like them. The evidence of a disciple of Christ is not mere church attendance or blind obedience to leadership, or they adhere to the rules of their organization, but that they are now making disciples using their own life's failures and successes as examples of growth in God. The AA sponsor spends as much time with the initiate wanting to change from their old life to a radically new one as they can. It takes more than *"fellowshipping"* for a few minutes during a meeting.

Jesus told us to go into all the world and teach (to make disciples- learners and pupils by being transparent) and the best way to learn is by watching others do it, this teaches what we now know far more effectively. This also solidifies what we are teaching. How can we learn from someone or something we only see once or twice a week for a few hours?

If all teaching is done by one or in some cases a few so-called ministers, then once again, this enfeebles the majority of saints and turns them into spectators sitting in an auditorium listening to one man usually behind a podium/pulpit. The audience has no ability/chance to ask questions or have any input, neither will they know how to apply said information to their lives in a daily, personal, and meaningful way.

The ability for the body of Christ to minister to their neighbourhood is in direct correlation to how much the body of Christ has been allowed to minister to itself. Teaching becomes ingrained into their psyche by repeating the teaching to others. As new believers come into the body, they must not only be welcomed but be immediately placed in the care of an older believer (not necessarily a class. This is just church in a smaller form). Both benefit from this pattern as it has been proven to work for over four millennia.

AA calls them sponsors who are accountable to their charges. The bible calls them disciples and elders who are accountable to their charges but also accountable to God for how they handle these babes in Christ. The format of AA does not address the issue of sin, salvation, sanctification, righteousness, or redemption but they have never claimed to do so. They address the issue of alcohol abuse, its many dangers and effects on families and the community in general. They have been extraordinarily successful at doing what their charter states. The charter of the Ecclesia is to make disciples and preach to the lost the gospel of the Kingdom of God only. We, particularly the Apostolic Church, have become so enamoured by the revelation of Acts 2:38, one God and holiness, that we have forgotten why we are here. We have been busy building a system which neither allows freedom of speech nor to teach unless sanctioned by leadership. We have been so focused on outward appearances, belonging to the right organization, and building education through official bible colleges or their offshoots, that we have failed our communities at large. We have failed to communicate to others the purpose of why we're still here (hint: it is not to attend church services and pay money to keep the church doors open, rather it is to obey our Lord's greatest commands: to love God, to love one another, to preach the good news of the royalty, rule, and realm of God and to make disciples of this new Kingdom).

None of the churches in the bible had names let alone putting *First Church of* (insert name of town here), then focusing on getting more people to come. Naming a church makes as much sense as naming your hand Bob and your foot Sophie. The Ecclesia was one group and were known (not named after) by what city, town, village or even household they happened to be in (Ecclesia in the house of... or the church of a city etc. See **Romans 6:15, 1 Corinthians 16:19, Colossians 4:15**). The Ecclesia in Antioch became known by their closeness in actions of Christ Himself, therefore the sinners named then *Christians.* Everyone was anonymous and they all met for one purpose; to help strengthen one another through, not only teaching of the Torah and how to live the Torah, but care for each other's needs (this is what helped them live in one accord). The letters written to one Ecclesia were circulated to the Ecclesia in their regions. It was not until circa 120 AD that the letters written to those same churches began to be collected and compiled. What did the early church do for nearly 90 years? They handed down the commandments of Christ via personal teaching and example to whomever wanted to seek and live for God who then added daily to the church such as should be saved (see **Acts 2:47**). The epistles were shared amongst each gathering and this wisdom spread throughout the entire Ecclesia (**Colossians 4:16**). I believe if Paul was alive today, the western church would have gotten several epistles.

Paul tells Timothy that one must rule his own house before he can take care of the church of God (**1 Timothy 3:5**). Notice two important phrases in this passage- *rule his own house* and *take care of the church.* Today, we have reversed these two criteria, we take care of our families and try to rule the church. To rule here speaks of Proistēmi- to stand before, to preside and practice. A man must be able to Proistemi his own household in order to *take care of* (Epimeleomai- to care for physically or otherwise) the church. We have come to assume that the preacher is also the teacher, pastor, administrator, chief cook, and bottle washer and so on and because he does all this, he has a right to rule like a small king over his fiefdom (the lives of the saints). The only singular man that was all things to all men was the God/Man Jesus Christ and He has not put that kind of responsibility on one man as He knows that is what the Ecclesia is for. Paul starts off in **1 Corinthians 9:19** *For though I be free from all men, yet have **I made myself servant unto all*** (not just those who submitted to him, agreed with him, or paid their tithe), *that I might gain the more.* He had made himself a servant to all men. A servant cares for the needs of others first. He goes on to explain that he relates to others where they are and ends with **1 Corinthians 9:22** *To the weak became I as weak, that I might gain the weak: **I am made** all things to all men, that I might by all means save some.* **Paul did not say he *was* all things to all men.** Paul related to the weak by showing his weakness, he related to the hurt by sharing in their hurt. We all can relate to the struggle we have to sin in our weaknesses, because we were all born in sin, and though we have been delivered from the power of sin, we must still relate to the sinner. When a sinner or a struggling saint comes in, we are to relate to their plight and show them that they can be victorious over sin or their struggle through the Christ that dwells in us. Thus, God *makes us all things to all men.*

I believe we must have people who are wise guides (not wise guys) and people with whom the body can truly relate to. How can people relate to people whom they only see once or twice a week for a couple of hours at a time? How can people relate to someone who won't park their feet under the kitchen table unless there's a problem? How can people relate to believers when they don't really know from personal experience what they believe? How can people relate to so-called ministry who are so far above the masses, because of their position, or that there are so many people that the leadership are run off their feet? How can they relate to those who have been in *ministry* so long they have forgotten where they have come from? Unrelatable people in pulpits and pews have negated their purpose for being in the Ecclesia. The *Ecclesia is the ministry* and as it fulfills its purpose of discipling (not disciplining) one another, we will see that the need for hovering overseers will diminish for the older and wiser saints over time. If we operate within the purpose we were made for, a new influx of saints will be constantly coming in, thus the need for biblically oriented leadership will never diminish.

If a normal mentally healthy fifth grader still needs a fifth-grade teacher after several years, it shows the teacher has not done their job. As the student moves on in life and learns more from others, they become proficient members of society. They then put into practice life skills taught to them by skilful life teachers. If a student sits under the same preacher/teacher for years and has not grown past the preacher/teacher, we have an anomaly. The reason is because most are taught what to think not how to think, thus impeding their own growth and not becoming a discipler themselves. They are forever tied to the pastor's apron strings (if it's wrong for a fully grown man or woman to be tied their mother's apron strings, why would it be right for a spiritually grown man or woman to be tied to the pastor's/bishop's apron strings?) rather than growing, going, and sowing into the Kingdom of God and the world at large themselves.

The greatest difference between Alcoholics Anonymous and the church today is that AA tries to get people to learn to fend for themselves as quickly as possible while they remain in contact with their sponsor and the people that helped them. At the same time these new members are told, that to make what they have learnt stick, they must, as soon as is practicable, begin to impart what they have learnt through soul searching, changes they have made and through life's ups and downs to others. The person wanting to change does not go to one meeting a week, because they know they are weak. AA gives the addresses of other meetings in an area so the new member can get as much time as possible around others also trying to better themselves. Disciples learn from other disciples how to implement the word of God in a practical way. Rarely will a disciple practically learn from what is heard from a pulpit (they will gain valuable information given under inspiration, but who then do they have for daily imitation?). If they are told they must learn from the leadership of their church *only*, it limits the type of input and regular fellowship required to grow into a mature disciple of Christ. As they learn from the word and spirit of God and humble, wiser, and older disciples, they find that they will grow faster as they teach others what they have learnt. This is the way we learn in the natural and the way the early church taught also. The Ecclesia Jesus filled with His spirit did not limit learning, fellowship, and sacrifice of time to one or two days a week. It was a daily affair that involved all in the gathering, once again, not limited to elected or appointed leadership.

Unlike the simple AA structure, the church holds all the teaching within the hierarchy and doles it out piecemeal with very little if any follow-up on how each member is actually doing with the teaching. We do not teach the people how to feed themselves (we just tell them to), but keep them reliant, as long as possible, on the hierarchy telling them what to do almost exclusively from behind a pulpit, bible schools (for those who have the financial wherewithal or necessary academic knowhow) or conferences and camp meetings. Many times, the new convert does not have one person they can call on anytime (mainly because all the saints have busy lives and cannot spare the time, yet this is exactly what the word sacrifice means) and so they try to attend whatever meetings they can. They are told that that particular church is where they must attend and cannot leave until given permission from the pastor. However, not everyone can receive the help they need in one or two meeting a week especially when they have the demonic realm constantly buffeting them or beckoning them back to the pseudo-normal life they had. After all, better the devil you know, than the devil you don't, right?

The church must adopt the format of disciple making handed down through God's people, the Jews, which has proven to be successful for over 4,000 years. Though AA does not claim to be a spiritual or political organization, they seem to be able to help those who no longer wish to let that type of spirit run their lives. Isn't that the same mandate of the Ecclesia? To be a living, sacrificing witness to people who no longer want to live for the spirit of the world and are looking for someone to help them by showing (not just telling) them of a better way?

Recently on social media I have been seeing '*praise reports*' that many people are being filled with the Holy Ghost and baptized in His name, and I am thrilled and fearful at the same time. I have preached in many of these churches, and I know how they operate. Who is going to take these new-borns and daily feed them, teach them how to study the bible for themselves, show them how to use a concordance and how to study the bible in context, visit with and pray for them? The pastor? He is so busy running the church and trying to '*win souls for Jesus*' that he has very little time past the initial and obligatory few visits at the new convert's home. Many pastors are working a secular job also and have families they must cater to and rightly so. If we follow the AA structure (which copied the Jewish and early Ecclesia's structure) we would keep ninety percent instead of losing ninety percent in the first two years.

Many readers will feel offended by this last paragraph, but as Ben Shapiro loves to say, *'facts don't care about feelings'.* Truth is truth and if it is presented in a manner designed to make the hearer search deeper, the hearer would be a fool's fool to not do so. It is not and never has been about numbers, but about being fellow sinners redeemed by God helping other sinners find their place in the Commonwealth of the Kingdom and being a living sacrifice unto God allowing Him to use **ANYONE** to further His Kingdom. If we do this, the numbers will come.

Section 4

Chapter 33

Some Don'ts.

Before I get to the greatest of these one another commands (love), I feel it is my duty to also address some **do not do** *to one another* commands. We find that in God's word there are many commandments: those that command an action (love and serve God and each other) and those the forbid an action (don't steal, lie, backbite, withhold mercy, grace, and love). God does not command us to feel something or forbid us from feeling something before we do or do not do something. This is because our feelings are almost always a result of an action or inaction either done by us or to us.

It is important to note that the word of God has considerably many more dos' than don'ts, therefore, if we spend our time doing the do's, we will have considerably less time, and eventually the inclination, to do the don'ts.

Once again, I stress, that this is by no means an exhaustive list and further study should be undertaken by the reader in order to reach the level of maturity that God requires of us all (see **1 Corinthians 3:2, Hebrews 5:12, 6:1-2**). We are told by Peter to, *grow in grace, and in the knowledge of our Lord and Saviour Jesus Christ. To him be glory both now and for ever. Amen* (**2 Peter 3:18**). We grow in the knowledge of God so that we might fulfil God's will within the Ecclesia and the world at large.

First, we should understand that doing those things that God forbids not only inhibit the growth of the Kingdom of God, but also tears it down from within. When we do that, we are doing the work of His enemy and still calling ourselves Christians/Apostolics/Pentecostals. This is the epitome of hypocrisy (Hupokritēs- an actor under an assumed character, a stage player). These types of people are spoken of with much malice in Exodus and Deuteronomy. God calls them *a stiffnecked people* (Qâsheh- severe, churlish, hardhearted, obstinate, stubborn). For example, *Circumcise therefore the foreskin of your heart, and be no more stiffnecked. Now be ye not stiffnecked, as your fathers were, but yield yourselves unto the LORD, and enter into his sanctuary, which he hath sanctified for ever: and serve the LORD your God, that the fierceness of his wrath may turn away from you* (**Deuteronomy 10:16, 2 Chronicles 30:8**. See also **Exodus 32:9, 33:3-5, Deuteronomy 9:6**). Peter is giving his audience (the Jews) a history lesson and rounds it by quoting from Moses' speech to the people, *Ye stiffnecked* (Sklērotrachēlos- obstinate, harsh, or severe) *and uncircumcised in heart and ears, ye do always resist the Holy Ghost: as your fathers did, so do ye* (**Acts 7:51**). This is an abomination and a stench unto God's metaphorical nostrils.

Having a large group of people gathering in one place is by no means proof that God is fulfilling His will in a town region or state. With enough money and influence (and a good amount of food) I can fill a large hall with people, and though they will be at the same place, at the same time, they will not all be in one accord with Christ at the centre. Generally speaking, a large group is, in most instances, a hindrance to the personal and interpersonal growth of its members for two main reasons.

1. It is much easier to hide in the crowd and remain lukewarm where we will not challenge nor be challenged to change our paradigm.
2. In a large crowd, everybody is busy trying to live their lives and do not have time to be involved in any meaningful depth in the lives of others.

This is why dispersal was commanded in **Acts 1:8** *But ye shall receive power, after that the Holy Ghost is come upon you: and **ye shall be witnesses unto me both in Jerusalem, and in all Judaea, and in Samaria, and unto the uttermost part of the earth**.* To do the things that God commands, we must do them to, for and with one another, which takes the power and wisdom of the Holy Ghost. The Lord knew how we tend to brag about how big our crowds are, so He circumvented this trait by commanding us to go and take the power of God out of our Jerusalem. It is hard to have a big crowd if we are always on the move. This does not mean we must all move around like modern day nomads, but that as we continue to congregate into ever larger crowds, we tend to pass by hungry, hurting, sick and lonely people on our way to have church. If large numbers and signs and wonders were truly the criteria for that we should have large numbers going to a central point to worship God, it would have been prudent for Jesus to stay in the wilderness where He fed the multitude. John the Baptist was in the wilderness and thousands came to see him (some travelled over 200 miles to go and see John) yet after 6 months where were those people? They went back to their lives, in their towns and villages and Jesus had to go back to those same towns and villages to give the message again.

Saying large number is God's will because we have large numbers is circular reasoning. It is starting with the conclusion then searching for evidence that proves the conclusion. Read the stories of Jesus in the wilderness again. Thousands came to hear the word; Jesus healed them all and there were many deliverances. But when God's will was fulfilled for that time, (they were fed, heard the word, got healing and devils gone and showed compassion. In **Matthew 14:14, Mark 6:34, Luke 9:11, John 6:2**) we read, they went home with more than what they came with. Please note, no one invited them, they followed God and the disciples anywhere they went, not to a building or back to the Temple, but to the wilderness. When it came time for the disciples to go through these towns after the resurrection, (from Jerusalem to Judea, Samaria then the rest of the world), many already believed, they just needed to be baptized and be filled with the Spirit of God. Instant gatherings in homes in these towns and villages. Today, we would have set up a church in the wilderness. Today a church is considered somewhat successful if it has stayed in one area for a long time and has a large group of people attending. In the early days of the Ecclesia, the opposite was true. People left their comfort zones and took the message to the world. The world may have meant down the street, across the village or another region.

That is one reason God put it on Caesar's heart to destroy the Temple. People were coming to Jerusalem to hear the Gospel in direct contravention to Christ's commands to, *go into all the world, to preach the Kingdom of God* [only] *and teach His commands* (make disciples **Mark 16:15, Matthew 28:18-20**). What of those who did not have the wherewithal to go to Jerusalem? Easy, no Temple, no need to go to Jerusalem. The disciples were forced to go further afield to where the lost and hungry were.

We must take the things written in God's word and use the lessons in this book and others like it to where it matters most. In **Acts 2:46** *And they, continuing daily with one accord in the temple...* (Hieron- precincts of the city, neighbourhood to neighbourhood and from household to household). This is where the gospel of the Kingdom of God is to be preached and lived out; where it is not hidden behind bricks and mortar, given from pulpits in the hope that unsaved people came to our services and hear it, and not doled out in a tiny 35–45-minute spoonful to those who are hungry for more.

Jesus warned the religious leadership of His time of withholding the word of God from the people in **Luke 11:52** *Woe unto you, lawyers! for **ye have taken away*** (Airō- keep the mind in suspense,) *the key* (Kleis- to close up, as shutting a lock) *of knowledge: ye entered not in yourselves, and them that were entering in ye hindered.* I am not saying that we are purposefully withholding God's word, I'm saying that we have created a system where this is the only way to get God's word to the people.

It is difficult to catch real Christianity when the world and so many believers are being inoculated with small doses of it on a weekly basis. If we are to emulate our Lord and Master, then we must put aside our petty differences, both organizationally and individually and be about our Father's business. By removing the middle wall of partition that separate saints from leadership, mature saints from baby saints, and begin the task of searching our souls, repenting for our selfishness and start healing the fractured Ecclesia and treating each other with love and respect, giving each other the time, grace and mercy God has given to us to grow at His pace. We will soon see exponential growth God's way. Remember, what He grows, He is able to keep.

Chapter 34.

Speak not evil one of another.

James 4:11 *Speak not evil* one of another, brethren. He that speaketh evil of his brother, and judgeth his brother, speaketh evil of the law, and judgeth the law: but if thou judge the law, thou art not a doer of the law, but a judge.

This, in the plainest of terms, is to be a slanderer, defamer, backbiter, one who speaks ill of the absent. Read what Paul says of those who are partakers of such behaviour. The Greek for backbiter is Katalaleō- to slander with no recourse, to be a traducer which means one who attacks the reputation of another by slander or libel, (a traducer is one of the traits of Satan). They are a defamer, maligner, vilifier. It also means a depreciator, detractor, disparager, knocker - one who belittles the worth of something or someone. Check out the definition of what *Satan* is. It will be eye opening. Being a backbiter and slanderer is the work of our enemy and when we engage in such behaviour, we have changed kingdoms, then cry foul when things fall apart.

To speak evil of another saint is to speak evil of one of God's children and we are treading on very shaky ground indeed. I have been on the receiving end of such vilification many times and it never bodes well for those who have chosen to speak evil of me, not because I am someone special or have not made mistakes in my life or in the service God has given me (as Paul would say, *God forbid*), but because I am a child of God doing his best to advance the business of his Father. Whether the accusations have an element of truth in them or not, we do the Kingdom of God no favours by trying to destroy anyone's reputation or malign their character especially to family and friends. When we think that we are the instrument of God to punish or destroy someone (and most pitifully, we have convinced ourselves that we are doing it for God and His Kingdom like Saul, who thought he was doing God a favour), we have deceived ourselves and we will reap the rewards for such self-deception.

Those who gloat over or desire the fall of a saint have removed themselves from the presence of God (they fool themselves into believing otherwise) and have opened themselves up for judgement of the most severe kind. These types of people erroneously believe they are doing God a favour by trying to teach someone a lesson, to malign or destroy their reputation, to get others to disfellowship someone, to get a husband, wife, son, or daughter to leave, ignore or belittle their loved ones. Sadly, it is usually done under the guise of protecting the Ecclesia. Remember Saul, when he was arresting and imprisoning the believers just for obeying what God Himself had commanded them to do? These misaligned and misguided people have convinced themselves they are still relevant in the Kingdom of God, and that they continue to hear His voice. The deception of such people goes deep, and their actions carry no weight except to justify themselves and their feelings before others. They use scripture out of context and believe that only they are hearing from God regarding any matter.

Schadenfreude is the experience of pleasure, joy, or self-satisfaction that comes from learning of or witnessing the troubles, failures, or humiliation of another. The Ecclesia is not to participate in schadenfreude nor rejoice over the fall of anyone, but to be broken hearted and begin the process of restoration in meekness and humility because this could easily have been them had the tables been turned (see **Galatians 6:1-3**). Solomon writes, *Rejoice not when thine enemy falleth, and let not thine heart be glad when he stumbleth:* (**Proverbs 24:17**).

Even when people were being self-willed and attempting to take glory from God in **2 Peter 2:10** we are told in the next verse, *Whereas angels, which are greater in power and might, bring not **railing accusation** against them before the Lord* (**2 Peter 2:11**). Is the Lord blind that He cannot see what is going on in His Ecclesia? This speaks of all saints not just leadership.

To speak evil of someone for whom Christ died to redeem unto Himself, is to tell God He does not know what He is doing. Many have used **1 Corinthians 5:5** completely out of context when they perceive a sin that they do not consider repented of as a reason, *To deliver such an one unto Satan for the destruction of the flesh, that the spirit may be saved in the day of the Lord Jesus.* Yet Paul is not writing of any sin, but of a specific sin that was not even mentioned amongst the heathens, *It is reported commonly that there is fornication among you, and such fornication as is not so much as named among the Gentiles, that one should have his father's wife* (**1 Corinthians 5:1**).

To use **1 Corinthians 5:5** to justify cutting someone off from the fellowship or praying for their demise (under the guise of saving their soul) shows the ignorance these venomous and vile pseudo-saints have of scripture as well as the absolute depravity of their soul. They are, in essence, behaving like reprobates themselves. Even Paul, when he mentioned Alexander the coppersmith, who did him much evil (**2 Timothy 4:14**), would not go into detail and just said the Lord will reward him according to his works. Where was the maligning, the publishing what he had done 'to protect the saints', the shaming and name calling or the belittling of his worth? He did not call the saints together and tell them Alexander was a bad man and wrote no letters to tell others to have nothing to do with him. He just let it go. If we feel the need to destroy someone on God's behalf, to protect His reputation or so-called covering of the saints, we are in dire need of a good dose of milk of magnesia for a cleaning from a prideful spirit. We may not agree with their doctrine or may not agree with the results they get, but to malign them personally and destroy their character to their friends and family is siding with the great traducer himself, Satan, and is not a biblical way of being the Ecclesia of the Kingdom of God. We are saying God is not capable of taking care of it Himself and that we are the mighty hammer of God to punish evildoers. Did not the disciples repeat the teachings of Christ Himself by telling us not to reward evil for evil, (**Romans 12:17, 1 Peter 3:9, 1 Thessalonians 5:15**). The disciples in their haste to protect Christ's reputation as the Messiah, were willing to call fire down from heaven on a village that did not submit to their Lord, and Jesus's response was to rebuke them by telling them ... *Ye know not what manner of spirit ye are of. For the Son of man is not come to destroy men's lives, but to save them.* Luke then goes on to tell us what Christ's response was ...*And they went to another village* (**Luke 9:55-56**).

No promise of future retribution or judgement. It was just not their time. The way Jesus tells us to mind our own business when it comes to trying to force others to follow us is remarkably different from today's churches. Let us look at **Mark 9:38-40** again, *And John answered him, saying, Master, we saw one casting out devils in thy name, and he followeth not us: and we forbad him, because he followeth not us* (the church people today). The response from the Master was priceless ...*But Jesus said, Forbid him not: for there is no man which shall do a miracle in my name, that can lightly speak evil of me. For he that is not against us is on our part.* Which part of this is difficult to understand? I find it refreshing that the word *forbid* means to not hinder, withstand, keep from, or prevent and yet when we backbite someone, that is exactly what we are doing. We are preventing someone else from seeing things for themselves by inserting something into other's thinking that is slanderous with no recourse. Rarely have these weak and spineless backbiters gone to those whom they are telling us about and spoken to them about it, yet they expect us to take their word as gospel, a typical messiah complex. These are dangerous people infiltrated into the body of Christ by our enemy. These insufferable people are what God calls, 'sons of Belial'- without profit, worthless; by extension destructive, and wicked (see the story of the sons of Eli the high priest. They were in the ministry, but the people thought them worthless and destructive **1 Samuel 12:12-17**).

Even if someone did what these backbiters say they did, the backbiters are still wrong because they are exacting revenge on others. The bible expressly puts vengeance into the hands of God alone, and to exact punishment on someone, is to foolishly try to remove power from God Himself, a most fanciful and futile deed and if this does not show the height of their utter stupidity and their asinine views, I do not know what does.

Speaking evil contradicts **Philippians 4:8** *Finally, brethren, whatsoever things are **true**, whatsoever things are **honest**, whatsoever things are **just**, whatsoever things are **pure**, whatsoever things are **lovely**, whatsoever things are of **good report**; if there be any **virtue**, and if there be any **praise**, think on these things.* These people will quote **Philippians 4:19** *But my God shall supply all your need according to his riches in glory by Christ Jesus,* all day long, while neglecting what Paul wrote only eleven verses earlier. As mentioned earlier, to *think on* means to take an inventory of these things. What things? The bad things? No! Take inventory on the things mentioned above. If we feel someone has wronged us then we are to take an inventory of what is true, honest, just, pure, lovely, and good report, of the virtuous and praiseworthy things and think on, contemplate, meditate, understand, get to know these things. These are the things we are to focus on with one another and let God deal, in His time and fashion, with those things that are contrary to His word.

These types of people remind me of Muslims who kill if someone speaks against allah or if someone maligns their dead and buried prophet, Muhammad, and they will do it in the name of allah. As if allah is not big enough to care for his own reputation. These snakelike pretenders masquerading as saints and leadership who claim they love God but treat any of the brethren maliciously, are no different to murderers according to God. In **Matthew 5:21** the Messiah says, *Ye have heard that it was said by them of old time, Thou shalt not kill; and whosoever shall kill shall be in danger of the judgment: But I say unto you, That whosoever is angry with his brother without a cause shall be in danger of the judgment: and whosoever shall say to his brother, Raca,* (worthless, empty, a term of utter vilification) *shall be in danger of the council: but whosoever shall say, Thou fool* (Mōros- to call dull, or blockhead, to shut up or to silence), *shall be in danger of hell fire.*

When Jesus was in the Garden of Gethsemane, Peter had perceived that there was a threat to his Lord and Master. To protect Him, Peter pulls out a sword and cuts off Malchus' ear, all in the name of protecting God. Jesus told him to, *Put up thy sword in its sheath…* Does this sound like God needs protection from a mere human? (He has 36,000 angels prepped and ready to destroy these mere humans in the name of protecting God). God has bigger fish to fry, and He will deal with each one of us at the appointed time and in His appointed manner (**Matthew 26:52** and **John 18:11**). Peter tried to hurt the source of his anger, but Jesus turned around and healed that same source. Just the opposite to what Peter wanted. It would not be a stretch of the imagination that Malchus would have been amongst the 120 in the upper room if not the 3,000 on the day of Pentecost, don't you?

To those who have deluded themselves (and many times, also deluded their gullible and spineless followers) into believing that they must destroy others whom they consider have done wrong, I can only point them back to what God says in **1 Thessalonians 5:14-15** *Now we exhort you, brethren, warn* (Noutheteō- to put in mind, that is, to caution or **reprove gently**: a mild rebuke) *them that are unruly,* (not others) *comfort the feebleminded, support the weak, be patient toward all men. See that none render evil for evil unto any man; but ever follow that which is good, both among yourselves, and to all men.*

These people who speak evil of others rarely if ever take their concerns to the person or persons involved. They will recruit others to their cause in the vain and pitiful attempt to justify their own existence and how they feel about what they consider to be wrong. They are the epitome of the word *cowardice.* They make accusations and will not allow their accusations to be challenged openly. They are blowhards who in almost all cases speak from second or third hand sources. The more people they recruit to their so-called cause, the more justified they feel and the more fools they have garnered to their self-righteous cause the happier they seem to be. Then they will say things like *'Look how many agree with us.'* We could say the same for the Nazi Party in Germany or for the spurious and malcontented leaders who garnered the multitude to their cry, *'Crucify Him, give us Barabbas'.* The people that join these ignorant fools in their second-hand criticism are just as guilty as the perpetrators of the evil speaking. They have tied themselves to the fate of those who refuse to forgive and hold grudges. Even if there is some truth to the accusation, it will be blown out of all proportion or it will be from a past situation which God Himself has forgiven and placed under the blood of the sacrificial Lamb. Who are they to dig up the sins of others? Are they not aware that they are in danger of having their own sins dug up also and placed upon themselves? Have they not read, *For with what judgment ye judge, ye shall be judged: and with what measure ye mete, it shall be measured to you again?* (See also **Matthew 18:32-35**).

This is equivalent to the modern-day phenomenon of the cancel culture that has permeated the Western church and has destroyed the lives of many people, families, and careers, only we do it in the name of Christ. Perhaps another reread of, *And why beholdest thou the mote that is in thy brother's eye, but considerest not the beam that is in thine own eye?* is in order (**Matthew 7:2-3**). They will be vehement in their criticism and totally neglect any good the other person may have done and then they will turn around and preach the love and grace of God to others. Are they not aware that they have just condemned themselves by their own hypocrisy? Have they not understood the scripture in **Matthew 12:36-37**, *But I say unto you, That every idle word that men shall speak, they shall give account thereof in the day of judgment. For by thy words thou shalt be justified, and by thy words thou shalt be condemned.*

The brother of the Lord (James) warns us of such people in his writings to the Jews in Jerusalem, *Doth a fountain send forth at the same place sweet water and bitter? Can the fig tree, my brethren, bear olive berries? either a vine, figs? so can no fountain both yield salt water and fresh* (**James 3:11**).

This speaking evil of one another is being pushed as righteous indignation under the guise of helping the person involved even though many times the person involved has yet to hear from the offended party. This would be tantamount to having your case heard in absentia and found guilty without getting a summons to stand before a judge. Not even evil sinners do that within the laws of evil man. In a worldly court, if someone is tried and found guilty in absentia, all efforts have been taken to allow the accused person to defend themselves, but the alleged offender has refused to show up.

In the book of **Titus 3:2-3** we are commanded, *To speak evil of no man, to be no brawlers* (quarrelsome), *but gentle* (Epieikēs- appropriate, mild, moderation patience), *shewing* (Endeiknumi- to indicate by word or act) *all meekness unto all men. For we ourselves also were sometimes foolish* (Anoētos- unintelligent and sensual), *disobedient* (Apeithēs- contumacious, unpersuadable), *deceived* (Planaō- roamed from safety, truth, and virtue), *serving divers lusts and pleasures, living in malice and envy, hateful* (Stugnētos- unpleasant and offensive), *and hating one another.* These railers, gossips and backbiters have a bad memory and have forgotten that they themselves were foolish, disobedient, deceived, serving divers lusts and pleasures, living in malice and envy, hateful, and hating one another and have not had their dirty laundry aired for all to see, but have received grace and mercy which they now refuse to give to the same extent they had received it.

We are not capable of doing any good of eternal value outside of what we allow God to do through our feeble lives through the guidance of His spirit. We all struggle in different ways, but grace and mercy are available to all, and available for all to give in the same manner it was received-FREELY. Those who speak evil of one another and refuse to give grace and mercy to others will find that they will soon run out of both themselves. They will eventually be stripped of all they have and reduced to nothing until they repent and bring forth meet worthy of repentance and forgive others (**Matthew 3:8**). Solomon tells us of the givers and withholders in **Proverbs 11:24** *One gives freely, yet gains even more; another withholds what is right, only to become poor* (Berean Study Bible). This has nothing to do with money but an attitude of the heart.

To speak evil of one another especially within the Ecclesia is to deny the saving and regenerative power of God in a brother or sister in Christ. We must be very wary of those who speak evil of other saints especially to or around us, especially when they do not live close by, and we cannot see the other person to verify what we hear. Warning: if these malodourous people tell you not to contact the object of their vilification, then it is time to be suspicious. They will infect those of an insipid mind and weak spine and poison the hearts of members of the Ecclesia against someone who has done the hearer no harm. These people have *a form* (Morphōsis- an appearance) *of Godliness but deny* (Arneomai- contradict, reject, or abnegate [renounce]) *the power thereof. From such turn away* (**2 Timothy 3:5**). In almost all cases, those that speak evil of others *to* you, will in due time speak evil to others *of* you.

If we have indulged in this type of cancerous behaviour, then we must forget what the other person has done and focus on our own repentance and leave the brother or sister in the hands of the Lord. If we truly want to help, let us get along side of them, talk things out and see if we can agree, using the word of God as our guide, on how we can all move forward and grow from our experiences and how we can use them to help others for the sake of the Kingdom of God. We had better heed the words of Jesus, *Thou hypocrite, first cast out the beam out of thine own eye; and then shalt thou see clearly to cast out the mote out of thy brother's eye* (**Matthew 7:5**).

The fruit of the spirit is what we are to exhibit to the world, but as **James 3:10-12** tells us of trees and water, *Out of the same mouth proceedeth blessing and cursing.* **My brethren, these things ought not so to be**. *Doth a fountain send forth at the same place sweet water and bitter? Can the fig tree, my brethren, bear olive berries? either a vine, figs? so can no fountain both yield salt water and fresh.* **The fruit of love cannot grow on the same tree as the tree of the works of the flesh. The only fruit it will bear is bitterness, anger, envy, pride, arrogance and so on and this does nothing to grow the Ecclesia.** Having a large gathering where the above are also operating is undoing all the good we think we are trying to do.

So, if we are to show the world what the fruit of the spirit is, but we have the works of the flesh going on in our lives, we are Pharisees and Sadducees of the highest order. The Lord Himself rebuked them for being hypocrites and white-washed tombs (actors and good looking on the surface but full of death on the inside).

We may believe we are not under the law, but James contradicts this fallacy for those whose heart is evil. Please remember, he is not writing this to the world at large, but to those who claim the name of Christ as Lord. He clearly states that... *But if ye be led of the Spirit, ye are not under the law* (**James 3:18**). Only those who are led of the spirit have been released from the curse of the law. But as usual there are two sides to every coin and James does not mince words when he openly rebukes those who claim to be spirit led but truly manifest the works of its nemesis (the flesh).

Read on and see what James describes as a hypocrite. Hypocrisy and flesh work hand in hand. *Now the works of the flesh are manifest, which are these; Adultery, fornication, uncleanness, lasciviousness. Idolatry, witchcraft, hatred, variance, emulations* (jealousy, malice, indignation), *wrath, strife* (causing factions, forcing people to take sides), *seditions, heresies* (forming a sect). *Envyings, murders, drunkenness, revellings, and such like: of the which I tell you before, as I have also told you in time past, that they which do such things **shall not inherit the kingdom of God*** (**Galatians 5:19-21**). James tells us the works of the flesh are the deeds, the actions, the doings, and labours of our own thinking. When we do what we think is right by trying to turn one against another, it is labouring in the flesh and showing our own carnality which eventually leads to calamity.

Many Christians would never commit adultery or fornication or dabble in witchcraft, commit murder, drunkenness, or idolatry but have regularly indulged in hatred, wrath, strife, heresies and revellings to enter and run their daily lives. They act as if these sins are less destructive to the soul of man and in the eyes of God. They will quickly condemn someone who has told a lie or not been as ethical as they should have been or who has left their church/organization, but their hearts are in a much more condemned state with God than the ones they rail against. They have built up a calloused resistance to the grace, mercy, and sovereignty of God.

These evil things in the heart of people who call themselves by His name, contradict all the positive they attempt to do or think they are doing for the Kingdom of God. All their efforts to show God with their degrees, doctorates, positions, preaching, singing, giving or real estate acquisition in the name of God will come to nought. They have judged the saints to be unworthy of their love, even though they are commanded to love the unlovable as Christ loved them, thus they have negated and relinquished their own citizenship and voided their passport into the Kingdom of God. They are illegal immigrants who try to use the new Kingdom for their own benefit. To speak evil of the saints is to speak evil of God and His people. Is this really what God intended for those who are called by His name?

Chapter 35.

Be not puffed up one against another.

1 Corinthians 4:6 *And these things, brethren, I have in a figure transferred to myself and to Apollos for your sakes; that ye might learn in us not to think of men above that which is written,* ***that no one of you be puffed up for one against another.***

What does puffed up mean. Do you know someone who is a braggard, know-it-all, a vaunting person, blowhard, self-aggrandizing, and big-talker or truly believe they are right on any and all subjects? These are just a few of the words that aptly describe a puffed-up person. There is a great misconception about what it means to be ignorant. Many have come to believe it means stupid or dumb. Ignorant just means to not know something because we are not aware of certain facts. In other words, we are uninformed on a particular subject or piece of data.

People can be ignorant concerning something about themselves, others, or the word of God, but when they are made aware of their ignorance by God or others and they remain in that state, they move from ignorance to arrogance and there is a fine line between the two. As educator and author, Balroop Singh once said, *Arrogance is the armour of the weak. They are always at war to hide their real self.* Those who claim to be right in everything and all words that come out of their mouths are truly gospel, ought to read **1 Samuel 2:3** *Do not boast so proudly, or let arrogant words come out of your mouth, for the Lord is a God of knowledge, and actions are weighed by Him* (Holman Bible) or perhaps **Romans 12:16** *Be of the same mind one toward another. Mind not high things, but condescend to men of low estate.* ***Be not wise in your own conceits*** (selves).

With the advent of public libraries, the internet, more higher education facilities than ever before, we have become puffed up with knowledge and pride, yet we lack basic common sense and wisdom. With the advent of computers and cell phones, we have a wealth of knowledge, but a dearth of wisdom. We have come to believe that if we know something it must be true, and we must not be challenged on it. The problem is that we have just enough knowledge on a particular subject to think we are right, but not enough to know we may be wrong. There is always more to learn. It took Albert Einstein ten years to figure out the theory of general relativity and we think we have all the bible figured out because of four years of bible school where we learn by rote what has been taught with no further research on our behalf? We must just believe what has been repeated over the last one hundred years, then we will get our piece of paper which only proves we can read, listen, and remember? Bible schools, like the overwhelming majority of universities and colleges today, tell us what to think, not how to think nor allow thinking that challenges current understanding. They do not greatly encourage further research and deeper revelation as this may contradict the status quo. Challenging a teacher or a professor is considered bad form if not downright rebellious. Jesus did not mind being challenged and dealt with all challenges by contextual scripture citation, then living the scripture in front of them. He did not say, '*because I told you so*'.

Of you be puffed up is a phrase that I believe was written with today's churches in mind. Why is this? The vast majority of people in the first and second century church populace were illiterate and knew very little of Torah writings. They only knew what was told to them at synagogue and Temple. It was usually those very few with a higher education that became puffed up. To be puffed up is the

Greek word Phusioō and it means a sense of blowing; to inflate, that is to make proud (haughty): [arrogantly superior and disdainful]. They equate education with wisdom or intelligence with understanding. I personally know of several people with more degrees than a thermometer but are as wise as a two-year-old in a lolly shop. Solomon gives us a clue as to what being puffed up really is in **Proverbs 16:18** *Pride goeth before destruction, and an haughty spirit* (Gâbahh- lofty, arrogant, self-grandeur- *look at me, I'm the boss, do as you're told*) *before a fall.* This speaks of people who are arrogant because of what they think they have achieved.

Having a revelation from God does not make us superior, only more responsible to live out that revelation before God and man. Mistakes and failures are covered under RAFL (repentance and forgiveness law). To know something of the Kingdom of God puts us in greater danger of being prideful which eventually turns into arrogance unless we strive to remain humble and teachable.

Paul tells us... *For I say, through the grace given unto me, to every man that is among you,* **not to think of himself more highly than he ought to think;** *but to think soberly, according as God hath dealt to every man the measure of faith* (**Romans 12:3**). He is warning that we are susceptible to Huperphroneō- (to esteem oneself overmuch, be vain or arrogant). To think soberly is Sōphroneō, from Sōphrōn which means to be moderate in thought, opinion, and self-control, in other words, holiness. One may dress to holiness standards, but if they think more highly of themselves than they ought, they are just modestly dressed arrogant people. One of the problems the spiritual leaders mentioned in the gospels had, was that they had esteemed themselves into their lofty positions. *And the Pharisees also, who were* **covetous** (greedy), *heard all these things: and they derided him* (Jesus). *And he* (Jesus) *said unto them, Ye are they which justify yourselves* (Dikaioō- to render, to show high regard for self), *before* (Enōpion- in the face of, in front of) *men; but God knoweth your hearts: for that which is highly esteemed* (Hupsēlos- lofty in place or character) **among men** *is* **abomination** (Bdelugma- a detestation and idolatry) *in the sight of God* (**Luke 16:14-15**). Read that last part again, S-L-O-W-L-Y. This is not just a malady of leadership, but a malady of some people who have sat in the pews for a long time also.

Did you catch that? Being lofty is as detestable to God as idolatry and women dressing in men's clothing or murdering babies. There are very few things that are an abomination (disgusting, detestable, obscene, an atrocity) unto God, amongst them are homosexuality, unjust measures and weight, hands that shed innocent blood, a false witness, offering the imperfect unto God and prayers offered by hypocrites just to name a few, and in the midst of this, the Lord puts esteeming oneself highly, being lofty in thought which is pride (see also **Proverbs 6:16-19, Leviticus 18:22**).

Solomon again writes **Proverbs 11:2** *When pride cometh, then cometh shame: but with the lowly is wisdom.* Solomon knew what it was to be prideful. The Book of Ecclesiastes confirms this and he warns that with pride comes Qâlôn- disgrace, confusion and eventually dishonour. When these puffed-up people within the Ecclesia are shown for who they really are and what spirit they have, they will be ashamed and hopefully repent and humble themselves in the sight of God and reconcile with those they have damaged and lorded over and have lauded themselves. We are exhorted by Paul regarding false teachers, *He is proud* (Tuphoō- to inflate with self-conceit: high-minded, to be slowly consumed without flame), *knowing nothing* (Epistamai Mēdemia- understand not even one thing), *but doting* (Noseō- to hanker after, to have a diseased appetite) *about questions* (Zētēsis- disputings just for the sake of disputing) *and strifes of words* (being pedantic: an insulting word used to describe someone who annoys others by correcting small errors, caring too much about minor details, or emphasizing their own expertise especially in some boring or narrow subject matter), *whereof cometh envy* (ill will), *strife* (quarrelling), *railings* (blaspheme), *evil surmisings* (always suspicious of motives) (**1 Timothy 6:4**). He says that these types of people are ***false teachers*** who do not adhere to the words of the Lord according to godliness (see verse 3). Why are we even listening to these sad imitations of human beings masquerading as Christians.

To be puffed up is to look big but filled with nothing but air. Look at a balloon for example. It can be inflated to many times its original size, but it has very little if any weight or substance. At a festive gathering, many balloons seem to brighten up the place, but after the show is over, they are either deflated or burst and cast into the rubbish. Balloons are designed to attract the eye from one area to another, to attract attention so to speak, to be showy.

When I was in the auto industry in California, and Australia in the 90's and early 2000's, before we opened to the public on weekends, we inflated hundreds of big, bright balloons with helium (even lighter than air) and placed them on cars that we were trying to sell. The purpose was to get people's attention, to stop and come in for a look at what we had to offer (*Our Cars are better than their cars. Come and see us, we have better deals*). We were intentionally trying to distract people from what they were doing and where they were going, so we could do mutual business. But at the end of the weekend, we would burst the balloons or deflated then discard them. I don't know how many people came in and purchased a car just because they saw the balloons over the years, but I'd venture to guess it was rather miniscule.

In my humble opinion (yes, I see the irony), people who are easily distracted and led will continually follow these puffed-up buffoons/balloons (notice how similar the two words are). But when these overly self-absorbed people are pricked (confronted or challenged) through their thin skins, they have precious little substance, make weird sounds, and fly off into a rage, then disappear. They get angry, accusing the confronter of usurping their authority or trying to sow discord. When the deflation happens, their followers are left with nothing of any real substance or value. We are warned of these arrogant and oppressive people by the prophet Isaiah, ***For the leaders of this people cause them to err***; *and they that are led of them are destroyed* (**Isaiah 9:8-16**). Once the puffed-up ones have been deflated, they fill themselves with themselves once again, move on and find others they can attract to themselves or their cause. They appear to be godly but contradict God's power to change people (for the think they are the ones to change people according to their understanding and timetable) and sadly and most importantly, all they have succeeded in doing is contradicting their own testimony (**2 Timothy 3:5**).

These puffed-up ones take no correction from anyone nor do they think they have done anyone any wrong or on the rare occasion they do admit they may have been wrong, it is downplayed by pointing out that others are worse than themselves. Getting an apology from these people is harder than getting a black eye from a nun. It takes a major catastrophe to get these types of people to admit they are wrong and when they do, it is usually with a motive of smoothing things over so they can get back to being puffed up. Even Paul tells us through his warning to the Corinthians, *But what I do, that I will do, that I may cut off occasion* (Aphormē- take opportunity) *from them which desire occasion* (Aphormē); *that wherein they glory* (Kauchaomai- boast and vaunt), *they may be found even as we.* ***For such are false apostles, deceitful workers, transforming themselves*** (Metaschēmatizō- transfigure or disguise themselves) *into the apostles of Christ* (**2 Corinthians 11:12-13**). Did you see that people who glory in themselves are false apostles and deceitful?

Now some are puffed up, *as though I would not come to you. But I will come to you shortly, if the Lord will, and will know, not the speech of them which are **puffed up**, but the power. For the kingdom* *of God is not in word, but in power* (**1 Corinthians 4:18-20**). Paul here is not in the least interested in the speech of those that are puffed up but in the power of God that is working through them, not once or twice a week or the occasional miracle, but over their whole daily operational lifetime by example. One cannot be puffed up and yet remain a humble vessel of the Lord as these two are diametrically opposed. *Let no man beguile you* (Katabrabeuō- defraud of salvation) *of your reward in a voluntary humility and worshipping of angels, intruding into those things which he hath not seen,* **vainly puffed up** *by his fleshly mind* (**Colossians 2:18**).

The Pharisees, Sadducees, chief priests and elders, scribes and lawyers were extremely puffed up by their own self-importance and education and, much to their consternation, Jesus deflated them many times in the presence of the ordinary folk. No wonder they hated Him so much. When Nicodemus, a Pharisee, came to Jesus privately and admitted he did not understand what the Master was saying, Jesus didn't publicly correct him. Why? Because he admitted he did not know something. Look at the parable of the Pharisee and the publican (tax collector). *And he spake this parable unto certain* **which trusted in themselves that they were righteous, and despised others** (Exoutheneō- to set at nought or esteem less. Jesus was speaking to the leadership): *Two men went up into the temple to pray; the one a Pharisee, and the other a publican. The Pharisee stood and* (here's the puffed-up part) **prayed thus with himself**, *God, I thank thee, that I am not as other men are, extortioners, unjust, adulterers, or even as this publican. I fast twice in the week, I give tithes of all that I possess.* Notice the term, *prayed thus with himself*; the Pharisee was talking to himself about himself. God was not even listening. He was bragging of all his achievements and did not give God any of the glory but bathed in his own self-righteous magnificence wrought through his own works, self-importance, and education. He trusted in himself and despised the tax collector.

Billy Cole, the Apostle to Thailand is known to have said in a conference, *"For every ONE that is puffed up because people bragged on them, there are 100 that died from a lack of encouragement'.* It is very difficult to be puffed up and encourage someone else at the same time. If there is encouragement, it is usually given to do as they are told because these puffed-up ones know best.

Enter the lowly publican, a man from a notorious and nefarious group of people, hated by all and sundry, yet still a Jew who has the nous to go to the temple to seek forgiveness. He was hated by the Jews because he collected hard earned money to give to their oppressors, and hated by the Romans because he was a sell-out to his own people. Knowing this, he came to the outer courts (for he did not feel worthy to enter the temple) and beat his chest with remorse for the kind of life he had led. The story continues with, *And the publican, standing afar off, would not lift up so much as his eyes unto heaven, but smote upon his breast, saying, God be merciful to me a sinner.* Jesus then tells the moral of the parable... *I tell you,* **this man** (the one looked down by everyone) *went down to his house justified rather than the other: for every one that exalteth himself shall be abased; and he that humbleth himself shall be exalted* (**Luke 18:9-14**).

Notice who was justified and who was not. The puffed up one went away just as lost as when he arrived, though he was a leader and had done good things written in the Torah (God's word. He tithed, he fasted, he even gave a few coins to the poor), yet he had deceived himself into believing because of his education (one could not be a Pharisee unless one was educated and well connected) and obedience to the traditions of the elders (see **Matthew 15:2, Mark 7:3-5**) that God not only heard his prayer, but that he was alright with God. The one who knew he was nothing but a miserable wretch, who had lived a life devoid of faith in God and service to his countrymen but came to realize his need for God and forgiveness and beat his chest in repentance, was the one that God not only heard but also acted on. Being **puffed up for one against another** is one way of saying *I'm better than you and I'm going to show you just how big I really am*. These people use statements like, *we wield a lot of power, or do you know who I am?*

Who knows himself a braggart, let him fear this, for it will come to pass that every braggart shall be found an ass.

William Shakespeare. All's Well, That Ends Well. Act 4, Scene 3.

Nature is a great teacher, and there is much we can learn from the Puffer fish (Tetraodontidae). These creatures, ranging in size from the 1-inch-long dwarf or pygmy puffer fish to the freshwater giant puffer fish, which can grow to more than 2 feet in length. They are scaleless fish and usually have rough to spiky skin. On a humorous note, the Torah calls fish with no scales or fins an unclean fish (**Leviticus 11:9-10** *These shall ye eat of all that are in the waters: whatsoever hath fins and scales in the waters, in the seas, and in the rivers, them shall ye eat. And all that have not fins and scales in the seas, and in the rivers, of all that move in the waters, and of any living thing which is in the waters, they shall be an abomination unto you*).

The Puffer fish has a rather distinctive feature in that when it is threatened it gulps seawater to make itself look bigger and badder than what it really is. It warns potential threats that it is not to be trifled with. Many of these fish add another dimension in their protection bubble by being venomous. The venom (tetrodotoxin) makes them foul tasting and often lethal to other fish. To humans, tetrodotoxin is deadly, up to 1,200 times more poisonous than cyanide. There is enough toxin in one pufferfish to kill 30 adult humans, and there is no known antidote. This effectively stops anything getting close enough to possibly hurt it. This, however, makes it a very solitary fish. Puffer fish are highly territorial and don't like to dwell close to each other as they will usually try to out-puff (out-pride) one another.

People who are puffed up with knowledge (somehow, we seemed to have confused knowledge and intelligence with understanding and wisdom) who think only they can hear from God and are under the mistaken concept that only their opinion actually matters (the overwhelming majority surround themselves with sycophants). Though they are surrounded by people they are actually pretty lonely creatures. They are the puffer fish of the Ecclesia.

In my home country of Australia, the Bufo Marinus (cane toads) are an amphibian plague, which puffs up to ward off any potential predators and adds toxicity to its list of anti-predator weaponry. If ingested, its venom can cause rapid heartbeat, excessive salivation, convulsions, paralysis and can result in death for many native animals. Mammals that try to incorporate cane toads into their diet get a mouthful of toad toxin that is at first distasteful, and very often fatal.

Having toxic people in our lives is unfortunately just a part of living on this planet, however, having toxic people who have puffed themselves up operating within the Ecclesia, can and must be dealt with, for they will eventually poison us and, in many cases, cause a spiritual death that will not have a remedy. Poison only harms once it enters the body. There are anti-toxins that may be administered; however, this must be done quickly, and in many cases, there will be lingering after effects and possibly scars.

Not being puffed up against one another is a safety mechanism God has incorporated into the body. These puffed-up ones tend to cause chaos and split the body into factions (*if you're not with us, then you must be with them*), and will eventually bring about its demise from within. Nothing kills the unity of the body faster than factions and comparing oneself with others (whether it is with a view to superiority or inferiority). There will always be others who have travelled further in life than us, and others who have yet to either begin their journey or are still in the early stages of their journey. Rarely is one puffed up by comparing oneself to someone who has achieved more than they have as this usually leads to feelings of inadequacy which are then projected onto others whom they feel are inferior to themselves. Being puffed up comes from looking at others who have yet to reach a level of maturity we think we have achieved. It is allowing the air of vanity to inflate ourselves to over importance and to believe that only we have the answer to everyone's dilemmas.

Very rarely will a puffed-up person ever say they don't know something or suggest you seek counsel with someone else. They continually tell people they know pretty much everything. They must surround themselves with people whom they have mesmerized into believing that they (the superior) are the only hope they (the inferior) have. The puffed-up ones will separate family members from each other on the pretext that they know better. They must remain the inferior's rescue ranger, or the game is over.

We are **commanded** to not be puffed up one against another and just like any commandment, if we break it there will be consequences which will reverberate throughout eternity. If we love as Paul tells us to, then we must also understand that not being puffed up is also a command. *Charity suffereth long, and is kind; charity envieth not; charity vaunteth not itself,* (Perpereuomai- braggart, to boast) **is not puffed up** (Phusioō- to inflate [oneself], to be proud or haughty), *Doth not behave itself unseemly, seeketh not her own, is not easily provoked, thinketh no evil* (**1 Corinthians 13:4-5**).

Other than using education (degrees, certificates, honorariums, and doctorates etc.) they are constantly introducing themselves as pastor, bishop, doctor and so on) as if this gives them the authority to speak on any subject. A degree only qualifies someone to speak to a matter they have read and studied about, a degree does not equal authority. Another thing that puffs these people up is having knowledge of a situation, **1 Corinthians 8:1** *Now as touching things offered unto idols, we know that we all have knowledge.* **Knowledge puffeth up**, *but charity edifieth.* They think that the more knowledge they have of a situation the more important they are. A higher education is no guarantee of wisdom or intelligence, neither does it prove one's ability to lead, love or carry a burden. There are many people with PhD's, DDL's, MA's, BA's and such who are just plain stupid, should never be placed in charge of a parking booth let alone people who have issues or cannot think for themselves. Like a peacock spreading its tail and strutting about to impress the peahens in their own tiny barnyard, knowledge both in education and of situations alone does nothing but attract attention to themselves. When knowledge is coupled with humility, love, and sacrifice, it may be useful to the body of Christ.

Like the Pharisees and Sadducees, those with big heads are usually the ones with the smallest minds. They lose perspective and the only reality they have is from their own miniscule and mostly insignificant world. They are so busy looking at how others have failed in their attempt at life that they neglect to see their own shortcomings and failures (this is mote and beam time). They involve themselves into things that don't concern them all under the guise of *"knowing better"*.

Let us look at the business world as an example of knowledge puffing up. With the right degree from the right college or university, and the right letters of introduction from the right people in a particular field, a person will stick out in the crowd of people vying for the same position in a company. They can command a higher salary or better perks and with even more knowledge they can command respect by having more titles conferred upon them (usually by others who have the same knowledge and titles). But none of these things teach us how to be better citizens or to love, respect and honour one another, pray for, give, serve, sacrifice, or bear one another's burdens. University/college professors obtained their knowledge through schooling and continued to learn then became teachers. Very few actually have real world knowledge or have been a part of real-world solutions. They only teach what they have learnt. They command high salaries and demand respect. They struggle for tenure and peer recognition. But respect for what, knowing how to read and talk? Their knowledge on a particular subject has puffed them up.

Puffed up and lightweight.

A balloon filled with air weighs extraordinarily little and is easily blown about by a light breeze. It serves no real purpose other than the *ooh aah* factor at parties and conventions. A balloon filled with water, however, has much more mass but is not much more useful than one filled with air. Other than some fun science experiments, they are used for games to distract and entertain children at parties and............., That's it, I got nothing else.

Air and water are like excessive pride and arrogance and at this point I must give a definition of both. Pride is an emotional state deriving positive affect from the perceived value of a person or thing, while arrogance shows itself as an attitude of superiority manifested in an overbearing manner or in presumptuous claims or assumptions and an offensive display of superiority or self-importance. Whether someone is puffed up with air (pride) or water (arrogance) they have no place on the battlefield for the souls of man. Arrogance usually has many accompaniments such as wealth, power, parentage, tenure, or education (these may also be perceived). These people distract the weak minded from God's purpose within the Ecclesia and do much harm to seeking saints who want to fulfill their purpose in the Commonwealth of the Kingdom of God. How may you ask? They demand that people conform to their way of thinking. They judge people based upon what actions they would have done in any given situation (though they never bother to ask what options the other person had). This in turn hinders the seeker from seeking God for their own salvation's sake. The bigger a balloon gets the more attractive and sometimes, even intimidating it looks to others and so these timid and ignorant souls submit out of terror rather than out of a willing deference to the word of God to humble elders made wise (but not arrogant) from years of service to the Commonwealth of the Kingdom of God.

The Dunning-Kruger Effect is a type of cognitive bias where people with little expertise or perceived expertise assume they have superior expertise or ability. This overestimation comes about as a result of the fact that they do not have enough knowledge to know they don't have enough knowledge. They know enough to be of a little use, but not enough to know how dangerous they are.

The story of the three little pigs and the wolf (James Orchard Halliwell-Phillipps 1820-1889) coming to blow their houses down is a perfect example of a person/people who are walking around huffing and puffing their valuableness and perceived invincibility to the Kingdom. They will huff and puff and blow your house down if it is made of weak materials, but the house built not just **on** stone but **of** stone, (for the Ecclesia is made up of lively stones- real disciples (people), *Ye also, as lively*

stones, are built up a spiritual house, an holy priesthood, *to offer up spiritual sacrifices, acceptable to God by Jesus Christ* **1 Peter 2:5**), where every stone strengthens the stone next to it, will withstand all trials. The real Ecclesia cannot be affected by these blowhards (pun intended) and these airbags will eventually give up and go find another set of ignorant victims to threaten with their foolhardiness. As a side note, even the world uses the term, *"air of superiority"* as a substitute for the phrase puffed up. Air of superiority is defined as, *a manner, affectation, appearance, or behaviour indicative of self-importance and condescension.* Same thing, different words.

The best way to deflate a puffed-up person is to pray for them and follow the leading of the Holy Ghost. This is like a pin in their soft and very thin outer casing and soon we will see what they are filled with.

Hitler defeated most of Europe in under a year. He mesmerized the people with his speaking ability, false promises and used gifts to friends to win even more friends to his nefarious plans for domination of what he considered weaker nations. He blustered and blew his way into superiority, made alliances with Italy, and ruled with an iron fist. All became subject to his demented will. Winston Churchill convinced the allies that to bring Hitler down, they should invade Europe through the soft underbelly (Italy), the weakest part of Hitler's defence. Every proud and arrogant person has one. The Holy Ghost will tell a praying saint what and how to pray for these puffed up ones, so they may repent.

Love for one another never displays an air of pride or arrogance. The hope is that eventually they will run out of air or water and will finally submit to the conviction of the Holy Ghost. This should be our prayer. Real love is submitting to the Holy Ghost and to each other for the benefit of the Commonwealth of the Kingdom of God, not so that our authority will not be challenged, but so our humility would be emulated. God's purpose of deflating a puffed-up person is so they will repent of their pride and arrogance and become the humble servant God called them to be. In this manner the world may see a viable option to the death and darkness they now walk in.

Chapter 36.

Grudge not one against another.

James 5:9 *Grudge not* one against another, brethren, lest ye be **condemned**: behold, the judge standeth before the door.

Condemned is a rather harsh word with bad connotations in our modern language. It is the word Stenazō- to make or put in straits, to put pressure on. A condemned criminal is put in restraints (cuffs and prison) and is pressured to behave in a manner that will be safe for the community. The modern word *grudge* has a different meaning today than what was written centuries ago; its form is a persistent feeling of ill will or resentment resulting from a past insult or injury (whether real or perceived), to give or allow reluctantly or resentfully (Oxford Dictionary). The original meaning is from the Middle English (circa 1150-1500) *grutch*, which meant to overly complain or grumble. Though the modern version of grudge is not good either (to reluctantly give or admit), we will stick with the biblical version of this destructive trait within the Ecclesia. James is telling us that when we grudge against (hold a grudge, complain or grumble) we are actually condemning ourselves.

The Hebrews left Egypt because Moses had convinced them, the Egyptians and the surrounding nations with signs and wonders, that God was who He said He was (the world got to see the I AM, not who Moses was). With all the miracles that God performed (ten plagues), how He took them away from their slave masters with cart loads of treasure, these people still murmured (had a grudge) against God and Moses. These former slaves to a tyrant king (representative of Satan) had a grudge against God and Moses because things weren't going as smoothly as they thought it would or should, after all, they were God's people, right? With the attitude of the exiled generation that came out of Egypt, they condemned themselves. *I will therefore put you in remembrance, though ye once knew this, how that the Lord, having saved the people out of the land of Egypt, afterward destroyed them that believed not* (**Jude 1:5**).

They may have been mistreated in Egypt, but hey, at least they had food, shelter, and water, right? Their plan was that they would leave Egypt, walk for about eleven days, maybe a month or two, and enter merrily into the land of Canaan which flowed with milk and honey. Piece of cake, right? They couldn't have been more wrong.

They had no concept of God's timing and what He had planned for them to know before they entered into their promised land. God had some rules that He required to be strictly followed in the promised land. For example, Egypt had multiple gods and the Hebrews were also worshipping these gods whilst living there, hence the first commandment. Not sure if this is true? What was the first thing the Hebrews did when Moses did not come back from the mountain top in a timely manner? They built themselves a golden calf and danced around it. One of the Egyptian gods was represented as a calf (Apis) and the ritual was to dance around it, hoping their dancing would please Apis. The one true God was not happy with their idolatry (and ticking off God is never a wise move by anyone's standard). After impatiently waiting for Moses for forty days, the people (with no evidence, just feelings based on their impatience) began murmuring and accusing God of killing Moses. According to **Exodus 32:6** they reverted to their old ways ...*And they rose up early on the morrow, and offered burnt offerings, and brought peace offerings; and the people sat down to eat and to* *drink, and rose up to play* (to laugh outright (in merriment or scorn), mock, make sport). They went against God's plan and murmured because they did not expect things to go the way they did.

The Egyptians allowed multiple spouses and sexual partners, but God told them not to commit adultery or fornication. Theft was illegal in Egypt but forbidden in the promised land. Disobedient children were not going to be tolerated in the land of Canaan as they were in Egypt. See where this is going? The Ten Commandments were a direct correlation to what the Hebrews were living with in Egypt.

The seed of a grudge is planted when something we expect to happen doesn't go the way we want. The first emotion we feel is mostly disappointment, followed quickly by anger and if held onto long enough, bitterness will soon be nipping at our heels. Shortly thereafter, we become hostile to the person or thing that caused the disappointment. A constant murmurer has had these traits for a long time and many times is unable to extricate themselves from it. One who constantly complains is addicted to the feelings of self-pity they have in their minds. Like a drug addict must be delivered from the thing that gives them the high, so must constant complainers, in a sense, be delivered (not that there is a demon of complaining. That is the human spirit that indulges in this activity) from the high they receive when they feel justified or proved right. These people look for problems when solutions are just around the corner, they create mountains from ant hills, and find a problem for every solution. When there's an answer ready to be given, by their own negativity, they snatch defeat from the jaws of victory. Therefore, we need the body of Christ to help in these disappointing times. The Ecclesia reminds us of the Sovereignty of God and that *our* appointments do not always match *His* appointments, thus we have dis-appointments.

Genesis 27:41 *And Esau **hated** Jacob because of the blessing wherewith his father blessed him: and Esau said in his heart, The days of mourning for my father are at hand; then will I slay my brother Jacob.* Esau hated Jacob because his brother conned him out of his birthright. Without a doubt Esau was wronged, but how he reacted to the wrong showed what was in his heart. The word *hated* is the word Sâṭam, which shows that he lurked for, persecuted, and opposed himself against his brother and it comes with the idea of obsessing for revenge. Here we see a man who was wronged and for several decades had a grudge against his brother (see Genesis chapters 25 and 32). In the end though, he allowed God to soften his anger ridden heart. At the same time God was working on Jacob (now Israel) who had also repented of his conning ways. Because both had submitted to God, their relationship was restored. This is what God expects from His Ecclesia.

A grudge between the brothers and sisters in the Ecclesia is precisely what the enemy wants to slow down the work of God. The only way a grudge can be dealt with is repentance and if possible (by God's standard, not ours) biblical restoration (see **Galatians 6:1-3**). When people fail to meet our standards and needs, and fail they will, as we will for others, disappointment sets in and if this disappointment is nursed long enough, like silverfish in the closet, it will eat away at the very fabric of our soul. God must be our supply, not just for finances, material, and joy, but also for our peace. Yes, He uses people, but we must remember, people are prone to failure and grace and mercy is the only salve that works. A grudge, they say, is like drinking poison, then hoping the other guy dies a slow and painful death, when in reality, the only ones experiencing death is the one holding the grudge.

The Gilead Balm.

A true paradox is that as we repent and give grace and mercy to those who have failed us (not necessarily wronged us), we receive the same healing balm of Gilead for ourselves. Jeremiah speaks of a balm, one that heals the hurting heart. He writes, *For the hurt of the daughter of my people am I hurt; I am black; astonishment hath taken hold on me. Is there no balm in Gilead; is there no physician there? why then is not the health of the daughter of my people recovered?* (**Jeremiah 8:21-22**). Certain false prophets and fake or domineering pastors (**8:10**) were telling people that all was well with Israel when things were definitely not well. It led the people into a time of much sorrow and disillusionment. *For they have healed the hurt of the daughter of my people slightly* (offering temporary peace), *saying, Peace, peace; when there is no peace* (**8:11**). These false pastors (God's words, not mine, **23:1-2**) were not even sorry for how they had let the people down with their trickery and fed them with platitudes. They just told the people what they wanted to hear with the same old messages about the same old subject and caused them not to grow. He asks the question, *Were they ashamed when they had committed abomination? nay, they were not at all ashamed, neither could they blush: therefore shall they fall among them that fall: in the time of their visitation they shall be cast down, saith the LORD* (**Jeremiah 8:12**).

Between verses thirteen and seventeen, the people take time to repent for trusting in man rather than in God. There is still much lamenting and disappointment between verse eighteen to twenty, but then God mentions the balm of Gilead. The people were hurting, and they were in dire need of a physician. They had a long time to let disappointment set in, that led to anger which led to erroneous thinking that their God had abandoned them. Skip forward about 570 years and the answer to Israel's pain and suffering shows up in an insignificant town next to the capitol, shown through a man called Yeshua (a common name at the time), who would answer the call to be their servant/shepherd and great physician. Yeshua healed their diseases, put their false teachers (man appointed and self-appointed leaders) in their place and restored the nation's chance of salvation.

He *was* and *is* the Balm of Gilead to those hurting people, but His medicine was not easy to take. He said that if we followed Him, we would more than likely experience being hurt, disappointed, even be hated, then die for His name's sake (**Ephesians 4:26, Acts 1:8**). He would make himself available to heal the hurt others have intentionally or unintentionally inflicted upon us (see **Hebrew 4:15-16**). He told us we would be misunderstood, hated, ostracized, cause us to flee from one city to another (**Matthew 10:22-23**), but that if we endured, we would be saved.

Not doing things for and with the Ecclesia is wrong but doing them grudgingly is equally wrong. Peter tells us with what attitude we are to minister to one another, *And above all things have fervent charity* (passionate love without ceasing) *among yourselves: for charity shall cover the multitude of sins. Use hospitality one to another* **without grudging** (grumbling or murmuring). *As every man hath received the gift, even so minister the same one to another, as good stewards of the manifold grace of God* (**1 Peter 4:8-10**). As we have received the gifts of grace and mercy, so we ought to minister these gifts freely. Grace and grudges are like oil and water, though after much turmoil it is difficult to separate the two, when the quiet time comes, we will see them separate and which one comes to the fore.

God didn't give us the book of revelations so we could build bigger buildings or bomb shelters in our backyards stocked with supplies. He gave us the book so we could build bigger dinner tables and invite people over to share our Lord and lives.

Author Unknown.

Chapter 37.

Do not go to law with one another.

1 Corinthians 6:7 *Now therefore there is utterly a fault among you,* **because ye go to law one with another.** *Why do ye not rather take wrong? why do ye not rather suffer yourselves to be defrauded?*

This does not necessarily mean that we take a brother to the local shire or county courthouse (though that is not right either). At first glance it seems to say one thing, however a further look will see that it has another meaning. This is known as a Double-Entendre (double meaning). Here are some famous Double-Entendre headlines, *Miners refuse to work after death* or, *New obesity study looks for larger test group* or perhaps, *Children make nutritious snacks*. We must look deeper than what we initially see. To not *go to law with one another* also has a double meaning and we will see that both meanings go directly against the word of God for His Ecclesia. First, as mentioned earlier, there is only one law maker, God, and His law is not only just and impartial, but also eternal. What God says about any issue is purely from heaven's point of view where righteousness reigns and truth is not filtered through feeble human thinking or our ever-changing feelings.

Hebrews 9:26 tells us that God had to suffer via us mere mortals denying Him, cursing His name, being rejected for the simple act of showing Himself for who He really is. Much of the Ecclesia in western society, have been using Him as some jolly old rich grandpa who is there to bring the goodies, make us feel good when we are sad and to help us build little empires in His name. He sadly has become like the grandpa we visit regularly and keep up appearances because we are in His will to get the mansion. What God requires for entry into His Kingdom is just as valid for today's Ecclesia as it was on the first Pentecost post resurrection and for those prior to His arrival on earth as a man. Loving Him above all, loving our neighbour as ourselves, sacrificial obedience to His will until death. Obedience, not just referring to the Fantastic Five, standards and obedience to the right organization. We read, *For then* **must he often have suffered** *since the foundation of the world: but now once in the end of the world hath he appeared to put away sin by* **the sacrifice of himself** (**Hebrews 9:26**).

How did He suffer often? Because we have broken His laws with such monotonous regularity and hubris that it begs description. But there is coming a time when all will be revealed and judged by God, based not on how our feelings were hurt or who broke our puny and fickle laws and traditions, but upon His Holy law. *And as it is appointed unto men once to die, but after this the judgment* (**Hebrews 9:27**) and *...I saw the dead, small and great, stand before God; and the books were opened: and another book was opened, which is the book of life: and the dead were judged out of those things which were written in the books,* **according to their works** (**Revelation 20:12**). For a judgement to be made, there must be a solid reference which does not change, and all is measured with a plum line, otherwise there could be no just punishment nor reward.

God is not interested in all our extra canonical laws and prescriptions, rules and regulations, traditions, protocols, and ethics we place on ourselves and each other to keep us from sinning. When we are biblically discipled and led by and obey the Holy Ghost, breaking God's commands will soon become abhorrent. The more laws we make, the more laws we cannot help but break. Though I do not subscribe to Russian American writer and philosopher, Ayn Rand's general philosophy, I believe she put it perfectly when she wrote, *"There's no way to rule innocent men. The only power any government has is the power to crack down on criminals. Well, when there aren't enough criminals, one makes them. One declares so many things to be a crime that it becomes impossible for men to live without breaking laws."*

These manufactured laws more often than not create a situation in which the concerns or aims of two different parties are incompatible, otherwise known as a conflict of interest. What does God want and what do we want? Overwhelmingly, they are not the same. That is where submission to the Holy Ghost is imperative. If someone has offended us and we mention the law, which the breaking of brings a curse, what do we do with **Galatians 3:11** *But that no man is justified by the law in the sight of God, it is evident: for, The just shall live by faith. And the law is not of faith: but, The man that doeth them shall live in them.* **Christ hath redeemed us from the curse of the law**, *being made a curse for us: for it is written, Cursed is every one that hangeth on a tree:* **By bringing up the law, we try to justify ourselves by the law, however, we will be judged in the same manner when we break God's laws.**

To invoke the law on one another places the invoker under the same scrutiny and removes the gift of grace from the accuser. Let me give an example. **James 2:8-10** tells us, *If ye fulfil **the royal law according to the scripture**, Thou shalt love thy neighbour as thyself, ye do well: But if ye have respect to persons* (show partiality amongst the saints)*, ye commit sin, and are convinced* (Elegchoŝ- rebuked and convicted) *of the law as transgressors. For whosoever shall keep the whole law, and yet offend in one point, he is guilty of all.* There are two laws at work here, the royal law and the Mosaic law. The law of God is not like a smorgasbord where we get to pick and choose which laws we want ourselves or others to adhere to. If we invoke the law on one another in an area we deem as sacrosanct, the entire law will be used as a magnifying glass to highlight our own weaknesses and failure. Read on, *For he that said, Do not commit adultery, said also, Do not kill. Now if thou commit no adultery, yet if thou kill, thou art become a transgressor of the law* (**James 2:11**). Let us follow this thought through to its logical conclusion, shall we?

Before you go off on a screaming fit and say you haven't murdered anyone, sincerely search your soul, see if you have done any of the following that are yet to be placed under the blood sacrifice of the Messiah. Injustice (unfairness or unrighteousness), harlotry, idolatry, plotting (whether in the heart or mind, even if it's not carried out) to bring someone down, malice, avarice, greediness, withholding help from those in need, injurious, wished harm, jealousy, quarrelling, contentious, being crafty, bad character traits, gossiping, slander or talking against someone whilst they are not in your presence, not giving someone a chance to answer charges, impious, insulter, mal-treater, appearing above others, becoming worthless, foolishness, promise breaker, hard-hearted towards any saint, trucebreaker, lacking human and divine mercy. It's okay, put the book down and self-examine for a little while, then you can see what true grace you have been given. Put plainly, we may not have committed murder, but if we have killed someone (with our mouths or in our hearts) we are held to the same standard as one who has taken a life. Killing someone's reputation or their fellowship with others is just as bad as the mortal death of another to God.

Here is just one scripture where all the above (in general terms) are mentioned and they were written to the church of Rome (believers in the Messiah, the One true God, all baptized in His name, filled with the Holy Ghost, and spoke in tongues). These people had God, but did not retain God in their knowledge (did not recognize or have full discernment), *Being filled with all unrighteousness, fornication, wickedness, covetousness, maliciousness; full of envy, murder, debate, deceit, malignity; whisperers, Backbiters, haters of God, despiteful, proud, boasters, inventors of evil things, disobedient to parents, Without understanding, covenantbreakers, without natural affection, implacable, unmerciful:* **Who knowing the judgment of God, that they which commit such things are worthy of death, not only do the same, but have pleasure in them that do them** (Romans 1:29-32). Once again, I want to make it perfectly clear, this was NOT written to the world, but to believers. When we bring up the law and invoke it upon others, we also place ourselves under the same law with the same punishments.

Second, as mentioned previously, we tend to enforce laws we make on our own, and only when it suits us. Let me give you an example. We dole out judgment with such impunity based solely on how we feel at a particular time and who has caused the infraction of our own laws. This is contrary to the word of God (it is partial, and it goes against the very character and word of God (see **James 3:17, 1 Timothy 5:21, Romans 3:6-9, Acts 10:34-35, Colossians 3:25**). One of our friends or loved ones may do something today and it does not faze us, but tomorrow, because we are preoccupied with something, or not feeling well, we blow up at them and they are wondering what's going on. If a non-family member or stranger does those things, we apply a harsher sentence. This is just a small example of breaking a mini law which last only as long as we want it to.

Jesus tells us that He is not a judge between two brethren (who owes who) in a squabble about money, *And one of the company said unto him, Master, speak to my brother, that he divide the inheritance with me* (**Luke 12:13**). Jesus answers with, *Man, who made me a judge or a divider over you? And he said unto them, Take heed, and beware of covetousness: for a man's life consisteth not in the abundance of the things which he possesseth* (**Luke 12:14-15**). Jesus told them to sort out their own squabbles as we in the Ecclesia are meant to do. These *'brothers'* were not interested in right or wrong, they wanted judgment based on their wants and desires. Jesus will not step in on our petty little squabbles because He is more interested in judging righteously based upon His actions, His character and how closely we align ourselves to them. He tells us to swallow our pride and sort out our messes as much as we can. This would be like two church soccer teams going to prayer just before the game and asking God to help them win. Whose prayer does He answer? Neither. Just play the game to the best of your abilities and let the chips fall where they may.

Jesus speaks of issues between the brethren and sorting it out between ourselves, *Therefore if thou bring thy gift to the altar, and there rememberest that thy brother hath ought against thee; Leave there thy gift before the altar,* **and go thy way; first be reconciled to thy brother, and then come and offer thy gift.** *Agree with thine adversary* (Antidikos-opponent) *quickly, whiles thou art in the way with him; lest at any time the adversary deliver thee to the judge, and the judge deliver thee to the officer, and thou be cast into prison* (**Matthew 5:23-25**). As we can see, God does not jump in and make it all better. He expects us to do all in our power to reconcile with one another, not sue each other either in man's court or the court of opinions of the saints in our churches. How can we reconcile the world unto Christ if we cannot reconcile with each other or are taking each other before the courts of man or God?

Matthew 7:2 *For with what judgment ye judge, ye shall be judged: and with what measure ye mete, it shall be measured to you again.* The law of God was not made to suit ourselves, to fit into our time frame or busy schedule, our whims or to protect you and me. The laws were given to protect the Commonwealth of the Kingdom of God as a whole. God put into place a mechanism against false accusations made against a member of the Kingdom. *Thou shalt not bear false witness* (**Exodus 20:16**) which forbids:

1. Speaking falsely in any matter, lying, equivocating, and any way devising and designing to deceive our neighbour.

2. Speaking unjustly against our neighbour, to the prejudice of his reputation, which involves the guiltiness of both.

Exodus 23:1 explains this very well. *Thou shalt not raise a false report* (Shâv'- morally destructive for the cause of ruin and subjective [based on how we see things or what we choose to believe]): *put not thine hand* (don't join in) *with the wicked to be an unrighteous witness*. If we join in with others who are trying to ruin someone's reputation, then we are just as guilty as the one who makes the accusation.

If justice is not done with the restoration of the so-called wrong doer as the final result, then we become an *unrighteous witness* (claiming they want restoration is not good enough, for words are cheap. What are the visible proofs of their claim?). The Pharisees who brought the woman caught in adultery to Jesus, claimed they wanted justice, to fulfil the word of God. If they truly wanted justice, they would have brought the man as well. But the Lord saw they had ulterior motives in judging her. Jesus never did condone her actions but brought to light their own wicked hearts which even they could not refute. **John 8:6-7** *But Jesus stooped down, and with his finger wrote on the ground, as though he heard them not. So when they continued asking him, he lifted up himself, and said unto them, He that is without sin among you, let him first cast a stone at her.* When it seemed the message was not getting across, He continued to write in the dirt, but this time He must have spoken some of the things He wrote. Because in verse 9 we read, *And they which **heard it**, being convicted by their own conscience, went out one by one, beginning at the eldest, even unto the last: and Jesus was left alone, and the woman standing in the midst.* Their own heart sunk their attempt at judgment (please note that they used the word of God out of context to justify their action. They even quoted from **Deuteronomy 22:22** and **Leviticus 20:10**), but had they been using the word correctly, they would have brought the man as well as the woman before Jesus). Jesus then dealt personally with the woman by forgiving her sin and then commanding her not to do it again. This by the way shows mercy above judgement, *For he shall have judgment without mercy, that hath shewed no mercy; and **mercy rejoiceth against judgment*** (James 2:13). I do not think it would be a stretch of the imagination to assume that she would be one of the 120 on the day the Ecclesia was manifested in the upper room, if not one of the 3000 born again on the first Pentecost after the resurrection.

What can we learn from this situation? When a brother or sister falls (not necessarily in what *we* call sin), we are to search our own hearts, admit we have failed our Lord countless times, bring them to Jesus and trust that the Lord will do that which is right in His sight. If we truly had restoration in mind, we would also ask God if there was anything we could do to help in the restoration. Judgemental prayer never gets past our ceilings. David does a very courageous thing in **Psalm 139:23-24** when he says, *Search **me**, O God, and know my heart: try **me**, and know **my** thoughts: And see if there be any wicked way in **me**, and lead **me** in the way everlasting.* He wrote this when God made him king over *all* Israel. He wanted to care for God's people, God's way and he knew that if there was any malice in his heart for the Northern Kingdom, he would not rule righteously. He lays himself bare before the Lord and asks the most Holy One to search his heart to see what is really in there. Will we do the same today? Will we ask God to search our hearts before we invoke some archaic man-made law of our church or organization, or a law of God filtered through our own fickle feelings.

Leviticus 19:17-18 *You shall not hate your kinsfolk in your heart. Reprove your kinsman* (family, brothers, and sisters) *but incur no guilt because of him. You shall not take vengeance or **bear a grudge against your countrymen**. Love your fellow as yourself: I am the Lord* (Jewish Study Bible). If Christ redeemed us from the curse of the law, why would we invoke the law of God upon one another?

Back in 1995 I was driving from Stockton, California to Grass Valley, in the foothills of the Sierra Nevada Mountains to meet with a pastor. I was running late and about an hour and half into the trip I stopped to call the pastor to inform him of my late arrival. The use of cell phones was not prevalent at the time. The only place I could find with a working phone was in a bar, so I went in to call. There was no answer, so I left to continue my journey. I met with him, and we arranged for me to preach in a couple of months. A week later I get a call cancelling the engagement and when I asked why, he told me that one of the elders of his church had seen me come out of the bar and had told him that it was not a good witness. He proceeded to quote **1 Thessalonians 5:22** *Abstain from all appearance of evil* while totally ignoring the previous verse; *Prove all things; hold fast that which is good.* The elder and pastor had prejudged (using scripture, no less, unfortunately out of context) without further investigation. Ironically, the pastor, a few years later, was accused of an affair (based on circumstantial evidence, what people thought they heard and saw) that he did not commit and was forced to resign. It was only years later that it was proven an affair did not take place. This is what Jesus meant when he said in **Matthew 7:1-2** *Judge not, that ye be not judged. For with what judgment ye judge, ye shall be judged: and with what measure ye mete, it shall be measured to you again.* Judgment can only happen when a law is invoked, then all involved will be held to the same standard.

Do not go to law with one another. It is just not worth it. Go to God on behalf of one another. The results will be far more pleasing and everlasting.

Chapter 38.

Do not bite and devour one another.

Galatians 5:15 *But if ye **bite and devour** one another, take heed that **ye be not consumed** one of another.*

Many of us have seen the old 1920's silent pictures of Dastardly Dan's foiled attempt to get the deed to Miss Darlene's gold mine or the cartoon where the superhero defeats the super villain's nefarious plans to take over the world, and the bad guy says in the end, '*Drats, thwarted again!*". Their plans were thwarted, foiled, by someone or something. When we bite and devour one another we foil our own plans or as Paul puts it, we become consumed one of another.

Let us look at what it means to *bite and devour*. The term *Daknō kai Katesthiō* means to thwart and wear down, to foil an attempt. When someone is trying to live for and with God and another prevents that from happening whether it is through backbiting, gossip (or as I like to call it- "*Christian sharing for prayer*"), disfellowshipping because of disagreements etc, we no longer are an instrument in the hand of God to increase His Kingdom, but a tool in the hand of God's enemy to do his bidding. Many a true work of God has been hindered, delayed, or minimized because other saints have put the kybosh on it. We think that all must agree with us, or it cannot possibly be God. These kinds of pseudo-saints are so closed minded, it would take a team of horses to pry it open.

Mistakes are Good.

I believe there are two types of education leading to wisdom. They are, learnt and earnt wisdom. For example, *"There have been dark places from my past where lessons were learnt and wisdom was earnt"*. People must be free to learn from their mistakes as this is what brings about personal wisdom. I feel a definition of mistake is in order. First, it is an error or fault resulting from defective judgment, deficient knowledge, or carelessness. Second, it is a misconception or misunderstanding. If someone makes a mistake, and we nail them to that same stake (pun intended) for ever, we are biting and devouring one another. We have taken on the mantle of judge, jury and executioner based on our own fallacious thinking of what we would have done and not the mind of Christ (although I admit every now and then, by pure coincidence, they are the same). We make children feel bad at school because of mistakes they've made rather than praising them on their attempts and using those same mistakes to build correct understanding.

Sadly, we do the former with one another in the Kingdom of God also. If somebody attempts to do something for God and it doesn't work out, we tell them it failed. Who said it failed? We then make them sit down until they earn our trust. What hypocrisy! So what, there doesn't seem to be a long line of people standing outside our churches willing to do the will of God. When the disciples could not cast out the demon in **Matthew 17:14-21**, though they tried, do we see Jesus scolding them and not trusting them until they've paid their dues in the sin bin? No! Not at all. He corrected them and moved on.

To bite and devour is an animalistic trait given to non-sentient beings like viruses, lions, wolves, hyenas, jackals, bugs. They devour because it is in their nature to do so. They cannot help it, it is the only way they can survive and grow the pack, pride, or culture. To feast on the weak is their sole reason for survival and if there are no weak ones, they will gather in ever bigger hunting groups to take down the stronger ones. This thinking would have members of the Ecclesia turn on one another for the smallest of infractions to their code of ethics or traditions. However, we have been given a promise by Peter in his second letter, *Whereby are given unto us exceeding great and precious promises: that by these **ye might be partakers of the divine** (Theios- godlike) **nature** (Phusis- disposition or constitution, growth (by germination or expansion)), having escaped the corruption that is in the world through lust* (**2 Peter 1:4**). We have been made into something that has never existed on earth before, and Peter concurs with his fellow apostle, Paul, *Therefore if any man be in Christ, **he is a new creature**: old things are passed away; behold, all things are become new* (**2 Corinthians 5:17**). A new creature has a new nature. It does not think like its former self, like no other creature. There are many different breeds of dogs, but their natural instincts are the same.

There will always be a leader in every pack of biters and devourers. They will be the ones with the loudest mouths, hardest hearts and smallest minds, the least amount of compassion, mercy, and grace, usually taking scripture out of context and with the wrong spirit. They will be the ones who cite the rule book and keeping count as to how many times the rules were broken. They will be the ones that will think they have their act together and expect others to be as 'spiritual' as they think they are. They will be the ones who will write off (rather quickly I might add) those that do not measure up or are taking too long to get their act together. They will be the ones who constantly speak in pithy platitudes and have a one size fits all mentality to every problem (*well, you just need to fast more, pray more, have more faith, give more in offerings, read your bible more, go to church more* etc.). They will also be the ones who will *not* sacrifice their time, talents, and treasures, nor will they come down to the level of those who are hurting to be a part of the restoration of a fallen one back into the Ecclesia, not grudgingly or with pride, but with humility and a broken heart for the saint. They belong to the ATNA group (all talk and no action) and in so doing they nullify their own witness that they belong to the Commonwealth of the Kingdom of God. They bite and devour in the name of unity, and oxymoron at best and an abomination to God at worst.

Each time we take a bite into a steak it gets smaller, the same happens when we bite into each other. There's an old quip that goes, *How do you eat an elephant? One bite at a time.* The enemy knows he cannot destroy us in one fell swoop, so he employs situations and people to try to destroy our lives, one bite at a time. His greatest tool is not the system of the world, most of us are far too smart for that. If we have even a modicum of spirituality, we would see through that. No, instead, he uses so-called self-appointed or man-appointed spiritual leaders or saints who have bought their pew by dint of time in the church and who are more interested in tithing on their *mint and rue and all manner of herbs, and* (Kai- yet) *pass over judgment* (Krisis- justice- the divine law) *and the love of God: these ought ye to have done, and not to leave the other undone* or uber-spiritual brothers and sisters in the Lord who think they are holier than Swiss cheese (see **Luke 11:42, Romans 12:3**). These have caused many more to leave the Ecclesia than poverty, disease, or persecution.

I refer you to an earlier comment about pain caused by those closest to us. David experienced this same pain, and he described it in rather sombre tones in **Psalm 55:13-15** *It is not an enemy who reviles me, I could bear that; it is not my foe who vaunts himself against me- I could hide from him; but it was you, my equal, my companion, my friend; sweet was our fellowship; we walked together in God's house* (Jewish Study Bible). We see the hurt and anguish David felt from his own son Absalom. His enemies have always looked to do him harm, but he was blindsided and flabbergasted when it was one of his own, one who claimed the name of Jehovah, his equal, his companion, his sweet friend, one with whom he went to the *house of God.*

Resorting once again to Shakespeare, we see in the play *Antony and Cleopatra,* act 3, scene 1, that Caesar was assassinated by the senate of Rome. Caesars were well known to be assassinated on a regular basis and almost always by those closest to them (whether it was from members of his family, the senate, or the praetorian guards, it was always those that he trusted the most that did most of the damage). The tragedy, and what is infinitely more important, is not that Caesar is assassinated by the senate, but that the assassination took place at the hands of his intimate friend. Therein lies the term, *Et Tu, Brute? (You too Brutus?).* Caesar, like David, expected this type of treatment from his enemies and that is what makes the pain excruciating. It was not the physical death that bothered David or Caesar, but the personal nature of the betrayal.

Not so friendly, friendly fire.

Fratricide (the killing of a friend, in military terms it is also known as *"friendly fire*) is a term given to an act of negligence where troops fire on troops from their own side. This happens in what is called the *fog of war.* When the lead is flying, the smoke is thick and hard to see through, the smell of cordite and corpses is strong, fear grips the heart of men and rash decisions are made. Not knowing where a unit of troops is on a map or in comparison to another, and indiscriminate panic shooting, can kill many more than the enemy would have in one area. One-or-two-degrees incorrect sighting from an artillery barrage 7 kilometres (4.5 miles) away can mean the destruction of an entire unit of troops until someone halts the fire. This is very disturbing and the cause of much grief and introspection on behalf of the offending party and more training is involved to ensure it does not happen again.

However, when a deliberate and well-planned act to destroy, damage, or obstruct something or someone occurs, it is no longer called friendly fire but sabotage. When sabotage is perpetrated upon one's own people it is called treason. Friendly fire can be forgiven and corrected. Sabotage is expected from the enemy, but treason is aimed at fellow citizens and during times of war, the latter is usually punishable by summary execution. No-one accidently turns on a brother or sister or turns them in to the enemy. Neither can one accidently take a bite from a steak. It is a deliberate act to devour said steak.

Another example of biting and devouring one another and the loss that the Commonwealth of the Kingdom of God incurs is when someone in the Ecclesia does something that you or the leadership disagrees with. It may or may not be against God's word, but you have decided that person should be made aware that they have crossed the line and that their actions will not be tolerated. Has anyone spoken to them to find out what options they had when the choice was made? Did you or the leadership see if there was a way to help the situation or were they forced to go through it alone because there was no one to talk to without the fear of recrimination or ostracization? Is the situation really as bad as it is purported? Was there anyone who went alongside and helped them look for other options or to help mitigate some of the fallout? Was there even an option for that to happen?

Yet, in many cases that person will be ostracized, brow beaten, or removed from ministry and or fellowship without any recourse. We have taken small chunks from them, devoured them, reduced them to nothing over time and in many, but not all cases, lost them from the Ecclesia. To show how insane we can be, when they do leave and go to another church, we call them backsliders, prideful or reprobates. We will give account to God for this type of treatment, and a high price will be paid, mark my words. Those in the Ecclesia who practice such things have lessened the effectiveness of the Commonwealth of the Kingdom of God and it has consumed us.

We must exercise spiritual restraint when dealing with members of the Ecclesia with whom we disagree and remember that we are not as far along as we think we are, nor are others at the same level that we are. We must allow God to change the person as God has changed us, in His will, time, and manner. We must be there when the members of the Ecclesia need us, not to change them, but to walk through the change with them.

Two men on a deserted island will have different ideas of how to survive. If they do not work together but fight over how to find food, water, and make shelter, both will be hungry, thirsty, and exposed to the elements. If they bite and devour one another because each one thinks their way of survival is superior, they will soon be consumed (worn away and depleted) of one another and both will needlessly suffer and die.

Those in the body who have differing views are not our enemy. They may challenge our paradigm, but this is not evil. Paul, Peter, Thomas, the Pharisees, and Sadducees all had their paradigm challenged, but all received truth from a source they were not used to. By biting and devouring one another we may inadvertently be cutting off our own noses to spite our faces. All truth does not come from the same pipeline, though it does come from the same source (the Holy Ghost inspired word of God).

Chapter 39.

Do not envy one another.

Galatians 5:26 Let us **not be desirous of vain glory**, *provoking one another,* ***envying one another***.

Exodus 20:17 Thou shalt not **covet** thy neighbour's house, thou shalt not covet thy neighbour's wife, nor his manservant, nor his maidservant, nor his ox, nor his ass, nor any thing that is thy neighbour's.

The ugly green-eyed monster of envy can cause many to question God as to why they do not have something or someone that others may have. Envy is a want to have a quality, possession, or other desirable attribute belonging to someone else, it is also known as jealousy and it manifests itself as bitterness, discontent, and resentment, all of which are highly poisonous to the soul of man. It robs us of peace and oft times, much sleep.

Before we dig into this chapter, I think a quick understanding of the differences between envy and covet is necessary. The main differences are that envy is a feeling of discontent and resentment based on someone else's possessions, abilities, or status, while covet is wishing, longing, or craving for something that belongs to someone else. Envy allows someone to feel displeasure or hatred towards another person for their good fortune or possessions, and to covet is to wish for their good fortune or possessions with eagerness; to burn with this desire possession of said good fortune, often enviously. Both, in context with the Ecclesia, are dangerous and tend to lean toward destruction of relationships rather than godly edification.

Strangely, Paul tells the Corinthian church to ...**covet** *earnestly the best gifts: and yet shew I unto you a more excellent way* (**1 Corinthians 12:31**). This word is a mistranslation of the phrase *be zealous for*. After speaking of the importance of the gifts for the operation of the Ecclesia, Paul tells the reader to Zēloō from Zēlos- to have zeal (in a favourable sense) ardour, eagerness, and a fervent mind toward the best gifts for the Ecclesia. Whatever gift the Ecclesia needs at any given moment, that is the best gift, and we are to be zealous to work in the gifts that benefit the Ecclesia whether it is prophecy, healing, hospitality, administration, giving, exhortation, tongues, working of miracles, teaching, helps, government, words of knowledge, words of wisdom, teaching, that is what we are to desire.

Envy is the opposite of Commonwealth in that it seeks to get for self rather than to give to others. It robs us of fellowship because we usually cannot stand to be near the one's we are envious of. Envy also makes us think the other person could not have possibly deserved said blessings, after all, doesn't God know what we know of that person? It robs us of peace because we spend more time complaining about what we do not have rather than thanking God for what we do have. It robs us of time spent on the things of God. Envy takes away from what we can give and receive from others because of what they have or what we do not have. The only thing we can be envious of, is someone else's walk with God, in that it should provoke us to emulate what they did to get that close to God. We are not to imitate them (robotically) but emulate them. To emulate is to strive to equal or excel; to vie with successfully. This allows for individual growth or conviction but still has the same results. This is not to be confused with imitate; to copy the actions, appearance, or mannerisms of another, to ape, to produce an object identical to a given object.

We (the Ecclesia) are all created different but with the same goal, to do all in our power to obey God's word, as revealed by God's spirit and by loving Him with all our being, manifesting that love to one another, thus finding ourselves to be citizens of the Commonwealth of the Kingdom of God. We are to imitate Christ but emulate others. *followers* (Mimētēs- imitators) *of me, even **as*** (Kathōs- in as much and according to) *I also am of Christ*, says Paul, not once but three times (**1 Corinthians 11:1, 4:16** and **Philippians 3:17**). Paul is requiring us to imitate Christ's life in him, but not necessarily imitate him. He is not saying that all should become tent makers and travel the world, remain single and be an apostle. I have heard many a preacher who leans heavily to speaking on prayer, that they pray from 5-7 am every day for example. Others wanting to have a powerful prayer life then set their alarms for 5 am and try to pray for two hours. That is imitating. However, God may have enough people praying from 5-7 am and He requires you to pray from 9-11 pm. You are still praying but at a different time. This is using a principle to get the same result. That is emulating.

When we envy one another, we are distracted from what God is trying to do in us for the benefit of the Kingdom of God. Many church goers will not like the next statement but, truth is truth, whether we like it, understand it, accept it or not. All that God does is for His Kingdom not to *bless* an individual. If we are members indeed one of another, each blessing is for the Ecclesia and as members one of another, we are blest. So, what distracts us mere mortals from fulfilling our purpose? It is not always something that stands out, the shiny, the big or the beautiful, though this is what Satan uses many times to distract the immature believers. Sometimes we get distracted by our routines, the stuff we do day-in, day-out with monotonous regularity. Yet often it is the mundane and dull thing that God has chosen to use to show who He really is. Thanks to the law of entropy, shiny things will always lose their lustre, tall things will eventually crumble or fall into disarray and the beautiful will always lose its outward appeal. Those things however, which cannot be seen, the eternal things that God is trying to impress upon us that we should be looking at, will last forever.

The first part of **Galatians 5:26** tells us, *Let us not be **desirous of vain glory**...* The highlighted part is four words which is a compound of one Greek word, Kenodoxos, and it comes from the word Doxa meaning the glory of God. Here Pauls warns us that taking glory for ourselves turns any kind of glory into vain glory. It makes it empty or self-conceited. Whenever we take any glory, it is glory that destroys our souls. The only one excited about it is the one taking it. God views it as theft. In fact, when Jesus called the people at the temple, *a den of thieves*, He was telling them in essence... *My house is called a house of prayer (Proseuche- worship) and you have made it a den of thieves, you have stolen the purpose of my house and used it for your edification, your financial gain, to lift yourself up.* (**Matthew 21:13, Mark 11:17, Luke 19:46**). The Temple was where they were meant to give God the glory, honour, and worship due only to Him, but when they gloried in their own wisdom, might, understanding and money-making programmes, they robbed God of the glory due to Him, even in His own house.

Vain glory in the modern sense goes like this: We (as a group) or you and I have inordinate pride in ourselves or our achievements, which leads to excessive vanity. It is also classed as ostentatious pride. Have you seen some of our buildings lately? As if these vain-glorious buildings actually lift God up or help one soul to enter into the Kingdom of God, let alone help disciple them. On the other hand, just because we do not have big buildings and fancy ministries, doesn't mean we don't have excessive pride. We sometimes strut around acting like we personally won World War 2 because we believe in Acts 2:38, baptism in Jesus' name, we know there is one God, and preach *'holiness'*. Because of this, we have somehow come to believe we are special and that anything else we say must also be right. The only way the above makes us special is that by obeying them, we are born again, and we understand the singular nature of God. End of story. It does not guarantee greater revelation or a deeper understanding of God's word from now on without deeper searching. As mentioned earlier, ***Acts 2:38 is a birth certificate, not a diploma***. Being born again only gets us to see the Kingdom of God according to **John 3:3**, it is only the beginning of a life of endurance and cross bearing, of denying ourselves for the Kingdom of God and His people, not the be all and end all. If we are not moving on to perfection then we remain babes in Christ, and our born-again experience does us no good (see **Hebrews 6:1-2, 1 Corinthians 3:1-8**).

I have learnt more about God in the last ten years by listening to and reading humble men and women from many generations ago who were not what we call apostolic in manner or beliefs, than I have listening to the same old, tired, and rehashed sermons of late that have no substance in teaching how one is to live in and for the Kingdom. Do not misunderstand me, I am Apostolic in my belief and preaching that Acts 2:38 is the way to become born-again, and I believe there is only one God who manifested Himself in a man we know as Yeshua (Jesus) and that all the ways He showed us to live must be lived today. Now what? Holiness? Yes, but by which organization's standard? Teaching has all but disappeared from much of the western style churches and we rely almost solely on preaching, the louder and more effected our speech, the more anointed we say it is. We shout, and run the aisles, and speak in tongues every chance we get and almost every sermon is the same (containing the Fabulous Five- Acts 2:38, one God, pay tithes and obey the man of God, with a regular serving of holiness living), but these things, once we already believe in them, rarely last past the church service into real life in a real world full of real people with real problems looking for real solutions from a real God. Form over function never holds up where the metal meets the meat.

When it is all about me and mine and how we are blessed because we have had another one or two souls born-again this month and how we convince them to come to the services and show them our buildings and family programmes, God does not get any glory, because they were attracted by what we offered rather than just the Kingdom of God only and what He commands them to do (past being born again, such as being despised, persecuted, reviled, martyred, being poor in spirit, taking up the cross, obeying the word of God straight from God, and buffeted even more by the demonic realm than before. All for the sake of His righteousness and the Kingdom of God. Tell them these things and see how many will come to the front). I truly believe that we have inadvertently turned the altar into a sort of confessional. It is where we tell people they can confess their sins to God and seek forgiveness. I believe a study of the purpose of an altar is well overdue in a vast majority of our western style churches. We will be surprised how far we have strayed from God's word, and we don't even know it. We do not know it because tradition blinds us from truth.

When we boast about our increasing numbers but don't have anyone to personally disciple them, we are desirous of vain-glory, and we should not envy those who do such things. I feel we should pity them for their delusional understanding of God's Ecclesia.

People are always attracted to glory whether it is vain or not. Look at Hollywood actors, sports stars, flamboyant politicians, opinionated news casters, big tech moguls and television preachers. The more ostentatious they are, the more they seem to attract. There is something that draws the mindless sheeple to their cause. The more people a pastor has in *his* church, the more other pastors will sit up and listen to what he has to say. They have big offices, certificates and diplomas from the right schools, pictures of themselves with prominent leaders of their organizations or local politicians on their walls. They have many preaching engagements and much glory from ardent admirers and peers in their organization, but their glory is vain, empty, and pretentious. It is not God's glory, because He will not share His glory with anyone. *I am the LORD, that is My name; And My glory I will not give* (Nâthan- bestow or appoint) *to another, Nor My praise to carved images* (**Isaiah 42:8**). In fact, He tells us seven times that He is a jealous God- **Exodus 34:14** *For thou shalt worship no other god: for the LORD, whose name is Jealous, is a jealous God* (see also **Nahum 1:2, Joshua 24:19, Deuteronomy 5:9, 6:5, Exodus 20:5**). He is the only one that has a right to have glory.

Paul says that we are, *not to be desirous* which comes with the connotation of longing for or reaching for *vain glory*. Even Solomon warns us, *And put a knife to thy throat, if thou be a man* **given to appetite** (Nephesh- discontentment, greed, or pleasure). *Be not desirous* ('âvâh- wish for or covet) *of his dainties* (Maṭ'ammâh- delicacies, the finest cut, the best of things)*: for they are deceitful meat* (**Proverbs 23:2-3**). It means to get for ourselves what we feel we deserve. It is using statements like, '*Do you know who I am?*' or '*We wield a lot of power in the organization*' or the worst one of them all '*because I said so*' (this elevates their word to the same status as God's word thus making them as gods: which is the lie Satan told Eve in the Garden), *For God doth know that in the day ye eat thereof, then your eyes shall be opened,* **and ye shall be as gods**, *knowing good and evil* (**Genesis 3:5**).

This sets up an *us versus them* class system which is as abhorrent to God as the slaughter of innocent babies. It is what got Satan kicked out of the presence of God in the first place; he wanted glory. He wanted it before the Garden, in the wilderness with Jesus and still wants it today. He gets it vicariously through us when we envy something God did not mean for us to have or have right now. We cannot allow others to glorify us and not correct them as Peter and John did in **Acts 3:12** *And when Peter saw it, he answered unto the people, Ye men of Israel, why marvel ye at this? or why look ye so earnestly on us, as though by our own power or holiness we had made this man to walk?* Or perhaps Peter's command when *...Cornelius met him, and fell down at his feet, and worshipped him. But Peter took him up, saying,* **Stand up**; *I myself also am a man* (**Acts 10:25-26**).

Earlier we saw how we are to provoke one another to *love and good works*, but have you ever met someone who just provokes you? This is also a no-no in the Kingdom of God. Smack in the middle of do not seek glory and do not envy one another is *don't provoke one another*. We all seem to do this from time to time because, let's face it, we are human, and we tend to get on people's nerves (though many may be too polite to mention it) but this kind of provoking is for people who do it in a bad way and with monotonous regularity. However, we must once again look to the original meaning and context this was written. The word provoking is Prokaleomai meaning to irritate, to call to oneself. The Aramaic English New Testament defines it as- to ridicule. It is easy for those who have reached a certain level of maturity, whether in career, sports, familial or in church, to ridicule those who are lower on the totem pole or who are struggling with certain issues. We laugh at their sometimes-misguided attempts to serve God and view their lives as if they had the knowledge we have right now and forget all the dumb things we thought and did until we got some hard earned and scarring wisdom.

To ridicule someone is to subject them through contemptuous and dismissive language or behaviour. If we ridicule someone, it is not giving them the time, space and grace given to us. All we have was given to us by others who have gone before us, so that we may stand a little higher than we stood before. Sir Isaac Newton (1642-1726), noted mathematician, scientist, author, physicist, theologian, and astronomer once wrote, *"If I see further, it is because I have stood on the shoulders of great men"*. The great Sir Isaac Newton got his greatness because of what other men had done and gone through before him. When we ridicule (provoke) one another, we in essence, forget where we came from.

We are to do the opposite of ridicule when it comes to the saints. We must respect and commend them even if some of their customs or convictions are strange to us or we disagree with some things they believe. We must respect their convictions as much as we want our convictions, beliefs and opinions respected. This creates dialogue and fresh ideas can be discussed in a civil and profitable manner as long as growth in God for both parties is the reason for the discussion. We must remember that each member of the Ecclesia comes with a unique set of life experiences and perspectives, all of which are useful and employable in the Kingdom of God, whether in the doing or withholding of doing.

If they are in the Ecclesia, God put them there (see **Acts 2:47**), not for us to change them, but to be an example of what change looks like and to learn from each other. If we listen to them, it doesn't mean we must agree with every little thing they say, nor that they must agree with every little thing we say, but by listening to each other, we will gain a fresh perspective on life so that when we are interacting with the world, we can see things from a different point of view. In doing this, we will have greater success in allowing God to use us as a tool to bring others to the point of repentance. After all, that is why God donned flesh and came to earth, to see things from our perspective (**Hebrews 4:15-16**). If we only respect those with whom we agree, then we are nothing more than religious bigots living in echoing caves and as useful to God as a braille menu at a fast-food drive through. A bigot is defined as a person who is obstinately or unreasonably attached to a belief, opinion, **or faction**, especially one who is prejudiced against or antagonistic toward a person or people on the basis of their belief or association with another group.

Jesus spoke to the Pharisees and Sadducees, though they were from different factions and neither believed as He believed. Yet, He showed them the right way in the same manner as the woman at the well, the centurion, the governor, the blind, lame, the woman caught in adultery and demon possessed. He played no favouritism with any man or group.

We can listen and learn from others by asking the right questions, really listening to the other's point of view (not just waiting for our turn to speak). Jesus did this regularly. We must remember that when we disagree with a person about a certain topic, we're not trying to go to battle against a brother or sister in God. Being aggressive in our opinion is a quick way to shut down the other's capacity to hear what we're trying to say. Listening builds rapport with other members of the Kingdom of God and who knows, we may actually learn something that will help us. If we think we have all the answers, then we are truly enchanted with ourselves and entrenched in vain glory.

As we no longer covet what others have, whether it be time, talents, treasures, revelations, or positions, and begin to rejoice and weep with them, others outside of the Ecclesia will see and will be able to make an informed and revelatory decision as to what we have to offer.

Chapter 40.

Do not hate one another.

Titus 3:3 *For we ourselves also were sometimes* **foolish, disobedient, deceived, serving divers lusts and pleasures, living in malice and envy, hateful, and hating one another.**

Do not hate one another? Well, *duh*, that is a bit obvious, don't you think? Yes, but sometimes we get so caught up in our daily lives, we neglect to look at what we are doing, the obvious. The result of our actions to search God's word for a deeper meaning and how we can incorporate it into our lives will determine where we end up in the Kingdom of God.

Sometimes we get so busy trying to prepare for *'the rapture'* that we are unable or unwilling to live the life we have here and now. When we pray and ask God to show us His will and how we are to go about fulfilling it, we must also cease focusing our eyes and hearts on the faults and failings of our brothers and sisters and become a part of their growth in Him. The world rarely sees such love and altruism, so when it is displayed it catches the eyes and ears of our communities. The problem arises when we remain self-centred and anybody who gets in our way, we tend to look at them as a distraction or an obstacle to getting what we want. So, we end up hating those whom we perceive as getting in our way or messing with our paradigm. We are told to hate the world (its system, not the people) but to love one another. Sometimes, we slip up and reverse the polarities and our compasses are thrown out of alignment.

Let us look at what Paul was conveying with the above scripture (**Titus 3:3**). Here are the Greek to English translations for the words in bold. He was saying that in our lifetime we have been unintelligent, unpersuadable, seduced, a slave to various forbidden longings and sensual delights, living in depravity, jealousy, ill will, odious (we stink) and loving others less than some (partiality). Not a great track record for standing up and pointing the finger at other's faults, is it?

Thank God for such mercy that God did not obliterate us at the first sign of our stinky, lustful, jealous, stupid, stubborn, deceived, and hateful lives. But hey, that's God for you. Now, He says that we are to be like Him in all we say and do. *So, how's that working for you*?

Here is the thing, now that we are filled with His spirit, not many actually go around hating each other. Unfortunately, we have used today's definition of hating and applied it to an almost 1900-year-old group of letters and then walked around like a rooster in a hen house, prideful that we are not like those people in Titus' letter. I hate (I see the irony) to burst your bubble, but we are more like them than we think.

Let us break down what Paul was saying to his half Jewish/half Gentile disciple, co-worker in Christ and brother in the Lord, shall we? Paul was not using the word hate with its first 2 definitions of Miseo, which are to detest or persecute. Allow me to give you a personal example of detest and persecute. When I was growing up, my mother used to play a game with me called, *how much artichoke can I cram down my son's throat*. It was not fun, believe me. You see, I vehemently hate artichoke (aptly, the word choke is in its name). I detested it and felt persecuted while she was giving it to me. It tasted like a cross between a Harlem Globetrotter's gym sock and six-week-old dead shark that suffered from halitosis. When my mum made me eat it, I felt persecuted and proclaimed that the Geneva Convention on prisoners of war had been violated or that the U.N. should be contacted, and asylum should be sought.

This was my definition of *hate and persecute,* and to this day I still use it to gauge how I feel about certain things. For example, *is this thing as bad as artichoke*? This will determine my reaction. I was in hospital, for three weeks when I was in the Royal Australian Army after I was hurt. I was bored out of my gourd and had lots of pain; however, it wasn't as bad as artichoke. When someone does something that hurts me or my wife, I pull out the old artichoke and see whether they deserve the artichoke treatment. You get the point, I'm sure.

However, the third definition of Miseo (hate) is far more subtle (and this is where many of us fall flat on our faces) but has the same consequences in the long run. It means to love less. Yes, to love a person less than God loves them is as much a crime as me shoving artichoke down a fellow artichoke hater's throat. This is where partiality brings down many people, many churches, and many organizations. We treat some better than others, we give priority to some people in the church while placing others who do not seem to have anything of value to offer us or are lower on the hierarchical totem pole, whether it be spiritually, economically, socially, mentally, or educationally, little to no attention at all. When we say we will give this person our time, talents, or treasures because we like them or they have something to offer the church but, withhold our giving of these same things because we don't like others or *'don't really know them'*, biblically speaking, we have fallen into the trap of artichoke hatred.

We have divided God's love based on our human emotion and intellect, which is about as useful as bull with an udder (it will produce nothing) and then we have the audacity to go around saying we want souls in our churches. Can someone say *Hypocrite*! John understood this concept when he quilled, *But whoso hath this world's good, and seeth his brother have need, and shutteth up his bowels of compassion from him, how dwelleth the love of God in him?* He goes on, *If a man say, I love God, and* **hateth** (Miseo- to love less) **his brother, he is a liar:** *for he that loveth not his brother whom he hath seen, how can he love God whom he hath not seen? And this commandment have we from him, That he who loveth God love his brother also* (**1 John 3:17, 4:20-21**). Hypocrite or liar, those are the only two choices we have when we love the brethren less than we love God.

If we will be brutally honest for one moment, we would like to see souls in the church who can become like us, and can contribute to the church, whether it is in time, talent, or treasure. Some readers would be horrified at this statement, but look at who most of us invite, or hang around, are they not those of our station? Look at the people Jesus *'hung around with'*. He went to sinner's houses, walked, and ate with beggars and sick people, ate with leaders (religious as well as political). He met with them in the temple, at night, by the sea, on the road, in villages and cities, on mountains and in wildernesses. The beggar on the street, though they could contribute very little to the synagogue, was just as important as the high priest, the woman caught in adultery was given the same forgiveness as Peter. Malchus (the arresting officer in the Garden of Gethsemane) got just as much a healing as Jairus' daughter. He fed the multitude with spiritual as well as natural food and cared not what town they came from, whether they were spiritual or not.

In our business of life, we sometimes forget Jesus was all human as well as all God and that He displayed that humanity to others. He wants us to use our humanity (which we are changing daily to be transformed in His image. We are still human, only now with a new nature) to display His love and share His Kingdom in a way that the natural man and woman can understand. We sometimes get caught up in being spiritual so we can prepare for heaven, that we forget to show our humanity.

Sadly though, when we do show our humanity, we get criticized and ostracized. Jesus wept, laughed, joked around, He got angry, frustrated, hungry, sad, lonely, disappointed, and scared (in the garden), yet somehow, we (and especially the leadership) have to put on this façade that we are superhuman and never make mistakes or fail. Are we *better* than Jesus?

Wait, what?

Like many statements we make, the context in which they are spoken determines their meaning. For example, when Jesus said, *If any man come to me, and **hate not his father, and mother, and wife, and children, and brethren, and sisters, yea, and his own life** also, he cannot be my disciple* (**Luke 14:26**). He used the word Miseo, that we should love God more than others (including our own families) or we cannot be His disciple. This means that we are to love God more than our families, but not love them less than God loves them. I know it sounds like a contradiction, but really, it's not. John takes it one step further, that we are to love each other equally, without partiality. We are to love others with the same passion as God. I understand that we love our families very much, but God doesn't differentiate between blood family and His family. *A new commandment I give unto you, That ye love one another; **as I have loved you**, that ye also love one another, This is my commandment, That ye love one another, as I have loved you.* (**John 13:34, 15:12**). It is not to love them as we think, feel or they deserve. This will be hard to take for the western style church people, but this is just as important to love others **as Christ loves others** as *ye must be born again.*

If Uncle Joe or Aunt Mimi are in our family because of our spouses after marriage, and we treat them as family (or should), what is the difference when it comes to God's family? God is not partial. When we hate one another (love one another less), we are saying that this one or that one is inferior and does not deserve our love or not as much anyway. God comes along and says that we were just as much a sinner as they were/are and that we were going to the same *Lake of Fire* as they were/are. His grace and mercy must be equally applied to both and yet, sometimes we deem our love and attention greater than God's. As Jethro Clampett from the Beverly Hillbillies used to say, *"Whee doggy, their cornbread ain't done in the middle, granny".*

To hate one another (whether detest, persecute, or love less) does the body of Christ great harm. The world may be stupid, but they are not dumb or blind. They can see through our partiality from a mile away. They can see us leaving our church services, some leaving in nice cars and others have to take a bus or have to walk, they can see when we go for *'fellowship'* at the restaurant and how we treat each other and segregate into our little cliques. They can see when they come to visit our church buildings and how we congregate with those of the same socio-economic status or sit sparsely apart from each other. And then we have the audacity to tell them that they should come to our church because we *'have the truth'* or argue that we are God's representatives here on earth. I have spoken to many waiters, waitresses and hotel clerks who secretly laugh at all these phony *'church goers'* after they leave their establishment. They see how certain members of the group are neglected or put to one side, they leave a mess, complain the most, many times tip the worst and all with a smile on their faces while handing out church cards and inviting them to come and meet God.

F.B. Meyer wrote in his expository on James 2:1-13, *AVOID SERVILITY TO THE RICH. "This sin of making distinctions in God's house is as rife today as ever; and wherever it is practiced the divine Spirit departs. God's love is impartial, so far as outward appearances might affect it; and in His Church the only real differences must be those of humility, purity, and righteousness."*

"Blessed are the poor in spirit," whether they be rich in this world's goods or not. But it is easier for a poor man to be rich in faith and an heir of the Kingdom, because he can give more of his attention to the things of the Spirit."

"The law of love must be supreme with us; and we must love our fellows, whatever their position or property, as ourselves, for Christ's sake. If we fail in this, we show that we have never entered into the heart of the Christian faith. A man may observe all the laws of health; but if he inhale one whiff of poison he may die; so we may be outwardly obedient to the entire Decalogue (or our church/organization's understanding of holiness. Author's note), *but delinquency in love will invalidate everything."* (Publisher: Hodder Stoughton. 1912).

Our disobedience to God brings about the same curses as when Israel disobeyed God. We can read of these in **Deuteronomy 28:15-36** which resulted in God people becoming a byword (Sheniynâh- a taunt or gibe, a scorn or ridicule) to the surrounding nations in verse 37. No wonder the church has become a derision and a byword to much of the world today. We have not shown those within our own ranks the true love of God, let alone the world. We can, should and must love one another as Christ loved you and me. How is this accomplished? With sacrifice and impartiality which the Oxford Dictionary defines as, *the fact of not supporting one person or group more than another.* Partiality (favouritism, picking and choosing what or who we like, while ignoring or neglecting others) is contemptable to God, *Therefore have I also made you contemptible and base before all the people, according as ye have not kept my ways, but have been partial in the law* (**Malachi 2:9**). They were partial in their treatment of the people and God made them base (Shâphêl- humiliated, debased and bring lower). This scripture as with all of Malachi was written to the priests (the leadership) not the masses and whatever they did, the people followed. The law of God demands we treat no-one partially. I can have a partiality to certain foods, what type of music I listen to or a particular type of vehicle I like to drive and that is fine, because they do not have a soul. However, to treat a living soul, especially in the household of faith (**Galatians 6:10**) with partiality, places me at odds with the Commonwealth of the Kingdom of God.

The propitiation of Christ's death for us is not based on anything we have done, thus nullifying the erroneous thinking that some are better than others. As Paul puts it, *There is neither Jew nor Greek, there is neither bond nor free, there is neither male nor female: for ye are all one in Christ Jesus. And if ye be Christ's, then are ye Abraham's seed, and heirs according to the promise* (**Galatians 3:28-29**). As His death, burial and resurrection was given freely and equally to all, so must we give the very love that took Him to the cross and held Him there, without partiality, freely, and sacrificially to all.

For those who treat some better than others, what do you do with **Romans 2:11** *There is no respect of persons* (partiality) *with God,* or perhaps the words of David will strike a chord when he says, *Before the LORD; for he cometh to judge the earth: with righteousness shall he judge the world, and the people with* **equity** (Mêyshâr- evenness, that is, prosperity or concord, straightness, equal, sweetness. **Psalm 98:9**). To call on the name (Onoma- character and authority) of Jesus for our supply and healing but not take on His nature is to behave in a manner that contradicts or undermines our claims that we know Him and is incompatible with His word. This can be boiled down to one word- hypocrisy.

And here is an open rebuke to those who will have respect of person (a Hebraic term meaning partiality amongst the people), *For the LORD your God is God of gods, and Lord of lords, a great God, a mighty, and a terrible,* **which regardeth not persons**, *nor taketh reward: He doth execute the* *judgment* (He does right by) *of the fatherless and widow, and loveth the stranger, in giving him food and raiment. **Love ye therefore the stranger: for ye were strangers in the land of Egypt*** (Deuteronomy **10:17-19**). God reminds them where they came from. If we are going to claim that we are holiness people and are becoming holy as He is holy, then we had better step up our game and start acting as He would act and we can start by not loving one another less than others, or as Titus admonishes us, stop hating one another.

Section 5

Chapter 41.

Love one another.

(Romans 13:10) *Love worketh no ill to his neighbour: therefore love is the fulfilling of the law.*

We must stop telling people we are no longer under the law, but under grace. Paul clearly states that there is a law and our loving one another is fulfilling this law. *We must love each other* is not just a true statement, but a command, and unless it is backed up with who, how, when, where and why, then it becomes just another nebulas declaration like, *we must be on fire for God* or Paul's oft unexplained and out of context statement like, *I die daily.* Many parents often tell squabbling siblings to *'just play nice',* but whose definition of nice are we talking about, child #1 or child #2? The reason there is conflict is because two children have a differing opinion of nice, and they do not know how to navigate around those difference in order to achieve their goal of happily playing together.

I would like to interject a fine definition of *opinion* attributed to George Eliot (Mary Ann Evans. 1819-1880) which will explain the above statement on being nice. *"Opinion is really the lowest form of human knowledge. It requires no accountability, no understanding. The highest form of knowledge... is empathy, for it requires us to suspend our egos and live in another's world. It requires profound purpose larger than the self-kind of understanding."*

Our opinions carry no weight in the courts of heaven let alone here on earth. We have a saying back in Australia, *opinions are like noses, everybody has one and they have at least two holes in it.* Because we do not know the heart of men and women, we can only judge by what we see and even then, unless we are in constant contact with the Master, what we see will be filtered through the lens of flesh and our past experiences (the latter is not intrinsically evil, but it cannot be relied upon as the mainstay of our judgements). To give up self for another is to live as Christ lived, die like He died and rise in newness of life as He did. This ought to be the goal of everyone who claims to be born again of water and spirit and has done so in His name. Numbers in pews are not a biblical sign of a successful gathering this side of eternity, sacrificial love, and empathy, however, are.

George Müller (1805-1898) the Prussian/German evangelist wrote, *"There was a day when I died; died to self. My opinions, preferences, tastes and will; died to the world, its approval or censure; died to the approval or blame even of my brethren or friends; and since then, I have studied only to show myself approved unto God".* When we give up our own self-interest for the Kingdom of God, we no longer need platitudes to keep going nor the approval of *any* man and most importantly we will not *care* if man approves of us or not.

Platitudes sound very religious and have many people shouting a hearty *amen* when they are spoken, whether in passing or from the pulpit. But how to do those things takes much more than just saying those things. I would venture to guess that those who speak in platitudes do not actually live them. A platitude is a statement or a cliche, especially one with a moral content, that has been used too often to be interesting or thoughtful, for example- *God is good, just pray about it, get on fire for God,* or the ever popular but out of context, *don't worry, God will supply.* If they lived them, they would not be speaking in such a manner and would know how hard it is to be a normal human and just love each other or how hard it is to 'die daily' to the flesh (see the story of the rich young ruler, **Matthew 19:26, Mark 10:27**). Remember, we are wrestling against an enemy who desires our downfall and unless we submit to the word of God and help each other grow, we would needlessly struggle and lose heart in our purpose. Many in our pews are torn in different directions every day and have no idea how to go to God or even search His word then obey it. They have not been shown. They may have been told countless times, every week by the myriad of sermonizers that fill our pulpits, but shown? Sadly, very few have been biblically discipled and thus they seek a god that does not exist other than in their mind. When we love one another, we experientially share this one God with each other in both the natural and spiritual sense and growth occurs naturally. No need of coercion or flattery.

Enter the revealed and manifested word of God, which not only gives a commandment but also gives us a way of fulfilling that command, then to top it all off, the author of the same command gives us two ways (the former being only a little more important than the latter), those being the Holy Ghost, and elders (older and mature saints) in the Ecclesia to disciple us on fulfilling those commands.

Club love or agape Love.

There are several types of social clubs our society engages in, like knitting, crocheting, Boy and Girl Scouts, 4H, Lion's Club, car club, sports club, night club, bowling club etc. There is a difference between the relationship one has for people with the same interests and those who have experienced near death together such as a heart transplant club (also known as the *zipper club*), fireman's club, police club, base jumping club etc. Humans are an extremely social creature, and the oxymoronic thing is that we want to retain our individualism within these social structures (there's a difference between retaining our individualism and retaining our uniqueness). In other words, let me join your group, but I want to remain singular. Almost without exception we are drawn to others of like passions or interests, whether religious, secular, political or ideological. This, however, does not mean that the members of these social groups love one another. To love as God loves takes considerably more than the social or occasional weekly or twice weekly interaction. To love as we are commanded to love (without hesitation, reservation, or partiality) means becoming vulnerable and exposed to possible rejection or challenged on our doctrines, beliefs, or paradigms.

We cannot say we are committed to something if we are not willing to sacrifice ourselves for it. Loving parents would readily sacrifice themselves for their children, loving spouses will lay down their lives for each other. They will disregard the voices of others and give the benefit of the doubt to their spouse as disciples do for one another. Unfortunately, this type of sacrifice for one another is not preached in many of our pulpits and manifestly shared within our pews. Going to church when we don't feel like it is not sacrificing for the church, neither is putting extra money into the offering for the building or missionary fund. We will get money again next week or next month. Doing something because we don't feel like it is NOT a sacrifice. A true sacrifice is when something inside of us dies with no chance of resurrection for the benefit of the Kingdom of God (i.e., each other). For example, sacrificially giving of our time, talents, and treasures directly to another human being sitting next to us in the pew has a far greater impact on the Kingdom of God than impersonally giving to a government registered entity. Sacrificing our lives for another life is what proves our love, not how much offering we give. Should we give? Yes, the scripture commands it, but that is the lowest form of giving. God did not send someone else to sacrifice for humanity's sin, He came

Himself. He could have created a special creature not seen before on earth, endowed it with special powers to remove sin and guilt and yet it would not have the same amount of love God has for the world. Loving vicariously or by proxy is nowhere near as impactful as personally loving one another. Love dies for the loved one. Love surrenders sleep, food, time for the loved one. Love puts in the greatest effort for the object it loves. It goes beyond feelings, beyond pain and beyond common sense for the object of its love. Love sees that there is one greater than self that must be catered to, it is zealous for good works (not just good thoughts) and burns with manifest passion to forgive, it shows grace and mercy and craves for restoration of relationships to become paramount. With these, we will conquer the world.

The church is freedom from the world.

The Dordrecht Confession (1632)-9 sums up some of the basic principles that form part of the

teaching of the Classic Free Churches concerning ecclesiology thus:

"We also believe, and confess a visible Church of God, namely of those who, as explained above truly repent, believe rightly, and receive true baptism. They are united with God in heaven and incorporated into the fellowship of the saints on earth. These persons we hold to be the chosen race, the royal priesthood, the holy people, who have the witness that they are the spouse and bride of Christ. Indeed, they are children and heirs of eternal life. A tent, a tabernacle, and a house of God in the Spirit, built upon the foundation of the apostles and prophets– Christ being the chief cornerstone. This Church of the living God he bought and redeemed with his own precious blood. According to his promise, he will always stand by this church: to comfort and protect her even to the end of the world. He will dwell and walk with her and keep her so that neither floods nor tempests nor even gates of hell shall ever move or conquer her. This church is to be known by her Scriptural faith, doctrine, love and godly life; also by a fruitful living up to, use, and observance of the ordinances of Christ, which He so highly commended and enjoined upon his followers."

(Pelikan and Hotchkiss, 2003:778)

When we go to a place and meet the same people at the same time and do the same things for five, ten or twenty years and we still do not really know them, we can rest assured we have a club kind of love, and that's okay if that is all we want. But this kind of love is not freedom, for we must act in a certain manner, go through protocols, and not offend anyone in order to have and receive club love. There is another kind of club, a deep and more intense kind of love, one where the heart pounds, the adrenaline rushes and one never knows what's going to happen. Where death could be just around the corner. The people in this kind of club share something different. They share themselves. God's greatest gift was the gift of Himself, and if we truly are followers of God, then the greatest gift we have to offer other (especially those of the household of faith) is ourselves.

When we transfer this kind of love to the flesh and blood Ecclesia, we tend to live life to the fullest, we suffer the lowest of lows and experience the highest of highs. We tend to be fearless because we have made ourselves vulnerable to one another, but most of all, a bond is forged that will outlast most *earthly* relationships. This is a love that goes beyond the sane, the ordinary, or the predictable. This kind of love is death defying and changes lives. This is God's love, lived through the Ecclesia, shown to the world and only this kind of love draws the sinner to Christ and not our structures, our programmes, and organizations.

Our Lord, Master and King came to perform a death-defying act. He first created mankind with the view of voluntary love and obedience to its creator. This failed miserably because power and knowledge became the focus of man rather than trust and humility with God. Satan tempted mankind with two main things in the Garden of Eden, *For God doth know that in the day ye eat thereof, then your eyes shall be opened,* **and ye shall be as gods** ('ĕlôĥîym)*,* **knowing** *good and evil. And when the woman saw that the tree was good for food, and that it was pleasant to the eyes,* **and a tree to be desired to make one wise,** *she took of the fruit thereof, and did eat, and gave also unto her husband with her; and he did eat* (**Genesis 3:5-6**). Power and knowledge.

Then came the first great reset in the form of a flood, starting with a family that loved and obeyed him. He commanded them to go forth and multiply (same command as Adam and Eve). He gave His creation a new world in which they could fellowship with Him and share in His love with one another. Once again, He was disappointed, and they began to ignore or try to replace Him. This led them into bondage. After this came the greatest jailbreak in history, where millions of Hebrew slaves were thrust into a desert, cared for in clothing, food, water, and protection and still they were not satisfied, so that generation was destroyed by God Himself, and the second generation entered into the promised land (see **Jude 1:5**). Once again, God's people became idolatrise and were taken captive into the hands of the Babylonians, Assyrians, Persians, and Midianites. This time He waited about 800 years and showed up in the flesh to give His love personally. He risked rejection but still gave anyway, but this time it cost Him His earthly life. Jesus said to follow Him. Are we prepared to risk it all for the object of our love as God did for us? If not, then how can we say we are followers of Christ?

God joined the human club, which came with death, sickness, disease, hatred, murder, and all kinds of dangers, something He had never experienced before. Though He did not sin He came to know sin by vicariously experiencing humanity at its finest and its worst. He became the President, CEO, and chairman of the board of the largest single-minded group on earth. He named it the Ecclesia, and if we choose, we can come to know Him through His people and our personal efforts, but only if we learn and do what He did. We determine how much we know Him and become like Him. Pastors, preachers, bible schoolteachers are not the masters of our destiny nor of how much growth we determine we want in God.

Which club are we in? Is it a club where, becoming vulnerable is a prerequisite to join with the possibility of getting hurt and disappointed? Or does the thought of this type of vulnerability scare us into inaction. It seems we have inadvertently joined a club where we can only show our good side. Only one club will help us become fit for the future Kingdom of God, while the other, like an illicit drug, is designed to make us feel good for another week.

To cite C.S Lewis once again, *"To love at all is to be vulnerable. Love anything and your heart will be wrung and possibly broken. If you want to make sure of keeping it intact you must give it to no-one, not even an animal. Wrap it carefully around with hobbies and little luxuries; avoid all entanglements. Lock it up safe in the casket or coffin of your selfishness. But in that casket, safe, dark, motionless, airless, it will change. It will not be broken; it will become unbreakable, impenetrable, irredeemable. To love is to be vulnerable."* The Four Loves (Harcourt Publishing, 1960)

I have seen Christians treat their beloved pets with more tender-heartedness and kindness than they treat their fellow believers. They spend inordinate amounts of time and money on their pets, while the lonely, sick, depressed, brokenhearted, and sometimes lost, sitting next to them in the pews get little to no attention at all. When I hear these hypocrites say how they want to win the lost, my blood boils. We expect God to do all the work while we sit and *enjoy the service.* Look at what God said to Ezekiel, *Again he said unto me, Prophesy upon these bones, and say unto them, O ye dry bones, hear the word of the LORD. Thus saith the Lord GOD unto these bones; Behold, I will cause breath to enter into you, and ye shall live: And I will lay sinews upon you, and* **will** *bring up flesh upon you, and cover you with skin, and* **put breath in you, and ye shall live**; *and ye shall know that I am the LORD. So I prophesied as I was commanded: and as I prophesied, there was a noise, and behold a shaking, and* **the bones came together, bone to his bone** (Ezekiel 37:4-7).

Please note what God says here, *I will* (future tense) *breath in you*. In verse seven the bones came together, there was sinew, flesh, and skin, but still not breath (Rûach- exhalation, life spirit, rational being). Just because we gather does not mean there is life. A gathering of bones would never have received God's breath (animated life for purpose), It was when the bones were connected to each other with sinew, flesh, and skin, (a skeleton does not make a human body) that God could breathe life into those bones.

Ezekiel 37:9 *Then said he unto me, Prophesy unto the wind, prophesy, son of man, and say to the wind, Thus saith the Lord GOD; Come from the four winds, O breath, and breathe upon these slain, that they may live.* Why did God revive this valley of bones? *So I prophesied as he commanded me, and the* **breath came into them** (past tense)*, and they lived, and stood up upon their feet,* **an exceeding great army** (Ezekiel 37:10). We are to take this Gospel of the Kingdom of God into a foreign land as an invading army of the servants of the Most High God.

Ezekiel goes on to prophecy, *And shall put my spirit in you, and ye shall live, and I shall place you in your own land: then shall ye know that I the LORD have spoken it, and performed it, saith the LORD* (**Ezekiel 37:14**).

As an evangelist, I go from church to church and see a valley of dry bones with no breath of God's life into them because they won't come together as the bones in the valley did. Yet, we knowingly and falsely sing songs like, *'Holy spirit breath on me'* or *'I am a friend of God'* or *'I could sing of your love forever'* or *'God will make a way'*. Why would God intervene where His love for one another is willingly abandoned for self?

I think at this point the words of Paul to the Romans are rather poignant, *Owe no man any thing, but to love one another:* **for he that loveth another hath fulfilled the law.** Hold the phone! I thought we were no longer under the law? You can see how we repeat things without first checking in God's word.

It can be said that Paul is telling us that we are to owe no man anything but to be vulnerable, to show who we really are, to lay down our lives for one another as commanded by Jesus, *This is my commandment, That ye love one another, as I have loved you. Greater love hath no man than this, that a man lay down his life for his friends. Ye are my friends, if ye do whatsoever I command you* (**John 15:12-14**). There is a huge risk of being hurt, just ask David, Jesus, Joseph, any loving parent, spouse, or anyone whose heart *you* may have broken. Imagine your world without some kind of risk. A coma would be a better alternative. A ship may not experience raging seas and be safer in a harbour, but is that what a ship is built for?

For this, Thou shalt not commit adultery, Thou shalt not kill, Thou shalt not steal, Thou shalt not bear false witness, Thou shalt not covet; and if there be any other commandment, it is briefly comprehended in this saying, namely, Thou shalt love thy neighbour as thyself. Love worketh no ill to *his neighbour: **therefore love is the fulfilling of the law** (Romans 13:8-10).* This dispels the insane concept of, *not being under law, but under grace, doesn't it?*

To paraphrase journalist and author Hunter S. Thompson in question form, *who is the more fulfilled man, he who has braved the storms of life and lived, or he who has not left the safety of shore and merely existed?* To love the brethren is a debt incurred when we become born again in His name, and this debt must be paid daily.

Chapter 42.

The Bond Between the Scriptures and the Ecclesia.

There seems to be an uneasy relationship between the Ecclesia and the scripture in our modern western society. As Leonard Ravenhill says, *"The word of God is either absolute or obsolete"*. We want the usability of the scriptures but struggle with the totality of those same scriptures. We eagerly embrace, *we must be born again of water and spirit* and *one God* but, will not embrace *restoring a fallen saint thus fulfilling the law of Christ,* or that *we are to submit to one another.* We are unable to do anything that pleases God without faith (**Hebrews 11:6**), this is apparent, but there's another important aspect to pleasing God, *sine scripturis, ibi est fides,* meaning *without scripture there is no faith*. We desire to have faith to move mountains, do miracles, cast out demons and raise the dead, and so we should. But what about faith to do the other scriptures that don't lead to anything we can see or feel? What about the scriptures that seemingly contradict what we have been told is truth? Will we search as diligently for the answers to those questions or continue to rely solely on what we are told from a bible schoolteacher or pulpit preacher?

Everybody has faith (whether they are religious, agnostic or atheist). They have faith that what they believe is truth, that it works and that it will make their life better. We have faith when we set the alarm to wake up that we will, in fact, wake up. We have no guarantees that we will arise. We have faith that the chair we are about to sit in will hold our weight and we have faith that our bosses will pay us at the end of the week or month. We also have an unknown faith for more long-term things. For example, we hear an ad extolling the wonders of the latest model cars and we believe what they say. We then action that belief by going out and test driving the car, doing our research and then (and this is where belief turns into faith) we plonk down the deposit. We have no guarantee that we will have a trouble-free life with the car (in fact we are fully aware we will have some troubles), we cannot see into the future and touch what the car will be like in four years' time, but we go ahead anyway. We are committing and risking the next four to six years of monetarily gifting a company for the use of a car we will not own until we make the last payment. Yet, we will be responsible for its upkeep, fuel, maintenance, and insurance, even though we do not own it. Please don't tell me we all don't have faith of some kind. Risk and faith are synonymous. Please, for the sake of all that is holy and righteous, let us stop singing of our faith in God if we will not risk all we have to prove it.

For those who are born-again, we have gone through the same process as buying a car. We heard (**Romans 10:14-15**), we checked it out (**Luke 14:26-30**), we believed (**John 6:35-40**), and we followed through (**Acts 2:37-38**). You see, the word of God and our faith in it is our connection to an unseen God. Scripture alone or faith alone is like driving a nail with a glass hammer. We must constantly gauge what we are doing or should be doing by what God has written in both the Old and Renewed Covenant and the personal revelation (not personal translation, interpretation, explanation, or application (for me only- Epilusis) we receive through the Holy Ghost (**2 Peter 1:20**). *That the God of our Lord Jesus Christ, the Father of glory, may give unto you* **the spirit of wisdom and revelation in the knowledge** *of him* (**Ephesians 1:17**). To those who are already born of water and spirit, what we hear from a pulpit should only be used as a motivator to search the scriptures daily for ourselves or confirmation of what God has already shown us. As the scriptures are being revealed (Apokalupsis- being disclosed, coming to light) we obey them. If we only do what we are told to do because it came from the pulpit, then we are buying a car because the advertiser or salesman said it was great. Sadly, many people just buy what they are told to buy, then buyer's remorse grips their hearts, but all too often, it is too late, they've bought the package and now must deal with it. Have we become identical to other believers in the hundreds of denominations we claim we are different to?

To begin the massive flesh killing task of loving one another as we do ourselves, and as Christ loves us, we must look to the scriptures, not what we feel or are told to think or believe. We will begin with four verses (though there are many more) which give us an enormous clue as to what Jesus was saying would be the greatest denominator between falsehood and reality concerning the Kingdom of God. They are **John 13:34-35** *A new commandment I give unto you, That **ye love** one another; **as I have loved you**, that ye also **love one another**. By this shall all men know that ye are my disciples, if ye **have love** one to another.* On the same night He tells His disciples in **John 15:12** and **17**; *This is my commandment, That ye **love** one another, as I have loved you… These things I command you, that **ye love** one another.* Surely there is no ambiguity to these verses concerning what we are to do to one another?

As mentioned in the last chapter, the Lord boldly proclaims who our friends should be and who His friends are, *Greater love hath no man than this, that a man lay down his life for his friends. Ye are my friends, **if ye do whatsoever I command** you* (**John 15:13-14**). Singing *I am a friend of God* over and over and over and over again does not make us one, keeping His commandments, however, does. Christ has told us that we are His friends *if we obey His commandments* and that we should lay down our lives for His friend (the Ecclesia). I believe we complicate church by picking and choosing who will be our friends and loving them, but Christ told us to love *His* friends. There's an old saying that goes, *any friend of God is a friend of mine* (paraphrased). Simple, isn't it?

We see that, just as the Ten Commandments were not suggestions on how to live right with God and man, neither are the above verses on loving one another, optional or suggestions, dependant on feelings, reciprocation, or circumstances (how convenient it is to show love) nor on how others treat us. The Lord calls them commandments which in both the Old and Renewed Covenant are rather strong in their description: In Hebrew the word Tsâvâh- meaning to constitute, enjoin, appoint, **to give a charge**, put or **set in order**. In Greek, the word is Entolē- an injunction (a warning or order), an authoritative prescription, a precept (a general rule intended to regulate behaviour or thought).

As we can see, these words were not lightly spoken, and because the Kingdom of God and its inhabitants would be known by this particular attribute, He made it abundantly clear that it was a commandment to love in order to be considered a Citizen of His Kingdom. To love one another is just as much a commandment as *You shall have no other Gods before me, You shall not make for yourselves an idol, You shall not misuse the name of the LORD your God, Remember the Sabbath day by keeping it holy, Honour your father and your mother, You shall not murder, You shall not commit adultery, You shall not steal, You shall not give false testimony, You shall not covet* (**Exodus 23:3-17**). To show us how important it is to love one another and our neighbour, He made it the eleventh commandment in **John 13:34-35.** Can it be any clearer?

He did not say we are to love others by the world's definition nor to love them as they love us, because this creates a dichotomous society. Our problem is that we live in a post-fallen world, so our "*love for ourselves*," unlike Adam and Eve, is complicated at best. Because, how we love ourselves depends so heavily on what has happened in the past or how we feel at the moment. Many people struggle to accept who they are, who don't like what they see (this is why we have such a growing transgender and homosexual community, they are not satisfied with who and what God made them), so if we love others as we love ourselves, it becomes a very fickle standard to base this commandment on. He commanded us to LOVE ONE ANOTHER, by one standard only, AS I HAVE LOVED YOU. If I love myself as God loves me, now I can love others as I love myself.

God's love attracts those who truly seek him, they cannot help themselves. Like a moth to a flame, they will be irresistibly drawn to those who display and offer God's love, proving by showing, not just preaching or classroom teaching, what the Kingdom of God is like. It is a Kingdom where love of and for the Ecclesia is as important as our love of and for God, for we cannot love one without the other (*If a man say, I love God, and hateth* (Miseo- love less) *his brother, he is a liar: for he that loveth not his brother whom he hath seen, how can he love God whom he hath not seen?* (**1 John 4:20**). It is so important, that those that either do not have it or have relinquished it, are not allowed in the Kingdom (see **Revelation 2:1-5**). No-one can prove God's love by scripture alone, and to attempt to do so would be as futile as holding back a river with a colander. If God *gave* (an act or deed) His only begotten Son to a sinful world to *show* His love (**John 3:16, Romans 5:8**), what makes us think we can do any less than by *giving* to the world the same type of love (complete and sacrificial), thereby *showing* we also have this same God dwelling in us?

Love has become such an ambiguous word these days, it means many things to many people. To say "*I love ice-cream*" and "*I love my spouse*" in the same sentence is weird to say the least. So, how do we know what kind of love Jesus is telling us to display? Yes, I said display, for love that is not displayed is not love, it is a concept, a nebulas theory attempting to masquerade as something solid, an idea that masquerades as reality. The answer to *what is love,* is what we will delve into in this section. Love, like justice, must not just be done, but seen to be done. Not seen for vain glory but seen that others may see God in us. Closed door sessions where justice is dispensed, will always leave doubt in the minds of the people if it truly was justice and not tainted by any bias or bribery. Peter writes, **Seeing** *ye have purified your souls in obeying the truth through the Spirit* **unto unfeigned love of the brethren**, *see that ye love one another with a* **pure heart** *fervently* (**1 peter 1:22**). Love and purity are tested or judged in public.

Rabbi and psychiatrist specializing in substance abuse, Abraham Twerski once said, '*we don't give to those whom we love, we love those to whom we give.* This has stuck with me and has altered my perception and my course in the Commonwealth of the Kingdom of God. Giving of money is the lowest form and least risky way to be involved in the Kingdom of God. Why? Because money is something we can all get back within a relatively short space of time by our own efforts. But to give of our very being to another human who has been broken by this world and its system of dog eat dog or crushed by authoritarian leadership whether secular or religious and selfish saints, is one of the most amazing gifts we can give. That is why the reward is so great, for where the risk is the greatest, so, the reward will be equally as great. The greatest reward we have in the Kingdom of God is to love those whom God loves and to be with them and Him, both now and for all eternity.

Hollywood has broken the phrase '*I love you*' and robbed it of its original meaning. They have polluted it with casual sex, affections, and perverted ways of showing it. It used to mean that the hearer could rely on having someone there through thick and thin to share their life with, of faithfully putting the object of their love in highest regard. Now-a-days it means '*I'll be there as long as it is convenient, as long as you love me back* or *as long as I feel it*'. The love of man has become purchasable and cheap, transient, and manipulative. God's love has never changed, it cannot be bought, extorted, or manipulated to get what we want.

Too many times today, *I love you* is a rather selfish phrase, and it means *I love how you make me feel*. How about when we do not feel anything, will we still love? I hear so many of today's Christians say things like, *I love my pastor, I love my church, I love my organization, I love my car, I love my job, I love my boat, I love my house, I love my* (insert item here). The list is endless. We give up a little bit of time and even 10% of our income (which we are told we will get back anyway in the form of blessings and healings), and some of us will even give up a day or two in a year to help clean the church building, all for the things we say we love. But when it comes down to giving up our lives (literally and figuratively) for the people who make up the Ecclesia, (not just the pastor, bishop, or organization) where is the love then? How come we do not hear '*I love the least loved saints in the church, I love the guy in the gas station down the road or that sad lady at the checkout in the grocery store I see week in week out*'? Where is the love for a disciple struggling with unforgiveness, anger, smoking, or depression? Where is the love for the husband and wife who struggles with deep seated issues or the child dealing with loneliness or despair?

Fish love.

To quote Rabbi Abraham Twerski once again, "*A Rabbi asks a young man why he was eating the fish? The young man tells him it is because he loves the fish. The Rabbi replies, "Oh, you love the fish? That's why you took it out of the water, killed it and boiled it? Don't tell me you love the fish; you really love yourself. Because the fish tastes good to you, you took it out of the water, killed it and boiled it*".

Rabbi Twersky goes on to explain: "*So much of what is love is fish love. For example: A young couple fall in love, but what does that mean? It means that he saw in this woman someone that can provide him with all of his physical and emotional needs and she felt the same. To them, that was love. But each was looking out for their own needs, it was not love for the other person. They became the vehicle for their own gratification*".

"*Too much of what is called love is fish love. An external love is not, 'what am I going to get. But what am I going to give?*"

Rabbi Twersky goes on to quote Ethicist Rabbi Dessler, '*People make a serious mistake in thinking that you give to whom you love, and the real answer is you love the one to whom you give*'. His point is, if I give something to you, I've invested myself in you, and since self-love is a given (because everyone loves themselves to one degree or another), now that part of me has become in you, there's a part of me in you I love. True love is a love of giving, not a love of receiving."

I don't often cite Friedrich Nietzsche, but truth is truth, no matter who's mouth it comes out of. He wrote that, '*We don't really love other people. We love our version of other people*'. We create a version of our spouses, our friends, or the believers in our mind, and that is what we love and give to. Consider this, how often do we make (not find) the time and energy to get to know one another (the saints) for who they really are (not the façade most of us portray at our church services), and if we do and find they are not what we had in our minds, do we still fellowship with them? Do we love them through their annoying times, their frustrating times, their fearful times, the times they struggle with a particular sin? Or, as I have observed over the last 35 years in ministry on all five continents, we only love or fellowship with them if they don't burst our image of them, or they believe and behave in a manner that pleases us? If we love those in the Ecclesia with the understanding of love the world has handed us, then we will only receive the reward that earthly love can give us, fleeting, temporal and unsatisfying. However, when we love according to the words of Christ and His apostles, then there is a reward that lasts into eternity in the presence of God.

The hearts of the religious leaders in Christ's time, were so far removed from the heart of God, that the Lord showed the hypocrisy of their false love by placing pure love right in front of them. He said to them, *But woe unto you, Pharisees! for ye tithe mint and rue and all manner of herbs, **and pass over** (neglect) **judgment and the love of God**: these ought ye to have done, and not to leave the other undone* (**Luke 11:42**). In Matthew's version we read, *... and have omitted the weightier matters of the law, judgment, **mercy, and faith**...* (**Matthew 23:23**). Jesus said they omitted (Aphiēmi- left or laid aside, sent away, or yielded up) the weightier (Barus- grave) matters of God's word. The Church of Ephesus also left, laid aside and yielded up their first love and were commanded by the Master Himself to go back to it so they would not lose their light (revelation. See **Revelation 2:4**). We can give to the penny what God requires of us but if we neglect true judgement, the love of God, mercy, and faith, we are just fooling ourselves (as the Pharisees and the Ecclesia in Ephesus did) into thinking our little group is right with Jehovah.

Elie Wiesel, Romanian-born American writer, professor, Nobel laureate, and Holocaust survivor is quoted as saying, *"The opposite of love is not hate, it's indifference. The opposite of art is not ugliness, it's indifference. The opposite of faith is not heresy, it's indifference. And the opposite of life is not death, it's indifference*." There is no doubt that we can tell if someone loves us by the way they treat us, make time for us, and listen to our sometimes-inane babblings as we eliminate some of our baggage with the help of God's word, His Spirit, and godly, humble, and wise elders. What hurts more than being hated or mistreated in matters of the heart is being ignored, thought of as superfluous or just someone to fill a space (pew). We may not say these things with our mouths, but our lack of actionable and visible love leads to only this conclusion.

If love cannot be seen with the naked eye, there will always be doubt that this love exists. Saying it and showing it are as different as chalk and cheese. Just as God transcends all space, time, and matter, (it takes faith to believe in God through His word) so love transcends all manner of difficulties (it takes faith to believe that actionable love will eventually conquer all things). Love looks for ways to express God for the benefit of others especially to those of the household of faith (the Commonwealth of the Kingdom of God, **Galatians 6:10**), whereas selfishness looks for ways to express oneself for the benefit of self.

God did not sit in heaven and have warm fuzzy feelings for His creation. He loved, and that love needed an outlet to express itself. He got off His throne, robed Himself in flesh and showed us His love in that, *while we were yet sinners, He died for us* (**Romans 5:8** and **John 3:16**). That is why Jesus said the world will see our love and will know to whom we belong. *By this shall all men know that ye are my disciples, if ye have love one to another. Herein is my Father glorified, that ye bear much fruit; so shall ye be my disciples* (**John 13:35, 15:8**). This is the only place where seeing is believing is permissible.

We have been given a major understanding of how to show love to the saints and the world at large in **Luke 10:25-37**, when a lawyer comes and asks Jesus what he must do to inherit eternal life. Jesus answers him with a question, *what do you think?* The lawyer replies by quoting from **Leviticus 19:18** and **Deuteronomy 6:5**, which boils down to loving God and your neighbour. Please note, this highly educated and well-connected lawyer in God's word quoted scripture, but still had no idea what it really meant nor how to fulfil it. All his education and degrees still could not help him in his quest for the answer to the ultimate question of life after death. He knew the scripture and where it was, but no personal revelation of it, that's why, he was not sure of how to inherit eternal life. Jesus being fully aware of this man's heart, digs into his spiritual piety and shows it for what it was, empty. He takes what this man already knows, commends him on his answer, then begins to show him the practical side of the scripture he just quoted. This is why preaching alone (the giving of scripture from a pulpit) does not solidify someone into the body. There must be a practical application which we can take home and do immediately.

This man then questions Jesus with *'Who is my neighbour?"* Notice, Jesus did not get mad at this man questioning Him. He truly wanted to know. Jesus gives a practical application via a parable of a man who gets robbed, beaten, and left for dead. Two men, one pseudo-religious and the other hyper-religious, who had seen this maltreated man left dying on the side of the road, went their way and also left him. Note: they were a priest and a Levite who ignore the battered man. One could not be a priest without being a Levite, but one could be a Levite and not be a priest. The point is, that it was those of the religious clan (the Levites) that left the man. They were no better than the ones who robbed and beat the man. Jesus illustrated what the Kingdom of Heaven was like by using a Samaritan, a man hated by the pseudo and hyper religious, to show what true love is. He ended the parable by turning the lawyer's question right back on to him, *who is this man's neighbour?* (**Luke 10:36**).

The lawyer rightly said, *He that shewed mercy on him* (**Luke 10:37**). Jesus then uses the original question to illustrate what he must do (not just what he must believe) ...*Then said Jesus unto him,* **Go,** *and* **do** *thou* **likewise** (once again a command to do something about what he now knows/believes. Neither the priest or the Levite would have wanted to be left for dead on the side of the road, but would have wanted someone to show love, kindness, and mercy). So, the answer to what and how do we show love is as simple as the Golden Rule. *Therefore all things whatsoever ye would that men should* **do** *to you:* **do** *ye even so to them: for this is the law and the prophets* (**Matthew 7:12**). Please note also: Jesus used the original law of the Old Covenant to display what He wanted to be done in the Ecclesia today. Everything we need to confirm the Renewed Covenant can be found and revealed in the Old Covenant, and if we will only make the time to seek, God will ensure we find what we are looking for (see **Jeremiah 29:12-13**). Remember, the word and God are synonymous. By seeking Him through His word, we find the Kingdom of God and His righteousness.

We can read in the Talmud of a man who came to Hillel, a Jewish sage (110BC-10AD) and said to him that he would convert to Judaism if Hillel could tell all he needed to know about being Jewish as long as he could hop on one foot. Hillel accepted the challenge and told the man, **"What is hateful to you, do not do to your fellow: this is the whole Torah; the rest is the explanation; go and learn."** Paraphrased it says, *"The essence of being Jewish is, 'Love your neighbour as yourself. Do not do to someone something you do not want done or do to someone those things which you want done to yourself'. All the rest is commentary'.* How can we show this today? We can show it by going out of our way to do something for another person and do it in the name of God. People throughout history have stolen, killed, waged war, and argued in the name of God, but the Ecclesia is to love, give and sacrifice in the name of God. We love not just those with whom we agree, but someone who (as the story above indicates) may have a different way of living than we do. In other words, our neighbour.

The Hebrew word for neighbour is Rêya`, which means an associate (more or less close): a brother, companion, fellow, friend, husband, lover. The Greek defines it as Plēsion meaning a fellow (countryman, Christian or friend), someone nearby. As we can see a neighbour is not necessarily someone who lives next door to us, but taking these definitions, it is anybody we have dealings with (whether regular or occasional) as written in **Galatians 6:10**, *As we have therefore opportunity, let us do good unto **all** men, **especially** unto them who are of the household of faith*. We must first display this love for and to one another before we can say we love the lost in the world (see also **1 Peter 4:17**). Weeping for the lost, if we can't weep for our neighbour in our church, is wasting our time!

It is truly an unnecessary difficulty to try to be at peace with those whom we do not love in the world if we will not be at peace with each other. As mentioned earlier, to be at peace is not the absence of conflict, but the pushing past conflicts, our own offenses and hurt feelings and pursuing a peace that would show others who the Prince of Peace really is. Amid human struggles, there will always be a chance to make peace. It is these *peacemakers* that Jesus said would be a part of and inherit the Kingdom of God, not *peacekeepers* (**Matthew 5:9**).

Why are we asking God to bring in new saints if we cannot or will not care for, love and be at peace with the ones we already have? This is the attitude we must have, that of God's love shown God's way will strengthen the body to receive any new saint God sends our way. The old Stephen Stills song from 1970 comes to mind. In it he writes that, *'if you can't be with the one you love, love the one you're with'*. Paul wrote something similar in **Philippians 1:23-24** *For I am in a strait betwixt two, having a desire to depart, and to be with Christ; which is far better: Nevertheless to abide in the flesh is more needful for you.* It was clear he would rather have been at rest after years of trials and persecutions, of walking thousands of miles and to eventually be in the loving presence of the Lord, but instead, he resigns himself to stay and show love to the people of God, which was far better for them both, while he was here on earth.

Peace with one another is a worthwhile ambition but we must first have this peace within ourselves. If we are lacking this peace, we MUST seek it from God and get help from the Ecclesia. The way peace is distributed is by the pure, unadulterated, unbiased, and unfeigned love of a God who showed us how to give until it hurts (even unto death) by His example.

Paul tells us that to love is a debt to our fellow man in **Romans 13:8** *Owe no man anything, but* (Ei Mē- except) ***to love** one another: **for he that loveth another hath fulfilled the law***. The law of God is bound by love, shown by love, and spread by love. Please don't quote from your rule book, minister's manual, articles of faith, organization's magazine, or code of ethics if you're not going to lay down your life for me and allow me to do the same for you. Your rules, traditions, and minister's manuals come infinitely short of the word of God and serve only to force compliance for compliance's sake. We give because we love, we serve because we love, we sacrifice because we love. We grow in this love because we give, serve, and sacrifice for those whom we choose to love. We can only do so because He first loved us. Our service, giving and sacrifice is a response to what He has already done for us, and we give like for like (100% for 100%). That is the very definition of relationship.

The love of God is planted in our hearts as a seed, and it will remain a seed until it is cultivated as any seed in the Garden of Eden was (see **Genesis 1:11**). What fruit we have today is a direct result of the seed we have inside of us and the work we are doing to cultivate it. We cannot bare anything else. James gives us a perfect analogy of like for like when he asks us, *...can the fig tree, my brethren, bear olive berries? either a vine, figs?...* (**James 3:12**).

Paul tells us how to show this kind of love, *Forbearing one another, and forgiving one another, if any man have a quarrel against any: even as Christ forgave you, so also do ye* (**Colossians 3:13**). James gives a practical example of how to show God's love, *Confess your faults one to another, and pray one for another, that ye may be healed* (Iaomai- made whole, cured). *The effectual fervent prayer of a righteous man availeth much* (**James 5:16**).

Loving as God loves is extremely difficult for the flesh, in fact it is downright impossible, that is why it must be crucified daily and ruled by the indwelling Spirit of God. I refer you to **Psalm 11:5** *The LORD trieth* (Bâchan- to test, examine and prove) *the righteous: but the wicked and him that loveth violence his soul hateth*. If it were easy, everybody would be doing it. God tests us to show us whether we will love without dissimulation (Anupokritos- sincere and without hypocrisy. **Romans 12:9**). This kind of love is not, nor cannot be shown by the squeamish or faint of heart, but by the valiant of spirit and determined of mind. Why? Because there is no guarantee on earth that this kind of love will be returned. And yet, by so doing, as we imitate Christ's death to self and continued adherence to the command to love as He loves, it guarantees sharing in His resurrection into newness of life (**Romans 6:4**). He gave this kind of love knowing full well that the majority of people would reject it, and yet, here we are, beneficiaries of the most powerful force on earth.

It was not three nails that held Him on that cursed tree, but love. He took the nails because humanity could not see His love with the naked eye. Sin is man-made, so were the nails. It was man-made sin that put Him on the cross, but it was God's love that took Him there and God's love that kept the angels from destroying mankind for their sin, (**Matthew 26:53-54** *Thinkest thou that I cannot now pray to my Father, and he shall presently give me more than twelve legions of angels? But how then shall the scriptures be fulfilled, that thus it must be?*). A love only a God who is completely enamoured with His own creation could show. This kind of love has no bounds and cannot be taken from us, we can however, relinquish it or neglect it. As this kind of love is freely received it must be freely given, or it is not God's love. This kind of love destroys strongholds, tears down middle walls of partitions (that separates us from one another **Ephesians 2:14**), reunites husbands and wives, children and parents, long lost families and friends and saves communities. It cares for those who for *WHATEVER* reason cannot care for themselves and submits to the unseen (but not unknowable) God for the sake of the Commonwealth of the Kingdom of God (**2 Corinthians 10:4, James 1:27**).

Far too many times we show a modicum of this kind of love and even then, we usually wait for the *feelings of love* to manifest before we act on it. Nowhere in the canon of God's word does it say that we are to *feel* love before we show love or show it when it is convenient. In fact, by acting only when we feel like it or when it is convenient, shows how carnal we are and how little we really understand of God's love. If we show love only when the feelings are present, it is really selfishness disguised as piety because we are doing it based on how *we* feel rather on what it will do for others. We behave just like the sinners around us and the sinners we once were. We do it to placate our emotions rather than as a sacrifice and to satisfy a holy and righteous God.

I heard Rabbi Manis Friedman tell a story of an old man who fought with his wife very often and pretty much everybody knew it. One day he was seen going to the drug store with much haste and when someone stopped him and asked him what is going on, he said his wife was extremely ill and he had to get to the drug store to get her medicine and rush home and give it to her. The other person commented on how much he must love his wife for doing that so quickly. His response was *'what's love got to do with it?'*

This couple was angry with each other but still did things for each other because their love for each other transcended their feelings at the time. It is not a matter of feeling, but a matter of doing and many times, the feeling follows. We place way too much emphasis on signs and wonders before we do things and one of those signs we rely on heavily is *feeling* love before we give love.

When two people are courting, it is said that they have *fallen in love*. They almost constantly *feel* love, the butterflies in the tummy, the sleepless nights, the hours long phone calls, the little gifts and so on. When they mistakenly believe that these feelings are so strong that nothing will stop them, they get married and foolishly expect the feelings to continue forever. When real life hits them square in the face as well as the bank account, when misunderstandings and offences arise, when tiredness has crept upon them and the feelings are not there every day, they either blame the other or settle for a drudging life of co-habitancy. Sometimes when the *feeling* is missed so badly, they will seek it out in a third person or in family members. When the feelings come back via the third person (which they will, because it's new and fresh) during this time of seeking, and it is fondly remembered, many will take drastic measures to continue thinking that putting their hopes of continued feelings of love in the new object of their seeking will make them *feel* better.

I am not saying that we should forego the feelings of love nor that we should show love out of some robotic sense of duty. Love *is* a duty, but it is a duty we fulfil with the utmost of joy and freewill, feelings or not. True love will eventually come with feelings and are to be enjoyed when they come. However, to seek out feeling love as a sign that one must have before one loves is like sliding down a slippery slope laced with razorblades into a vat of alcohol, an unbelievably bad ending indeed (little cuts all along the way, with sudden disaster in the end). When we love God's ways, many times our emotions cannot help but gush out. We must enjoy those times, cherish those times, and very much share those times, but we do not live for those times nor hold back loving someone until we have those times.

The kind of love God is commanding us to have (one toward another) is called AGAPE love. The love that is exclusive to God and His people who are led of the spirit thus making themselves the sons and daughters of God (**Romans 8:14**). In its purest form, it is doing what is right and best for the object of our love, even if it involves unpleasant feelings and/or is inconvenient. These are the times that prove we love one another as Christ has loved us.

The Lord said in **Luke 6:32-33** *For if ye love them which love you, what thank have ye? for sinners also love those that love them. And if ye do good to them which do good to you, what thank have ye? for sinners also do even the same.* Giving love to only those whom we hope at some time in the near future will give back to us, has little to no value in the Kingdom of God or within the Ecclesia. God may allow it to happen and uses such people and situations for His will, but in order to enjoy the Agape love of God in eternity, it will require us to show the Agape love of God in the temporal.

Church attendance, giving to the church and obeying your pastor, belonging to the right organization, having a heritage from a Christian dynasty does nothing for our soul if we do not love one another as He loved us. Paul tells us of temporal things and their complete valuelessness in 1 Corinthians chapter thirteen. In fact, these things if we are not vigilant, could actually work against us. Reliance on these *things* lead us into the *Valley of False Security* which eventually brings us to the *Wall of Self-Deception*. This has us believing all is well when, indeed, it is far from well. Our Lord and Saviour told us three times in one conversation, *A new commandment I give unto you, That ye love one another; as I have loved you, that ye also love one another* (**John 13:34, 15:9, 12**). It could not be any clearer.

The Longest Twenty-Four Hours.

If we read the gospel of John carefully, we can see that it is written in three distinct sections. Chapters one through twelve relate to Christ's ministry, chapters thirteen through nineteen were about one twenty-four-hour period, while the remainder (death, burial, resurrection, manifesting Himself and commanding them to be filled with His spirit) are over ten days. The words of a man on death row are rather important and we can see that loving and sacrificing one for another weighed rather heavy on the heart of Christ before His death. The Master showed love to a group of men and women He knew would shortly leave him, one would betray Him with a kiss, and all would deny knowing Him or at least stand back and helplessly watch.

What God said about love during this time was not a brand-new commandment, as God has been telling us throughout human history to do this. For example, *If there be among you a poor man of one of thy brethren within any of thy gates in thy land which the LORD thy God giveth thee, thou shalt not harden thine heart, nor shut thine hand from thy poor brother* (**Deuteronomy 15:7**), and Solomon tells us, *A friend **loveth at all times**, and a brother is born for adversity* (Tsârâh- tightness, affliction, anguish, distress, tribulation, trouble. **Proverbs 17:17**).

If the people at our church gatherings are not our friends (as Jesus described friends), then who is? Mostly, it seems, it is people with whom we agree, or we like. This is a very childish view of friendship as opposed to the biblical view. A 4-year-old only likes those who like them, but this ought not to be so amongst the mature brethren in the Ecclesia. For example, little Brian and Amy know that Aunt Becky and Aunt Diedre are coming to visit. Aunt Becky is wealthy, and Aunt Diedre is barely making it. They both bring gifts commensurate with their income, who do we think the children will gravitate to, Becky or Diedre?

The reason why we do not sacrifice for others is because we do not deem them as friends in the biblical sense, *Greater love hath no man than this, that a man **lay down his life for his friends*** (**John 15:13-14**). To *lay down* is to Tithēmi- to commit; to place (in the widest application, literally and figuratively), properly in a passive or horizontal posture, to kneel down or lay aside. This is the same word Jesus used when He told the disciples that He ordained them, *Henceforth I call you not servants; for the servant knoweth not what his lord doeth: but I have called you friends; for all things that I have heard of my Father I have made known unto you. Ye have not chosen me, but I have chosen you, and **ordained you*** (Tithēmi- to commit, to place (in the widest application, literally and figuratively), properly in a passive or horizontal posture, to kneel down or lay aside. It has been erroneously taught in Western churches that ordained means to be lifted up, clearly it does not), *that ye should go and **bring forth fruit, and that your fruit should remain**: that whatsoever ye shall ask of the Father in my name, he may give it you. These things I command you, that ye love one another* (**John 15:15-17**).

This is what Christ expects us to do for those within His Ecclesia. *Do not call me your friend* (or brother) *if you are not willing to lay down your life for me. You and I must adhere to the same standard.* Many militaries and universities have a motto for which they strive to achieve. The SAS Regiment of Australia's motto is *Qui Audet Suscipit*, meaning *Who Dares, Wins*. The motto of Oxford College in England is *Dominus Illuminatio Mea*, meaning *Lord, Enlighten Me*. The motto for the Ecclesia ought to be, *Ad Sacrificium Pro Amico,* To Sacrifice for a Friend.

To show love is to prove we know love, but what about those people who grew up in abusive homes, orphanages or on the streets? They do not know the love of parents who would do all in their power to protect and nurture them. What do they do? They look to the heavenly Father and the real Ecclesia (a type and shadow of a mother) to show them what love looks like and teach them how to replicate it.

It would take volumes to write on the minutia of how to love one another as Christ loved us, so I will not foolishly attempt to do so. I will, however, give you a few biblical and earthly examples of what it looks like and trust that it will suffice to whet the reader's appetite to search out how to apply them to their own life. I will set them out in story form from the word of God, through history and my own personal experience. It does not matter if you cannot do them all. God is interested in your initial steps and passion to continue regardless of earthly returns, then He will not only show you more but will join you in your journey to love others as He loves them and loves you. To fulfill the greatest commandment comes with many difficulties and many sacrifices but also with some amazing rewards, chiefest of these is to hear …*well done thou good and faithful servant, thou hast been faithful over a few things, I will make thee ruler over many things: enter thou into the joy of thy lord* (**Matthew 25:21-23**. See also **Luke 19:13-25**).

There are several ways one can show love and receive love other than God's Agape. Family, friend, brotherly/sisterly, master/servant, charitable and spousal, each of these can be shown without any relationship with God. However, the love that flows through a servant of God via the above avenues has the power to eternally change a soul. That is the point of giving and receiving Agape love, to make an everlasting difference.

Love breeds hope. If someone is loved without reservation, hesitation, or partiality, hope springs eternal. It gives a brightness to one's smile and puts a bounce in one's step. It shines a light into the darkest of days and brings the finish line into view. Hope that is deferred makes a person sick in the heart and soul, but when God's love is displayed, the stormiest night brings a hope of calm days ahead (see **Proverbs 13:12**).

Hope gives strength, endurance, and passion to finish a task. When God's love, grace and mercy are applied, hearts are filled with hope and the tough times don't seem so insurmountable. Hope lifts the body's ability to produce endorphins which reduces the sensation of pain and affects emotions. Hope heals the heart and restores calm in the worst situations. *Be of good courage, and he shall strengthen your heart, all ye that hope in the LORD* (**Psalm 31:24**). To love as Christ loves, gives hope, both for this life and eternity.

Chapter 43

Some fine examples.

The examples you are about to read are true and factual. None of the names have been changed (although a couple have been made up) because they would not have wanted them to.

From gleaner to owner.

The story of Ruth and Boaz conjures up all kinds of romantic thoughts. However, the story of Boaz marrying Ruth is more than an allegorical story of love between God and mankind and it would not have happened if Ruth had taken a slightly different path and followed her sister-in-law, Orpah. To get the full impact, I urge you to read all four chapters and immerse yourself in this romantic love story with a happy ending both in the natural and the supernatural.

A synopsis of the Book of Ruth.

Naomi, a widow from *Bethlahemjudah* (**Ruth 1:1.** Yes, it really is one word) living in Moab during a time of famine. Naomi also lost her two sons to the grave, and had no reason to stay in Moab, so she decided to take the perilous 7-10 day journey to go back to her hometown where there was much food. As a widow she had no source of income and felt that the charity of her own people and access to the tithe given to the storehouse would sustain her until she too passed away. Naomi told her daughters-in-law to go back home (Moab) to be with their people. Orpah, though sad and weeping to be parted from her beloved mother-in-law, relented, and took her journey to the land of her fathers.

However, Ruth, Naomi's other daughter-in-law, because of her love for her late husband and his mother, refused to leave Naomi and pledged to stay by her side and care for her. This in and of itself was an amazing act of kindness, but it did not stop there. Ruth also pledged that she would dedicate herself to Naomi's people and most astounding of all, to Naomi's God. This was an out of the box thing to do. Ruth had the freedom and opportunity to go to the land of her people (Moab), find a new husband, settle down and raise her children, just like any other wife, but she chose to go to an unknown land, to be with an unknown people and serve an unknown God, all for the love of her husband's mother. This love was not coerced nor given as a result of a promise of future happiness, she had no angel visitation nor did a prophet speak to her of the will of God.

When Ruth and Naomi arrived in *Bethlahemjudah*, there was no welcome wagon with baskets of food and offers of shelter flooding in. Ruth was a stranger to all but Naomi. Where and how were they going to live would have been questions that crossed Ruth's mind. The Israelites had a form of social welfare (the tithe) but there was another law written in the Torah of the God of Israel, that if someone was harvesting a crop, they were to leave some of the crop around the edges for the poor to glean. Ruth worked hard to feed Naomi and herself by gleaning in a field owned by Boaz, a wealthy landowner. Ruth was not looking for a husband or to make money by selling some of the excess wheat. Her life was wrapped around caring for her mother-in-law, a Jewess.

This is the epitome of love one for another, willing to forsake your people and any chance of having the *"good life"* in order to care for someone else. This is radical love and if it is done because of our love for God, then it will never be unrequited. This type of love did not immediately change their situation, but it did change her future and created history (read that again, SLOWLY). Notice that Ruth was not a Jewess, she was not in any way connected to the God of Israel except through marriage and her unfeigned love for Naomi. This is what Peter wrote about, *Seeing ye have purified your souls in obeying the truth through the Spirit* **unto unfeigned love** *of the brethren, see that ye love one another with a pure heart fervently* (**1 Peter 1:22**). This type of love (Anupokritos- speaks of being sincere and without dissimulation- partiality, or hypocrisy) is what God expects from the Ecclesia, those called (Hebrew- Qârâ'- pronounce, publish or are bidden. Greek- Epikaleomai- invited, invoked for aid and worship) by His name, not just baptized in it. Because of this amazing life, all the children Ruth was carrying inside herself, were inserted into the lineage of King David and eventually the King of kings, the Lord Jesus Himself (...*And Salmon begat Booz of Rachab; and Booz* **begat Obed of Ruth***; and Obed begat Jesse; And Jesse begat David the king*... **Matthew 1:5-6**).

Back to the field. When Boaz saw Ruth gleaning in his field and enquired of the reapers who she was, they told him the story of not just who she is, but of what she was doing for a fellow citizen of the land of Israel. Ruth was already beautiful, but I'm sure in Boaz's eyes, her beauty had just multiplied. So much so, that he ordered that the reapers should leave extra sheaves for Ruth. After her continued service to Naomi, Boaz finally got the nerve to talk to her. When he got the complete story of what had happened, he loved her all the more. Ruth had no idea of Boaz's love because he had yet to speak of it. All she knew was from that day and every day from then on, there was more wheat than usual. God's love is never unrequited if we will just be persistent.

Though she had opportunities to marry other men during her time with Naomi, she chose to remain faithful to her commitment to her mother-in-law. This is evidenced by Boaz's praise of her, ...*Blessed be thou of the LORD, my daughter: for thou hast shewed more kindness in the latter end than at the beginning,* **inasmuch as thou followedst not young men, whether poor or rich** (Ruth 3:10).

The story follows up with Ruth and Boaz getting married and Ruth going from a gleaner of the field to owner of the field. She was now able to care for her mother-in-law even better. We never hear of Orpah again after chapter one. Though she wept, had deep feelings of pity and sorrow and no doubt loved and even wished the best for her mother-in-law, she goes off into obscurity. We can safely assume she remarried a nice man and had lots of children and died a happy woman, but she was never inserted into God's Kingdom. Obscurity is where many who claim the name of the Lord will go if the Agape love of God is not in them for the children of God (brothers and sisters in His Ecclesia).

Ruth and Orpah both had a choice. One chose the easier path which led to only visible benefits, while the other chose the more difficult path of sacrificial love which eventually led to an unseen Kingdom and where the King welcomed her into His bloodline. Which one will you be, Orpah or Ruth?

Chaim and Ezra the bankrupt.

The story of a love slave.

The next example may throw some people for a loop because the term *slave* comes with such a bitter taste in the mouth of modern people. It has to do with being a slave by choice rather than a slave by conquest. I was once asked by a friend '*what kind of person chooses to become a slave?*'

The answer is as simple as it is revelatory. We are or were a slave to Satan and his dog-eat-dog system in this realm. However, the good news is that another Master has shown up on the scene with another option. The choice, to leave or stay, as always, is ours and ours alone. No man can make this choice for us. **Romans 6:16** *Know ye not, that **to whom ye yield yourselves** servants* (Doulos- slave) *to obey, his servants ye are to whom ye obey; whether of sin unto death, or of obedience unto righteousness* (Dikaiosunē- equal with God in character and actions)*?* Notice: *to whom ye yield?* We must yield ourselves to someone, whether to Christ or to sin. We all must yield in one form or another. To yield is to Paristanō- to stand besides, to be at hand ready to assist, to proffer (to present for acceptance), to aid or provide to others. We choose to yield to God in this manner or to our old nature in this world. There is no middle ground. We decide to remain a slave to sin or transfer our slavehood to a new Master who expects us to become a slave to righteousness (Dikioasune- equal with God in character and action).

This story begins with a man up to his ears in debt with no way of extricating himself. He has already sold everything of value he had, and it is still not enough. He now has no lock, no stock, and no barrel, no money, no home and seemingly no hope. He is pretty much scraping the bottom of the metaphorical barrel and it looks like he's going to be sold at auction to pay back a little bit more, but still nowhere near enough to remain a free man for the rest of his life.

But wait, there is one last option. It's not pretty but it's a way out that won't cause a lifetime of pain and suffering. It's called *Peonage*, or debt slavery. This is a pledge of a person's services as security for the repayment for a debt or other obligation, a worker bound in servitude to a landlord/creditor. In Hebrew law (**Exodus 21:1-6**) the terms of the repayment are clearly and reasonably stated, and the person who is holding the debt thus has some control over the labourer but is also obligated to care for the basic needs of the peon/servant. Freedom is assumed upon debt repayment which cannot be more than six years. *And if thy brother, an Hebrew man, or an Hebrew woman, be sold unto thee, and serve thee six years; then in the seventh year thou shalt let him go free from thee. And when thou sendest him out free from thee, thou shalt not let him go away empty: Thou shalt furnish him liberally out of thy flock, and out of thy floor, and out of thy winepress: of that wherewith the LORD thy God hath blessed thee thou shalt give unto him* (**Deuteronomy 15:12-14**).

This bankrupt man needed a miracle and one showed up in the form of a fellow Hebrew (a compatriot, a friend) willing to pay his debt in order to stay off the slave market. This is a reciprocal arrangement. It is not a handout but a hand up. He would work for a set number of years then be given his freedom to try again. If you were given these two options only (sold as property in a slave market or peonage, which would you choose?)

God gave specific rules on how to treat people who are in debt. We are not to be cruel nor condescending, neither are we to punish them but to remember who paid *our* debts. We are to be compassionate and show mercy in the form of helping in any way we can without charging usury (interest). Solomon gives us God's will in these matters, *He that hath pity upon the poor lendeth unto the LORD; and that which he hath given will he pay him again* (**Proverbs 19:17**). The word *lendeth* is a severe mistranslation of the Hebrew word Lâvâh which means to be intertwined, to unite or remain unto the Lord. By helping the brothers and sisters in this manner it helps us to be united and remain in God. In the overwhelming majority of bankruptcies, people never intended to go broke. Circumstances beyond their control, bad financial advice or lack of understanding had caused their financial downfall. Let us see what the rules for peonage are shall we?

These are the rules that you shall set before them (the people of God)*: When you acquire* (buy the debt of) *a Hebrew slave, he shall serve six years; in the seventh year he shall go free, without payment. If he came single, he shall leave single; if he had a wife, his wife shall leave with him. If his master gave him a wife, and she has borne him children, the wife and her children shall belong to the master, and he shall leave alone.* This is where the story would normally end, but as usual, there's always more if we will only look deeper.

But if the slave declares, "I love my master, and my wife and children: I do not wish to go free," his master shall take him before God. He shall be brought to the door or the doorpost, and his master shall pierce his ear with an awl; and he shall then remain his slave for life (**Exodus 21:1-6**. Jewish Study Bible, Oxford University Press, Second Edition). Israel was given many laws on how to treat each other, and God, knowing the propensity of man to get into debt, made a way of escape with consequences and restoration in mind.

This is a powerful story of two men, one a master and the other a bankrupt (we will call the master Chaim, meaning Life, and the bankrupt Ezra meaning Help) and how both their lives were inextricably changed due to a series of unfortunate circumstances. It is about a man who not only helps a brother out, but also feeds, clothes, and shelters him, and to top it off, he gave this brother/servant a wife and allowed him to have children. Chaim was under no obligation to do anything but the bare minimum, yet somehow Ezra came to love his brother/master. One does not fall in love with someone who only gives the least amount possible to maintain a relationship. This story of Chaim and Ezra is the personification of love between two fellow citizens of the same kingdom. To the best of our knowledge, Chaim and Ezra were not blood family but citizens of Israel, and when one citizen was in need another citizen stepped in.

Chaim's life would not have been much different had he not helped Ezra. He wasn't in need of another servant. He could have hired one from anywhere and possibly even cheaper, but a brother in need meant more than saving a few shekels. Hebrew law forbade charging a fellow citizen usury (interest or taking financial advantage of another member of the Commonwealth of Israel) and this is lived out in the core commandments of Judaism, "*Love your neighbour as yourself*" (**Leviticus 19:18**). This commandment stands at the core of the Torah. Chaim was, in fact, fulfilling the Torah by caring for Ezra in love as we have been commanded to do by the Lord of the Torah (**Matthew 22:35-40, Luke 10:27** and **Mark 12:28-38**).

After many years, it came time for Ezra's release, and he must decide, does he go back out to the world alone and start again with virtually nothing but a few shekels or does he stay where he and his family are loved, cared for, and have a purpose?

We see in verse 5, there was so much love for Chaim that Ezra, when given the option to leave after having his debt manumitted (released from servitude), he willingly and openly, before God and the judges of the city, refuses to leave Chaim's service. His thinking would have been something like this: "*When Chaim stepped in to help me, I had lost everything, my house, livestock, and friends. I was homeless, hapless, and hopeless. He saved me from a life of slavery to outside forces. Chaim paid my debt and cared for me in ways I have never been cared for in my whole life. Yes, I have to work hard, but it beats begging and being homeless. He saw how lonely I was, and he gave me a wife who bore me children. I now have a great friend, the love of a family, shelter, food, clothing, and a purpose, much more than I've ever had before*".

Ezra must have considered long and hard, for when the day came for his release, he chose to *...plainly say, I love my master, my wife, and my children; I will not go out free:* (**Exodus 21:5**). To *plainly say* is a Hebraic double positive ('âmar, 'âmar); Ezra avowed, avouched, declared, and was determined to stay with Chaim. Why? The answer is because Ezra *Loved his master.* Chaim, (the master- meaning 'âdôn- sovereign, controller, and owner) not only showed mercy by paying off Ezra's debt, but he showed him love ('âhêb- to show affection) in that he kept on giving, not just to Ezra's need (food, water, and shelter) but to Ezra's desire for family and purpose.

In Hebrew, Ezra's declaration went somewhat like this, 'âmar 'âmar 'âhêb 'âdôn- *I avow this day that because of my master and how he loved me, I also love him and will not leave. I will stay a slave because of love- I will be a love slave.*

A formal declaration had been made and a ceremony was performed to ratify the declaration. We read in **Exodus 21:6** *Then his master shall bring him unto the judges; he shall also bring him to the door, or unto the door post; and his master shall bore his ear through with an aul;* **and he shall serve him for ever**. Look at the last seven words of the above verse. **And he shall serve him for ever**. The term *for ever* is 'ôlâm and it means time out of mind and perpetual. In other words, Ezra could not envisage a time where he would not serve Chaim and his interests. From this point on he would be about Chaim's business, not because Chaim saved him from a bad situation but because of his love for Chaim. I am sure you can see the parallel with the Lord and us. There comes a time when we mature in the Lord, and we stop just praising Him for getting us out of hell and begin worshipping Him because we love Him and willing to serve Him for no other reason than because of who He is.

To understand why Chaim bored a hole in Ezra's ear, we must look at how slaves and ownership (peonage) was viewed in the early years of the Nation of Israel. A Hebrew covenant must have blood involved or it is not enforceable (see **Hebrews 9:18, 20-22, Exodus 12:22, Luke 22:20** for example). In usual terms an animal was sacrificed to seal the covenant, but in Ezra's case, as he was the promise, a small amount of blood was required. Ezra made a blood covenant with Chaim which is why the term *he shall serve him for ever* was used. This love was not paid back in kind. Ezra could not give Chaim any money but chose to serve in love as a sign of his gratitude. Blood covenants were a normal part of many civilizations and continued even until recent times. We've all heard of blood brothers, where a small cut was made in the hands of two people, and they shook hands (signifying their blood was now mixed) and that they were now committed to each other until death. This was the covenant between Ezra and Chaim, until death.

Because of the mercy shown to a penniless and bankrupt man, a bond was forged in love, and it lasted for ever ('ôlâm- time everlasting, perpetual). Love of this kind (Agape) will last for ever. This is the eternal love of one citizen of the Commonwealth of Israel (the Kingdom of God) to another. We, on this side of the cross, have been grafted into that same Commonwealth of Israel (**Romans 11:17-24**) by our obedience to the biblical order of salvation (**Acts 2:37-46**). We are to use Israel as an example of how to live for God (**1 Corinthians 10:11** *Now all these things happened unto them* (Israel) *for ensamples: and they are written for our admonition, upon whom the ends of the world are come*), we must also love in this manner and if we continue to love each other in this manner, we will end up serving God together for ever.

Covenantal love.

This is a love, in many aspects, similar to Ruth's love for Naomi, but it takes it one step further. *Then Jonathan and David made a covenant, because he loved him as his own soul* (**1 Samuel 18:3-4**). Ruth loved Naomi because she was her late husband's mother (familial/agape love), however, Jonathan loved David as he loved his own soul, for no other reason other than he could recognize someone with the anointing of God on them, which takes us back to love your neighbour as yourself. In this display of love, we see Jonathon willing to go against his own king (his leadership) because he recognized the anointing of God on David. Jonathon swore an oath of allegiance to David, and not even his leadership, his father, the King nor the priests could make him break his promise.

Today, when someone becomes a citizen of a country other than the country of their birth, they must swear allegiance to their new country usually through a naturalization ceremony. This is especially important in times of conflict, for the government and its citizens must be able to count on the love and loyalty to their new country more than anything else and will commit to die for it if necessary. This breeds loyalty and strength in their chosen country amongst its citizens.

Jonathon had seen the evil deeds of King Saul (his father), and recognized the injustices being perpetrated on David, who had done nothing but serve Jonathon's father with fidelity and honesty. Jonathon made a promise to protect David whenever and wherever possible and he would even go against the king and his government officials in order to do so. This placed Jonathon in, not just a precarious position with his leadership, but also, a very special place in God's and David's heart as we will soon see.

A friendship, like David had never known, blossomed because one man had promised to honour and protect the anointing on David's life. Remember, David was not one of the high society elites or borne of the right parentage, neither was he born into a religious heritage, he held no association with the right group nor did he belong to a tribe that was wealthy. These were the people Jonathan was used to rubbing shoulders with.

Randy Alcorn, founder, and director of Eternal Perspective Ministries (EPM) writes of shepherds, "*In general, they were considered second-class and untrustworthy.*" *Jeremias, the prophet who authored the book of Jeremiah, documented that shepherds were deprived of all civil rights. They could not fulfill judicial offices or be admitted in court as witnesses.*" David came from obscurity to fulfil a promise made to Ruth.

David was a shepherd who not only knew how to use a sling, but how and when to use the name of God. Jonathan acknowledged that if his promise were going to be kept, it meant that even though he was next in-line to the throne, he would relinquish that right in order to see the Kingdom of God (Israel) set up God's way. This was a love for God and His Kingdom manifested in Jonathon's love for David. Jonathon loved God and His choice of king more than he loved the people's choice of king. The Kingdom of God and His government was paramount to Jonathon and his proof was that he not only covenanted with God's choice but gave up his rights to be a part of the elite and rule his own kingdom.

How does that work today? If we have a desire to do a certain thing in the Kingdom of God and we see an anointing on someone within the Ecclesia (not necessarily the pastor or bishop), we will honour God's choice and help them fulfil their purpose for the Kingdom of God. This is what I said earlier, *Be kindly affectioned one to another with brotherly love; in honour **preferring one another***.

(**Romans 12:10**). This is loving God's choice and doing all in our power to see the will of God fulfilled. Remember, its not always about us, but about God's choice for the Kingdom. Sometimes we are David and sometimes we are Jonathon. It matters not to God. It only matters to Him whether we will covenant with God and others to see His purpose fulfilled in their lives. This is what is meant by, seeking *first the Kingdom of God and His righteousness* (**Matthew 6:33**).

David loved Jonathon in return so deeply, that it transcended that of his love for his wife (Michal who was a bad wife and she was put aside for deriding David's dancing when the Ark of the Covenant returned to Israel. Michal was more worried about how David would look to the people than being happy the Ark of the Covenant was returned to Israel). This meant that this love between David and Jonathon went beyond normal limits or boundaries. It was not a bromance or a homosexual love, but a love that went into a deeper realm. Jonathon loved Israel (God's Kingdom) so much that he was willing to forego his place in line to rule it. The kind of love men have for one another who have come through the thick of battle, who have faced the dragon and won, whose desire to see the other live and succeed is covenantal love.

One did not place someone else above their own father let alone if their father was the king. David's only desire was to serve God by serving the king, who, for his service wanted to kill David one day only to want to adopt him the next. When the king was in one of his crazy moods, David walked or ran away. We live in a world full of troubled people and some are in our churches, but God has chosen out of them, a people who will help His Ecclesia fulfil its purpose. How we love the saints within the Ecclesia is how God sees our love for Him. Only when we determine to show this kind of covenantal love, can we truly say we love God.

More often than not, these people whom God brings across our paths will not be in the '*ministry*' so-to-speak, they will come from obscurity, but they will be anointed by God, they will be shepherds, uneducated, unknown, and unappreciated and if we will only take our eyes off the shiny, man-qualified, and credentialed people, we will see what God sees. These people will not be perfect, (as David was imperfect, yet he was still a man after God's own heart), they will have problems like all of us do, but they are still chosen of God to fulfil a purpose. Those who love God will covenant with these '*nobodies*' to see the will of God fulfilled, even if they have to go against the status quo. They look past the natural and see in their brothers and sisters something that others do not see, and they will forego their own rights, pleasures, and desires to climb the ministerial ladder or pad their bank accounts to see others become whom God has called them to be. They do it for the love of God, the love of the Kingdom of God and for the love of the one they want to see succeed in God.

Jonathon knew that God chose David for the benefit of His Kingdom, and the saints of the Ecclesia (like Jonathon) will give up their ambition and place in the church, for the benefit of the church. Once again, because it is important, they will, in essence, be fulfilling the command in **Romans 12:10** *Be kindly affectioned one to another with brotherly love; in honour* **preferring** *one another.* Notice, Paul did not say preferring the pastor or bishop, presbyter, or superintendent, he says we are to Proēgeomai or show deference to ***one another***.

What about Jonathon? What did he get for all this love? It is important to note that Jonathon did not lose out in this relationship. How was Jonathon's love toward David rewarded? After Saul and Jonathon were killed in battle and David became king (as prophesied by the prophet Samuel), all of Saul's children and grandchildren were rounded up and killed, except Mephibosheth, Jonathon's own son, whose name by the way meant *dispeller of shame*. We read in **2 Samuel 9:6-7** *Now when Mephibosheth, the son of Jonathan, the son of Saul, was come unto David, he fell on his face, and did* *reverence. And David said, Mephibosheth. And he answered, Behold thy servant! And David said unto him, Fear not: for I will surely shew thee kindness **for Jonathan thy father's sake,** and will restore thee all the land of Saul thy father; and thou shalt eat bread at my table continually.*

Because of the kindness and promise made and kept by Jonathon to David, Mephibosheth became the adopted son of King David and had all rights and responsibilities due to Jonathon restored unto Him. He even sat continuously at the king's table, an extremely high honour indeed. Remembering the words of the Master, *he that humbles himself shall be lifted up,* Mephibosheth *fell on his face, and did reverence* (Shâchâh- crouched, bowed down, prostrated himself) to king David. Sometimes our rewards for the love and kindness we show to others, does not come directly to us but to our children and grandchildren. Because Jonathon stood against an evil leader (his own father, the king) and the status quo (it was his turn to rule), his bloodline became a member of the household of David (Israel) which placed him into the genealogy of the Christ. Our love one for another has repercussions for generations to come.

Stephen and the stoners.

John MacArthur makes a statement that reveals another aspect of what true love is and how it is shown in ultimate sacrifice. *"Forgiveness is the most godlike act a person can do. Nothing is more godlike than forgiving someone and we are never more godlike than when we forgive".* The love of God protects us, heals us, delivers us from ourselves, feeds, clothes, and shelters us, but the greatest way that He shows His love is when He has done all of the above, even though we disobey Him sometimes, yet He still forgives a truly repentant heart.

Christ gave us a command on several occasions that in order to be considered His disciples we were to follow Him to resurrection unto eternal life via the cross of self-denial. He told us in **John 15:9,12** and **13:34** that we are to love as He loved. I believe that the greatest act of self-sacrifice Christ did was not that of dying for us (though that was an amazing thing to do), but that he forgave those that crucified Him. He sought no retribution for their crime of Theocide, but rather chose to forgive them.

Among those who took the words of the Master seriously regarding forgiveness was a young man by the name of Stephen and we read his incredible testimony in Acts chapter 6. He was doing all that was expected of him in the Ecclesia, preaching the Kingdom of God only and making disciples (yes, believe it or not, these are the only two things God commanded the Ecclesia to do. Not start churches, raise up ordained ministers or raise money. These are all man's attempt at building small 'k' kingdoms hoping this will please God). Stephen was chosen to distribute food to the widows and orphans because he was, an honest and wise man and most importantly, he was full of the Holy Ghost (**Acts 6:1-3**). This was a part of his discipleship to the believers. Stephen was doing what James wrote of 27 years later, *Pure religion and undefiled before God and the Father is this; To visit the fatherless and widows in their affliction, and to keep himself unspotted from the world* (**James 1:27**). Basically, what every believer in the Messiah should be doing.

Stephen had heard the parables of the Master as told by the disciples and took them to heart. He heard how, on the cross, the Messiah had prayed for those who were killing Him and that he stood as a born-again man because of it. He only waited for his chance to show how the Master had changed his life. By the time we get to verse eight of chapter six we see he has progressed from being an honest and wise man, full off the Holy Ghost, to being a man *...full of faith and power, did* *great wonders and miracles among the people.* He started out serving food, God saw his heart and began using him in a deeper way. I've said it before to many young people wanting to sing for God on the platform or preach the gospel behind a pulpit, if you won't sing for God during the 166 hours in the week, why would you want to sing for him on a platform for 2 hours a week. If you won't share the gospel with your life with the people you come in contact with in 166 hours in the week, what makes you think you should share it for two hours a week from a pulpit.

Satan couldn't care less that we attend church services, pay tithes, run the aisles, jump, shout amen, how much victory we sing we have or go to every conference we can afford. He couldn't care less that we know how to quote the Fabulous Five of our tenets. Satan gets mad when we progress in God through personal study, are obedient to the revelations we receive from God's word and loving others as God loves them like Stephen. Satan was having none of this upstart who was only supposed to hand out food. Stephen's growth represented a threat to Satan's kingdom, so ol' slewfoot went to the religious folk (the church goers) and stirred up strife because Stephen was making them look bad in the eyes of the people. He wanted to grow in God, they wanted to remain in their status quo. They tried to argue with him, but remember, he had the Holy Ghost and wisdom (many today just have the Holy Ghost but lack wisdom). When they brought him before the council, God had given him in that self-same hour that which he needed to say as promised, *And when they bring you unto the synagogues, and unto magistrates, and powers, take ye no thought how or what thing ye shall answer, or what ye shall say: For the Holy Ghost shall teach you in the same hour what ye ought to say* (**Luke 12:11**). When they could not win by the word, they resorted to rumours and innuendos about him. In all of this, Stephen just stuck with the word of God (**Acts 6:11-15**).

The love of God in the heart of Stephen for his detractors was evident when he finally asked to speak his mind with the hope of turning their hearts towards God. For the next 52 verses he tries to show them all God has done for Israel and how it all culminated in God loving them so much that He came to walk amongst them in order to restore their relationship with their Mighty Jehovah (**Acts 7:2-53**). Their response was unloving to say the least, but Stephen's response showed who his Lord and Master was.

Stephen had shown the same love for the people of God, as Christ Himself had shown on the cross. He did not try to win them with miracles, signs, and wonders, or to prove he was right by arguing scripture, or by showing his Holy Ghost by speaking in tongues nor by superior knowledge of Torah. He spoke to the people, *things pertaining to the Kingdom of God,* the same as His Master did in **Acts 1:3**. Why did Stephen try so hard? Because they were the ones that His Master had died for, and the command of the Lord was to love them as His Master loves them, to sacrifice his life for theirs. He gave the ultimate for someone else's benefit.

When the crowd called for his death (**Acts 7:54**) he stood firm in his belief that God would be with him until the end (notice, his belief was not *'until God got him out of the situation'*). We continue, *But he, being full of the Holy Ghost, looked up stedfastly into heaven, and saw the glory of God, and Jesus standing on the right hand of God, And said, Behold, I see the heavens opened, and the Son of man standing on the right hand of God* (**Acts 7:55-56**).

This did nothing to reduce the anger of the mob (I call them sheeple because they were led by a few ex-slaves who formed their own organization called The Synagogue of the Libertines), and though he had the face of an angel (**Acts 6:15**), they still wanted nothing to do with this fresh and restored way of looking at God.

In the end, as they were stoning Stephen and as he was on his knees praying for his executioners, God was standing up for His son. It was at this point, he remembered and repeated the words of Christ from the cross... *and cried with a loud voice, Lord, lay not this sin to their charge. And when he had said this, he fell asleep* (**Acts 7:60**).

This is love for a group of misguided malcontents, who wanted to see this faithful servant's demise. He was rocking their paradigm (as they were casting rocks at him). He challenged their doctrine, and they would have none of it, especially from some upstart who was not from their organization nor had their education level. In amongst all these verses is an obscure line which reads *...And cast him* (Stephen) *out of the city, and stoned him:* **and the witnesses laid down their clothes at a young man's feet, whose name was Saul** (Acts 7:58). The same Saul, who in the next chapter was consenting to (Suneudokeō- thought well of and feel gratified with) Stephen's death (and all those insignificant people who believed and lived the same as Stephen). We note that only one chapter later Saul would become Paul the disciple, who had witnessed not only just Stephen's death, but also his willingness to show the love of God by forgiving his detractors/executioners. Saul the disciple, soon to become Paul the apostle, had been a recipient of that forgiveness prayed for by Stephen. Stephen was only obeying God's word and being a witness (Martus- martyr. **Acts 1:8**) in Jerusalem, and for that he paid with His life. However, his manifestation of God's love was also instrumental in paving the way for Saul's eventual meeting with God on the road to Damascus four years later. There's no time limit on what God can do when we show His love.

We never really know what affect our love for God's people will have. Saul had experienced God's love and forgiveness long before his Damascus-road experience. With each one he imprisoned, beat, and had executed, their forgiveness was gnawing on his heart. Stephen's love for God and His people, allowed for two thirds of the Renewed Covenant to be written. We must never underestimate what God's sacrificial love for His people will do through you and I and how that love shown through forgiveness can and will affect many who witness it in our lives.

The grenade and the glory.

Romans 5:6-7 *For when we were yet without strength, in due time Christ died for the ungodly. For scarcely for a righteous man will one die: yet peradventure for a good man some would even dare to die.*

Jacklyn Harrell "Jack" Lucas (February 14, 1928 – June 5, 2008) was an American soldier in World War II who was awarded the highest military decoration for valour (The Medal of Honour) at the age of 17 as a private first class in the Marine Corps during the Battle of Iwo Jima (2/19/45-3/26/1945), a lonely island in the Philippines Sea, where almost 7000 U.S. soldiers died, and many acts of bravery were committed (27 out of 427 Medals of Honour awarded during WW2 were won on that island alone).

During a close firefight in two trenches, between Lucas, and three marines against 11 Japanese soldiers, Lucas saved the lives of the other three marines from two enemy hand grenades that were thrown into their trench. He unhesitatingly threw himself on one grenade, while in the next instant pulling the other grenade under him. One grenade he covered with his body exploded and wounded him severely; the other grenade failed to explode. He is the youngest Marine and the youngest serviceman in World War II to be awarded the Medal of Honour.

We all marvel at this kind of heroics and wonder what was going through a person's mind while in the heat of battle, killing the enemy and trying not to get killed, the stench of death and the deafening sounds of gunfire, in the blink of an eye, with very little if any forethought, they sacrifice their own lives for a comrade? This makes no sense, does it? Yet thousands put their lives on the line for strangers every day and we don't even think about it. Strangers laying down their lives for strangers. How much more should the Ecclesia do so for each other, not just for strangers, but especially for fellow citizens of the Commonwealth of the Kingdom of God? **Ephesians 2:12** *That at that time ye were without Christ,* **being aliens from the commonwealth of Israel, and strangers** *from the covenants of promise, having no hope, and without God in the world.*

Jack Lucas' love for his comrades has gained him an everlasting gratitude from those whom he saved by giving all to them when they needed it, and a splendid example to other soldiers of courage and sacrifice. His name will forever be on the lips of those who witnessed and benefitted from his bravery and sacrifice and in the hearts of their children and grandchildren. If this is so in the natural, should it not be so in the spiritual?

The Love of God took us from the kingdom of darkness where we lived for ourselves and headed for certain death and separation from the eternal God, and brought us into His marvellous light, where we live and die for God and one another. But how can we do so if we don't know one another and how can we know one another if we only superficially connect with each other once or twice a week for a few hours (**1 Peter 2:9, 1 John 3:16**)? If we are not involved in each other's lives (not in a prying or meddlesome way) how will we know how we can be of service? Many times, God will not tell us things about each other, because He wants us to get to know one another and use common sense. The purpose of any basic training in any military is not just to learn how to toughen up soldiers to fight but also how to fight together. One would scarcely die for a stranger but for someone who has locked horns with the enemy together with us and has come through the other side alive? This builds a special bond. A bond that brings courage in tough times and looks to strengthen others in times of conflict, whether it be national, or personal.

Love that lays down itself for the good of another is not natural to man. On the contrary, this type of love, when seen in operation, usually makes the headlines of the press. So, why is it so rare? Mainly because man has been forced into fending and tending to our own needs with reckless abandon. We have been taught to blow our own trumpet, get all we can, hold onto it, get to the top no matter who we have to step on, and if we're feeling generous, give a little away, and rest in the false peace we've helped the world a little in our own special way (don't forget to get that tax exemption receipt).

People like Mother Theresa, Mahatma Gandhi (who was known to have said *'If Christians would live as the bible and their God commanded them, all India would be Christian today'*), Oscar Schindler, Nelson Mandela, Karl Plagge (a German Army officer who rescued Jews during the Holocaust in Lithuania), and others have become icons of goodness and self-sacrifice and the subject of books and movies. We see them as someone special, but from God's point of view their acts of self-sacrifice for the good of others is meant to be the norm within the Commonwealth of the Kingdom of God.

A brother or sister in the Ecclesia is fighting in the same war, but just as war has many battlefronts and many casualties, so does the Ecclesia, and just as in any war, when a soldier falls, they are replaced as soon as possible in order to hold the line. The tired and slightly wounded are encouraged to keep fighting, while those who are severely wounded are taken off the front line and cared for by those who have a healing touch. These wounded warriors are fed, and restored so they can either go back to the front or stay back and train new and willing people with their years of experience on the front line. They will use both their wisdom and empathy gained on the battlefront, being cared for, and caring for others.

There is no greater bond forged in humanity than that of two or three men in a fox hole, who have fought off the advances of a determined enemy. The fear in the heat of battle is real, the stench of corpses and cordite surrounds the warriors, but as long as they have their comrades in arms with them, knowing that they would lay down their lives for one another, the fight continues with victory in sight. The women are not excluded. They have fought and suffered much in wars, but as they banded together to help one another, they gained strength and determination to see the battle through.

One cannot understand this type of brotherhood unless one has trained and fought tooth and nail for the same goal and has come through with many scars and sleepless nights. This can only happen when we love to the death, those with whom we share a common goal, (such as a foxhole), so to speak. The furtherance of the Kingdom of God here on earth is being violently and relentlessly resisted by Satan and those who live in his kingdom. Yet, the apostle John admonishes us, *Ye are of God, little children,* **and have overcome them**: *because greater is he that is in you, than he that is in the world* (**1 John 4:4**). John says we have Nikaō- conquered, prevailed and gotten the victory of them (the spirit of the world, not flesh and blood). Are we really that foolish to believe that we can do this on our own? Yet it is this sacrificial love that conquers and confounds an enemy.

Left, not lost, or forgotten.

The Lord told the Ecclesia in the city of Ephesus that even though they had done many good things, they had left (not lost or forgotten, but left) their first love (**Revelation 2:4**). The same love which Christ had died to redeem mankind unto Himself. The love that lays down its own life for that of a friend (**John 15:13**). The love that goes beyond superficial words and meetings and goes deep into the hearts of sinners and saints alike. All the good works the Ephesians had done amounted to nothing because they did not have His love for one another. The kind of sacrificial love that sees a need and acts before the flesh has a chance to influence the outcome in the negative.

Seventeen-year-old Jack Lucas did not weigh up the odds of survival, he did not contemplate if his actions would one day be returned to him by his fellow trench mates. He acted instinctively and for that, his peers awarded him the highest honour in the land. How much more will we, when we act in like manner for one another (instinctively and without hesitation) be rewarded with the highest honour in the universe, to be given a crown of righteousness (greater than any medal) by our Lord, Master, and Saviour. What greater honour is there than to hear the greatest words to be uttered throughout eternity, *Well done, thou good and faithful servant: thou hast been faithful over a few things, I will make thee ruler over many things: enter thou into the joy of thy lord* (**Matthew 25:21**).

I think the apostle John summed up what it means to be a child of God in his first epistle. I would like to submit the importance of Christ's command to love one another through his writing. *And hereby we do know that we know him,* **if we keep his commandments**. *He that saith, I know him, and* **keepeth not his commandments, is a liar**, *and the truth is not in him. But whoso keepeth his word, in* *him verily is the love of God perfected: hereby know we that we are in him. He that saith he abideth in him ought himself also so to walk, even as he walked.*

The New Commandment.

Brethren, I write no new commandment unto you, but an old commandment which ye had from the beginning. The old commandment is the word which ye have heard from the beginning. Again, a new commandment I write unto you, which thing is true in him and in you: because the darkness is past, and the true light now shineth. **He that saith he is in the light, and hateth** (Miseo- to love less) **his brother, is in darkness even until now.** *He that loveth his brother abideth in the light, and there is none occasion of stumbling in him.* **But he that hateth** (Miseo) **his brother is in darkness,** *and walketh in darkness, and knoweth not whither he goeth, because* **that darkness hath blinded his eyes** (1 John 2:3-11).

This commandment is to be taken as seriously as our determination to live 'holiness' lives. Dressing right, speaking right, belonging to the right church, paying tithes, all our tongue talking and praying for the pastor all pale into insignificance, if we do not love one another as Christ loved us. If we do not love as Christ loves, then we have only become a tinkling cymbal or sounding brass (see **1 Corinthians 13:1**).

Section 6

Chapter 44

The lunacy of love.

We can never comprehend what kind of love leaves a place of heavenly rest and repose, a place where all one's desires are fulfilled with just a thought and where all creation bows down at the feet of its creator, to come to a place where the giver of this love was not recognized but by a handful of He's own creation, to walk amongst the filth and deprivation of fallen humanity, to view the degradation of His creation's misery and to then make known that all will be well to those who follow Him. We must follow Him, not just in word or belief, but in becoming like Him in all ways, through the Garden of Gethsemane, the ridicule, the false accusations, then the humiliation of the cross all the while denying himself vindication from heaven.

This is love in its purest form; unfeigned, untainted, and uncorrupted, to leave the known for the unknown, not for self but for others. And yet, this is exactly what God expects of those whom He has called and have answered the call, those of His Ecclesia, who have been baptized in His name, filled with His spirit, and surrendering as servants of righteousness. Those who do so will one day wed and rule a Kingdom with Him. Those whose passion to emulate their Lord, Master, and Saviour in love and service, and have this kind of love is only found in heavenly places (*And hath raised us up together, and made us sit together in heavenly places in Christ Jesus* **Ephesians 2:6**) for only in heavenly places can a love like this conquer the assaults and ambushes of a wicked world.

This love gives up things, time, talents, and treasures for the brethren without a second thought. It is not for gain but to be Holy for, as and because, He is Holy (**1 Peter 1:15-16**). It is the only thing that strengthens not only the receiver but the giver at the same time. It is the only thing that replenishes as quickly as it is given. When given freely, the heart expands beyond normal, and it requires no medical attention. The world is waiting with bated breath to see a church that displays this kind of love one for another. If pure fentanyl (an extremely toxic and deadly synthetic opioid, which only takes about two milligrams, approximately the size of ten grains of salt) can kill an adult, what can a show of pure love do to a hurting man, woman, teenager, or child? Selfishness and egotism under the guise of seeker friendly Christianity, where we cater to the comforts and needs of the church populace without expecting their lives to be transformed via discipleship, is toxic and destroys thousands of hurting hearts daily, but God's love shown through sacrificially willing servants saves many more. The former ruins and kills, the latter heals, and restores.

Giving up things for the brethren (all the brethren, not just the leadership or from our little cliques) is all a part of being in the Ecclesia. Even a cursory reading of Romans chapter fourteen shows that we give up certain things for the brethren if it will help them in their walk with God. A love that does not cost us dearly is more than likely an emotional response to certain external stimuli. We feel loved, therefore we love back. To give from our excess is a start, however, to give sacrificially from the inner most parts of our being proves that God and His love resides within us.

Tongues only proves God once entered into us, loving as He loves proves He still resides and abides, but more importantly, rules. Every person is different, that is why we must have ongoing communication with the one who loved us first, through worship, prayer, study and discipling one another, for only He knows the heart of man and what each heart needs in order to get closer to Him. God is a tough task master, but His demands are not grievous. **1 John 5:3** *For this is the love of God, that we keep his commandments: and his commandments are not grievous* (Barus- burdensome). He is also a loving God, one who knows how far He can push us (for it is in the pushing that we grow). He requires that those who wish to enter into His presence must endeavour to become like Him in every aspect (failures are covered through repentance and moving forward) for in His presence there is only righteous love. Even when God shows His fierceness it is shown in love. We would do well to leave the fierceness to God and be about His business of preaching the Kingdom of God only and making disciples. As we do both in love for those in our pews then the lost, we will see the Kingdom of God regain its influence in earth as it is in heaven.

Chapter 45

Do the crime, do the time.

Galatians 5:14 *For all the law is fulfilled in one word, even in this; Thou shalt love thy neighbour as thyself.*

To love our neighbour as we love ourselves is the lowest form of love allowed in the Kingdom of God. This was given to all saints in order to live peacefully within society. Don't steal, don't lie, don't cheat etc. are all laws made to benefit society in general. These laws were made by God to keep order in His Kingdom and when those laws are broken, there is a penalty to pay. It is so in any society, why would it be any different in God's society? There were two laws given in the Garden of Eden (to procreate and tend the Garden (not to eat of the tree of knowledge of good and evil was a part of tending the garden) and while the law was kept, the relationship between God and man was strong; but when the law was rejected in order to fulfil a lust for power and knowledge (outside of what God deemed necessary) to become like gods, the maker of the law had no choice but to pass judgement which unfortunately was banishment. Let us look at 3 different ways in which breaking laws effects each and every one of us not just the one who breaks the law.

Case 1.

A person gets drunk, and on the drive home runs a stop sign and hits a pedestrian. They are maimed for life and can no longer function as they used to or would do in society. A man-made law now severely limits the driver's ability to function in society due to a long prison sentence and the one who was maimed can no longer function as planned within the local community. Copious amount of time and money are spent in rehabilitation and lifelong care is put into place. Cause and effect. One breaks the law, but more than one is affected eventually. Society suffers the loss of input of two contributing members which has a ripple effect on future generations. A study of the *Butterfly Effect* (which is the outsize significance of minute occurrences) is well worth doing to see the ripple effect of each person on earth.

Case 2

A husband and wife, struggle in their marriage and after a long time call it quits. They use a manufactured law such as divorce (it was never God's idea. Moses only gave it to them because of their hard hearts **Matthew 19:8**) in order to no longer honour the marriage vows. Their children now must deal with two angry and hurt people trying to live a normal life (extremely difficult at best, but now it is impossible) with all the pain and suffering that goes with it. They now function at a reduced capacity as people, their children have half parents trying to do the job of two which causes further breakdown in the children's ability to function in the greater society. The input into society by those children has now been diminished and society is the loser.

Case 3

A brother or sister in the Lord is struggling with a deep-seated issue in their lives. They constantly fall and though genuinely repentant they still struggle. The church rejects them or no longer spends time with them and uses man-made rules and traditions to begin the process of ostracization so they would not taint others with their sin. All of life's experiences God has allowed and placed in them is now outside the church and unable to help anyone in the church. They were not loved as the Lord had commanded (because of man-made rules) and others will not be able to see the victory that God would eventually bring and draw on the experiences of the shunned ones.

The word calls the idea of loving one another the *Law of Christ*. When we keep the law, the Ecclesia functions as purposed, when we break the law and withhold love, we function at a reduced rate which eventually leads to the Ecclesia malfunctioning. The prefix *mal* means *not, badly, opposite, faulty as in malfunctioning, maladjusted, malcontent, or malodourous-* (smelling bad). When we do not love one another as Christ loved us, we can pretend (rather well I might add) that we are the Ecclesia of the one true God, however, we are not fooling anyone, least of all God. We begin to function at far less than optimal. The world will know that we are His disciples by the fact that we obey the law of Christ and love one another.

This love is not shown when things and people are behaving in a manner that pleases us. This law of Christ is tested and becomes ingrained when we have the ability and opportunity to break the law of Christ yet choose not to.

I am usually not tested in areas I already excel, but in areas I struggle, and usually when no-one is looking, that is my bugbear. One night in 2002, I was driving on the Warrego Highway (from Wallumbilla to Charleville in the Queensland outback); I had not seen another vehicle around for about 300 kilometres, I saw some road signs that said 100 kilometres per hour (70 mph). I struggled with this because I was in a hurry and the conditions seemed safe for me to drive about 115 kilometres per hour (80 mph). The powers that be (The Shire of Murweh) clearly stated what was considered safe for both driver and community. I had broken a law that was meant to keep the community safe and had I have been caught by the local constabulary, I would have lost a considerable amount of money via a hefty fine and four points from my license. I would not have had the right to complain about the whys and wherefores of my fines because the signposts were clearly marked, and I understood my actions.

If a shire council is within its rights to fine a person breaking a law made for the safety of the local community, is not God also within His rights to punish those who break the Law of Christ (to love one another) meant for the safety of His community? Yet, we continually, and seemingly with impunity, break the Law of Christ on a daily and sometimes even hourly.

To obey His commands to love one another is not where it stops. It goes substantially further than that. The Law of Christ states we are to love one another *as Christ loves us.* It is not good enough for a husband to love His wife. He must love her *as Christ loved the church and gave Himself for it.* It is not good enough for a wife to submit to her husband, she must submit to him *as unto the Lord.* It is not good enough for children to just obey their parents, they must do so *in the Lord* (**Ephesians 5:22, 25, 6:1**). Neither of the above statements lessens the IQ, uniqueness, or power of the person, it just means that we acknowledge that God's word is right, and we will obey it no matter how we feel or think. We trust that when God gives a command that it is in our best interest. Those in the Ecclesia have a higher calling than the rest of the world. The law of the land is the same for an ordinary citizen and a Supreme Court Justice, but the justice is held to a higher standard, and more is expected of that person. They will be judged harsher when they break the law than anyone else. According to the words of the Master... *And that servant, which knew his lord's will (Thelēma-determination or decree), and prepared (Hetoimazō- adjusted, made fit) not himself, neither did according to his will, shall be beaten with many stripes. But he that knew not, and did commit things worthy of stripes, shall be beaten with few stripes. For unto whomsoever much is given, of him shall* *be much required: and to whom men have committed much, of him they will ask the more* (**Luke 12:47-48**).

To quote the ancient Chinese philosopher and writer, Lao Tzu, *Being deeply loved by someone gives you strength, while loving someone deeply gives you courage.* Courage is sorely lacking in the western style churches today because as soon as hardships come, the vast majority ask for prayer to take the hardships away, cut themselves off from the ones they consider are the source of the hardships or retreat into themselves and let their minds play havoc with all sorts of scenarios. Yet, the very definition of courage (which is what we are commanded to have in the midst of the hardship and to give to others), is the state or quality of mind or spirit that enables one to face danger, fear, or the vicissitudes of life with self-possession, confidence, and resolution. When we love one another as He loves us, we have the same courage that took our Lord all the way to the cross, to the grave and to the resurrection.

Why do we tell people a half truth when we say He will never leave or forsake us, when the condition is that we are to have courage and not fear what man can do, *Be strong and of a good courage* ('âmats- alert, steadfastly minded, established, fortified and hardened)*, fear not, nor be afraid of them: for the LORD thy God, he will not fail thee, nor forsake thee* (**Deuteronomy 31:6**). Note: God doesn't go instead of us, He goes when we go, if we don't go, neither does He. If all things are meant to be easy because we are born-again, what need is there for courage?

There is absolutely no acceptable reason for members of the Ecclesia not to display the kind of love required to remain in the Ecclesia. If we say we live for the Lord and not follow His greatest commandment, then we of all men are most deceived and miserably wretched. Below are 14 verses (though there are multitudes more) that will solidify the premise of this book. To love one another was not a Renewed Covenant concept, so I have included just a few from the Old Testament.

Deuteronomy 15:7-8, 11 *If, however, there is a needy person among you, one of your own kinsmen in any of your settlements in the land that the Lord your God is giving you, do not harden your heart and shut your hand against the needy kinsman. Rather, you must open your hand and lend him sufficient for what he needs.* **11** *For there will never cease to be needy ones in your land, which is why I command you: open your hand to the poor and needy kinsman in your land.* (Jewish Study Bible- JSB). **Proverbs 17:17** *A friend loveth at all times, and a brother is born for adversity.* **Zechariah 7:9** *Thus said the Lord of Hosts: Execute true justice; deal loyally and compassionately with one another* (JSB).

1 John 3:11 *For this is the message that ye heard from the beginning, that we should love one another.* **1 John 3:23** *And this is his commandment, That we should believe on the name of his Son Jesus Christ, and love one another, as he gave us commandment.* **1 John 4:7** *Beloved, let us love one another: for love is of God; and every one that loveth is born of God, and knoweth God.* **1 John 4:11** *Beloved, if God so loved us, we ought also to love one another.* **1 John 4:12** *No man hath seen God at any time. If we love one another, God dwelleth in us, and his love is perfected in us.* **2 John 1:5** *And now I beseech thee, lady, not as though I wrote a new commandment unto thee, but that which we had from the beginning, that we love one another.* **1 Thessalonians 4:9** *But as touching brotherly love ye need not that I write unto you: for ye yourselves are taught of God to love one another.* **1 Thessalonians 3:12** *And the Lord make you to increase and abound in love one toward another, and toward all men, even as we do toward you:* and once again we read how love is visible in **1 Peter**

1:22 *Seeing ye have purified your souls in obeying the truth through the Spirit unto unfeigned love of the brethren, see that ye love one another with a pure heart fervently:*

This next verse points to loving one another as a debt incurred when we become a part of the body of Christ; **Romans 13:8** *Owe no man anything, but* (Ei Mē- except, save only) *to love one another: for he that loveth another hath fulfilled the law.* We are to owe (Opheileō- be under obligation, indebted to, must, ought and should) love one to another. Once God made the promise never again to destroy mankind with a flood, He became indebted to His own word. He placed a reminder (the rainbow) of His promise as a witness between God and man. We have that same kind of reminder of our promise to love and serve Him daily. It is called the day of our spiritual birth and His word. Once we submit to God's way of being born again, we have also become indebted to obey His commands, the greatest of these is to love the Lord our God with all our heart and mind and strength and the second is likened unto it, that we love one another as He has loved you and I (**Matthew 22:36-40**).

To love as He loves, we must first know how spiritually poor we really are and that we cannot walk this walk alone. God has provided an entire body, the world's largest and greatest group of likeminded people, to help us follow Him and His commands.

To be a part of this body, one must give up all pretence of individual rights and comforts as their primary focus and submit to the head (*For the husband is the head of the wife,* **even as Christ is the head of the church:** *and he is the saviour of the body* **Ephesians 5:23***, And he is the head of the body, the church:** *who is the beginning, the firstborn from the dead; that in all things* **he** *might have the preeminence* **Colossians 1:18**). He (Christ, not man) will direct us into the safest place on earth, His body.

Chapter 46

Final thoughts.

The purpose of a lighthouse is not to keep ships safe. If safety is the primary purpose, ships would not leave the safety of the harbour. No, my friends, the purpose of the lighthouse is to guide ships in the darkness and storms. The lighthouse is not what ships head towards. The purpose of God's light is not keep us safe, but to guide us through our storms to our final destination.

At the end of the Master's earthly ministry, He asks Peter a curious question, one that must apply to all who call Him Master. In **John 21:15-17** we read, *So when they had dined, Jesus saith to Simon Peter, Simon, son of Jonas, lovest thou me more than these? He saith unto him, Yea, Lord; thou knowest that I love thee. He saith unto him, Feed my lambs. He saith to him again the second time, Simon, son of Jonas, lovest thou me? He saith unto him, Yea, Lord; thou knowest that I love thee. He saith unto him, Feed my sheep. He saith unto him the third time, Simon, son of Jonas, lovest thou me? Peter was grieved because he said unto him the third time, Lovest thou me? And he said unto him, Lord, thou knowest all things; thou knowest that I love thee. Jesus saith unto him, Feed my sheep.*

Peter's heart was full of joy, for His Master had returned from the dead (in a glorified body no less) and he was forgiven for cursing God. The Master even served him by cooking him a breakfast of fish. As a side note, how can we tell we have forgiven someone? When we can sit and eat together. Peter did not know it, but he was about to be asked a question which, when answered correctly, was to be followed by a command and when that command is obeyed, it would reverberate into eternity.

The Lord asked Peter, *'Lovest thou me?'* We tend to skip over this little suffix- *est,* but please note the word the writer of this Gospel was compelled to use in this question. *Lovest;* the suffix *est* denotes the highest or the most. We use the words greatest, humblest, busiest, choicest to say it is the most or best of something or someone. The Greek for lovest is Agapaō meaning much or to love in a social or moral sense and it comes from the Hebrew ʿâgab meaning to breath after or dote over (to bestow or express excessive love or fondness habitually, to adore, to spoil). The Lord did not ask Peter if he loved or had love for Him. This is past and present tense as in *did you love me yesterday* or *do you love me now*? He asked *Lovest thou me?* He was asking Peter if he had love for Him more than anyone or anything else. He even added the word *more* (Pleiōn- in quantity, quality, a major portion or more excellent) *than these.* The Lord did not question Peter's love for Him but whether his love for Him was greater than his love for his family, friends, and the disciples he had grown so dear to.

He gushes out in typical Peterian style, *Of course I do, you know I love* (present tense) *you.* Jesus immediately followed Peter's answer with a command to prove his love. The great Shepherd was about to pass on to Peter (and all those that follow him, *Neither pray I for these alone, but for them also which shall believe on me through their word;* **John 17:20**), how we who call on Him as master can prove whether we *lovest Him.*

We are to feed His lambs/sheep. We are to pasture, to keep *His* sheep/lambs safe from the enemy of their souls. Not by placing them in bubble wrap of rules and regulations trying to protect them from normal life, or by telling them they can't do anything until someone tells them they can. Not by trying to be someone's Holy Ghost or by pressuring them into submission. Like the great commission, this was not written to 'the ministry', but to all who claim His name. We are to imitate the great Shepherd who, as mentioned in **John 10:11** ...*giveth his life for the sheep.* Being a disciple/leader in the church requires us to give our lives for His sheep. We are to show our love for the great shepherd by emulating Him. *He giveth* (Tithēmi- to place in the widest sense in a horizontal posture, to lay down, same as the word ordained) *his life* (Psuchē- breath, spirit, heart, mind, and soul. **John 10:15**). We have been incorrectly conditioned to think that the work of the '*elected or educated ministry*' is to take care of the sheep, when in fact it is the work of all who claim to love the Lord and have been filled with his spirit.

I have noticed recently that we Apostolics try to use scripture to prove that we love each other, when in the Kingdom of God, He commands us to show love to one another to prove the scriptures. We can argue the oneness of God, the baptism in Jesus' name and the necessity of the infilling of the Holy Ghost pretty much better than anyone else, we can prophecy with the best of them, have revelation coming out of our ears, faith to spare and even willing to let go of some of our goods and ten percent of our income, but if we do not love each other the way we are commanded, we have become nothing but noise, just another voice in the cacophony of voices claiming they have the truth. This just shows we are nothing (see **1 Corinthians 13:1-3**).

The Lord made it clear in His last few days on earth, that we are all to be *witnesses* (Martus- martyrs, to be a record), to lay down our lives as a witness to whom we belong **Acts 1:8**). Jesus also made it unmistakably clear as to whose sheep we are and whose sheep we are to feed. I will put it in bold so that you will not forget it. Feed **MY SHEEP.** We love Him? Prove it! Tend, care for, lay down all you have and are, for **His** lambs. Our shoutings, long winded prayers, dancing, altar calls, running the aisles, bible quizzing, sermons, choirs and fancy gowns, beautiful platforms, prayer meetings, conferences, buses, ministries, organizations, board meetings, camp meetings (oddly enough, where nobody actually camps), and all other man-made attempts to show we love Him, all come to bupkis and pale into irrelevance if we do not personally lay down our lives for His sheep (the Ecclesia) by feeding them with our whole lives.

When ewes feed their lambs, they do not shove grass or hay down the baby's throats. They feed them with milk. Milk they have produced by eating food meant for older sheep, digesting it, and converting it into food for the young ones. The sheep allow the lambs to get really close and suckle from their teat, to smell them, lay on them, feel their heartbeat and a bond is formed between ewe and lamb. In the pasture when lambs are inadvertently separated from their mothers, all that is necessary to gather their lambs is for the ewes to give a distinctive sound and the lamb knows where to go just by that sound. To us, it is a cacophony of sound, but to the lamb who has fed from the breast of a loving mother, who has gotten close enough to memorize her scent, it is a specific call known only to the lamb. When rams sense danger, they place themselves between the danger and the lamb. Their life is in their progeny and will risk everything to see it grow.

Today, we have no trouble birthing new saints. Where we struggle is in letting them get close enough to hear our heartbeat and suckle from the nutrients God has given us. We expect the shepherd to feed them (by corralling them into pens twice a week and shoving hay or grass down their collective throats) when it is the responsibility of every member of the flock to teach them how to feed themselves. The term *wet-nurse* comes to mind. The definition is as follows, *A wet nurse is a woman who breast feeds and cares for another's child. Wet nurses are employed if the mother dies, or if she is unable or chooses not to nurse the child herself.* Have we inadvertently hired wet-nurses and are now calling them pastors, because we are unable or unwilling to feed the ones God brings in? The responsibility lays at the feet of the Ecclesia to feed and care for the young in the body, thus showing them how to feed and care for the next generation. This is the kind of love our Lord and Master has commanded us to have. Anything less is disobedience and rebellious.

Obeying Acts 2:38 is likened to a baby's first breath; this is the first look into the Kingdom of God, but as a normal baby must grow in order to become a functioning member of society, so must the believer in Christ grow in order to function properly in the Commonwealth of the Kingdom of God. Paul tells us that we are to go beyond what we learnt when we first came to a saving knowledge of Christ, ***Therefore, leaving*** (Aphiēmi- to go from) ***the principles of the doctrine of Christ, let us go*** (Pherō- be driven, endure, bring forth. See **Matthew 10:22**) *on unto perfection;* (Teleios- complete of labour, growth, mental and moral character, of full age [become fully grown]), *not laying again the foundation of repentance from dead works, and of* **faith** *toward God, Of the* **doctrine of baptisms***, and of* **laying on of hands***, and of* **resurrection** *of the dead, and of* **eternal judgment***. And this will we do, if God permit* (**Hebrews 6:1-3**). It seems when we have a room full of believers, we still preach the same things. Why? Because it gets many more *amens* and *preach it pastor,* but does it help us to grow? It only confirms what we already know. We preachers, pastors and bible schoolteachers need fresh revelation, answering the congregation's everyday questions about everyday things every day. We need to go back to teaching more than preaching to the choir what they already know.

These principles Paul mentions in **Hebrews 6:1-2** are laid down in the first few weeks or months of a newly born-again believer. If we are still majoring on these after years, we truly have missed the mark and become like the church of Corinth and those to whom Paul wrote the Letter to the Hebrews. We have remained babes in Christ when we should be teachers. To the Corinthians he wrote, *And I, brethren, could not speak unto you as unto spiritual, but as unto carnal, even as unto babes in Christ. I have fed you with milk* (The Fabulous Five)*, and not with meat: for hitherto ye were not able to bear it, neither yet now are ye able. For ye are yet carnal: for whereas there is among you envying, and strife, and divisions, are ye not carnal, and walk as men?* (These were daily issues that were not being dealt with **1 Corinthians 3:1-3**). Paul says the same thing, *Of whom we have many things to say, and hard to be uttered, seeing ye are dull* (Nōthros- sluggish, lazy, and stupid [not my words, but Paul's]) *of hearing. For when for the time* ***ye ought to be teachers*** (Didaskalos- instructors)*,* ***ye have need that one teach you again which be the first principles of the oracles of God;*** *and are become such as have need of milk, and not of strong meat. For every one that useth milk is unskilful* (Apeiros- inexperienced and ignorant) *in the word of righteousness: for he is a babe* (Nēpios- a simple minded person, an immature Christian). *But strong meat belongeth* ***to them that are of full age*** (Teleios- complete in labour and growth, in mental and moral character)*, even those who by reason of use have their senses* (Aisthētērion- organs of perception, judgement) *exercised* (Gumnazō-trained) *to discern both good and evil* (**Hebrews 5:11-14**).

We must obey the Law of Christ and of the prophets, such as, *Bear ye one another's burdens, and so fulfil the law of Christ,* and, *On these two commandments hang all the law* **and** *the prophets* (**Galatians 6:2, Matthew 22:40**). Everything else is commentary (an expression of opinions or offering of explanations about an event or situation). We must be who the Creator of heaven and earth called us to be within the Ecclesia for when the Ecclesia operates properly, there we will find our purpose, our contentment, and our joy. God is not in the least interested if we become successful in

354

the world via our careers or how high we rise in our particular organization. God couldn't care less how far we have climbed on the ministerial ladder if we do not, with love, sacrifice our desires and wants for one another we seek the mind of Christ as we are commanded. He could not care less how many churches we '*plant*' or degrees we can accumulate if we do not sacrificially love as He loves those under our care. He does, however, deeply care about how many disciples we are personally making and how much of the love of God we display. As Paul writes in **Romans 5:5** *And hope maketh not ashamed; **because the love of God is shed abroad** (Ekchunō- poured out, bestowed, gushed out) in our hearts by the Holy Ghost which is given unto us.* For those who claim to be filled with the Holy Ghost but are not shedding abroad this same love which Jesus commanded, we are propagating a false narrative to an unsuspecting world. *Yes, Jesus loves me, for the bible tells me so.* So what? He loves you so we can share that same sacrificial love within the Ecclesia then to the world, we don't keep the love of God for ourselves. We get it so we can shed it abroad, starting with those in our homes, our pews, our neighbourhoods, our cities then our nation or as Jesus so poignantly put it *...and ye shall be witnesses unto me both in Jerusalem, and in all Judaea, and in Samaria, and unto the uttermost part of the earth* (**Acts 1:8**).

As we come to the close of this book, I want to reiterate the purpose of the Ecclesia. For a long time, we have been placing the cart before the horse in much of our lives. For example, the purpose of a company is not to make money. The purpose of a company is to advance something or to do something for a greater cause. The purpose of a car is not to buy gas, but to go somewhere. Will a good company make money? Yes. Does a car need gasoline? Yes, but those things are not its purpose. The purpose of the Ecclesia is not to win souls, but to proclaim a Kingdom and King so powerful, that the earth is His footstool and heaven is His throne (**Acts 7:49**). It is to make and grow disciples of the souls that are drawn to this powerful Kingdom by the King through us (**John 12:32, Romans 8:29**). Will we win souls? Of course, we will, it will be as a natural outcome of our growth in God that others will see and want the same. Do we put inordinate pressure on the saints to win souls? Unfortunately, many times, yes, and it must be stopped at once. When a believer grows and becomes like their Lord, their hearts will automatically be burdened to be a light to the lost, salt in the earth and souls will become born-again as a natural consequence of their love for God and each other. If these things are not present, then we must ask the hard questions. Are they really committed? Do they want to be but don't know how? Perhaps it is because the older saints have not poured themselves into the newer saints and helped them grow.

Our priorities are skewwhiff and hence, our results are lop-sided. The early church did not grow as a result of soul winning programmes, but as a result of prayer and fasting for one another, of eating together, of sacrificing themselves for the Kingdom of God, of selling their stuff and giving to those in need and of learning how to walk in the spirit and be led the same way (**Galatians 5:16, 25, Romans 8:14, Acts 2:42-26, 4:32-25**). In so doing and allowing the Spirit of God to correct all the things given to them through their walk by the same spirit and by letters from older believers regarding their motivations, attitudes, doctrines, and love for one another. It was as they did these things, the numbers followed. Why? Because God had a place He could bring a seeker to, that would love and care for them as He wanted.

Distractions.

The apostle Peter gave some great advice when he wrote, *Casting all your care upon him; for he careth for you* (**1 Peter 5:7**). Unfortunately, we have misunderstood this verse and preached it as we are to cast our concerns and worries onto God, because He is concerned for us. A deeper look at this verse shows a remarkable disconnect between what we believe and what God is trying to convey. The word *care* actually means- through the idea of distractions, to part or divide (Merimna). We become distracted from our purpose and then wonder why God is not moving in our lives as He did in the early church or even when we first surrendered to Him. Paul writes in **2 Corinthians 11:3** *But I fear, lest by any means, as the serpent beguiled* (deluded or cheated) *Eve through his subtilty* (Panourgia- sophistry [use of fallacious arguments, especially with the intention of deceiving] cunningness), *so your minds should be corrupted from the simplicity* (Haplotēs- singleness and generosity) *that is in Christ*. He also asked those in Galatia, *Are ye so foolish? having begun in the Spirit, are ye now made perfect by the flesh?* (**Galatians 3:3**). We all start out well, then after being subtly distracted from our purpose we fall into a rut of church attendance, paying the tithe, going to conferences (for those that can afford it) and lunch after church for even more pseudo-fellowship where we talk about everything but God in most cases. We have been distracted from our journey by something good that happened along the way.

To paraphrase a story told by Frank Viola, winning souls is likened to going on a journey from Houston Texas to Bangor Maine. Along the way the car breaks down in Knoxville Tennessee. I stay there for several days awaiting parts for the car. While I'm getting my car fixed, I see how beautiful the area around Knoxville is. I'm meeting wonderful people in Knoxville and the food is tremendous. I become so enamoured by Knoxville that after a while I forget that my goal was to go to Bangor. So now I stay in Knoxville and spend all my time trying to fix other people's broken cars. I tell people on their way to Bangor how awesome Knoxville is, I extol the wonderful things they can do or get in Knoxville, and so, many join me in extolling the wonders of Knoxville. Before long I have a large crowd in Knoxville and have come to believe that Knoxville was my destination because God would not let me have such a large crowd if it was not His will, right? That, my dear brothers and sisters, is what has happened to modern day Christianity. We have forgotten our goal, our raison d'être, the most important reason for our existence. Jesus tells us why we exist in **Matthew 28:18-20** *And Jesus came and spake unto them, saying, All power is given unto me in heaven and in earth. Go ye therefore, and teach all nations, baptizing them in the name of the Father, and of the Son, and of the Holy Ghost: Teaching them to observe all things whatsoever I have commanded you: and, lo, I am with you alway, even unto the end of the world. Amen.*

The sole purpose of the church was to be a vehicle to carry the spirit and love of God and manifest the word of God to a lost and dying world. How did Jesus say we would manifest it? By our love for one another (**John 13:35**) as we disciple one another. We do this via preaching (Kerusso- proclaiming and publishing) the Kingdom of God only, to the lost (allowing God to draw them) and then making disciples of those who choose to follow. We have become focused on winning souls (saving the world) and lost sight of our destination to prepare those within the Ecclesia for the Kingdom of God.

Have we become distracted, like Abraham and Terah in Haran? What was meant to be a short stop to refresh the animals and resupply of food, ended up being many years. It took the death of Terah and a mighty move of God to get Abraham to leave this comfortable place and head back on his journey, to go to his final destination. It was only in Canaan Abraham was to see the promise fulfilled.

Instead of praying for a move of God in our next church service, how about we become the move of God in our church community and trust that God would use us and our lives as a vessel to show the lost what His Kingdom is all about. A move of God in our church *service*, but not in our homes, our workplaces, our schools, and neighbourhood, is like a self-licking ice-cream cone (*a self-perpetuating system that has no purpose other than to sustain itself*). Is this really how we want to portray the Commonwealth of the Kingdom of God? We (the Ecclesia) see the word lived daily and we learn, when we learn, we grow, and we retain what we learn when we do and teach what we know. As we do, the ones that are looking for God will see, when they see, they will receive the same opportunity to obtain grace and mercy as we did.

This reminds me of the story of Abram and Sarai, who desired to see a miracle child come to pass. Unfortunately, they used earthly means to fulfil a promise by Sarai giving her maid, Hagar, to Abram as a concubine (a normal thing in those days). Abram's purpose was to go where God told him to go, say what God told him to say and take care of his extended family. If they would have been patient and just waited for God to do what God said He would do, there would be peace in the Middle East today. When we try to do God's job (trying to win souls and foolishly using man's methods and programmes) instead of loving and discipling one another, we will end up with another man-made construct (which, like the Middle East, only causes friction and fractions) instead of the church Christ said He would build. Our job mirrors that of Abram. Go where God tells us to go (into all the world, starting close to home, then the neighbourhood, then the state, then the nation (**Acts 1:8**), say what God tells us to say (preach the Kingdom of God only), and make disciples of all nations (Ethnos- races, tribe; specifically a foreign (non-Jewish- gentiles) by implication pagan, heathen, people), **teaching** them (Didaskō- causing to learn) to *observe Christ's commandments* (**Matthew 28:19-20**). Unbelievably, that is all that is required of the Ecclesia and as we do this, God steps in with His wisdom, power and Spirit and draws the seeker, causing them to ask what they must do. It is only then that we give them the keys to becoming born again and the discipleship pattern starts all over again.

As we love and care for the ones we have sitting in our pews first, God will bring in the lost and hungry. *And they continued stedfastly in the apostles' doctrine and fellowship, and in breaking of bread, and in prayers. And fear came upon every soul: and many wonders and signs were done by the apostles.* **And all that believed were together** (Epi- superimposition (of time, place, order, etc.), as a relation of distribution, the same direction, on behalf of), **and had all things common** (Koinos- shared by all or several); *And sold their possessions and goods, and parted them to all men, as every man had need. And they, continuing daily with one accord in the temple, and breaking bread from house to house, did eat their meat with gladness and singleness of heart, Praising God, and having favour with all the people.* **And** (De- but, moreover, now) **the Lord added to the church daily such as should be saved**. (Acts 2:42-47).

We were never meant to add people to the church through special social programmes, gimmicks, block parties, festivals, singsperations, plays, invite a friend to church day, more comfortable or newer pews, more attractive platforms and pulpits, better technology, buses, more ministries, food bank drives, parties, or special dinners. When we do what we're created and called to do (to show the world what *love one another as I have loved you* looks like and how we obey the word of God through sacrifice), NOW, THE LORD ADDS TO THE CHURCH **DAILY**. If we add them through our own means the enemy can take them through his means. But when God adds them, and we disciple them in love, very few will leave. The reason? Their initial relationship was with

Christ, their Lord and Saviour not with the church building and our programmes. Jesus said, *While I was with them in the world*, **I kept them in thy name: those that thou gavest me I have kept, and none of them is lost**, *but the son of perdition; that the scripture might be fulfilled* (John 17:12).

God uses us, not gimmicks to get His message of the Kingdom across and when we do our part, to preach the Gospel of the Kingdom, love, and disciple one another, the chance of them *"backsliding"* become almost negligible.

To build community requires vigilant awareness of the work we must continually do to undermine all the socialization that leads us to behave in ways that perpetuate domination.

Bell Hooks, Teaching Community: A Pedagogy of Hope.

The vast majority of people only change when change is the only option they have. We must all change. If not now, then when? If not here, then where? If not you and I, then who? Let us not become this generation's ATNA's- All Talk and No Action. Worship services without sacrifice have little to no impact in the Commonwealth of the Kingdom of God let alone the world. While seeking to be comfortable in our homes, our church buildings and our communities seems right, it is, in fact, the antithesis of the Commonwealth of the Kingdom. If we cannot or will not emulate Christ's walk here on earth, then we will not follow Him into the New Heaven and New Earth.

Addendum.

What is an addendum? It is a supplement to a document that further adds definition and clarification in a concise form, such as a contract for the sale of a business. An addendum clarifies, for example, what stock, staff, or equipment is to remain with the company and how the company name is to be used. The Renewed Covenant is an addendum to the Old Covenant. As approximately two thirds of the Renewed Covenant is directly or indirectly cited from the Old Covenant, it can be safely said the Renewed Covenant is an addendum, a refining not a redefining of God's word. It is a reiteration of God's commands and manifestation of how to live those commands and fulfil His desires in a manner that pleases Him and is beneficial to His Ecclesia.

Below is a list of seventy-seven commands that Christ gave us to do while we walk this earth in obedience to His spirit. This list is not in any particular order, only that they are things God commands of all those who claim to be His. We may *think* we are serving God, but are we serving Him according to His will or ours?

Remember a commandment, when it concerns coming from God is Entolē, meaning injunction, that is, an authoritative prescription, and just like a prescription from a doctor it must be followed based upon the doctor's extensive knowledge of the body if it is to have the desired benefit. If we follow the list below, we will do well in both this life and the one to come.

The Universal Law of God (The Law of Christ):

1. The greatest is to love God first.

2. Love all other people the same as yourself (Matthew 22:39).

The Ten Commandments:

3. Have no other gods.

4. Make no graven images.

5. Don't take His name in vain. Keep the seventh day Holy.

6. Honour your mother and father.

7. Don't commit murder.

8. Don't commit adultery.

9. Don't steal.

10. Don't give a false witness.

11. Don't covert your neighbour's wife or possessions.

The Golden Rule:

12. Treat others as you would have them treat you.

The Commandments to the Ecclesia as a whole:

13. Do not be angry with you brother without a cause.

14. Rejoice when they persecute you.

15. Forgive those who have trespassed against us in the same manner we have been forgiven by God for trespassing against Him.

16. We must be born again.

17. Abide in Him.

18. His word is to abide in us.

19. Let people see our good works so that they may glorify God.

20. Let our light shine (don't hide God in our hearts or in our church buildings).

21. End disputes quickly.

22. Whatever causes us to sin, cut it off.

23. Don't swear any oaths.

24. Turn the other cheek.

25. Give when people ask of us and don't expect anything in return.

26. Give more than what is required (go the extra mile).

27. Love our enemies and those that would despitefully use us.

28. Give to the poor (not so that we would gain approval from God or people).

29. Pray privately (not to impress others).

30. Give privately (so no-one but God knows).

31. Fast privately (so no-one can see you).

32. Store up your treasures in heaven.

33. Strive to enter into the strait gate.

34. Seek first the Kingdom of God and don't be concerned with your material needs.

35. Don't worry about tomorrow.

36. Judge righteously.

37. Show mercy.

38. Give grace as we've been given grace.

39. Don't cast our pearls before the swine.

40. Give and it shall be given (whole of life, nothing to do with money).

41. Feed the hungry.

42. Clothe the naked.

43. Visit the sick.

44. Visit the prisoners.

45. Watch out for false prophets.

46. Cast out demons,

47. Raise the dead.

48. Lay hands on the sick.

49. Love the children.

50. Don't take on titles (Rabbi, Master or Father, pastor, bishop, presbyter, superintendent, first lady, Mother of the church etc).

51. Don't oppose other believers who are not in our group.

52. Have faith in God.

53. Be like the Good Samaritan (go and do likewise).

54. Love people like God loves people (as I have loved you).

55. Whenever we eat and drink, do it in remembrance of Him (not once or twice a year. More than a twenty second prayer).

56. Wash one another's feet.

57. Go and teach all nations to obey my commands.

58. Go and wait for the Holy Ghost and be my witnesses (This does not mean go witnessing).

59. Be ready for His return.

60. Bear one another's burdens.

61. Speak to the mountain.

62. Take the beam out of our own eye.

63. Go feed the multitude.

64. Come follow me.

65. Bring the child to me (after we can't do anymore).

66. Go into all the towns and proclaim the Kingdom of God is at hand (preach to the lost).

67. Do my works and greater than these.

68. Go and tell your friends (demoniac)

69. Go and show your healing to others (lepers).

70. Go and prepare a feast for the disciples (the last supper).

71. Go and tell John what you've seen (the despondent).

72. Search the scriptures for in then we have salvation.

73. Take up you bed and walk.

74. Bring the blind to me.

75. Put away you instrument of death (sword)

76. If we remember a brother or sister has something against us, leave our gift and go make it right.

77. Rejoice when men revile you.

Acceptable to God.

Wherefore we receiving a kingdom which cannot be moved, let us have grace, whereby **we may serve God acceptably** *(Euarestōs- quite agreeably, to please well) with reverence and godly fear: For our God is a consuming (Katanaliskō- utterly destructive) fire* (**Hebrews 12:28-29**). *I beseech you therefore, brethren, by the mercies of God, that ye present your bodies a living sacrifice, holy,* **acceptable unto God**, *which is your reasonable service. And be not conformed to this world: but be ye transformed by the renewing of your mind, that ye may prove what is that good, and acceptable, and perfect, will of God.* (**Romans 12:1-2**). *Let the words of my mouth, and the meditation of my heart,* **be acceptable in thy sight**, *O LORD, my strength, and my redeemer* (**Psalm 19:14**). *Is it such a fast that I have chosen? a day for a man to afflict his soul? is it to bow down his head as a bulrush, and to* *spread sackcloth and ashes under him? wilt thou call this a fast, and **an acceptable day to the LORD?*** (Isaiah 58:5).

Many have a proclivity to focus on the commands that bring us to where we must be born-again (a once in a lifetime experience), and after this we focus on receiving blessings or miracles. After we have got the blessings and miracles, what then? Sadly, we spend an inordinate amount of time on quasi-spiritual matters (where church attendance, holiness standards, obeying the pastor, paying tithes is all there is to this walk with the Master. This is where we have a form (Morphōsis- formular or appearance) of godliness but deny/contradict our testimony) by neglecting the weightier matters of God, such as righteous judgement, love, and mercy (**Matthew 23:23**). The number of times I have seen the believers strictly adhering to church attendance, holiness standards (each church has their own), obeying the pastor and paying tithes while they have no prayer or worship life, are stingy with their money to others, holding onto goods, withholding of time or talents, harbour bitterness, unforgiveness or malice in their hearts, do not personally study let alone obey the word, engage in backbiting, gossiping or have domineering or authoritarian spirits, is mind boggling to say the least. We cannot say we love God while living with such things in our lives.

Please, for the love of God and His holy people, let us not preach, speak, or sing of heaven while our deeds promote the kingdoms of this world (see **Matthew 4:8, Luke 4:5**).

The above seventy-seven commands from the lips of our Lord are a necessity if we are to remain born again until we are saved, *And ye shall be hated of all men for my name's sake: but **he that endureth to the end shall be saved*** (**Matthew 10:22**). This is what Jesus meant when He told us in the great commission, *...teaching them to observe all things I have commanded you...* (**Matthew 28:20**). Paul was concerned with doing what God had called him to do or else it would not bode well for him, *But I keep under my body, and bring it into subjection: **lest that by any means, when I have preached to others, I myself should be a castaway*** (Adokimos- unapproved, worthless, or rejected). Just as migrating to another country has its privileges, it also has its responsibilities and so have we, when we are born-again according to Jesus' and Peter's words in **Mark 16:16, Luke 24:47, Acts 2:38-40**.

Everything God's word tells us about heaven, we are to mirror here on earth (*As it is in heaven, so in earth.* **Luke 11:2**), and those who do the works (commands) of the King here, will be allowed to rule and reign with Him in the New Jerusalem on the New Earth under the New Heavens. *It is a faithful saying: For if we be dead with him, we shall also live with him: If we suffer, we shall also reign with him: if we deny him, he also will deny us* (**2 Timothy 2:11-12**).

Finally, my brothers and sisters, let us meditate on John's letter to the church where he tells us a harsh fact, *In this was manifested the love of God toward us, because that God sent his only begotten Son into the world, that we might live through him. Herein is love, not that we loved God, but that he loved us, and sent his Son to be the propitiation for our sins. **Beloved, if God so loved us, we ought also to love one another*** (1 John 4:9-11).

Kieth (Bashar) Fansa.

2023 ©

ledofgod@ymail.com

+1 361-676-0882

Made in the USA
Columbia, SC
06 January 2025

49336344R00198